Using
Windows NT®
Server 4

Drew Heywood

Contents at a Glance

A Division of Macmillan Computer Publishing, USA
201 W. 103rd Street
Indianapolis, Indiana 46290

Using Windows NT® Server 4

Library of Congress Catalog No.: CIP data available upon request.

ISBN: 0-7897-1612-7

00 99 98   6 5 4 3 2 1

Interpretation of the printing code: The rightmost double-digit number is the year of the book's printing; the rightmost single-digit number, the number of the book's printing. For example, a printing code of 98-1 shows that the first printing of the book occurred in 1998.

Credits

Executive Editor
Laurie Petrycki

Acquisitions Editor
Sean Angus

Development Editor
Jim Chalex

Technical Editor
Dave Bixler

Managing Editor
Sarah Kearns

Project Editor
Christopher Morris

Copy Editors
Keith Cline
Gayle Johnson
Kate Givens
Kate Talbot

Cover Designers
Dan Armstrong
Ruth Harvey

Book Designers
Nathan Clement
Ruth Harvey

Indexer
Craig Small

Production
Jeanne Clark
Christy M. Lemasters
Sossity Smith
Heather Stephenson

Contents

About the Author

Drew Heywood has been involved in the microcomputing industry since he purchased an Apple II in 1978. For the past eleven years, he has focused on networking. After spending several years in government and the private sector as a network administrator, Drew came to New Riders Publishing as a product line manager for a new line of networking books. From 1991 to 1995, Drew expanded the New Riders title list to include some of the most successful networking books in the industry. In early 1995, Drew left New Riders to become a full-time author. He has written or contributed to several New Riders books, including *Inside Windows NT Server*, *Networking with Microsoft TCP/IP*, *Inside NetWare 3.12*, and several books on NetWare certification.

About the Technical Editor

Dave Bixler is a senior infrastructure consultant with a large systems integrator. He is also a contributing author of *The Windows NT 4.0 Server Security Handbook* and has done technical editing on a number of Que projects. Dave has been working in the networking arena for the last ten years, working on network designs, NT Server implementations, and network management, as well as Internet connectivity and security. Dave is MCSE certified, and has certifications from a number of other industry leaders, including Novell, IBM, 3Com, and Check Point. He can be reached via email at dbixler@art-deco.net.

Acknowledgments

To Sean Angus, thanks for the opportunity and the support.

To Jim Chalex, thanks for a great edit.

To Dave Bixler, thanks for one of the best tech edits I have ever had.

To Blythe, thanks as always for patience in the face of deadlines.

To everyone at Macmillan, thanks for giving me yet another chance to do a Macmillan book.

Dedication

For Blythe and for our future together

We'd Like to Hear from You!

Que Corporation has a long-standing reputation for high-quality books and products. To ensure your continued satisfaction, we also understand the importance of customer service and support.

Orders, Catalogs, and Customer Service

To order other Que or Macmillan Computer Publishing books, catalogs, or products, please contact our Customer Service Department:

Phone: 1-800-428-5331

Fax: 1-800-835-3202

International Fax: 1-317-228-4400

Or visit our online bookstore:

`http://www.mcp.com/`

I WROTE MY FIRST Windows NT Server book about three years ago. Ancient history! In those early days of Windows NT, every book started out like a Microsoft sales pitch. We authors thought we had to sell you readers on the features of Windows NT. Maybe 30 pages in, we'd decide we had extolled enough virtues of Windows NT and we would move on to actually teaching you to do something.

Those days have changed. Selling you on Windows NT is as unnecessary as selling you on personal computing or networking. Windows NT is part of the computer landscape, its features on everyone's lips. So no sales pitch. Let's get to work.

Windows NT Server is both simple and complex. Simple considering everything it does, but complex because it does so much. When you commit to learning Windows NT Server, you take on a big task but not an impossible one. With perseverance and the right help, you will have no trouble reaching your goal of Windows NT mastery. I've tried to do several things in this book to help you along the way.

For one thing, I've cut out a lot of jargon and theory. You can drive a car without knowing its compression ratio or how to adjust the wheel alignment, can't you? Well, you can learn to do an incredible amount of networking without knowing about packets or protocol analysis. In this book, we won't be looking under the hood any more than necessary. There won't be any layered protocol models, whatever those are, or long discussions about how Windows NT's security innards work. It's enough that you can install and configure the protocols, or that you can set up user accounts and give users the permissions they need to do their jobs. Later, when you are more comfortable with Windows NT, you can turn to more advanced tomes or to Microsoft's documentation and get down to the gory details (if you are curious). For now, the focus is on teaching you how to perform your job as a Windows NT Server administrator.

Organization of This Book

Enough preliminaries. You know why we're here. Now let's see how we are going to work together to enable you to become a Windows NT Server network administrator.

Part 1: Laying the Foundation (Chapters 1 Through 12)

If you are new to Windows NT Server, you will find it profitable to use the chapters pretty much in the sequence found in the book, at least for the first 12 chapters. Those chapters provide a foundation that you will build on in later chapters. Material in these chapters is carefully sequenced, and you should try to work through the chapters in the order they appear (although readers with some networking experience can probably skip Chapter 1 without missing anything).

Part II: TCP/IP (Chapters 13 Through 19)

TCP/IP is everywhere. You can't avoid it, but it might be best if you put off working with TCP/IP for a bit. After you know how a Windows NT Server network functions with simpler protocols, you will be better able to set up and troubleshoot a TCP/IP network. So, if possible, don't start these seven chapters until you are familiar with the preceding 12.

If you can't avoid TCP/IP, you might wind up in Chapter 13 before you complete the earlier material. That's okay. There's nothing about TCP/IP that will kill you. But I have to give you more theory with TCP/IP than with other protocols. There's even a complete (short!) chapter devoted to theory. Be sure you read Chapter 13 before you attempt to install or configure that first TCP/IP computer.

Part III: Advanced Topics (Chapters 20 Through 26)

The remainder of the book is a bit of a grab bag. You will learn everything from setting up a dial-up server, to editing the Registry, to setting up communication between Microsoft and NetWare servers.

By the time you reach these chapters, you will have a thorough grounding in Windows NT basics and you can pick and choose the topics you require.

So, Let's Get Started, Already

An efficient book should have an efficient Introduction, and I've done my best to be brief. So dig in. You will be amazed at how quickly you can arrive at a working Windows NT network.

Laying the Foundation

Setting Up Your Network

Components of a network

Characteristics of local and wide area networks

Networks and internetworks

Building an Ethernet LAN

Networks are no longer new, and you probably have some networking experience. But I want to ensure that you know some basic concepts and definitions and that you will start with a working network. You can't learn about Windows NT Server if you don't have a network.

If you think your knowledge of networks is past the basics, by all means skip to Chapter 2, "Installing Windows NT Server 4," where I plunge into NT Server installation. But if you need to brush up on the fundamentals, please read on. I promise it won't take long.

You don't need to know the details of how networks work in order to manage a network. For example, you need to know what a protocol is, but you don't need to know how protocols work. Eventually, as you grow, you will be faced with troubleshooting situations in which a knowledge of the inner secrets of networking will be required. But there is a tremendous amount you can do before you are initiated into the inner circle.

This chapter is my attempt to briefly describe what everyone should know about networking. You will learn the components of a network and how to wire a basic network. Then you will be ready to really get wrapped up in networking.

What Makes a Network?

At its heart, a network is simple enough, consisting of just four types of components:

- Servers
- Clients
- Media
- Protocols

That's it. Really! Of course, there are several types of servers, clients, media, and protocols, but the basics of one type apply to the others. Figure 1.1 shows a generic network so that you can acquaint yourself with the graphic elements I will use throughout this book. I've chosen to draw an Ethernet-style network because Ethernet is the most common network medium by far. Unfortunately, protocols manifest themselves as electrical signals in computers and on the network medium, so I can't very well depict them in a figure.

Now, let's aim for some high-level definitions of these components.

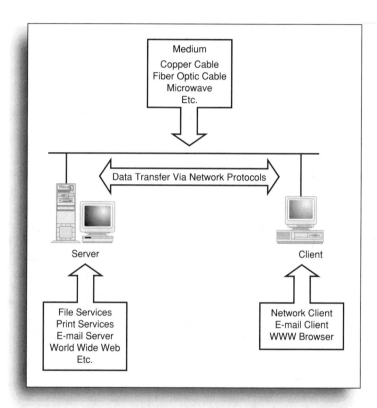

FIGURE 1.1

Components of a network.

Servers

Any computer that can share resources with other computers is a *server*. Servers can share many different things. Perhaps the most prominent examples of shared resources are files, printers, email distribution, databases, and World Wide Web documents. A server can be dedicated to providing a single service, or it can serve many functions.

In the Microsoft world, many types of computers can be servers. Windows NT Server computers are nearly always servers, as you would expect. Windows NT Workstation, Windows 95, Windows 98, and Windows for Workgroups computers can easily be configured as servers—you just check a box in a Control Panel applet.

SEE ALSO

➤ *You'll learn how to set up Windows NT Server in Chapter 2, starting on page 21.*

➤ *Chapter 6 shows you how to set up Windows NT as a file server, starting on page 183.*

➤ *In Chapter 7 you'll learn how to set up Windows NT as a print server, starting on page 213.*

➤ *To set up a World Wide Web server, see Chapter 19, starting on page 563.*

Clients

A *client* is a computer that uses resources that are shared by servers. To become a client, a computer must load a software component that knows how to communicate through the network. It is this component that is typically referred to when the word *client* is used. Some general-purpose clients let computers access file- and printer-sharing services. Electronic mail servers typically require their clients to have specialized email client software. The client for a World Wide Web server is a Web browser, such as Microsoft's Internet Explorer. A computer can be a client for many types of services all at once.

Windows NT was designed with networking in mind. When you install a network adapter on a Windows NT computer, the computer automatically becomes capable of functioning as a client on a Microsoft network.

SEE ALSO

➤ *Chapter 8, starting on page 247, explains how to configure Windows 95, Windows 98, Windows for Workgroups, Windows 3.1, and MS-DOS computers as network clients.*

A computer can simultaneously function as a server and as a client. If you turn on the file and printer sharing feature of a Windows 95 computer, for example, the computer appears on the network as a server. But a user of that computer can continue to work as a network client.

Media

Servers and clients need to communicate in order to exchange data. This communication takes place through a *medium*.

Computer networks use many types of media. The most common medium is copper cable, but you will also encounter optical fiber, microwave, and light media.

Protocols

Any time two entities communicate, they must use a language that both understand. The languages of network communication are called *protocols*. Think of protocols as vocabulary and rules of grammar, and you'll get the idea. You will never see a protocol (they're hard to show in figures), but as a network administrator you will be intimately connected with selecting and configuring protocols. Don't be afraid of protocols. Yes, if you dig down far enough, they are intensely technical beasties, but that's true of everything that has to do with computers. You don't need to know how a microprocessor works in order to use a computer, and you don't need to know many of the technicalities of protocols to learn the skills presented in this book. So relax.

SEE ALSO

➤ *Windows NT supports three network protocols. NetBEUI and NWLink are simple to set up. Chapter 3 has everything you need to know, starting on page 83.*

➤ *TCP/IP is a more complex protocol. You'll learn the basics in Chapter 13, starting on page 425, but it takes several more chapters—14 through 18, to be exact—to fully cover TCP/IP configuration.*

Local and Wide Area Networks

You will encounter two types of networks: local and wide area. Although a wide area network typically covers a larger geographic area than a local area network, that is only one characteristic that distinguishes LANs from WANs.

Local Area Networks

A *local area network* or LAN is typically fast and inexpensive and has a limited communication range. Once LANs are hooked up, you can pretty much take them for granted. LANs move data quickly and have gotten so cheap that any office can afford one. A LAN can cost less than $100 per computer, and that's primo-quality networking at 10 million bits per second. But LAN

Network speed

When I talk about network speed, I don't mean that data gets to its destination faster. All networks move signals at about the speed of light.

By network speed, I mean the number of bits that can be pumped through the network in a given time. A 10-megabit-per-second (Mbps) network moves about 10 million bits past a given point in a second.

The capacity of a network to move a certain number of bits in a certain period of time is often called *bandwidth*.

technologies typically have very limited ranges, and they fall apart when they are stretched more than a few miles.

The most common type of LAN is Ethernet. A typical Ethernet has a maximum bandwidth of 10 Mbps, but you can now buy 100 Mbps Ethernet equipment at many computer stores. The recent buzz is about 1 gigabit Ethernet—that's right, one *billion* bits per second. Ethernet has proven that it can meet increasingly demanding networking requirements.

SEE ALSO

➤ *I'll introduce you to Ethernet later in this chapter in the section "Building an Ethernet Network," on page 14.*

Wide Area Networks

A *wide area network*, or WAN, is typically slower than a LAN, very expensive, and can span any geographic area. WANs are slower than LANs not because they have to be but because speed and distance cost money. It's expensive to put up communications satellites and microwave stations or to stretch optical fiber cable for thousands of miles. Consequently, with a WAN you typically buy what you absolutely must have, not what you want. And what you buy, you pay for—every month. WAN bandwidths typically range from about 128 kilobits per second (Kbps) to about 4.5 Mbps, although much higher speeds are available if you have very deep pockets. You don't have to look very far for a WAN; you probably use one almost every day. It's called the Internet, and it's the world's biggest WAN.

Unless you are IBM or a telecommunications provider such as AT&T, a WAN isn't something you own. It's something you lease. You work with a provider to determine your needs. It's then up to a vendor to bring the appropriate lines into your site and install the equipment you need in order to connect. You then run a cable from your LAN to the WAN equipment, and you're hooked up. Your big decisions involve how much bandwidth you require and how you will pay for it. To familiarize you with the symbols, Figure 1.2 shows two LANs communicating through a WAN connection. The lightning bolt is the conventional symbol for a connection that involves a commercial telecommunications link.

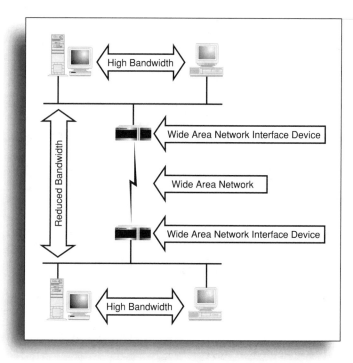

FIGURE 1.2
Two LANs connected by a WAN link.

The big point I want to make about WANs is that bandwidth is a precious commodity. You will frequently encounter situations in which you must take particular care when designing your network to ensure that you don't overwhelm a WAN connection.

SEE ALSO

➤ *See the section "Connecting to a Wide Area Network" in Chapter 15, starting on page 482, for a discussion of some wide area network options.*

Networks and Internetworks

Any network technology has limitations. A 10 Mbps Ethernet has a limited maximum size and a maximum number of computers it can support. So it's very common to have to break networks into several smaller networks.

Consequently, it's often necessary to build a "network of networks," that is, several networks that are connected. Such a network is shown in Figure 1.3. The devices that connect the networks are called *routers*. A router is a device that has the intelligence to forward messages from one network to another as required.

FIGURE 1.3
A network with routers.

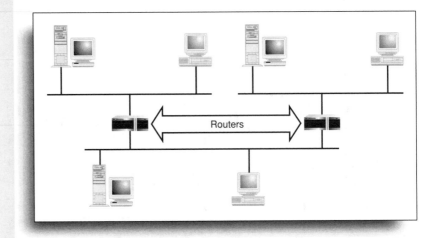

Now, here's some terminology:

- An *internetwork* is a network of networks and is sometimes an *internet*, which is not to be confused with *the* Internet.

- A *subnetwork* or *subnet* is part of an internetwork that is bounded by routers.

As you might have noticed, the term *network* is used pretty flexibly. It can refer to a complete corporate network and mean the same thing as *internetwork*. Or it can be used to describe part of an internetwork, a subnetwork. In other words, the word *network* is not rigidly defined. I'll try to make it clear throughout this book which sense of the term I'm using. If I simply use the term *network*, you can be pretty sure that the discussion applies to internetworks or subnetworks.

SEE ALSO

➤ *Chapter 3 discusses routing with the NWLink protocol. See the section "Configuring IPX Routing" on page 99 for more information.*

➤ *Chapter 15, starting on page 471, is devoted to routing on TCP/IP networks.*

Building an Ethernet Network

Okay, you need to network your office, and you're starting from scratch. Besides computers, what else do you need?

Let's assume that you're going to put in an Ethernet. That's what nearly everyone chooses. In fact, you'll have to work hard to buy anything else. So Ethernet it is.

I'll assume you're hooking up a 10 Mbps Ethernet. 100 Mbps Ethernet is readily available, but the components are more expensive, and the cabling is a bit more temperamental to install.

Cabling

You have several choices of cabling for Ethernet, but the over-whelming choice is 10Base-T. This cable is a lot like the cables you use to connect your phone to the wall. It has telephone-style modular connectors at each end, and it snaps in just like a telephone cord. You can't actually use the same cords you use to hook up your phone. But if you can plug a phone into the wall, you can hook up an Ethernet.

The T in 10Base-T stands for *twisted pair*, a type of cable in which pairs of copper wires are twisted together. The twisting reduces sensitivity to electronic noise. Figure 1.4 shows an example of a 10Base-T cable with a connector, which is called an *RJ-45 connector*.

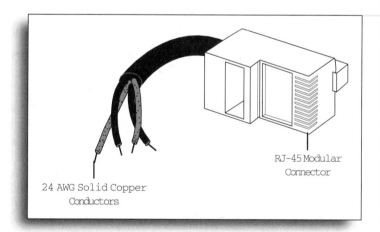

RJ-45 Modular Connector

24 AWG Solid Copper Conductors

FIGURE 1.4
10Base-T cable with an RJ-45 connector.

You will need a special type of 10Base-T cable called Category 5, or CAT5 for short. This is a high-performance cable that you can use at speeds up to 100 Mbps. If you ever need to upgrade to 100 Mbps Ethernet, your cables will be ready.

If you want to run cables through your walls or ceilings, I recommend that you hire a cabling contractor to do the work for you. He will have the equipment and expertise required to do a

Premade CAT5 cables

Unless you want to buy expensive tools and spend time learning to use them, you should plan on buying premade CAT5 cables. Many computer stores stock suitable cables, and some will make custom cables to order. These cables will be professionally made and tested, and they're probably the best way for you to connect your equipment. The following are two catalog sources for cables and other network components. Both companies offer excellent technical support for their products.

Data Comm Warehouse
(800) 642-3064
www.warehouse.com

Black Box Corporation
(800) 552-6816
www.blackbox.com

good job. It's easy to damage CAT5 cable when pulling it through tight places.

A cable contractor will know how to terminate your cable runs with nice, neat plug-in boxes, and he will have the equipment needed to test your cable after it's installed. A good network cable tester is a pricey piece of equipment. And after you've gone to the trouble of hiring a contractor, you should insist on having the cable tested before you sign off on the job.

Network Adapters

Every computer must have a network adapter. Some computers now ship with adapters already installed. Others require installation on your part.

I recommend that you buy dual-speed Ethernet adapters. They can work at 10 Mbps now and at 100 Mbps in the future if you ever need more performance. You will be surprised at the small difference in price between a 10 Mbps adapter and a 10/100 Mbps adapter. It will be much cheaper to buy dual-speed adapters now than to swap out 10 Mbps adapters in the future.

If your computers have PCI slots, by all means buy PCI network adapters. In theory, at least, these adapters are entirely self-configuring. Just plug them in and turn on the computer. In reality, you might need to tweak your computer's BIOS configuration to ensure that the PCI cards pick up the right interrupts. But the fact remains that PCI devices are almost always easier to configure than their ISA counterparts.

If you must install your network adapters in ISA slots, you need to take into consideration interrupts, I/O addresses, DMA settings, and other things that allow a card to work properly with a computer.

SEE ALSO

➤ *If you aren't comfortable with interrupts and other settings, Appendix C, starting on page 807, will give you some guidelines.*

After you install the adapter, you need to install the network driver software. You can install network drivers when you install Windows NT, or you can install them after NT is installed.

SEE ALSO

➤ *Chapter 3 explains in detail the procedures for installing and configuring network adapter drivers on Windows NT computers. See the section "Adding and Removing Network Adapters" on page 90.*

Windows 95 and 98 automatically detect most network adapters and install the drivers automatically.

Consult the product documentation for the procedures used to install network drivers on Windows for Workgroups.

The Microsoft client for MS-DOS will install drivers for some older network adapters. You will need to manually reconfigure the driver files to set up more-recent adapters.

Hubs

The heart of a 10Base-T network is the hub, a box that accepts cables from several computers. Hubs typically have capacities between 5 and 24 computers. You simply run a CAT5 cable between each computer and the hub to establish a network connection (see Figure 1.5). The cable connecting a computer to a hub can't be longer than 100 meters (about 330 feet).

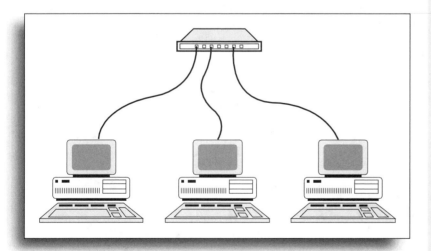

FIGURE 1.5

Connecting computers to a 10Base-T hub.

A hub is a very simple device that lets all the attached computers communicate. There is practically nothing to worry about with a hub. In most cases, there isn't even a power switch.

Each computer port will usually have two status lights. One light, always green in my experience, glows to indicate that a connection has been established with a remote computer, indicating that the hardware and network drivers are working at both ends of the connection. (10Base-T network adapters also have a connection status light, allowing you to confirm the connection status at the computer and hub ends.) Another light, typically amber, flashes when traffic is detected on the port. Some inexpensive hubs might have a single activity light for the entire hub.

One light on the hub flashes in response to Ethernet events called collisions. Some collisions are normal on an Ethernet, and a flashing collision light indicates that the network is functioning. If the collision light is on most of the time and the network slows down, you have too much traffic. (I'm purposely not explaining what a collision is, because you don't need to know how Ethernet works in order to run your network.)

If you have too many computers for one hub, you can add hubs and connect them, but you have to use special ports intended for hub-to-hub connections. Don't just run a cable between two computer ports. Hub-to-hub ports are labeled differently on different brands of hubs. Some are labeled "crossover" ports. The manuals included with your hub will show you how to make the required connections.

Building large Ethernets gets pretty involved. You might need repeaters to boost the signal, fiber-optic cable segments to increase the range, and routers to segment network traffic. The information I've given you will help you set up an Ethernet in a small office. If your network is more than about 300 meters in diameter (the distance between the two computers that are farthest from each other), you should bring in a network consultant to ensure a proper network design.

Now Your Computers Can Talk

I have deliberately kept things simple in this chapter. My goal was to help you network your computers, not to turn you into an electrical engineer. As you can see, setting up a basic LAN is quite a simple proposition these days.

If you have set up a network as described in this chapter, keep in mind that no communication takes place until your servers and clients are configured with network software. That's the real job, and it will take the next 25 chapters to cover the topic thoroughly.

Now that your network is up, you're ready for Windows NT Server. Let's move on to the next chapter and perform your first NT Server installation.

Installing Windows NT Server 4

The actual process of installing NT is extremely simple. The Setup program is highly automated and prompts you every step of the way. Assuming that your server and network hardware are correctly configured and are working properly, you should experience few difficulties.

Nevertheless, this is a fairly large chapter, for a variety of reasons. Here are just some of the issues that complicate this chapter:

- NT supports more than one file system. How will you set up the file partitions on the server?

- Are you upgrading? If so, do you want to replace the old operating system or retain it and set up a multiboot configuration?

- NT can communicate using three different network protocols. Which will your network use?

- Windows NT computers can play several domain security roles. How will the computer you are installing participate in the network?

- The setup process can be started from MS-DOS, Windows 95, Windows 98, or Windows NT, or from boot floppies. Which method should you choose?

- The installation CD can be placed in a local or shared network CD-ROM drive. How can you use each option to your best advantage?

- The Setup program is also used to repair damaged NT files and to upgrade older Windows versions to NT 4. When do you repair, and what's the procedure?

- Windows NT can set up multiboot configurations with other operating systems. Is that what you want?

By the end of this chapter, we will have looked at all these issues. Before looking at setup procedures, however, we need to look at some planning issues. After that, we'll step through the installation procedure. Then we'll consider some variations on the basic setup process.

Planning the Server File Partitions

If your computer will be running only Windows NT Server 4, it takes practically no effort to plan your server file partitions. If, however, the computer must also support a multiboot configuration with MS-DOS or Windows 95 or 98, you must consider two issues:

- Will NT share a file partition with another operating system?
- Which file system will be used to format the various file partitions?

Let's look at the file system types first.

Supported File Systems

A *file system* determines how files are stored in the hard drive partition. NT supports two file systems: the older FAT system used by MS-DOS, and the NT File System (NTFS) specifically designed for NT.

FAT

FAT (file allocation table) is an old and inefficient file system that is still the only file system that MS-DOS can use. Perhaps the most significant headache with FAT has to do with the way files are stored in allocation units called *clusters*. When a cluster is assigned to a file, the entire cluster is allocated. If the cluster size is 4 KB and a file requires 4100 bytes of storage, two 4 KB clusters are allocated, with most of the second cluster simply wasted.

This inefficiency gets worse when hard disk partitions grow, because large partitions are formatted with larger clusters. With large partitions, which make the most sense on today's huge hard drives, clusters can grow to 32 KB, and file storage becomes terribly wasteful. If you want to use disk space efficiently, you must keep partitions below 1 KB in size to maintain a reasonable cluster size.

FAT-16 and FAT-32

Microsoft has introduced two versions of FAT:

- 16-bit FAT (FAT-16) is used by MS-DOS, retail Windows 95, and Windows NT.

- 32-bit FAT (FAT-32) was distributed only with new OEM versions of Windows 95. You had to purchase a new computer in order to obtain a version of Windows 95 that supports FAT-32. Windows 98 includes a FAT-32 converter.

Windows NT doesn't support FAT-32. It can't be installed on a FAT-32 partition or read data in a FAT-32 partition.

To improve storage efficiency, FAT volumes are frequently compressed. Compression utilities are included with later versions of MS-DOS, with Windows 95 and 98, and from third-party software vendors. Windows NT is not compatible with compressed FAT volumes.

NTFS

NTFS is an improved file system that offers several advantages:

- **Support for Windows NT security.** User access can be restricted at the file and directory levels, improving the level of security control. This is highly desirable on shared file servers.

- **Support for long filenames.** NTFS doesn't restrict you to the 8.3 filename format required for MS-DOS. (MS-DOS users can still access files with long names using special name abbreviations.)

- **Greater fault tolerance.** Disk actions are logged so that they can be backed out of or tried again when errors or hardware failures interrupt write operations. This allows NTFS to survive problems that would corrupt FAT files or entire FAT volumes.

- **Fault-tolerant storage volumes.** NTFS disks can be configured in multidisk arrays that offer better performance, fault tolerance, or both.

SEE ALSO

➤ *For more about file storage, see Chapter 10, "File Storage Systems," starting on page 319.*

Unless you're installing a multiboot computer that must share files with MS-DOS or Windows 95 or 98, NTFS is clearly the file system of choice for Windows NT Server.

But a file server is supposed to run all the time, serving files! So it's difficult to imagine many instances when you will install Windows NT Server in a multiboot configuration. Perhaps you might in a laboratory or an experimental setting, but never on a production network file server!

Partitions

Hard disks can have two types of partitions:

- *Primary partitions* are used for booting operating systems. MS-DOS supports only a single primary partition on a given hard disk. If more than one primary partition exists on a hard disk, MS-DOS can read files only in its boot partition (drive C:). NT, however, can use primary partitions for file storage and supports up to four primary partitions on a hard disk (three if an extended partition is also found on the hard disk).

- *Extended partitions* were invented to allow MS-DOS computers to have multiple storage volumes on a hard disk. An extended partition is subdivided into one or more spaces that are designated as logical storage volumes.

If an MS-DOS (or Windows 95 or 98) computer has drives C:, D:, and E: on a single hard disk, drive C: is in the single primary partition that MS-DOS supports. D: and E: are logical drives created in an extended partition.

If you will be running only Windows NT on a computer, you will probably create a single primary partition on your first hard disk, formatting the partition with NTFS. The storage inefficiency of NTFS doesn't increase as volume size increases, so large volumes are preferred.

If you're creating a multiboot system, the computer must be booted using a primary partition that is formatted with FAT. NT can be installed in the boot partition, or it can be installed in its own partition (in which case the boot partition is used only during the boot process).

The Windows NT system requires a boot partition (used to boot the computer) and a system partition (which stores the Windows NT operating system). The boot and system partitions can be the same (in which case both are drive C:), or they can be separate partitions (in which case the boot partition is drive C:).

Viewing NTFS partitions in FDISK

If you view an NTFS partition with the MS-DOS **FDISK** utility, it will be identified as an HPFS volume. HPFS is the *high-performance file system* that was developed for OS/2 and was recognized by NT prior to NT version 4.

Although NT can use C: as the boot and system partitions, the system partition can be located on another hard disk. Here is one example of hard disk partitioning for a multiboot computer:

- **C:**. This is the MS-DOS primary partition used to boot the computer and is formatted with FAT. The system boot files for all operating systems are stored in this partition. MS-DOS and Windows 95 or 98 can be installed in this partition. NT can read files stored in this partition.

- **D:**. This is a Windows NT primary partition, created when NT is installed, and it is formatted with NTFS. The Windows NT system files are stored in this partition. Applications and files used under NT can also be stored in this partition. These files can't be accessed by MS-DOS or Windows 95 or 98 (even if the partition is formatted with FAT) because MS-DOS and Windows 95 and 98 can't access a second primary partition.

There are a few special requirements for the Windows NT system partition:

- At least 90 MB must be available to receive the Windows NT system files. That's a bare minimum, of course. You need more to accommodate applications, log files, and additional Windows NT components you might install in the future.

- The system partition can't be configured as a volume set or a stripe set.

SEE ALSO

➤ *For information on volume sets or stripe sets, see page 319.*

Upgrade Considerations

Nearly any Microsoft operating system can be upgraded to Windows NT 4; MS-DOS, Windows 3.x, Windows for Workgroups, and Windows 95 or 98 can all be upgraded. You can choose either to replace the old operating system or to keep the old with the new and set up a multiboot computer.

Two things must be done to set up a multiboot Windows NT computer:

- The boot partition must be formatted with FAT.
- Windows NT must be installed in its own directory, separate from other operating systems.

When you install Windows NT Server 4 in the same directory as an older version of Windows, the older Windows version is replaced. Some of the old Windows settings will be migrated to Windows NT Server 4. What you keep depends on the version of the old operating system.

For Windows NT version 3.5x, the default system directory was C\Winn35. When you install Windows NT 4 on a computer running Windows NT 3.5x, you have several options on the installation directory:

- You can install Windows NT 4 in its own directory, which is typically C:\Winnt, in which case you are configuring a computer that will dual-boot Windows NT 3.5x and 4. None of the settings from Windows NT 3.5x will be migrated to Windows NT 4.
- You can install Windows NT in C:\Winnt35. This is an upgrade installation, and compatible settings will be migrated from Windows NT 3.5x to Windows NT 4.

Planning the Network Protocols

Network protocols are the rules and codes that computers use to communicate through a network. Windows NT supports three sets of network protocols:

- **TCP/IP.** These are the protocols of the Internet and are the most widely used protocols in the world. However, they are a bit complex, and you need some background knowledge before you can set them up.
- **NWLink.** This is Microsoft's implementation of Novell's IPX and SPX protocols. NWLink is easy to set up and works well, but it can't be used to connect to the Internet or to other TCP/IP networks.

- **NetBEUI.** This is a simple protocol that has long been used on Microsoft network products. NetBEUI is suitable only for small networks that don't require routers.

NWLink and NetBEUI require a bit of explanation but aren't very difficult to understand or manage. I will use NWLink as an example in this chapter.

SEE ALSO
➤ *Both NWLink and NetBEUI are described in greater detail on page 83.*

You will almost certainly work with TCP/IP sometime in the future, but it takes several chapters to properly cover TCP/IP configuration.

SEE ALSO
➤ *Since you're probably eager to get NT up and running, we'll defer discussion of TCP/IP until Chapters 13 through 17.*

Planning the Server's Domain Security Role

Windows NT Server networks use domains to simplify network management and use. A domain is an administrative grouping that collects the shared resources of many computers.

SEE ALSO
➤ *Starting on page 103, you will learn how Windows NT uses domains to organize resources on large groups of computers.*

Within a domain, a Windows NT Server can function in one of three domain security roles:

- Primary domain controller
- Backup domain controller
- Standalone server

The computer's security role is determined when Windows NT Server is installed. You can swap roles between a primary domain controller and a backup domain controller. You can also promote a backup domain controller if the primary domain controller is lost. However, a server can't be turned into a domain controller unless you reinstall NT Server. Therefore, it's important to know the computer's planned role before you start to install Windows NT Server.

Each domain has one or more *domain controllers* that maintain a database defining the resources in a domain. There will always be one *primary domain controller* (PDC) that stores the master copy of the domain database. Additionally, there should be one or more *backup domain controllers* (BDCs) that store extra copies of the domain database. A Windows NT Server can function as a PDC or as a BDC; this is determined when NT Server is installed.

Besides domain controllers, a Windows NT Server computer can function as a *stand-alone server* that shares resources with the network but doesn't store a copy of the domain database.

Options for Starting Setup

When you acquire Windows NT, you receive an installation CD-ROM and three setup floppy disks. The CD-ROM can be either a full license or an upgrade version. The upgrade version can upgrade Windows NT Server 3.5x to 4.0.

NT Setup can be started in several ways; each technique has its advantages. Here's the list of options:

- If you're installing on a computer that has a supported CD-ROM drive, you can initiate setup by booting from the three setup floppy disks that are included with Windows NT.

- If the computer has a CD-ROM drive and is running MS-DOS, Windows 95 or 98, or Windows NT, you can execute the Setup program directly from the installation CD-ROM.

- If the computer is connected to a network, you can install the installation CD-ROM in a shared network drive. MS-DOS, Windows 95, and Windows NT computers can then run the Setup program from the shared CD-ROM drive.

Installing from the Setup Boot Floppy Disks

When you obtain a Windows NT Server license, you receive three Setup floppy disks. To install using the Setup disks, the computer must be equipped with a 3^1/$_2$-inch floppy disk and a CD-ROM drive that is supported by Windows NT. IDE and SCSI CD-ROM drives are supported.

To begin installation, insert the Windows NT CD-ROM into the CD-ROM drive. Then boot the disk labeled "Setup Boot Disk" and follow the prompts.

SEE ALSO

➤ *For details on the setup steps, see the section "Installing Windows NT Server" on page 35 later in this chapter.*

Installing Directly from the CD-ROM

When you initiate installation by executing the Setup program from the installation CD-ROM, there are two versions of the Setup program:

- **Winnt32.exe** is a 32-bit program that you use when running Windows 95 or 98 or Windows NT.
- **Winnt.exe** is a 16-bit program that can be used to initiate Windows NT Setup on a computer that is booted with MS-DOS.

These executable files are stored in the installation CD-ROM in a directory that corresponds to the hardware platform on which NT will be installed. Look for them in the following directories:

- **/Alpha.** Digital's Alpha RISC processor.
- **/I386.** Intel 80386 and later processors.
- **/Mips.** MIPS RISC processor.
- **/Ppc.** Power PC processor.

Each of the setup programs supports two installation methods: rebooting from floppies and rebooting from the hard disk. Let's see how each method works.

Rebooting from Floppies

When you run Winnt32.exe or Winnt.exe, the first installation phase copies all the required installation files as follows:

Changing partitions during setup

If you want to change the partition structure on the hard disk, you must start Setup by booting from the Setup Boot disks. You can't change the partition structure or reformat the partitions when you install directly from the CD-ROM because setup files are copied to the system partition as the first installation step.

■ The files required to reboot the computer and begin the setup process are copied to three floppy disks. These floppy disks are *not* the same as the floppies included when you buy Windows NT Server. They can be used only to continue an installation that was started with the `winnt32` or `winnt` command.

■ All other required installation files are copied to a temporary directory, usually on the computer's C: drive.

After files are copied, you restart the computer and continue the Setup program by booting the system from the boot floppies. Setup then uses the files in the temporary directory to complete the installation process. Because all required files were copied to the temporary directory, the CD-ROM isn't required during the remainder of the setup process. After Setup completes, the temporary directory is deleted.

Rebooting from the Hard Disk

When `Winnt32.exe` or `Winnt.exe` is executed with the `/b` option, the boot files are copied to the hard disk, allowing Setup to continue by booting to the hard disk without needing the boot floppies. This requires more disk space, but it eliminates the need to create the boot floppies. In general, I prefer to install with the `/b` option and skip creation of the boot floppies.

Setup Program Options

When you initiate Setup by running `Winnt32.exe` or `Winnt.exe`, a number of options are available that let you customize the setup process. Some of them are summarized in Table 2.1.

TABLE 2.1 Winnt32.exe and Winnt.exe options

Option	Function
/b	Causes Setup to copy the boot files to the computer's hard disk rather than to floppy disks. With this option, you don't need to boot the system with floppy disks to continue installation.
/ox	Causes Setup to create a set of installation boot floppy disks. These disks are the same as the disks included with the product.

continues…

Time requirements for WINNT and WINNT32

`Winnt.exe` takes about 45 minutes to copy the temporary files. `Winnt32.exe` is much faster. So don't use `Winnt.exe` for setup when you're installing from a 32-bit operating system.

If you already have startup floppies, here's how to skip the floppy creation step

If you already have a set of restart floppy disks, you can skip the step that creates them by including the `/t` flag with the `winnt32` or `winnt` command (for example, `winnt32 /t`).

Understanding the free space requirements for WINNT32 and WINNT

Because `Winnt32.exe` and `Winnt.exe` copy all the required installation files to the temporary directory on the boot partition, you must ensure that considerable free space is found on the drive that will receive the temporary files before starting Setup with one of these commands. You can use the `/t` option to direct the temporary files to a storage volume other than C:. See Table 2.1 for a description of the `/t` option.

TABLE 2.1 **Continued**

Option	Function
/s:*pathname*	Specifies an alternative pathname for the directory that contains the installation files.
/t:*drive_letter*	Forces Setup to place temporary files on a specific drive.
/x	Disables the creation of boot floppies. Use this option when you already have a set of boot floppies.

Options for Locating the CD-ROM Drive

Because Winnt32.exe and Winnt.exe can be executed from the command line, you have a lot of flexibility for locating the installation CD-ROM. This section discusses three options.

Installing from a Windows CD-ROM

If you're running a version of Windows on a computer that has a supported CD-ROM, you can install from the local CD-ROM drive. To perform an installation with a floppy disk reboot, you can simply browse the CD-ROM with your favorite disk utility and run Winnt32.exe or Winnt.exe.

If you want to use any of the setup options, you will need to open a command prompt. Here is an example of a setup command:

```
f:\i386\winnt32.exe /b
```

This example does the following:

- Accesses a CD-ROM that is set up as drive F:.
- Accesses the version of Winnt32.exe that is appropriate for an Intel x86 computer.
- Performs a floppy-free installation where boot files are copied to the C: drive.

Installing from a Shared Network CD-ROM

If you are installing on a computer that has a network connection, you can install from a CD-ROM drive that is shared on the network.

SEE ALSO

➤ *You will learn how to share CD-ROM drives on page 183.*

Suppose that you need to install Windows NT to a computer that doesn't have a CD-ROM drive. The quickest way to connect the computer to the network is to install MS-DOS and to use the Network Client for MS-DOS. You can even put MS-DOS and the network client software on a bootable floppy disk.

Installing Windows NT on an MS-DOS computer using a shared network CD-ROM

1. Insert the Windows NT CD-ROM into the network CD-ROM drive.

2. Share the CD-ROM drive as described in Chapter 6, "Sharing Files."

3. Install MS-DOS on the computer that will receive Windows NT Server. Be sure to create a C: drive with sufficient free space to receive the temporary installation files.

4. Install the MS-DOS client software.

SEE ALSO

➤ *Installing MS-DOS client software is described on page 247 in Chapter 8.*

5. Restart the computer and log on to the network. Connect a drive letter to the shared CD-ROM and make that drive your current drive.

6. Change to the directory that contains the installation files appropriate for your computer. For an Intel x86 computer, you would execute the command CD \i386.

7. Execute the command Winnt.exe /b to begin installation.

8. Proceed to the section "Installing Windows NT Server" for the remainder of the installation procedure.

SEE ALSO

➤ *The section "Installing Windows NT Server" is on page 35.*

Installing from a Shared Network Volume

Actually, the installation files don't even need to be on a CD-ROM. If you have a network server that has sufficient room for the installation files, you can copy the files to the server's hard disks, share the hard disks, and install from there. The setup procedure is simple.

Installing from a shared network volume

1. Create a directory on the server to receive the master installation files. Let's name the directory \NTMaster.

2. Copy the appropriate directory or directories from the installation CD-ROM to \NTMaster. If your clients are equipped with Intel x86 processors, for example, you would copy the directory \I386 from the CD-ROM to \NTMaster.

3. Share \NTMaster as described in Chapter 6, "Sharing Files and Managing File Security."

SEE ALSO

➤ *The procedures for sharing files can be found on page 183.*

4. Install MS-DOS on the computer that will receive Windows NT Server. Be sure to create a C: drive with sufficient free space to receive the temporary installation files.

5. Install the MS-DOS client software as described in Chapter 8, "Activating Network Clients."

SEE ALSO

➤ *Information on activating network clients can be found on page 247.*

6. Restart the computer and log on to the network. Connect a drive letter to the share that contains the installation files, and make that drive your current drive.

7. Change to the directory that contains the installation files appropriate for your computer. For an Intel x86 computer, you would execute the command CD \i386.

8. Execute the command winnt.exe /b to begin installation.

9. Proceed to the section "Installing Windows NT Server" for the remainder of the installation procedure.

SEE ALSO

➤ *The section "Installing Windows NT Server" is on page 35.*

Installing from an Unsupported CD-ROM Drive

Before the industry standardized IDE and SCSI CD-ROM drives, a number of proprietary CD-ROM interfaces were used under MS-DOS. None of these proprietary interfaces are supported under Windows NT. But because the CD-ROM drive is required only when the temporary files are copied, you can even install Windows NT on an MS-DOS computer equipped with a CD-ROM drive that is not supported by Windows NT.

Installing using an unsupported CD-ROM drive

1. Install MS-DOS on the computer. Be sure to create a C: drive with sufficient free space to receive the temporary installation files.

2. Install the necessary CD-ROM drivers and reboot the computer.

3. Insert the Windows NT CD-ROM into the CD-ROM drive.

4. Change the default drive to the CD-ROM drive.

5. Change to the directory that contains the installation files appropriate for your computer. For an Intel x86 computer, you would execute the command CD \i386.

6. Execute the command winnt or winnt.exe /b to begin installation.

7. Proceed to the next section for the remainder of the installation procedure.

Installing Windows NT Server

To simplify this discussion, I have made several assumptions:

- The system partition will be on drive C:.
- This will be a new installation, not an upgrade.
- Windows NT Server will be installed in the directory C:\Winnt.
- The server will be configured as a Primary Domain Controller.

The procedures discussed in this section apply regardless of the method used to start the setup process. Despite the number of steps, Setup is pretty straightforward, and you might find that you can skip much of the discussion.

1: Choosing Installation or Repair

The Welcome to Setup screen branches in two directions:

- Press Enter to continue. This is what you'll do in this section.

- Press R to repair the server. Later in the setup procedures, you will create an Emergency Repair Disk, which lets you use this repair option if crucial server files are damaged and the server can't be started. Repair procedures are described later in this chapter.

SEE ALSO

➤ *See the section "Making Emergency Repairs" later in this chapter on page 58 for the procedure.*

2: Selecting Disk Controller Drivers

Next, Setup must select a disk controller driver. You can do the following:

- Press Enter to have Setup examine your hardware to detect mass storage devices and identify required drivers. I recommend having Setup scan for devices unless you have unsupported hardware.

- Press S to skip detection and select a driver from a list.

If your disk controller is on the supported hardware list, it's easy to allow Setup to detect your hardware and select a driver for you. The only disadvantage is that detection takes a few minutes because Setup loads every available driver and tries them to see if your hardware responds. All the available drivers are tried, even after a match is found, because you might have two or more disk controllers of different brands or models.

Choose to skip detection if either of the following is true:

- You know which driver(s) you need, and it would be faster to choose the driver(s) from a list.

- You are using unsupported hardware and you need to supply drivers on a disk.

Special keys used during setup

In most steps, press Enter to take Microsoft's preferred path through the setup procedure.

Throughout the setup, you have these options:

- Press F1 for help tailored to the step you're executing.

- Press F3 to exit the setup procedure.

2a: Detecting Mass Storage Devices

While Setup scans for mass storage devices, you are prompted to insert Setup Disk 3.

Setup can detect a wide variety of SCSI adapters. If Setup identifies one or more mass storage systems, you will be presented with a list that you can accept or reject. Devices such as IDE and ESDI hard drives don't appear in the list; these drivers are installed in a later step. You have a choice of the following:

- Press Enter to accept the list and continue.
- Press S to specify additional devices. If you choose this option, you will go through the manual driver selection procedure.

2b: Selecting Drivers Manually

If you press S to specify additional devices, Setup presents a scrolling list containing a wide variety of drivers for SCSI host bus adapters.

Loading a driver

1. Scroll through the list by pressing the up and down arrow keys.

2. If the required driver is in the list, highlight it by pressing Enter.

3. If the required driver is not in the list and you have the driver on disk, select the bottom choice, Other (requires disk provided by a hardware manufacturer).

   You are prompted as follows: `Please insert the disk labeled Manufacturer-supplied hardware support disk into drive A:`. Do so and press Enter to load the driver.

4. The driver you selected will be added to the mass storage devices list. You may add other drivers by pressing S.

5. When all required drivers appear in the list, press Enter to continue the installation.

3: Loading More Device Drivers

Setup now test-loads every device driver on the CD-ROM, including IDE, ESDI, and CD-ROM. By the end of this process, Setup will know almost everything about all of your mass storage devices unless you have something really unusual.

4: Choosing Upgrade or New Installation

If Setup detects an existing version of Windows NT on your computer, you will be given the option to upgrade. Make one of the following choices:

- Press Enter to upgrade to Windows NT version 4. Most old configuration options will be retained.
- Press N to replace the existing copy of Windows NT with a new installation of version 4. The old configuration will be lost.

The following discussion assumes a new installation.

5: Identifying Computer Hardware

Next, Setup examines your system to determine its basic hardware configuration. The following characteristics are typical for Intel x86 servers:

Computer: Standard PC

Display: VGA or compatible

Keyboard: XT, AT, or Enhanced Keyboard (83 to 102 keys)

Keyboard Layout: U.S.

Pointing Device: Microsoft Serial Mouse

Setup will probably be right about all this information, but you can change any item by using the up and down arrow keys to select an item and pressing Enter. A list of options will be presented.

If you aren't located in the United States, for example, you might want to select a different international standard for the keyboard layout. You can choose from a considerable number of nationalized keyboard layouts.

When this list is correct, select **The above list matches my computer** and press Enter.

6: Partitioning the Hard Drive

Next, Setup shows a list of the hard drives on your server, along with the partitions on each drive. The first partition on the first drive (Drive 0) is highlighted. This is the default partition for installing Windows NT. You must designate or create a primary partition on this drive to be used as the system partition for Windows NT.

6a: Deleting Existing Partitions

You might want to delete an existing partition by highlighting the partition entry and typing D. This lets you create new partitions if required. You will be asked to confirm your request to delete the partition.

6b: Creating a Partition

Creating a partition

1. Select any area labeled **Unpartitioned space**. When you do so, a new option, **C=Create Partition**, appears at the bottom of the screen.

2. Press C to create a partition.

3. A new screen is presented that declares the minimum size for the new partition (1 MB) and the maximum size (the full capacity of the unpartitioned space).

   In the box labeled **Create partition of size (in MB)**, enter a size for the partition that is in the minimum-to-maximum range.

4. Press Enter.

When you return to the partition list after creating a partition, you will see an entry similar to the following:

```
C:  New (Unformatted)               1016 MB
```

Creating a multiboot configuration by placing the Windows NT system files on a different partition

If you create a new drive such as D: and specify that NT should be installed on the new drive, the Windows NT boot files will be installed on drive C:, and the system files will be installed on the drive you specify.

If drive C: is a FAT volume that contains an existing operating system, you are creating a multiboot configuration.

6c: Selecting a System Partition

You can select either of the following as a Windows NT Server system partition:

- A partition marked `New (Unformatted)`.
- An existing primary partition. Windows NT can be installed over existing software in a FAT or NTFS partition provided that the partition is of sufficient size. (RISC-based servers must start from a FAT partition.)

Select a partition from the partition list and press Enter.

7: Formatting the System Partition

The options you see next depend on whether you have designated a New (Unformatted) partition or a partition that was previously formatted.

7a: Formatting a New (Unformatted) Partition

If you selected a New (Unformatted) partition, you have two choices on the next screen:

- Format the partition using the FAT file system
- Format the partition using the NTFS file system

Select one of these options and press Enter.

7b: Formatting an Existing Partition

If you selected an existing formatted partition in step 7, you will see the following four options:

- Format the partition using the FAT file system
- Format the partition using the NTFS file system
- Convert the partition to NTFS (visible for FAT partitions only)
- Leave the current file system intact (no changes)

Choose the third option to convert a FAT partition to NTFS without losing any files currently stored on the partition. The fourth option retains current files and doesn't change the file system.

Converting FAT partitions to NTFS

NTFS partitions are first formatted with the FAT file system. The first time the server starts after Setup has been completed, the FAT partition will be converted to NTFS.

FAT partitions can also be converted to NTFS at a later time. See "Converting File Systems" in Chapter 10 for the procedure.

8: Selecting a Directory for Windows NT

After the partition is selected and formatted, files can be installed. You will be asked to specify a directory for Windows NT. The default directory is \WINNT. Files will be installed on the system partition that you designated in step 7.

If an existing Windows NT installation is found on the system drive, you have the option of installing in the same directory or designating a separate directory for installation.

9: Examining the Hard Disks

Next, Setup gives you the option of performing an exhaustive secondary examination of your hard disks. For first-time installations in particular, this test should always be performed, even though it can take quite a while on systems equipped with large hard drives.

- Press Enter to have Setup examine your hard disks.
- Press Esc to skip disk examination.

It is unwise to skip the disk examination unless the disk has been tested lately either by Setup or by a third-party testing utility.

10: Copying Files

After the hard disks have been examined, Setup copies files to the system partition.

If you are installing from floppy disks, you will be prompted to change disks as needed.

11: Restarting the Computer

When files have been copied, the computer must be restarted. Remove any floppy disk from drive A and press Enter.

12: Accepting the Software License Agreement

After the computer restarts, you will be shown the first window using the new user interface. If you are familiar with

Place Windows NT in a new directory to multiboot Windows NT and the old operating system

If you retain the existing Windows NT installation and install in a new directory, both versions will be entered into the boot menu, allowing you to multiboot the old OS as well as Windows NT Server 4.

The %SystemRoot% directory

The directory you specify in step 8 will be the root directory for the Windows NT operating system. This directory is often referred to as the %SystemRoot% directory. If you specify \WINNT as the directory for Windows NT system files, %SystemRoot% refers to the directory C:\Winnt.

Windows 95, you will recognize the screen format. If the interface is new to you, you might want to consult the bonus chapter on the CD-ROM called "Making the Transition to the New Interface."

The first window to appear is titled Software License Agreement. Read the license agreement and click **Yes** to continue the installation. If you click **No**, the installation will be halted.

Files are now copied to the installation drive.

Navigating back through Setup

Starting from this point, you can move both forward and backward through the installation procedure. In most cases, you can click **Back** to return to an earlier step and make changes.

13: Continuing Installation

As the next screen explains, the rest of the installation takes place in three stages:

- Gathering information about your computer
- Installing Windows NT Networking
- Finishing Setup

Click **Next** to begin the first stage—gathering information about the computer.

14: Entering Identification Information

After the system restarts, a Windows dialog box appears (see Figure 2.1), requesting the following information:

- **Name** (required)
- **Organization** (optional)

Complete these free-form text entries and click **Next** to continue.

15: Selecting Server Licensing

The next window determines the server licensing mode, which is covered in greater detail later in this chapter. You have two options:

- Choose **Per Server** if you want to license based on concurrent connections to this server. If, for example, you want to support up to 100 concurrent connections to this server, you must purchase 100 client access licenses.

- Choose **Per Seat** if you want to license based on the number of client computers on the network.

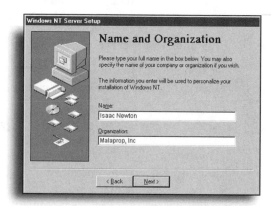

FIGURE 2.1

Installation: Entering identification information.

You might want to take the time to determine the relative costs of these two methods for your network. In general, per server licensing might be the most cost-effective if you have a single server. With per server licensing, however, a client that connects to two or more servers must be equipped with a client access license for each server being accessed concurrently.

If you have two or more servers, per seat licensing might work out better. A client can use a single license to access any number of servers that are configured for per seat licensing.

After selecting a licensing mode, click **Next** to continue.

16: Specifying a Computer Name

Each computer on a Windows network must be assigned a unique name. This can be the name of the primary user of the computer, a designation of the computer's function, or some other meaningful name.

Enter a name in the **Name** box and click Continue. Click Continue to confirm.

Licenses must be configured in the License Administration utility

You must use the License Administration program to specify the number of licenses that have been purchased for your server or network.

17: Selecting a Server Type

Windows NT Server can be installed with one of three configurations. Specify one of the following types in the next dialog box:

- **P̲rimary Domain Controller**
- **Back̲up Domain Controller**
- **S̲tand-Alone Server**

Click **N̲ext** to continue. (The rest of this example assumes that Primary Domain Controller was chosen.)

18: Specifying an Administrator Account Password

If you are installing a PDC, you must specify a password for the Administrator account, which will be given full administrative permissions for the domain that is being created. In the next window, complete the following fields with the password to be assigned to the Administrator user account:

- **P̲assword**
- **C̲onfirm Password**

These entries must match.

The password is optional; you can get away without entering one, which is fine while you're experimenting with Windows NT Server. (Because Setup regards no password as a questionable choice, you will be asked to confirm your decision.) You should be sure to enter a password for any in-service server, however, because the Administrator account has full control over all resources on the server.

Because domains have a global account database, installing a backup domain controller doesn't require you to create an Administrator account. The Administrator account for the domain is used. When installing a BDC in a domain, you must enter the user name and password for a user account that has administrative privileges in the domain.

If you're creating a standalone server (the computer is not joining a domain), you're asked to specify both a user name and a password for the server's administrator account.

Click **N̲ext** to continue.

19: Creating the Emergency Repair Disk

An Emergency Repair Disk contains information about your server's hardware configuration. It can be used to recover the server from corruption in system files that prevents the server from starting up.

When Setup asks you if you want to create an Emergency Repair Disk, you should select **Yes, Create an Emergency Repair Disk (Recommended)** and follow the prompts.

Choose **No, Do Not Create an Emergency Repair Disk** to skip this step. You can create an emergency repair disk later using the RDISK utility.

20: Selecting Components

The next window lets you specify which optional components will be installed. Options are organized into five categories:

- **Accessibility options.** Options that let you configure the cursor, keyboard, sound, display, and mouse. Some of these options are decorative, but some let you make the computer easier for handicapped users to use. For example, you can use sticky keys to help users who can't hold down two keys simultaneously.

- **Accessories.** Here are 14 optional accessories, such as the Calculator and Character Map utilities familiar from Windows 3.x. Also included are new utilities such as the Internet Jumpstart Kit, which provides a World Wide Web browser. All are briefly described in the Description box.

- **Communications.** Here you select from the following utilities: Chat, HyperTerminal (a modem communication program), and Phone Dialer.

- **Games.** Four games are available: Freecell, Minesweeper, Pinball, and Solitaire. By default, none are selected.

- **Microsoft Exchange.** Installs client software for Internet Mail, Microsoft Exchange (an integrated mail and messaging application), and Microsoft Mail.

■ **Multimedia.** A variety of applications for playing multimedia sound and video clips. None of these should be required for a dedicated server.

It is recommended that you install Windows NT Server on a computer that will be dedicated to providing network services. Users should not be playing games, sound, or video on a dedicated server computer. Therefore, the options you will require from this window are very limited. Pick and choose carefully.

Click **Next** when components have been selected.

21: Beginning Network Installation

Next, you will be shown an installation status screen. The next task, which will be highlighted, is **2) Installing Windows NT Networking**. Click **Next** to continue.

22: Specifying the Network Connection

In the next window, shown in Figure 2.2, you specify how the computer will connect to the network. The following choices are given:

■ **Wired to the network**. The computer can connect to the network through a network adapter card (such as Ethernet or token ring) or via an ISDN connection.

■ **Remote access to the network**. The computer connects to the network through a modem. If you choose this option, you will be required to install Remote Access Service (RAS).

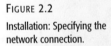

FIGURE 2.2
Installation: Specifying the network connection.

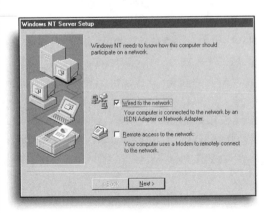

SEE ALSO

➤ See Chapter 20, "Setting Up a Remote Access Server," on page 595, for information about RAS configuration and usage.

You can check either or both of these options. Click **Next** to continue.

23: Installing the Internet Information Server

The Internet Information Server (IIS) includes a variety of components that let a Windows NT Server provide services on TCP/IP networks. World Wide Web, FTP, and Gopher servers are included.

In the next window, select **Install Microsoft Internet Information Server** if you want to set up an Internet server. Click **Next** to continue. This chapter assumes that the IIS is not installed.

SEE ALSO

➤ See Chapter 19, "Setting Up a World Wide Web Server," on page 563 for information about IIS.

24: Setting Up Network Cards

A primary or backup domain controller must have a network card because it must attach to the network before its domain security role can be established. Servers don't require network cards during setup, but you will need to install one later to enable network communication.

Setup has a sophisticated capability to scan your computer, identify network cards, and determine their settings. You can take advantage of this capability in the next dialog box.

It is recommended that you choose **Start Search** to use automatic card detection, which is described in step 24a.

Choose **Select from list** to skip card detection and go to step 24b or to skip card detection altogether.

24a: Using Automatic Card Detection

If Setup is able to identify your adapter card, the name of the adapter will be added to the **Network Adapters** box, as shown in Figure 2.3.

TCP/IP is required for IIS

The Internet Information Server requires the TCP/IP protocols. If you choose to install IIS, be prepared to configure TCP/IP as described in Chapter 16. This requires some planning, so don't install the IIS without doing the necessary up-front work.

- Click **Next** to accept the entry and continue with the next installation step.

- Remove the check mark to ignore the entry.

- Click **Find Next** to find another card if more than one is installed. (If your cards all use the same drivers, you don't need to click **Find Next**.) You can activate only one card at this stage in the setup. Additional cards can be installed in step 24: Setting Up Network Cards.

- Click **Select from list** to select another card manually.

FIGURE 2.3

Installation: A network adapter has been selected for installation.

24b: Selecting Network Adapters Manually

If you chose **Select from list** in step 24a, you can use the Select Network Adapter dialog box, shown in Figure 2.4, to select a driver from the **Network Adapter** list. In addition to seeing drivers for supported hardware, you can click **Have Disk** if you have a floppy disk that includes drivers for your adapter. You will be prompted to specify the drive letter and path where the driver files can be found.

After you select a network adapter, click **OK**. Click **Cancel** to skip manual adapter selection. Either option returns you to the network adapter setup screen, where you click **Next** to continue.

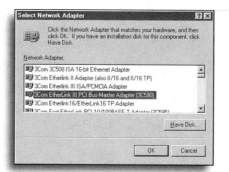

FIGURE 2.4

Installation: Selecting a network adapter manually.

25: Selecting Protocols

Next, Setup presents the dialog box shown in Figure 2.5, which has check boxes for three protocols:

- **TCP/IP Protocol**. This option is checked by default. If you choose it, you must be prepared to configure the adapter.

- **NWLink IPX/SPX Compatible Transport**. This option is checked by default.

- **NetBEUI Protocol**. This option is not checked by default and is not required. Enable it only if you require NetBEUI compatibility with existing systems.

Check your drivers

Windows NT 4 has been out for quite a while now, and new versions have been issued for many of the hardware drivers. You should check with the vendor to determine if you are installing the latest drivers for your hardware. Fortunately, this is easy to do in most cases, because most manufacturers now publish their drivers through their Web sites.

FIGURE 2.5

Installation: Selecting protocols to be installed.

SEE ALSO

➤ *TCP/IP adapter configuration involves many parameters, and you should be familiar with Chapters 13 through 18 (Part II) before you start configuring TCP/IP on your own.*

➤ *NWLink and NetBEUI configuration procedures are discussed in Chapter 3.*

You can click **Select from list** to obtain additional choices:

- **DLC Protocol**. This option supports printing to HP printers that are connected directly to the network.

- **Point-to-Point Tunneling Protocol**. This protocol is used to support secure private communication on public networks such as the Internet.

SEE ALSO

➤ *Point-to-Point Tunneling Protocol is explained in Chapter 20, "Setting Up a Remote Access Server."*

- **Streams Environment**. This option supports applications written to the AT&T application programming interface. Check this option if you are running applications requiring streams.

- **Have Disk**. Click this button if you want to install another protocol from a disk.

Check the desired protocols and click **Next** to continue the installation.

26: Adding Network Components

The next dialog box, shown in Figure 2.6, lists the network components that will be installed. You can't remove components at this time, but you can add them by clicking **Select from list**.

27: Installing Network Components

In the next dialog box, click **Next** to install the network components you have selected.

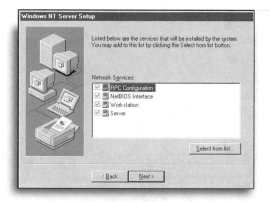

FIGURE 2.6
Installation: Selecting network services.

28: Configuring the Network Adapter

Next, you will be shown the Network Card Setup dialog box. Here, you must specify the hardware settings for your adapter card, such as the IRQ and I/O port address.

Be careful when making these settings. Incorrect settings prevent the computer from communicating with the network and can cause installation to fail. Setup is unable to verify that the settings you enter are correct. (Windows NT does not provide support for Plug and Play devices and can't automatically configure these devices or determine their settings.)

Click **OK** when the settings are correct. The driver will be installed for the network adapter.

29: Copying Files

All required files are now copied to the computer.

30: Review Bindings

You can now review the bindings that have been established. A binding is a chain of drivers that are linked to a given service. You can disable a binding by selecting it and clicking **Disable**.

Click **Next** to continue.

You can't back up after the driver is installed

You can't back up once the driver is installed because Setup can't unload the driver.

If you want to use DHCP

If TCP/IP protocols are being installed, you have the option of having the IP address and other settings established by a DHCP server. If your network already includes a DHCP server and you want to obtain settings from DHCP, click **Yes** at the TCP/IP Setup prompt. DHCP is discussed in Chapter 17, "Simplifying Administration with DHCP."

If you select "Remote access to the network"

If you selected **Remote access to the network** in step 22, RAS must be installed and configured at this time. See Chapter 20, "Setting Up a Remote Access Server," for RAS installation procedures.

31: Start the Network

Next, you have two choices:

- Click **Next** to start the network and continue the setup.
- Click **Back** to stop the network if it is running.

You must click **Next** to continue the setup.

32: Configuring the Computer Name

The contents of the next window depend on the server type. Figure 2.7 shows the window used to configure a primary domain controller. Three sets of options can appear:

- If you're configuring a primary domain controller, you must enter values in the **Computer Name** and **Domain** fields. If the domain you specify doesn't exist, it will be created and this computer will be established as the PDC. If the domain already exists, you must specify another domain name.

- If you're configuring a backup domain controller, you will see four fields: **Computer Name**, **Domain**, **Administrator Name**, and **Administrator Password**. The administrator name and password you specify will be used to add this computer to the domain you specify, where it will be configured as a BDC. If the username and password you enter do not have administrator privileges in the domain, the computer can't be added.

- If you're configuring a standalone server, you will see four fields: **Computer Name**, **Domain**, **Administrator Name**, and **Administrator Password**. The administrator name and password you specify will be used to add this computer to the domain you specify, where it will be configured as a standalone server. If the username and password you enter do not have administrator privileges in the domain, the computer can't be added.

Click **Next** to continue.

FIGURE 2.7
Installation: Entering the computer identification.

33: Finishing Setup

The next window informs you that you are at **step 3, Finishing Setup**. Click **Finish** to continue. The computer will be configured to run Windows NT.

34: Entering Date and Time Properties

The next window is titled Date/Time Properties.

Select the **Date & Time** tab to configure the system clock.

Select the **Time Zone** tab and choose a time zone from the list provided. Be sure to check the box **Automatically adjust for daylight saving changes** if that's appropriate for your locale. This check box will be deactivated for some time zone choices, such as **Indiana (East)**.

Click **Close** to accept the settings and continue.

35: Configuring the Display

Setup won't let you configure a video display setting that is nonfunctional with your equipment. Setup attempts to detect your video card, and the Detected Display information box shows you the hardware it identifies. Click **OK** to continue.

The next dialog box, Display Properties, is shown in Figure 2.8. It lets you select settings that are appropriate to your display type.

FIGURE 2.8
Installation: Configuring the display.

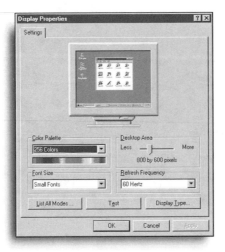

Setting the video display mode

1. Confirm that the adapter that Setup has identified is correct. If not, choose **Display Type** and select a different video adapter.

2. Select the video display modes you want by setting appropriate values in the **Color Palette**, **Desktop Area**, **Font Size**, and **Refresh Frequency** fields. Be sure that the settings you choose are supported by your monitor. Incorrect settings can damage your monitor circuitry.

3. Click **Test**. Setup displays a grid that tests the display mode you have selected. After a few seconds, the grid is cleared.

4. After the test, you will see the prompt Did you see the test bit map properly? If the display appeared to be correct, click **Yes** to confirm that it functioned properly. Then click **OK**. This mode can then be selected for the display adapter.

5. Some trial and error might be required to identify the best settings for your monitor. Keep going until you find a mode that passes the test. You can't select a mode that you haven't identified as OK.

6. After selecting a video display mode, click **OK** in the Display Properties dialog box.

Setup now saves the configuration for the server and proceeds through several configuration procedures.

36: Creating the Emergency Repair Disk

If you clicked **Yes** to create an emergency repair disk (recommended) in step 19, you will be prompted to insert a floppy disk labeled Emergency Repair Disk. Any information on this disk will be overwritten.

Insert a floppy disk in the floppy drive and click **OK**. The Emergency Repair Disk will be created.

37: Restarting the Computer

Next, you will need to restart the computer. Remove all floppy disks and click **Restart Computer** to continue.

The first time a new server restarts, the process might be lengthy. For one thing, if you specified that the system domain should use NTFS files, the FAT partition that was created during setup must be converted to NTFS.

Installation is now complete. The server will restart.

Logging On and Off, Restarting, and Shutting Down the Server

After the server restarts, the Begin Logon box invites you to press Ctrl+Alt+Delete to log on. Unless you have used NT before, it might seem odd to use Ctrl+Alt+Delete for a purpose other than booting the computer, but this is actually an important NT security feature. Pressing Ctrl+Alt+Delete always directs NT to a place in the Windows NT kernel that can't be modified by outside programs, and consequently to a place that is immune from viruses, Trojan horses, and other nasties. This makes it impossible (theoretically, at least) for an intruder to install program code that intercepts your username and password when you log on to Windows NT.

After you give the computer this "three-finger salute," you will see a Logon Information dialog box.

To log on, supply the following information:

- **User name.** If this is the first time a primary domain controller has been started, only the Administrator account will exist.

- **Password.** For new PDCs, this password was declared during step 17 of the setup.

- **Domain.** This is the domain you want to log on to. By default, this will be the domain you declared in step 17.

The first time you log on, you will see the Welcome to Windows NT dialog box. If you don't want to see it again, remove the check mark from the box **Show the Welcome Screen next time you start Windows NT**.

To log off, press Ctrl+Alt+Delete any time when you are logged on. Unlike with DOS, the Ctrl+Alt+Delete key sequence doesn't immediately reboot the system. Instead, it produces the Windows NT Security dialog box, shown in Figure 2.9. This dialog box has the following options:

- **Lock Workstation.** Choose this option to lock the station when you're logged on. You will stay logged on, so processes will continue to run, but you will have to enter your user password to regain access to your session.

- **Change Password.** Choose this option to change your password.

- **Logoff.** Logs out of the current session and displays the Welcome banner.

- **Task Manager.** Displays a list of running tasks and lets you switch to a task or end a task. This option is especially useful to cancel a task that has hung or malfunctioned.

- **Shut Down.** This option gives you two further options:

    - **Shutdown.** After Windows NT performs a controlled shutdown, the server doesn't restart. Use this option if you need to turn the server off.

- **Shutdown and Restart.** Use this option if you have made changes that require a server restart to be activated.

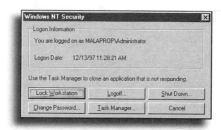

FIGURE 2.9
The Windows NT Security dialog box.

Initiating a shutdown from the Start menu

1. From the **Start** menu, choose **Shut Down**.

2. In the Shut Down Windows dialog box, select one of the following options:

- **Shut down the computer?**
- **Restart the computer?**
- **Close all programs and log on as a different user?**

3. Click **Yes** to execute the selected action. Click **No** to return to Windows.

Reinstalling Windows NT

There are many times when you will need to reinstall Windows NT. Here are a few examples:

- You need to upgrade Windows NT to a newer version.
- You need to change a computer's domain role. You can't upgrade a server to a domain controller without reinstalling Windows NT, for example.
- You need to repair some damaged files.
- You need to establish a computer as a backup domain controller in a different domain.

A reinstallation isn't that different from a new installation. The chief difference is that Setup detects the presence of an existing

Computer names and security IDs

When a Windows NT computer is installed in a domain, it is identified by two different things:

- A name, which is provided to simplify the network for users. The computer name can be specified by the network administrator, during installation or at a later time.

- A *security ID* (SID), a long number that is the identifying characteristic actually used in the domain to regulate security. The SID is established by the Setup program. It can't be modified or re-created.

When you perform a New Version installation, a new SID is created for the computer. Therefore, even though the computer might retain its old name, the SID changes and the computer has a new identity.

To repeat, *any time you perform a New Version installation, a new SID is established and the computer's domain ID changes.*

Because of this, any New Version installation of a Windows NT computer essentially creates a new computer. The computer's old identity can't be recovered. Therefore, you should perform a New Version installation only after carefully considering the impact of the change on the computer's SID.

copy of Windows NT. After that, you can go down two distinct paths:

- You choose **New Version** to replace the current operating system. All old settings are lost. This is a destructive reinstallation. A New Version installation is required to make certain changes—for example, to change the computer's domain security role.

- You choose **Upgrade installation** to upgrade an existing copy of NT, retaining the settings of the old version. This is a nondestructive reinstallation. An Upgrade installation can be used to repair files and to upgrade the operating system version. It can't be used to change the computer's security role or to make fundamental changes such as the location of the system partition.

Making Emergency Repairs

During setup step 32, you have the option of creating an Emergency Repair Disk (ERD). This is a special disk containing a variety of files that can be used to repair Windows NT when files are corrupted or lost.

The ERD contains copies of various critical configuration files, including some of the most important information in the Registry. The Registry is the central configuration database for Windows NT. Although the Registry is very robust, it can be damaged, and an updated ERD can be used to restore the Registry to a pristine, working condition.

SEE ALSO

➤ *You will learn all about the Registry in Chapter 22, "Editing the Registry."*

Your system configuration changes fairly frequently, and many of these changes affect files that are stored on the ERD. Therefore, before showing you how to use the ERD to repair your system, I want to show you how to create an up-to-date ERD.

Updating the Emergency Repair Disk

Windows NT includes the Repair Disk Utility (Rdisk.exe), which is used to create and update the ERD. As vital as it is, Rdisk doesn't have an entry on the **Start** menu. You can run it from the **Run** entry on the **Start** menu, but you will probably choose to add a shortcut to your desktop or to the **Start** menu so that you can start Rdisk easily.

SEE ALSO

➤ *For more information on how to create program shortcut icons, see page 783.*

You should update the ERD whenever the system prompts you to (for example, when file volumes are changed) or when any significant change is made to the system configuration (such as a change to the hardware or a manual change to a Registry setting).

Updating the Emergency Repair Disk

1. Start Rdisk.exe. The Repair Disk Utility is shown in Figure 2.10.

FIGURE 2.10
The Repair Disk Utility.

2. Click **Update Repair Info**. This creates a directory named %SystemRoot%\repair that contains duplicate Registry repair information as well as information that can't fit on the ERD floppy disk.

3. When prompted, insert a floppy disk to receive the emergency repair information. The disk will be formatted, and files will be copied to it.

4. Label the disk, identifying the computer on which it was created and the date. Place the disk in a secure location. (The disk contains critical security information and should be carefully guarded.)

Now that you have a current ERD, you can repair the NT installation should the need arise.

Performing an Emergency Repair

To repair the Windows NT installation, you need an up-to-date ERD and the Windows NT CD-ROM.

Repairing the Windows NT installation

1. Start a Windows NT installation using your choice of methods. Perhaps the easiest to use are the Setup boot disks.

2. When the prompt is offered, press R to repair the system.

3. Select the actions you want the repair to perform. Here are your choices:
   - Inspect Registry Files
   - Inspect startup environment
   - Verify Windows NT System Files
   - Inspect boot sector

   After checking the actions to be performed, click **Continue** and press Enter.

4. Setup is now at step 3, as described earlier in this chapter. Proceed through step 5.

5. You will be prompted to supply an Emergency Repair Disk. At this point, you have two options:
   - Press Enter if you have an Emergency Repair Disk.
   - Press Esc if you don't have an Emergency Repair Disk. Setup will do its best to repair Windows NT by looking for files on the hard drive. (At this point, it will attempt to use files in the %SystemRoot%\repair directory.)

6. Insert the Emergency Repair Disk when you are prompted to do so. Then follow the prompts.

7. When Setup is prepared to restore Registry files, select which of the following Registry areas you want recovered:
   - SYSTEM (System Configuration)
   - SOFTWARE (Software Information)

- DEFAULT (Default User Profile)
- SECURITY (Security Policy) and SAM (User Accounts Database)

Click **Continue** and press Enter to restore Registry settings.

8. If Setup identifies a version problem with a file, you are given the following options:

- Press Esc if you don't want to repair the file. You might want to skip the repair if you have installed an updated copy of the file since Windows NT was initially set up.
- Press Enter to repair the file. The file will be restored to the version on the Windows NT Server CD-ROM.
- Press A to repair all files.

9. When repairs are complete, remove the ERD and restart the system.

Installing Service Packs

Microsoft occasionally issues updates for products in the form of Service Packs. Service Packs can be obtained in several ways:

- They can be downloaded from Microsoft's Web site (http://www.microsoft.com).
- The are included in the Microsoft TechNet subscription CD-ROMs.
- In some cases, a Service Pack is included with a new Windows NT add-in that requires a certain Service Pack level.

Windows NT 4 is quite stable as it ships, so you don't necessarily need to install any Service Packs. When a new Service Pack ships, review its technical description to determine whether it is required in your installation. Some new Windows NT add-ins require Service Packs. Internet Information Server version 4 requires Windows NT Service Pack 3, for example.

Don't rush to install the latest Service Pack as soon as it becomes available on Microsoft's Web site. Wait a few weeks

How emergency repair affects the Registry

The Emergency Repair process restores the Registry to its state when the ERD was last updated. Any changes made to the Registry since the last ERD update will be lost.

for bug reports to filter out through the media. Service Pack 2 for Windows NT introduced numerous bugs and quickly earned a bad reputation.

Each Service Pack seems to have its own installation procedure, so I can't provide general guidelines here. Review the documents included with the Service Pack for instructions.

To determine the Service Pack level for a computer, open My Computer. Then, from the **Help** menu, choose **About Windows NT.** The About Windows NT box, shown in Figure 2.11, describes the operating system version level, including any installed Service Packs.

FIGURE 2.11

The About Windows NT box describes the Windows NT version and Service Pack level.

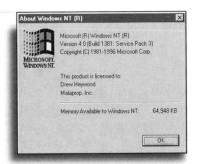

Managing Windows NT Client Licenses

Microsoft's licensing agreement requires you to purchase licenses for clients who connect to your Windows NT Servers. Licenses are not included when you purchase a copy of Windows 3.x, 95, 98, or Windows NT Workstation, and you must purchase an appropriate number of licenses. How many licenses you need depends on the licensing method you select.

When you install Windows NT Server, you are asked to declare a licensing method (see step 15). You have two choices:

- **Per server**. You declare the maximum number of users who can log on to each server and buy that number of licenses.

- **Per seat**. You must purchase a license for each user on your network.

With per server licensing, you declare a maximum number of users who are permitted on a given server and then purchase that number of licenses. Per server licensing is typically chosen when the organization has a single server or, if there are multiple servers, when each user logs on to one and only one server. Under per server licensing, a user who logs on to two servers requires an available license on each server.

Per seat licensing is typically chosen when many users simultaneously access two or more servers. In such cases, one license permits one user to access any number of Windows NT Server computers. If per seat licensing is chosen, you must purchase a license for each user on your network, regardless of the number of servers that are accessed by a given user.

The License Database

Windows NT Server maintains a distributed database that records the licenses that have been obtained for a network. Licenses can be recorded on any Windows NT Server computer, but that makes it difficult for the administrator to keep track of the number of licenses that have been obtained and how those licenses are being used.

To centralize license administration, you can choose to maintain an *enterprise license server*. If the network has more than one domain, license information for each domain is replicated to a *domain license server* that is located on the PDC for the domain. Then the license information is replicated from the domain license server to a single enterprise license server that has a complete record of the licenses for the entire organization. Figure 2.12 shows how licenses are collected first to the domain license servers on the domain PDCs (WIDGETS1 and DOODADS1) and then to MALAPROP1, which is functioning as the enterprise license server.

Selecting a licensing mode

If you can't decide which licensing method to use, start with per seat licensing. You can make a one-time switch from per server to per seat licensing if you decide that per seat licensing is preferable.

Licensing other Microsoft products

Other Microsoft products require their own licenses, such as SQL Server and Exchange Server. These licenses are managed similarly to client licenses for Windows NT Server.

FIGURE 2.12

Licenses can be replicated to maintain a centralized license database.

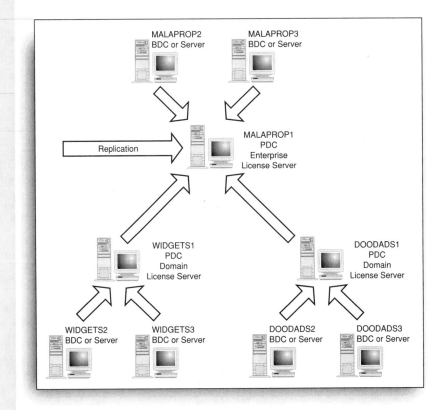

Managing Per Server Licensing

When per server licensing is used, licenses are installed "from the bottom up." Licenses are installed on each individual server, and a license can be used only on the server on which the license is installed. If you purchase 50 licenses for server WIDGETS2, a maximum of 50 people can log on to WIDGETS2 at any given time. After licenses are installed on the individual servers, license replication can then be used to maintain a central domain or enterprise license server database. When installing per server licensing, perform the following procedure on each server.

Installing per server licensing

1. Open the Licensing applet in the Control Panel. You see the dialog box shown in Figure 2.13.

FIGURE 2.13
The licensing applet.

2. If multiple licensed products are installed on this server, select the desired product from the **Product** list.

3. The **Per Server for** *x* **concurrent connections** radio button must be selected. This setting is determined when Windows NT Server is set up.

4. To add licenses, do the following:

    a. Click **Add Licenses** to open the New Client Access License dialog box, shown in Figure 2.14.

    b. Enter the total number of licenses you have purchased in the **Quantity** field and click **OK**. A licensing agreement will be displayed.

    c. Check the **I agree that** check box to consent to the licensing agreement, and click **OK** to return to the Choose Licensing Mode dialog box.

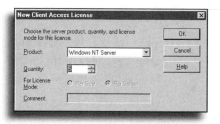

FIGURE 2.14
Adding new client licenses.

5. To remove licenses, do the following:

    a. Click **Remove Licenses** to open the Select Certificate to Remove Licenses dialog box, shown in Figure 2.15.

    b. Select a product from the **Installed Certificates** list. Notice that the **Quantity** column indicates the number of licenses that have been added for this product.

c. Enter the total number of licenses to be removed in the **Number of Licenses to remove** field.

d. Click **Remove**.

e. Close the dialog box.

FIGURE 2.15

Removing per server licenses.

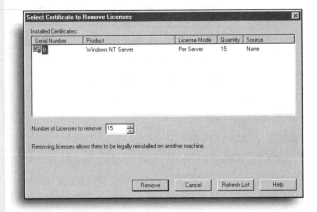

6. If necessary, configure license replication as described in the section "Managing License Replication."

Managing Per Seat Licensing

If you have chosen to use per seat licensing, you must purchase a Windows NT Server client license for each client computer on your network. If you have purchased 100 licenses and you configure per seat licensing, 100 users can simultaneously access an unlimited number of servers.

When per seat licensing is used, licenses are installed "from the top down." Licenses are installed on a license server, after which they are added to individual servers on a per seat basis. As licenses are used, utilization data is replicated up to the license server, which ensures that maximum license counts are not exceeded.

Selecting the per seat licensing mode

1. Open the Licensing applet in the Control Panel.

2. If multiple licensed products are installed on this server, select the desired product from the **Product** list.

3. If the **Per Server** radio button is selected, select the **Per Seat** radio button.

4. Read the License Violation dialog box, shown in Figure 2.16. If you still want to change to per seat licensing, click **No**. Click **Yes** to revert to per server licensing.

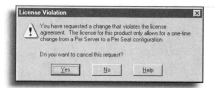

FIGURE 2.16
Verifying the change from per server to per seat licensing.

After you have configured per seat licensing on the desired servers, configure license replication as described in the next section. Then add licenses as described in the section "Monitoring Your Licenses."

Managing License Replication

If you have more than one Windows NT Server computer on your network, license replication can be used to coordinate licenses across your network. When per server licensing is used, license replication collects information about your licenses on a central computer, where they can be conveniently monitored. When per seat licensing is used, license replication collects information about how those licenses are used across the network.

Before you configure license replication, you must do some planning. In any domain, the PDC will function as the domain license server, collecting license data from other servers in the domain. If your organization has more than one domain, the PDC for one domain will function as an enterprise license server, collecting license data from all the domain license servers on your enterprise network.

Configuring license replication for a server

1. Open the Licensing applet in the Control Panel.

2. Click **Replication** to open the Replication Configuration dialog box, shown in Figure 2.17.

FIGURE 2.17

Configuring license replication.

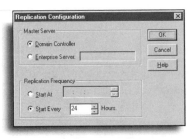

3. If this computer is the enterprise license server, select **Domain Controller**. Also select **Domain Controller** if this computer is the PDC in a single-domain network. (The **Domain Controller** setting specifies that this computer is the end point of the replication chain and doesn't need to replicate licenses to any other computer.)

4. If this computer is a BDC or a standalone server, select **Enterprise Server** and enter the name of the PDC for the domain.

5. If this computer is a PDC that replicates its database to an enterprise license server, select **Enterprise Server** and enter the name of the enterprise license server.

6. You have two options for scheduling license replication:

   - **Start at** *time*. Select this radio button to specify a time at which replication will take place. Then enter a time in the time field. This option lets you replicate once per day at a time when the network is experiencing little use.

   - **Start Every** *x* **Hours**. Select this radio button if replication should take place at specified intervals during the day. Then specify an hour interval in the spin box. (The default interval is 24 hours.) This option lets you replicate licenses once or more throughout the day.

7. Click **OK** when replication has been configured.

Monitoring Your Licenses

The Administrative Tools Group contains a shortcut for the License Manager, which is used to monitor the status of your

Microsoft licenses. This utility has four tabs that let you view different aspects of your licenses.

The Purchase History Tab

The **Purchase History** tab is shown in Figure 2.18. This tab lists the licenses purchased for your network.

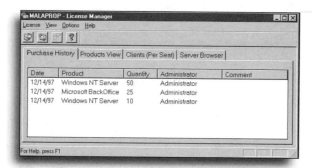

The Products View Tab

The **Products View** tab, shown in Figure 2.19, lists licenses organized by product. Use this information to determine whether you have purchased sufficient licenses for per seat licenses or whether you are running out of licenses on a particular server.

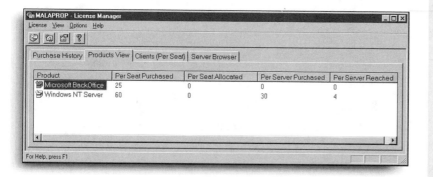

The Clients (Per Seat) Tab

The **Clients (Per Seat)** tab is shown in Figure 2.20. This tab focuses on per seat licenses and describes the licensed and unlicensed usage for each user.

FIGURE 2.20

Viewing per seat licenses.

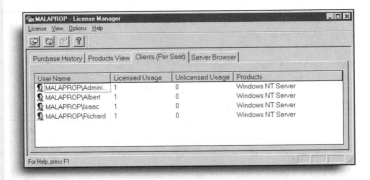

FIGURE 2.20

Viewing per seat licenses.

The Server Browser Tab

The Server Browser tab, shown in Figure 2.21, lets you examine the licenses installed on any server in the enterprise. You can also add per seat licenses and configure license groups.

In Figure 2.21, the Enterprise tree has been expanded. You can select any server in the tree to display the server's license status.

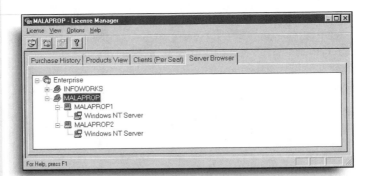

FIGURE 2.21

Viewing the licenses for a particular server.

Adding Per Seat Licenses

Adding per seat licenses from the Server Browser tab

1. From the **License** menu, choose **New License** to open the New Client Access License dialog box, shown in Figure 2.22.

2. Select the product to be licensed in the **Product** field.

FIGURE 2.22
Adding per seat licenses.

3. Specify the number of licenses to be added in the **Quantity** field.

4. When the license agreement is presented, accept it by checking the **OK** box.

5. If desired, enter a descriptive statement in the **Comment** field.

6. Click **OK.**

Setting Up License Groups

Ordinarily, license usage is reported on the basis of one license per user. But what if users share a computer? You don't want those users taking up two of your client licenses, do you?

License groups allow your users to share licenses. When users are members of a license group, they can use the same license and take turns using the network.

You can't work with user accounts until some user accounts have been created. I put this section here for completeness. If you need to create license groups, see the procedures described in Chapter 5, "Adding Users and Groups." Then return here after you have created the user accounts that will be affected.

Creating a New License Group

Creating a license group

1. Open the License Manager utility.

2. From the **Options** menu, choose **Advanced** and then **New License Group**. This opens the New License Group dialog box, shown in Figure 2.23.

FIGURE 2.23
Adding a license group in
License Manager.

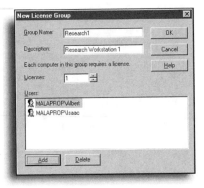

3. Enter a name for the license group in the **Group Name** field.

4. Enter a description for the group in the **Description** field (optional).

5. Enter the number of licenses allocated to this group in the **Licenses** field.

6. Click **Add** to open an Add Users dialog box like the one shown in Figure 2.24.

FIGURE 2.24
Adding users to a license
group.

7. Pull down the **List Users from** list box to select the source of the user accounts that should be listed in the **Users** list:

   • Choose <Enterprise Server> to list users known to the domain managed by the enterprise license server.

- Choose a domain name to list users who have accounts in a specific domain.

The **U**sers list lists all user names that are recorded in the domain you specify.

8. To add a user to the group, select the user name in the **U**sers list and click **A**dd.

9. To remove a user from the group, select the user name from the **Add Us**e**rs** list and click **D**elete.

10. Click **OK** to add the users listed in the **Add Us**e**rs** list to the license group.

Editing a New License Group

Editing a license group

1. From the **Options** menu, choose **Advanced**, and then choose **E**dit **License Group** to open the License Groups dialog box, shown in Figure 2.25.

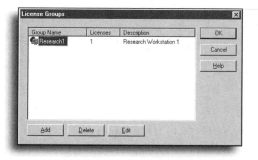

FIGURE 2.25
Editing license groups.

2. To change the members of the group, select a group and click **E**dit.

3. To remove a group, select a group and click **D**elete.

4. To add a new group, click **A**dd and follow the instructions in the preceding section.

Customizing the Windows NT Boot Process

The Windows NT boot process is controlled by entries in the following places:

- The boot.ini file, used on Intel x86 platforms
- The Registry, used on all Windows NT platforms

This section will show you how to modify these resources to customize the boot sequence.

The *boot.ini* File

boot.ini is a text file that is stored in the root directory of drive C. boot.ini is created by the Setup program and is assigned the Read Only and System attributes.

To modify the boot.ini file, use Explorer to remove the Read Only and System attributes. The file can then be modified with any text editor, such as Notepad.

Here is a typical boot.ini file:

```
[boot loader]
timeout=30
default=multi(0)disk(0)rdisk(0)partition(2)\WINNT35
[operating systems]
multi(0)disk(0)rdisk(0)partition(2)\WINNT35="Windows NT
➥Server Version 3.51"
multi(0)disk(0)rdisk(0)partition(2)\WINNT35="Windows NT
➥Server Version 3.51 [VGA mode]" /basevideo /sos
```

Before the boot.ini file can be examined in detail, you need to examine the ARC (Advanced RISC Computer) names that are used to identify partitions on hard drives in the boot.ini file and how the ARC names are used to identify the startup directories for operating systems.

ARC Naming Conventions

Partitions on Intel x86 Windows NT computers are identified in the boot.ini file by ARC naming conventions, which define the hard disk and partition on which the operation system resides. An example of an ARC name is `multi(0)disk(0)rdisk(0)` `partition(2)`. Before examining the details of the `boot.ini` file, you need to take a look at how devices are identified using ARC names.

ARC Name Syntax

All Intel x86 SCSI systems use a BIOS that translates the internal format of the SCSI drive to the format understood by the computer. From the computer's viewpoint, the SCSI drive looks like a conventional drive, such as an IDE drive. Therefore, the settings used in `boot.ini` are the same for all drives installed on x86 systems.

On x86 computers, all devices, including devices attached to SCSI adapters whose BIOS is enabled, are defined in `boot.ini` using the following format:

```
multi (a) disk (b) rdisk (c) partition (d)
```

RISC computers are more comfortable with SCSI devices, and a SCSI BIOS is not required. When the BIOS is not enabled for a SCSI adapter, devices attached to the SCSI bus are identified by ARC names with the following format:

```
scsi (a) disk (b) rdisk (c) partition (d)
```

When the BIOS is disabled for a SCSI adapter, the `scsi` keyword is used in the ARC names for devices serviced by the adapter. NTLDR can't use the SCSI adapter's BIOS to access attached devices; NTLDR loads `NTBOOTDD.SYS` to access the devices.

ARC Name Examples

Consider the first SCSI hard disk (the one with the lowest SCSI address—typically address 0), attached to the first SCSI adapter on a system, whose BIOS is enabled. If this disk has three partitions, the partitions would have the following ARC names:

```
multi(0)disk(0)rdisk(0)partition(1)
multi(0)disk(0)rdisk(0)partition(2)
multi(0)disk(0)rdisk(0)partition(3)
```

ARC name keywords and parameters

Here are descriptions of the keywords and parameters in an ARC name:

- `scsi`/`multi` (*a*) identifies the hardware adapter, where *a* is the ordinal number of the adapter. The first adapter is assigned the ordinal number 0, the second is assigned the ordinal number 1, and so on.

- `disk` (*b*) identifies the device's address on the SCSI bus. When the `multi` keyword is used, *b* will always be 0.

- `rdisk` (*c*) identifies the ordinal number of the disk when the `multi` keyword is used. For the first disk, *c* will be 0. When the `scsi` keyword is used, *c* will always be 0.

- `partition` (*d*) identifies the partition on the drive that is specified by the preceding parameters. The value of *d* will be 1 for the first partition on the hard disk, 2 for the second partition, and so on.

Next, consider a hard disk with SCSI address 2, attached to the second SCSI adapter on a system, whose BIOS is disabled. If this disk has three partitions, the partitions would have the following ARC names:

```
scsi(1)disk(2)rdisk(0)partition(1)
scsi(1)disk(2)rdisk(0)partition(2)
scsi(1)disk(2)rdisk(0)partition(3)
```

Finally, consider a slave IDE drive (the second drive on an IDE controller) that is attached to the first IDE controller in a computer. If this drive is configured with three partitions, the partitions would have the following ARC names:

```
multi(0)disk(0)rdisk(1)partition(1)
multi(0)disk(0)rdisk(1)partition(2)
multi(0)disk(0)rdisk(1)partition(3)
```

Specifying Operating System Startup Directories in *boot.ini*

ARC names are used with directory paths to specify system startup directories. The directory \WINNT35 on the first partition of the first (master) IDE drive on the first IDE controller would be identified as follows:

```
multi(0)disk(0)rdisk(0)partition(1)\WINNT35
```

In the case of MS-DOS, the startup partition is identified using a conventional drive letter. Within the boot.ini file, the DOS boot directory is identified by the path c:\.

The Structure of the *boot.ini* File

The boot.ini file consists of two sections: [boot loader] and [operating systems]. This section examines how these sections are organized.

The *[boot loader]* Section

This section establishes the default operating system and determines whether it will be loaded if the user doesn't select an operating system after a timeout interval. The [boot loader] section accepts two optional parameters:

- **timeout=***n* This parameter establishes a timeout interval of *n* seconds. If the user doesn't select an operating system within the timeout interval, the operating system specified by the default parameter will be loaded. If the timeout parameter is omitted, the system will wait indefinitely for the user to select an operating system. If the parameter is entered as timeout=0, the default operating system will be selected immediately without user action.

- **default=***partition\directory* This parameter specifies the partition and directory of the default operating system that will be loaded when the timeout interval expires. If the default parameter is omitted, the first entry in the [operating systems] section will be taken as the default.

SEE ALSO

➤ *The* [boot loader] *parameters can also be modified using the Startup/Shutdown tab of the System utility in the Control Panel, as described in Chapter 19.*

The *[operating systems]* Section

Each entry in the [operating systems] section specifies a directory from which an operating system can be started. Entries in the [operating systems] section accept the following optional switches:

- **/basevideo** This switch compels the system to be configured to use standard VGA video with 640×480 resolution. Setup always adds an option to the boot.ini file that includes the /basevideo switch. This option can be used to boot the system if video has been misconfigured for the adapter.

- **/sos** This option causes the boot loader to display the names of drivers being loaded as the system boots. If this option is omitted, NTLDR.EXE displays progress dots (....) as the boot process progresses but doesn't display filenames.

- **/noserialmice=[COM***n*¦**COM***x,y,z***]** This switch disables checking for pointing devices on the specified serial ports. /noserialmice=COM1 disables checking on COM1. /noserialmice=COM2,3,4 disables checking on COM2, COM3, and COM4. If the COM parameter is omitted, mouse checking is disabled on all ports.

Modifying entries in the [operating systems] section

You can modify entries in the [operating systems] section only by directly editing the boot.ini file.

Use this switch if NTDETECT tends to incorrectly identify a serial device as a mouse. Unless the port is excluded, the mouse driver will be bound to the wrong port, and the device on the serial port will be unusable.

- **/crashdebug** Include this switch to enable the Automatic Recovery and Restart capability.

- **/nodebug** Include this switch to suppress monitoring of debugging information. Debugging information is useful to developers but slows system performance under normal circumstances.

- **maxmem:***n* Use this switch to specify a maximum amount of RAM (*n* KB) to be used by Windows NT. This switch can be used to reduce the memory allocation for some hardware platforms and is useful if bad memory chips are suspected to be causing problems.

- **scsiordinal:***n* If a system is equipped with two identical SCSI adapters, use this switch to distinguish the adapters. For the second adapter, the parameter *n* should be 1.

The Registry's Role in the Boot Process

Many entries in the Registry are used to configure Windows NT when the operating system is loaded. First, you will look at some specific Registry keys. After that, you will examine the use of the LastKnownGood configuration.

SEE ALSO

➤ *Chapter 22, "Editing the Registry," starting on page 657, tells you more about the structure of the Registry and its role in controlling the Windows NT configuration.*

Registry Keys Related to Loading Windows NT

Figure 2.26 shows the Registry Editor, focusing on the HKEY_LOCAL_MACHINE subtree. Several of the subkeys deserve special mention with regard to the Windows NT loading process.

- **HKEY_LOCAL_MACHINE\SYSTEM\Clone.** This subkey is the temporary repository for Registry values that are collected while Windows NT is loading. Following initialization and a successful logon, values in the Clone subkey are copied to a control subset, such as ControlSet001. This control subset is identified as the LastKnownGood configuration by the Select subkey.

- **HKEY_LOCAL_MACHINE\SYSTEM\ControlSet00x.** These subkeys define control set configurations. Value entries in the Select subkey define the function of each of the control sets. As many as four control sets may be defined by the system, but it is most common to see two control sets in the Registry.

- **HKEY_LOCAL_MACHINE\SYSTEM\CurrentControlSet.** This subkey stores the Registry entries that define the current (running) system configuration. After system startup, the CurrentControlSet is identical to the LastKnownGood configuration. System configuration changes are reflected in the CurrentControlSet, but the LastKnownGood configuration retains the settings last used to successfully start the system.

- **HKEY_LOCAL_MACHINE\SYSTEM\Select.** This subkey stores value entries that define the functions of the various control sets. See Figure 2.26 for examples of the value entries for this subkey. Each value entry includes a hex value that points to a control set. The value 0x00000001, for example, maps to ControlSet001. Four values appear in the Select subkey:

  - **Current** points to the control set that was actually used to start the system.

  - **Default** points to the control set that will be used to start the system the next time the computer is booted.

  - **Failed** identifies the control set that was replaced when the LastKnownGood control set was used. This key can be used to identify a bad control set so that it can be corrected.

  - **LastKnownGood** points to the control set that is a clean copy of the last control set that was successfully used to start the system.

FIGURE 2.26

The Registry Editor,
focusing on the
HKEY_LOCAL_MACHINE
subtree.

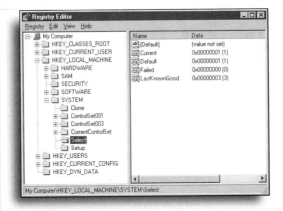

FIGURE 2.26

The Registry Editor,
focusing on the
HKEY_LOCAL_MACHINE
subtree.

Using the *LastKnownGood* Configuration

When Windows NT is booted, the user always has the option of invoking the LastKnownGood configuration, a copy of the control set that was used when Windows NT was last started successfully. (A successful boot is not achieved until a user logs on to the system. At that time, the LastKnownGood configuration is created.)

The system will attempt to load the LastKnownGood configuration under two circumstances:

- If the system must recover from a severe or critical error encountered when loading a device driver.

- If the user requests that the LastKnownGood configuration be used during startup. During system startup, NTLDR presents the option **Press spacebar NOW to invoke the Hardware Profile/Last Known Good menu**. If the user does not invoke the LastKnownGood configuration, the system uses the Default control set.

Use the LastKnownGood configuration to recover from severe system startup problems. For example:

- You have installed a new driver and restarted the system to load the driver, but the system will not boot successfully. The LastKnownGood configuration will not invoke the new driver and can start successfully.

- You have introduced errors when editing the Registry. Use the LastKnownGood configuration to back out of the changes. Of course, the LastKnownGood configuration can correct only entries that were made to the CurrentControlSet; it can't recover from errors made in other areas of the Registry.

- You want to back out of *all* configuration changes made during the previous session.

You're Up and Running

You now should have your first server up and running. That's a big step. It means that the hardware is working and that NT has installed properly. So give yourself a pat on the back and play a little Solitaire.

If you have a simple network, you can probably move on to Chapter 4, where you will begin to create the domains that you will use to manage your network.

If your network is a bit more complex, however, you need to proceed to the next chapter, where you will learn how to manage the NetBEUI and NWLink protocols. There you will learn the limitations of each protocol and see how to set up more elaborate networks using NWLink.

Configuring Network Adapters, Services, and Protocols

Characteristics of Microsoft Network protocols

Using the Network applet

Building networks with NWLink

As you have learned, Microsoft has designed Windows NT to support multiple protocols—simultaneously if necessary. This chapter gives you further information on your primary network protocol options and explains how to select and configure NetBEUI and NWLink. TCP/IP configuration is a much bigger topic, and Chapters 13 through 18 are devoted to the various technologies required to set up a Microsoft TCP/IP network.

Microsoft Network Protocols

The life of a network server is not an easy one. As if it doesn't have enough to do serving files and printers, it must be multilingual as well. This requirement has several sources.

Before the Internet explosion, there wasn't a dominant protocol. Until fairly recently, vendors actually sought to develop proprietary network protocols, sometimes for competitive reasons and sometimes because no existing protocol met their requirements. In the early 1980s, when LANs were beginning to emerge as a networking technology, there were no established LAN protocols. TCP/IP was in its infancy and was regarded as a complex protocol for large networks. In keeping with the "simpler" LAN environment, the industry emphasis was on simpler protocols that reduced processing requirements, eased administration, and simplified the user environment.

Two of the protocols that found their way into Windows NT originated in the LAN environment. NetBEUI was specifically developed as a protocol for small LANs. Novell's IPX/SPX protocols were intended as versatile and robust LAN protocols that were easy to administer. Riding the wave of Novell's successful NetWare product, IPX/SPX became one of the dominant protocols, although it has been eclipsed by TCP/IP in recent years.

You need to select one or more protocols for your network. To help you make your decision, let's briefly review your options and their advantages and disadvantages.

Characteristics of NetBEUI

NetBEUI is also called the NetBIOS Frame (NBF) protocol because it was designed as a basic network protocol that could service NetBIOS network clients. NetBEUI requires no configuration and is fast and efficient. So why not use NetBEUI on every network?

The chief reason is that NetBEUI messages don't include network numbers, which are used to identify network destinations on routed networks. Consequently, it is impossible to route NetBEUI messages through an internetwork, preventing you from constructing NetBEUI networks that have more than a couple hundred computers, all of which must be at the same location. You can't use NetBEUI to build a network that includes a WAN link.

If all of the following statements apply to your network, you might consider using NetBEUI:

- Your network is small and will remain so.
- Routing isn't required.
- You don't require connectivity to NetWare servers.
- You don't require connectivity to the Internet or to other TCP/IP networks.

But there is nothing you can do with NetBEUI that can't be accomplished with NWLink or TCP/IP. If you have either alternative protocol installed, there is little reason to include NetBEUI in the system configuration.

Characteristics of the NWLink IPX/SPX-Compatible Protocol

NWLink is a robust, powerful protocol that remains easy to configure. Not much more difficult to configure than NetBEUI, NWLink is routable, allowing you to build internetworks consisting of multiple LAN and WAN elements.

NWLink is required in only one situation: if you need to connect to NetWare networks using the Gateway Service for NetWare client. But even that requirement might diminish in significance as Novell continues to adapt NetWare to TCP/IP. All in all, it is becoming a TCP/IP world.

You might want to choose NWLink when any of the following conditions apply:

- Your network is large or will become large, and routing is required.
- You require connectivity to NetWare IPX/SPX networks.
- You don't need to support TCP/IP services.
- You don't want to undertake the planning and management required to configure TCP/IP.

Characteristics of TCP/IP

TCP/IP is becoming the preferred protocol on Microsoft networks and will be the default protocol when the next generation of Windows NT ships. TCP/IP supports networks of any size and has excellent WAN and routing support.

If there is a disadvantage to TCP/IP, it is that it provides few services automatically. Host naming is handled automatically on NetBEUI and NWLink networks. On TCP/IP networks you need to configure auxiliary name services such as Windows Internet Name Service (WINS) and Domain Name Service (DNS). This results in added complexity and management for services that require no effort at all with NetBEUI or NWLink.

SEE ALSO

➤ *WINS is covered in Chapter 16, "Supporting Windows Naming with WINS," starting on page 485.*

➤ *DNS is covered in Chapter 18, "Supporting the Domain Name Service," starting on page 529.*

But automated services often generate higher levels of network traffic, because it is necessary for computers to exchange data frequently to keep service databases current. Consequently, NWLink is not a "lean" protocol. TCP/IP, on the other hand, is extremely efficient and generates relatively little network overhead traffic.

Consider TCP/IP for your network if any or all of the following conditions apply:

- Your network is large or will become large, and routing is required.

- You require connectivity to the Internet.

- You require support for TCP/IP services, such as World Wide Web servers.

- Your staff has the time and expertise required to manage TCP/IP.

If your network is configured with TCP/IP, there should be little need for other protocols. A possible exception might be a requirement for NWLink if the network must communicate with NetWare servers. If in doubt about selecting network protocols, choose TCP/IP.

Using the Network Applet

The Network applet in the Control Panel is the primary tool for installing, removing, and configuring protocols. We will return to the Network applet throughout this book. Figure 3.1 shows the Network applet dialog box. As you can see from the different tabs, the Network applet configures a wide variety of network features. In this section we will review the primary operations you will perform with the Network applet.

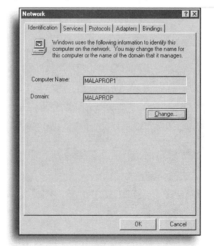

FIGURE 3.1

The Network applet.

Changing the Computer Name and Domain Name

The **Identification** tab displays two key items that define the computer—its computer name and its domain. The **Computer Name** field defines the computer's NetBIOS name—the name by which the computer is identified throughout the Microsoft Network environment. The **Domain** field defines the domain that the computer uses to log on to the network.

You can change the computer name and domain on a workstation or stand-alone server. If the workstation or server is sharing resources, however, changing identification can be time-consuming, because many users' computers might be referencing shared resources on the computer. If you change a server's name or domain, all clients that access the server must change their references to the shared resources on the computer.

To change the computer's identification, click **Change** in the **Identification** tab. This will open the Identification Changes dialog box, shown in Figure 3.2. You can change the values of the **Computer Name** and **Domain Name** fields. The computer must be restarted in order for the changes to take effect. If you want to change the computer name and the domain, you must change the name first and then restart the computer. Then you can change the domain.

FIGURE 3.2

Changing a computer's identification information.

Adding, Removing, and Configuring Services and Protocols

Windows NT includes a wide variety of services and protocols that you install as they are required. The procedure is essentially the same for services and protocols, so we can consider them together.

To add a service or protocol, follow these steps:

Adding a service or protocol

1. Open the Network applet and select the **Services** or **Protocols** tab. Figure 3.3 shows the **Protocols** tab.

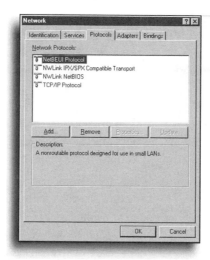

FIGURE 3.3

The Protocols tab in the Network applet.

2. To remove a service or protocol, select the item and click **Remove**. Close the Network applet and restart the computer to complete the operation.

3. Some services and protocols can be configured within the Network applet. To configure an item, select it and click **Properties** to open dialog boxes specific to the item.

SEE ALSO

➤ *Several examples of service and protocol reconfiguration are included in this book. For example, configuration of NWLink is discussed later in this chapter, in the section "Building Networks with NWLink."*

➤ *Configuration of the TCP/IP protocol is discussed in Chapters 14 through 18, starting on page 455.*

4. To add a service or protocol, click **Add** to open a list of services or protocols that can be added. A sample list of protocols is shown in Figure 3.4.

Changing the identification of a Windows NT computer

In Chapter 4, "Building a Domain," you will learn that Windows NT computers can't simply log on to a domain. The computer must first be given a domain account by an administrator. If you need to change the computer name or the domain of a Windows NT computer, you must coordinate with the domain administrator to ensure that the computer account is properly established.

Changing the identification of a domain controller

Domain controllers present special cases because they are closely tied to the domain security system both by name and by domain. You should review the material in Chapter 4 before you attempt to change the identification information for a Primary or a Backup Domain Controller.

FIGURE 3.4
Selecting a protocol to be added.

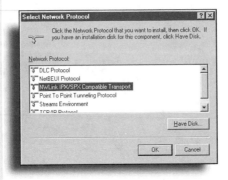

5. If the item you want is in the list, select it.

   If you are adding a service or protocol that is on a vendor's floppy disk or CD-ROM, click **Have Disk** and follow the prompts.

6. Click **OK**. In most cases, files will be copied, and you will be asked to supply a path to the installation files. If the files are on the Windows NT CD-ROM, the path will be *driveletter*:*platform*, where *platform* is i386, alpha, mips, or ppc, depending on your hardware. On an Intel x86 computer, a sample path is F:\i386.

7. Click the **Close** button to close the Network applet. In many cases, dialog boxes will be presented so that you can enter configuration parameters for the service or protocol you are installing.

8. In most cases, you must restart the computer to activate the changes.

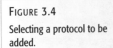

Removing services and protocols

You might need to remove a service or protocol. Simply return to the Network applet, select the appropriate tab, select the item to be deleted, and click **Remove**. You will need to restart the computer to complete the removal.

Adding and Removing Network Adapters

You might need to add, remove, or reconfigure network adapters. This is also performed using the Network applet.

To manage adapters, open the Network applet and select the **Adapters** tab, shown in Figure 3.5. This figure was prepared on a computer that is equipped with two network adapters.

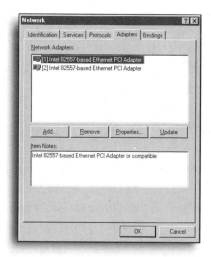

FIGURE 3.5
The Adapters tab in the
Network applet.

To remove an adapter, select the item and click **Remove**. Close the Network applet and restart the computer to complete the operation.

To configure an adapter, select it and click **Properties** to open dialog boxes specific to the item. Some adapters have configurable properties. Newer Plug-and-Play adapters are self-configuring, and typically the dialog boxes don't have editable fields.

To update the drivers for an adapter, select the adapter, click **Update**, and follow the prompts. You will need to supply a disk from the manufacturer that includes the updated drivers.

To add an adapter, follow these steps:

Adding an adapter

1. Click **Add** to open the Select Network Adapter dialog box, shown in Figure 3.6.

2. If your adapter appears in the **Network Adapter** list, select the entry and click **OK**.

   If your adapter doesn't appear in the **Network Adapter** list, click **Have Disk** and follow the prompts to load the adapter drivers from a manufacturer's disk.

FIGURE 3.6

Selecting a network adapter.

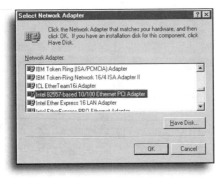

3. If you're installing a second adapter of a type that is already installed, you will see the prompt A network card of this type is already installed in the system. Do you want to continue? Click **OK** to confirm your selection.

4. Next, an adapter-specific dialog box appears, allowing you to review and modify the setup parameters for the card you're installing. Be sure to read the manufacturer's documentation when setting up an unfamiliar adapter.

5. Close the Network applet.

6. If NWLink or TCP/IP protocols are installed, you will see dialog boxes where you should review the protocol-specific properties related to the adapter. If TCP/IP is installed on the computer, every new adapter requires configuration to work with TCP/IP.

7. Restart the computer to activate the new adapter.

The adapter you added will now appear in the **Network Adapters** list. If multiple adapters are installed, they are identified by numbers—[1], [2], and so forth. If more than one adapter is installed, you might want to configure routing support.

SEE ALSO

➤ *To configure routing for NWLink, see the section "Building Networks with NWLink" later in this chapter.*

➤ *To configure routing for TCP/IP, see Chapter 15, "Building TCP/IP Internetworks," starting on page 471.*

Managing Bindings

Network drivers, hardware, and protocols are associated by *bindings*. The **Bindings** tab in the Network applet can be used to review and adjust the bindings that are in effect on a computer. Figure 3.7 shows the bindings on a typical computer.

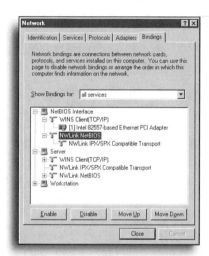

FIGURE 3.7
Bindings on a typical computer.

Bindings display document linkages between network components. You can change the way the bindings are presented by selecting one of the following settings in the **S̲how Bindings for** field:

- all services
- all protocols
- all adapters

Figure 3.7 shows bindings organized by services. A + in the left-most column indicates that the entry can be expanded to display additional binding levels. In this figure, several entries have been expanded fully.

Active bindings are identified by a network icon. You can enable and disable bindings by selecting the entry and using the **Enable** and **Disable** buttons.

When an object is bound to more than one protocol, the binding priority is indicated by the order of the entries in the hierarchies displayed in the **Bindings** tab. Figure 3.7 shows two protocols bound to the NetBIOS interface. In this case, the protocol with the highest priority for the NetBIOS interface is TCP/IP, so NetBIOS applications will first attempt to access network resources using TCP/IP. If the required resource is not available through TCP/IP, the computer attempts to access the resource using NWLink.

That would be inefficient if most of the resources required by this computer were accessed through NWLink. In such cases, you might want to adjust the binding priority. To raise the priority of a bound object, select the object and click **Move Up**. To lower the priority of a selected object, click **Move Down**.

A better approach, however, would be to eliminate one of the bound protocols if at all possible. With few exceptions, it should be possible to satisfy all network communication requirements using a single protocol. Certainly, most communication needs can be met by TCP/IP.

Building Networks with NWLink

It's extremely easy to configure networks with the NWLink protocols. On simple networks, no configuration is required. When routers are added, configuration is quick and simple.

NWLink Network Characteristics

When you set up an NWLink network, there are only a few configuration considerations. To see what they are, examine the internetwork in Figure 3.8. This internetwork consists of two network segments. One issue with internetworks is how frames are to be routed to the correct destination network. Most of the configuration required for IPX has to do with network routing.

NWLink, IPX, and SPX

NWLink consists of two protocols developed by Novell: Internetwork Packet Exchange (IPX) and Sequenced Packet Exchange (SPX). It isn't really necessary for you to be aware of the characteristics of these protocols. I'm explaining because I want you to understand why NWLink is described as an IPX/SPX-compatible protocol.

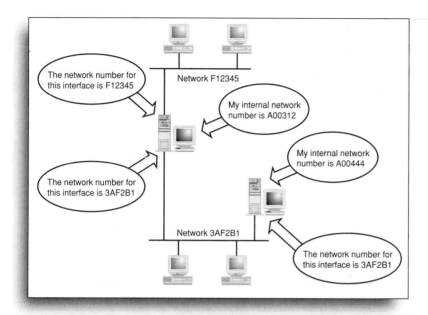

FIGURE 3.8
An example of an IPX internetwork.

When a network interface card on a server is configured to connect to an IPX network, the configuration for the interface must declare a *network number* that is associated with the network segment. This network number can consist of up to eight hexadecimal digits. The network number that is declared for the interface becomes the network number for that network segment. Clients connected to that network learn the network number and include it in the destination fields of frames they transmit.

Two things should be noted about the network numbers in Figure 3.8:

- Each network segment must be assigned its own network number, which must be unique throughout the IPX internetwork.

- All computers attached to the same network must agree to use the same network number; otherwise, errors are generated.

Installing NWLink on an existing IPX network

All servers attached to an IPX network must use the same network number for the network. If you're installing an NWLink computer on a network that already includes NetWare or NT servers using IPX, you must determine the existing network number and configure the new server to match.

Besides the network number assigned to its interface, each NetWare server is also configured with an *internal network number*. Also an eight-digit hex number, the internal network number is used to deliver data to the correct process within the NetWare server. The internal network number must also be unique and can't conflict with any other network numbers or internal network numbers on the internetwork.

Declaration of network numbers is the only essential task when setting up an IPX network. With Windows NT, you have the choice of specifying the network numbers to be used. In most cases, however, you can configure Windows NT to discover the network numbers that are active on the attached networks and configure itself appropriately.

Configuring NWLink Protocol Properties

After installing the NWLink protocols, you can configure them as follows:

Configuring NWLink protocol properties

1. Open the Network applet and select the **Protocols** tab.

2. Select NWLink IPX/SPX Compatible Transport from the **Network Protocols** box and choose **Properties** to open the NWLink IPX/SPX Properties dialog box, shown in Figure 3.9.

3. NetWare servers also support an internal network number that supports interprocess communication among servers. An internal network number must be configured if this server will be an IPX router or will be running File and Print Services for NetWare. The default internal network number is 00000000, which instructs Windows NT to examine the network number and select one that doesn't conflict with numbers already in use. If you change the default number of 00000000, be sure that the number you enter doesn't conflict with other internal NetWare network numbers on the network.

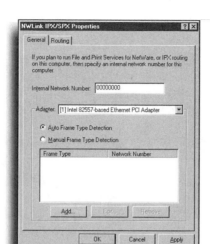

FIGURE 3.9
Configuring NWLink.

4. If this computer is configured with two or more network adapter cards, select the adapter to be configured from the Adapter field.

5. Select **A̲uto Frame Type Detection** if Windows NT should examine the network to identify the frame type in use. Unless your IPX network is using multiple frame types, this setting will typically let the server communicate with the network. With automatic frame type detection, only one frame type will be used.

In step 6, you will observe that a network number must be specified when a manual frame type is added to the configuration. When you select **A̲uto Frame Type Detection**, Windows NT will detect the network number that is associated with the frame type that is selected; it is unnecessary to specify a frame type.

6. Select **M̲anual Frame Type Detection** if you want to specify the frame type(s) that IPX will use. Manual frame type selection is necessary to prevent confusion in networks with multiple frame types, or to bind multiple frame types to an adapter. If you select **M̲anual Frame Type Detection**, you must add at least one frame type to the configuration. To add a frame type, do the following:

Selecting IPX network numbers

If your organization's network includes existing IPX segments, chances are that they are configured with low-order network numbers such as 00000001. That's an easy choice, and servers are often installed without defining a long-term plan for numbering networks. To avoid address conflict, define a network numbering scheme for your entire organization and keep a central registry of IPX network numbers.

   a. Click **Add** to open the Manual Frame Detection dialog box.

   b. In the **Frame Type** field, select one of the frame types that is offered. You will be shown only frame types that are compatible with the network adapter card being configured.

   c. In the **Network Number** field, specify the network number that is used for this frame type on the attached network segment. All computers that use the same frame type on a given network segment must be configured with the same network number. If you add two or more frame types, each frame type must be associated with a unique network number.

7. Click **OK** when configuration is complete. Restart the computer to activate the configuration changes.

NWLink and Frame Types

One configuration item that you might need to attend to is the frame type for Ethernet or token-ring networks. A frame type is a variation on the basic frame format for a network. Novell NetWare supports four frame types for Ethernet and two for token ring. The primary reason for changing the frame type is to allow the Windows NT network to be compatible with another network.

Current Novell networks run the following default frame types:

- **Ethernet_802.2 for Ethernet networks.** This frame type fully conforms to the IEEE 802 standards and is the default frame type for current NetWare versions.

- **Token_Ring for token ring networks.** This frame type conforms to IBM token ring and to IEEE 802.5 standards and is the default token ring frame type on NetWare networks.

The following frame types are also supported:

- **Ethernet_802.3.** An older Ethernet frame type Novell developed before the IEEE 802.2 standard was set. This frame type continues to be supported on Novell networks but is not preferred.

- **Ethernet_II.** The frame type that predated the IEEE 802.3 standard. This frame type is used on TCP/IP networks.

- **Ethernet_SNAP.** A variation used to support Macintosh EtherTalk networks.

- **Token_Ring_SNAP.** A token-ring variant that supports Macintosh TokenTalk networks.

Because Novell networks can bind multiple protocols, the best course of action is to have all networks bind to the Ethernet_802.2 or Token_Ring frame types. If your NetWare administrator is unable or unwilling to do that, you can add frame types to NWLink in the Protocol Configuration dialog box.

When you set NWLink to the recommended setting of Auto Frame Type Detection, NWLink examines the network and selects an active frame type. If Ethernet_802.2 frames are detected or no frames are detected, the Ethernet_802.2 frame type is selected. Otherwise, NWLink selects the frame type that is observed on the network.

Configuring IPX Routing

If you are configuring more than one network adapter on a computer, you probably want to use the computer as a router. Windows NT can function as a router for the NWLink protocols. Figure 3.10 shows a network that requires routing. The computer shown is equipped with two network adapters and connects to two NWLink networks.

FIGURE 3.10

IPX routing must be enabled on computer A.

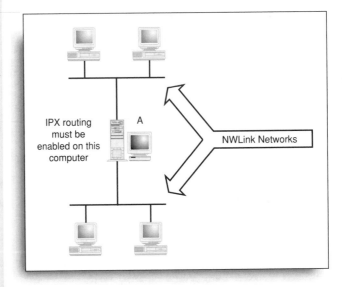

To configure the computer in the figure as an NWLink router, you would do the following:

Configuring a computer as an NWLink router

1. Install and configure two or more network adapter cards of either the same or different types. When you have more than one network adapter card in a computer, you will be prompted to specify a unique internal network number.

2. In the Network utility, select the **Services** tab.

3. Click **Add** to open the Select Network Service dialog box.

4. In the **Network Service** list, select the entry RIP for NWLink IPX/SPX Compatible Transport and click **OK**.

5. When prompted for the source file location, specify the path of the directory where the installation files can be found. Typically, this path points to the installation CD-ROM.

6. When you see the prompt Netbios Broadcast Propagation (broadcast type 20 packets) is currently disabled. Do you want to enable it?, click **Yes**.

7. Close the Network applet and restart the computer.

8. Open the Network applet and select the **Protocols** tab.

9. Select NWLink IPX/SPX Compatible Transport and click **Properties**.

10. Select the **Routing** tab and ensure that the **Enable RIP Routing** check box is checked.

11. If the **Enable RIP Routing** check box isn't checked, select it and click **OK**. Restart the computer to activate routing.

Note

When computers communicate using the NWLink protocol, browsing and name resolution are supported by NetBIOS over NWLink, which is dependent on Type 20 packets. Type 20 broadcasts are broadcast on the network so that all computers receive the NetBIOS naming information. If NetBIOS Broadcast Propagation is disabled, type 20 broadcasts will not be forwarded by routers, and users will be prevented from browsing or resolving names for computers that are not attached to the local cable segment.

When NetBIOS broadcast propagation is enabled, type 20 packets propagate for only eight hops from the computers that originate the packets. A hop occurs each time a packet crosses a cable segment. Therefore, when NWLink is the only protocol on the network, clients can't communicate with servers that are more than eight hops away. As a result, no more than seven routers can separate computers on a network that is running only NWLink. (Networks of up to 15 hops can be implemented using TCP/IP.)

The Network's Up; Let's Build a Domain

You have now set up the highway that lets your computers communicate, but a highway isn't much use without somewhere to go. Now you need to set up some destinations on that highway by establishing domains and servers. We'll start by looking at a single-domain network.

Building a Domain

At this point, you have accomplished a lot—you have installed Windows NT Server on at least one server and you have set up a network communication infrastructure that enables your computers to exchange data. Basically, you have created the highways and the interchanges that enable your users to travel around on your network. But because highways are worthless without somewhere to go, you now need to start building the shopping malls and businesses that provide users with destinations and things to do.

Ultimately that means installing applications and other services on the network. After the applications and services are in place, you must also provide your users with the access to those applications. Access means the ability to log on to the network, and logging on means *security*—enabling users to connect with the resources they need without being able to connect with resources they shouldn't have.

The cornerstone of Windows NT Server security is the *domain*, which provides a way of coordinating the security on multiple Windows NT Server computers. This chapter shows you how to set up a network with a single domain, which is as complicated as most of us need to get. Before you administer a domain for the first time, it will be useful for you to have an understanding of how domains compare to the other means of managing shared network resources.

Managing LAN Resources

Broadly speaking, resources are shared on the network in two ways: by placing the resources on centralized computers called *servers*, and by sharing resources on users' personal computers— a process called *peer-to-peer* resource sharing. Over the years, network developers have evolved several means of managing the resources being shared on a network. This section looks at the following resource control methods:

- Peer-to-peer workgroups
- Stand-alone servers

- Domains
- Directory services

Peer-to-Peer Workgroups

One of the oldest methods of sharing resources on LANs is
still supported by several Microsoft products: Windows NT
Workstation, Windows for Workgroups 3.11, and Windows 95
and 98. (Windows NT Server can also network in a peer-to-peer
environment, but why would you want to?) Under the peer-to-
peer approach, every user's computer can be both a server and a
workstation. The term "peer-to-peer" makes the point that every
computer on the network is essentially equal, able to share and
be shared with every other computer. Take a look at how that
works on Windows 95.

Figure 4.1 shows a departmental network. Several users have
resources on their computers that must be shared with other
users. For example:

- Albert needs to share some engineering specifications that
  are on his computer at C:\specs. His fellow engineers need
  to be able to retrieve and update these files.
- Marie has a color laser printer. Her coworkers in the
  Marketing department need access to this printer.
- Richard's computer has a copy of Excel that is shared with
  other users in the Finance department.

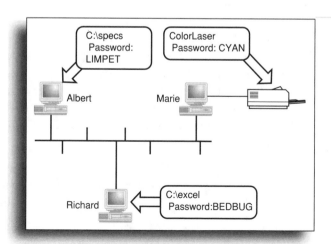

FIGURE 4.1

Sharing resources on a peer-
to-peer network.

Figure 4.2 shows the dialog box Albert uses to share `C:\specs`. Albert has shared the directory, and users access the shared directory using a process called *browsing*. Figure 7.3 shows a user browsing the network to locate Albert's shared files.

FIGURE 4.2

The dialog box Albert uses to share `C:\specs`.

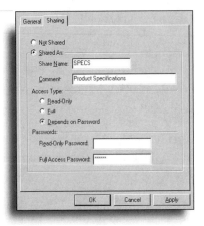

FIGURE 4.3

Browsing a network to locate shared files.

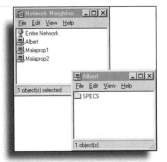

It is quite easy to share the directory, but sharing raises some issues. Who should be able to read the files? Who should be able to modify them? Who should not be able to access the files at all? If Albert needs to restrict access, notice that he can assign two passwords: a **Read Only Password** and a **Full Access Password**. That would appear to solve Albert's problem, wouldn't it?

Well, it happens that Marie needs to restrict access to her printer, which is expensive to operate and shouldn't be used to print off Web pages. And Charles' copy of Excel has a limited license, and he needs to restrict its use to a limited number of individuals. So both Marie and Charles add passwords to their shared resources as well.

Without a whole lot of trouble, we have gotten up to four passwords! If it is necessary to restrict passwords on a peer-to-peer network, passwords proliferate and the peer-to-peer proposition soon becomes preposterous. When critical files are spread out willy-nilly on user's personal workstations, how do users find the files they need? Do they keep crib sheets with the file locations and passwords? Crib sheets that go out-of-date and that list passwords for everyone to see?

There are some other problems with peer-to-peer networks. Who is going to back those files up? Do you put a tape drive on each computer and hope each user will diligently start the backup software and rotate tapes when he or she leaves? Do you still believe that the tooth fairy brings quarters?

Finally, what happens when users reboot their workstations while files are being shared? Oh, that's right, Windows is so reliable that it's never necessary to reboot anymore. Right?

So, peer-to-peer works, but its a ponderous solution suitable for small offices and non-critical files. If the stuff you need to share is really important, a better sharing solution is needed.

Central Servers

The extreme opposite of peer-to-peer resource sharing is the central server. The idea of the central server is that you put everything important in one basket and watch that basket very carefully. All the shared files go on a single server from which they are shared. The server is carefully protected with an uninterruptible power supply and a big, fat tape drive that can back up everything. Figure 4.4 shows a network with a central server.

All users log on to the central server to access files, printers, and other shared resources. Because everything is in one place, shared resources are easy to find. If need be, users can even use the MS-DOS DIR command to find files. A single server means that access control is simple. A user has one name and password that gets him or her into the server. Management software on the server is used to maintain a database of users and of the resources users are authorized to access.

FIGURE 4.4

A network with a central server.

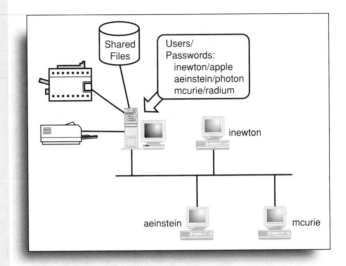

It doesn't take much for a network to outgrow a single server, however. Many offices just have too many users to make a single server practical. Some services, such as SQL databases and electronic mail, are resource hogs that practically cry out for their own servers. If you have enough users, even file sharing may be too much for a single server. You may need to distribute the files on several servers just to spread out the workload.

The simple centralized server model begins to break down when a second server is added. That's because each server has its own security database. Figure 4.5 illustrates the problem. To have access to Server A and Server B, a user must have a separate username and password on each computer, raising many of the objections examined for peer-to-peer workgroups. It's a bit easier now because passwords are assigned to users rather than to shared resources. Therefore a single password gets a user access to all the resources shared on a single server. But now the user has user accounts on two servers, and keeping the same password on both servers becomes a hassle.

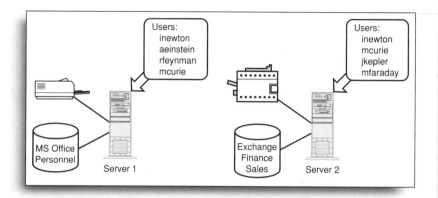

FIGURE 4.5

Two servers complicate network administration.

Now that there are multiple servers, users need to remember which server has the files they want. To access a printer, the user needs to remember which server the printer is connected to. All in all, two servers are at least four times as complicated as one.

What is needed is a system that treats multiple servers as a single, easily-managed resource. There are two common solutions to the multiple-server quandary: *domains* and *directory services*. Domains are simpler, so look at them first.

Domains

Domains are, in fact, the solution employed on Windows NT Server 4. A domain is just a database that handles the resource sharing security for multiple servers. Each user has one domain username and password. After logging on to the domain, the user can browse the network and access any services on any server for which the user is authorized.

Domains borrow concepts from both workgroups and centralized servers. Like workgroups, domains can be informal. Although the user database is maintained centrally, the shared resources can reside on many different computers and can be administered by different people. If a user's workstation is running Windows 95 or NT, the user can share files and printers using the domain user database to provide security. Therefore domains can evolve fairly easily, with a minimum of centralized control.

But domains also place a stronger emphasis on dedicated servers than you will find in typical networks organized around peer-to-peer workgroups. In most cases, some computers are set up to function solely as servers. When a computer is dedicated as a network server, it is easier to justify a more reliable, better-performing computer and it is easier to protect the computer with things such as uninterruptible power supplies and tape backup.

Domains make network administration easier, but they leave the user with the problem of locating network resources. A user still must know which server has a required file, printer, service, or application. They can browse the network using the same technique that applied to workgroups, but nothing about a domain directs users to where they want to go. To direct users you need, well, a directory.

Directories

A *directory* is a comprehensive index of all the resources being shared on a network. Working much like a telephone yellow pages, a network directory enables the user to search the network for categories of services without worrying about where the service is actually located. When you dial an 800 number, you aren't concerned with the location of the person on the other end of the line, are you? You just want to reach the company that offers the product you require. In much the same way, a network directory makes it unnecessary to worry about which server has a particular file or printer. You just find what you want in the directory and connect up.

At present, two directories dominate the industry:

- Novell offers the Novell Directory Services (NDS). Although NDS has been focused on Novell's NetWare servers, Novell is making efforts to make NDS a universal directory, providing a central directory for services on many different types of computing platforms.
- X.500 is an international standard directory service. X.500 has been slow to catch on, but recent innovations suggest that it will grow in prominence.

A directory service greatly simplifies the use of a large network. A user logs on to the network once and is granted access to services by the directory service, no matter how many servers there may be or how large the network. In that regard, a directory service is much like a domain, offering a single logon to many servers.

But a directory also provides a uniform way to locate resources in the network. That is an important advantage these days as networks grow in scope, often spanning continents. Particularly as organizations integrate the Internet into their network operating strategies, there are just too many network resources— changing too rapidly—for users to commit everything to memory. They might as well try to memorize the telephone book.

Microsoft does not yet offer a directory for Windows NT Server, but is moving in that direction. Windows NT version 5.0 will include the Active Directory, a directory service tailored to work on top of Microsoft's domain architecture. Active Directory is based on the X.500 standard. Until recently, X.500 wasn't very practical for LANs. The software required for a full X.500 is big—so big that it has been restricted to mainframe computers. But the industry is starting to take notice of the Lightweight Directory Access Protocol (LDAP), which has reduced the horsepower needed to provide X.500 directory services. LDAP can run on LAN servers and is being incorporated into many common products such as Internet browsers. Novell has adapted their Novell Directory Service to make it LDAP compliant; Microsoft's Exchange mail system is also LDAP compliant.

Directories are not nirvana. For one thing, directory management is a pretty complex thing. The simplicity that directories offer the user is compensated for by additional administrative complexity. The network managers must understand the intricacies of the directory database, and directory databases can be pretty intricate. But that task is not for this book. (I'm simply describing directories to give you a view of the future.) The actual implementation of the Microsoft Active Directory can wait for the next edition.

Structure of a Domain

To keep things simple, this chapter focuses on single-domain networks. In practical terms, that's not as big a restriction as you might suppose. Probably the majority of networks can be implemented using a single domain.

SEE ALSO

➤ *If yours is a large organization that can't fit in a single domain, Chapter 12, "Extending Multi-Domain Networks," will show you how to grow your network using a multi-domain model.*

The SAM Database

The heart of a domain is the domain security database that contains information about the users and groups recognized by the domain together with the permissions assigned to the users and groups. The database is maintained by a component of Windows NT Server called the Security Access Manager, and is typically referred to as the SAM database. Information in the SAM database regulates the activities users can perform in the domain. Because the domain security database is so important, the domain administrator will typically arrange to keep extra copies that are synchronized with the master database.

The Roles of Servers in Domains

A server in a domain can have one of three roles, depending on its responsibility for the domain security database:

- Primary Domain Controller
- Backup Domain Controller
- Server

Take a look at each type of server to see how it contributes to the domain's functionality.

The Primary Domain Controller

The first server in a domain is always a *Primary Domain Controller* (PDC). In fact, creating the PDC for a domain creates the domain. The PDC contains the master SAM database.

When a user logs on to the domain, the PDC examines the SAM database to verify the user's name and password. If the name and password match the user's account information, the user is *authenticated*—that is, the user is given a set of credentials that enables him or her to access resources in the domain.

The PDC is critical to proper domain function, and changes to the SAM database cannot be made unless the PDC is running. The User Manager for Domains utility is used to create and manage the users and group entries found in the SAM database.

Backup Domain Controllers

On a network, one of anything is a recipe for disaster. If the PDC has the only copy of the SAM database, the domain grinds to a halt if the PDC goes down. Users cannot log on, and administrators cannot change user or group permissions.

Consequently it is highly desirable to have at least one Backup Domain Controller (BDC). Periodically, in a process called *synchronization*, the PDC gives each BDC a copy of the master SAM database. This benefits the domain in several ways:

- User logons can be authenticated by PDCs and BDCs, so logon performance is improved. This is particularly advantageous when many users are logging on, as at the beginning of the business day.

- Users can log on when the PDC is down.

- If the PDC crashes, a BDC can be promoted to make it the PDC for the domain.

A BDC is not a substitute for a PDC, however. All changes to the SAM database are made on the PDC and are then replicated to the domain BDCs. Therefore you can only add, remove, or change users or groups when the PDC is operating. If the PDC is down and cannot be restarted promptly, however, normal domain function can be restored by promoting a BDC to PDC.

Servers

It is not necessary for every Windows NT Server computer to function as a domain controller, and there are good reasons why you might want to configure a computer as a stand-alone server. Here are a few:

- You may want to dedicate a server to a particular task, such as running a database or email server.

- A stand-alone server can be administered by a separate group of staff members. A database server, for example, might be managed by a database administrator rather than the network administration staff.

- You might want to retain the flexibility to move the server to a different domain. In most cases, you must reinstall Windows NT Server to move a domain controller to a different domain, but stand-alone servers can change domains at any time. Even though a stand-alone server is not a domain controller, it can participate in a domain and recognize users and groups that have been established in the SAM database. Users and groups in the domain can be assigned permissions to resources on the stand-alone server.

Synchronizing the SAM Database

Changes made to the SAM database are first stored on the PDC, after which they are replicated to the domain BDCs in a process called *synchronization*. Changes to the PDC database are recorded in a *change log*. When an existing BDC requests updates from the PDC, the BDC will receive a *partial synchronization* consisting of all database changes that have taken place since the last time the BDC was synchronized.

The change log has a limited capacity. It operates as a *circular buffer*, purging older changes as new changes are recorded. If a BDC is offline for an extended period of time, it may miss some changes that have been purged from the change log. In such cases, the BDC will receive a *full synchronization* consisting of a complete copy of the PDC's domain database.

BDCs are synchronized by the NetLogon service, typically at five-minute intervals. In most cases, this frequency is sufficient to ensure that the BDC will not miss updates made to the PDC's change log, which has a default capacity of approximately 2,000 changes. If changes are being lost and full synchronizations are frequently required, the update schedule and the size of the change log can be adjusted by editing Registry settings.

Full synchronization of a BDC can generate significant network traffic. That isn't usually a problem when the PDC and BDC are connected by a high-bandwidth LAN. But when the PDC and BDC connect through a WAN, full synchronizations should be avoided. In such cases, you may want to increase the size of the change log and schedule synchronization to take place during periods of low WAN traffic.

SEE ALSO

➤ *For Registry settings that affect domain synchronization, see the section titled "Configuring Domain Synchronization" later in this chapter.*

➤ *For information about the Registry see Chapter 22, "Editing the Registry."*

Estimating the Capacity of a Domain

Although most organizations can probably function with a single Windows NT Server domain, that begs the question, "Just how large can a domain get?" Like so many such questions, the answer is, "It depends." And the main thing it depends on is the processing horsepower of your domain controllers.

One factor that regulates domain size is the size of the SAM database. The entire SAM database is loaded into the RAM of the domain controller, so clearly there's a link between the size of the SAM database and the server RAM requirements. Because of the RAM requirement, you must consider the time required to load the SAM database into RAM when the server boots.

The SAM database contains four types of objects, listed here with their storage requirements:

- Each user has a *user account*, at 1,024 bytes (1 KB) each.
- Each Windows NT client requires a *computer account*, at 512 bytes (0.5 KB) each.
- Each *global group* requires 512 bytes plus 12 bytes per user.
- Each *local group* requires 512 bytes plus 36 bytes per user.

SEE ALSO

➤ *Global and local groups will be explained in Chapter 8, "Activating Network Clients."*

To see how these requirements play out, assume a network with 1,000 users and 1,000 Windows NT computers. Users are organized using 10 global groups, with an average membership of 200 users per group. The network also has 10 local groups with an average membership of 20 users. Here are the calculations to determine the size of the SAM database:

1,000 users × 1,024 bytes = 1,024,000 bytes

1,000 computer accounts × 512 bytes = 512,000 bytes

10 global groups × 512 = 5,120 bytes

2,000 global group members × 12 = 24,000 bytes

10 local groups × 512 = 5,120 bytes

200 local group members × 36 = 7,200 bytes

Total SAM database size = 1,577,400 bytes

The total size for the SAM database would be a bit over 1.5 MB. That's not a particularly large SAM database, and it could easily be accommodated by a single domain.

Server hardware has a lot to say about the size of the SAM you should try to load on a domain controller. Table 4.1 gives some hardware recommendations taken from Microsoft literature.

TABLE 4.1 **Selecting domain controller hardware**

Users	SAM Size	Minimum CPU	Minimum RAM
10,000	<15 MB	Pentium or RISC	48 MB
15,000	<20 MB	Pentium or RISC	64 MB
30,000	<30 MB	Pentium or RISC	128 MB
45,000	<20 MB	Pentium or RISC	192 MB

I consider these figures to be optimistic. I can't, for example, imagine running Windows NT Server with only 48 MB of memory. But the table does give you a sense of the server hardware you should be contemplating, and it does make clear that memory is at least as important as the CPU in determining a server's domain capacity.

Depending on the server hardware, Microsoft suggests that a single domain controller can support between 2,000 and 5,000 users. That might be, but it could only work if the users aren't logging on at about the same time. But you know the reality. Everyone arrives at about 8 o'clock and wants to log on immediately. So the practicality of the matter is that you probably need more domain controllers than the Microsoft recommendation requires. If users complain about logon performance, add a domain controller.

Managing Domain Controllers

During the discussion about installing Windows NT Server in Chapter 2, you saw how a server's domain security role is defined during the setup process. But there's much more to managing domain controllers and servers than just declaring the security role during setup. This section shows you the ins and outs of domain controller management.

Introduction to Server Manager

The Server Manager utility is used to perform many of the tasks of managing domain controllers, servers, and computers. Figure 4.6 shows the Server Manager focused on the domain MALA-PROP, which presently consists of a PDC and a BDC, but does not include any user workstations or stand-alone servers. The remainder of the chapter explores several of the functions of Server Manager.

Microsoft's SAM database size recommendation

Microsoft recommends a maximum SAM database size of 40 MB, which would accommodate approximately 26,000 users, 26,000 NT clients, and 250 groups. Clearly, it would take high performance server hardware to handle a domain that large.

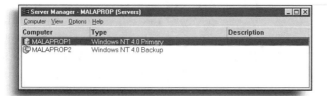

FIGURE 4.6

Server Manager showing a domain with a PDC and one BDC.

Determining which computers will be listed in Server Manager

The **View** menu has several options that determine which computers will be listed in Server Manager:

- **Servers.** Only Windows NT Server computers are displayed.

- **Workstations.** Only workstation clients are displayed (MS-DOS, Windows 3.x, Windows 95 and 98, and Windows for Workgroups).

- **All.** All servers and workstations are displayed.

- **Show Domain Members Only.** Only computers logged on to this domain will be displayed.

Finding Server Manager

The shortcut for Server Manager is found in the **Start** menu under **Programs|Administrative Tools (Common)**. Most of the other Windows NT administrative tools are located in that folder as well.

Domain Controllers and Security IDs

Human administrators identify domains and computers by the names we assign to them. But the names are only for human consumption. Inside the guts of Windows NT, an object is known by its *security ID* or SID, a long number established when the object is created.

When a PDC is created, a SID is established that identifies everything in the domain managed by the PDC. In fact, when a BDC is added to a domain, the domain SID is added as a prefix to the BDC computer's SID to identify the BDC. Because a SID identifies a domain or a computer, some network management operations can get pretty troublesome.

Suppose that the PDC for domain WIDGETS crashes. You decide to fix the problem by getting a new computer and reinstalling Windows NT Server, giving the computer the same name and specifying that the new computer is the PDC for the WIDGETS. But after you install NT Server, you find that none of the clients recognize the new PDC. Why?

The explanation is that the new PDC has a different SID, even though it has the same computer name and manages a domain with the same name as before. Because the SID has changed, the new domain is not the same as the old domain, and there is nothing you can do about it.

That's why it is important to have at least one BDC in a domain. If the PDC crashes, you can promote the BDC to PDC. The domain remains intact because the SID does not change.

You should remember a couple of important rules when installing PDCs and BDCs:

- Never perform a New Version installation on an existing PDC. Specifying the same domain configuration during setup will not help because Setup will create a new SID for the PDC. Computers that have already been added to the domain will be unable to communicate with the PDC because the computers are still using the old SID. As a result, computers will be mysteriously unable to communicate with their domain.

- Never install a domain controller when the PDC for a domain is down or unavailable due to a broken network connection. Suppose you attempt to install a new PDC when the existing PDC is down. Setup cannot find the current PDC, so it will permit you to create a new PDC with the same domain name. But the two PDCs will have different SIDs. Although the computers belong to domains with the same name, the domains are distinct because they have different SIDs. If you wish to install a new computer as the PDC of an existing domain, first install the new computer as a BDC in the domain. Then promote it to PDC while both domain controllers are running.

Creating a Primary Domain Controller

A PDC can only be created during the setup process. After you select Primary Domain Controller during setup, you specify a domain name. Domain names cannot contain spaces.

Setup then searches the network to see whether the domain name you entered is already in use. Setup continues only if a matching domain is not found.

When the domain is first configured, Setup creates an account with the username Administrator. This is a special account that has complete administrative authority for the domain being created. You are asked to enter a password for the Administrator account. Although a blank password will be accepted, this is such an important account that you should definitely create a password. Don't enter an easy-to-guess password. The password represents the keys to your network.

Creating a Backup Controller

BDCs are also created during setup. If you instruct Setup to create a Backup Domain Controller, you receive a prompt to enter several pieces of information:

- The name of the computer
- The domain to which the computer is being added

Warning: Don't forget the Administrator password

Don't forget the password for the Administrator account! The password is encrypted in the SAM database and cannot be recovered. If you lose the password, you will need to perform a New Version installation to establish a new password for the Administrator account.

- A username that has Administrator permissions in the domain the BDC will join
- The password for the Administrator account

Managing Domains

Creating the BDC computer account before setup

If you prefer, you can use Server Manager to create the BDC computer account before you run Setup. The procedure for creating a computer account is described later in this chapter.

This section examines several of the domain management tasks you may need to perform. Thanks to the way SIDs operate, some domain management operations are a bit tricky, so you will need to learn what you can and cannot get away with.

Promoting a Backup Domain Controller

Figure 4.5 introduced you to Server Manager, the primary tool you will use for managing computers in your domains. You use Server Manager to promote a BDC so that it is the PDC for its domain, for example, something you should do whenever the PDC will be shut down for very long.

When you promote a BDC, the events differ somewhat depending on whether the PDC is running:

- If the PDC is operating, a current copy of the domain's SAM database is synchronized to the BDC, after which the BDC can be promoted to become the PDC for the domain. Finally, the old PDC is demoted to a BDC.
- If the PDC is not available, the BDC's current SAM database will be established as the domain database. If any changes made to the PDC have not been synchronized to the BDC, the unsynchronized changes are lost. When the old PDC is reactivated, it must be demoted to make it a BDC.

Assuming that the PDC is online, the procedure to promote a BDC is as follows:

Promoting a BDC with the PDC online

1. Log on using a user account that has Administrator permissions.

2. Start Server Manager and choose **Servers** from the **View** menu.

3. Select the BDC to be promoted.

4. In the **Computer** menu, choose **Promote to Primary Domain Controller**.

5. Read the warning shown in Figure 4.7. As the warning makes clear, you should not promote a BDC while users are active in the domain.

6. Choose **Yes** to promote the BDC.

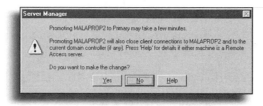

FIGURE 4.7
You see this warning when you begin to promote a BDC.

In Figure 4.8, server MALAPROP2 has been promoted and is now the PDC of the MALAPROP domain.

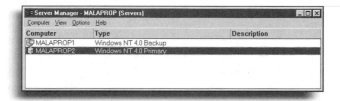

FIGURE 4.8
MALAPROP2 has been promoted to the domain PDC.

Demoting a Primary Domain Controller

Confusion can arise if you promote a BDC while the PDC is offline and you encounter some differences during the promotion process:

- You receive a warning that the PDC is unavailable and that promoting the BDC might result in errors when the PDC is returned to service.

- When the old PDC comes back online, its status is uncertain. (In similar situations I have seen the old PDC come online as a workstation or as an inactive PDC.)

When the old PDC attempts to rejoin the domain, it is not permitted to do so if another computer has been promoted to the PDC role. While Windows NT Server starts on the old PDC, you will see the message At least one service or driver failed during system startup, and error records are stored in the Events log. One record in the Events log has the source of NetLogon. The Detail Description reads, A Primary domain controller is already running in this domain.

SEE ALSO

➤ *You can examine records in the Events log using the Events Viewer, which is described in Chapter 23, "Managing the Server."*

In Server Manager, the old PDC will show as inactive (its icon is shown as an outline). If you wish to bring the old PDC back into the domain, it must be demoted to a BDC.

To demote the computer to a BDC, follow these steps:

Demoting a PDC to a BDC

1. Log on as an administrator.

2. Start Server Manager and choose **Servers** or **All** from the **View** menu.

3. Select the old PDC to be demoted.

4. In the **Computer** menu, choose **Demote to Backup Domain Controller**. (This option appears only if the selected computer is a duplicate PDC.)

Synchronizing Domain Controllers

Under most circumstances, Windows NT Server ensures that BDCs are synchronized with their PDCs at frequent intervals. In rare instances, however, BDCs may lose synchronization and you may need to resynchronize an individual BDC or the entire domain.

To synchronize an individual BDC, do the following:

Synchronizing an individual BDC

1. Log on to the domain as a domain administrator.

2. In Server Manager, choose **Servers** in the **View** menu.

3. Select the BDC to be synchronized.

4. In the **Computer** menu, choose **Synchronize with Primary Domain Controller**.

To synchronize all BDCs in the domain, do the following:

Synchronizing all BDCs in the domain

1. Log on to the domain as a domain administrator.

2. In Server Manager, choose **Servers** in the **View** menu.

3. Select the PDC.

4. In the **Computer** menu, choose **Synchronize Entire Domain**.

Creating a New Domain

A new domain is created when a PDC is established for the domain. To a very real extent, the PDC *is* the domain. You can create a new PDC during the setup process.

SEE ALSO

➤ *Creating a new PDC during the setup process is described earlier in this chapter in the section titled "Creating a Primary Domain Controller," page 119.*

You can also create a new domain by moving an existing PDC to the new domain. The procedure is as follows:

Creating a new domain by moving an existing PDC

1. Log on to the domain as a domain administrator.

2. Open the Network applet in the Control Panel and select the **Identification** tab, which is shown in Figure 4.9.

3. Click the **Change** button to open the Identification Changes dialog box shown in Figure 4.10.

4. In the **Domain Name** field, enter the name of a domain that does not already exist on your network.

5. Read the warning that is shown in Figure 4.11 and choose **Yes** to continue with the change. After a pause, you are greeted with a message welcoming you to the new domain.

FIGURE 4.9

FIGURE 4.9

The Identification tab in the Network applet.

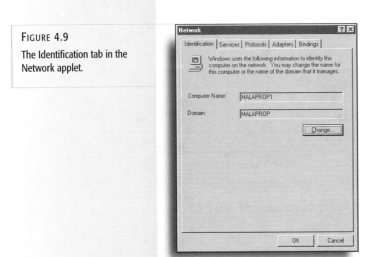

FIGURE 4.10

Changing the domain name for a PDC.

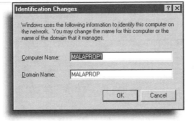

FIGURE 4.11

You receive this warning when changing the domain of a PDC.

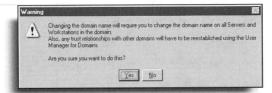

6. Restart the computer to put the change into effect.

7. If the old domain will remain active, you should promote a BDC in the old domain so that the domain has a working PDC.

Moving a Domain Controller to a New Domain

As you learned in the preceding section, a PDC can be moved to a new domain fairly easily, although extensive cleanup may be required. A limitation on the procedure is that a PDC can be moved only to a domain that does not already exist.

A BDC cannot change its domain, but its domain can be renamed if the PDC's domain is renamed first. This works because the PDC retains the same SID it had before and continuity is maintained. Unless you are careful, however, renaming a PDC's domain can result in two domains where one existed before.

An effective way to move a domain controller to a new domain is to reinstall Windows NT Server with a New Version setup. But you can reinstall a PDC to a domain only if the domain does not already exist. If a domain exists, it already has a PDC, and you cannot use Setup to create another PDC in the domain. Instead, you must install the computer as a BDC and promote it after installation.

To move a BDC to a different domain, you must reinstall Windows NT Server on the computer using a New Version setup. Unfortunately, a New Version setup overwrites all the configuration settings on the computer.

Renaming a Domain

You can use the Network applet to rename a domain, but the procedure is neither simple nor foolproof. To rename a domain, you must change the domain name for every computer in the domain. First change the PDC, followed by the BDCs. Finally, change the domain for all the stand-alone servers and computers. Because domain services will be disrupted, the entire procedure must be performed while no users are connected to the domain.

Go through this example of renaming a domain. Domain ALPHA is to be renamed BETA. ALPHA's PDC is named PDC1, and there are two BDCs named BDC1 and BDC2. Here is the procedure:

1. Change the domain of PDC1 (the PDC) to BETA and restart PDC1. This establishes the domain BETA.

Warning: Moving PDCs to new domains

Changing the name of a domain is a lot more involved than it looks. The computers in the old domain will not follow the change, so you will have a lot of cleanup to do. All the BDCs must be reinstalled to change them to the new domain. Servers and computers can be moved to the new domain more easily by changing their domain so that they log on to the new domain. On a large domain, however, you must change the configurations of quite a few computers.

2. Change the domain of BDC1 (a BDC) to BETA and restart BDC1, which will be established as a BDC of BETA.

3. Change the domain of BDC2 (the second BDC) to BETA and restart BDC2.

This procedure works because neither BDC1 nor BDC2 was promoted to a PDC before it was moved to domain BETA. Therefore, PDC1 was the only PDC and the same SID was used throughout the procedure.

If you are not careful, the BDCs will lose their association with the domain controlled by PDC1. Between step 1 and 2, there is a period when the PDC and BDCs belong to domains with different names. To get an idea of how things can go wrong, consider the following:

1. PDC1's domain is changed to BETA. After PDC1 is restarted, domain ALPHA does not have a PDC.

2. BDC1's domain is changed to BETA. BDC1 is now a BDC for domain BETA.

3. BDC2 is promoted to make it the PDC of domain ALPHA.

4. The administrator attempts to change the domain of BDC2 to domain BETA but is unsuccessful. When BDC2 was promoted, ALPHA and BETA became two distinct domains, and BDC2 can no longer be moved.

Now, to move BDC2 to domain BETA, it is necessary to reinstall Windows NT Server on BDC2. A New Version installation is the only procedure that will enable BDC2 to acquire the SID of domain BETA.

Stand-alone servers and workstations can change their domains at any time, however. The computer is just added to the new domain by an administrator in the new domain (a procedure described in the following section).

Adding Workstations and Servers to a Domain

Windows NT servers and workstations cannot simply log on to a domain. They must be recorded in the domain database before they are permitted to access domain resources.

Two steps are necessary to add a Windows NT computer to a domain and enable it to log:

- A domain computer account must be created for the computer.

- A user must log on to the domain to complete the registration of the computer with the domain.

These two procedures can be performed together or separately, using one of three procedures:

- The domain computer account can be created using Server Manager, after which a user logs on to complete the registration. The log on can take place during Windows NT setup or afterward.

- Both steps can be performed while Windows NT is installed.

- Both steps can be performed using the Network applet of the Control Panel.

Each of these methods has its value, so all three procedures are examined.

Using Server Manager to Add a Computer Account to a Domain

This procedure creates a computer account in a domain. After the computer account has been created, a user can log on to the domain using the computer associated with the computer account.

It often makes sense to separate the tasks of creating the computer's domain account and logging on to register the computer with the domain. Although an administrator is required to create the computer account, any user who has a user account can log on and complete the registration after the computer account exists. In such cases, it is not necessary for an administrator to visit the computer to complete the computer registration.

To add a computer to a domain, follow these steps:

Adding a computer to a domain

1. Log on to the domain as an administrator and open Server Manager.

2. Select **All** in the **View** menu so that all computers will be listed.

3. Select the command **Add to Domain** from the **Computer** menu. Figure 4.12 shows the dialog box titled Add Computer to Domain. This dialog box is used to add workstations, servers, and BDCs to a domain.

4. In the **Computer Type** box, select the type of computer being added to the domain. You have two choices:
   - **Windows NT Workstation or Server**
   - **Windows NT Backup Domain Controller**

5. Enter the computer's name in the **Computer Name** field.

6. Choose **Add** to add the computer to the domain.

7. Choose **Cancel** when all required computers have been added.

After you add a computer to a domain, it will be listed in the Server Manager computer list. Figure 4.13 shows an example of a workstation that has been added using Server Manager.

The Computer's icon changes in Server Manager following a successful logon

In Figure 4.13, the computer ISAAC has not yet logged on to the domain. Notice that the icon is shown in outline form. After a user logs on from the computer, the icon will be filled in.

FIGURE 4.12

Adding a computer to a domain.

FIGURE 4.13

Workstation ISAAC has been added to the domain, but has not yet logged on.

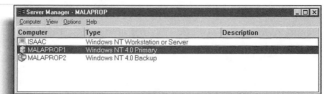

Completing Computer Registration While Installing Windows NT

After a computer account has been added to a domain using Server Manager, any user can install Windows NT Workstation or Server on the computer and complete the registration of the computer with the domain.

During Windows NT Server setup, you can choose to install a Primary Domain Controller, a Backup Domain Controller, or a server.

SEE ALSO

➤ *The procedure is described in step 32 of the installation procedure in Chapter 2.*

If the computer was previously added, it is unnecessary to enter an administrator's username and password when installing the Windows NT software. Just specify the computer name, and Setup will configure the computer to access the domain.

Completing Computer Registration While Logging On to the Computer

After the computer account has been added to the domain, users can join the domain from the computer. To join a domain from a Windows NT Workstation client, do the following:

Joining a domain from a Windows NT Workstation client

1. Open the Network applet in the Control Panel and select the **Identification** tab.

2. Check the **Computer Name** field to ensure that the name matches the name that was added to the domain in Server Manager.

3. If the computer name does not match:
   a. Choose the **Change** button to open the Identification Changes dialog box shown in Figure 4.14
   b. Enter the correct name in the **Computer Name** field.
   c. Close the Network applet and restart the computer to activate the name change
   d. Begin this procedure again.

Only Windows NT clients need to be added to a domain

Clients running MS-DOS, Windows 3.x, or Windows 95 and 98 can just log on to a domain. You don't need to use Server Manager to add the computers to the domain.

FIGURE 4.14

Changing a computer's network name.

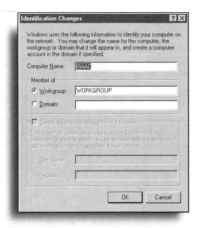

4. Choose **Change** to open the Identification Changes dialog box. In Figure 4.15, the Identification Changes dialog box is being used to add the computer ISAAC to the domain MALAPROP.

5. To join a domain when the workstation was previously added:

   a. Verify that the **Computer Name** field reflects the computer name that was added in Server Manager.

   b. Select the **Domain** radio button.

   c. Enter the domain name in the **Domain** field.

   d. Choose **OK**.

6. Exit the Network applet and restart the computer when you are prompted to do so.

7. When the computer restarts, press Ctrl+Alt+Delete to log on again.

8. In the Begin Logon dialog box, change the entry in the **Domain** field to the name of the domain you specified in step 5c.

9. Complete the **User Name** and **Password** fields with valid user account information.

10. Choose **OK** to log on.

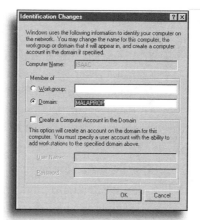

FIGURE 4.15
Adding computer ISAAC to the domain MALAPROP.

Adding Workstations, Servers, and BDCs to a Domain During Installation

Windows NT computers can also join a domain during installation. When this is done, the installation must be performed by an administrator, who must enter a valid administrator name and password.

SEE ALSO

➤ *The procedure for adding Windows NT computers to a domain during installation is described in step 32 of the installation procedure in Chapter 2.*

Adding Workstations or Servers to a Domain Using the Network Applet

Workstations and stand-alone servers can change their domains at any time. If the procedure is performed by an administrator, the entire procedure can be performed using the Network applet on the computer that is changing domains.

To change the domain of a Windows NT workstation or server, follow these steps:

Changing the domain of a Windows NT workstation or server

1. Log on to the computer using an account that has administrator permissions in the domain the computer will be joining.

2. Open the Network applet in the Control Panel and select the **Identification** tab.

3. Verify that the **Computer Name** field matches the name that the computer will have in the new domain. If the name is incorrect, click **Change** to open the Identification Changes dialog box. Enter a new computer name and restart the computer. Then repeat this procedure beginning at step 1.

4. Select the **Domain** radio button.

5. In the **Domain** field, enter the name of the domain that the computer will be joining. In Figure 4.16, a computer named RICHARD is being added to the domain MALAPROP.

6. In the **User Name** field, enter the name of a user that is an administrator of the domain the computer is joining.

7. Enter the user's password in the **Password** field.

8. Exit the Network applet and restart the computer.

9. When the computer restarts, press Ctrl+Alt+Delete to log on again.

10. In the Begin Logon dialog box, change the entry in the **Domain** field to the name of the domain you specified in step 5c.

11. Complete the **User Name** and **Password** fields with valid user account information.

12. Choose **OK** to log on.

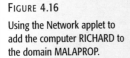

FIGURE 4.16

Using the Network applet to add the computer RICHARD to the domain MALAPROP.

Removing a Computer from a Domain

A Windows NT computer account is a permanent feature of the domain and does not disappear when a computer stops using the domain. When you move a computer to a new domain, you should remove the computer's account in the old domain.

To remove a computer account from a domain, follow these steps:

Removing a computer account from a domain

1. Log on to the computer's old domain as an administrator.
2. Start Server Manager.
3. Select the computer to be removed.
4. Choose **Remove from Domain** from the **Computer** menu. You will be required to confirm your decision.

It may take several minutes before the computer is removed from the list of computers shown in Server Manager.

Configuring Domain Synchronization

When the PDC determines that a BDC must be synchronized, the PDC sends a signal called a *pulse*. Synchronization is initiated by the BDC when it responds to the pulse. The PDC staggers pulses to limit the number of BDCs that attempt to synchronize at a given time.

Synchronization is a function of the NetLogon service, which is also responsible for validating user logons. Several characteristics of the synchronization process can be customized through the Registry. The relevant values are found under the following Registry key:

```
HKEY_LOCAL_MACHINE
    \System
        \CurrentControlSet
            \Services
                \Netlogon
                    \Parameters
```

SEE ALSO

➤ *Chapter 22, "Editing the Registry," explains how to locate and modify values in the Registry.*

The following Registry parameters can be added to the Registry or modified using the Registry Editor. All parameters are of type REG_DWORD.

- **ChangeLogSize**. This value entry determines the size in bytes of the Change log, which is stored in memory and on disk in %SystemRoot%\netlogon.chg. Partial synchronizations are performed using entries in the Change log. If partial synchronizations are performed at infrequent intervals, increase the Change log size to ensure that changes will remain in the Change log. If changes have been scrolled out of the Change log, a full synchronization will be necessary. A typical Change log entry consists of 32 bytes, enabling a 65,536 byte change log to store approximately 2,000 entries. Default value: 65536 (64 KB); range: 65536 to 4194304 (64–4,096 KB).

- **Pulse**. This value entry determines the pulse frequency in seconds. At the expiration of the pulse interval, the PDC sends a pulse to BDCs that need the changes accumulated since the last pulse. Default value: 300 (5 minutes); range: 60—3600 (1 minute to 1 hour).

- **PulseConcurrency**. This value entry determines the maximum number of BDCs that will be pulsed at any one time. In large networks or WANs, it may be desirable to pulse a limited number of BDCs at any one time to minimize network traffic and load on the PDC. Increasing PulseConcurrency increases LAN traffic and load on the PDC while synchronizing BDCs more rapidly. Decreasing PulseConcurrency reduces load on the PDC, but prolongs synchronization. Default value: 20; range: 1–500.

- **PulseMaximum**. This value entry determines the maximum interval at which BDCs will be pulsed, regardless of whether changes have been made to the domain database. Default value: 7200 (2 hours); range 60–86400 (1 minute to 1 day).

- **PulseTimeout1**. This value entry determines how many seconds a PDC will wait for a BDC to respond to a pulse before declaring the BDC to be non-responsive. Non-responsive BDCs do not count against the PulseConcurrency count. This mechanism enables the PDC to stop attempting to update non-responsive BDCs and accelerate updates of the remaining BDCs. If a domain has a large number of non-responsive BDCs, a large value for this parameter may result in slow partial synchronization of the domain. A small value may cause the PDC to mistakenly classify BDCs as non-responsive. Default: 5 (5 seconds); range 1–120 (1 second to 2 minutes).

- **PulseTimeout2**. This value entry determines how many seconds a PDC will permit for a BDC to complete a partial synchronization. When this timeout is exceeded, synchronization process is presumed to be stalled and the BDC will be declared to be non-responsive. The BDC is given PulseTimeout2 seconds to complete each partial synchronization attempt. If this value is too large, a slow BDC may consume an excessive portion of a PulseConcurrency slot. If this value is too small, the number of BDCs that fail to complete a partial synchronization may rise, increasing demand on the PDC. Default: 300 (5 minutes); range: 60–3600 (1 minute to 1 hour).

- **Randomize**. This value entry specifies the time a BDC will wait before responding to a pulse. Each BDC will wait a random number of seconds in the range of 0 through Randomize before calling the PDC. Randomize should always be smaller than PulseTimeout1. Default: 1 (1 second); range: 0–120 (0 to 2 minutes).

The time to synchronize all changes to BDCs in a domain will be greater than:

((Randomize / 2) × NumberOfBDCs) / PulseConcurrency

- **Replication Governor**. This value entry specifies the size of the data packets transferred from the PDC to the BDC during synchronization, as well as the frequency of calls from the BDC to the PDC. A value of 100 establishes the maximum size data buffer of 128 KB. Smaller values specify a percentage of 128 KB; for example, a value of 50 specifies a data buffer of 64 KB. Reducing the value of Replication Governor also reduces the frequency with which the BDC will request data from the PDC. If the value is 66, the BDC will have an outstanding synchronization call no more than 66% of the time. Range: 0–100.

To activate changes in these Registry parameters, you must use the Service tool in the Control Panel to stop and start the NetLogon service.

Deploying a Domain on a Wide Area Network

When a domain includes a slow WAN connection, you need to take special precautions when deploying the domain controllers. Your goal is to minimize the amount of traffic that traverses the WAN link simply to maintain the domain.

Figure 4.17 shows a domain that includes WAN connections to two remote sites. Notice that each remote site is equipped with a BDC that enables local users to log on without generating logon traffic through the WAN connection. The local BDC also supports network browsing, enabling users to browse the network without the need of contacting computers at other sites.

It is necessary to synchronize the BDCs with the PDC at periodic intervals. In a LAN environment, synchronization takes place at five minute intervals, but this would generate too much WAN traffic. Consequently, the administrator will want to increase the time interval between synchronizations by editing Registry parameters described in the preceding section. You may, for example, wish to increase the pulse interval by adjusting the value of the Pulse parameter.

You may also wish to add the ReplicationGenerator parameter to the Registry of the remote BDC and assign a value less than 100. This will reduce the packet size and the frequency of requests the BDC makes to the PDC, reducing synchronization traffic through the WAN.

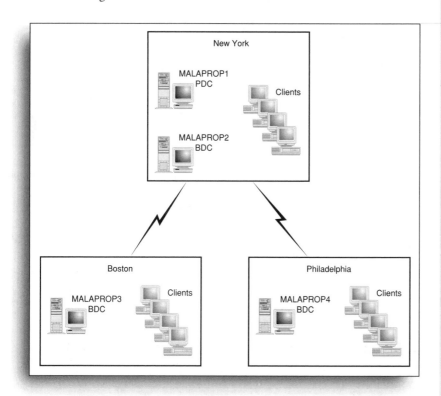

A "Simple" Domain?

This has been a fairly long chapter about a pretty simple thing, the Windows NT domain. Setting up domains isn't all that difficult, and you may never need some of the procedures included in this chapter. But domains have their shares of gotchas, and this chapter has been swollen by the need to cover the various problems you may encounter.

Now that you have a domain, you need to put some users in the domain. Otherwise you may have a very attractive domain, but nobody can do any work in it. Fortunately, users and groups are the topic of the following chapter.

Adding Users and Groups

Built-in user accounts

Built-in groups

What changes when a computer joins a domain?

Introducing User Manager for Domains

Managing user accounts

Managing the account policy

Managing groups

A network without users would be pristine, easy to manage…and useless. Without users, your network can't pay its freight, so you have to let them in. The trick is to let users into your network in ways that are easy to manage and that don't compromise security.

It would be easy to add users if everyone could be trusted with administrator permissions, but that's clearly not a good idea. You need to put up barriers so that everyone can't read everyone else's latest performance review, for example. Or so that an irate employee can't erase critical files on his way out the door on his last day.

To put up the proper barriers, restrictions that keep users away from what they shouldn't access without preventing them from doing their jobs, takes a lot of the jiggling and fussing over the permissions users are assigned. Security is one of your most sensitive responsibilities as a network administrator, and you need to become quite comfortable with the security tools Windows NT Server has to offer.

This chapter examines the first of those tools: user and group accounts. Every user who uses the network must have a user account, and in theory everything you need to do with security could be done with user accounts alone. But when you have more than two users, it is genuinely cumbersome to assign all permissions to individual users. That's where groups come in. In most cases, several users will have the same network access requirements. Groups enable you to manage users collectively, and the effective use of groups will go a long way toward simplifying your life as a Windows NT Server administrator.

Our first job in this chapter is to learn about users and groups, which come in a variety of flavors. And we need to look at the built-in users and groups that Windows NT Server creates for you. After that, we will look at how you can create your own private user and group accounts.

User and Group Accounts

To complicate things just a bit, Windows NT Server supports two types of users and two types of groups. Specifically, Windows NT Security is based on the following:

- **Global user accounts.** These are user accounts that originate within the Windows NT environment.
- **Local user accounts.** These are user accounts that originate in other server environments, such as LAN Manager and NetWare.
- **Global groups.** These are used to manage groups of users within a domain and also to export groups of users to other domains.
- **Local groups.** These are used to manage groups of users within a domain and also to import global users and global groups from other domains.

As you might suspect, each has specific uses, so you will need to explore their uses in considerable detail. The following sections examine the types of users and groups.

Global User Accounts

When you create a user account within Windows NT Server, it has a global scope. Global user accounts can be referenced in any domain that trusts the domain in which the user account was referenced.

You can assign network security permissions to individual user accounts, but it is more common to make users members of groups and to assign permissions to the groups. Group memberships enable you to administer the permissions for many users with single security operations.

In this book, you will be working only with global user accounts, so when I use the expression *user account*, I am referring to a global user account.

Global versus local

In Microsoft terminology, a *global entity* can be used by domains other than the domain in which the entity was created. Global entities are also said to have a *global scope*.

A *local entity* can be used only in the domain in which it is created. Local entities are also said to have a *local scope*.

SEE ALSO
➤ *Multi-domain networks and trust relationships are the subjects of Chapter 4, "Building a Domain," starting on page 103.*

Local User Accounts

Local user accounts originate in network environments other than Windows NT Server. A user account on a Microsoft LAN Manager network might be given access to resources on a Windows NT Server network through permissions assigned to a local user account, for example. Local user accounts can also originate on IBM LAN Server and Novell NetWare networks.

You won't be using local user accounts in this book to any great degree. I regard mixed-vendor networks as pretty advanced stuff, because local groups are a bit tricky to manage. If you are focused on Windows NT Server networking, you won't encounter local user accounts at all.

Global Groups

Groups are lists of users who share a common set of network permissions. Global groups can contain only user accounts that originate in the same domain as the global group. Global groups cannot contain other groups.

Group membership

The contents of a group are frequently referred to as the *members* of the group.

A global group has a global scope, meaning that it can be used in domains other than the domain in which the global group was created. That doesn't mean much at present, when you are considering only single-domain networks, but the capability for one domain to reference groups in another domain is crucial to the task of building multi-domain networks. You will see how valuable global groups are when you examine multi-domain networks in Chapter 12.

Local Groups

Local groups can be assigned permissions only in the domain in which the group was created. Local groups can include both user accounts and global groups, from the local domain and from other domains as well. This makes a local group a good way to collect users and groups from several domains so that they can be assigned common permissions.

Let's picture a simple example that shows how local groups and global groups work together. Figure 5.1 shows a two-domain network. The domain Malaprop is the primary domain on the network, and all user accounts are created in it.

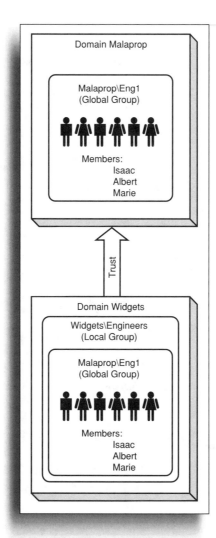

FIGURE 5.1

The global group
`Malaprop\Eng1` is a member of the local group
`Widgets\Engineers`.

Widgets is a domain that includes resources used by the Widgets division. The administrator of Widgets could have created separate user accounts for the Widgets domain, but that would have required users to maintain passwords in both Malaprop and Widgets. That's a practice to be avoided devoutly, so the Widgets administrator has chosen a different approach.

The Widgets administrator has said that the Widgets domain will *trust* the Malaprop division. Any user who successfully logs into Malaprop will be trusted by Widgets. They don't have a wide-open door to Widgets, however, and they are subject to the permissions the Widgets administrator has assigned.

The Widgets administrator asks the Malaprop administrator to create a group consisting of Widgets engineers. The Malaprop administrator creates the global group Eng1 in the Malaprop domain.

Because Widgets trusts Malaprop, the Widgets administrator can bring the Eng1 group into Malaprop. This is done by adding the global group Eng1 to the local group Engineers. The practical upshot is that any user in the domain Malaprop who is a member of Eng1 is given the permissions assigned to the group Engineers in the Widgets division.

Built-In Users and Groups

Local versus global

It's worth emphasizing the following distinctions between local and global groups:

- Global groups can be members of local groups

- Local groups *cannot* be members of global groups

When you install Windows NT, Setup creates several user and group accounts. These built-in users and groups greatly simplify the task of setting up access security. In addition, several of the built-in users and groups have special capabilities, either for using or administering Windows NT.

Built-In User Accounts

Every Windows NT Server and Windows NT Workstation computer has two default user accounts: Administrator and Guest.

The *Administrator* user account has a full set of permissions to manage the server or workstation on which the account is created. To prevent you from being locked out of a computer, the Administrator user cannot be deleted or disabled, although it can be renamed. Because it is so powerful, the Administrator account should be given an especially secure password. Store a record of the password in a very safe place, and put the Administrator account into semi-retirement. Later in this chapter, you will learn how to create user accounts that have capabilities similar to the Administrator account; these accounts can be used for day-to-day administration.

The *Guest* user account cannot be deleted, but it can be disabled or renamed. The idea is that users who don't have their own accounts will log on using Guest, which has a limited set of permissions. By default, however, Guest is disabled, and in most cases that's the way it should stay.

A valid use for Guest might be in a public access environment. Suppose you work for a government agency that wants to make specific information available to the public. It would be impossible to assign user accounts to unknown users, but careful design of a Guest account could solve your problem. Just be sure that Guest users can access only the files they should.

Built-In Groups

There are quite a few built-in groups of local and global varieties. Most of the built-in groups have a special capability, often a capability that can only be assigned by making a user a member of the group. Members of the Backup Operators group, for example, can back up any file to tape, but they don't have the keys to the LAN as administrators do.

The following sections discuss the built-in groups. Notice that there are a few differences between the built-in groups on Windows NT Server domains on and Windows NT Workstation computers and standalone servers. Five attributes are described for each group:

- **Scope.** Whether the group is local or global.
- **Managed By.** Users or groups who have authority to manage the group.
- **On NT Server Domains.** Whether the group is automatically created in Windows NT Server domains.
- **On NT Workstations and Servers.** Whether the group is automatically created on Windows NT Workstations and standalone servers.
- **Automatic Members.** Users or groups that are automatically given membership in the group.

Account Operators

- Scope: Local
- Managed By: Local Administrators
- On NT Server Domains: Yes
- On NT Workstations and Servers: No
- Automatic Members: None

Members of Account Operators can manage most user accounts and groups in the domain. They can create, delete, and modify most user and global group accounts. They cannot, however, assign access permissions. Nor can they manage the accounts of administrators or modify the following local groups: Administrators, Server Operators, Account Operators, Backup Operators, or Print Operators. Use the Account Operators group to delegate routine users and group maintenance tasks. For example, a department head who is a member of Account Operators could make user account changes as employees change assignments.

Administrators

- Scope: Local
- Managed By: Local Administrators
- On NT Server Domains: Yes
- On NT Workstations and Servers: No
- Automatic Members: Administrator (user), Domain Admins

Members of the Administrators local group have administrative authority over the domain, workstation, or server where the account was created. To enable a user to function as an administrator, simply add the user's account to the appropriate Administrators group.

Administrators are restricted in one area: They don't automatically have access to files on NTFS file systems. Each NTFS file or directory has an *owner* who has full authority to administer the file or directory. The owner can grant or restrict Administrator access to those files or directories. Even an Administrator cannot access files or directories without the necessary permissions. An administrator can, however, take ownership of any file or directory.

SEE ALSO

➤ *For more about file ownership, see page 197.*

➤ *For more about NTFS permissions, see page 197.*

Backup Operators

- Scope: Local
- Managed By: Local Administrators
- On NT Server Domains: Yes
- On NT Workstations and Servers: Yes
- Automatic Members: None

File backup is a task that is often delegated, perhaps to overnight operators in a computer room. In such cases, you don't want the backup operator to have full Administrator privileges. The Backup Operators group enables users to perform routine backup tasks without giving them the keys to the LAN. Members of Backup Operators can back up and restore files, log on to the server locally, and shut down the system. They cannot, however, perform administrator functions such as changing file security.

Domain Admins

- Scope: Global
- Managed By: Global Administrators

- On NT Server Domains: Yes

- On NT Workstations and Servers: No

- Automatic Members: Administrator (user)

Domain Admins is a global group that is automatically made a member of the Administrators local group. Thus every member of Domain Admins is an administrator.

Users don't gain any special permissions as members of the Domain Admins account. So why is there a Domain Admins account when users who need to be administrators can simply be added to the Administrators group?

As a global group, Domain Admins can be imported to other trusting domains. Suppose that domain Widgets trusts domain Malaprop, and you want the administrators in Malaprop to also administer Widgets. Thanks to the global nature of Domain Admins, you can include the Malaprop\Domain Admins group in the Widgets\Administrators group. Now, when an administrator assignment changes, you simply update the membership of Malaprop\Domain Admins, which changes the administrators for both the Malaprop and Widgets domains.

When a Windows NT Workstation or a standalone server is brought into a domain, the Domain Admins group is automatically added to the Administrators group on the workstation or server. If you don't want members of Domain Admins to manage a particular workstation or server, you must manually remove the Domain Admins group from the computer's Administrators group.

Domain Guests

- Scope: Global

- Managed By: Global Administrators, Account Operators

- On NT Server Domains: Yes

- On NT Workstations and Servers: No

- Automatic Members: Guest (user)

The Guest user is a member of the Domain Guests global group, which is in turn a member of the Guests local group. The

Guests group is assigned permissions that should be given to guests, who log on without a personal user account.

In multi-domain networks, you can include the Domain Guests group in the local Guests group of other domains that trust the logon domain. This is an easy way of granting users guest permissions in multiple domains.

Domain Users

- Scope: Global
- Managed By: Global Administrators, Account Operators
- On NT Server Domains: Yes
- On NT Workstations and Servers: No
- Automatic Members: All domain users

All user accounts are automatically added to the Domain Users global group. The Domain Users group is in turn included in the Users group, establishing all users in Domain Users as users in the domain. The Users group is assigned permissions that apply to all users in the domain.

Domain Users serves much the same purpose as Domain Admins, making it easy to import a group of users from one domain to another. If Widgets trusts Malaprop, simply add the group Malaprop\Domain Users to Widgets\Users to make all users in the Malaprop domain members of Widgets.

Guests

- Scope: Local
- Managed By: Local Administrators, Account Operators
- On NT Server Domains: Yes
- On NT Workstations and Servers: Yes
- Automatic Members: Domain Guests

The Guests group is used to define the permissions that should be available to users who log on as guests. Members of the Domain Guests group have guest permissions in the domain.

Members of the Guests group on workstations and servers have limited permissions, appropriate to users who have not been authenticated during logon. Guest users can maintain a profile on a Windows NT Workstation computer, but they cannot manage local groups or lock the workstation.

Power Users

- Scope: Local
- Managed By: Local Administrators, Account Operators
- On NT Server Domains: No
- On NT Workstations and Servers: Yes
- Automatic Members: Domain Guests

Members of Power Users can perform user functions on workstations and standalone servers. They can create user accounts and modify the accounts they have created. They can add user accounts to the built-in groups Users, Guests, and Power Users. They can start and stop printer and file sharing on the workstation or server.

If a Windows NT Workstation or a standalone server is added to a Windows NT domain, a recommended strategy is to add user's domain user accounts to the Power Users group. This enables the user to be a user in the domain and to administer the workstation or server.

Print Operators

- Scope: Local
- Managed By: Local Administrators
- On NT Server Domains: Yes
- On NT Workstations and Servers: No
- Automatic Members: None

Members of Print Operators can share, stop sharing, and manage printers running in a Windows NT domain. They are permitted to log on to servers locally and can shut servers down.

Replicator

- Scope: Local
- Managed By: Local Administrators
- On NT Server Domains: Yes
- On NT Workstations and Servers: Yes
- Automatic Members: None

Members of the Replicator group can perform replication of files in a domain or on a workstation or server.

SEE ALSO

➤ *Replication is discussed in Chapter 25, "Managing Directory Replication," starting on page 727.*

Server Operators

- Scope: Local
- Managed By: Local Administrators
- On NT Server Domains: Yes
- On NT Workstations and Servers: No
- Automatic Members: None

Each domain controller has a Server Operators local group, whose members can perform many nonsecurity management tasks on the server. They can share and unshare files and printers, format server disks, back up and restore files, log on locally to servers, and bring down servers.

Users

- Scope: Local
- Managed By: Local Administrators, Account Operators
- On NT Server Domains: Yes
- On NT Workstations and Servers: Yes
- Automatic Members: None

Most users will be members of the Users local group, typically through membership in the Domain Users group which is a member of Users. Members of Users are not permitted to log on locally to primary or backup domain controllers, and can access domain resources only by logging on to a client workstation. Users maintain a profile on a Windows NT Workstation.

SEE ALSO

➤ *Windows NT profiles are described in Chapter 8, "Activating Network Clients," starting on page 247.*

What Changes When a Computer Joins a Domain?

As you learned in Chapter 4, "Building a Domain," Windows NT computers must be added to a domain before they can log on to the domain. Adding a computer to a domain creates a SID for the computer and establishes a computer account in the SAM database.

Domain controllers (PDCs and BDCs) fully participate in domain security. You can see the link by examining the Administrators group. Any user who is a member of the Administrators group (or of the Domain Admins group that is a member of Administrators) is an administrator for the domain controllers in the domain. In other words, the Administrators group for the domain also functions as the Administrators group for each domain controller.

Stand-alone servers and Windows NT Workstations are not as intimately tied to the domain. Each computer maintains its own security database that regulates access to resources on the local computer. And each computer has its own set of local groups (Administrators, Backup Operators, Power Users, Replicator, and Users). Consequently, members of the domain don't automatically have membership in the corresponding groups on the servers and workstations. A member of the domain Backup Operators group isn't a member of the computer Backup Operators group, for example.

When a server or workstation joins a domain, it can be managed by domain administrators and used by domain users. This is accomplished by making two group membership assignments when the computer is added to the domain:

- The domain Domain Admins account is added to the Administrators account on the server or workstation.
- The domain Domain Users account is added to the Users account on the server or workstation.

These changes enable the server or workstation to participate in the security established for the domain. If you need to assign permissions that are not assigned to the Administrators or Users groups, you can assign additional permissions to any of the following:

- Individual users of the domain the server or workstation belongs to
- Individual users of domains trusted by the domain the server or workstation belongs to
- Global groups of the domain the server or workstation belongs to
- Global groups of domains trusted by the domain the server or workstation belongs to

You cannot, however, assign permissions to domain local groups. All groups on servers and workstations are local groups, which cannot have domain local groups as members.

SEE ALSO
➤ *For a description of the SAM database, see page 103.*
➤ *For a description of SIDs, see page 118.*

Introducing User Manager for Domains

The tool for managing users and groups is User Manager for Domains, which is started from a shortcut in the Administrative Tools group. Figure 5.2 shows User Manager for Domains, which has two panes. The upper pane lists user accounts, whereas the lower pane lists groups.

Before looking at the procedures for managing users and groups, let's briefly examine some specialized User Manager operations.

FIGURE 5.2

User Manager for Domains.

1 Upper pane: User Accounts

2 Lower pane: Groups

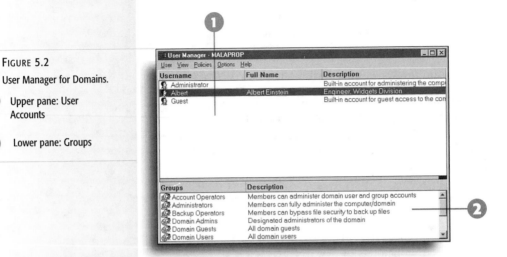

Selecting a Domain or Computer

You can change the domain or computer being managed by User Manager for Domains. The procedure is as follows

1. Choose **Select Domain** from the **User** menu.

2. In the Select Domain dialog box, specify a domain using any of the following techniques:

    • Enter a domain in the **Domain** field.

    • Enter a computer name in the **Domain** field. Computer names are specified with two preceding backslashes, for example \\malaprop1. If the computer you name is a PDC or a BDC, you will select the domain to which the domain controller belongs.

    • Select a domain in the **Select Domain** list box.

3. Select **Low Speed Connection** if you will be accessing the domain or computer through a low-speed connection, a process that is described in the next section.

4. Click **OK**.

Working with Low-Speed Connections

A substantial amount of data flows between User Manager for Domains and the domain or computer that is being managed.

This network traffic isn't a problem on a LAN, but it can cause problems if you are managing a domain or computer through a wide area network.

When managing through a WAN, you can improve performance by selecting **Low Speed Connection** when you choose the domain or computer to be managed. This restricts the data flowing through the network in several ways:

- User accounts are no longer listed in the main window, and the **Select Users** option in the **User** menu is inactive. You must specify user accounts by name to manage them.

- Groups also are no longer listed in the main window. Local groups can be created or managed using options from the **User** menu, but you cannot create or manage global groups. Global group memberships can be managed by changing group memberships in the user's accounts.

- The **View** menu commands are inactive.

User Manager for Domains will remember the connection speeds for the last 20 domains that have been administered. The **Low Speed Connection** check box will be checked appropriately after you specify a domain to be managed.

Low-speed communication can also be enabled by choosing **Low Speed Connection** from the **Options** menu.

Refreshing the User Account List

Changes you make to user accounts are posted immediately. If other administrators are managing user accounts, their changes are posted at intervals, and you will not see their changes until User Manager for Domains examines the network.

You can force User Manager for Domains to refresh its user list by choosing the **Refresh** command from the **View** menu. The **Refresh** command is unavailable when a low-speed connection is selected.

Sorting User Accounts

User accounts are normally sorted in alphabetical order. The **View** menu has two commands that you can select to change the sort order:

- **Sort by Full Name**
- **Sort by Username**

These options are unavailable when a low-speed connection is selected.

Managing User Accounts

User Manager for Domains is a versatile tool that enables you to manage individual user accounts or groups of user accounts. This section will examine the techniques required.

Notes on Managing the Administrator and Guest User Accounts

As you have learned, two accounts are built-in to each Windows NT installation: Administrator and Guest. You need to be aware of some special considerations when managing these accounts.

The Administrator Account

Administrator is a member of the following built-in groups, from which it cannot be removed:

- Administrators
- Domain Admins
- Domain Users

To create other users who are equivalent to Administrator, you must include them as members of these three groups.

You cannot remove the Administrator account, but you can rename it. In fact, it is a good idea to rename the Administrator account as a security precaution.

Many attempts to attack computer systems make use of built-in user accounts that are known to exist. Anyone trying to break into your network knows that Windows NT has an Administrator account, which gives them half the information they need to log on. All they must guess is the password.

Most accounts can be configured to lock up if several bad logon attempts are made, but you can't afford to have Administrator locked up because it is your ultimate management tool when all else fails. Because Administrator isn't subject to a maximum number of bad logon attempts, a hacker can try forever and you won't know a thing about it.

There are things you can do to protect the Administrator account:

- Create other accounts to perform network administration tasks.

- Rename Administrator to make it harder for an intruder to guess its name.

- Assign an especially secure password that would be very difficult to guess.

- Don't use the built-in Administrator account, even after it is renamed, so that an intruder who is snooping the data on your network can't learn the new name you have assigned.

The Guest Account

The Guest account can be disabled, and you should do so unless Guest access is appropriate for your system. By default, the Guest user doesn't have a password. Unless a password is assigned, any user can use Guest to log on, even from untrusted domains.

Guest is more powerful than its name implies. Guest is a member of the special group Everyone, and Everyone typically has read and execute permissions for all newly created directories and lots of other things besides. So unless you are very careful, Guest can enable an unauthenticated user to access a surprising amount of your domain.

Avoid using your administrator account

Because it is so powerful, you should use an administrator account only when it is necessary to do so. When logged on as an administrator you can easily delete critical files. Also, any virus that you introduce to the system will have administrator access, enabling it to infect more files.

Therefore, you should have two accounts: an administrator and a user account. Use the user account whenever possible. Use the administrator account only when necessary.

Decoying intruders

Typically, one of the first things an intruder will do is attempt to break in to the Administrator account. You can frustrate break-ins and detect intruders by renaming the real Administrators account. Then create a dummy Administrators account that has no permissions but a very tough password. Hackers will bang on this account without success and might tip you off by locking up the account with excessive failed log ins. Account lockouts are described later in this chapter in the section "Changing User Account Properties."

Unless you intend to be very careful, you should disable Guest and create user accounts. Even if a user will be temporary, it is worth the effort of creating a user account.

Creating a User Account

Users are created in the New User dialog box, shown in Figure 5.3. To open the New User dialog box, choose the **New User** command from the **User** menu of User Manager for domains. Figure 5.3 shows the New User dialog box after it has been completed to create a user.

FIGURE 5.3

Adding a new user account.

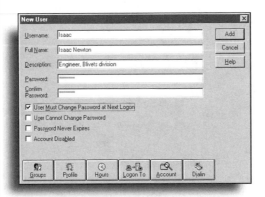

After you complete the fields in the New User dialog box, click **Add** to create the user account. The following sections discuss the various fields.

Username

Each user account is identified by a username, which must be unique in the domain in which the user account is created. A username can include up to 20 characters, including upper- and lowercase letters, numbers, and many punctuation characters. The following characters, however, are not permitted:

= + [ ] \ / < > ; : ' " ?

Username assignment is surprisingly tricky. Except in very small organizations, you can't use first names, because they will be duplicated surprisingly quickly. So you need to establish a username policy that will be consistent throughout your organization and that allows for sufficient variety to avoid duplication.

There are many schemes for assigning usernames. Here are three:

- First initial, plus last name. For example, Richard Feynman's username would be RFeynman. Again, a digit can be added to distinguish names when duplications arise, for example RFeynman1 and RFeynman2.

- First name plus last initial, such as IsaacN. Numbers can be added if there are duplicates—for example, IsaacN1 and IsaacN2.

- First name, plus a number. For example, Marie821. Generally speaking, users don't care for these names because they are difficult to remember, particularly if usernames are also employed in email addresses.

Personally, I prefer the first option. That's why it is first. The pool of first names is surprisingly limited and soon results in duplications in an organization of any size. Last names tend to be more varied.

Full Name

The **Full Name** field is optional, permitting you to enter a more complete name for the user. The full name appears in several lists that are presented to users by network utilities. This field is especially valuable if your conventions for usernames don't produce names that are easy for users to remember.

You should establish a convention for full names, just as for usernames. In some cases, full names will be used by network programs, perhaps in the address directory for an email program. In such cases, it is often preferable to enter full names with the last name first (for example Curie, Marie rather than Marie Curie) so that names will be sorted in lists alphabetically by last name.

Description

The **Description** field is optional. Use it to further identify the user, perhaps giving the user's job title or department.

Username format suggestions

If your network includes MS-DOS or Windows 3.x users, it is convenient to restrict usernames to eight characters. This makes it convenient to create user home directories, which can have the same name as the user's network name. With some name schemes, this might mean truncating a user's full name. For example, Jim Anderson's username would be Janderso. When names are constructed to include a differentiating digit, the name portion would be truncated to seven characters, for example RFeynma1 and RFeynma2.

If your network includes only Windows 95 and Windows NT and files are stored on NTFS volumes, then filenames are not restricted to 8.3 format. In such cases, you can match usernames of any length to filenames. It is a good idea to create usernames that don't include spaces, however, because spaces complicate things when you are including a filename in a path specification.

Password and Confirm Password

If you want, you can enter an initial password for the user account, in which case you must enter it in both fields. Passwords are never displayed in open text when they are entered, and the **Confirm Password** field verifies that you have entered the password correctly.

Passwords can consist of up to 14 characters and *are* case sensitive. Administrators can place some restrictions on the types of passwords that are permitted.

SEE ALSO

➤ *For more about password management, see page 174.*

User Must Change Password at Next Logon

If this box is checked, the user must change the account password the next time he or she logs on. The box is checked by default. You should always check this box if the password fields are left blank when the account is created to ensure that the user doesn't use an empty password.

Because even administrators can be restricted from accessing files, it is useful to prevent administrators from knowing users' passwords. That is easy to accomplish if you force users to enter passwords the first time they log on.

User Cannot Change Password

There are at least two reasons you might want to prevent users from changing their passwords:

- Two or more users share a user account
- Passwords are defined and entered by an administrator, whereas users are not permitted to enter passwords

The second reason makes sense if you ponder users' tendency to choose passwords that are easy to remember and type. Unfortunately, most easily remembered passwords are also easy to guess. (I own a commercial book that is a guide to hackers.

One appendix contains two pages that list common passwords.) It is surprising how many intruders gain access to a system simply because they have the perseverance to enter hundreds of passwords until one clicks.

Therefore, some organizations that require high levels of security assign passwords centrally, enabling administrators to choose passwords that are not easily guessed. On Windows NT, that is the only way to supervise the content of users' passwords, because passwords are encrypted after they are entered and cannot be examined by the network administrator.

Password Never Expires

In the Account Policy, described later in this chapter, you can force passwords to expire at specified intervals. In rare instances, you might want to override password expiration for a specific account.

If you check **Password Never Expires**, it overrides the value of **User Must Change Password at Next Logon**.

Account Disabled

Check this box to disable an account without deleting it. Some situations when it is useful to disable an account include

- Disabling the account of an employee who is on extended leave

- Disabling an account that is used by a person filling a particular role when the position is vacant

- Creating a template account that is used to create other accounts

Groups

Click the **Groups** button to open the Group Memberships dialog box, shown in Figure 5.4. This dialog box is used to determine which groups a user belongs to.

Creating more secure passwords

A common technique for cracking into computer systems is to use a *dictionary attack*, simply trying, perhaps with the help of automation, every word in the dictionary until a password is found. You can reduce vulnerability to dictionary attacks and other brute force cracking techniques by making up your passwords. An easy way to do that is to combine two unrelated words, such as "fatrock." Or try including a non-letter character such as "gimme5." And remember that Windows NT passwords are case sensitive, so you can improve things by mixing case, for example "HigHHo."

FIGURE 5.4

Adding a new user account.

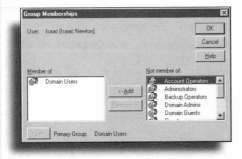

Selecting multiple list items

You can select multiple groups in the Member Of list (or in most Windows lists, for that matter) by holding down the Ctrl key while clicking each group you want to select.

Adding a Group Membership to a User Account

The **Member Of** box lists groups to which the user account already belongs. To add a group membership to the user account, select the group name in the **Not Member Of** list box and click **Add**. The group name is removed from the **Not Member Of** list box and is added to the **Member Of** list.

Removing a Group Membership from a User Account

To remove a user account from the membership list for a group, select the group in the **Member Of** list and click **Remove.** The group name is removed from the **Member Of** list box and is added to the **Not Member Of** list.

You are not permitted to remove the user's primary group. If you want to remove that group, you must first select a different primary group as described in the next section.

Selecting the Primary Group for a User Account

Each user account has a primary group, a feature that is used only by users who are accessing Windows NT Server from a Macintosh. When a Mac user creates a folder, the user's primary group is associated with the folder.

In deference to Mac users, a primary group must be designated for each user account. To change the primary group, select a group in the **Member Of** list and click **Set**.

Profile

The **Profile** button in the New User window opens the User Environment Profile dialog box, shown in Figure 5.5. This dialog box is used to configure user profiles, home directories, and other features of a user's network environment.

FIGURE 5.5
The User Environment Profile dialog box.

User Profile Path

Users of Windows NT have *user profiles* that store their desktop environments from session to session. A profile stores settings in the Start menu, the desktop, and a variety of applications. In most cases, users manage their own profiles, which are stored on the local workstation.

When they log on to a network, users have the option of keeping a copy of their profile on a network server. The advantage of having a *network profile* is that a user can move to different workstations and still work with the same profile. Setting up user profiles is a bit elaborate, so I have postponed discussion until Chapter 9, "Advanced Client Features."

SEE ALSO

➤ *User profiles receive detailed discussion on page 291.*

Logon Script Name

Users of Windows NT, MS-DOS, Windows for Workgroups can be assigned a *logon script*, a batch file that is executed when the user logs on to the network. Logon scripts are less versatile than profiles, and you will probably want to use profiles for Windows NT users.

A logon script is simply a batch file (.BAT extension). By default, logon script files are stored in the directory c:\Winnt\system32\ repl\import\scripts, although you can specify a different directory if desired. The advantage of the default directory is that it can be easily replicated to other servers using the Windows NT Replicator service. A master copy of the logon script is placed on the PDC and the Replicator service is used to copy the script to other domain controllers, enabling users to find their logon scripts on any server they happen to log on to.

SEE ALSO

➤ *The Replicator service is discussed in Chapter 25, "Managing Directory Replication," starting on page 727.*

The logon script path is entered in the **Logon Script Name** field, and can be entered in any of the following ways:

- Enter the filename only (such as `ISAAC.BAT`) if the file is in the default logon script directory.

- Enter a relative path (one that doesn't begin with a drive letter or backslash) to specify a directory path relative to the default logon script directory. If you enter `WIDGETS\ALBERT.BAT`, the `ALBERT.BAT` file is stored in the WIDGETS subdirectory of the default logon script directory. The full path would be `C:\Winnt\system32\repl\import\scripts\WIDGETS\ALBERT.BAT`.

Users can be assigned individual logon scripts, or users with similar needs can share logon scripts.

SEE ALSO

➤ *Logon scripts are discussed in on page 291.*

Home Directory

Each user who logs on from a Windows NT computer has a *home directory* which is the default directory for many user activities. For example, when a user opens a command prompt, the initial directory in the command prompt window will be the user's home directory.

The home directory can be located on the user's personal workstation, but it will not be available if the user logs on from another computer. In many cases, therefore, it makes sense to place the user's home directory on the network.

In Figure 5.5, the user's home directory is on a local workstation.

Placing a home directory on the user's local workstation

1. Open the user's account properties in User Manager for Domains and select the **P**r**ofile** button to open the User Environment Profile dialog box.

2. Select the **Local P**a**th** radio button.

3. Enter a local directory path in the **Local P**a**th** field—for example, `C:\Home`.

Figure 5.6 shows a User Environment Profile that assigns the user a home directory on a network server. To place the home directory on a network server, do the following:

Replacing the home directory on a network server

1. Create a directory on a network server in which users' home directories will be located.

2. Share the home directory.

3. Open the users' account properties in User Manager for Domains and select the **P**r**ofile** button to open the User Environment Profile dialog box.

4. Select the **C**o**nnect** radio button.

5. Specify a drive letter in the **C**o**nnect** spin box.

6. Enter the UNC path to the home directory. UNC paths are described in a nearby note.

Automatically created home directories

If in step 6 you specify a home directory that doesn't exist, it will be created. Permissions for the home directory are configured so that only the user who owns the home directory has access.

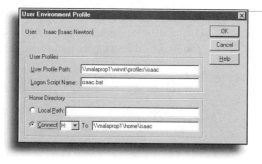

FIGURE 5.6

This user's home directory is on a network server. After you configure a home directory, when a user logs on, the drive letter you specify will be connected to the home directory you name. The user can access his or her personal network files by changing to the home directory.

Within Windows NT domains, resources are often identified using the *universal naming convention* (UNC). A UNC name consists of three parts:

- **A computer name**, preceded by two backslashes—for example, \\MALAPROP1.
- **A share name**, preceded by a single slash.
- **A directory path** relative to the directory indicated by the share name.

An example of a UNC name is \\MALAPROP1\home\isaac. This UNC name is interpreted as follows:

- The directory is on computer MALAPROP1.
- The directory is located in a directory that has the share name home.
- The directory isaac is a subdirectory of the directory with the sharename home.

SEE ALSO
➤ *Directory sharing is discussed on page 183.*

Hours

The **H**<u>o</u>urs button in the New Users dialog box opens the Logon Hours dialog box, shown in Figure 5.7. This dialog box can be used to restrict the hours during which the user can be logged on to the network. In the Logon Hours dialog box, a white square represents an hour when the user isn't permitted to be logged on. In Figure 5.7,

- The user is permitted to log on daily from 4:00 a.m. to midnight.
- The user isn't permitted to log on between midnight and 4:00 a.m. because that is when daily backups are performed.
- The user isn't permitted to log on Sunday because that day is reserved for comprehensive backups and system maintenance.

To permit logon during a time period, select the hours and click **A**<u>l</u>low.

To prevent logon during a time period, select the hours and click **D**<u>i</u>sallow.

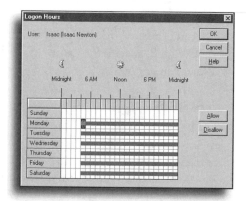

FIGURE 5.7
The Logon Hours dialog box.

You can select hours using any of the following techniques:

- Click a specific hour block.
- Drag the cursor through a block of hours.
- Click a day label to select that entire day.
- Click the top of an hour column to select that hour for all days.
- Click the square above Sunday to select the entire week.

Click **OK** to save the logon time configuration to a user's account profile.

Logon To

The **Logon To** button in the New Users dialog box opens the Logon Workstations dialog box, shown in Figure 5.8. This dialog box can be used to restrict the workstations a user is permitted to log on from.

Forcibly disconnecting users

Users will be forcibly disconnected when their logon hours expire only if you check **Forcibly Disconnect Remote Users from Server When Logon Hours Expire.** See the section "Disconnection Policy" later in this chapter for a discussion of this parameter.

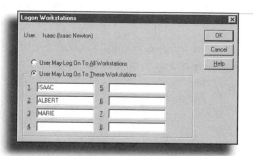

FIGURE 5.8

Assigning workstation logon restrictions. By default, the **User May Log On to All Workstations** radio button is selected, and no workstation restrictions are in effect.

To impose workstation selections, select the **User May Log On from **T**hese Workstations** radio button. Then, in fields **1** through **8**, specify the names of workstations from which the user can log on.

Account

The **Account** button in the New Users dialog box opens the Account Information dialog box, shown in Figure 5.9. This dialog box configures two aspects of a user account: when and if the account expires and whether the account is a global or local account.

FIGURE 5.9

Assigning account information.

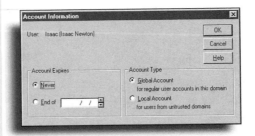

Observations on workstation logon restrictions

Workstation logon restrictions are most effective with Windows NT clients because the computers are registered with the domain and are assigned a SID. A Windows NT computer cannot impersonate another Windows NT computer because they have different SIDs.

Non-Windows NT clients are not assigned SIDs and can change identities with little effort, making it easy to evade logon restrictions based on workstation names.

Account Expiration

In most cases, user accounts remain active until they are manually deactivated by an administrator. Occasionally, however, you might want to configure an expiration date. Suppose that a contract programmer has joined your organization for a specific period of time. If you configure an account expiration date when the user's account is created, you cannot forget to deactivate the account at the appropriate time.

By default, the **Never** radio button is selected and the account has no expiration date.

To assign an expiration date, select the **E**nd Of radio button and enter a date in the date spin box.

Account Type

You will need to configure the user account type only if your network admits users whose accounts exist in another domain that isn't trusted by this domain. This might be a nontrusted

Windows NT domain, or it might be an account in another network environment such as Microsoft LAN Manager, IBM LAN Server, or Novell NetWare.

By default, the **Global Account** radio button is selected and the user is expected to log on to a Windows NT domain controller to gain access to a network.

If you decide to permit a user from a nontrusted network environment to access the domain, select the **Local Account** radio button. Users with local accounts can be granted permissions to domain resources but cannot log on to the domain interactively. Local accounts created in one domain cannot be used in a trusting domain. Because local accounts are seldom required in a Windows NT Server network, they receive no further consideration in this book.

Dialin

The **Dialin** button in the New Users dialog box opens the Dialin Information dialog box, shown in Figure 5.10. This dialog box works with the remote dialin capability of Windows NT, which is covered in its own chapter.

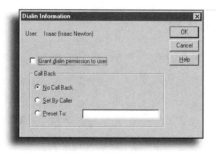

FIGURE 5.10
The Dialin Information dialog box.

SEE ALSO

➤ *For information about the Windows NT dialin service, see page 596.*

Changing User Account Properties

Changing a user account is very similar to the process of creating it in the first place. The dialog boxes are very similar, but there are a few changes that should be noted.

Modify a user account

1. Select the user account in the User Manager user list.

2. Open the User Properties dialog box by pressing **Enter** or by choosing the **Properties** command from the **Users** menu.

The User Properties dialog box is shown in Figure 5.11. Notice that you cannot change the **Username** field after the user account has been created. Otherwise, the process of changing a user's account properties is the same as the process of creating the user account in the first place.

FIGURE 5.11

Changing user properties for an existing user.

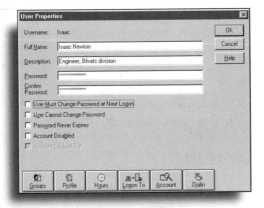

Copying User Accounts

If you are creating a new user account, you can save a bit of effort by copying an existing user account that has the configuration required for the new account.

Copying a user account

1. Select the user account to be copied in User Manager for Domains.

2. Choose the **Copy** command from the **User** menu.

This creates a Copy of the *User* dialog box that is similar to the New User dialog box, except that the copy of the *User* dialog box is filled out with many of the settings that were established in the user account that was copied. You still must fill out fields such as **Username**, **Full Name**, and so forth, but you will save quite a bit of work.

The Account Locked Out Property

The **Account Locked Out** property in the User Property dialog box cannot be selected by the administrator. This property is selected when the account is locked out due to a violation of a logon security restriction or to an expiration of the account. After this property is set, an administrator must clear the check box to unlock the account.

Deleting User Accounts

Built-in user accounts cannot be deleted, but you can delete user accounts that have been created by administrators or account operators.

Like many other objects, a user is identified by a SID. Therefore, once deleted a group cannot be re-created. Although a new group might have the same name as a previous group, the new group will have a different SID. So think twice before you delete a group.

Deleting a user account

1. Select the user in User Manager for Domains.

2. Choose **Delete** from the **User** menu, or press the Delete key.

3. Read the warning shown in Figure 5.12. Click **OK** to delete the group or **Cancel** to cancel the action.

4. You will be asked to confirm your decision a second time. Click **Yes** to delete the group.

Managing Multiple User Accounts

After several user accounts have been created, you might find it useful to manage several user accounts at once. Suppose that you have created a new group and want to make 30 users members of the group. It would be a nuisance to have to change each user's account properties individually.

To manage several user accounts, you must first select them in the User Manager user list.

Besides the mouse techniques described in Appendix A, you can select the users who belong to a group (or groups) by doing the following:

Template accounts

It is frequently useful to create template accounts that contain the settings appropriate for a department. You can then easily copy the template account when setting up a new user in the same department. Check the **Account Disabled** field of the template account so that the account cannot be used to log on to the system.

FIGURE 5.12

You see this warning when deleting a user.

1. Choose the **Se**lect Users command in the **U**ser menu to open the Select Users dialog box, shown in Figure 5.13. Notice that this box lists groups, not individual user accounts.

FIGURE 5.13

Selecting users based on group memberships.

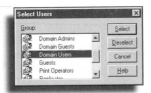

2. To select the users who belong to a particular group, select the group in the **Group** list. Then click **Select**.

3. To deselect the users who belong to a particular group, select the group in the **Group** list. Then click **Deselect**.

4. Choose **Close** to return to User Manager. The users who belong to the groups you selected will be selected in the User Manager users list.

When you are managing several users at once, you will notice a few changes in the properties dialog boxes. The User Properties dialog box, for example, lists the users being managed, as shown in Figure 5.14.

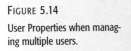

FIGURE 5.14

User Properties when managing multiple users.

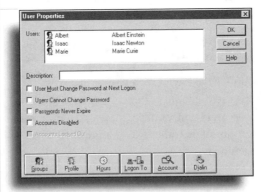

SEE ALSO

➤ *To learn some techniques for selecting multiple items in a list, turn to page 783.*

Changes Encountered When Managing Multiple Users

When two or more users are selected, you can only manage properties that are common to all users. This restriction has the following effects:

- In the User Properties dialog box, you cannot modify the following fields: **Full Name**, **Password**, **Confirm Password**, and **Passwords Never Expire**.

- In the Group Memberships dialog box, you can manage only group memberships that are common to all users you have selected.

- In the User Environment Profile dialog box, you can assign common or custom profile assignments.

- The Logon Hours dialog box can be used only to set the same logon hours for all selected users.

- The Logon Workstations dialog box can be used only to set the same logon workstation for all selected users.

- The Account Information dialog box can be used only to set the same properties for all selected users.

Configuring User Environment Profiles for Multiple Users

There is a trick you can use in the User Environment Profiles that makes it easier to specify profile and home directory paths for multiple users. The trick involves the %username% environment variable, which refers to the *current user*. When you include it in a path or UNC name, it supplies the appropriate username as properties are configured for each user account.

Let's see how %username% makes it easy to make mass assignments of user profile paths, logon scripts, and home directories. Figure 5.15 shows examples of all three techniques.

The key in each case is to create usernames consisting of eight characters or fewer, which enables you to use the username to specify a directory or filename that is suitable for users of MS-DOS, Windows 95, and Windows NT workstations.

FIGURE 5.15

Using %username% to configure profiles, logon scripts, and
home directories.

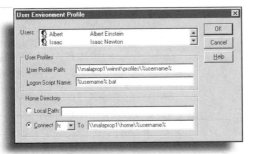

Specifying User Profiles for Multiple Users

You can include the %username% variable as the directory in
the **User Profile Path** field. If the profile path is being configured for user Isaac, the user profile path will be `\\malaprop\`
`profiles\isaac`.

Specifying Logon Scripts for Multiple Users

To specify a logon script for several users, you can use
%username% in the filename. In Figure 5.15, the **Logon Script
Name** field contains the value `%username%.bat`. For user Marie,
the resulting profile path would be `marie.bat`.

Creating Home Directories for Multiple Users

To specify home directories for several users, you can include
%username% in the home directory UNC name. In Figure
5.15, for user Richard, the home directory name would be
\\malaprop\home\richard.

Managing the Account Policy

The account policy sets several restrictions that affect all users in
the domain. Figure 5.16 shows the Account Policy dialog box,
which you open in User Manager for Domains by choosing the
Account command from the **Policies** menu. This figure doesn't
show the default settings. Instead, I have configured the dialog
box with settings that I recommend. The following sections
describe these settings in detail.

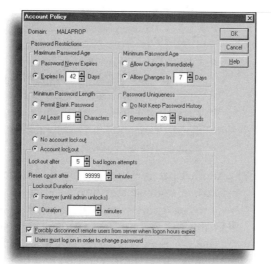

FIGURE 5.16
The Account Policy dialog box with suggested settings.

Password Restrictions

You can define four password restrictions:

- **Maximum Password Age**. Settings in this box specify the lifespan of a password. If you select **Password Never Expires**, users will never be forced to change their passwords. In nearly all situations, however, passwords should expire in no more than 60 days. I recommend that you select **Expires in...Days** and specify an expiration time of 60 days or fewer.

- **Minimum Password Age.** Fields in this box set a minimum password life span. If users can change their passwords immediately, they will tend to revert to an old, favorite password, making the password easier for a potential intruder to guess. If you select **Allow Changes In...Days**, users must wait the number of days you specify before again changing their passwords. I recommend a minimum password age of seven days.

- **Minimum Password Length.** You have the option of permitting users to have blank passwords, but this is seldom desirable. In nearly all cases, you should select **At Least...Characters**. Most security experts recommend that passwords should have a minimum length of six characters or greater.

- **Password Uniqueness**. These settings determine how many times a user must change his or her password before an old password can be reused. If you select **D**o Not Keep **Password History**, users can reuse passwords almost immediately. I recommend that you select **R**emember... **Passwords** and enter a value of 10 or greater.

Another parameter, mysteriously hidden at the bottom of the Account Policy dialog box, also relates to users and their capability to change passwords. If you check **Users M**ust Log On in **Order to Change Passwords**, a user whose password has expired cannot change the password without contacting an administrator. If the field isn't checked, a user can change his or her password even when the password is expired.

Account Lockout Policy

What happens when a user enters a bad password when logging on? In most cases, you want the system to permit a limited number of failed logon attempts, after which the user account should be locked.

I recommend that you select the **Account Loc**kout radio button. Here are my recommendations for the settings:

- **Lockout After...Bad Logon Attempts.** In my opinion, a user who cannot successfully log on in five attempts has either forgotten his or her password, or is trying to break in. In either case, you want to lock the account so that the matter will be brought to an administrator's attention.

- **Reset C**ount After... Minutes. This field specifies the interval (from 1 to 99999 minutes) in which the minimum number of bad logon attempts will lock the account. I recommend that you set a high value to ensure that the user will contact an administrator when the account is locked out. Otherwise, an intruder can make several bad attempts that will never become known because they will be purged

Hacker myths

There is a myth that computer intruders are exceptionally clever computer geeks who know how to crack their way into the most secure systems. Although a few such people exist, most intruders simply exploit known loopholes such as weak password enforcement. Restrictive account lockout policies can considerably improve the security of your network.

from the system before the legitimate user again attempts to
log on.

- **Lockout Duration.** If you select **Duration...Minutes**, the
user can attempt to log on again after the interval you specified. However, if the user can't log on after five attempts, it
is very likely that an intruder is trying to log on. I recommend that you select **Forever (Until Admin Unlocks)** to
make intruders' lives more difficult.

Disconnection Policy

The last setting in the Account Policy dialog box is **Forcibly
Disconnect Remote Users from Server When Logon Hours
Expire.** If this box is checked, users are forced off the system
when their logon hours expire. See the "Hours" section earlier
in this chapter for a discussion of logon hours properties.

Some users often leave at night without logging out. Selecting
this option is one way to ensure that they will log off at the end
of the business day.

Managing Groups

The bottom pane of the main window in User Manager for
Domains lists groups that have been defined in the domain.
Earlier in the chapter, it was explained that a number of built-in
groups are created when a Windows NT domain is established.
In Figure 5.17, the panes in User Manager for Domains have
been adjusted to show all the built-in groups.

Take a moment to examine the groups appearing in User
Manager for Domains. Notice that global groups (such as
Domain Admins) are tagged with an icon that includes a world
globe. Local groups (such as Admins) are marked by an icon that
includes a workstation in the background. Now let's see how you
can create your own groups.

Local and remote users

In Windows NT Server terminology, a *local user* is working with
files that reside on the local
computer. A *remote user* is
accessing files through the network via shares. Only remote
users are affected by the
account disconnection policy.

FIGURE 5.17

Note the icons that identify global and local groups in User Manager for Domains.

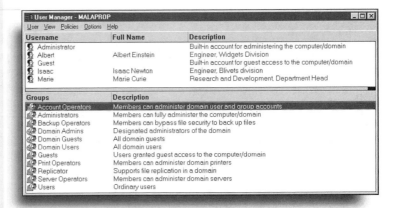

Creating a Global Group

Creating a global group

1. Log on as an administrator or as an account operator and start User Manager for Domains.

2. Choose the **New Global Group** command in the **User** menu to open the New Global Group dialog box, shown in Figure 5.18.

FIGURE 5.18

Creating a global group.

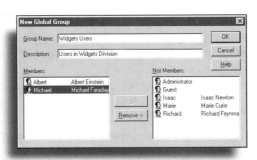

3. You must complete the **Group Name** field. Enter a name for the group, which can consist of up to 20 characters.

4. The **Description** field is optional. You may choose to enter a note that further explains the group.

5. Only user accounts can be members of global groups. To add members to the group, select the usernames in the **Not Members** list. Then click **Add**.

6. To remove users form the group, select their names in the **Members** list. Then click **Remove**.

7. Click **OK** to create the group.

Creating a Local Group

Local groups are a bit more involved because they can contain both users and groups, which can be taken from the local or from remote domains.

Creating a local group

1. Log on as an administrator or as an account operator and start User Manager for Domains.

2. Choose the **New Local Group** command from the **User** menu to open the New Local Group dialog box, shown in Figure 5.19. (This figure was prepared after members were added to the group.)

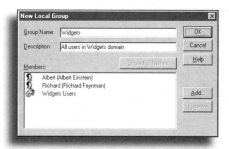

FIGURE 5.19
Creating a local group.

3. You must complete the **Group Name** field. Enter a name for the group, which can consist of up to 20 characters.

4. The **Description** field is optional. Descriptions are especially useful on networks that have large numbers of groups.

5. To add user and group names to the group, click **Add** to open the Add Users and Groups dialog box, shown in Figure 5.20. This window has a lot of options:

- **List Names From.** Local groups can contain users and groups from the local domain and from domains trusted by this domain. To select a different domain, click the arrow to open a domain list and select the domain.

- **Add.** To add a user account or group, select the entry in the **Names** list, then click **Add**. The name will be copied to the **Add Names** list.

- **Members.** To view the members of a global group, select the group in the **Names** list and click **Members**. You can choose specific group members to add to the group you are creating.

- **Search.** The list of names can be quite long. In some cases, you might want to click **Search** to find an entry. After you find what you want, it can be added to the members of the group.

FIGURE 5.20
Selecting members for a local group.

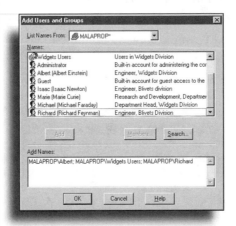

6. Click **OK** when the group is defined as you want.

Changing Group Properties

To change the properties of a group, double-click the group entry in the Groups list of User Manager for Domains. Or select a group name and choose **Properties** from the **User menu**. The Global Group Properties and Local Group Properties windows enable you to manage group properties.

Copying a Group

If you are creating a group that will have properties similar to an existing group, you can copy the existing group. Select the existing group in User Manager for Domains. Then choose **Copy** from the <u>U</u>ser menu. A New Group Window enables you to configure the new group, which initially will have the same members as the group that was copied. You must specify a unique name for the new group.

Deleting a Group

Built-in groups cannot be deleted, but you can delete groups that have been created by administrators or account operators.

Like many other objects, a group is identified by a SID. Therefore, once deleted a group cannot be re-created. Although a new group might have the same name as a previous group, the new group will have a different SID. So think twice before you delete a group.

Deleting a group

1. Select the group in User Manager for Domains.

2. Choose <u>**Delete**</u> from the <u>U</u>ser menu, or press the Delete key.

3. Read the warning, which is similar to the one shown in Figure 5.12. Click **OK** to delete the group or **Cancel** to cancel the action.

4. You will be asked to confirm your decision a second time. Click **Yes** to delete the group.

All Dressed Up and Nowhere to Go

You now have users and groups with which to manage them. But at present, there isn't much your users can do except log on. To make the network useful, you must share files and printers with your users, tasks that are covered in the next two chapters.

In the next chapter, you learn how to set up file shares that enable users to access shared data files and applications. Then, in Chapter 7, you see how to share printers. After you have finished those chapters, you will actually be the proud owner of a working Windows NT Server network.

Sharing Files and Managing File Security

Your network now has users with nowhere to go. They can log on, but they can't access any files through the network. That's where sharing comes in. *Sharing* is the technique used on all Microsoft networking products to make directories, and the files in them, available to network clients. If you have networked any Microsoft product, from Windows for Workgroups to Windows 95, you are familiar with sharing.

But sharing is considerably more robust with Windows NT Server than with other Microsoft network-capable operating systems. You can establish very high levels of security, and files can be stored on centralized servers that are more reliable and better-performing than most users' workstations.

It is easy to share directories and files. The trick is to share without compromising security. Windows NT Server supports four levels of security that enable you to tightly control user access to shares:

- **Abilities**. Users gain abilities by being assigned to built-in groups.
- **Rights**. Rights initially are assigned to built-in groups but can be assigned to groups or users by an administrator.
- **Shares**. Shares are directories that are shared on the network. Shares can be assigned share-level permissions.
- **Permissions**. Users and groups can be assigned permissions for directories and files on NTFS volumes.

In Chapter 5, "Adding Users and Groups," you learned the capabilities that are assigned to built-in groups, capabilities that arise from the abilities and rights held by the groups. You also learned how to establish users as members of groups. So, you already know that users' memberships in built-in groups define much of users' access to network resources.

This chapter focuses on shares and permissions, two security features that extend the capabilities users gain as a result of their memberships in built-in groups. We'll start with shares, because shares apply to files on both FAT and NTFS volumes. Then we'll look at the permissions that can be used to protect files on NTFS volumes.

File Sharing

Files can only be accessed through the network if they are shared. Before going into the details about sharing, let's look at a simple example.

File Sharing Basics

Figure 6.1 shows a server's file system as viewed in Windows NT Explorer. Note the folder icons. A plain folder indicates that the directory has not been shared. A folder in an outstretched hand indicates that the folder is shared.

You will probably find that Windows NT Explorer will be your preferred tool for managing directories, files, and shares. If you are not too comfortable with Explorer, take a few minutes to look at Appendix A, "Tips on the Windows NT User Interface." The section "Tips on Using Windows NT Explorer" will briefly introduce you to the capabilities of Explorer.

FIGURE 6.1

A Windows NT directory tree with default shares.

When Windows NT Server is installed, several shares are established:

- Each volume is assigned an administrative share. For example, C: is given the share name C$. Administrative shares are for use only by administrators.

- `C:\Winnt` is also shared as an administrative share.

- A share named NETLOGON is publicly available so that users can access the files they need to log on.

Most of the default shares are administrative shares and can't be used by ordinary users. The NETLOGON share isn't good for much besides logging on. So, before users can do anything useful with the network, you must create shares that give them access.

Every Windows NT computer has a Program Files directory. Suppose you have installed applications in Program Files that you want to share with network users. The following procedure assigns the share name Programs to Program Files.

Sharing a directory

1. Open Windows NT Explorer and expand the tree in All Folders until you can see Program Files.

2. Right-click the folder to be shared to open its context menu.

3. Choose **Sharing** from the context menu to open the *folder* Properties dialog box shown in Figure 6.2. Notice that the **Sharing** tab is selected.

4. Select the **Shared As** radio button to activate sharing for the folder.

5. In the **Share Name** field, enter the name that will be used to advertise the share on the network.

6. If you want, you can include a description of the share in the **Comment** field. These descriptions appear in browse lists and help users identify shares.

7. By default, the **Maximum Allowed** radio button is selected, indicating that the share can be accessed by an unlimited number of users.

   To limit access to the share, select the **Allow...Users** radio button and indicate a maximum number of users in the spin box.

8. By default, the special group Everyone is given Full Control permissions to the share. Because Everyone includes, well, *everyone*—all users who have been authenticated to access the domain, whether local or remote—all users can use the share.

Folders and directories

Microsoft uses the terms *folder* and *directory* interchangeably, and indeed they both refer to the same thing. There is a tendency to use "directory" when working in a non-graphic environment or when at the command line and to prefer "folder" when working in a GUI such as Windows NT Explorer. But Microsoft and everyone else, including this author, are inconsistent.

It really doesn't matter which term you use. Both terms refer to a special file in the file system that serves as a logical container for other files.

Shares and MS-DOS users

If a share will be accessed by MS-DOS or Windows 3.x users, the share name must conform to the 8.3 naming convention. MS-DOS and Windows 3.x users cannot see longer share names.

Windows 95 and 98 and Windows NT users can use longer share names.

The **Permissions** button opens a dialog box where you can configure custom share permissions. Share permissions will be discussed in detail in the section "Share Permissions," later in this chapter.

9. Click **OK** to save the share. The Program Files folder icon is now tagged with a sharing hand.

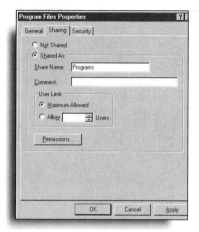

FIGURE 6.2
Editing share properties.

Connecting with File Shares

Now that the folder has been shared, users can log on to the domain and access files in the shared folder. Shares are accessed differently from different network clients:

- Windows NT 4 and Windows 95 or 98 clients can access shares through Explorer or through the Network Neighborhood, tasks that are described in the next two sections. Shares can also be accessed from the command line by using the net use command.

- Windows 3.x and Windows NT 3.x clients access shares through File Manager or the net use command.

- MS-DOS users access shares through the net use command.

You can browse shares using Explorer, Network Neighborhood, or File Manager. After browsing, you will in most cases map a drive letter to the share, enabling you to use files in the share as though they are stored on a local hard disk.

SEE ALSO

➤ net use *and several other commands are discussed on page 278.*

Connecting Through the Network Neighborhood

Let's peruse an example of share browsing using Network Neighborhood.

Connecting to a share through Network Neighborhood

1. Double-click Network Neighborhood.

2. In Network Neighborhood, double-click the server that is hosting the share. At this point, Network Neighborhood resembles Figure 6.3.

FIGURE 6.3

Browsing for a share in Network Neighborhood.

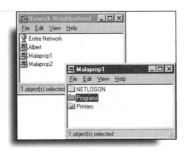

3. Right-click the Programs share to open its context menu.

4. Choose **M**ap **N**etwork **D**rive from the context menu to open the Map Network Drive dialog box shown in Figure 6.4.

FIGURE 6.4

Mapping a drive letter to a share.

5. In the **D**rive field, select a drive letter that will be used to access the share.

6. The **P**ath field is already completed with the UNC name of the share.

7. If you don't have permission to access the share, but have use of another user account that has the required permissions, you can specify the other user account in the **Connect As** field.

8. If this drive connection should be reestablished each time you log on to the network, check **Reconnect at Logon**.

9. Choose **OK** to create the connection.

The user can now access drive J: in My Computer or in Explorer just as he or she would access a local drive. Figure 6.5 shows Explorer after a user has connected drive J: to `\\Malaprop1\Programs`. Notice that the folder `Program Files` isn't visible to the user. The `Program Files` folder displays as the root directory of drive J:.

Connecting Through Explorer

Connecting to a share with Explorer

1. Choose the command **Map Network Drive** in the **Tools** menu to open the Map Network Drive dialog box shown in Figure 6.5.

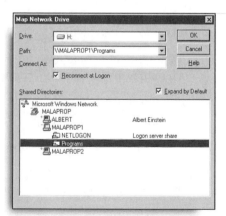

2. Select an unused drive letter in the **Drive** field.

3. Complete the **Path** field with the UNC name of the share. There are two techniques for defining the share path:

■ Browse the tree in the **Shared Directories** window, as was done in Figure 6.5. When you locate the share you

---

A note regarding MS-DOS users

The `\Program Files` directory has a long name that exceeds the MS-DOS 8.3 format requirement. Won't that mess up MS-DOS and Windows 3.x users? No, because the share name Programs conforms to the 8.3 rule. Users don't see the name of a directory that is the root directory of a share, so the long file name has no impact on MS-DOS and Windows 3.x users.

FIGURE 6.5

Mapping a network drive in Explorer.

want, double-click the share to copy its UNC name to the **Path** field.

- Manually enter a UNC name in the **Path** field.

4. If you don't have permission to access the share, but have use of another user account that has the required permissions, you can specify the other user account in the **Connect As** field.

5. If this drive connection should be reestablished each time you log on to the network, check **Reconnect at Logon**.

SEE ALSO

➤ *UNC names are discussed on page 166.*

➤ *The procedure for connecting to a network share with Windows 3.x or Windows for Workgroups is described on page 393.*

Share Permissions

You can fine-tune share access by assigning *permissions* to the share. Permissions establish upper limits on the operations a user can perform on files in the share. You can further limit the actions users can perform by assigning directory and file permissions on NTFS volumes, but users cannot perform any actions that are not permitted by the permissions of the share they are using to access the file.

Four types of permissions can be assigned to shared directories. Here they are, arranged from most to least restrictive:

- **No Access.** No permissions are granted for the share.
- **Read.** Share users can do the following:

    Display subdirectory names and file names.

    Open subdirectories.

    Display file data and file attributes.

    Run program files.
- **Change.** In addition to actions permitted by Read permissions, users can do the following:

    Create subdirectories and files.

    Modify files.

Connecting to shares with `net use`

Many network operations can be performed from the command line with options of the `net` command. For example, `net use` establishes drive connections with shares. Even though you might be addicted to GUI utilities, the command-line `net` utility can be a blessing because it enables you to perform network operations in batch files and logon scripts.

To connect drive M: with `\\malaprop1\apps`, you would enter the following command at a command prompt: `net use m: \\malaprop1\apps`.

If any part of the UNC path name includes a space, enclose the entire UNC name in quotation marks, for example: `net use o: "\\widgets1\data files"`.

Change subdirectory and file attributes.

Delete subdirectories and files.

- **Full control.** In addition to actions permitted by Change permissions, users can do the following:

Change permissions.

Take ownership.

Share permissions can be assigned to user accounts, groups, and the special identities Everyone, SYSTEM, NETWORK, INTERACTIVE, and CREATOR OWNER. Special identities are described in a sidenote on this page.

Special identities

In addition to users and groups, permissions can be assigned to objects called special identities or special groups. Windows NT Server supports five special identities:

- **Everyone.** Includes all users and can be used to assign permissions that all users of a domain hold in common. Everyone includes guests and users from other domains.

- **SYSTEM.** Represents the operating system. Setup assigns initial permissions to SYSTEM. Administrators will seldom, if ever, be required to modify permissions assigned to SYSTEM.

- **NETWORK.** Includes all users who access a file or directory through the network. Permissions assigned to NETWORK are in effect only when the user accesses a resource remotely.

- **INTERACTIVE.** Includes users who log on locally to the server. Permissions assigned to INTERACTIVE are in force only when the user logs on to the server computer directly.

- **CREATOR OWNER.** Represents the user who creates a directory or file. Permissions given to CREATOR OWNER for a directory are assigned to any files or subdirectories that are created in the directory. As a result, users are given the rights assigned to CREATOR OWNER for any subdirectories they create.

SEE ALSO

➤ *NTFS permissions are discussed on page 197.*

Changing Share Permissions

To view permissions assigned to a share, choose the **Permissions** button in the **Sharing** tab of the *folder* Properties dialog box (see Figure 6.2). This opens the Access Through

Share Permissions dialog box shown in Figure 6.6. In this dialog box, you can examine the permissions that are assigned for the share. You can also modify permissions as required.

FIGURE 6.6

Setting share permissions.

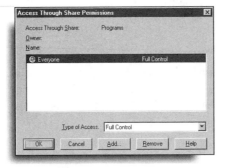

Adding a User or Group to the Share Permissions List

You can also add users or groups to the permissions list for the share as required.

Adding a user or group to the permissions for a share

1. Right-click the shared directory in Windows NT Explorer.

2. Choose the **Sharing** command in the context menu.

3. Click **Permissions** in the **Sharing** tab of the Properties dialog box. This opens the Access Through Share Permissions dialog box shown in Figure 6.6.

4. Click **Add** to open the Add Users and Groups dialog box shown in Figure 6.7. In the figure, the group Blivet Engineers has been selected for addition to the share permissions list, with Read permissions.

5. To view a different domain, click the down arrow in the **List Names From** field. Select a domain from the list that is presented.

6. By default, only groups appear in the **Names** list. To include user accounts in the **Names** list, click **Show Users**.

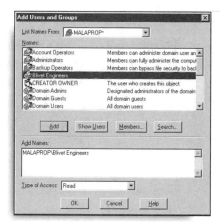

FIGURE 6.7
Selecting names for addition to
a share permissions list.

7. To add a user or group to the share permissions list, select
an entry in the **Names** list and click **Add**. The name is
added to the **Add Names** list box.

Repeat this step for each user or group that is to be assigned
permissions to the share.

8. Choose **OK** to return to the Access Through Share
Permissions dialog box. The names you entered in the **Add
Names** list will now appear in the **Name** list, together with
the permissions you specified.

Modifying Permissions

Modify share permissions already assigned to a user or group

1. Right-click the shared directory in Windows NT Explorer.

2. Choose the **Sharing** command in the context menu.

3. Click **Permissions** in the **Sharing** tab of the Properties dialog box. This opens the Access Through Share Permissions
dialog box shown in Figure 6.6.

4. Select an entry in the **Name** list box.

5. Pull down the **Type of Access** list box and select the access
permissions to be assigned to the objects in the **Add Names**
list.

6. Click **OK**.

Removing a User or Group from Share Permissions

Remove a user or group from the permissions list for a share

1. Right-click the shared directory in Windows NT Explorer.

2. Choose the **Sharing** command in the context menu.

3. Click **Permissions** in the **Sharing** tab of the Properties dialog box. This opens the Access Through Share Permissions dialog box shown in Figure 6.6.

4. Select an entry in the **Name** list box.

5. Click **Remove**.

6. Click **OK**.

Stopping Sharing

Stop sharing a directory

1. Right-click the shared directory in Windows NT Explorer.

2. Choose the **Sharing** command in the context menu.

3. Select **Not Shared** in the **Sharing** tab of the Properties dialog box.

Creating a New Share for a Shared Directory

Add a new share to a directory that is already shared

1. Right-click the shared directory in Windows NT Explorer.

2. Choose the **Sharing** command in the context menu.

3. Choose **New Share** to create a new share.

Each share must have its own unique name. When multiple shares exist for a directory, it is especially useful to add a comment to each share that explains its purpose.

Guidelines for Assigning Share Permissions

For a newly created share, Full Control permissions are assigned to the special identity Everyone. If the share is on an NTFS volume, you can leave the default share permissions in place. You can restrict effective user permissions using NTFS permissions, as described later in this chapter.

If the share resides on a FAT volume, share permissions are your only tools for limiting user access to files. (Remember that share permissions only restrict remote users!) Here are some suggestions for selecting share permissions:

- Users often need only Read permissions in application directories because they don't need to modify files.

- In some cases, applications require users to share a directory for temporary files. If that directory is the same as the application directory, you can enable users to create and delete files in the directory by assigning the Change permission to CREATOR USER.

- Users typically require the Change permission for a directory that contains shared data files.

- Often users will be assigned Full Control permissions only for their home directories.

Permissions are cumulative. Suppose that user Isaac belongs to the group Engineers. If Everyone has Read permissions to the Specs share but Engineers has Change permissions to Specs, then Isaac has Change permissions for the directory.

Administrative Shares

Windows NT Server automatically shares some directories. These shares, called *administrative shares*, are not advertised to users who browse the network. In some cases, administrative shares support network functions of the operating system. In other cases, administrative shares are defined for the convenience of administrators.

The following administrative shares are automatically established:

- **ADMIN$.** An ADMIN$ share is added to each server and is associated with the Windows NT Server system directory, which is usually `C:\WINNT`.

- *driveletter***$.** An administrative share is created for each hard disk. For example, the administrative share for drive C: has the share name C$.

Administrative share security

You might think that users who discover the existence of administrative shares could use them to gain access to areas of the server they cannot ordinarily access. Simply knowing the existence of C$ will not permit a user to remotely access the root of C:, however. To access the root of a drive, you must be logged on as a member of the Administrators, Server Operators, or Backup Operators groups.

The NETLOGON share

In addition to the administrative shares, one other share named NETLOGON is created when Windows NT Server is installed. The NETLOGON share is used by the NetLogon service to process logon requests and should not be removed or modified.

- **IPC$.** This share supports the named-pipes mechanism that provides *inter-process communication* between programs. IPC$ supports remote administration of computers.

- **PRINT$.** This share supports printer sharing.

- **REPL$.** This share is established when a replication server is configured, and is used to support export replication.

Notice a common thread in administrative share names: they all end with a $. Any share that ends with a $ will not be advertised in network browse lists.

Connecting to an Administrative Share

Because administrative shares don't appear in browse lists, you must make an extra effort to connect with them.

Connecting to an administrative share

1. Choose the **Map Network Drive** command in the **Tools** menu to open the Map Network Drive dialog box shown in Figure 6.8.

FIGURE 6.8

Connecting to an administrative share.

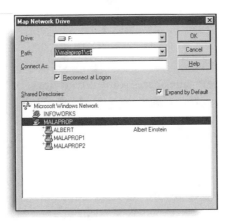

2. In the **Drive** field, select a free drive letter.

3. In the **Path** field, enter the UNC name for the desired share. For example, drive C: on server Malaprop1 would have the UNC name \\malaprop1\c$, as shown in Figure 6.8.

4. Click **OK**.

Creating Your Own Administrative Shares

It is often useful to create shares that are available to administrators but are not advertised to users. To create a non-advertised share, simply include a $ as the last character of the share name.

To use a non-advertised share, a user must be aware of the share's existence and must specify the share path name manually.

Understanding Ownership

Ownership is a very important concept in Windows NT security. Every object—directory, file, or printer—has an owner who is usually the user who created the object. The owner of an object has a special status, conferred by the CREATOR OWNER special identity, and typically has complete authority over the object.

The owner of an object controls the permissions of all users, even members of the Administrators group. This enables owners to configure home directories that are completely private, or to set up directories that can be accessed on a strict need-to-know basis.

The owner of an object cannot give ownership away. Owners can give permission to take ownership, however. This approach prevents a user from creating an object and then making it appear to belong to another user.

Administrators can take ownership of any file directory. This provision is necessary, because administrators must have the ability to manage objects owned by users who leave an organization or change departments. An administrator has difficulty abusing this privilege; once taken, a file cannot be given back. An administrator cannot, therefore, take ownership without leaving behind evidence of the action.

Managing NTFS Permissions

Directories and files stored on NTFS volumes can be assigned permissions that are more elaborate than the permissions available for shares. Administrators and owners have considerable freedom to fine-tune security down to the level of individual files. By contrast, share permissions apply uniformly to the shared directory and to all subdirectories and files in the shared directory.

How NTFS Permissions Work

NTFS security supports six individual permissions, which can be applied to directories and files. In permission lists, each permission is indicated by an abbreviation. Here is a list of the permissions, their abbreviations, and their effects on directories and files:

- **Read (R)**

  Directory: Permits viewing the names of files and subdirectories

  File: Permits reading the file's data

- **Write (W)**

  Directory: Permits adding files and subdirectories

  File: Permits changing the file's data

- **Execute (X)**

  Directory: Permits changing to subdirectories in the directory

  File: Permits executing the file if it is a program file

- **Delete (D)**

  Directory: Permits deleting the directory

  File: Permits deleting the file

- **Change Permissions (P)**

  Directory: Permits changing the directory's permissions

  File: Permits changing the file's permissions

- **Take Ownership (O)**

  Directory: Permits taking ownership of the directory

  File: Permits taking ownership of the file

Standard Directory Permissions

To simplify the task of assigning directory permissions, Microsoft has defined a series of standard permissions that can be used to assign useful sets of permissions in a single operation. Table 6.1 summarizes the standard permissions for directories.

TABLE 6.1 **Standard permissions for NTFS directories**

Standard Permission Name	Individual Permissions for Directory	Individual Permissions for File	Explanation
No Access	None	None	No access to directory or to files
List	RX	Not Specified	List directory contents, change to subdirectories, no access to files unless otherwise given
Read	RX	RX	List directory contents, change to subdirectories, read data from files, execute programs
Add	WX	Not Specified	Create subdirectories, create files, no access to existing files unless otherwise given
Add & Read	RWX	RX	List directory contents, create subdirectories, change to subdirectories, read file data, execute programs
Change	RWXD	RWXD	List directory contents, create subdirectories, change to subdirectories, delete subdirectories, read file data, create and modify files, execute programs, delete files
Full Control	All	All	All directory permissions, all file permissions, change directory and file permissions, take ownership

Notice that each standard directory permission defines two sets of permissions:

- Permissions that are applied to the directory, shown in the second column of the table.
- Permissions that are applied to files created in the directory, shown in the third column of the table. When permissions are applied to a directory, you have the option of applying file permissions to existing files as well.

To represent standard directory permissions, the directory and file permissions are typically shown in two pairs of parentheses. For example, the Add & Read standard permission is represented as (RWX)(RX).

In two cases (List and Add), the third column of Table 6.1 indicates that file permissions are not specified. In these cases, no file-access permissions are assigned. If users are to have access to files created in directories having these permissions, you must assign permissions to the files separately from the standard directory permissions.

Standard File Permissions

Standard permissions are also defined for files. The standard file permissions are

- No Access
- Read (RX)
- Change (RWXD)
- Full Control (All)

How Permissions Accumulate

Except for the special case of the No Access permissions, a user accumulates permissions from the permissions assigned to his or her user accounts and to all groups he or she belongs to. To see how permissions accumulate, let's look at an example.

Marie needs to access a directory named \engspecs. She belongs to several groups that have permissions for the \engspecs directory:

- **Blivets.** Members have Read permissions (R)(R).
- **Eng.** Members are assigned (W)(W) permissions, enabling them to add and update documents.
- **Eng_Mgt.** Members have (D)(Not Specified) permissions, enabling them to delete documents.

In addition, Marie's personal user account is assigned (X)(XD) permissions for the directory.

Marie inherits permissions from all three groups in addition to her personal permissions. Here is a summary of her permissions:

```
(R   )(R   )  from the group Blivets
( W  )( W  )  from the group Eng
(   D)(    )  from the group Eng_Mgt
(  X )(  XD)  from her personal user account
```

Summing permissions from all four sources, we find that Marie has working permissions of (RWXD)(RWXD).

The No Access Permission

There is a significant deviation from the rule of accumulated permissions. The No Access permission overrides all other permissions and denies the user access to the directory or file for which the No Access permission is assigned.

The No Access permission has this effect regardless of how the permission is assigned. If it is assigned to the user's personal user account or to any group to which the user belongs, the user is denied access. Even administrator access is blocked by the No Access permission.

Try an experiment. Create a directory named \Test. Edit the permissions for the \Test directory, assigning the No Access permission to Everyone. Now, log on as an administrator and try to access the contents of the \Test directory. You will not be able to do so. Clearly, misapplication of the No Access permission could be disastrous and has the potential to cause irreparable damage to a computer, locking out even administrators so that they cannot access files or correct the problem.

If the No Access permission is assigned to a directory, only the owner of the directory can revoke the No Access permission. In a pinch, an administrator can take ownership of the directory and revoke the No Access permission. Because you created the \Test directory, you are the owner of the directory, enabling you to remove the No Access permission and delete the directory.

Assigning Standard Directory Permissions

Assigning permissions to a directory

1. Right-click the directory in Explorer, My Computer, or Network Neighborhood and choose **Properties** from the context menu.

2. Select the **Security** tab in the Properties dialog box. Figure 6.9 shows the **Security** tab.

FIGURE 6.9

The **Security** tab in the Properties dialog box.

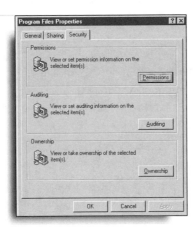

3. Click **Permissions** in the **Security** tab to open the Directory Permissions dialog box shown in Figure 6.10.

4. If a group or user is already listed in the **Name** list, you can change permissions as follows:

   a. Select the group or user in the **Name** list box.

   b. Pull down the **Type of Access** list (shown in Figure 6.11) and select the permissions to be assigned to the selected group or user.

FIGURE 6.10

Permissions assigned to directory.

FIGURE 6.11

Selecting directory access permissions.

5. To add a group or user to the **Name** list:

a. Choose **Add** to display the Add Users and Groups dialog box shown in Figure 6.12.

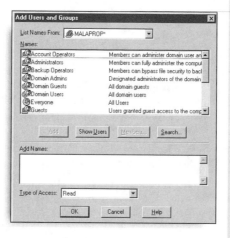

FIGURE 6.12

Adding a group to directory permissions.

b. To display names from another domain, open the list in the **List Names From** field and choose a domain.

c. To show names in the **N**ames list, click the **Show Users** button.

d. In the **N**ames list, double-click the groups or users to be added. The names you double-click will be copied to the **A**dd Names list.

e. Pull down the **T**ype of Access list box and select the permissions to be assigned.

f. Click **OK** to add the names to the Directory Permissions dialog box.

6. Determine whether file permissions should be applied to files already existing in the directory for which you are defining permissions. If file permissions should be assigned, check **Replace Permissions on Existing Files** in the Directory Permissions window. If you don't check this box, existing files retain their current permissions.

7. Determine whether the permissions you are assigning should be applied to subdirectories of the directory for which you are defining permissions. If permissions should be assigned to subdirectories, check **Replace Permissions on Subdirectories**. If you don't check this box, subdirectories retain their current permissions.

8. Click **OK** to save the directory permissions.

Assigning File Permissions

The procedures for managing file and directory permissions are similar.

Assigning permissions to a file

1. In Explorer, My Computer, or Network Neighborhood, select the file or files to be managed.

2. Right-click one of the selected files and choose **Properties** from the context menu.

3. Select the **Security** tab in the Properties dialog box.

Warning! Use No Access with caution

Remember that the No Access permission can have far-reaching and unforeseen effects. If a user holds the No Access permission for a file or directory, all access is denied, regardless of other permissions the user might have.

4. Choose **Permissions** in the **Security** tab to open the File Permissions dialog box shown in Figure 6.13.

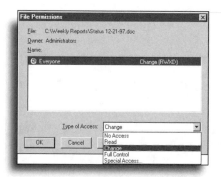

FIGURE 6.13
Permissions assigned to files.

5. Manage names and permission assignments as described for directories.

Assigning Special Access Permissions

You might find that none of the standard permissions meets your requirements. In such cases, you can assign custom permissions, referred to as *special access permissions*.

Assigning special access permissions to a directory

1. While defining access permissions, pull down the **Type of Access** list and choose **Special Directory Access** to display the Special Directory Access dialog box shown in Figure 6.14. The permissions currently assigned to the directory will be checked.

2. Check the permissions you want to assign.

3. Click **OK** to assign the permissions.

Assign special access permissions

1. While defining access permissions, pull down the **Type of Access** list and choose **Special File Access** to display the Special File Access dialog box shown in Figure 6.15. The permissions currently assigned to files will be checked.

If you selected two or more files, permissions that are not held in common by all selected files are shown with gray Xs.

2. Check the permissions you want to assign.

3. Click **OK** to assign the permissions.

FIGURE 6.14

Assigning special access permissions to a directory.

FIGURE 6.15

Assigning special file access permissions.

Changing Ownership of Directories and Files

As we have seen, every directory and file has an owner. There are occasions when it is necessary to change ownership of an object, but an owner cannot simply give an object away. There are two ways to change ownership of a file:

- The owner can give another user permission to take owner-ship, after which the other user takes ownership.

- An administrator can forcibly take ownership.

Both scenarios are described in the following sections.

Giving a User the Right to Take Ownership

Use the procedures described in the section "Assigning Special Access Permissions." In the Special Directory Access or Special File Access dialog boxes, assign the Take Ownership permission to the desired user or group.

Taking Ownership

Taking ownership of a directory or file

1. Right-click the directory or file in Explorer, My Computer, or Network Neighborhood and choose **Properties** from the context menu.

2. Select the **Security** tab in the Properties dialog box.

3. Choose **Ownership** in the **Security** tab. The dialog box you see depends on whether you have permissions to view the directory.

4. If you selected a directory for which you have the Take Ownership permission, you will see the dialog box shown in Figure 6.16. Click **Take Ownership** to take ownership of the directory and its contents.

FIGURE 6.16

The ownership information for a directory.

5. When taking ownership of a directory, you will see the warning shown in Figure 6.17. Click **Yes** to take ownership.

6. If you don't have the permissions required to view the owner, you will see the message in Figure 6.18. If you have the Take Ownership permission or if you are an administrator, click **Yes** to overwrite the existing permissions and take ownership.

An Example: Setting Up User Access

Now, let's seen how shares and NTFS permissions play out in some real-world situations. Consider drive C: shown in Figure 6.19. This drive has several directories that will be shared on the network:

- **\Applications.** This directory contains all shared applications. Users must be able to read and execute files in the \Applications directory subtree, but don't need to create or modify files because their personal configuration files will be stored in their home directories. The List standard permission provides the required Read and Execute permissions.

- **\Applications\Personnel.** This subdirectory contains applications and files that should be accessed only by members of the Personnel department. No other users should have access. A Personnel group will be created and will be assigned the required permissions for this directory. Permissions are revoked for all others.

- **\Home.** This directory contains users' personal home directories. It is shared with the share name Home. Personal directories are secured so that only the directory owner has access to directory contents.

- **\Weekly Reports.** In this directory, all employees maintain their weekly status reports. The directory is shared with the share name Reports. Users must be able to modify their own files, but only engineering managers should be able to read all files. Therefore, a special Reports group is created to control access to this folder.

FIGURE 6.19
This directory tree is used to illustrate directory permissions.

Creating the Shares

The first step is to share each directory. Three shares are required:

- **\Applications** is shared with the share name Apps.

- **\Home** is shared with the share name Home.

- **\Weekly Reports** is shared with the share name Reports.

Why no share name for the Personnel subdirectory? Because Personnel is a subdirectory of the \Applications directory, which is already shared, a separate share isn't required. Users in Personnel are required to map a single drive to the Apps share.

Because these directories will be further secured with NTFS file permissions, we can use the default share permissions. The default share permissions, you will recall, grant Full Control permissions to Everyone. After we create groups, we will tighten up access controls with NTFS permissions.

Create the Groups

Two groups will be created:

- **Personnel.** Membership is restricted to members of the Personnel department.
- **ReportManagers.** Membership is restricted to managers who have full access to the \Weekly Reports folder.

Assigning Permissions

First, let's look at the permissions for the \Applications directory. Recall that standard List permissions are appropriate for this directory. Because all employees can use these applications, List permissions can be assigned to the Everyone special identity.

Figure 6.20 shows the Directory Permissions dialog box used to establish permissions for \Applications. Notice that both check boxes have been selected so that permissions propagate to files and subdirectories.

FIGURE **6.20**

Permissions assigned to the \Applications directory.

Next, the permissions for the `Personnel` subdirectory must be established. Figure 6.21 shows the Directory Permissions dialog box for this directory. In this case, group Everyone has been removed from the permissions list, and Change permissions have been granted to the Personnel group.

To secure the `\Weekly Reports` directory, we make use of the CREATOR OWNER special identity. By assigning Change permissions to CREATOR OWNER, we permit users to modify status reports they create. The group Everyone is given Add permissions to enable all users to create new status reports. The group ReportManagers is given Change permissions. Figure 6.22 shows the Directory Permissions dialog box.

Besides sharing the `\Users` directory, we don't need to do anything special in terms of permissions. When home directories are created from User Manager for Domains, the correct permissions are assigned to each home directory. Each user is established as the only user of his or her home directory with Full Control permissions. By default, no other users, including administrators, have permissions to users' home directories.

Now We Can Get Down to Work

You have users, you have shared files, and everything is nicely secured. Now users can begin to work on the network. Except for one minor problem, that is. Unless they have a personal printer, they can't print. But one reason we have a network is to make it easier for users to access printers. So we need to take sharing one step further and look at printer sharing. On to the next chapter!

Where'd those permissions come from?

You might be surprised that five groups have permissions for the `\Applications` directory. How were all those permissions assigned to the directory that I created?

When a directory is created, it inherits the permissions of the directory in which it is created. If you examine the permissions for the root directory of C:, you will find the same permissions that Figure 6.19 shows for Administrators, CREATOR OWNER, Server Operators, and SYSTEM. Initially, Everyone had Full Control permissions for `\Applications`, but that was changed to List permissions before the figure was prepared.

Doing things in the right order

When assigning permissions to directory trees, it's important to work from the topmost directory down, because permissions propagate to lower-level directories. When I assigned permissions to the `\Applications` directory, the permissions propagated to the subdirectories of `\Applications` including the `\Personnel` directory. After that, I assign the permissions I want to `\Personnel`.

Had I started with the `\Personnel` directory and then done `\Applications`, the permissions assigned to `\Applications` would have overwritten `\Personnel`, and Everyone would have had access to the `\Personnel` directory. That is definitely not what I want to wind up with.

FIGURE 6.21

Permissions assigned to the
`Personnel` directory.

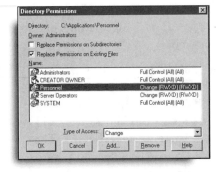

FIGURE 6.22

Permissions assigned to the
`\Weekly Reports` direc-
tory.

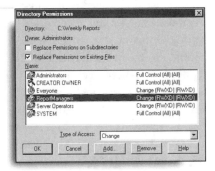

Sharing Printers

How network printing works

Installing printer hardware

Creating printers

Managing printer operation

Creating separator files

When you install a network, it makes considerable sense to share printers. Although printer prices have fallen dramatically in recent years, a wide variety of features are found only on expensive printers, such as photo-quality black-and-white printing, duplexing, and top-quality color. Better printers also tend to be less expensive to operate, because those printers attract vendors' best technologies.

We've established that it's often a good idea to share printers. But just how difficult is it? You probably think network management is complicated enough; printer sharing isn't all that desirable if it is much more complicated than hooking up a parallel cable. As you'll soon see, sharing printers on Windows NT networks isn't very complex at all.

How Network Printing Works

A printer on a network has a more difficult job than a printer that serves a single computer. Users want to print to the network just as if they had a personal printer, so a printer must simultaneously receive multiple print jobs from multiple users. To let printers equitably serve many users, network printers use a mechanism called *spooling*.

Figure 7.1 illustrates the spooling process, which works like this:

1. When a user prints a job, the job is not sent directly to the printer. Instead, the print job is sent to a *print server*, a computer that receives the jobs and is responsible for having them printed.

2. The print server stores the print jobs in a *spooler*, typically a file store on a hard disk, although large RAM buffers can also be used. Jobs are held in the spooler until a printer becomes available.

3. The print server tracks print jobs. When a printer becomes available, the print server *despools* the job.

4. The print server sends the print job to the printer.

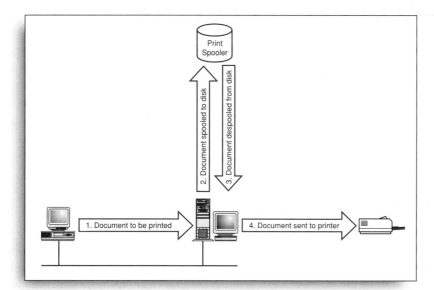

FIGURE 7.1
How spooled printing works.

The spooler is essentially a large, smart buffer. Not only can it track many jobs from many users, but it can also handle jobs based on a variety of criteria, such as the following:

- **Scheduling.** Jobs can be scheduled for printing at a particular time. It might be most appropriate to print a large job overnight, for example, to avoid tying up the printer.

- **Permissions.** Printer permissions can be used to restrict access to printers.

- **Printer availability.** Printers can be assigned to printer pools. The spooler will direct a print job to the first available printer that meets the requirements of the print job.

As just mentioned, the user prints to a printer (software) that directs the document to a print device (hardware). Printers and print devices can have several relationships, as shown in Figure 7.2:

- **One-to-one.** One printer can be associated with a single print device.

- **One-to-many.** One printer can send documents to several print devices, despooling documents to print devices as

---

A note on Microsoft terminology

Microsoft printing revolves around *print devices* and *printers*. In Microsoft terminology, a print device is the actual hardware that we typically refer to as a printer. Microsoft refers to the software component as printers—the print drivers and other software that are loaded on a user's PC. A print server provides the software component that Microsoft calls a printer. I apologize for the confusing terminology; it's Microsoft's, not mine.

Here's another bit of terminology: A *document* is a print job that is in the printer queue, either being printed or waiting its turn to be sent to a print device.

hardware becomes available. This arrangement is often called a *printer pool*.

- **Many-to-one.** Several printers can send documents to one print device. Each printer will be associated with different print criteria. For example, one printer might only print documents at night, queueing jobs until after hours. Another printer might operate at all times, servicing routine print jobs.

FIGURE 7.2

Relationships between printers and print devices.

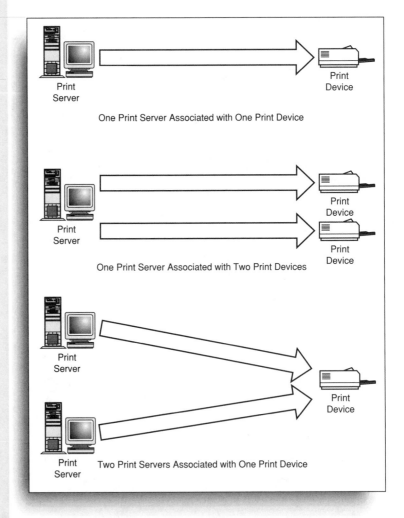

Installing Printer Hardware

In most cases, your printer devices will connect with the print server through a parallel interface or through the network. In rare instances, printers are connected through serial interfaces, but serial connections are too slow to support all but the slowest printers.

Parallel Ports

Parallel printers are easy to set up, so there's not much to say. Most Intel PCs are equipped with two parallel ports:

- LPT1, which uses IRQ 7
- LPT2, which uses IRQ 5

Windows NT automatically recognizes available parallel ports, and no port setup is required. A third parallel port can be added if required. You will need to install an adapter card and find a free interrupt. Parallel printer cables should not exceed a length of about 25 feet.

SEE ALSO

➤ *If you aren't comfortable with interrupts, see Appendix C, "Configuring Servers and Clients," which briefly reviews some hardware basics.*

SEE ALSO

➤ *Because serial ports are most often used for modem communication, they are covered in Chapter 20, "Setting Up a Remote Access Server."*

Supporting Network-Attached Printers

A few printers, including some from Hewlett-Packard, connect directly to the network. To communicate with these printers, the print server must be configured with the Data Link Control (DLC) protocol. To install DLC, do the following:

Installing the Data Link Control protocol

1. Open the Network applet in the Control Panel.

2. Select the **Protocols** tab.

3. Click **Add**.

4. Select DLC Protocol from the **Network Protocol** list.

5. Click **OK**.

6. Provide disks and path information as requested.

7. Restart the computer.

Creating Printers

Recall that a *printer* is the print spooler, the software component of the printing process. The process of installing a printer is called *creating a printer*.

Printers are created and managed using the Print Manager utility. You must be a member of one of the following groups to create printers:

- **Administrators** (Windows NT Workstation and Server)
- **Server Operators** (Windows NT Server)
- **Print Operators** (Windows NT Server)
- **Power Users** (Windows NT Workstation)

When you create a printer, the procedure you follow depends on whether the printer device is connected directly to a port on the computer or connected through the network. Network and local connections are created somewhat locally, so the procedures will be covered separately.

Creating a Printer for a Local Print Device

After the print device has been connected to a local port, the steps to set up the printer are as follows:

Creating a printer for a local print device

1. Open the Printers icon in the Control Panel. (It is also found in My Computer and Windows NT Explorer.) This opens the Printers window, shown in Figure 7.3. The Printers window contains an icon for each printer that has been created on the computer. It also contains an icon for the Add Printer Wizard.

FIGURE 7.3
The Printers window.

2. Double-click the Add Printer icon to open the Add Printer Wizard, shown in Figure 7.4.

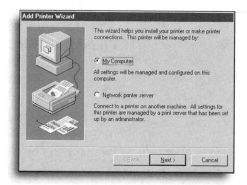

FIGURE 7.4
The Add Printer Wizard.

3. The initial window of the Add Printer Wizard has two options:

- **My Computer**. Select this option if the printer is physically attached to a port on this computer.

- **Network printer server.** Select this option if the printer is attached to a remote network print server.

In this example, we are installing a locally-attached printer, so we select **My Computer**.

4. The next dialog box is shown in Figure 7.5. This is where you specify the port that is used to communicate with the printer.

a. If the printer is attached to an LPT or COM port, select the port. You can also select FILE: to create a printer that stores printer-ready output in a file.

b. To add a port, click **Add**. The ports that can be added depend on your installation. Here are some examples:

- **AppleTalk Printing Devices.** This option is available when AppleTalk protocol support is installed. It enables printing to AppleTalk printers.

- **Digital Network Port**. This option is available when TCP/IP or DECNet protocols are installed. It enables printing to DEC print devices.

- **Hewlett-Packard Network Port.** This option is available when the DLC protocol is installed, enabling printing through the network to printers equipped with HP JetDirect adapters.

- **LPR Port.** This option is available when the TCP/IP Printing service is installed. It supports printing for applications that use the LPR protocol.

c. To configure a port, select the port and click **Configure Port**. The configuration options depend on the type of port you have selected.

d. After you have selected one of the ports in the **Available ports** list, click **Next**.

FIGURE 7.5
Selecting a printer port.

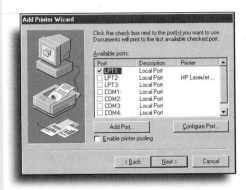

7. The next dialog box, shown in Figure 7.6, is used to select a printer driver.

a. If your printer is listed, select an entry in the **Manufacturers** list and then choose a printer in the **Printers** list.

b. If your printer drivers are on a diskette, click **Have Disk** and follow the prompts.

c. Click **Next** to continue.

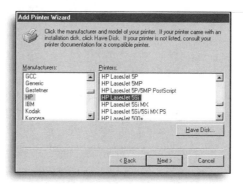

FIGURE 7.6
Selecting a printer driver.

8. Next, specify a name for the printer. The name you enter will identify the printer to users who browse the network.

9. In next dialog box, shown in Figure 7.7, you configure the printer for sharing on the network.

Select **Not shared** if this printer will be used exclusively by users of this computer.

Select **Shared** if users will be permitted to access this printer through the network.

Unlisted Drivers

If your printer isn't listed and you don't have drivers on diskette, consult the printer vendor for the best driver to use. At the present time, Microsoft provides all printer drivers for Windows NT. You can download Microsoft-supported drivers from `http://support.microsoft.com/support/downloads/`.

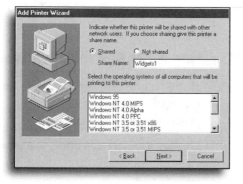

FIGURE 7.7
Configuring printer sharing.

Print servers

If you configure a Windows NT computer to share a printer on the network, the computer functions as a *print server*. The only significant difference in configuring a stand-alone computer and a print server is the choice of **Shared** or **Not shared** that is made during setup.

10. If you selected **Shared**, a share name will be suggested in the **Share Name** field. Change this name if you wish. Remember that MS-DOS and Windows 3.x users can access shares only if the share name conforms to the 8.3 name format.

11. Windows NT print servers can supply drivers to Windows NT and Windows 95 or 98 clients, eliminating the need to install the drivers directly on the clients.

    If you selected **Shared**, select the drivers that should be installed on this print server. By default, the Add Printer Wizard copies drivers for Intel x86 computers. Other printer drivers are installed only if they are selected.

    The Windows NT Server 4 setup CD-ROM includes drivers for Windows NT 4 clients only. If you select another operating system, you will need the installation disks for those operating systems in order to copy the required printer drivers. Be sure that you have the disks available and that you know the paths to the installation directories before you request installation of the drivers.

12. Click **Next** to continue.

13. The next prompt asks Would you like to print a test page? To test the printer, click **Yes**. To skip the test, click **No**.

14. Click **Finish** to complete the installation. Supply disks and file paths as requested to install the drivers and configure the printer.

Creating a Printer for a Network Print Device

If you will be printing to a print device that is attached to a print server, the printer setup procedure is slightly different from the procedure you just examined.

Creating a printer that prints to a network print device

1. Open the Printers icon in the Control Panel.

2. Double-click Add Printer.

3. Choose **N**etwork printer server and then click **N**ext.

4. The next dialog box is Connect to Printer, as shown in Figure 7.8. Browse the network. Locate a print server and select one of the shared printers.

FIGURE 7.8
Selecting a network printer.

5. Click **N**ext.

6. Click **Finish** to complete the installation.

Did you notice something different, perhaps even shocking? You didn't need to specify the type of printer or install a driver! If the print server and client are both Windows NT computers, network printing offers an interesting twist: It is unnecessary to install printer drivers on the client computer. Printer drivers are installed on the print server, and the client obtains the drivers as required.

The printer now appears as an icon in the Printers window and can be selected in applications. Figure 7.9 shows the printer being selected in Microsoft Word.

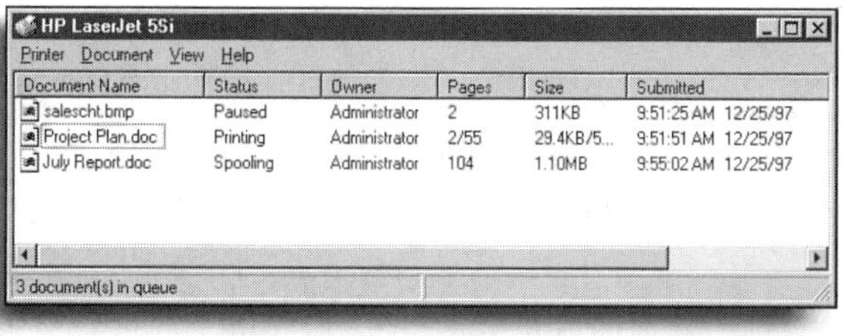

FIGURE 7.9
Documents are in the spooler queue for this printer.

Connecting to a Printer from MS-DOS

Many MS-DOS applications require that a printer be configured with a port assignment. On Microsoft clients, the net use command is used to establish printer connections from the command line.

To connect LPT3: to printer Laser1 on server Malaprop1, you would enter the following command:

```
net use lpt3: \\malaprop1\laser1
```

Selecting a Default Printer

Although a user can have several printers installed, at any given time there will be one *default printer*, which is used unless the user specifies otherwise.

If you have multiple printers, you can change your default printer as follows:

1. Open the Printers icon in the Control Panel.
2. Right-click the printer that you want as your default.
3. Choose **Set as De_f_ault** from the context menu.

Managing Printer Operation

You can view and manage the spooler queue for a printer and manage jobs in the queue in a variety of ways. There are some restrictions on the jobs you can manage:

- Users can always manage the jobs they originate.
- Members of the Administrators, Server Operators, and Print Operators groups can manage any job.
- Users can manage documents on a printer if they have been given Full Control permission for the printer.
- Users have limited management capabilities if they have been given Manage Documents permission for the printer.

To open the Printer Manager for a printer, double-click the printer icon in the Printers folder. Figure 7.9, shown a moment ago, shows a typical Printer Manager window.

The following information is displayed for each document:

- **Document Name.** The detail you see depends on the environment that originated the document. In some cases, you see the filename, along with the application that created it.

- **Status.** Printing, Spooling, Paused, and Deleting are the most common messages. If no status is displayed, the document is waiting to be printed.

  If a document is waiting to have a form mounted, the name of the form is shown in the **Status** field.

- **Owner.** The user name of the document owner.

- **Pages.** The number of pages in the document.

- **Size.** The document size in bytes.

- **Submitted.** The date and time the job was submitted.

Managing Printers

The **Printer** menu has several commands that can be used to manage how the printer handles documents:

- **Pause Printing.** You might want to pause a printer, perhaps when the printer device requires attention. When a printer is paused, users can continue to spool jobs, but none will be printed. When a printer is paused, the word Paused appears in the window's title bar, and a check appears beside the **Pause Printing** command. To resume printing, choose the **Pause Printing** command again.

- **Purge Print Documents.** Choose this command to purge all print documents that are currently in the spooler queue. Purged documents can't be recovered.

Managing Documents

Several commands on the **Document** menu are used to manage the printing of individual documents:

- **Pause.** You can pause an individual document. You might want to pause a large document for printing later, or you might want to hold a document that requires a special form until the form is loaded to the printer. To pause a document, select the document and choose the **Pause** command.

- **Resume.** To resume printing of a paused document, select the document and choose **Resume**.

- **Restart.** Sometimes a printer can malfunction, damaging some of the pages of a print job. If you detect the damage before a print job has been removed from the spooler, you can restart the printing of the document from the beginning. To restart a document, select the document and choose **Restart**.

- **Cancel.** You can remove any document that is waiting to print. Select the document and choose **Cancel**.

Managing Document Properties

Documents have a variety of properties that can managed while they are waiting to be printed. To display the properties for a document, do one of the following:

- Double-click the document icon.
- Right-click the document icon and choose **Properties** from the context menu.
- Select the document and choose **Properties** from the **Documents** menu.

Figure 7.10 shows the document properties window.

The General Tab

The **General** tab is shown in Figure 7.10. You can manipulate the following properties on this tab:

- **Notify.** Specifies the name of the user who will be notified when the job has printed.
- **Priority.** Specifies the priority for printing the document, ranging from 1 to 99, where 99 is the highest priority. This option can be used to rearrange the order in which jobs will be serviced by the spooler.

FIGURE 7.10
Document properties: the
General tab.

- **Schedule.** By default, **No Time Restriction** is selected, which means that jobs will print as soon as possible. To delay a document, select **Only From** and specify a time interval. This provides a way to delay printing of large jobs until night hours so that they won't tie up the printer.

The Page Setup Tab

The **Page Setup** tab contains printer-specific options such as paper size, paper source, and so forth. If you are printing from a Windows application, this tab is informational only. In most cases, the settings are specified by the Windows application that printed the document and can't be modified once the document is in the print queue. These settings are discussed in the section after this one, "Configuring Document Defaults."

The Advanced Tab

The **Advanced** tab contains printer-specific options. If you are printing from a Windows application, this tab is informational only. In most cases, the settings are specified by the Windows application that printed the document and can't be modified from Print Manager. These settings are discussed in the next section.

Configuring Document Defaults

Most Windows applications specify the printer settings for documents when a document is printed. In the rare instances when applications don't specify printer settings, you can configure default document settings that will be used on a printer. These settings will be used when you're printing from a non-Windows application or when you're using the PRINT command to print a document from the command line.

To open the Default Document window, shown in Figure 7.11, double-click the printer icon in the Printers window and choose **Document Defaults** from the **Printer** menu.

FIGURE 7.11

Document default settings: the Page Setup tab.

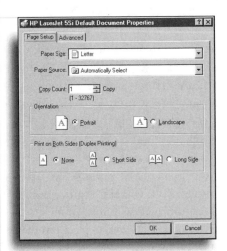

The Document Properties window has two tabs. The specific settings depend on the capabilities of the printer device that is being configured, so the accompanying figures are examples only.

A typical **Page Setup** tab is shown in Figure 7.11. Here are common settings on this tab:

- **Paper Size.** Specifies the paper size to be used by default.
- **Paper Source.** If a printer has more than one paper source, selects the paper source that contains the default paper.
- **Copy Count.** Specifies the default number of copies to be printed.

- **Portrait** and **Landscape.** Specifies the default printing orientation.

The **Advanced** tab presents a hierarchical view of the document's features. Many of its options are the same as those on the **Page Setup** tab. The features you see will depend on the printer hardware's features. Figure 7.12 shows the **Advanced** tab for a Hewlett Packard LaserJet 5Si printer.

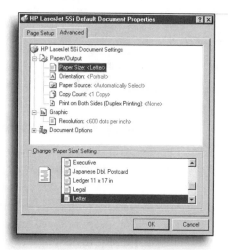

FIGURE 7.12

Document default settings: the Advanced tab.

To change a setting, select the entry and change the setting in the box below. In Figure 7.12, the default paper size is being specified.

Configuring Printer Properties

In many cases, you won't need to configure a printer beyond the default settings that are established when the printer is created. However, you can configure a printer in a variety of ways. To manage properties for a printer, right-click the desired icon in the Printers window and choose **Properties** from the context menu. Or open the printer's window and choose **Properties** from the **Printer** menu.

A sample printer Properties window is shown in Figure 7.13. The various tabs are discussed in the following sections.

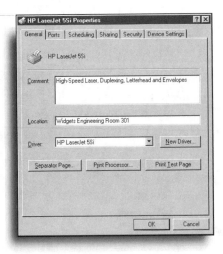

FIGURE 7.13

Printer properties: the General tab.

Printer Properties: the General Tab

The **General** tab is shown in Figure 7.13. This tab supports a potpourri of general configuration functions.

Configuring Comment and Location Information

The first property in the **General** tab is **Comment**. This field accepts a freeform comment. Perhaps the best use is to provide contact information identifying the person who is responsible for maintaining the printer hardware. If the printer has special features, such as a letterhead paper bin or an envelope feeder, those features might be worth a mention as well.

The **Location** field accepts freeform text that describes the printer's location.

Changing the Printer Driver

The **Driver** field describes the driver that is currently assigned to the printer. If other drivers are installed, you can use this field to change the driver. Or you can click **New Driver** to install a new driver.

Specifying a Separator Page

A *separator page* is a file that is printed prior to a print job. The separator page can contain text and commands. If a separator page is to precede each job, click **Separator Page** and enter the path to the separator page file in the **Separator Page** field of the dialog box that is provided. Three standard print separator files are included with Windows NT:

- **PCL.SEP**. For use with Hewlett-Packard printers and other printers that use the HP Printer Control Language (PCL). In dual-protocol printers, PCL.SEP switches the printer into PCL mode.

- **PSCRIPT.SEP**. For use with HP printers equipped with PostScript. In dual-protocol printers, PSCRIPT.SEP switches the printer into PostScript mode.

- **SYSPRINT.SEP**. Prints a separator page on PostScript printers.

Each of these files can be edited, and you can create custom separator pages easily.

SEE ALSO

➤ *The later section "Creating Separator Files" describes this procedure.*

To cancel the use of a separator file, select the text in the **Separator Page** field and delete it.

Configuring the Print Processor

The **Print Processor** button opens the dialog box shown in Figure 7.14. This dialog box specifies the driver that is responsible for processing print jobs for this printer. Windows NT includes only one print processor, named WINPRINT. You need to change the entry in the **Print Processor** box only if you install software that provides its own print processor. Consult the software documentation for details.

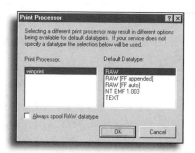

FIGURE 7.14
Specifying the print processor.

In rare instances, you might need to change the **Default Datatype** entry. Choices for this field include the following:

- **RAW.** Data is passed to the printer as raw bit streams. This is required for printing graphics jobs, for PostScript, and for printing with Windows TrueType fonts. In fact, this setting is required for most printing and works for most other printing as well. You seldom will need to use other options.

- **RAW [FF appended].** Used in rare instances when an application doesn't force a form feed at the end of a print job.

- **RAW [FF auto].** Data is passed to the printer as raw bit streams. A form feed will be sent if WINPRINT determines that one was not sent to terminate the job.

- **NT EMF 1.003.** A special Windows NT format to be used if your applications require it.

- **TEXT.** Use this choice for printing with applications that print only ASCII text. A form feed is forced at the end of the print job. Some text-mode DOS applications print more effectively with this setting.

Printing a Test Page

After you configure changes on a printer, you should test them by printing a test page. Click **Print Test Page** to do so.

Configuring Ports Properties

The **Ports** tab, shown in Figure 7.15, configures several port-related configuration characteristics.

A printer can send jobs to several print devices. This arrangement is called a printer pool and was described earlier in this chapter. Two conditions apply:

- The printer devices must be connected directly to the same print server, although you can mix different types of ports.

- The printer devices must be identical. Otherwise, the configuration information entered into Print Manager won't apply to all printers. If printers differ, configure the printer so that it matches the specifications of the most limited printer hardware.

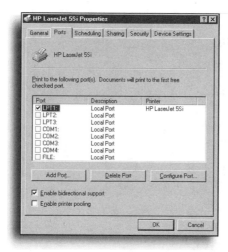

FIGURE 7.15

Printer port properties.

To create a printer pool or to add a print device to an existing pool, select the ports by clicking their entries in the **Ports** tab.

To deselect a port, remove the check mark.

To delete a port from the list, select the port and click the **Delete Port** button. You might want to remove a port if it isn't available in the print server's hardware configuration.

To add a port to the list, click **Add Port** to open the Printer Ports dialog box, which is shown in Figure 13.9. See Chapter 13, "Essential TCP/IP Concepts," for the procedures and options when adding ports.

To configure a port, select the port and click **Configure Port**. A dialog box will be displayed with configuration options for the type of port that has been selected.

Many new printers are capable of engaging in a two-way dialog with the driver software. For example, they can tell the driver when they are low on toner. If your printer supports bidirectional communication, check **Enable bidirectional support**.

Configuring Scheduling Properties

Not all the options on the **Scheduling** tab have to do with scheduling, but that is the first topic to be considered (see Figure 7.16).

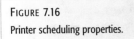
F IGURE 7.16
Printer scheduling properties.

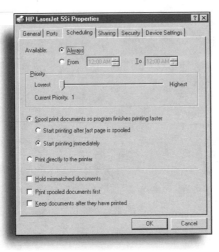

Scheduling Printer Availability

It can be extremely useful to delay print jobs for later printing.
This is most commonly done so that large or low-priority jobs
can print overnight when printers ordinarily are idle.

You can establish several logical printers, associating them with
the same printer. Each logical printer can be configured with different scheduling properties, allowing you to have distinct
restrictions for different users, priorities, or types of jobs.

If the logical printer is to be available at all times, select **Al**w**ays**.

To restrict the availability for the logical printer, select **From**
and specify a time interval in the **From** and **To** boxes.

Setting Printer Priority

The **Priority** control determines the printing priority associated
with this logical printer. If several printers are serviced by the
same print device, the printer with the highest priority will be
given preference in the order of printing jobs.

Configuring Spooler Operation

You can tune spooler operation using several options on the
Scheduling tab, as shown in Figure 7.16.

By default, you enable spooling by selecting the option **Spool print documents so program finishes printing faster**. When spooling is enabled, you have a choice of two modes of operation:

- **Start printing after last page is spooled.** This option ensures that the entire print job is available in the spooler, but printing can't begin until the entire job has been spooled.
- **Start printing immediately.** By default, jobs start printing as soon as the first page of the job has been spooled. Printing can begin earlier in the print cycle, and print jobs are completed more quickly.

To disable spooling, select **Print directly to the printer**. The following choices are available only when spooling is active:

- **Hold mismatched documents.** When this option is checked, the print server will hold jobs that don't match the form that is currently mounted on the printer. When this option isn't checked, jobs of the same priority are printed in the order submitted, and form changes must be performed as required. Although this isn't checked by default, check it to minimize the frequency of form changes.
- **Print spooled documents first.** When this option is checked (the default), a job that has completed spooling will be printed before a job in the process of spooling, even when the spooling job has a higher priority. The default is typically the better choice.
- **Keep documents after they have printed.** If you're printing documents that can't easily be recreated, check this option. The document will remain in the spooler after printing is completed. If a printing problem occurs, you can reprint the spooled jobs. Because jobs must be deleted manually when this option is enabled, you should use this option only in special instances.

Configuring Printer Sharing

The **Sharing** tab, shown in Figure 7.17, is used to determine printer sharing characteristics. If a printer is not to be shared, select **Not Shared**.

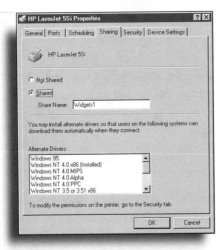

FIGURE 7.17

Printer sharing properties.

Concealing printer shares

Just as you can create file shares that don't appear when users browse the network, you can conceal printer shares by adding a dollar sign ($) to the end of the share name. Users who want to access the printer must enter the share name manually when connecting to the printer.

Installing other drivers

The Windows NT Server 4 installation CD-ROM includes drivers for Windows NT version 4 only, including I386, MIPS, Alpha, and PPC drivers. Drivers for prior versions of Windows NT or for Windows 95 must be copied from the installation disks for those operating systems. Be sure that you have the disks available and that you know the paths to the installation files before you try to install these drivers.

To share a printer, select **Shared** and specify a shared name. Windows NT and Windows 95 users can operate with long share names, but you must restrict the name to 8.3 format if the printer is to be shared by MS-DOS and Windows 3.x users.

Drivers for Windows NT 4.0 x86 computers are installed by default. If other Windows NT platforms must be supported, select the platforms in the **Alternate Drivers** list so that drivers will be copied for those computers.

Configuring Printer Security

The **Security** tab has three buttons addressing different areas of security:

- **Permissions**
- **Auditing**
- **Ownership**

Auditing is addressed in Chapter 23, "Managing the Server." Permissions and ownership are discussed in the following sections.

Taking Printer Ownership

The user who creates a printer is the printer's owner and can administer all characteristics of the logical printer. The owner can let other users administer the printer by giving the users Manage Documents or Full Control permission.

Any user who has Full Control permission can take ownership of the printer by selecting the **Ownership** option on the **Security** tab. This opens the Owner box, which includes a **Take Ownership** button. Click this button to assume ownership of the printer.

Managing Printer Permissions

Printer permissions can be managed by the owner of the printer or by users who have Full Control permission. Four permissions can be assigned to printers:

- No Access
- Print
- Manage Documents
- Full Control

Users with the Manage Documents permission can perform the following actions:

- Controlling document settings
- Pausing, resuming, restarting, and deleting documents

Users with Full Control permission can perform the actions permitted by Manage Document permission. They also can perform these actions:

- Changing document printing order
- Pausing, resuming, and purging logical printers
- Changing logical printer properties
- Deleting logical printers
- Changing logical printer permissions

The document owner

The user who creates a document is established as the document's owner. All users can perform Manage Document operations on documents they own.

The procedure for setting printer permissions is nearly identical to the procedure for setting file permissions. Follow these steps:

Setting printer permissions

1. Select the **Security** tab. Then click **Permissions** to open the Printer Permissions dialog box, shown in Figure 7.18.

FIGURE 7.18

Configuring printer permissions.

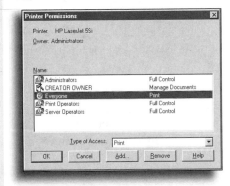

SEE ALSO

➤ *For more information on setting file permissions, see Chapter 6, "Sharing Files and Managing File Security."*

2. To change permissions for a user or group, do the following:

   a. Select a name in the **Name** box.

   b. Pull down the **Type of Access** list and select the desired access.

3. To add a user or group to the permissions list, do the following:

   a. Click **Add** in the Printer Permissions dialog box. The Add Users and Groups dialog box appears, as shown in Figure 7.19.

   b. If required, select a different domain from the **List Names From** drop-down list.

   c. To display user names in the **Names** box, click **Show Users**.

   d. Add names to the **Add Names** box by double-clicking entries in the **Names** box or by selecting entries in the **Names** box and clicking **Add**.

e. In the **Type of Access** box, select the permissions to be assigned to the names you have selected. All selected users and groups receive the same permissions.

f. Click **OK** to add the users or groups to the permissions list for the printer and return to the Printer Permissions box.

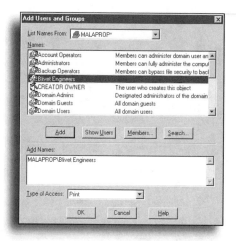

FIGURE 7.19

Adding users and groups to printer permissions.

4. To remove a name, select the entry in the **Names** box of the Printer Permissions dialog box and click **Remove**.

5. Click **OK** to save the permissions.

Configuring Printer Device Settings

Figure 7.20 shows the **Device Settings** tab. It presents a hierarchical list of the printer's hardware features. The details you see depend on the printer driver that is being used for this printer. To view or change a setting, select the property from the list. In some cases, options will appear on the **Settings** tab for changing settings. In other cases, a button will be displayed that opens a secondary dialog box. An example is the Soft Fonts option, selected in Figure 7.20.

FIGURE 7.20
The printer's Device Settings
tab.

Identifying Available Forms for a Printer

You can assign a different type of form to each paper tray on the printer. If a print job requests an available form type, the appropriate paper tray will be accessed. If a print job requests a form that is unavailable, a printer operator can load the form in a paper tray and modify the printer properties to show that the form type is available.

In Figure 7.21, the Form To Tray Assignment category has been opened to reveal the trays available on this printer. To assign a form, select one of the paper trays that is listed to open the **Change...Setting** list. Scroll through this list and select the form type that is to be associated with the paper tray you have selected.

Specifying Printer Memory

It is particularly important for Windows NT to know how much memory is installed in a laser printer. When graphics are printed to a laser printer, the entire page must be imaged in memory before the page is printed. This can't be achieved if the memory installed in the printer is insufficient for the graphics being printed.

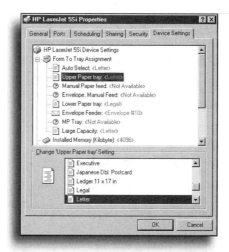

FIGURE 7.21
Changing printer form assignments.

If the printer has insufficient memory to image the entire page, Windows NT might resort to *banding*—sending the page in sections.

To configure the amount of memory, select **Installed Memory (Kilobyte)** and then choose a memory amount from the list that is provided, as shown in Figure 7.22.

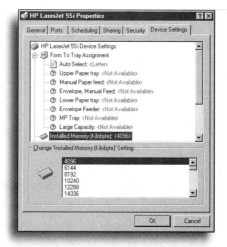

FIGURE 7.22
Specifying printer memory.

Setting Page Protection

For some page printers, such as laser printers, you have the option of enabling or disabling page protection. Page protection instructs the printer to image the entire page in memory before printing. Page protection ensures that complex pages can be printed correctly. If the printer supports this feature, select **Page Protect** and change the setting to **On**.

Specifying Fonts

Some printers can accept additional fonts in the form of font cartridges or soft fonts. Two options on the **Device Settings** tab relate to fonts.

If font cartridges are installed in the printer, select a font cartridge under **Installed Font Cartridges** and specify the installed cartridges by choosing them from this list. The number of cartridges you can select depends on the printer model.

To install soft fonts, select the **Soft Fonts** item to reveal a button that displays the Font Installer window. Use this window to install drivers for soft fonts.

Printing devices can use three types of fonts:

- **Hardware fonts.** The font data resides in the hardware of the printing device, either built into the printer or in plug-in cartridges.
- **Screen fonts.** These are fonts that Windows NT can translate into printer-specific output. The standard screen font technology for Windows is called TrueType. Screen fonts are installed using the Font utility in the Control Panel. This is the printing font technology most commonly used with Windows applications.
- **Soft fonts.** These fonts can be downloaded to the printer. Soft font files are stored on the print server, and Windows NT will download the fonts to printers as required. DOS and Windows computers must have their own copies of soft-font files and are responsible for downloading the fonts to printers. The time required to download soft fonts can slow printing performance.

Setting Up Halftone Printing

The **Halftone Setup** item reveals a button that displays a Device Color/Halftone Properties window. This window lets you fine-tune the printing characteristics of printers that support these features. Halftone and color properties can be set only by users who have Full Control access for the printer (Administrators, Server Operators, Print Operators, and Power Users). Discussion of these features is beyond the scope of this book.

Managing Print Servers Remotely

Users who are logged on as members of the Administrators, Server Operators, or Print Operators groups can manage printer operations remotely. Users who have Full Control permission for a printer can also manage the printer remotely.

To select a printer for remote management, follow these steps:

Selecting a printer for remote management

1. On the remote computer, create a network printer that connects to the network printer that is to be managed.

2. Open the icon for the remote printer in the Printers window. You can either double-click the printer icon or right-click the icon and choose **Properties** from the context menu.

3. Manage the printer as though it were local.

Creating Separator Files

You can create custom separator pages, or you can edit the standard separator pages that are included with Windows NT. A separator page file is a standard text file that has a .SEP extension. .SEP files are created with a text editor, or you can use Windows Write, which is included with Windows NT.

Storing separator pages

Separator page files must be stored on the print server. By default, files are stored in \Winnt\sys-tem32.

Table 7.1 lists the codes that are used in separator files. These codes are called *escape codes*, because they begin with an escape character that signals the start of a script command. Any character that will not appear in the text of a file can be used as the escape character. Microsoft uses the \ character as the escape character in standard .SEP files, so \ is used in Table 7.1.

TABLE 7.1 **Escape Codes Used in Windows NT Separator Files**

Escape Code	Function
\B\M	Starts printing in double-width block characters. Block printing continues until \U occurs.
\B\S	Starts printing in single-width block characters. Block printing continues until \U occurs.
\D	Prints the date. The date format is determined in the International section of the Control Panel.
\E	Forces a page eject. Remove this code if you are getting extra blank separator pages.
\F*pathname*	Starts a new line and prints contents of a file specified by pathname.
\H*nn*	Sends a printer control code where *nn* is a hexadecimal number. Codes are defined by the printer's control language. Consult your printer documentation for information.
\I	Prints the job number.
\L*cccc*	Prints the string of characters represented by *cccc*. The string is terminated by the next occurrence of an escape character.
\N	Prints the user name of the user who submitted the job.
\T	Prints the time the job is being printed. The time format is set in the International section of the Control Panel.
\U	Terminates block-mode printing.
\W*nn*	Sets the page width, where *nn* is a width from 1 to 256. The default width is 80.
n	Creates *n* line feeds where *n* is in the range of 0 to 9. Use \0 to end the current line of text and start a new line. Otherwise, printing continues on the same line.

The following is a custom separator file that I created by modifying PCL.SEP. This file ensures that a PCL printer is switched into PCL mode and then prints identification information on the separator page. Line numbers have been added to assist discussion.

```
1     \
2     \H1B\L%-12345X@PJL ENTER LANGUAGE=PCL
3
\L**********************************************************
4     \1\B\S\N\U\1
5
\L**********************************************************
6     \4\D\L     \T\1
7     \LJob #  \I
8     \E
```

Here is a line-by-line explanation of the file:

1. This line establishes the character that will serve as the escape character for the rest of the file. The character on this line can function only as an escape character and may not appear in any other text in the file.

2. \H1B sends a hexadecimal 1B code to the printer. This is the ASCII escape character that is used as the escape character in PCL. This code readies the printer to accept a command sequence.

   The text following \L is the PCL command. This text contains the command that puts the printer in PCL mode.

3. This line uses the \L (literal) command to print a line of asterisks above the user name.

4. After skipping one line (\1), this line switches into block mode (\B\S) and prints the user's name.

5. Same as line 3.

6. This line first skips four lines and then prints the date (\D) and time (\T). The \L command inserts some spaces between the two items.

7. \L is used to print the text Job # and is followed by an \I to print the actual job number.

8. \E forces a page eject so that the print job starts on a new page.

Here is an example of the separator page that would be printed by this file:

```
*************************************************************

HH   HH                                    111      ddd
HH   HH                                    11       dd
HH   HH    aaaa    rr rrr    oooo          11       dd
HHHHHH       aa    rrr rr  oo   oo         11       ddddd
HH   HH    aaaaa    rr  rr oo   oo         11     dd  dd
HH   HH   aa  aa    rr       oo   oo       11     dd  dd
HH   HH    aaa aa rrrr        oooo         1111    ddd dd



*************************************************************



12/23/97      8:29:21 AM

Job #  9
```

It's Working...But Someone's Been Left Out!

Your Windows NT Server is now working with a basic set of services. Users can log on, access files, and print. That is, they can if they are using Windows NT clients, which are the only clients we have covered so far. Since most people use something other than NT, this leaves out a lot of users.

Therefore, it's time to take up the subject of non-NT network clients. In the next chapter you will see how to enable MS-DOS, Windows 3.x, Windows for Workgroups, and Windows 95 and 98 clients to be clients on a Windows NT Server network.

Activating Network Clients

Enabling Windows 95 and Windows 98 as network clients

Windows for Workgroups 3.11 client configuration

Configuring MS-DOS computers as Microsoft network clients

Using Windows 3.1 as a Microsoft network client

Although Windows 95 has been available for about three years, the computer world still contains a broad mix of Microsoft operating systems. Windows 3.1 and Windows for Workgroups remain in widespread use, often mixed with Windows 95 clients. Even the introduction of Windows 98 may not change the product mix soon because many organizations are hanging on to older hardware that won't run newer versions well. And some organizations just don't want the upgrade and training costs that an operating system upgrade entails.

You need to know how to configure a wide variety of Microsoft network clients. This chapter covers four:

- Windows 95 and Windows 98
- Windows for Workgroups 3.11
- Windows 3.1
- MS-DOS

This discussion starts with the latest Windows version first and works back in time to the Stone Age.

SEE ALSO

➤ *Windows NT 4 client configuration is covered in several places in this book, so this chapter doesn't repeat the configuration procedures.*

➤ *See all of Chapter 3, "Configuring Network Adapters, Services, and Protocols," starting on page 83, for the basic procedures used to configure Windows NT Server and Workstation computers as Microsoft networking clients.*

➤ *Chapter 9, "Advanced Client Features," starting on page 291 discusses some advanced client features that apply only to Windows NT clients, including user profiles and account policies. You also learn some logon script capabilities that apply only to Windows NT clients.*

➤ *See Chapters 13 through 18 for information about configuring Windows NT clients for use on TCP/IP networks.*

Enabling Windows 95 and Windows 98 as Network Clients

Windows 95 and 98 are intended to be Plug-and-Play operating systems. They are designed to detect the hardware in your computer and configure it appropriately. Self-configuration extends to networking. If either operating system detects a network card, it will attempt to load the driver and get a network client running.

Windows 98 is particularly aggressive about self-configuration. It simply won't let you delete the driver for a network adapter. If an adapter is installed, it will usually be detected and the drivers will be re-established when you restart the computer. So there's a degree to which it is unnecessary for me to cover client configuration for Windows 95 and 98. A lot will be done for you, whether you want it or not.

Nevertheless, a time will come when you need to add an adapter driver, change a protocol, or reconfigure some network characteristic; so this section covers the procedures.

Installing Windows 95 and 98 Networking

If you have a network adapter installed, it will probably be detected as you install Windows 95 or 98—unless it is a newer adapter that isn't in the software's repertoire.

Windows 95 gives you the option of detecting the network adapter. If you check the **Network Adapter** check box, the Setup Wizard scans your system for an adapter, which it will probably identify successfully. Windows 98 detects the adapter without prompting you.

Some network adapters have multiple personalities that can confuse the setup programs, making them latch on to the wrong personality. Be sure that you confirm the adapter setup during setup.

After setting up Windows 95 or 98, you use the Network applet in the Control Panel to make changes to the network configuration. Figure 8.1 shows the Network applet as it appears in Windows 95 and 98.

FIGURE 8.1

The Windows 95 and 98
Network applet.

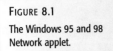

FIGURE 8.1

The Windows 95 and 98
Network applet.

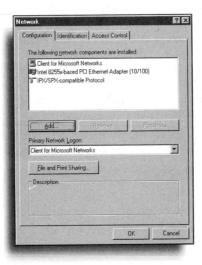

Configuring Network Components

Windows 98 is very aggressive about setting up hardware, and it is unlikely that you will need to manually add a network adapter unless you are using hardware that is introduced after Windows 98 ships. Windows 95 is less aggressive and is older, so it is more likely that you will need to add network adapter drivers after installing new hardware.

If Windows 95 or 98 fails to detect a new adapter and to install the correct driver, or if you need to install updated drivers for an adapter, add the network driver as follows:

Adding a network adapter driver

1. Open the Network applet and select the **Configuration** tab.

2. Click **Add** to open the Select Network Component Type dialog box shown in Figure 8.2.

FIGURE 8.2

Selecting a network component to install.

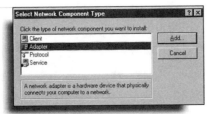

3. Select Adapter in the list box labeled **Click the type of network component you want to install**. Then click **Add** to open the Select Network Adapters dialog box shown in Figure 8.3.

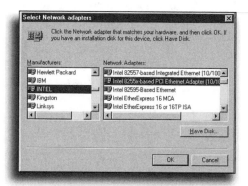

FIGURE 8.3
Selecting a network adapter.

4. In the Select Network Adapters dialog box, do one of the following:

   - If you are installing a listed product, select an entry in the **Manufacturer** list box. Then select a product in the **Network Adapters** list box.
   - If you are installing an unlisted product, or a product for which you have new drivers, click **Have Disk.** When prompted, specify a path where the drivers are located, typically on a floppy disk in drive A:.

   Windows will install the driver for the network adapter, Client for Microsoft Networks, and default network protocols.

5. The majority of Plug and Play adapters are completely self-configuring. Some network adapters, however, have configurable properties. If you double-click the network adapter in the list of installed network components, you will open a dialog box that enables you to configure the adapter properties. The contents of this dialog box will be specific to the network adapter being configured, so it is not possible to present a generic example here.

Plug and Play adapters

If you select a Plug and Play adapter, Windows 95 and 98 will insist that you restart the computer so that the driver can be installed in official Plug and Play fashion. But it's unlikely that you will have the opportunity to select a Plug and Play adapter because it would have been configured when you last booted the computer. See what I mean about Windows 95 and 98 being aggressive?

Default protocols

Windows 95 and Windows 98 install different default protocols:

- For Windows 95, the default protocols are NWLink (IPX/SPX) and NetBEUI.

- For Windows 98, the default protocol is TCP/IP, reflecting Microsoft's increasing emphasis on TCP/IP in the age of the Internet.

6. If you do not like the default protocols Windows has selected, you can delete a protocol. Select a protocol in the list titled **The following network components are installed**. Then click **Remove**.

7. To add a protocol to the configuration:

   a. Click **Add** in the Network applet dialog box.

   b. Select **Protocol** in the Select Network Component Type dialog box. Then click **Add** to open the Select Network Protocol dialog box shown in Figure 8.4.

   c. Select a manufacturer in the **Manufacturers** list.

   d. Select a protocol in the **Network Protocol** list.

If you select a protocol that requires configuration, you will see the required dialog boxes when you exit the Network applet. Enter the appropriate properties in the dialog boxes.

FIGURE 8.4

Selecting a network protocol to be installed.

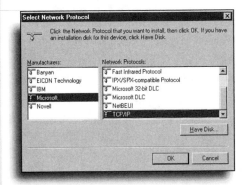

SEE ALSO

➤ *NWLink configuration is covered in all of Chapter 3, starting on page 83.*

➤ *TCP/IP configuration is covered in all of Chapters 13 through 18, starting on page 425.*

8. It is possible to install more than one network client on Windows 95 and 98. Windows 95 automatically installs Microsoft and NetWare clients. By default, Windows 98 installs the Microsoft client only. You can add or remove clients as you add or remove adapters or protocols.

9. If you have installed more than one network client, you should verify the selected client in the **Primary Network Logon** list box. When Windows 95 or 98 starts, it will use the client specified in this field to make an initial attempt to log on to the network.

10. Select the **Identification** tab, shown in Figure 8.5. This tab has the following fields:

- **Computer name.** Typically, this entry will be the same as your network username.

- **Workgroup.** This value matches the name of the workgroup or domain the computer will log on to. If the computer will log on to a domain, this field must contain the name of the domain.

- **Computer Description.** Here you can enter a brief message that identifies or describes the computer in greater detail. This description will appear with the computer name in browse lists.

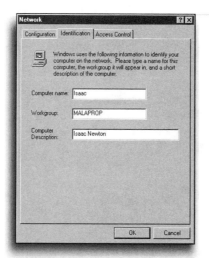

FIGURE 8.5

Configuring the computer's identification properties.

11. Return to the **Configuration** tab. You should check the properties of the Microsoft client. Double-click **Client for Microsoft Networks** to open the Client for Microsoft

Networks Properties dialog box shown in Figure 8.6. This dialog box has the following fields:

- **Log on to Windows NT domain.** If you check this field, Windows 95 and 98 will log on to a domain rather than a workgroup.

- **Windows NT domain.** If the field **Log on to Windows NT domain** is checked, this field must specify the name of the domain the computer is to log on to. The value of this field must match the value of the **Workgroup** field on the **Identification** tab.

- **Quick logon.** If this radio button is selected, Windows 95 and 98 will not attempt to re-establish persistent connections when the user logs on. A persistent connection is re-established only when the user attempts to access the shared resource. The logon process takes less time with this option, but the user experiences a delay when first connecting to a share.

- **Logon and restore network connections.** If this radio button is selected, Windows 95 and 98 attempts to re-establish all persistent connections when the user logs on. This option can prolong the logon process, but improves responsiveness when the user is logged on.

FIGURE 8.6

Configuring Microsoft network client properties.

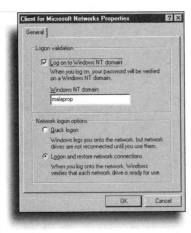

12. If this computer will share its files or printers on the network, click **File and Print Sharing** to open the File and Print Sharing dialog box. The following check boxes are available:

- **I want to be able to give others access to my files**
- **I want to be able to allow others to print to my printer(s)**

If you check either option, the option **File and printer sharing for Microsoft Networks** will be added to the list of installed network components.

13. After you have configured adapters, protocols, and clients as required, exit the Network applet. In most cases, you must restart the computer to activate changes.

Logging On

When Windows restarts, it will attempt to connect to the network. If you have specified a domain logon, you will be presented with the logon prompt Type your password to enter the Microsoft network. Windows 95 and 98 remembers your username from session to session, but you must enter your password with each logon attempt.

Mapping Drives to Shared Resources

If you are familiar with Windows NT 4, there is little need to describe the browsing and connection management features of Windows 95 and 98. After all, Windows NT 4 borrowed the Windows 95 user interface.

You follow these steps to map a drive to a file share:

Mapping a drive to a network file share

1. Browse network resources in the Network Neighborhood or in Explorer.

2. After you have found the share you want to connect to, right-click on the share to open a context menu.

3. Choose **M**ap Network Drive from the context menu to open the Map Network Drive dialog box. This dialog box has two data entry fields:

   * **D**rive. Select the drive letter you wish to map.

   * **Reconnect at logon.** Check this box to establish a persistent connection. Depending on the settings in the Client for Microsoft Networks properties dialog box, persistent connections are re-established when you log on (**Quick logon**) or when you first attempt to connect with a resource (**L**ogon and restore network connections).

Connecting to Shared Printers

Printer setup is managed by a wizard that is used to add a printer to your configuration. To add a printer, follow these steps:

Adding a printer for Windows 95 and 98

1. Open the Printers folder in My Computer.

2. Double-click Add Printer to start the Add Printer Wizard.

3. When asked to specify how the printer is attached to your computer, select **Network printer.**

4. When asked to specify the network path or queue name, click **Browse** to open a browse box, where you can locate and select the shared printer.

5. Complete the printer setup as for a normal printer.

6. Windows 95 and 98 can identify the printer type by examining the printer share. If Windows 95 or 98 printer drivers were installed on the print server, they can be accessed by Windows 95 and 98, and it is not necessary to install drivers on the local computer. If the required drivers are not installed at the print server, the required drivers will be installed on the local computer.

SEE ALSO

➤ *To learn how to install Windows 95 or 98 printer drivers on a Windows NT print server, see the section titled "Creating a Printer for a Local Print Device," page 218.*

Using Windows NT Server Tools for Windows 95 and 98

You may find it necessary to manage a Windows NT Server network from a Windows 95 or 98 workstation. For such situations, Microsoft includes with Windows NT Server 4 a set of network management utilities designed to run on Windows 95 or 98. Included are Server Manager, User Manager for Domains, Print Manager for Windows NT Server, File Manager, and Event Viewer.

To install the Server Tools for Windows 95 and 98, follow these steps:

Installing Server Tools for Windows 95 and 98

1. Open the Windows 95 Control Panel.

2. Start the Add/Remove Programs applet.

3. Select the **Windows Setup** tab.

4. Click **H**ave **Disk** and specify a path to the \Clients\Srvtools\Win95 folder on the Windows NT Server 4 installation CD-ROM.

5. Click **OK.**

6. Check the box next to **Windows NT Server Tools** and click **I**nstall. Files will be copied to the \srvtools folder.

7. Close the Add/Remove Programs applet.

8. Edit the PATH statement in the computer's AUTOEXEC.BAT file to include a path to C:\SRVTOOLS. This can be done by adding ;c:\srvtools to the end of the path statement.

9. Restart the computer.

A Windows NT Server Tools program group will be added to the Start/Programs menu. Also, the Explorer program will be extended to enable you to manage NTFS security properties as well as printers on Windows NT computers.

Windows for Workgroups 3.11

Windows for Workgroups (WfW) can be used by itself to build peer-to-peer networks that support file and printer sharing. The utilities included with WfW are network ready. Print Manager can share local printers and connect to shared printers elsewhere on the network. File Manager can share files and connect to shared files. Although you can network Windows 3.1, the utilities in Windows 3.1 cannot participate in the network with the same facility as the utilities in WfW.

Everything you need to configure a WfW 3.11 client is included with the product. This section shows you how to install networking software, connect to a domain, and access domain resources.

Installing WfW Network Software

When WfW is installed on a networked computer, Setup will normally install the network software and configure WfW to participate in a workgroup. If the WfW computer is already participating in a workgroup, the network software is already installed, and you can skip this section and go to the section titled "Connecting to a Domain."

Here are step-by-step procedures for adding network software to an installed copy of Windows for Workgroups:

Adding network software to Windows for Workgroups

1. Run the Windows Setup utility. The icon for Windows Setup is normally stored in the Main program group. In the Windows Setup dialog box, the **Network** field will indicate No Network Installed.

2. Choose the Change Network Settings command in the **Options** menu. The Network Setup dialog box will be displayed as shown in Figure 8.7. This box is the focus for most WfW network configuration procedures. In Figure 8.7, no networking features are enabled.

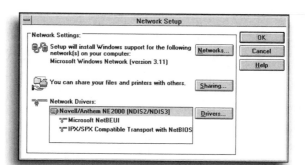

FIGURE 8.7
The Network Setup dialog box.

3. To install network support, click **Networks** to display the
Networks dialog box shown in Figure 8.8.

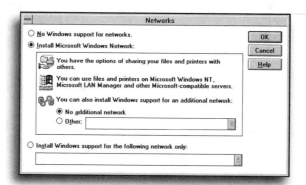

FIGURE 8.8
Selecting network support
options.

Although WfW can be configured with protocol stacks provided by other vendors, such as the Open Datalink Interface
(ODI) stack from Novell, you will probably want to use the
NDIS stack provided by Microsoft. NDIS supports multiple, simultaneous protocols including NetBEUI, NWLink
(a transport compatible with Novell's IPX/SPX), and
TCP/IP.

4. To install the protocols, click the radio button **Install
Microsoft Windows Network** and click **OK**. (If your network includes NetWare or other supported networks, you
will also need to select **Other** and follow the required procedures for the other network type.)

Problems with card detection

Some cards have multiple personalities that may fool the detection programs. If the card Setup detects is incorrect, you must click **No** to enter the Add Network Adapter dialog box.

You will be returned to the Network Setup dialog box, which now indicates that Setup will install the Microsoft Windows Network (version 3.11). Click **OK** to continue.

5. Setup attempts to discover any network cards in the PC. It will be successful with many older network adapters, but lacks the drivers required to support most modern adapters.

6. If you must manually select a network card driver, you will do so from the list in the Add Network Adapter dialog box, shown in Figure 8.9. In the figure, an NE2000 has been chosen.

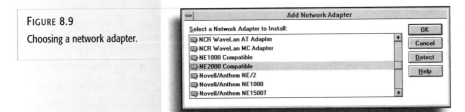

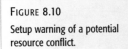
FIGURE 8.9
Choosing a network adapter.

7. Next, a series of boxes enables you to specify settings for your network card. In the case of the NE2000, the interrupt and the I/O port had to be confirmed.

If you select an interrupt that is normally dedicated to another resource, Setup warns you. Figure 8.10 shows the warning shown when **Interrupt 3** was selected.

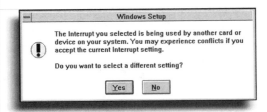

FIGURE 8.10
Setup warning of a potential resource conflict.

8. After specifying card settings, Setup presents the Microsoft Windows Network Names dialog box shown in Figure 8.1. Here you must specify the following:

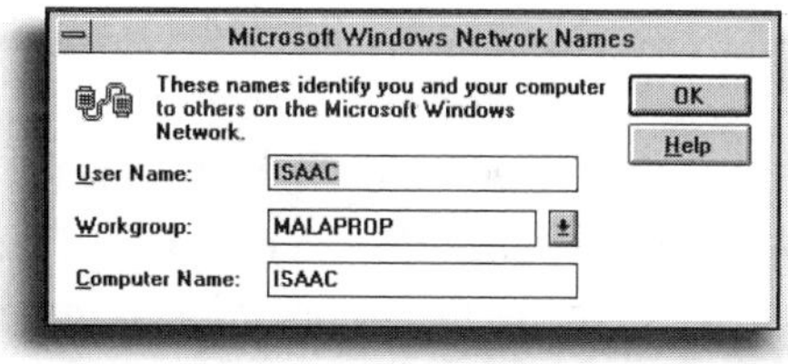

FIGURE 8.11
Specifying network names.

- **User Name**. This entry should match a username recognized by the domain this user will access.

- **Workgroup**. This can be a WfW workgroup (the default is WORKGROUP) or a domain. You should avoid using the default name WORKGROUP, especially if your network is connected to a WAN.

- **Computer Name**. This name should uniquely identify this computer on the network.

  Workgroup and computer names can consist of up to 15 characters and may include the following characters:

  ! # $ % ( ) - _ . @ ^ ' ~

  Spaces are not permitted.

9. Click **OK** when network names have been specified. Setup will begin to install files. Insert disks and specify file locations when prompted.

   You are notified that Setup will modify the files AUTOEXEC.BAT, SYSTEM.INI, and PROTOCOL.INI. The changes made to these files are discussed later in the chapter.

10. After files are installed, the computer must be rebooted to activate the network software. You are given the option Restart your computer now?. Click **Restart Computer** to activate the network.

11. When you restart Windows, you will see a Welcome to Windows for Workgroups dialog box. This dialog box has the following two fields:

    - **Logon Name**. This matches the name you specified in step 8.

    - **Password**. You should enter the password this user will enter to access the workgroup network.

Significance of the workgroup name

The entry specified in **Workgroup** determines which computers a WfW computer can share resources with. If the entry is the name of a workgroup, the WfW computer can share resources with other computers in the workgroup but not with Windows NT computers or with computers connected only to a domain.

If the entry in **Workgroup** is the name of a domain, the WfW computer can share resources with Windows NT computers, WfW computers, and with DOS computers running Microsoft Network software. The computer will not, however, enable the WfW computer to share resources with computers not logged on to the domain.

A WfW computer can share resources with a workgroup and log on to a domain by specifying a workgroup in the **Workgroup** entry and entering a domain, as described in the later section titled "Connecting to a Domain."

Windows for Workgroups passwords

WfW is capable of logging users on to a variety of resources while it is starting up. For this to work smoothly, a user should have the same username on each network. It is also useful to enter the same password on each network. There is no way to discover a password after it has been created, and one password is easier to remember than three or four.

12. Next you will see the message `There is no password list file for the user name. Do you want to create one now?`. Respond by clicking **Yes**.

13. A Confirm User Password dialog box requests that you enter the password a second time. Type the password again in the Confirm New Password dialog box and click **OK**.

WfW will encrypt the password you entered and store it in a file named `username`.`PWL` in the `Windows` directory (where `username` matches the user's logon name). The next time this user logs on to WfW, a password will be requested and checked against the password in the PWL file. If a blank password was entered, no password is requested when WfW starts.

The computer is now set up to participate on a network, but cannot yet log on to a domain. The next section covers the steps to connect the computer to a Windows NT domain.

Connecting to a Domain

After a WfW computer has been configured to connect to a network, you can enable it to log on to a domain. Start the Network utility in the Control Panel. The Microsoft Windows Network dialog box that is shown can be used to reconfigure many WfW network settings (see Figure 8.12).

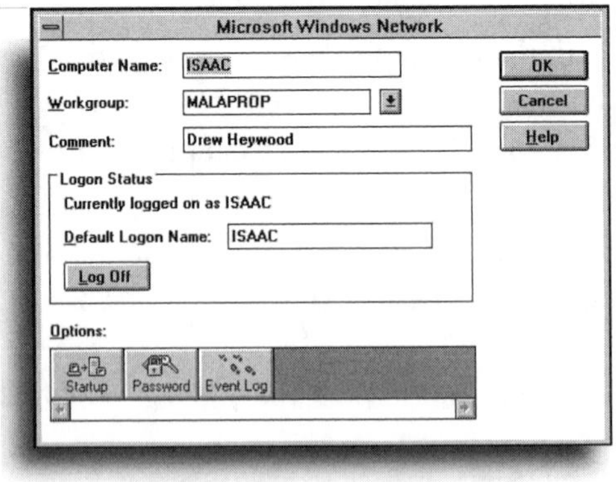

FIGURE 8.12

The Network applet in Windows for Workgroups.

To configure WfW to log on to a domain when starting, do the following:

Configuring WfW to log on to a domain

1. Click the **Startup** button to display the Startup Settings dialog box shown in Figure 8.13. Several check boxes are included:

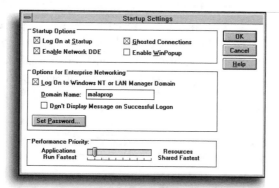

FIGURE 8.13

Specifying WfW network startup settings.

- **Log On at Startup**. Check this box to have WfW log you on automatically when it starts.

- **Enable Network DDE**. If you will be using network DDE with your applications, check this box. Check the box only if network DDE is required because enabling this option uses about 50 KB of memory.

- **Ghosted Connections**. Selecting this option saves time at startup by not establishing connections to resources until they are actually placed in use. Drive letters are reserved for persistent connections, but connections are not established.

- **Enable WinPopup**. WinPopup is a message display utility that displays network messages in Windows. If you will be broadcasting messages to users, enable this option. WinPopup also receives confirmation messages from domain print servers.

2. Check the box labeled **Log On to Windows NT or LAN Manager Domain** to enable WfW to log on to Windows NT Server when starting up.

3. Enter the logon domain name in the **Domain Name** box.

4. Click **Set Password** to enter the logon password at this time.

5. If you do not want to receive a message confirming a successful logon, check the box **Don't Display Message on Successful Logon**.

6. Click **OK**. You will be prompted to restart the computer.

7. When WfW restarts, you will be presented with the Domain Logon dialog box shown in Figure 8.14. Enter the password for the domain that was selected. If desired, you can change the domain, or click **Browse** to search for one.

8. If you check the **Save this Password in Your Password List**, WfW will encrypt the domain password and store it in this user's PWL file.

9. Following a successful domain logon, WfW displays a confirmation message similar to the one shown in Figure 8.15. (This box will not display if **Don't Display Message on Successful Logon** was checked in step 5.)

After workgroup and domain passwords have been stored in a password file, WfW will not request them when starting unless they are refused by the workgroup or the domain.

If a password has changed, or if you want to change your password, do the following:

- Change your domain password by selecting the **Set Password** button in the Startup Settings window (refer back to Figure 8.13).

- Change your workgroup password by selecting the **Password** button in the Microsoft Windows Network window, shown in Figure 8.12.

If you have not logged on to a domain and attempt to browse domain resources, you will be shown the logon message displayed in Figure 8.16, giving you the option of logging on to the domain.

FIGURE 8.16
Logging on to the domain in mid-session.

Connecting to Shared Directories

WfW computers can connect to shared directories on Windows NT computers, using File Manager.

Connecting WfW to a shared directory

1. Run File Manager.

2. Choose the **Connect Network Drive** command in the **Disk** menu.

3. Specify a drive letter and browse the network for a shared directory.

4. Specify whether the disk should be reconnected at startup.

5. Click **OK**.

The disk connection can be used as a virtual hard drive.

Connecting to Shared Printers

Unlike Windows NT, WfW computers cannot read print drivers from a print server. Before a WfW computer can use a printer shared by a Windows NT print server, the proper print drivers must be installed on the WfW computer.

To install a printer driver in Windows for Workgroups, follow these steps:

Installing a printer driver in Windows for Workgroups

1. Start the Print Manager.

2. Choose the **Printer Setup** command from the **Options** menu.

3. In the Printers dialog box, click **A**dd to display the **List of Printers** list box, shown in Figure 8.17. Browse the list to determine whether a driver is available to support your printer. If so, select the driver and click **I**nstall. You will be prompted to insert disks from the WfW installation set.

FIGURE 8.17

Installing a printer in Windows for Workgroups.

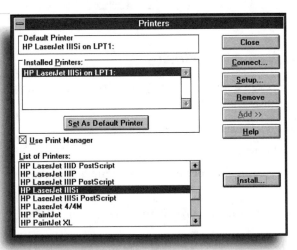

Unfortunately, the drivers included with Windows for Workgroups haven't been updated since the product was introduced several years ago, and many newer printer models are not directly supported. You might need to supply drivers on a floppy disk. To do so, click **Install Unlisted or**

Updated Printer from the **List of Printers** and then click **Install**. You will be prompted to enter a path where WfW can locate the print drivers, usually on drive A:.

4. The new printer will be automatically installed on LPT1: even if another printer already occupies that port. If you are sharing a workgroup printer on LPT1:, you must assign the network printer to a new port. To do so, follow these steps:

   • Click **Connect** in the Printers window. This will reveal the Connect dialog box shown in Figure 8.18.

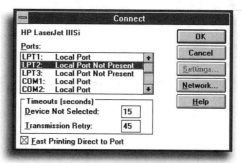

FIGURE 8.18
Connecting a printer to a port in Windows for Workgroups.

   • Select an unoccupied port in the **Ports** list box.
   • Click **OK**. You will be returned to the Printers dialog box. The printer will now be installed on the port you have selected.

To enable an installed printer to print to the network, you must connect it to a shared printer. This is also done in Print Manager.

Printing to a network printer

1. Start the Print Manager.
2. Select a printer that is labeled **(not shared)**.
3. Choose **Connect Network Printer** from the **Printer** menu. This will display the Connect Network Printer dialog box in which you can browse for a network printer (see Figure 8.19).

Background printing on the network

Windows uses background printing through the Print Manager to enable applications to print without waiting for a printer to become available. The approach works much like spooled printing on a network. Because printing on a network is already being spooled, you can improve network printing performance by enabling WfW to print directly to a port. To make the change, check the box **Fast Printing Direct to Port** in the Connect dialog box.

FIGURE 8.19

Browsing for printers in Windows for Workgroups.

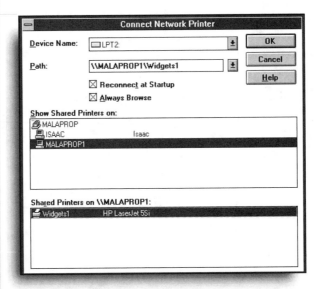

4. Browse for a shareable printer and select it to store the path in the **Path** box, or enter the path manually.

5. Check **Reconnect at Startup** if the printer connection should be re-established each time Windows for Workgroups starts up.

6. Click **OK** to return to the Connect dialog box. The **Ports** list box will now show that the port you specified is connected to the shared network printer.

7. Click **OK** to return to the Printer Manager. The printer list will now indicate the resource path to which the printer is connected.

Print Manager need not be running to print to the network unless you are sharing a local printer with a workgroup. WfW will open Print Manager if it is required.

MS-DOS

Windows NT Server includes software that enables MS-DOS and Windows 3.1 computers to function as clients on a Windows NT Server network. The client software is called Microsoft Network Client 3.0 for MS-DOS.

Creating an Installation Disk

You will need to create installation disks before the client software can be installed on the workstation. Disks are created using the Network Client Administrator utility, which is installed in the Network Administration program group.

When you start the Network Client Administrator, you will see the Network Client Administrator dialog box with several options, shown in Figure 8.20.

FIGURE 8.20

The Network Client Administrator options.

The DOS client can be installed in the following two ways:

- **Using a network installation startup disk that you boot on the workstation**. This disk has enough information to connect to the network and download client software from a directory on the server.

- **Using client installation disks that enable you to manually install the software on the workstation**.

Using a network installation startup disk has a number of catches:

- The disk must be formatted as a system disk using the same DOS version as the computer on which it will be installed. This can be problematic unless all your PCs have exactly the same DOS version.

- The disk must include a driver for the network card that will be on the workstation. Unless all your computers use the same network card, you will need several disks.

- It doesn't always work, and you might have to resort to manual installation in any case.

Therefore, the procedure I will describe involves use of a conventional client installation disk set.

To create the disk set, select the option **Make Installation Disk Set** and click **Continue**. This will take you to the Share Network Client Installation Files dialog box, shown in Figure 8.21.

FIGURE 8.21

Network Client installation options.

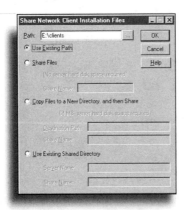

Network Client Administrator can copy the drivers for various network clients to the server, where they can be available to support client installation using network installation startup disks. Because the method described here uses the client installation disk set, it is not necessary to copy files to the server. They can be copied directly from the Windows NT Server installation CD-ROM to the floppies.

To create the installation disk set, follow these steps:

Creating an MS-DOS client installation disk set

1. Locate two high density disks. All files on these disks will be erased. Label these disks Network Client v3.0 Disks 1 and 2.

2. Start Network Client Administrator, select the **Make Installation Disk Set** option, and click **Continue**.

3. In the Share Network Client Installation Files dialog box, select **Use Existing Path**. Be sure that the drive letter in the **Path** field is correct for your CD-ROM.

4. Click **OK** to display the Make Installation Disk Set dialog box shown in Figure 8.22.

FIGURE 8.22
Preparing to create client instal-lation disks.

5. In the **Network Client or Service** list box, select **Network Client 3.0 for MS-DOS and Windows**.

6. In the **Destination Drive** field, select the disk drive you will be using.

7. Check the **Format Disks** check box. It is always a good idea to format. A quick format will be performed, if possible, to save time.

8. Click **OK** and follow the prompts to create the disks.

Installing Network Client for MS-DOS

Network Client requires MS-DOS version 3.3 or later. To install the Network Client on a DOS PC, follow these steps:

Installing the MS-DOS Network Client

1. Insert Disk 1 and, depending on the drive that holds the disks, type a:setup or b:setup from the C: prompt.

2. Press Enter once to reach a screen where you can enter a directory in which files will be installed. The default is C:\NET. Change this path if desired and press Enter.

3. Setup will examine your PC hardware. You might see the message shown in Figure 8.23. Network Client requires a substantial amount of DOS memory. Unless you will be using a memory manager to move programs to upper memory, you will need to do everything you can to conserve memory.

   Press Enter if Setup should maximize performance at the expense of higher memory overhead.

   Press C to conserve memory at the cost of reducing perfor-mance.

FIGURE 8.23

The Set Network
Buffers message.

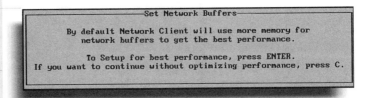

4. Enter a username of up to 15 characters. The name can include letters, numbers, and these characters: ! # $ % ^ & ( ) _ ' { } ~, but not spaces.

   After you enter a username, you will see the screen shown in Figure 8.24. This screen accesses three other screens that configure the Network Client. Use the arrow keys to highlight an option, and press Enter to select the option.

FIGURE 8.24

The main menu in Setup for
Network Client v3.0.

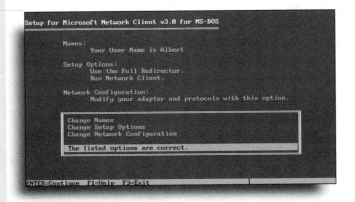

5. Select the **Change Names** option to display the screen shown in Figure 8.25. The computer name you entered in step 4 will appear in the **Change User Name** and **Change Computer Name** fields.

   The other fields will show the default entry of WORK-GROUP. In the figure, the domain name has been edited.

   To change a field, highlight it with the arrow keys and press Enter. Modify the entry in the **Change Domain Name** field to match the domain this computer will log on to.

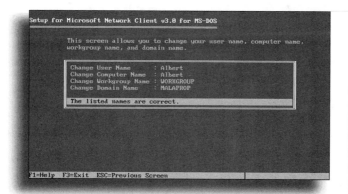

FIGURE 8.25
Changing Network Client names.

6. Click **The listed names are correct**, and press Enter to save the changes and return to the Setup menu.

7. Select **Change Setup Options**. This will bring up the screen shown in Figure 8.26. This screen has four options that you may choose to modify:

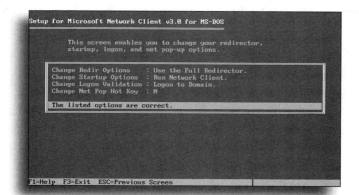

FIGURE 8.26
Entering Setup options.

- **Change Redir Options**. You can choose to use the **Full Redirector** or the **Basic Redirector**. The Basic Redirectory works for many users and saves memory. The Full Redirector is required to support Microsoft Windows, Remote Access Service, and other advanced functions.

- **Change Startup Options**. You can choose to:

  Run Network Client. The client runs when the computer is booted.

Run Network Client and Load Pop-Up. The pop-up is a utility that enables you to connect to network resources from a menu interface. It can be easily loaded later if needed.

Do Not Run Network Client. The client software must be started manually.

- **Change Logon Validation**. You can choose the following:

  Do Not Logon to Domain.

  Logon to Domain.

- **Change Net Pop Hot Key**. When the Net pop-up utility is loaded, it can be displayed with a hot key, normally Alt+N. You can change the letter for the hot key if it is used by another utility.

  When you have configured these options, choose **The listed options are correct**.

8. Click **Change Network Configuration** to display the screen shown in Figure 8.27, which is used to configure network adapters and protocols.

FIGURE 8.27
Configuring network adapter settings.

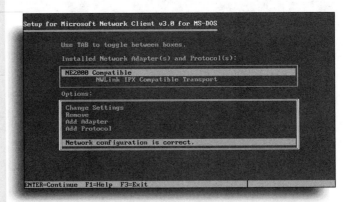

9. Examine the network adapter in the **Installed Network Adapter(s) and Protocols(s)** list box.

This screen has two boxes: **Installed Network Adapters and Protocols** and **Options**. To change the active box, press Tab.

10. If the listed adapter is incorrect, click **Remove** in the
    Options box. You will be asked immediately to add a net-
    work adapter. Select an adapter from the list provided.

11. To add an adapter, click **Add Adapter** and select an adapter
    from the list provided. To supply a driver for a card that is
    not listed, choose **Network adapter not shown on the list
    below**.

12. Click **Change Settings** and review the settings for your
    adapter. Figure 8.28 shows the settings screen. Change any
    setting by selecting it and choosing new values from a list.

    The default protocol NWLink is probably the only protocol
    you will require. If you want to install other protocols, click
    Add Protocol.

    * **Microsoft NetBEUI**. Add this protocol if you want
      to access shared resources on workgroup computers
      not running NWLink.

    * **Microsoft TCP/IP**. Add to support the TCP/IP
      protocol suite.

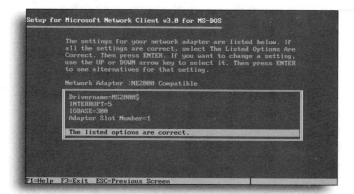

FIGURE 8.28
Settings for a network adapter.

SEE ALSO
➤ *See Chapters 13 through 18 for more information about configuring TCP/IP.*

13. Click **Network Configuration Is Correct** to return to the
    Setup menu.

14. After all settings are correct, continue installation by choos-
    ing **The listed options are correct in the setup menu**.

Reconfiguring network options

You may rerun the Setup utility in the network directory to reconfigure options. This is much more efficient than attempting to edit configuration files manually. Do not reconfigure by running Setup from the client installation disks.

15. You will be prompted to reboot the computer to activate the network software.

Logging On with Network Client

After the system boots, you can log on to the network as follows:

Logging on with the MS-DOS Client

1. The logon procedure depends on the option you chose for the **Startup Option** field in Setup.

    * If you chose **Run Network Client** and **Logon to Domain**, you will receive the prompt Type your user name. The username you entered during setup will be presented as a default. Enter a username, or press Enter to accept the default.

    * If you chose **Do Not Logon to Domain**, you must type the command NET LOGON at the DOS prompt when you want to connect to the network.

2. After you log on, you will be prompted for a workgroup password. Workgroup passwords might be stored in a file. You will be asked whether you want to create a password file for this user.

3. If the DOS client is logging on to a Windows NT Server domain, you will be prompted to enter a domain password.

4. If the Full Redirector has been loaded, after logging on, any commands in the user's logon script will be executed.

Network Client 3.0 memory requirements

Network Client v3.0 uses a significant amount of DOS memory. Unless you optimize memory, you might find that some applications will not run. You might also find that NET commands in logon scripts cannot be run due to memory limitations.

It is strongly recommended that you run a memory manager on all DOS clients. If possible, configure your system without expanded memory because EMS page frames occupy high DOS memory that could be used to relocate DOS TSRs and drivers.

Connecting Drives and Printers with the Workstation Connection NET Pop-Up

Network functions are accessed with the NET utility, which has both a command-line and a pop-up interface. The default hot key for the pop-up utility is Ctrl+Alt+N.

To connect a drive, follow these steps:

Connecting a network drive with the MS-DOS Client

1. Activate the NET pop-up by typing NET. If it is already loaded, press the hot key to display the Disk Connections

dialog box shown in Figure 8.29. Select fields in Disk
Connections by pressing the Tab key.

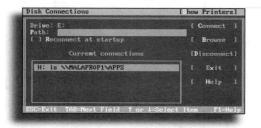

FIGURE 8.29
Connecting drives with the Net
pop-up utility.

2. If desired, change the drive letter in the **Dri̱ve** field.

3. Connect to a shared directory by entering a path in the **P̱ath**
field and clicking **C̱onnect**.

4. Click **Ṟeconnect at startup** if you want this connection to
be re-established when the Network Client starts up.

5. Press Esc when done.

To connect a printer, follow these steps:

Connecting to a network printer with the MS-DOS Client

1. Start the Net utility by typing NET or by pressing the hot key
if Net is already loaded.

2. Click **S̱how Printers** to display the Printer Connections
dialog box shown in Figure 8.30.

FIGURE 8.30
Printer connections in the
Network Client pop-up.

3. Select an entry in the **Port** field. No default value is
provided.

4. Enter a printer path in the **Path** field and click **Connect** to
make a connection.

5. Check **Reconnect at Startup** to have this printer connect when the Network Client is started.

6. Press Esc to leave the pop-up utility.

Using Network Client Commands

The NET command accepts several command arguments that control functions such as logon, logoff, and resource connections. These commands can be used interactively, but are probably most valuable when included in logon scripts. Examples of logon scripts are provided in the section titled "Logon Scripts" later in this chapter.

I've described several of the most useful NET commands in this section. A complete list of NET commands can be found in Windows NT Help; however, not all the commands listed in NT Help are supported by the MS-DOS Client.

To list available NET commands on the MS-DOS Client, enter the command NET HELP at a command prompt. To obtain detailed help about a specific command, enter the command NET HELP *COMMAND*, where *COMMAND* is the specific command you want to learn about.

NET HELP

NET HELP displays a summary of the NET command options. You can display details about any command by including a command as an option. To see a help listing on the LOGON command, for example, type the following:

```
NET HELP LOGON
```

NET LOGON

NET LOGON initiates a logon dialog. Entered alone, NET LOGON prompts you for a username and a password. You can also enter the name and password as parameters. For example, isaac would log on the default domain or workgroup with the password apple like this:

```
NET LOGON ISAAC APPLE
```

A different domain can be specified with the /domain:*domainname* option. For example:

```
NET LOGON MARIE RADIUM /DOMAIN:MALAPROP
```

NET LOGOFF

NET LOGOFF breaks your logon connection with the network. If you include the /YES option, you will not be asked to confirm your logoff request.

NET USE

Disks and printers are both connected and disconnected with the NET USE command. To connect drive C: to the APPS share on MALAPROP1, use this command:

```
NET USE C: \\MALAPROP1\APPS
```

The following command connects LPT1: to printer WIDGETS1 on server MALAPROP1:

```
NET USE LPT1: \\MALAPROP1\WIDGETS1
```

Add the option /PERSISTENT:YES to specify connections that should be made when the Workstation Connection starts up.

To see a list of your connected resources, enter the NET USE command without options.

NET VIEW

Use the NET VIEW command to list computers and shared resources. Enter NET VIEW without options to list computers that are sharing resources in your domain.

Include a computer name to list shared resources on the computer. NET VIEW \\MALAPROP1 lists shared resources on MALAPROP1.

NET TIME

NET TIME provides a convenient means of synchronizing a computer's clock with the clock on another computer. It is generally preferable to synchronize clocks in a share environment so that users can be assured that time and data stamps are meaningful.

To synchronize a client clock with the computer \\MALA-PROP1, you would use this command:

```
NET TIME \\MALAPROP1 /SET /YES
```

The /YES parameter carries out the NET TIME command without prompting you for confirmation.

NET STOP

The NET STOP command unloads services. To unload the pop-up, enter the following command:

```
NET STOP POPUP
```

You can stop the default redirector, which disconnects you from the network, by entering the following command:

```
NET STOP WORKSTATION
```

NET PASSWORD

Change your password with the NET PASSWORD command. Remember that users can have passwords in several places, including the password list file on the client and the username database on a domain or workstation.

Entered without parameters, the command prompts you for old and new passwords. You can also include old and new passwords as parameters. To change the password in the client password list file, the command syntax is as follows:

```
NET PASSWORD oldpassword newpassword
```

To change a password on a specific computer, include the computer name as a parameter. A username is also required:

```
NET PASSWORD \\WIDGETS1 MABEL oldpassword newpassword
```

To specify a domain, use the /DOMAIN option:

```
NET PASSWORD /DOMAIN:MALAPROP oldpassword newpassword
```

Windows 3.1

The Network Client can be used to enable Windows 3.1 computers to access Windows networks. Although Windows 3.1

workstations lack the workgroup features of Windows for Workgroups, they can become clients of Windows NT Server domains and of Windows workgroups.

Installing Networking for Windows 3.1

Network Client should be installed as described in the section titled "Installing Network Client for MS-DOS." This is a standard DOS installation, and no differences are required when Windows will be supported.

You might be tempted to install the Network Client files in the same directory as Windows, but this will not be permitted. The primary reason is probably that both Windows and Network Client rely on files named SYSTEM.INI, and Setup is not permitted to overwrite the Windows SYSTEM.INI file. (Windows for Workgroups is more fully integrated for networking, and one SYSTEM.INI file serves both WfW and the network drivers.)

After Network Client is installed, reboot the computer. Then start Windows and configure networking as follows:

Configuring Windows 3.1 networking

1. Start the Windows Setup utility in the Main program group.

2. Click **Change System Settings** in the Windows Setup **Options** menu. This will display the Change System Settings dialog box.

3. Pull down the **Network** box in Change System Settings to display a list of network options. From this list, choose the entry **Microsoft Network (or 100% compatible).**

4. Click **OK** to save the settings. Then close Windows Setup.

5. When you exit Windows Setup, you will be told that You need to exit Windows so that the changes you made will take effect. Click **Restart Windows** to activate networking.

6. You should check two settings in the Control Panel. Start the Network utility in the Control Panel.

   - If you want to have connections established in Windows re-established when Windows starts, check the box **Restore all connections at startup**.

- Normally you will receive warning messages if network services are not running. To eliminate these messages, check the box **D̲isable warning when network not running**.

Click **OK** when network settings have been made.

You are now ready to connect to network resources.

Connecting to Network Resources

You can connect to network resources in the following ways:

- By entering NET USE commands before starting Windows or from an MS-DOS prompt in Windows. These connections will be re-established if you include the /PERSISTENT:YES option.

- By connecting to files with File Manager and printers with Print Manager. These connections will be re-established when Windows restarts if you checked the **Restore all con-nections at startup** check box in the Network utility of the Control Panel.

Connecting Drives with File Manager

To connect a drive with File Manager, do the following:

Connecting a network drive with Windows 3.1 File Manager

1. Click **Network Clients** in the **D̲isk** menu. The Network Clients dialog box (see Figure 8.31) is somewhat different from the same box in Windows for Workgroups.

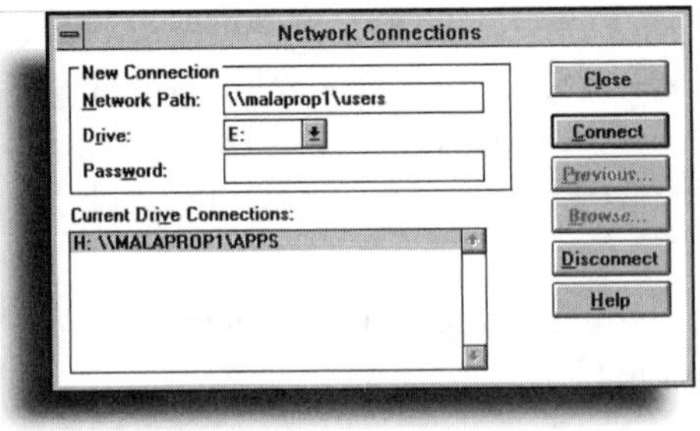

FIGURE 8.31

Connecting a drive in Windows 3.1.

2. Select an available drive letter in the **Dr̲ive** box.

3. Enter the path in the **N̲etwork Path** box. The Windows Networking driver does not enable you to browse for network resources.

4. If a password is required for this share, enter it in the **Passw̲ord** box.

5. Click **C̲onnect**.

6. Click **Cl̲ose** when all required connections are established.

The drives you have connected can now be used by any Windows program.

Connecting Printers with Print Manager

To connect a printer, follow these steps:

Connecting to a network printer with Windows 3.1 Print Manager

1. Choose **Network C̲onnections** in the **O̲ptions** menu. The Printers-Network Connections dialog box, shown in Figure 8.32, will be displayed.

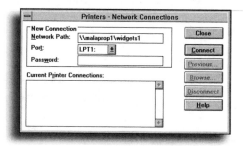

FIGURE 8.32

Connecting printers with Print Manager.

2. Enter a path in the **N̲etwork Path** field. As with File Manager, you will be unable to browse for resources.

3. If a password is required for this share, enter it in the **Passw̲ord** field.

4. Click **C̲onnect**. The printer connection will appear in the **Current Pr̲inter Connections** box.

5. Add other printer connections if desired by selecting other ports and entering the desired paths. Click **Connect** to complete each connection.

6. Click **Close** to return to the Print Manager.

The printers you have connected can now be used for printing with any Windows program.

Files Used with DOS and Windows Clients

When Microsoft network software is installed on a computer, several files are modified or added. Some of these modifications define parameters that you might need to modify. Therefore it is a good idea to take the time to familiarize yourself with the files discussed in the following sections.

CONFIG.SYS

Windows for Workgroups 3.11 and Network Connection 3.0 require two new lines in the CONFIG.SYS file:

```
LASTDRIVE=Z
DEVICE=C:\NET\IFSHLP.SYS
```

LASTDRIVE=Z configures DOS to support drive letters up to Z. (By default, DOS supports drives A through E.)

AUTOEXEC.BAT

If you have configured the computer to start the network automatically when booting, the NET START command will be added to the AUTOEXEC.BAT file, along with an appropriate path to locate the NET.EXE file. For example:

```
C:\WINDOWS\NET START
```

Windows for Workgroups performs most network functions within Windows. The Workgroup Connection must perform all network configuration functions from DOS. Therefore, Workgroup Connection 3.0 adds some other lines to AUTOEXEC.BAT.

With Network Connection, when protocols other than NetBEUI are loaded, the following command is added to the beginning of AUTOEXEC.BAT to load protocols and drivers without binding them to the Protocol Manager:

```
C:\NET\NET INITIALIZE
```

If you are using NWLink with Network Connection 3.0, you will see this line in the AUTOEXEC.BAT file, which loads the NWLink protocol:

```
C:\NET\NWLINK
```

Finally, Network Connection adds a NET START command. With Network Connection, NET START can be configured to log the user on to the network. Windows for Workgroups logs the user on after WfW starts.

PROTOCOL.INI

The PROTOCOL.INI file defines the configuration for the NDIS drivers. If several network card drivers or protocols are being loaded, PROTOCOL.INI can get quite elaborate; therefore this discussion examines only a simple example that loads an NE2000 adapter and the NetBEUI protocol. In general, you will find it much easier to let Microsoft setup programs build the PROTOCOL.INI file for the hardware you want to support. You will be required to make only small manual modifications to PROTOCOL.INI, if any are needed at all. The file can be modified by any text editor, including the Windows Notepad.

Windows for Workgroups places the PROTOCOL.INI file in the Windows installation directory (usually C:\WINDOWS). Network Client Setup places PROTOCOL.INI in the Network Client installation directory.

Here is a listing of a PROTOCOL.INI that was created by Network Client. I have added numbers to the lines to simplify discussion. This section won't go through the file line-by-line, but it will point out some significant features.

```
[network.setup]
version=0x3110
netcard=ms$ne2clone,1,MS$NE2CLONE,1
```

```
transport=ms$nwlink,MS$NWLINK
transport=ms$ndishlp,MS$NDISHLP
lana0=ms$ne2clone,1,ms$nwlink
lana1=ms$ne2clone,1,ms$ndishlp

[MS$NWLINK]
FRAME=ETHERNET_802.2
DriverName=nwlink$
BINDINGS=MS$NE2CLONE
[MS$NE2CLONE]
IOBASE=0x300
INTERRUPT=10
DriverName=MS2000$
[MS$AE2]
IOBASE=0x300
INTERRUPT=3
[MS$NE1CLONE]
IOBASE=0x300
INTERRUPT=3

[protman]
DriverName=PROTMAN$
PRIORITY=MS$NDISHLP

[MS$NDISHLP]
DriverName=ndishlp$
BINDINGS=MS$NE2CLONE
```

This file is divided into several sections, each beginning with a label in square brackets—for example, [MS$NDISHLP]. These labels enable network components to locate the lines relevant to them.

The [network.setup] section defines the basic characteristics of the network by cross-referencing other sections. The line beginning with netcard, for example, states that the driver to be used is MS$NECLONE and that parameters for the card can be found in the section [MS$NE2CLONE].

The [protman] section defines parameters for the Protocol Manager. If additional protocols are added to the NDIS protocol stack, this section tells the Protocol Manager which protocols have priority.

The [MS$NDISHLP] section supports configuration of the NDIS protocol stack and binds the NE2CLONE driver to the stack. You should not need to edit this section.

Each network board will have a section dedicated to it—in this example, [MS$NECLONE]. This is the only section likely to require manual attention if a card is reconfigured or if the Setup program will not permit you to enter a setting that your hardware supports.

SYSTEM.INI

A file named SYSTEM.INI is used by Windows and by Network Client. For Windows, this file is located in the Windows installation directory, which is C:\WINDOWS by default.

Network Client Setup will not permit you to install Network Client in the same directory as Windows, so you will have SYSTEM.INI files for both Windows and for Network Client.

SYSTEM.INI in Network Client

For Network Client, SYSTEM.INI has the following structure:

```
[network]
sizworkbuf=1498
filesharing=no
printsharing=no
autologon=yes
computername=ISAAC
lanroot=C:\NET
username=ISAAC
workgroup=WORKGROUP
reconnect=yes
dospophotkey=N
lmlogon=1
logondomain=MALAPROP
preferredredir=full
autostart=full
maxconnections=8
```

```
[network drivers]
netcard=ne2000.dos
transport=ndishlp.sys,*netbeui
devdir=C:\NET
LoadRMDrivers=yes

[Password Lists]
*Shares=C:\NET\Shares.PWL
HAROLD=C:\NET\ISAAC.PWL
```

You will recognize in this file many of the parameters that you entered when you set up the software. In fact, you can reconfigure most of the startup features of Network Client by editing this file. It is generally more prudent, however, to make changes with the Setup utility.

Each user who establishes a password list file (PWL extension) on the client will be given an entry in the [Password Lists] section.

SYSTEM.INI in Windows for Workgroups

Windows for Workgroups has a SYSTEM.INI file that contains settings both for Windows and for the network. The changes made to SYSTEM.INI are different for Windows for Workgroups 3.11 and network-enabled Windows 3. You will find it useful to scan SYSTEM.INI using either the Windows NOTEPAD or SYSEDIT utilities to identify features that are modified or added when networking is configured.

In WfW, you will find [network] and [Password Lists] sections that serve similar purposes to the sections defined for Network Client but might be more elaborate. WfW can share resources in addition to connecting to shares, and extra settings are required in the WfW SETUP.INI file.

Most of the network-related features of SYSTEM.INI can be reconfigured in Windows using the Control Panel or Windows Setup utilities. If you will be editing this file (or any configuration file for that matter), save a backup copy in case you introduce an error.

Logon Scripts

Logon scripts are an effective way to configure Windows NT Server clients when they are logging on to the network. Logon scripts are particularly effective for configuring a group of users so that they log on with the same set of drive and printer connections.

A logon script is usually a batch file, and has a BAT filename extension for DOS and Windows clients. Program files with the EXE extension can also be executed as logon scripts. The name of a user's logon script is specified in the user's account profile.

SEE ALSO

➤ *The procedure for specifying logon script names is described in Chapter 5, "Adding Users and Groups." See the section titled "Logon Script Name" on page 163.*

By default, logon scripts are stored in the directory `C:\Winnt\system32\repl\import\scripts`. In most cases, you won't want to change this location, particularly if you are operating a domain with more than one domain controller because you will want to use directory replication to copy logon scripts to all domain controllers in the domain.

When users log on to a domain, their logon can be authenticated by any active domain controller. If a logon script is specified for the user, the domain controller will look for the script on the local directory that matches the logon script directory location defined for the domain. In other words, each domain controller looks for logon scripts on its local C: drive.

You can use the Windows NT Server Replicator service to replicate copies of logon scripts from one domain controller to all other DCs in the domain.

SEE ALSO

➤ *The procedure for replicating files is described in Chapter 25, "Managing Directory Replication," starting on page 727.*

Logon Script Example

Logon scripts don't need to be elaborate. The following is an example of a logon script that defines resources by department. It might be set up for Widgets Engineering:

```
@echo off
net time \\keystone1 /yes
net use g: \\keystone1\apps /yes
net use s: \\widgets1\status /yes
net use lpt1: \\widgets1\laser1 /yes
```

This script uses NET TIME to synchronize each client workstation to the clock of KEYSTONE. By synchronizing all clients to the same clock, you know that you can rely on the time and date stamps on files.

The /YES option is included with each command and has two effects. First, /YES eliminates the need for users to respond to any prompts. Second, /YES ensures that these settings will replace any persistent settings that users have established.

Windows for Workgroups logon scripts

Because Windows for Workgroups users generally log on to the network after WfW has started, logon scripts execute in a virtual DOS session.

Now Your Network Is Ready to Go to Work

You have now added the client part of your client/server network, and any computer running a Microsoft operating system can now participate in your network. That, of course, means that your major network administration headache—dealing with users, their complaints and problems—is just around the corner. Take the time to master the intricacies of each type of network client before you turn the client software loose on your users' desktops.

Missing from this chapter are some advanced client capabilities that apply only to Windows NT computers. In the following chapter, you learn how to use user profiles, system policies, and advanced logon script capabilities to both simplify administration and enhance the usability of Windows NT clients.

Advanced Client Features

User profiles

The system policy

Windows NT logon script capabilities

When I speak of "advanced client features," I am really speaking of Windows NT clients, which have some special capabilities that are unavailable with other clients. Because Windows NT configuration is addressed throughout this book, I am not going to rehash the basic features of configuring Windows NT network clients in this chapter. Rather, I am going to look at some of the features that make Windows NT clients special.

For example, user profiles confer a special advantage only available with Windows NT clients. Profiles have two contrasting capabilities. They enable users to put their computer configurations on the network so that they work in their accustomed environment regardless of the computer they are working on. And profiles enable network administrators to preconfigure environments for users who perform similar tasks, ensuring that such users function in a uniform environment.

Administrators can establish system policies for Windows NT clients that greatly simplify workstation management. System policies restrict the actions users can perform on their network workstations by taking over control of certain areas of their Registries. Enforcement of system policies can greatly reduce the damage users can do to their workstations.

Logon scripts are batch files that can be configured to execute when clients log on to the network. You can use logon scripts to preconfigure users' environments, perhaps by mapping some network drives for them.

A final capability examined here is that of Windows NT Workstations to host network administration tools. This enables network administrators to work on Windows NT Workstation clients while having full access to the network management tools they require.

User Profiles

As you know, Windows NT retains your environment settings from one session to the next. When you log on, your desktop is restored to its state when you last logged off. Shortcut icons are in their accustomed positions, your Start menu has its familiar structure, your monitor has its accustomed settings, and your applications are configured as you like them. All this information is stored in a *user profile* created automatically and is identified with your user account. Table 9.1 summarizes the information stored in a user profile.

TABLE 9.1 Settings stored in user profiles

Source of Settings	Parameters in Profile
Accessories	User-specific settings for many Windows accessories (Clock, Calculator, Notepad, and so forth)
Control Panel	User-defined settings
Online Help	Bookmarks
Printer settings	Network printer connections
Taskbar	Personal program groups and program items with their properties, and all taskbar settings
Windows-aware applications	User-specific settings for applications that track settings on a per-user basis and update that information in the user profile
Windows NT Explorer	User-defined settings

Types of Profiles

All Windows NT computers, even isolated ones, support user profiles. *Local profiles* enable multiple users to share the same workstation while enabling them to regain their desktop settings when they log on. NT maintains local profiles automatically, and little administrative oversight is required. When a Windows NT computer is connected to a network, it becomes possible to establish *roaming profiles* and *mandatory profiles*, both of which are stored on a network server.

Even after a network profile is established, a profile is maintained locally on the workstation, enabling the user to establish a familiar desktop when the network is unavailable. When you log off the network, NT synchronizes your network and local profiles with copies of the current desktop configuration. This local profile is sometimes referred to as a *locally cached profile*. Regardless of the type of profile, all share a common database structure. Before putting profiles to work, it's important to examine the structure of a profile.

Profile Database Structure

The root folder for local profiles is `%SystemRoot%\Profiles` (by default `C:\Winnt\Profiles`). After a newly created user logs on for the first time, a profile folder structure is created for the user in the `%SystemRoot%\Profiles` folder. Network profiles, on the other hand, can be stored in any folder. Figure 9.1 shows an example of a `%SystemRoot%\Profiles` folder. Each user is assigned a sub-folder, named to match his or her username. Additionally there are two special profiles named `Default User` and `All Users`, which I'll get to in a bit.

FIGURE 9.1

Organization of local user profile folders.

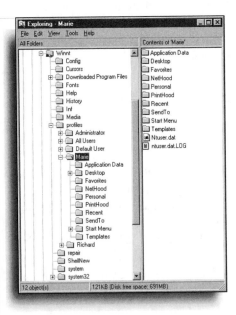

To show all the contents of a user profile folder, Figure 9.1 was prepared after configuring Explorer to display hidden files and file extensions. The various folders in the profile directory store shortcuts and application preferences that define the user's desktop. Table 9.2 lists the folders together with the settings stored in each. It should be noted that some applications may add their own folders to a user's profile.

TABLE 9.2 **Organization of profile folders**

Profile Folder	What It Stores
Application Data	Application-specific data for some Windows applications, such as user preferences for Word
Desktop	Non-system icons defined on the user's desktop, including shortcuts
Favorites	Shortcuts to favorite programs and locations, such as favorites defined in Internet Explorer (used by some applications)
NetHood	Shortcuts defined in the user's Network Neighborhood
Personal	Shortcuts to personal program items (used by some applications)
PrintHood	Shortcuts defined in the user's Printers folder
Recent	Shortcuts to documents used recently by some applications, such as files recently edited under Word
SendTo	Destinations available in the Send To option appearing in the context menus for files. Entries are defined by some applications
Start Menu	Entries in the user's personal areas of the Start Menu
Templates	Shortcuts to templates for some applications

Hidden folders in profiles

The NetHood, PrintHood, Recent, and Templates folders are hidden and do not normally appear in Windows NT Explorer.

The *Default Users* Profile Folder

When a user logs on for the first time, he or she does not yet have a user profile (unless an administrator has copied one into the user's profile folder). So, where does the user's initial working environment come from? It is initialized from a default profile stored in the Default Users profile folder. When a user first logs on, NT creates a personal profile folder and initializes the user's environment from the Default Users profile. Consequently, all profiles begin as a copy of the Default Users profile. When the user logs off, any desktop changes made by the user are stored in the user's personal profile.

The *All Users* Profile Folder

The All Users profile defines settings assigned to all users who log on locally to this computer and contains only two subfolders: a Desktop folder contains desktop shortcuts displayed for all users; and a Start Menu folder defines common program groups and their shortcuts. Common program groups and shortcuts are the ones that appear below the line that subdivides entries on the **Start** menu. (Users of Windows NT 3.51 are used to creating common program groups quite differently, by declaring the type when the program group is created. Under NT 4, a common program group is just a group stored under the Profiles\All Users\Start Menu folder.)

Profiles and the Registry

The folders in the profile store much of the data that constitute a user profile, but a profile also includes other personal settings that have been established in the Control Panel. These settings are stored in the Registry, so a different mechanism is required to include the settings in the user's profile.

SEE ALSO

> *Chapter 22, "Editing the Registry," explains the structure of the Registry. See the section titled "Registry Subtrees," on page 660.*

While working on an NT computer, a user's personal settings are stored in the Registry under the HKEY_CURRENT_USER root key. Figure 9.2 shows the HKEY_CURRENT_USER Registry subtree. As you can see, the subtree contains several entries tied to configuration of the user's working environment.

The data file associated with HKEY_CURRENT_USER is named Ntuser.dat, and the transaction log file is Ntuser.dat.LOG. You will find an Ntuser.dat file in each user's profile directory. You will also find the associated log file, named ntuser.dat.LOG. In Figure 9.1, hidden files are turned on to show you the Ntuser.dat and ntuser.dat.LOG files in the example user's profile. When a user logs on to NT, the data in Ntuser.dat is used to

---

Where do applications install?

In most cases, when you install an application the setup program places the icons in the Start Menu folder of your personal user profile. Occasionally, the icons may be installed in the All Users profile. In general, you cannot specify which profile should receive the icons, so it is always a good idea to verify the locations of the icons after an application is installed. Are the icons for your use only, or for the use of all users on the computer? You may meed to move them to the appropriate profile.

If applications are starting that aren't in your personal profile, check the All Users profile to see whether the icons are in the Startup folder for that profile.

initialize the HKEY_CURRENT_USER Registry subtree. When the user logs off, Ntuser.dat is updated from HKEY_CURRENT_USER.

FIGURE 9.2

The HKEY_CURRENT_USER subkey in the Registry.

As you can now see, a complete user profile consists of a folder structure in a profiles folder, together with numerous shortcut and other files, and capped off with the Ntuser.dat Registry file. The Ntuser.dat file turns out to have a crucial role in determining how profiles will function after they are stored on the network.

Some of the Control Panel settings stored in the Registry are hardware-dependent. An example is video display resolution. Consequently, profiles can be shared only among computers with similar hardware characteristics. It is unlikely, for instance, that you would be comfortable using the same profile on your 21-inch desktop monitor and your notebook. When profiles will be shared, they must be designed with consideration of the common capabilities of the workstations on which the profiles will be used.

Moving Profiles to the Network

Connecting a workstation to the network is a prerequisite to supporting network profiles, but it isn't the sole requirement. First you must create a folder on the server in which users' network profiles will be stored. Then you create a share for the profile folder. Finally, you configure users' accounts with a profile path.

A user's profile folder can be located on any network server that is accessible to the user. You can create one or more profile folders—often the best approach—to store profiles for groups

---

Updating Ntuser.dat

This is an important point that bears repeating: Ntuser.dat is updated only when the user logs off. As you will observe later, this behavior results in a couple of caveats where roaming profiles are concerned.

of users, enabling you to distribute profiles across multiple volumes and servers if necessary. You can store network profiles in the server's profile directory %SystemRoot%\Profiles, in which case users who are authorized to log on locally to the server will use their network profiles as local profiles. Or you can store each user's network profile in his or her network home directory, an approach that is complicated by the need to establish a network share for each profile directory.

To demonstrate network profiles, let's use a separately created profiles folder, which will be named C:\Profiles. After creating the folder, grant the group Everyone Change (RWXD)(RWXD) permissions for the directory, thereby enabling users to create and update their own profiles.

In this example, the profile directory is shared with the sharename Profiles$. The $ character makes this an administrative share that will not be advertised through network browsers. There is no reason users should connect to this share except through the profile mechanism.

SEE ALSO

➤ *Chapter 6, "Sharing Files," explains administrative shares in the section titled "Administrative Shares," page 195.*

The next step is to configure the user's account with the profile path. This is done in User Manager for Domains, as shown in Figure 9.3. The URL for the profile path specifies the server, share, and the name of the user's profile directory. For example:

```
\\malaprop1\profile$\Albert
```

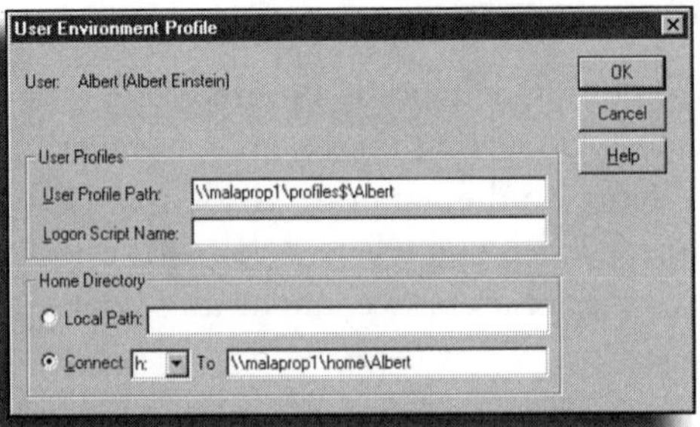

FIGURE 9.3
Adding a profile path to a user's account properties.

You can specify the user's profile directory by name, but an alternative that is especially useful if you are defining profile paths for multiple users is to use the system variable %Username% as was done in the example, enabling User Manager for Domains to supply the username for each user account being configured.

Logging On to a Network Profile

Assuming the previous steps have been performed to enable network profile support for a user, the events that take place when the user logs on depend on whether the user has previously logged on to the domain. First, assume the user has never logged on, in which case neither a local or a network profile exists. The sequence of events is as follows:

1. The user logs on.

2. Because a profile does not yet exist, the user's working environment is initialized from the Default User profile *on the user's local computer.*

3. A profile folder is created in the %SystemRoot%Profiles folder on the user's local computer. The local profile folder is populated with the required folders and data files. The folders and data files are time stamped with the logon date and time.

4. A profile folder is created in the server-based shared profiles folder. No folders or files are placed in the network profile folder at this time.

5. The user makes any desired changes to his or her environment.

6. The user logs off.

7. The profile is written out to the local profile folder. Changed files, including Ntuser.dat, are stamped with the logoff date and time.

8. The profile is written out to the network profile directory. All folders and files are stamped with the logoff date and time.

If the user has previously logged on to the network, things proceed a bit differently. The distinguishing factor is that if the user has previously logged on a local profile has been created for the user on his or her local computer. Consequently, in step 2, the user's environment is initialized from the user's local profile.

Okay, now the user has logged on and has created both a network and a local profile. Which profile will be used the next time the user logs on? That depends on which profile is more recent, as determined by the "last write time" stamps of the Ntuser.dat files. If the network profile time stamp is the same as or more recent than the time stamp of the local profile, the network profile will be used to initialize the user's environment. If the time stamp of the local profile is more recent, the local profile will be used.

The preceding procedures are all that are required to establish a roaming user profile. As you can see, it is not necessary for the network administrator to explicitly create the profile folders and files. All that is required is for the administrator to create the shared profiles folder, to establish the required security, and to add the path to the properties of the affected user accounts.

More Than One Profile

Because it is possible for a given username to be associated with more than one profile, profile confusion can arise. Within NT, a user account is known not by the username but by a Security ID (SID). Each time a user account is created, it is assigned a unique SID. Now, consider a possible scenario:

Albert's computer is assigned to a workgroup, and he has diligently created a profile that suits him to a T. His company decides to implement Windows NT Server and assigns Albert a domain account, equipped with a roaming profile. Albert logs on to the domain and gets his default profile, not the beautiful profile he has labored over. What happened?

The problem is that Albert's workgroup and domain accounts, although they share a username, have different SIDs. As far as

NT is concerned, they are distinct accounts with distinct profiles. If Albert logs on to the domain, he gets his domain profile; if he logs on to the workgroup, he gets his workgroup profile. When an administrator creates Albert's domain user account, the SID for the domain account is different from the SID for the workgroup account. Consequently, when Albert logged on to the domain for the first time, NT Server said, "Hmm, a new user. He doesn't have a profile, so he gets the default." Albert's desktop is initialized using the local `Default User` profile!

You can observe a user's various profiles in the System applet of the Control Panel. The **User Profiles** tab, shown in Figure 9.4, lists any profiles present on this computer. The **Name** column identifies the domain or workgroup the user belongs to. The **Type** column indicates whether the profile is **Local** (stored on this computer) or **Roaming** (stored on the network). We will return to this utility several times in the remainder of this chapter. Incidentally, although any user can view profiles in the System applet, standard users see only their own profiles. Administrators see all profiles stored on the local computer.

FIGURE 9.4

Managing profiles in the System applet.

Let's examine the protocols listed in Figure 9.4:

- Administrator has two local profiles. One is a local profile used when logging on to the MALAPROP domain. Another is a local profile used when logging on locally to this computer, which is named NTW1. The Administrator account does not have a roaming profile because it may be used to log on to machines with many different configurations.

- Albert has a local and a roaming profile. The administrator for the MALAPROP domain has configured Albert's user account with a roaming profile path. When Albert logs on locally, he uses a local profile for the computer NTW1.

- Marie has never logged on to this computer locally and has only a roaming profile for the MALAPROP domain.

Users often have several profiles and will access the appropriate profile depending on whether they are logging on to the domain or to the local machine. If they log on to the domain, they will access their roaming profile on the network server if it is available. Otherwise, they will access the locally cached copy of their network profiles.

Roaming Off the Network

A time stamp issue comes into play if you work on a computer that is isolated from the network, either due to a network outage or to an intentional disconnection. Suppose that your NT notebook is connected to the network and you are configured to use a roaming profile. You log off, disconnect the computer, and take a trip, during which the locally cached profile is used to set up your desktop. When you return and connect to the network, your local profile will have a time stamp that is more recent than the network profile. So, which profile will be accessed when you log on? To find out, take a look at the complete sequence of events.

Mabel fires up her notebook in her hotel room. She wants to use her familiar network profile, so in the Logon Information dialog box she logs on to the office domain. Here's what happens:

1. Because it takes too long for the workstation to connect with the network, NT assumes a slow WAN link and

displays a Slow Connection dialog box with the message
A slow network connection has been detected. Would you
like to download your profile or use the locally stored
copy? Mabel responds **Use Local**, which is also the default
choice if Mabel lets the counter expire. (The alternative is
Download, which of course would fail in the instance. The
Download option is provided for users who want to force
downloading of a profile over a working but slow WAN
connection such as a RAS modem connection.)

2. The next message informs Mabel, Your roaming profile is
not available, the operating system is attempting to log
you on with your local profile. Mabel clicks **OK**.

3. Next a Logon Message box proclaims, A domain controller
for your domain could not be contacted. You have been
logged on using cached account information. Changes to
your profile since you last logged on may not be
available.

4. Mabel works remotely, during which time her profile is
maintained locally.

5. Mabel returns to the office and jacks into the network. After
logging on, a Choose Profile message box proclaims, Your
locally stored profile is newer than your roaming profile.
Would you like to use the locally stored profile? Because
Mabel would like to retain profile changes she made on the
road, she clicks **Yes**. She would respond **No** to revert to the
network profile, losing any changes she made to the local
profile.

While working in her hotel (step 4), if Mabel looks at the **User
Profiles** tab of the System Control Panel applet (refer to Figure
9.3) she will see that her domain profile is being accessed from
the local copy.

WAN Issues

In general, NT profiles do not work well over slow WAN
links. In fact, Microsoft does not recommend using roaming
profiles across a slow network link. Not only does the profile
maintenance traffic chew up scarce bandwidth, but it also can

happen that local and roaming profiles get out of synchronization.

In one scenario, a user logs on via a WAN link slow enough to cause NT to time out. When that happens NT uses the local profile or initializes the user from the default profile if necessary. If when the session ends the remote server has become available, the local profile is used to update the roaming profile.

If users change locations frequently and wish to use roaming profiles, Microsoft recommends that copies of the roaming profiles be stored on servers at each site. You can use the directory replication capability of Windows NT Server to keep the various profile directories synchronized. Unfortunately, directory replication is one-way. You can update the remote profiles by copying the profile in the home office, but profile changes made at the remote site will not be replicated back to the main office.

SEE ALSO

➤ *Chapter 25, "Managing Directory Replication," covers directory replication, starting on page 727.*

Alternatively, you can switch users to mandatory profiles, which do not suffer from WAN update trouble because users cannot update them.

Even though you log on successfully through a slow link, such as a WAN or a RAS connection, it is usually preferable to switch from a roaming to a local profile. Doing so economizes on bandwidth utilization and eliminates synchronization errors. To switch to a local profile, open the **User Profiles** tab of the Control Panel System applet (refer to Figure 9.4). Select your roaming profile in the profiles list and click **Change Type**. A roaming profile will revert to local, as reported in the **Type** column. If desired, you can switch back to a roaming profile at the end of the session so that your network profile will be updated.

Administrator-Created Roaming Profiles

Suppose that you want to provide new users with predefined profiles. You could visit each workstation in the organization and modify user profiles, but there is a way to establish the user profile locally by copying a predefined profile to the new user's network profile directory.

The first step is to create the profile that will be distributed. To do that, you should create a separate user account specifically for profile maintenance. I call mine Profile Admin. Log on with this account on a workstation whose profile-dependent hardware characteristics are compatible with computers on which the profile will be used. Then design the profile as desired. Log off to save the profile.

While designing a profile, take care to ensure that any special files you incorporate into the profile—such as wallpapers, screen savers, and applications targeted by shortcuts—are present on the target computer. System files aren't usually a big deal because NT knows where to find them and most are installed by default. Applications are a different matter. If the profiles you distribute include shortcuts to applications, the shortcuts must point to valid folders and files. Consequently, you should ensure that organization standards specify how and where applications will be installed.

The profile you create will be a local profile. After the profile is designed, it is copied from the profile administrator's profile to the profile folder of the target user—a task performed on the **User Profiles** tab of the System applet in the Control Panel (refer to Figure 9.4). This tab lists local profiles as well as roaming profiles that are associated with users logging on on this computer. The procedure to copy a profile is as follows:

Copying a profile

1. In the **User Profiles** tab of the System applet, select the profile to be copied and click **Copy To**.

2. In the **Copy To** dialog box, shown in Figure 9.5, specify the UNC pathname of the destination profile directory. The **Browse** button enables you to browse for a local folder or for a remote folder in the Network Neighborhood.

3. In the **Permitted to use** box, click **Change** and select the user who is permitted to use the profile. Although you can specify a group in this field, groups should not share roaming profiles (as you will see later). However, it is feasible for groups of users to share a mandatory profile.

4. Click **OK** to copy the profile.

FIGURE 9.5

Specifying the destination folder and user when copying a profile.

SEE ALSO

➤ *UNC names are explained in the Note titled "UNC Names" in Chapter 5, "Adding Users and Groups," page 166.*

You can use this procedure to modify the Default User profile on any workstation. But don't try to update the All Users profile, which has a different structure and serves only locally logged-on users. To modify the All Users profile, use NT Explorer to create folders and shortcuts under the All Users folder.

When copying profiles for active users, the time stamps can get you into trouble. Suppose that you copy changes to Richard's profile while Richard is logged on. When Richard logs off, his profile will be saved, overwriting the profile you have copied.

Now, suppose that you update Richard's profile while he is working disconnected from the network. The profile you copy will be time stamped at the time it is saved. Richard is working with a locally cached profile, which is time stamped each time he logs off. Now Richard returns to the office and connects to the network. His local profile is now more recent than the network profile, and he will probably select the local profile, again discarding all the changes you put in his network profile. To prevent this sequence of events, you may need to update the time stamp on the profile you wish to have precedence. This can be done with the Touch utility that is included with the Windows NT Resource Kit.

Sharing Roaming Profiles

In one word, the guideline on sharing roaming profiles is, "Don't!" Yes, it is possible to share roaming profiles, but all sorts of confusion can arise. Any user sharing the profile can make changes to the environment, which is confusing enough. If you ever shared a Windows 3.1 computer with someone who loved to mess around with the desktop, you know how much pain and suffering sharing can entail.

To complicate matters further, suppose Albert and Richard are logged on simultaneously with the same roaming profile. Albert logs off first. Because Richard still has the profile open, any changes Albert has made to the profile cannot be written out. When Richard logs off, only his changes are written to the profile. Given the difficulties, it is hard to imagine a solid reason for sharing a roaming profile among multiple users.

Mandatory Profiles

Mandatory profiles cannot be permanently modified by the user. Although users can change their environments after logging on with a mandatory profile, the changes are not saved when the user logs off. Consequently, each time the user logs on the exact same profile will be used.

Because mandatory profiles cannot be modified by users, they can be shared. This is a great way to establish a standard desktop for large numbers of users, perhaps for dozens of employees who take telephone orders. Just assign the users the same mandatory profile in their user account properties.

Setting up a mandatory profile is embarrassingly easy. First create a profile, as described earlier in the chapter, and copy it to the desired directory. In the **Permitted to use** field, specify the user or a group of users permitted to use the profile. Then use your favorite tool to rename the `Ntuser.dat` file to `Ntuser.man`. That's it.

Windows 95 Profiles

Although Windows 95 supports profiles, they are incompatible with Windows NT profiles and are considerably less capable. Windows 95 profiles include only shortcut (`.lnk`) and program information (`.pif`) files. Windows 95 profiles are also less robust than their NT relatives because there is no fault tolerance mechanism similar to that provided by the `ntuser.dat.LOG` file. A file named `user.da0` provides a redundant copy of the `user.dat` file, which is the primary profile repository, but it does not provide fault tolerance through transaction logging and is used only when `user.dat` is lost or corrupted.

Windows 95 clients running the Microsoft Network Client or the Client for NetWare can access roaming user profiles, but these profiles must be stored in the users' home directories. The **User Profile Path** property of the user account is not used. Although mandatory profiles are supported for Windows 95 clients, mandatory profiles cannot be shared. It is necessary to create a separate profile for each user. To create a mandatory Windows 95 profile, rename the `user.dat` file to `user.man`.

The System Policy

If you want to tighten administrative control over users' working environments and the actions they can perform, consider setting up a system policy. You can control all Windows NT computers with a system policy, which is enforced by overwriting two areas of the Registry.

Windows NT Server includes a System Policy Editor, which is used to create a file named `NTConfig.pol`. This file is placed in the `Netlogon` subdirectory of the PDC. When a user logs on to a domain, the domain controller processing the logon checks with the PDC to see whether an `NTConfig.pol` file has been created. If `NTConfig.pol` is found, it is used to overwrite the appropriate sections of the user's local Registry. Two Registry subkeys are affected:

- `HKEY_CURRENT_USER` is overwritten with settings that affect the user's profile.
- `HKEY_LOCAL_MACHINE` is overwritten with settings that determine logon and network access settings.

System Policies and Domains

A system policy affects logon and network access settings. If a system policy is implemented, it should be implemented in all domains to which users log on. Consider the following sequence of events:

1. Isaac logs on to domain Malaprop, which enforces a security policy. The policy settings are downloaded to Isaac's computer and update his Registry.

2. Isaac logs on to the domain Blivets, which does not enforce a security policy. His Registry retains the policy settings that were established when he logged on to Malaprop.

This problem is avoided if a security policy is established for the Blivets domain as well.

Creating the System Policy

The system policy is created and managed using the System Policy Editor, which is installed in the Administrative Tools program group.

To begin creating the system policy, open the System Policy Editor and choose the **New Policy** command in the **File** menu. When a system policy has been opened, two icons will be displayed in the System Policy Editor, as shown in Figure 9.6.

FIGURE 9.6
Editing a system policy.

Adding Users, Groups, and Computers to the System Policy

You can create custom system policies for three groups of entities:

- Specific users
- Groups of users
- Specific computers

All users not covered by a custom policy in one of the previous categories are covered by the default system policy.

To add a custom system policy, do the following:

- To add a system policy for a specific user, choose **Add User** in the **Edit** menu and supply the name of the user to add. A user icon will be placed in the System Policy Editor window.

- To add a system policy for a specific group, choose **Add Group** in the **Edit** menu and supply the name of the group to add. A group icon will be placed in the System Policy Editor window. All members of the specified group will be affected by settings for this group system policy.

- To add a system policy for a specific computer, choose **Add Computer** in the **Edit** menu and supply the name of the computer to add. A computer icon will be placed in the System Policy Editor window. All users logging on to the specified computer are affected by settings for this computer system policy.

In all of these cases, a **Browse** button is provided, enabling you to browse for the desired resource. Figure 9.6 shows the System Policy Editor window after a user, group, and computer policy have been added.

Editing the User System Policy

To edit the System Policy Editor for a user, double-click the user icon to open the User Properties window (see Figure 9.7). The properties in this window are arranged in a hierarchical list. In the figure, the **Desktop** heading was opened to reveal two settings:

- **Wallpaper.** The check box for Wallpaper is gray, indicating that no setting has been established.
- **Color Scheme.** Here the administrator has clicked the check box to activate the setting. Doing so opened the Settings for Color Scheme box in which the administrator has selected the color scheme **Wheat 256**.

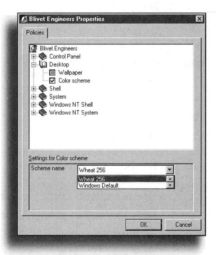

FIGURE 9.7

Changing properties for the desktop.

All other properties are configured in much the same way. Check the property heading to open a window in which settings are entered.

Users can waste a lot of time fiddling around with their desktops, playing with screen savers, and so forth. If you would like to put an end to that sort of thing, examine Figure 9.8. Under the **Control Panel** heading, you will find options that enable you to restrict the changes users can make to their displays. If you check **Restrict display**, five check boxes appear that enable you to block users from making changes to their displays. You can deny access to the Display icon entirely, or you can hide specific tabs in the Display utility.

Interpreting settings in System Policy Editor

If a check box is gray in the System Policy Editor, no policy has been specified for that property. A checked box indicates that the policy is in effect. An unchecked box indicates that the policy is not in effect.

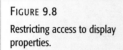

FIGURE 9.8

Restricting access to display
properties.

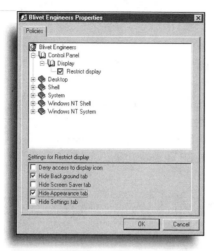

From the system administrator's point of view, much more interesting properties can be found under other headings. In Figure
9.9, the **Shell** heading has been opened to reveal a variety of
powerful properties. Here are just a few properties that can
prove valuable:

- **Remove Run command from Start menu.** Use this property to prevent users from running programs that are not
  defined as icons in the **Start** menu.

- **Remove Taskbar from Settings on Start menu.** This
  property can be used to prevent users from modifying the
  structure of the **Start** menu.

- **Hide drives in My Computer.** You can prevent users from
  running programs from icons in My Computer with this
  property. You can also prevent them from using My Computer to examine the contents of drives and from moving
  files and folders.

- **Don't save settings at exit.** Use this property to prevent
  users from making permanent changes to their environments.

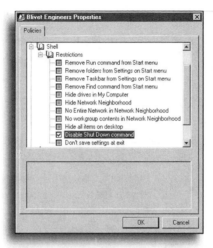

FIGURE 9.9
Restricting shell properties in a system policy.

As you can see, you can lock up a user's options pretty tightly using properties under the **Shell** heading.

As shown in Figure 9.10, two properties under the **System** heading enable you to prevent users from modifying the Registry or from running any but allowed Windows applications.

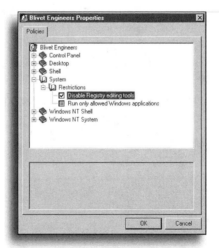

FIGURE 9.10
Restricting system properties in a system policy.

The Windows NT **Shell** heading has two subheadings:

- **Custom folders** contains properties that restrict users' ability to create and customize a variety of folders.
- **Restrictions** contains properties that restrict users from using custom shell extensions and from removing common program groups from the **Start** menu.

Because the User Properties list has so many settings, I'm going to leave it to you to take the time to scan the descriptions. You will find that most are self-explanatory. Use your imagination and ingenuity to establish the correct restrictions for your users.

Editing the Computer Policy

When you double-click a computer icon in System Policy Editor, you open the Computer Properties window shown in Figure 9.11. This window also presents a hierarchy of property categories. To illustrate, the Windows NT **Network** heading has been opened.

Once again, there are far too many properties to discuss here. The majority of properties are self-explanatory, so it's up to you to review the options.

FIGURE 9.11

Editing properties of a computer policy.

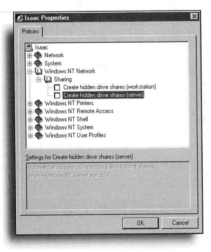

Saving the System Policy

After you have edited the system policy as required, save a new policy as follows:

Saving a new system policy

1. Choose the **Save As** command in the **File** menu.

2. Save the policy as `C:\netlogon\ntconfig.pol` on the Primary Domain Controller server. (Change the path if the system volume has been assigned a different drive letter.)

Using System Policy Editor to Edit the Registry

Choose the **Open Registry** command in the **File** menu to immediately write system policy changes to the Registry on the local computer. The changes are saved to the Registry when you choose **Save** in the **File** menu.

To connect with a Registry on another computer, choose the **Connect** command on the **File** menu. This option enables you to maintain users' Registries remotely.

Logon Scripts

Chapter 8, "Activating Network Clients," introduced you to logon scripts. You will use logon scripts less frequently when configuring Windows NT clients because profiles and system policies are more powerful tools for configuring users' environments. Nevertheless, logon scripts have their value where Windows NT clients are concerned. Indeed, some special logon script capabilities are only available for Windows NT clients.

SEE ALSO

➤ *Please review the section titled "Logon Scripts" on page 289 in Chapter 8, "Activating Network Clients."*

➤ *Also see the sections titled "Logon Script Name," page 163 and "Specifying Logon Scripts for Multiple Users," page 174 in Chapter 5, "Adding Users and Groups," for the procedures used to configure the logon script properties of user accounts.*

Although you can call an .EXE file as a logon script, typically logon scripts are batch files (.BAT extension) that contain executable commands. You will find the NET commands extremely valuable when creating logon scripts. A complete list of available NET commands is available in the Windows NT Help files. (Choose **Help** in the **Start** menu. Choose **Windows NT Commands** and look in the N's for the available NET commands.)

Logon scripts for Windows NT clients can make use of several logon variables. Table 9.3 lists these variables.

TABLE 9.3 Windows NT logon script variables

Variable	Description
%HOMEDRIVE%	The drive letter that connects to the user's home directory
%HOMEPATH%	The complete pathname of the user's home directory
%HOMESHARE%	The name of the share that contains the user's home directory
%OS%	The operating system running on the user's workstation
%PROCESSOR%	The processor type installed in the user's workstation
%USERDOMAIN%	The domain name in which the user's account is defined
%USERNAME%	The username of the user

The %USERNAME% variable was encountered in Chapter 5, "Adding Users and Groups," when it was used to specify logon script and profile names. (See the material cited in a cross reference earlier in this section.) Other variables can be used to enable logon scripts to adjust to changes in the user's environment when moving from computer to computer.

Variables also can be used to enable a single logon script file to service users in different departments. You could use the %USERDOMAIN% variable to enable the logon script to connect different printers, depending on the user's home domain, as in the following examples:

```
IF %USERDOMAIN% == WIDGETS NET USE LPT1: \\WIDGETS1\
➥LASER1 /YES
```

```
IF %USERDOMAIN% == ACCT NET USE LPT1: \\ACCT\ACCTLASR /YES
```

Another useful thing to do in a logon script is to synchronize client clocks with a given server, ensuring that all computers on the network will be set to approximately the same time. To synchronize client clocks with the server MALAPROP1, you would add the following command to the logon script:

```
NET TIME \\MALAPROP1 /SET /YES
```

Adding Windows NT Server Tools to Windows NT Workstation

You can easily install a set of Windows NT Server management tools on a Windows NT Workstation client. To install the tools, connect to the Windows NT Server installation CD-ROM and execute the SETUP.BAT file from the \Clients\Srvtools\Winnt directory. The following programs will be installed on the workstation:

- DHCP Manager
- Event Viewer
- RAS Administrator
- Remoteboot Manager
- Server Manager
- User Manager for Domains
- User Profile Editor
- WINS Manager

A program group and icons are not created by Setup; you must create these manually.

Now You've Got Users

Now you have user accounts and clients that can log on to the network. Your network is ready to see some serious usage, so you had better get ready. A good first step is to review your file

Setting the time on your master time server

If you are synchronizing clocks on the network, it would be nice if the master computer had the right time. The best way to set the master clock is to synchronize it with a standard time service, such as the US Naval Observatory or the National Institute of Standards and Technology. Such a program is included with the Windows NT Resource Kit. Read the "Time Service for NT" documentation file for more information.

systems. Do you have enough file storage to meet your users' needs? How should your storage be organized? Do you need to configure fault-tolerant storage to protect critical data? These are questions that will be asked and answered in the following chapter, in which you will take a close look at NT Server's file storage capabilities.

File Storage Systems

How NT organizes hard disks, partitions, and volumes

Managing disks and partitions

Managing volume sets

Managing stripe sets

Managing stripe sets with parity

Managing mirror sets

If you have only worked with MS-DOS or Windows 95 or 98, the file system capabilities of Windows are a breath of fresh air. Windows NT gives you considerably more freedom when setting up disk partitions and storage volumes. No longer are you limited to having a single primary partition per hard disk; Windows NT allows as many as four. Volumes can span multiple hard disks, growing to truly gargantuan size. Fault-tolerant disk configurations provide crash resistance while improving performance. NTFS has more robust error-recovery than FAT, and NTFS supports file-by-file compression that is far superior to any compression available for MS-DOS or Windows 95 or 98. File storage capabilities are among the chief advantages of Windows NT over its predecessors.

How Windows NT Organizes Hard Disks, Partitions, and Volumes

With Windows NT the relationships between hard disks and drive letters blur. A given hard disk can store many volumes, each with a distinct drive letter. Or a given volume can span as many as 32 hard disks—32 disks and only one drive letter! To take advantage of that versatility, you need to know something about how NT configures hard disks, partitions, drives, and volumes.

Hard Disks

Windows NT supports a wide variety of storage devices: conventional hard disks, read-only CD-ROMs, removable media such as read-write optical disks, and so forth. By far the most ubiquitous storage device is the hard disk, however. To this day, nothing rivals hard disks for their combination of speed, capacity, and low cost.

At present (late 1997), new hard disks range in capacity from about 1GB to 16GB. High-capacity drives also tend to be high-performance drives, with high spindle speeds and fast seek times, the two factors that most affect hard disk performance. Between 4GB and 8GB, you typically have a choice between standard hard disks suitable for workstations, and higher-performance drives intended for power users and servers. Hard disks with fewer than 4GB tend to target the needs of average end-users, offering good performance but not what you should demand for a network server.

SCSI hard disks are preferred for servers. Although a single IDE drive will perform as well or better than a single SCSI drive, when you add a second hard disk to the system SCSI gains the upper hand. Although only one IDE hard disk on a given controller can be active at a given time, a SCSI controller that supports *SCSI disconnect* can service many drives at once. SCSI is your only good choice if you are going to configure the multi-disk storage volumes that are described in this chapter.

Physical drives must be low-level formatted. SCSI drives can be low-level formatted using utilities that are included with SCSI adapter cards. IDE and ESDI drives cannot be low-level formatted by the users.

A disk is assigned a logical number by its hardware configuration. Disks on the primary disk controller are numbered starting at 0. Logical numbers are assigned differently for SCSI and IDE drives.

- SCSI hard disks on the primary controller are numbered from 0 through 6 (0 through 15 for wide SCSI) with 7 reserved for the disk controller itself. Drives on additional disk controllers are numbered where the previous controllers leave off. As many as four disk controllers can be accommodated.

- IDE hard disks on the primary controller are assigned disk numbers 0 and 1. Disks on a second controller are numbered starting where the first controller leaves off. A system can support a maximum of two IDE controllers for a maximum of four disks.

Disk sparing

Disk sparing is a technique employed by Windows NT to improve the reliability of disk storage. When Windows NT encounters a bad sector on a hard disk, the data in the bad sector are moved to a good sector. Windows NT notifies the disk driver of the bad sector and maps it so that it will no longer be used. Disk sparing is available only on SCSI hard disks.

Partitions

Before files can be stored, the hard disk must be configured with at least one *partition*. A partition is a logical division of the hard disk that can be formatted to contain storage volumes. There are two types of partitions: primary and extended.

A hard disk can contain up to four partitions, in the following combinations:

- One to four primary partition
- One to three primary partitions with one extended partition

A *primary partition* is a partition that can be configured to boot an operating system. MS-DOS/Windows 95 and 98 systems recognize only one primary partition on a given hard disk: the partition that was used to boot the system. Windows NT can make use of multiple primary partitions on a hard disk.

An *extended partition* is used on MS-DOS/Windows 95 and 98 systems to enable the system to have more than one storage volume on a hard disk. An MS-DOS/Windows 95 or 98 system can make use of one primary and one extended partition on each hard disk.

Extended partitions cannot be used for storage unless they have been configured to contain one or more *logical drives*. On Windows NT systems, extended partitions are used when it is necessary to assign more than four drive letters to a hard disk.

Volumes

After partitions are created, they must be formatted to establish volumes that can be used for file storage. These volumes correspond to the lettered drives you are familiar with: C, D, E, and so forth. The method of assigning drive letters differs on primary and extended partitions:

- A **primary partition** is formatted as a single volume. The entire primary partition is represented by a single drive letter.

- An **extended partition** can be subdivided into multiple logical volumes, each of which has a separate drive letter.

In Figure 10.1 the Windows NT Disk Administrator has been used to configure a system with the following characteristics:

- Disk 0 has one primary partition that is identified as drive C: and is formatted with NTFS.

- Disk 0 has one extended partition that has been formatted with three logical drives: F:, L:, and P:.

- Disk 1 has three primary partitions formatted as drives D:, G:, and H:.

- The CD-ROM drive is configured as drive E:.

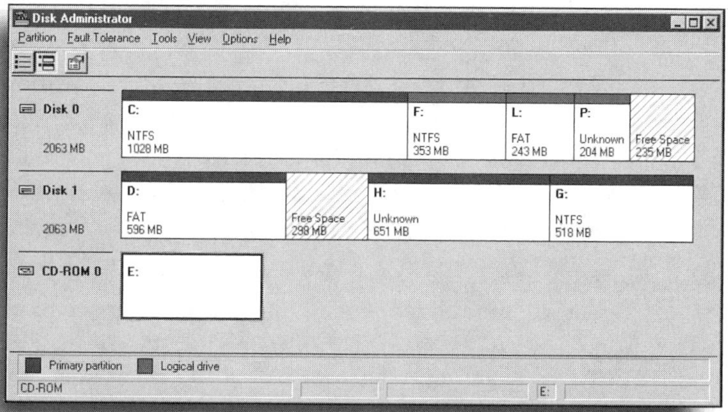

FIGURE 10.1

An example of a Windows NT disk configuration.

Some partitions are labeled Unknown, indicating that the partitions have not been formatted.

Each hard disk has a crosshatched area that is labeled Free Space. This space is available to be assigned to a partition.

Notice that the drive lettering doesn't follow MS-DOS conventions. With Windows NT you have the freedom to assign drive letters as you choose. Drive letters need not be in any predetermined order on any particular disks.

Drive Sets

Windows NT volume configuration capabilities go far beyond the limited capabilities of MS-DOS. Windows NT enables you to create volumes larger than a single hard disk, for example, or fault-tolerant volumes that are not damaged when a hard disk crashes. These special multipartition volumes are called *drive sets*. Windows NT supports the following types of drive sets:

- **Volume sets.** A volume set consists of two or more partitions that can be on the same or multiple disk drives.

- **Mirror sets.** A mirror set consists of two partitions on two drives that are constantly updated to contain the same data. If one drive of a mirror set fails, the mirror contains a replica of the data so that no data are lost and computer operation can continue.

- **Stripe sets.** A stripe set occupies two or more partitions on two or more drives. A technique called *striping* writes data to each volume segment in turn. Because multiple hard disks are used, the stripe set performs better than volumes that occupy a single hard disk.

- **Stripe sets with parity.** A stripe set with parity uses striping to create multidisk volumes, introducing parity error checking to create volumes that suffer no data loss in the event of a single hard disk failure.

Now that you know how Windows NT organizes disk storage, let's see how Disk Administrator is used to manage the disk storage subsystem.

Introduction to RAID

Redundant arrays of inexpensive disks (RAID) describes several methods of using multiple disks to improve performance, enhance reliability, or both. Several types of RAID configurations—called *levels*—have been developed, only three of which are of interest to microcomputer LAN users:

- **RAID 0.** Microsoft calls RAID 0 stripe sets.
- **RAID 1.** Mirror sets.
- **RAID 5.** Stripe sets with parity.

It is important to realize that RAID isn't a hierarchy. RAID 5 isn't inherently better than RAID 1. Both meet different needs, and have different advantages and disadvantages. You need to choose the RAID technology that is right for your network.

Windows NT makes it possible to implement RAID systems using only standard microcomputer hardware. When you don't use special RAID hardware, you give up several advantages:

- More robust hardware, possibly with fault-tolerant power supplies.
- The capability to replace failed hard drives without shutting down the server (hot swapping).

Microsoft also admits that a hardware-based RAID system should yield greater performance than the Windows NT Server software-based approach.

If RAID 5 meets your needs, you might want to consider a commercial RAID subsystem to obtain some extra fault tolerance and reduce the likelihood of down time.

Managing Disks and Partitions

First let's examine the basics of creating and managing primary and extended partitions. You should be comfortable with these procedures before you move on to the more advanced types of storage volumes supported by Windows NT.

All disk management procedures are performed using Disk Administrator. The shortcut icon is under Administrative Tools in the Start menu. You must be logged in as an administrator to change disk partitions.

Creating Primary Partitions

Primary partitions can be as small as 1MB or as large as the capacity of the hard disk.

Create a primary partition in Disk Administrator

Context menus

You can right-click a partition or free space area to open a context menu that contains commands for most of the operations that are appropriate for the area.

1. Select an area that is labeled Free Space. The area you select will be marked with a wide, black border.

2. Choose **Create** from the **Partition** menu to open the Create Primary Partition dialog box shown in Figure 10.2. Notice that the dialog box indicates the minimum and maximum sizes you can designate for the partition being created.

FIGURE 10.2

Specifying the size for a new primary partition.

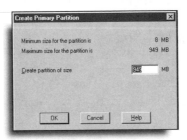

3. Enter the size that is desired for the partition in the **Create Partition Of Size** spin box.

4. Choose **OK**.

5. Choose the command **Commit Changes Now** from the **Partition** menu. After the partition is committed, it is marked as Unformatted.

MS-DOS computers can access only one primary partition on a given hard disk. If you attempt to create a second primary partition on a hard disk, Disk Administrator pops up the warning shown in Figure 10.3.

FIGURE 10.3

You see this warning when attempting to create multiple primary partitions on a disk.

Committing Partition Changes

Most changes you make to partitions don't go into effect until they are *committed*, an extra step that helps protect you from errors. Uncommitted changes to partition structures can be discarded. It's a bit like saving a file in a word processor. If you goof, you can retrieve your old file simply by not saving recent changes.

You must commit changes before you can actually work with a partition. You cannot format a new partition until it has been committed, for example, because the partition has not actually been created.

Partition changes accumulate until you choose the **Commit Changes Now** command; then Disk Administrator commits all changes that have been made since the last time changes were committed. If you exit Disk Administrator with uncommitted changes, you see the prompt, Changes have been made to your disk configuration. Do you want to save the changes? Choose **Y**es to commit changes, and **N**o to discard them.

Uncommitted changes

The text labels of uncommitted partitions are presented in a gray-colored font.

Updating the Emergency Repair Disk

In most cases, creating or deleting partitions affects information that is stored in the emergency repair configuration. You will often see reminders to update the Emergency Repair Disk. When you finish a session with Disk Administrator, take the time to use RDISK to update your Emergency Repair Disk.

SEE ALSO

➤ *The Emergency Repair Disk and the RDISK utility are discussed on page 59.*

Specifying the Active Partition

The first hard disk on a computer must have one partition that is designated as the *active partition*. This is the partition that is used to boot the computer. The Windows NT boot process is a bit unusual because it relies on two partitions, which can be the same or separate partitions:

- The *system partition* contains hardware-specific files that are used to load Windows NT. Files in this partition include `ntldr`, `osloader.exe`, `boot.ini`, and `ntdetect.com`. On Intel x86 computers, the system partition must be a primary partition that is marked as active. On RISC computers, the system partition is preconfigured by the setup software supplied by the computer vendor.

- The *boot partition* contains the bulk of the Windows NT operating system files, and can be formatted with the FAT or NTFS file system. The boot partition can be a primary partition or a logical drive in an extended partition.

Typically, the boot and system partitions will be the same partition. Separate partitions can be designated, however, which is particularly advantageous when setting up multiboot configurations. When Windows NT is installed, the system partition is created and designated as active.

Operating systems can boot only from a primary partition on Disk 0. You may want to install more than one operating system on a hard disk, in which case each operating system will be placed in its own primary partition. You must change the active partition to boot an alternate operating system. The active partition is marked with an asterisk (*) in Windows NT disk administrator.

Changing the active partition on an Intel x86

1. In Disk Administrator, select the primary partition on Disk 0 that contains the files required to start the desired operating system. The partition you select is identified by a bold, black border.

2. Choose **Mark <u>A</u>ctive** from the **<u>P</u>artition** menu.

3. Choose **OK** in the information box that is presented.

Creating Extended Partitions

A hard drive can have at most one extended partition, which can range in size from 1MB to the capacity of the hard disk. If you create an extended partition, a maximum of three primary partitions can co-exist on the disk.

Creating an extended partition

1. Select an area identified as Free Space. The area you select is marked with a bold, black border.

2. Choose **Create Extended** from the **Partition** menu. This opens the Create Extended Partition dialog box shown in Figure 10.4. The dialog box indicates the minimum and maximum sizes you can assign for the partition being created.

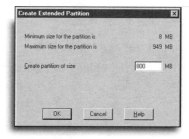

FIGURE 10.4
Specifying the size for a new extended partition.

3. Enter the size desired for the new partition in the **Create Partition Of Size** spin box.

4. Choose **OK**.

5. Choose **Commit Changes Now** from the **Partitions** menu to create the partition. No drives are created. The area containing the partition is still identified as Free Space. In Figure 10.5, the Free Space area with 800MB is the new extended partition. Notice that the crosshatching in a new extended partition is different from the crosshatching in non-partitioned free space.

FIGURE 10.5

The 800MB free space area is a newly committed extended partition.

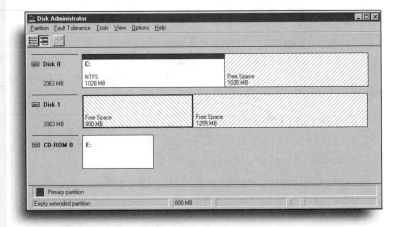

Creating Logical Drives

After you have created an extended partition you must create at least one logical drive in the partition.

Creating a logical drive

1. Select an area marked Free Space that is crosshatched to indicate that it is an extended partition. The area you select is marked with a bold, black border.

2. Choose **C**reate from the **P**artition menu. The Create Logical Drive dialog box appears. This box indicates the minimum and maximum size allowed for the logical drive you are creating.

3. Enter the desired drive size in the **C**reate **L**ogical **D**rive **O**f **S**ize spin box.

4. Choose **OK**. Figure 10.6 shows a new, unformatted logical drive.

5. To create the logical drive, choose **C**ommit **C**hanges **N**ow from the **P**artition menu.

Drives and volumes

Here is another place where Microsoft's terminology is muddled. Drives and volumes are the same thing, and the terms are interchangeable, although Microsoft tends to use each term in specific circumstances.

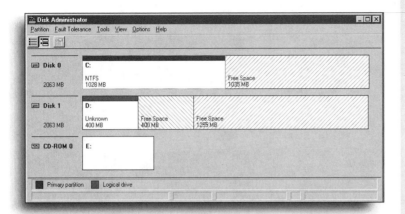

FIGURE 10.6
A new, unformatted logical
drive.

Formatting Drives

Formatting a primary partition or logical drive

1. If the drive is marked Unformatted it has not been committed. Choose **Commit Changes Now** in the **Partition** menu to commit changes. After changes are committed the partition or logical drive will be labeled Unknown.

2. Select the drive to be formatted. The selected partition is marked with a bold, black border.

3. Choose **Format** from the **Tools** menu. The Formatting dialog box is shown in Figure 10.7.

FIGURE 10.7
Formatting a drive.

4. The **Capacity** field can be left with the default value. It applies only when formatting floppy disks.

5. In the **File System** field, select Fat or NTFS.

6. The **Allocation Unit Size** field can be left with the default value. (This field enables you to change the cluster size of NTFS volumes, but the default cluster size is strongly recommended.)

7. The **Volume Label** field is optional. You can enter a description of the volume if desired.

8. Check the **Quick Format** check box if you want the partition formatted without checking for errors. (Quick formatting is unavailable for mirror sets or stripe sets with parity.)

   Normal formatting is a bit slower because Disk Administrator is very thorough about identifying and locking out bad spots on the disk.

9. If you are creating an NTFS volume, you can check **Enable Compression** if you want data compression to be active on the volume.

10. Choose **Start** to initiate the format.

11. Next you see the message Formatting will erase ALL data on the disk. Select OK to format the disk. Choose **OK** to proceed with formatting. As the partition is formatted, a bar graph charts the progress.

12. When the Format Complete message is displayed, choose **OK**. In Figure 10.8, D: is a formatted logical drive.

Volume Properties and Tools

Accessing volume properties

You can also access volume properties and tools by right-clicking the volume in Explorer or My Computer. Choose **Properties** from the context menu.

To view properties, select a volume on a drive and choose **Properties** from the **Tools** menu. The Properties dialog box is shown in Figure 10.9.

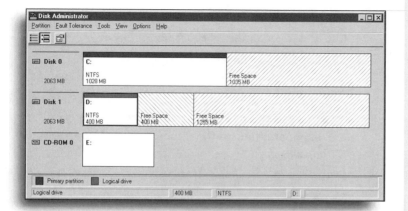

FIGURE 10.8
Formatting a drive.

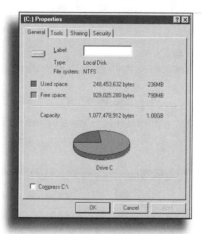

FIGURE 10.9
Drive Properties: The General tab.

Volume Properties: General

The General tab, shown in Figure 10.9, provides information about the use of the volume.

You can add a new volume label or change an existing one by entering a description in the **Label** field.

One of the most useful options on NTFS volumes is the capability of compressing files.

Compressing files on NTFS volumes

1. Check the **Compress** check box.

2. Click **OK** or **Apply**.

3. The information box shown in Figure 10.10 is displayed. The default action is to compress only files in the root folder. To compress files in all subfolders (in other words, to compress all files on the volume), check **Also Compress Subfolders**.

4. Choose **OK** to compress the volume.

FIGURE 10.10

You must specify that subfolders are to be compressed.

Volume Properties: Tools

The Tools tab is shown in Figure 10.11. This tab accesses some built-in and optional tools.

FIGURE 10.11

The Tools tab accesses auxiliary volume tools.

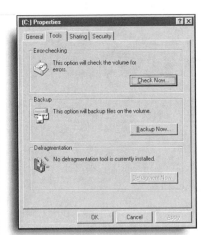

Command line check disk

Windows NT also provides the command-line Chkdsk utility, which has a few options that are not available in the GUI version. Consult the Windows NT Command directory in Help for more information.

FIGURE 10.12
Check Disk volume repair
options.

The **Check Now** button accesses a graphic interface for the
Check Disk utility, shown in Figure 10.12. Select the options
you want to apply to the volume.

The **Backup Now** button opens the Windows NT Backup utility, which is covered in the next chapter, "Protecting Files with
Backup."

The **Defragment Now** button accesses a third-party backup
tool if one is installed.

Volume Properties: Sharing

The Sharing tab is shown in Figure 10.13. You can use this tab
to configure sharing for the root directory of the volume. In the
figure, you see the C$ administrative share for drive C:.

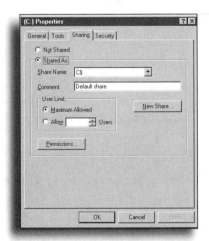

FIGURE 10.13
Sharing properties for a
volume.

Defragmenting disks

For best performance, a file should be stored in *unfragmented* form by storing the file on contiguous disk sectors. When Windows NT attempts to store a file it will search the volume for a block of available sectors that is large enough to receive the entire file. Disk fragmentation occurs when Windows NT cannot find enough contiguous sectors to store the file, forcing Windows NT to store the file in several places on the disk. Fragmented files are slower to read and write because the disk drive must perform extra head seeks.

Although Windows NT attempts to reduce the severity, fragmentation nevertheless occurs. Windows NT 4 doesn't include a disk defragmentation utility, so you should consider obtaining a third-party product. Ideally, you should be able to schedule disk defragmentation to take place automatically during a period when the LAN isn't in use.

Volume Properties: Security

The Security tab has three buttons:

- **Permissions.** This button opens a Directory Permissions dialog box.

SEE ALSO

➤ *Directory permissions are discussed on page 197.*

- **Auditing.** This button opens a Directory Auditing dialog box.

SEE ALSO

➤ *Auditing is discussed on page 701.*

- **Ownership.** This button opens a take ownership dialog box.

SEE ALSO

➤ *Ownership is discussed on page 197.*

Assigning Drive Letters

If you are new to Windows NT, a feature you will really appreciate is the capability of assigning drive letters to volumes. No longer are you at the mercy of the operating system where drive letters are concerned. Now your CD-ROM drive can be drive P: if you choose. Any volume on any disk can be drive D:.

Before you assign static drive letters, drive letters are assigned automatically according to rules borrowed from MS-DOS. Adding disks or volumes can change automatically assigned drive letters. System reconfiguration doesn't change static drive letters, however.

Assigning a drive letter to a volume

1. Select a volume.

2. Choose **Assign Drive Letter** from the **Tools** menu to open the Assign Drive Letter dialog box shown in Figure 10.14.

3. To assign a static drive letter, select the **Assign Drive Letter** radio button. Then select an available drive letter in the spin box.

4. Choose **OK**.

FIGURE 10.14
Assigning a drive letter to a volume.

Deleting Drives and Partitions

You may need to delete drives and partitions to reorganize your hard disk. To delete a partition or drive, do the following:

Deleting partitions of drives

1. Select the partition or drive.

2. Choose **Delete** from the **Partition** menu.

3. A confirmation dialog box is displayed. Choose **Yes** if you want to confirm the deletion.

4. Commit the change by choosing Commit Changes Now from the Partition menu, or by quitting Disk Administrator and choosing Yes.

Converting File Systems

You can convert a FAT volume to NTFS with the CONVERT.EXE utility.

Converting a FAT volume to NTFS

1. Open a command prompt.

2. To convert drive D: to NTFS, enter the following command: convert d: /fs:ntfs.

Managing Volume Sets

A *volume set* is a volume that is made up of several free space segments from as many as 32 disks. To see how a volume set is constructed, let's look at some before and after shots.

Deleting extended partitions

Before you can delete an extended partition, you must delete each logical drive that has been created in the partition.

Converting a boot partition

The boot partition cannot be converted while Windows NT is running. If you specify that CONVERT should process the active partition, you will see this message: Convert cannot gain exclusive access to the C: drive, so it cannot convert it now. Would you schedule it to be converted the next time the system restarts?

If you respond **Yes**, you can then shut down Windows NT and restart it. The partition is converted when the system starts backup. The system must boot several times in order to complete the conversion; be patient. Everything will work fine in the end.

Figure 10.15 shows a pair of disks that have several free space areas. These free space areas can be combined into a volume set.

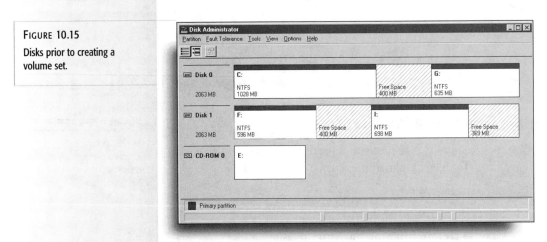

Figure 10.16 shows the disks after the volume set has been created. In the figure, volume D: is a volume set. It functions as a single, large volume.

A volume set functions much like a volume on a normal, primary partition. Figure 10.17 shows how files fill a volume set. Files are written starting with the first segment in the volume set. Then storage proceeds to the second, third, and subsequent segments.

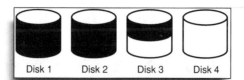

FIGURE 10.17
How volume sets store data.

Creating a Volume Set

Creating a volume set

1. Select an area labeled `Free Space`.

2. Hold down the Ctrl key and select another area labeled `Free Space`.

3. Repeat step 2 until all desired free space areas have been selected.

4. Choose **Create Volume Set** from the **Partition** menu. The Create Volume Set dialog box is displayed, as shown in Figure 10.18.

FIGURE 10.18
Specifying the size of a volume set.

5. Specify the size of the volume set in the **Create Volume Set of Total Size** spin box.

6. Choose **OK**.

7. Choose **Commit Changes Now** from the **Partition** menu to create the volume set.

8. Restart the computer to initialize the volume set.

9. Format the volume set.

In step 5, you specify the size of the volume set. If you select a size that is less than the maximum size available, space is proportionally deallocated from each of the free space areas. As Figure

10.19 demonstrates, this leaves a free space area for each segment that was added to the volume set.

FIGURE 10.19

Free space remains if you create a volume set that is less than the maximum size.

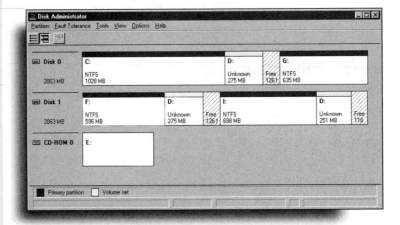

Formatting a Volume Set

To format a volume set, select any segment in the volume set. You will notice that all the segments in the volume set are selected. Then format the volume set as you would a primary partition or a logical drive. After formatting, all segments in the volume set will be identified by the same drive letter.

Extending a Volume Set

You can append additional segments to a volume or volume set. Be warned that, because files are stored throughout the volume set, free space cannot be recovered after it has been added to a volume or volume set.

Extend a volume or volume set

1. Select the volume or volume set.

2. Hold down the Ctrl key and select the free space area or areas to be added to the volume or volume set.

3. Choose **Extend Volume Set** from the **Partition** menu. This will open the Extend Volume Set dialog box.

4. Specify the size that is desired for the volume set by adjusting the **C̲reate Volume Set of Total Size** spin box.

5. You don't need to commit changes or format the new segment.

Advantages and Disadvantages of Volume Sets

Volume sets have at least two important advantages:

- They permit you to stitch small, noncontiguous free space segments into volumes of useful size.

- They enable you to create volumes that are larger than your largest hard disk. A volume set can incorporate all or part of the free space of as many as 32 hard disks, so very large volumes are possible.

Remember, however, that *there ain't no such thing as a free lunch*. The cost of a volume set is that reliability of a volume set is reduced somewhat by each disk that is added to it, and unfortunately, if one drive in a volume set fails, the entire volume set is damaged. So a volume set is less reliable that a volume that is stored entirely on a single disk.

The reliability of hardware is rated in a statistic called *mean time between failure (MTBF)*—the average number of hours the equipment is expected to operate without failure. When volume sets are created with two or more hard drives, the MTBF for the volume set is significantly less than the MTBF for the individual drives. The formula Microsoft provides follows:

$$MTBF_{set}=MTBF_{disk}/N$$

Where:

$MTBF_{set}$ is the MTBF for the volume set.

$MTBF_{disk}$ is the average MTBF for an individual disk.

N is the number of disks in the set.

As you can see, a four-drive set has one-quarter the MTBF of an individual drive.

Extending the system partition

Actually, the title of this sidenote is misleading, because the system partition, the one used to boot Windows NT, is the one partition you *can't* extend.

There is a trick, however. A third-party product named *Partition Magic* can extend the system partition, or any other FAT or NTFS partition, because it works while the computer is booted under MS-DOS. For information about *Partition Magic*, visit **http://www.powerquest. com**.

Managing Stripe Sets

Like volume sets, stripe sets enable you to construct volumes
from segments on multiple disks. But stripe sets store data in a
significantly different way than volume sets, using a technique
called *striping*. Figure 10.20 shows how striping works.

FIGURE 10.20

Data striping.

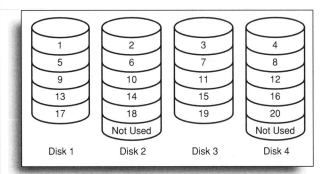

When files are written to stripe sets, the data are broken into
chunks that are written sequentially to each disk in the stripe set.
On a volume set, Windows NT attempts to keep files together
in physically adjacent segments. On a stripe set, Windows NT
intentionally distributes the file across multiple disks.

On the surface, striping doesn't sound like a very good idea, but
stripe sets have a significant edge over volume sets in one area—
performance. Hard drives spend considerable time just moving
their heads to seek data. When those head seeks are distributed
across multiple drives, the time required to retrieve a file is
reduced nearly by a factor of the number of drives. The performance improvement is particularly apparent when data are being
read from disk.

Because data are striped across multiple disks, the segments on
each disk must be approximately the same size. Figure 10.20
shows what happens when some segments are larger than others.
The excess space on the larger segments isn't used. Disk
Administrator ensures that space isn't wasted by adjusting all
segments in a stripe set to the same size.

Stripe sets have the same disadvantage as volume sets: reliability is reduced as you increase the number of disks in the set. Failure of any disk participating in the stripe set destroys all data in the stripe set. Therefore, stripe sets should be used when performance must be maximized and when adequate file backups reduce the risk of lost data.

Stripe Sets with Parity

Suppose you need to create a huge volume, larger than any hard disk in your inventory, but you can't afford the reduced reliability that is inherent in a volume set or a stripe set. Is there a technology that gives you the advantages of striping without the risks?

A technique called *striping with parity* is just such a compromise. Figure 10.21 shows how striping with parity works. When data are stored, they are striped across multiple drives. On one drive in the set, however, instead of writing data Windows NT writes a *parity record*. The parity record is created by performing a calculation on each "row" of stripes and storing the result in the parity record.

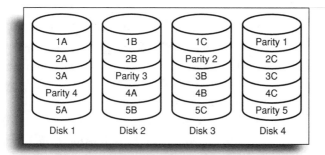

FIGURE 10.21
Data striping with parity.

In the event of a disk failure, the parity record together with the remaining disks can be used to recreate the data on the failed disk. This enables a stripe set with parity to continue functioning with a single disk failure. No data are lost, although performance is reduced because of the calculations required to compensate for the missing disk.

Disk striping with parity produces a fault-tolerant disk array that has less overhead than mirroring. Half the disk capacity of a mirrored pair is lost to overhead. With disk striping with parity, the overhead diminishes as drives are added to the stripe set. A stripe set with parity that is configured with four disks loses 25% of capacity to overhead. A five-disk stripe set with parity has 20% overhead.

Disk striping with parity typically has better read performance than mirroring when all disks in the set are functioning. When a disk in a stripe set fails, performance suffers until the disk is replaced. Therefore, you might want to invest in a commercial RAID system that enables you to "hot swap" disks, allowing you to replace a failed disk without shutting down the disk subsystem.

Creating a Stripe Set (RAID 0)

Creating a stripe set

1. Select an area of free space.

2. Hold down the Ctrl key and select additional free space segments. As many as 32 segments can be selected. Each segment must be on a separate disk.

3. Choose **Create Stripe Set** from the **Partition** menu.

4. In the Create Stripe Set dialog box, shown in Figure 10.22, Disk Administrator displays the maximum total size for the stripe set. This size is based on the creation of equal-sized segments on each disk. Specify the desired size in the **Create Stripe Set of Total Size** spin box.

   If you reduce the total size for the stripe set, a small amount of free space will be left on each disk, much as with volume sets.

5. Choose **OK**.

6. Choose **Commit Changes Now** from the **Partition** menu.

7. Restart the computer when prompted.

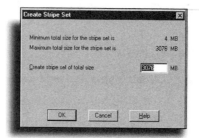

FIGURE 10.22
Specifying the size of a
stripe set.

8. Restart Disk Administrator and select any segment in the stripe set.

9. Choose **Format** in the **Tools** menu and format the partition.

Figure 10.23 shows a stripe set. Notice how Disk Administrator has constructed the stripe set of equally-sized partitions, based on the largest available free space area. (As in the figure, there may be a slight difference that results from the need to create disk partitions that fall on even storage boundaries, but waste is kept to a minimum.)

FIGURE 10.23
Drive D: is a stripe set.

Creating a Stripe Set with Parity (RAID 5)

At least three disks are required to establish a stripe set with parity.

Create a stripe set with parity

1. Select an area of free space on one disk.

2. Hold down the Ctrl key and select additional free space segments. As many as 32 segments can be selected. Each segment must be on a separate disk.

3. Choose **Create Stripe Set with Parity** from the **Fault Tolerance** menu.

4. In the Create Stripe Set with Parity dialog box, specify the size of the stripe set. The size that Disk Administrator displays takes all the selected free space into account. If you reduce the size, space is removed proportionally from each of the segments you have selected.

5. Choose **OK**.

6. Choose **Commit Changes Now** in the **Partition** menu.

7. Select any segment in the stripe set.

8. Choose **Format** in the **Tools** menu to format the stripe set volume.

Deleting a Stripe Set

A stripe set is invalidated if any drive in the stripe set fails. You must delete an invalidated stripe set, repair the hardware, and recreate the stripe set. Data must be restored from a backup.

To delete a stripe set, select one of the segments that makes up the stripe set. Then choose **Delete** from the **Partition** menu.

Regenerating a Stripe Set with Parity

If a disk participating in a strip set fails, the stripe set continues to function and applications can read and write data in the stripe set with parity volume.

After you replace the failed drive, you must regenerate the stripe set with parity volume.

Regenerating the stripe set with parity

1. In Disk Administrator, select one of the segments of the stripe set with parity.
2. Hold down the Ctrl key and select an area of free space that is at least as large as the members of the stripe set with parity.
3. Choose **Regenerate** from the **Fault Tolerance** menu.
4. Restart the computer. The fault tolerance driver will regenerate the failed member of the stripe set with parity.

Managing Mirror Sets (RAID 1)

A mirror set consists of two disk partitions, on separate disks, that are maintained as mirror images. Because two copies of the data exist, either disk can fail without resulting in data loss.

There are two ways of setting up the hardware for a mirror set:

- Both drives can be connected to the same controller, in which case a failed controller card causes the mirror set to fail.

- Each drive can be serviced by a separate controller, enabling the mirror set to survive the failure of either disk or either disk controller. You will sometimes see this configuration referred to as *drive duplexing*.

Mirror sets and disk stripe with parity sets are equally fault tolerant with regard to disks, with both able to survive failure of a single disk. Mirror sets typically write data faster than disk stripe with parity sets because it is unnecessary to generate the parity record for a mirror set. However, disk stripe with parity sets typically read data faster because data reads are distributed across more disks.

Mirror sets have a particular advantage, being the only form of fault tolerance that can be used with the system partition of a server. Stripe sets cannot be booted.

Creating a Mirror Set

To establish a mirror set, you designate a new partition that duplicates an existing partition on another drive. The same drive letter is associated with both partitions.

Creating a mirror set

1. Create and format a primary partition.

2. Select the primary partition.

3. While holding down the Ctrl key, select an area of free space on another disk that is at least as large as the partition created in step 1.

4. Choose **Establish Mirror** from the **Fault Tolerance** menu.

5. Choose **Commit Changes Now** from the **Partition** menu to create the mirror set.

6. Restart the computer when prompted. The mirror partitions will be synchronized as the computer restarts. Initial synchronization will take a several minutes.

Figure 10.24 illustrates a mirror set that has been established for drive C:.

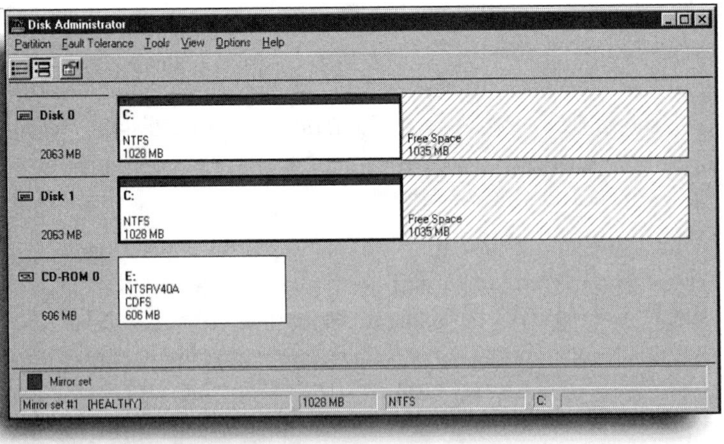

FIGURE 10.24

A mirror set has been established for drive C:.

Breaking a Mirror Set

Breaking a mirror set

1. Select a partition in the mirror set.

2. Choose **B**reak **Mirror** from the **F**ault **Tolerance** menu.

3. Disk Administrator presents the message `This will end mirroring and create two independent partitions. Are you sure you want to break the selected mirror?` Choose **Y**es to confirm breaking of the mirror.

4. You will see the message `Do you wish to continue with this operation?` Choose **Y**es to continue.

5. Choose **C**ommit **Changes Now** from the **Partition** menu to break the mirror set.

6. If you are breaking a mirror for the system partition, you will see the message `Changes have been made which require you to restart your computer.` Choose **OK**.

Repairing a Mirror Set

When a drive of a mirror set fails, you must break the mirror set. This exposes the working drive of the mirror set so that it can resume working as a standard volume. The working member of the mirror set retains the drive letter that was assigned to the set. You then can establish a new mirror set relationship with a replacement hard drive or with another hard drive on the system.

If the mirror set contains the system partition, the repair procedure is a bit more complicated. It also requires some foresight and planning, because you need to prepare an emergency boot disk as a precaution against disk failure.

Creating an Emergency Boot Disk

If the system partition is protected by a mirror set and the primary drive fails, you can use an emergency boot disk to start the server by using the mirror copy. First, you need to create a boot disk with the proper files. Then, you need to edit the `BOOT.INI` file so that it boots from another disk.

Using mirroring to duplicate a hard disk

One trick I have seen for replacing a hard disk (usually a small drive, one with intermittent problems, or one with a lot of bad sectors) is to set up mirroring, let the disks duplicate, break the set, and then remove the original drive, making the new drive the active one. This is particularly handy if you are replacing the primary with a larger drive—after the set is broken you can extend the volume.

To create the boot disk for an x86 computer, copy the following files from the root of the system partition to a floppy disk that you have formatted with Windows NT File Manager:

- NTLDR
- NTDETECT.COM
- NTBOOTDD.SYS (if present on your system)
- BOOT.INI

Editing *BOOT.INI*

Use File Manager to edit the properties of the BOOT.INI file on the floppy disk. Remove the System and Read Only properties from the file so that it can be edited.

Your BOOT.INI file will resemble this one:

```
[boot loader]
timeout=30
default=multi(0)disk(0)rdisk(0)partition(1)\WINNT
[operating systems]
multi(0)disk(0)rdisk(0)partition(1)\WINNT="Windows NT Server
➥Version 3.5"
multi(0)disk(0)rdisk(0)partition(1)\WINNT="Windows NT Server
➥Version 3.5 _[VGA mode]" /basevideo
```

The BOOT.INI file contains information that helps NTLDR find the system partition. The information is found in entries like this:

```
multi(0)disk(0)rdisk(0)partition(1)
```

This is called an ARC name—a format that is borrowed from Advanced RISC Computers. Each field in the ARC name defines a characteristic of the system partition:

- **multi(*n*)**. This field is multi(*n*) for non-SCSI systems and for SCSI systems using a SCSI BIOS. This field is scsi(*n*) for SCSI systems that don't use a SCSI BIOS. If the server has only one hard drive controller, then n will be 0. Additional hard drive controllers will be numbered 1 through 3. Edit this field if the mirror partition is attached to a different disk controller.

- **disk(o)**. For SCSI, *o* is the SCSI bus number for multiple-bus SCSI adapters. Edit *o* to reflect the SCSI address of the drive with the mirror partition. For multi, *o* is always 0.

- **rdisk(p)**. For scsi, *p* is always 0. For multi, *p* is the ordinal number of the disk on the adapter. Because IDE and ESDI adapters support only two drives, *p* will be 0 or 1.

- **partition(q)**. Edit *q* to indicate the primary partition number on the drive that contains the mirror of the system partition. Partitions are numbered 0 through 3. Extended partitions and unused partitions are not numbered.

When I was testing, the address for the mirror on disk 1 was as follows:

```
multi(0)disk(0)rdisk(1)partition(1)
```

After you edit the BOOT.INI file on the emergency boot floppy disk, use it to boot the system. It should fail, fill the screen with numbers, and include the following message:

```
***STOP 0x0000006B (0xC00000D,0X0000002,0X00000000,0X00000000)
PROCESS1_INITIALIZATION_FAILED
```

If this message fails to appear, your floppy disk isn't properly configured to boot your system.

I know that an error message is a strange way to tell you things are working as they should, but trust me, this error shows that everything is working fine. I tried it by replacing my disk 0 with an unformatted drive. The mirror of the system partition on disk 1 started up without a hitch.

SEE ALSO

➤ *ARC naming conventions are discussed on page 74.*

Recovering a Failed System Partition Mirror Set

If the primary drive of the mirror set fails, replace the failed hard disk.

Updating the BOOT.INI

The `BOOT.INI` file on the emergency boot floppy disk must be updated each time changes in partitions affect the ARC path of the partition that is mirroring the system partition.

Microsoft notes that this procedure works best when the drives in the mirror set have the same disk geometry: the same heads, cylinders, and sectors per track.

If you add a new hard drive to the system, you might see the message `No signature found on Disk n. Do you want to write a signature on Disk n so that Disk Administrator can access the drive?` Choose **Yes** to have the drive signature written.

Recovering a failed system partition mirror set

1. Boot the system with the emergency boot floppy disk.

2. Use Disk Administrator to break the mirror. Because you are breaking the mirror of the system partition, you must reboot the server.

3. Reestablish the mirror between disk 0 and the mirror partition, and exit Disk Administrator.

4. Boot again using the emergency boot floppy disk. The disk 0 mirror partition is rebuilt from the working mirror partition.

5. Use Disk Administrator again to break the mirror.

6. Change the drive letters of the partitions that were part of the mirror set so that the partition on disk 0 is drive C and the other partition from the mirror set is some other drive letter.

7. Exit Disk Administrator.

8. Remove the emergency boot floppy disk and reboot the system.

Volumes of Trouble

You now know how to create a wide variety of disk volumes on Windows NT computers. Each type of volume has advantages and disadvantages, so you need to choose your storage configuration carefully.

But there is one disadvantage all volumes share: no matter how carefully they are managed, all volumes can lose data. Whether files are damaged by malfunctioning hardware, software, or users, as administrator you must be prepared with a strategy that minimizes data loss. That brings us to backup, your primary insurance against data loss and the subject of the next chapter.

Protecting Files with Backup

Performing file backups is about as glamorous as paying for life insurance. Ninety-nine percent of the time, you make your nightly backup, or send off your hard-earned cash, and you get nothing in return. It's only when disaster strikes that there is a payoff. At least if you have been making good backups, you will be around when the beneficiary thanks you for retrieving a critical file from the nether regions. On the other hand, if the McKensie Proposal is lost (the day before it is due, of course) because you botched the backups, you may be banished to the nether-regions yourself.

It's easy to get lazy about backups, but nothing a LAN administrator does is more important than archiving data. When you think about it, the LAN *is* data. The hardware and software are just there so that the data has a place to be. LANs typically have a lot of data, and critical data at that.

Backup involves planning, execution, and testing. You need to plan an effective backup plan for your organization, you need to execute the plan faithfully, and you need to run frequent tests to ensure that the backups you are making are functional.

Planning a Backup Strategy

You need to make three decisions when planning your backup strategy: software, hardware, and scheduling.

Selecting Backup Software

This chapter doesn't look much at software selection. Instead, it focuses on the Windows NT Backup program. Nevertheless, you should take the time to examine other products that can back up Windows NT because Windows NT Backup is pretty rudimentary. It has limited automation or scheduling, does not keep a master catalog of tape contents, and can back up client computers only through file shares.

Unless your organization has network staff that works 24 hours a day, while you can initiate backup jobs using the Windows NT Schedule service, job automation is rudimentary at best. A particular shortcoming is that Windows NT Backup does not support tape autoloaders, a necessary feature if your backup jobs exceed the capacity of a single tape.

A master catalog keeps track of archived files in your entire tape library. You will often find that you don't know which tape holds a particular copy of a file. A master catalog is particularly useful if you do not perform a complete backup every night, in which case you may not know which tape holds a particular version of an archived file.

Windows NT Backup can archive clients through shares, but you must share the root directory of a share to back up an entire volume. In a large organization with many clients, backing up through shares is complex and trouble-prone. Third-party backup products include client backup software that makes the process much more convenient and reliable.

Here are a few products you may want to examine, with their Web sites:

- Backup Exec, www.seagate.com
- ARCserve, www.cheyenne.com
- UltraBac, www.ultrabac.com

But Windows NT Backup is free, it is reliable, and it meets the needs of many organizations. It may be a permanent or a temporary solution for you. I'll leave it up to you to decide which backup product best meets your needs. That leaves us with hardware and scheduling as planning considerations.

Selecting Backup Hardware

Given the size of today's hard disks, tape is the backup medium of choice for the vast majority of organizations. No other backup medium offers the combination of capacity and low cost that is available with tape.

LANs have backup needs that are distinctly different from user workstations. For one thing, there is more data on a LAN. For another, LANs are in use for a greater portion of the day. When an individual user goes home, he or she can start a backup job that can run for 12 hours if necessary. If you run a LAN, you may have trouble scheduling two hours a day for backup.

Therefore LAN backup hardware needs to be big and it needs to be fast. Before you buy any tape hardware, you need to carefully plan the capacity and speed you require. When you buy into a particular type of tape hardware, you are making a long-term commitment. In some cases, new generations of tape drives are not backward compatible.

I no longer attempt to describe specific hardware in my books because technologies, capacities, and performance levels change too rapidly. Basically, you will encounter four technologies:

- **Quarter-Inch Cartridge (QIC).** This format derives from work at 3M and uses a quarter-inch wide tape that shuttles back and forth through the cartridge as the head moves from track to track. The latest generation of QIC cartridges is called Travan, with the most recent drives having capacities in excess of 10 GB per cartridge (uncompressed). Some QIC drives are designed to connect to parallel ports or high-speed parallel interfaces, but these are far too slow to consider for LAN backups. SCSI devices are available and offer better speed, but lag behind other options. In general QIC hardware is too slow to consider for backing up LAN servers.

- **Digital Audio Tape (DAT).** This format is derived from the DAT format originally developed for audio recording. DAT uses technology similar to that of a video recorder to write data at high density on 4mm-wide tape that moves past the heads at a relatively slow pace. The latest generations of DAT drives can store 12 GB of data per cartridge. Transfer speeds range up to 1 MB/s—higher than QIC, but slower than 8mm or QIC.

- **8mm.** This format also uses technology derived from video recording to store data on 8mm-wide tapes. 8mm is a proprietary technology of Exabyte Corporation, which makes all 8mm drive hardware. Capacity of 8mm is very high, currently about 30 GB per cartridge, and very high transfer rates (up to 3 MB/s) are supported.

- **DLT.** DLT uses a half-inch tape in a unique cartridge that has a single take-up reel (the other reel is in the drive), resulting in very high capacities per cartridge—as much as 70 GB. Data transfer rates up to 5 MB/s are available.

For awhile, DAT held an edge as best compromise of capacity and throughput at moderate cost, but other technologies are beginning to chip away at DAT in terms of cost. Exabyte now offers 8mm drives that compare very favorably to the cost of DAT drives. Perhaps the chief disadvantage of DAT, 8mm, and DLT is that you can't trot down to CompUSA and buy one off the shelf. You need to do your research, find a qualified vendor, and order the hardware you need.

Because research is required, here are some Web sites that will get you started:

- `http://www.iomega.com/` For information about Iomega's line of QIC tape systems.

- `http://www.hp.com/tape/` HP now the Colorado line of QIC tape backup devices. They also produce the SureStore line of DAT and DLT drives.

- `http://www.ita.sel.sony.com/products/storage/` For information on Sony DAT and AIT tape backup systems.

- `http://www.exabyte.com/` For information about 8mm technology and descriptions of Exabyte's products.

- `http://www.quantum.com/` For DLT information, specifications, and product descriptions.

- `http://www.storage.digital.com` For more information about DLT from Digital, one of the originators of DLT technology.

Other Tape Backup Considerations

Tape backup can be a fairly involved process. Here are several miscellaneous topics you should consider when planning your backup strategy.

Open Files

Many applications and services keep files open at all times, and open files cannot be backed up because they are in a constant state of being modified. Windows NT Backup waits a bit to see whether an open file will be closed, skipping the file and reporting an error in the Backup log if the file cannot be backed up.

Some software packages, such as SQL database servers, have their own backup software. Other software packages, such as WINS, automatically create backup copies of their active data files so that the backup copies can be archived to tape. As you plan your backup strategy, identify the applications that maintain perpetually open files and ensure that you have taken them into account.

Multi-Tape Backups

In many cases, the data to be backed up exceed the capacity of a single tape, forcing you to either have multiple tape drives or to resort to *spanning*, the practice of continuing backup jobs on multiple tapes. All tape backup software packages support spanning.

But spanning means someone needs to be there to change the tape. Is someone in your LAN room during the night? If not, you can't span backup jobs. Unless, that is, you have a tape autoloader. These wonderful gadgets accept eight or more tapes and change them as required.

If, that is, your tape backup software supports autoloaders, which Windows NT Backup doesn't. If you have serious amounts of data to back up, you will need (a) a very big tape drive, (b) several tape drives—each of which must be managed separately—or (c) a tape autoloader.

Backing Up Clients and Multiple Servers

Ideally, all critical files should be stored on a LAN server where they can be backed up easily. Often, however, users store critical files on their network clients, files that should be included in your backup plan.

Windows NT Backup has only a limited capability to back up network clients and remote servers. To back up a remote computer—the computer that isn't running NT Backup—you must map a network drive to a share on the remote computer and back up the network drive. That means, of course, that a suitable share must exist on the remote computer, typically a share at the root directory. On Windows NT computers, you could use the administrative share that is assigned to each volume, but by default only administrators have access to the administrative shares. If backups will be executed by members of the Backup Operators group, that group must be enabled to connect with administrative shares. As you can see, backing up a large number of remote computers quickly becomes complex, what with assigning share permissions, mapping drive letters, and running the backups. And then, because backups are identified by drive letters, you need to remember which network drive was used to back up which computer. The record keeping can get complex indeed.

There's another problem with Windows NT Backup. It cannot back up the Registry on a remote Windows NT computer. If you can't back up the Registry, you are missing most of the computer's configuration data. I'll show you a workaround later in the chapter, but it is just a workaround, not a slick solution to the problem.

If you are committed to backing up several computers from a central server, you have an excellent excuse to investigate the third-party backup products mentioned earlier. All provide software that runs on the client and simplifies the process of performing remote backups. And all make it easier to track which files came from which computer.

Automation

You probably don't want to spend your evenings and weekends in the computer room running backups. If your company doesn't have an overnight computer staff, it would be nice to be able to automate the process so that it starts in the wee small hours when everyone has gone home.

The automation features of Windows NT Backup are pretty weak. Basically, you use the Schedule service to execute commands at specific times. There's no central console where you can track all the backup jobs. That's another thing third-party backup software can help you with.

Record Keeping

What record keeping? All NT Backup has is the storage log, which contains a lot of raw data but doesn't provide any summaries. If you want to know which tape ran when and what is on it, your best bet is to keep a manual log book. Again, a third-party backup package will do a better job.

In Summary

If your needs are simple, you can probably do fine with Windows NT Backup, which works reliably and has the advantage of being free. If you have a lot of data, want to back up several remote computers, or want convenient automation and record keeping, look at a LAN-capable third-party backup solution.

Nevertheless, we are going to focus on Windows NT Backup in this chapter because it's what everyone already has. If you know the capabilities and limitations of Windows NT Backup, you will be in a good position to evaluate your alternatives.

Planning Your Backup Schedule

Tape backups can be performed according to a variety of schedules, depending on your needs and goals. Before you buy any backup products, consider your options and your needs. Know how you want to back up files before you buy the wherewithal to do the job.

Types of Backups

Windows NT Backup can perform five types of backups. To understand how the backup types differ, you need to understand the file *archive bit* (also called the *archive attribute*). The archive bit is a marker on a file that can be turned on and off to indicate whether the file has been backed up since it was last modified.

Whenever a file is modified in Windows NT (or DOS), the archive bit is set. Some backup operations look only for files for which the archive bit has been set.

Backup operations do one of two things to the archive bit when the file has been backed up: They leave the bit in its current state, or they clear the bit to indicate that the file has been backed up.

The five types of backups are as follows:

- Normal
- Copy
- Differential
- Incremental
- Daily

The following sections discuss these types of backups.

Normal Backups

A *normal* backup does two things:

- Backs up all files that have been selected, regardless of the setting of the archive bit
- Clears the archive bit to indicate that the files have been backed up

Obviously, a normal backup performs a thorough backup of the selected files. By clearing the archive bit, a normal backup indicates that all files have been backed up.

Copy Backups

A *copy* backup does the following:

- Backs up all files that have been selected, regardless of the setting of the archive bit
- Leaves the archive bit in its pre-backup state

In other words, a copy backup does not alter the files that are backed up in any way, including changing the archive bit.

Differential Backups

Differential backups are so named because they record all the differences that have taken place since the last normal backup. A differential backup does the following:

- Backs up only files that have the archive bit set to show that the file has been modified
- Leaves the archive bit in its pre-backup state

Differential backups often are used in combination with normal backups. A normal backup of all files is performed each weekend to archive all files on the LAN, for example. Then a differential backup is performed each night of the week to back up all files that have been modified since the weekend. Figure 11.1 shows how this schedule works.

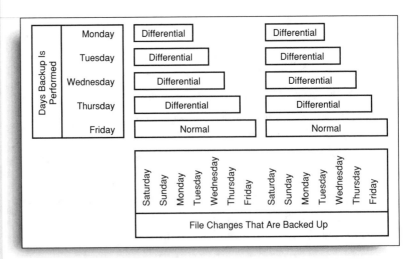

FIGURE 11.1

A weekly backup schedule using differential backups.

To restore all files on the LAN, you need to restore two sets of tapes:

- The normal backup for the preceding weekend
- The differential backup for the previous night

Differential backups commonly are used to reduce the amount of time in which backup jobs must run during the week. If you can schedule a normal (full) backup for the weekend but have limited time during the week, a differential backup still might fit into the weekday backup window.

Incremental Backups

Incremental backups record only the changes that have taken place during a preceding interval of time—often one day. An incremental backup does the following:

- Backs up only files that have the archive bit set to show that the file has been modified
- Clears the archive bit to indicate that the file has been backed up

Figure 11.2 shows how a combination of normal and incremental backups would work. The figure assumes that a normal backup is performed during the weekend, and an incremental backup takes place each week night. Notice that each incremental backup only records files that have been modified since the previous backup took place.

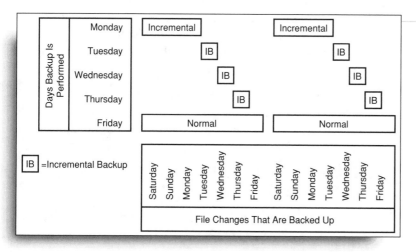

FIGURE 11.2

A weekly backup schedule using incremental backups.

Incremental backups are used to further reduce the time interval required to back up networks. If your LAN includes critical data, you might want to run incremental backups more than once a day so that an entire day's worth of work cannot be lost.

The disadvantage of incremental backups is that several tapes can be required to restore the network. If the LAN fails on Thursday, you must restore the last normal backup and the incremental backups for Monday, Tuesday, and Wednesday.

Daily Backups

Daily backups identify files to be backed up by examining the date stamp. If a file has been modified on the same day the backup is being made, the file will be backed up.

A particularly useful application for daily backups is to make checkpoint backups during the working day to capture changes at intervals shorter than 24 hours.

Limitations of Tape Backup

Notice that none of these backup types protects you against loss of data in files that have been modified since the most recent backup. What if you cannot afford to lose a single change that is made to any file, regardless of when the last backup was made? If you are running computers for a bank, how do you ensure that not a single transaction is lost?

There is no such thing as continuous backup, and open files can't be backed up. If your data is so critical that nothing may be lost, you need to be looking into one or more of the following options:

- RAID disk storage, so that a single hard drive failure will not lose data.
- Fault-tolerant hardware that has redundant power supplies, error-correcting memory, and other goodies that keep you from losing data.
- Fault-tolerant software that can rebuild damaged files. A good database system keeps a log file that can reconstruct all

transactions that take place. As long as the hard drives that contain the log file survive a disaster, you can restore last night's backup and roll the log forward to reconstruct the database to the point of failure.

Planning Tape Rotations

Tape rotation seeks to meet several goals:

- To spread wear across all your tapes
- To store data on and off site
- To have several copies of files where possible
- To retain files for a required minimum period

There are many different approaches to tape rotation, some of which are very complex. This chapter considers two approaches that are easy to manage manually.

Two-Set Rotation

If you don't need to archive files for extended periods of time, this is an easy-to-manage, simple rotation schedule. Essentially, you create two sets of five tapes and use each set in alternate weeks. Figure 11.3 illustrates the process.

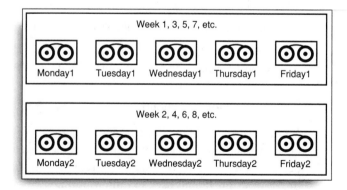

The tape labels in the figure assume that one tape will be required for each day. If your file volume requires spanning, you will need to create a set of tapes for each night—labeled, for example, Friday1A, Friday1B, Friday1C, and so forth.

My preference is to perform a normal (complete) backup each night, but you may need to perform partial backups if

- Your backup time window is too short to permit you to perform a complete backup on weeknights.
- Your files cannot fit on a single tape, but you don't have an attendant to change tapes. In such cases, you may want to schedule a normal backup once a week to minimize the hassle.

If you do not perform a normal backup nightly, you will schedule a normal backup once a week, probably on the weekend. Then a differential or incremental backup will be performed each weeknight.

Grandfather-Father-Son

The grandfather-father-son (GFS; or grandmother-mother-daughter, if you prefer) is a compromise between simplicity and the goal of establishing a long-term file archive. I will show you one variation on the GFS rotation concept, after which you may want to customize the schedules to more closely meet your needs.

For the GFS rotation shown in Figure 11.4, you need the following tapes:

- Four tapes for each weekday: Monday through Thursday
- Five Friday tapes, one for each Friday of the month, labeled Friday1 through Friday5 (because some months have five Fridays)
- One tape for each month

Monday through Thursday, a backup is performed using the tape for that night. These tapes are reused each week. You can perform a normal, differential, or incremental backup, depending on your needs and backup time window.

The first Friday of the month, the Friday1 tape is used to perform a normal backup. These tapes are rotated each week. Except for the tape required for the current week, these tapes are stored off-site, preferably in a facility specifically designed for the storage of data tapes.

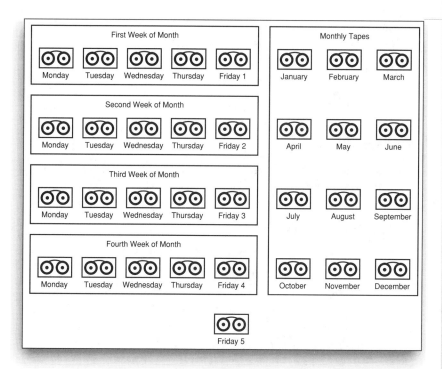

FIGURE 11.4
A grandfather-father-son tape rotation schedule.

On the last day of each month, a normal backup is performed on that month's tape. These tapes are stored off-site for at least one year. Legal requirements in certain industries may require a longer tape retention schedule.

If you own two tape drives, you can make on-site and off-site copies of the Friday and monthly tapes, enabling you to immediately access each night's backup in the event of an emergency.

Backing Up and Restoring Files

Now that you have an idea of the planning issues involved in establishing your backup strategy, let's get real and see how Windows NT Backup works. Despite the limitations noted earlier in the chapter, Windows NT Backup is quite a solid program. It is easy to use and reliable, and may be all your organization requires. Unless you know that you are going to select another software package, try working with Windows NT Backup for awhile. It will help you get comfortable with the backup process and experiment with some strategies before you plunk down big bucks for a third-party backup package.

Before you can back up files, you need to install the drivers that enable NT Backup to work with your tape drive. After looking at tape driver setup, we'll dig into the Backup program.

Installing Tape Drivers

Like every other hardware device, tape drives need drivers. Your first stop, therefore, is the Tape Devices applet in the Control Panel. Here's how to install the drivers for your tape drive:

Installing tape software drivers

1. Open the Tape Devices applet in the Control Panel.
2. NT attempts to detect any tape devices that are attached to the computer. If NT identifies a tape device, it presents a message similar to the one in Figure 11.5. Notice in the Tape Devices window that the tape drive is recognized but that the status is (driver not loaded).

FIGURE 11.5

NT has detected a tape backup device.

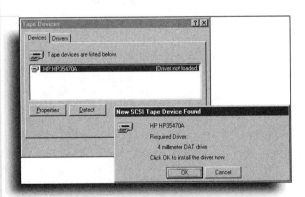

3. Click **OK** to install the driver for the device NT has detected.
4. When prompted, verify the path to the driver files on the installation CD-ROM (for example, E:\i386).
5. After the driver is installed, the Tape Devices window, shown in Figure 11.6, confirms that the tape drive has been configured.

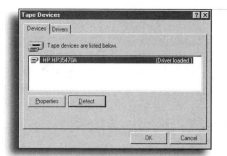

This is one of the rare instances when you don't need to restart NT after installing a new driver. You can go straight to the Backup program.

Backing Up Files

Figure 11.7 shows the Windows NT Backup program. You will find its shortcut in the Administrative Tools program group. Backup has two main windows:

- **Tapes** displays the status of tape drives configured on the computer and is used to select files to be restored from tape. When the Tapes window is selected, the **Restore** button on the toolbar is active.

- **Drives** displays disk drives known on this computer, including CD-ROM drives and mapped network drives. The Drives window is used to select files that are to be archived to tape. When the Drives window is selected, the **Backup** button on the toolbar is active.

We will first look at the process for backing up files, which turns out to have five steps:

1. Preparing the tape media
2. Selecting the files to be backed up
3. Selecting the backup options
4. Running the backup
5. Verifying the backup

The following sections examine these backup tasks.

Preparing the Tape Media

In most cases, new tapes require little or no preparation. If tapes have existing data from another backup system, they might need to be erased or formatted. Several tape options are found on the **Operations** menu. After inserting a tape, you can execute the following commands.

- **Erase Tape.** Choose this operation to erase records of previous backups. You have two choices:

  Quick Erase. Just erases the tape label and makes the tape usable with Windows NT Backup. Existing data remains on the tape and can be accessed.

  Secure Erase. Physically erases all data from the tape so that it cannot be accessed. You should perform a secure erase on tapes that will be discarded so that a third party cannot recover sensitive data from your files.

- **Retension Tape.** QIC data cartridges should be retensioned prior to first use and after every 20 backup operations. Retensioning fast forwards and rewinds the tape to equalize tension on the tape medium. 4mm, 8mm, and DLT tapes do not require retensioning.

- **Eject Tape.** Ejects a tape if a tape device supports software tape ejection.

Selecting Files for Backup

To select entire volumes, just enable the check boxes of the desired volumes in the Backup window. Here's a walkthrough of the procedure:

Selecting files to be backed up

1. To back up an entire drive, check the check box for the drive in the Drives window.

2. To back up specific files or directories, double-click a drive in the Drives window to open a drive tree window similar to that shown in Figure 11.7. This drive tree window works much like trees in utilities such as Windows NT Explorer. You double-click a directory icon labeled with a plus sign (+) to open the directory to the next level, for example.

Erase prior to unattended backups

You should erase any tapes that will be used during unattended operation because no one will be present to correct errors if Backup is unable to read the tape.

If Backup produces an error message such as `Tape Drive Error Detected` or `Bad Tape`, you might not be able to erase the tape with Backup in Normal mode. To erase a tape that causes these errors, start Backup by choosing **Run** from the **File** menu and add the `/nopoll` switch. (The command is **NTBACKUP /NOPOLL**.)

After you format tapes with the `/NOPOLL` switch, stop Backup and restart it normally. Do not attempt to execute normal operations with the `/NOPOLL` switch.

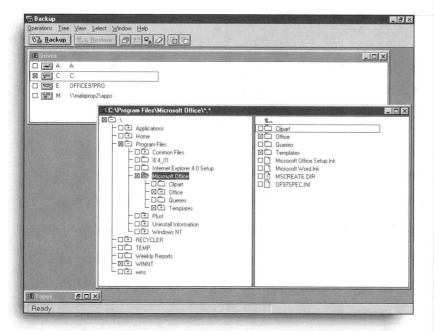

FIGURE 11.7
Selecting files and directories to be backed up.

3. Choose the files or directories to be backed up by checking the associated box. Checking a directory selects all subdirectories of that directory. You can, if you want, open the subdirectories and remove the check marks from specific subdirectories or files.

   Notice that a directory check box is filled with gray if any files or subdirectories under that directory are unchecked.

Specifying Backup Options

After you have selected the items to be backed up, choose the **Backup** command in the **Operations** menu, or click the **Backup** button in the toolbar. This displays the Backup Information dialog box shown in figure 11.8.

The options in this box follow:

- **Current Tape.** The name of the currently mounted tape, unless the tape is blank or has an unrecognized format.

- **Creation Date.** The date the first backup set on the tape was created.

Backing up removable media

Many computers are equipped with high-capacity removable storage devices. Unfortunately, the Windows NT Backup program does not permit you to directly select removable volumes for backup.

The trick is to share the drive that you want to back up; then connect a drive letter to the shared drive. You can then back up the storage device by selecting the drive letter connected to the removable drive.

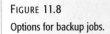

FIGURE 11.8
Options for backup jobs.

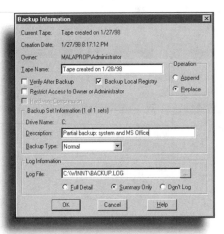

- **Owner.** The user who placed the first backup set on the tape.

- **Tape Name.** You can specify a tape name or permit Backup to use the default name "Tape created on date." This box is available only when you choose the **Replace** option.

- **Append.** Select this button to add the new backup set to the end of the tape.

- **Replace.** Select this button to overwrite existing backup sets on the tape with the current backup.

- **Verify After Backup.** Check this item to have Backup compare the tape contents to the original files to ensure that file data was written to tape without error.

- **Backup Local Registry.** The Registry is the heart and soul of Windows NT, and contains all the system's vital operational data. You should include the Registry in every backup of drive C: to ensure that you have a valid, recent copy in case the Registry files are damaged.

- **Restrict Access to Owner or Administrator.** Check this option to make the tape more secure. Data from the tape can be retrieved only by the tape owner, or by a member of the Administrators or Backup Operators group. This box is available only when you choose the **Replace** option.

Always back up the local Registry

You should always back up the local Registry. You just cannot have too many copies of the Registry because you always want to restore the most recent archived copy of the Registry when you are rebuilding a damaged system.

- **Hardware Compression.** This option is active only if your tape device supports hardware data compression. Check this box to activate the feature. Be aware, however, that using hardware compression can prevent you from restoring the tape from another brand of drive or from a drive that does not support data compression.

- **Drive Name.** This field displays the name of a drive that you checked in the Backup window. If you checked more than one drive letter, you see a scrollbar that can be used to display each of the drives. For each drive, you can enter a description and select a backup type.

- **Description.** Enter a brief description of the job.

- **Backup Type.** Choose the backup type from these options: Normal, Copy, Differential, Incremental, and Daily. Each type was discussed earlier in the chapter.

- **Log File.** Enter a path describing a file where log messages will be recorded.

  Full Detail. Logs all operations, including the files and directories that are backed up.

  Summary Only. Logs only major operations, such as starting and completing the backup and backup errors.

Running the Backup

When you have completed entries in the dialog box, click **OK** to continue with the backup.

Backup examines the tape that you have loaded to determine whether it already contains data. If Backup finds data and you have specified **Replace** as the backup operation, you will see an error message. Confirm that the files on the tape can be erased before you click **Yes** to continue.

Verifying the Backup

The Backup Status box displays a running commentary that informs you of the backup progress (see Figure 11.9). Pay particular attention to two statistics:

Backing up remote directories

Windows NT Backup does not back up Registries on remote computers.

If you want to back up your network from a central location, two utilities found in the Windows NT Resource Kit enable you to back up a Registry to files that can in turn be backed up through the network to tape. Use **REGBACK.EXE** to back up a Registry, and use **REGREST.EXE** to restore it.

- **Corrupt files.** High or increasing numbers of corrupt files might indicate hardware problems.

- **Skipped files.** These files were, of course, not backed up. If you see skipped files, check the log to ensure that missing these files is not a critical omission. You might need to force a user to log off to close the files.

FIGURE 11.9

The Backup Status box, shown after a backup job is completed.

Restoring Files

To restore files, first review your logs to identify the appropriate tape. If you are restoring a complete volume from a combination of several backup sets, be sure to restore the backup sets in the order they were made so that newer copies of files overwrite older copies.

Selecting Files to Restore

Prior to a restore, you must select the files to be restored. Backup enables you to restore entire tapes, specific backup sets, or individual files or directories. To select files to restore, follow these steps:

Selecting files to restore

1. Open the Tapes window by double-clicking the Tapes icon.

2. Insert the desired tape. After you insert a tape, Backup creates an icon for the tape in the Tapes window. If the tape contains more than one backup set, only the first set on the tape is listed in the Tapes window.

Coping with open files

Some files are skipped because they are held open by applications which must be shut down before the files can be backed up. Many database servers, such as Microsoft SQL Server, have their own backup routines that must be used to back up the database files.

Using backup logs

It is always a good idea to check the Backup log, especially to confirm that automated backup jobs completed successfully. The Backup log is a text file you can print or review with WordPad.

Apart from any record keeping you might do manually, the Backup log is your only record of tape contents. It is useful to retain the old logs until the tapes they describe are reused. You might want to name the Backup log file to reflect the name of the tape that it describes.

3. To see all backup sets on the tape, select the tape icon and choose **Catalog** in the **Operations** menu. In Figure 11.10, the tape that has been cataloged has backup sets for drives C: and M:.

4. You can load several tapes into Backup. Figure 11.10 shows a Tapes window with two tape catalogs loaded. If you insert several tapes in succession, the Tapes window will retain a catalog record for each tape volume.

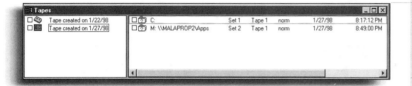

FIGURE 11.10

You can select entire tapes, volumes, or specific files to be restored.

5. To restore the entire contents of the tape, check the box next to the tape icon.

6. To restore the entire contents of a specific backup set, check the appropriate check box in the right-hand pane of the Tapes window.

7. If you want to select specific files or directories from a volume, double-click the folder icon (or select the folder icon and choose **Catalog** from the **Operations** menu). Backup will scan the tape and list detailed contents. You can browse the tape contents and select specific items to be restored. Figure 11.11 shows an example of a tape catalog.

8. You can restore entire tapes, specific backup sets, or individual directories or files by selecting the items you want in the Tapes window. You can open folders to locate subdirectories and files on a drive. Check all items that are to be restored.

Specifying Restore Options

After selecting items to be restored, choose the Restore icon in the toolbar or choose **Restore** from the **Operations** menu. Restore Information dialog box appears, as shown in Figure 11.12.

Files that are not restored

Windows NT Backup does not restore tape files that are older than the corresponding file on disk. You will be asked to confirm replacement of newer files.

Also, Windows NT Backup does not restore files that are to be restored to a directory for which the user does not have write permissions. Users are also prevented from overwriting files for which they do not have write permissions.

FIGURE 11.11

A catalog enables you to restore specific directories or files.

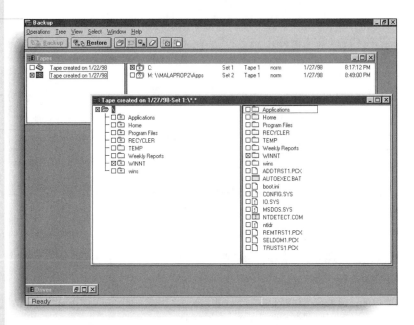

FIGURE 11.12

Selecting restore options.

The need for speed

Creating catalogs is a time when you will really appreciate the fast seek times possible with 4mm, 8mm, and DLT data cartridges. The catalog is stored as the last item on the tape, and Backup must search the entire tape. This can take considerable time with QIC cartridges, but takes less than a minute with a 4mm drive.

If you have selected two or more tape sets to restore, a scrollbar will be included in the Restore Information dialog box. You can select each set by moving the scroll handle.

For each tape set being restored, the following information and options are displayed:

- **Tape Name.** The name of the tape from which files are being restored for this set.
- **Backup Set.** The name you assigned to the backup set.

- **Creation Date.** The date the backup set was created.

- **Owner.** The user who created the backup set.

- **Restore to <u>D</u>rive.** Specify a different destination drive by entering the drive path here. This path can include local hard drives or drives created by network connections.

- **<u>A</u>lternate Path.** If files will not be restored to their original directories, specify the base directory to which the directory tree should be restored.

- **<u>V</u>erify After Restore.** Check this option to have restored files compared to the image on tape to ensure that errors have not occurred.

- **<u>R</u>estore File Permissions.** Check this box if you want to retain file permissions that originally were assigned to the directories and files. This option is available only if you are restoring to an NTFS volume.

- **Restore Local Re<u>g</u>istry.** Check this box to restore the server Registry. This option is active only if the Registry was backed up to the tape set and if it would be restored to the same volume on which it originally was located.

- **<u>L</u>og File.** Enables you to specify where messages should be logged. Options are the same as the options available in the Backup Information dialog box.

Restoring Files

After you have completed the Restore Information dialog box, begin the restore operation by clicking **OK**.

If you are restoring over existing files, Backup may discover that you are restoring a file that already exists on the target volume. When such conflicts are encountered, Backup seeks confirmation whether the existing file should be replaced, and displays the dialog box shown in Figure 11.13. You have the following choices:

- **<u>Y</u>es.** This option restores the specified file, but does not affect other files.

- **Yes to <u>A</u>ll.** This option replaces all conflicting files on disk with the corresponding files on tape.

- **No.** This option does not restore the specified file and continues with the remainder of the restoration. (Unfortunately, there is not a **No to All** option so that you can easily restore missing files.)

- **Cancel.** This option cancels the restoration completely.

A Restore Status box similar to Figure 11.14 displays the progress of the file restoration.

FIGURE 11.13

Backup requests confirmation to replace existing files.

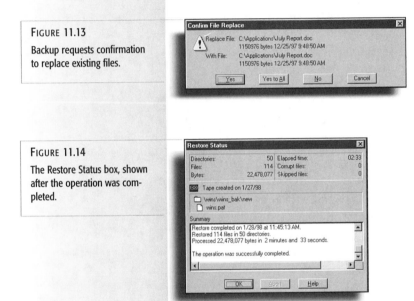

FIGURE 11.14

The Restore Status box, shown after the operation was completed.

Restoring from Spanned Tape Sets

If you are restoring a tape set that spans more than one physical tape, the catalog will be on the last tape on the set. Backup asks you to mount the appropriate tape so that it can read the catalog.

If a tape from the spanned set is missing or damaged, you might need to force Backup to rebuild a catalog by scanning each tape. To do this, start Backup by choosing **Run** from the **Start** menu and typing the command `ntbackup /missingtape`. Backup then scans each tape to build a catalog—a lengthy process, but one that is preferable to losing your data.

Restoring a Registry

You can restore only the Registry files to the volume from which they were archived, if you prefer. With the Windows Backup utility, you must select at least one file to activate the **Restore** button. Then you can check the **Restore Local Registry** check box in the Restore Information dialog box.

To restore from the command line, specify the following directory:

```
\Winnt\system32\config
```

You cannot restore the Registry directory to any disk other than the disk from which it was backed up.

Test Your Tapes

Don't take your backup procedures for granted. Test your tapes to ensure that files can be restored properly. If possible, try the procedure discussed at the end of this chapter and try to restore an entire server from tape backups. It's better to practice before you have a real emergency, because emergencies mean pressure. And who needs pressure when trying something for the first time.

It's also a good idea to run small restore jobs on a weekly basis to ensure that your files, directory structures, and security settings are being archived and can be recovered properly.

SEE ALSO

> *See the section titled "Recovering a Server" at the end of this chapter, page 391, for a procedure you can use to restore the entire contents of a server.*

Using Backup from the Command Line

A command-line interface is available for Backup. The primary use for the command-line interface is to build batch files that can be executed manually or by using the Windows NT command scheduler.

The syntax for the NTBACKUP command follows:

```
NTBACKUP operation path [/A][/B][/D"text"]
➥[/E][/HC:[ON¦OFF]]
[/L "filename"][/R][/T option][/TAPE:n][/V]
```

The command recognizes several options. (Square brackets indicate that a parameter is not required in Microsoft syntax diagrams.) The parameters and options for NTBACKUP follow:

operation	Always specify BACKUP.
path	Enter one or more path specifications of directories to be backed up.
/A	Include this option to have Backup append this job to tape. Omitting this option instructs Backup to replace the tape contents with the current job.
/B	Include this option to back up the local Registry.
/D *"text"*	Use this option to specify a description of the backup set. Place the description in quotation marks.
/E	If this option is used, the Backup log includes exceptions only. Without this option, a full Backup log is created.
/HC:[ON¦OFF]	Use this option to force a backup device to operate with hardware compression on or off. Specify the option as /hc:on or /hc:off. This option is effective only when the /A option is omitted, because the compression mode of the tape is determined by the mode used for the first set on the tape.
/L *"filename"*	This option specifies the name of the Backup log. Include the filename and path in quotation marks. The log created by NTBACKUP records only exceptions encountered as the backup job is executed.
/R	Secures the backup set by restricting access to the tape owner and to members of the Administrators or Backup Operators group. This option is effective only when the /A option is omitted.
/T *option*	Specify the backup type. Replace option with normal, copy, incremental, differential, or daily.
/TAPE:*n*	If the server has more than one tape drive, specify the drive to be used with a number *n* from 0 through 9 to reference the drive's number as listed in the Registry.

/V   Include this option to have Backup verify the
tape.

Now look at some examples. Following is a command that backs up the APPS directory of drive C:

```
ntbackup backup c:\apps /a/e/v /l "c:\winnt\Monday1.log"
/t differential
```

Notice that the order of the options does not matter. This command accomplishes the following:

- Backs up all files and subdirectories of C:\APPS
- Appends the tape set to the current tape
- Restricts tape log entries to exceptions only
- Verifies the backup
- Places the log in the file C:\Winnt\Monday1.log
- Performs a differential backup

Here is another example:

```
ntbackup backup c: d: h: /r/b /t normal /l:c:\March.log
```

This example does the following:

- Backs up drives C, D, and H
- Backs up the Registry on local drives
- Replaces contents of the tape (no /A option)
- Restricts access to the backup set
- Performs a normal backup
- Records a full Detail log (no /e flag) in C:\March.log

Because the interactive Backup utility is so quick and easy to use, you probably will use the command-line format primarily to create batch files. Because Backup does not support a macro language, however, the command-line approach is the only way to store backup procedures for repeated execution.

In the following section, you see how backup batch files can be scheduled for delayed or repeated execution. Here is a batch file that backs up drives on several servers:

```
net use g:\\widgets1\c$ /yes
net use h:\\widgets2\c$ /yes
net use i: \\acct\c$ /yes
```

```
ntbackup backup c: d: g: h: i: /e/v /l
➥"c:\winnt35\tuesday.log"
/t normal /d "Complete backup of Widgets1, Widgets2, and the
➥ACCT share"
```

Of course, a backup operator must be trusted on other domains before being permitted to back up his or her data in those other domains.

Scheduling Automated Backups

Windows NT has a Schedule service that can be used to schedule execution of commands. The Schedule enables you to schedule jobs to execute overnight or over the weekend, and to execute repeatedly without the need for rescheduling. This section shows you how to set up and use the Schedule to make tape backups.

SEE ALSO

➤ *To learn more about managing services, see the section titled "Server Manager" in Chapter 23, "Managing the Server," page 674.*

Starting the Schedule Service

The Schedule service can run in two modes:

- **As a system account.** In this mode, Schedule operates in the current logon session, using the permissions assigned to the logged-on user account. Schedule cannot operate when no user is logged on.

- **In its own logon session.** In this mode, Schedule uses permissions assigned to its own user account. Schedule can operate whenever the server is active and can function in the background when users are logged on to the server.

The first choice is useful when you are scheduling tasks that will take place while you are logged on.

In many cases, however, you will want to use the second approach with tape backups. By assigning a user account to the Schedule, you make it possible for backups to take place even when no one is logged on to the backup server.

Administrative shares and Backup Operators

The administrative shares such as C$ and D$ are available only to members of the Administrators local group. If members of Backup Operators will be backing up remote servers, you need to create shares that can be accessed by them.

Starting the Schedule Service as a System Account

Services are managed using the Service utility in the Control Panel. Open the Services applet to see a list of services, as shown in Figure 11.15. Notice that the Schedule service status is not started and its Startup mode is Manual. Services that are configured with an Automatic Startup mode are started when Windows NT Server is booted.

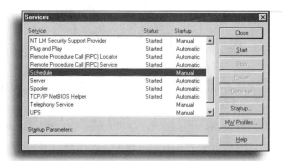

FIGURE 11.15
Service status, viewed in the Services applet.

To set up the Schedule service as a system account, follow these steps:

Setting up the Schedule service to work with a system account

1. Open the Service applet in the Control Panel.

2. Select the **Schedule service** in the **Service** box.

3. Choose **Startup** to display the Service dialog box shown in Figure 11.16.

FIGURE 11.16
Configuring the Schedule service to work with a system account.

4. Select **A**utomatic so that Schedule service will be started automatically.

5. Select **S**ystem Account.

6. Select **A**llow Service to Interact with Desktop if you want to monitor backup jobs as they run. (I recommend using this option when you are learning to schedule backups.)

7. Click **OK**. You will be returned to the Services window.

8. Choose **S**tart to start the Schedule service. It restarts automatically each time the server is booted.

9. Exit the Service applet.

Configuring the Schedule Service to Work with a User Account

If you configure the Schedule service to log on as a system service, you must remain logged on to the computer to enable scheduled jobs to be executed. If backups take place overnight, it can be risky to leave a server sitting while it is logged on. When automating overnight backups, in most cases you want backup jobs to run in Unattended mode, while no one is logged on to the server. To do that, you must enable the Schedule service to log on with its own user account.

Before you can configure the Schedule service to log on with its own user account, you must create a special user account that will be used by the service. Because the Schedule service will be running backup jobs, the user account must be made a member of the Backup Operators local group. Other group memberships might be required as well. Of course, proper trust relationships must be set up between domains before cross-domain memberships can be assigned.

SEE ALSO

➤ *To learn how to create user accounts, see the section titled "Creating a User Account," in Chapter 5, "Adding Users and Groups," on page 158.*

Before you go further, log on with the user account you have created and be sure you can back up the desired files.

Use a system account when testing

When you are experimenting, set up the Schedule service as a System service. You will find it much easier to learn the ropes and to set up your regular backup jobs.

Any time you change the settings for the Schedule service, you must stop and restart the service to have the changes take effect.

Don't use the Administrator account

Don't be tempted to use the Administrator account to enable the Schedule service. Doing so opens a security hole because the service is always logged on with the account you specify. Also, if you use the Administrator account, you must reconfigure the Backup service each time you change the account password.

To set up the Schedule service to log on with the user account you have created, follow these steps:

Configuring the Schedule service to log on with a user account

1. Open the Service applet in the Control Panel.

2. Select the **Schedule service** in the **Service** box.

3. Choose **Startup** to display the Service dialog box.

4. Select **Automatic** so that Schedule service will be started automatically.

5. As shown in Figure 11.17, select **This Account** and enter the user account name you have created for backups. You can click the **Browse (...)** button to browse the network and select the username.

FIGURE 11.17
Configuring the Schedule ser-vice to log on with a user account.

6. Enter the password for the user account in the two password fields.

7. Click **OK**. You will be returned to the Service dialog box.

8. Stop the service if it is running. Then choose **Start** to acti-vate the service with the changes you have made. If the ser-vice will not start, verify the configuration in the Service dialog box and ensure that the user account information has been entered properly.

9. Exit the Service applet.

The Log On As Service right

After you configure the Schedule service with a user account and click **OK** to exit the Service dialog box, a dialog box presents a message similar to this: `The account MALAPROP\BackerUpper has been granted the Log On As Service Right`. This right confers a special account capability you will not encounter elsewhere in the book, giving the user account the capabilities required to enable the Schedule service to execute tasks in the background.

When to configure the Schedule service with a user account

You only need to set up the Schedule service to log on with a user account if you are planning to have it run jobs in the background or when a user is not logged on. If the backup computer is located in a secure, locked area, you can do just as well by configuring Schedule as a system service and leaving it logged on with appropriate privileges. If you are concerned about security, install a password-protected screen saver so that the computer will be locked with a password when it is unattended.

Scheduling Jobs with the AT Command

Now that the Schedule service is started, you can enter scheduled jobs with the at command. at commands are entered at a command prompt. The syntax of the at command follows:

```
at [\\computer] [[id][/delete] ¦ /delete [/yes]]
```

or

```
at [\\computer] time [/interactive][/every:date[,...]
➥"command"
```

or

```
at [\\computer] time [/interactive][/next:date[,...]
➥"command"
```

The at command typed alone lists all currently scheduled jobs.

The command recognizes several options. (Square brackets indicate that a parameter is not required in Microsoft syntax diagrams.) The parameters and options for at follow:

\\computer	Specify the name of a Windows NT computer on which the command will execute. If this command is omitted, the current computer is assumed.
id	The identification number assigned to a scheduled command.
/delete	Include this option to cancel a schedule command. If an id is specified, only the jobs associated with that id are deleted. Otherwise, all scheduled commands are deleted.
/yes	When used to cancel all jobs, /yes eliminates the need to confirm the request.
time	Specifies the time in 24-hour format when the job should be scheduled.
/interactive	Include this option to enable the current user to interact with the job. Without this flag, the job operates in the background.
/every:date	Use this option to schedule repeating jobs. Specify one or more dates, where date is a day of the week (Monday, Tuesday, and so on) or a day

of the month (1 through 31). If date is omitted, the current day of the month is assumed.

/next:*date*   Use this option to schedule a job the next time date occurs. Specify one or more dates, where date is a day of the week (Monday, Tuesday, and so on) or a day of the month (1 through 31). If date is omitted, the current day of the month is assumed.

"*command*"   The command to be executed.

Assuming that BACKUP.BAT is a batch file, here are some examples of scheduling jobs with the AT command. This first example schedules the job once at 3:00 a.m. If it is later than 3:00 a.m., the job is scheduled for the morning of the next day.

```
at 3:00 "backup"
```

To schedule a job to happen regularly on Wednesdays at midnight, use the /EVERY option:

```
at 0:00 /every:Wednesday "backup"
```

If you want the job to happen every weekday, just add the extra days:

```
at 0:00 /every:Monday,Tuesday,Wednesday,Thursday "backup"
```

Particularly when you are debugging backup procedures, you might want to have the job operate in Interactive mode. Here is an example:

```
at 15:00 "backup" /interactive
```

After each job is scheduled, you see this message where *n* is the job number:

```
Added a new job ID=n
```

To delete a job, use the job ID with the /delete command.

Configuring Backup Jobs When the Backup Service Logs On with a User Account

It is a bit complicated to schedule jobs when the Backup service logs on with a user account because of the following:

The interactive option requires a logged-on user

Do not use the /interactive option with backup jobs that will run overnight without a user logged on to the desktop. Interactive jobs will attempt to connect with an active desktop and will fail.

- When the backup service is logged on with a user account, the Administrator cannot schedule jobs.

- The backup user is not authorized to schedule jobs.

Consequently, you must jump through some hoops to schedule automated backup jobs when the Backup service logs on with a user account. Here is a method that works:

Configuring backup jobs when the Backup service logs on with a user account

1. Log on as an administrator.

2. Open the Service applet in the Control Panel.

3. Stop the Schedule service.

4. Open the Schedule service properties and select **S̲ystem Account.**

5. Start the Schedule Service.

6. Schedule the desired backup jobs.

7. Open the Service applet in the Control Panel.

8. Stop the Schedule service.

9. Open the Schedule service properties.

10. Configure the Schedule service to log on with a user account.

SEE ALSO

➤ *Review the section titled "Configuring the Schedule Service to Work with a User Account" earlier in this chapter on page 384 for the procedures required in step 10.*

11. Start the Schedule service.

Unfortunately, you must go through this entire procedure each time you make a change to scheduled jobs.

Scheduling Jobs with Command Scheduler

The Windows NT Resource Kit includes a useful utility called Command Scheduler (the program file is `winat.exe`) that enables you to schedule and manage jobs in an interactive windows-based environment. If you start the Command Scheduler and the Schedule service is not started, Command Scheduler asks whether you want to start the service.

Figure 11.18 shows the main window of Command Scheduler. Each job executes a batch file. I prefer to place the backup commands in batch files because I can edit batch files more easily than I can schedule commands. Figure 11.18 shows three types of scheduled events:

- Every weeknight at 1:00 a.m., a batch file executes that starts the backup for that night.

- Every day, a batch file executes that backs up changed files, appending them to last night's backup tape. This is a checkpoint backup, capturing files that have changed that morning. It cannot back up open files, but it will capture some of the modified files, reducing the impact of a possible server crash.

- On day 31 of the current month, an end-of-month backup will occur. It starts before the regular backup job so that it preempts the Backup program on that day.

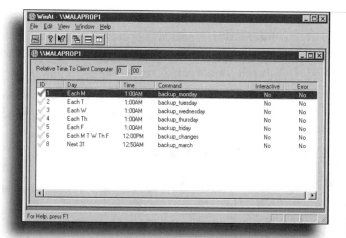

FIGURE 11.18
Command Scheduler.

Command Scheduler enables you to add and edit backup jobs with a graphic interface. To add a scheduled job, choose **Add** in the **Edit** menu to open the Add Command dialog box shown in Figure 11.19. The dialog box contains the following fields:

- **Command.** Enter the command to be executed.

- **This Occurs.** Specify whether the job should occur:

  Today. The command executes once only, at a time later today.

  Tomorrow. The command executes once only on the next day.

  Every. The command executes every day specified in the **Days** list box.

  Next. The command executes once only, on the next occurrence of the day or days selected in the **Days** list box.

- **Days.** If **Every** or **Next** is selected, select one or more days in this box. You can select days of the week or days of the month. Hold down the Shift key to select multiple days.

- **Time.** Enter the time. You can tab to each time field and enter a number, or select each field in turn and change the value with the arrow buttons.

- **PM.** When checked, the **Time** field indicates a time between noon and midnight.

- **Interactive.** Check this box if the job should be available on the desktop of the currently logged-on user. (See the earlier warning about interactive jobs.)

After you have completed the dialog box, click **OK** to add the job and return to the Command Scheduler main window.

FIGURE 11.19

Scheduling a job in Command Scheduler.

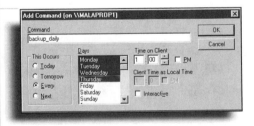

To change or remove a job, select the job and choose **Change** or **Remove** in the Command Scheduler main window.

Recovering a Server

If you experience total failure of a server's boot hard drive, the hardest part of recovery is restoring the system directory. You cannot just re-install NT and then restore the \Winnt directory tree because the running copy of NT holds files open that prevent the restoration of critical files. Often, attempting to restore the system directory just results in a non-working system.

I'm going to describe a procedure that works. The procedure assumes that you are backing up the Registry each time you run a backup job.

Recovering a server from backups

1. Reinstall Windows NT, *specifying a different system directory than the one used previously*. The normal system root directory is the default C\Winnt. In this example, I will assume that NT will be installed in the directory C:\NewNT.

2. Configure the tape drive.

3. Fire up Backup and obtain your most recent backup tape that includes the system directory.

4. Restore the most recent normal backup to the original file locations. Because the original system root directory is not being used, Backup can restore all files to that directory without conflicting with open files. Check **Restore Local Registry** and **Restore File Permissions** when restoring the files.

5. Restore any incremental or differential backups that were made since the last normal backup.

6. When prompted, select **Yes to All** to restore all files on the tapes, replacing existing files if necessary.

7. When satisfied the server is operating properly, delete the temporary system directory (C:\NewNT).

The preceding procedure assumes that you are restoring the following files:

- The entire system directory (C:\Winnt)

The Command Scheduler

The Command Scheduler is distributed with the Windows NT Resource Kit for Windows NT version 3.5. As I write this, I can't be sure it will be included in the Windows NT Resource Kit for version 4. If it is not included, it is worth doing some legwork to obtain a copy. The **at** command leaves just a bit to be desired.

- The Registry
- A boot.ini file that boots the operating system in C:\Winnt

If you are not restoring a boot.ini file that boots NT from the system directory you are restoring, you will need to edit boot.ini to boot the restored copy of NT.

SEE ALSO

➤ *See the section titled "The Structure of the boot.ini File" in Chapter 2, "Installing Windows NT Server 4," on page 76, for details about the boot.ini file.*

Here's Your Security Blanket

Reliable backups are among the best security blankets a network administrator can have. Nothing builds your credibility with users like the magic of pulling a lost file out of oblivion. It's a lot of work to establish good, tested backup procedures, but the reward will come. Sooner or later it will come. And you will be glad of every minute you spent on file backups.

The next stop is to begin to expand your network. In the following chapter you learn how to build really big networks by adding domains to your network infrastructure.

Extending Multi-Domain Networks

Trust relationships

Multi-domain models

Establishing trust relationships

Granting inter-domain permissions

Removing trust relationships

Planning multi-domain networks with WANs

Until now we have kept things simple, focusing on networks that have a single domain. In fact, many organizations will never need the material covered in this chapter. A single domain has room for quite a few users, particularly if it has enough domain controllers to speed user logons. But some situations call for additional domains. Here are a few:

- Every domain controller increases housekeeping traffic as it remains current on the state of the SAM and browsing databases. Eventually, domain housekeeping traffic may escalate to the point that it makes sense to add a second logon domain so that some users log on to different computers.

- Some departments want to retain a level of autonomy that comes with managing their own domains.

- Some organizations may have multiple, independent Windows NT networks that they want to stitch together into an enterprise network. When departments are used to having their own domains, they might not want to surrender their territorial rights, hence a multi-domain LAN becomes a political necessity.

Windows NT domains can be organized quite flexibly. In fact, there are three possible ways to configure multi-domain networks. After you see how domains can cooperate, using structures known as *trust relationships*, you will examine the available models for multi-domain LANs. Then you'll see how to configure trust relationships and inter-domain security.

Trust Relationships

A trust relationship is a one-way agreement consisting of a trusted and a trusting domain. It works like this:

- A *trusted domain* allows another domain to share its security database.

- A *trusting domain* assigns users' permissions based on user account and group memberships in the trusted domain.

Trust relationships can be one-way between domains, or they can be two-way. Let's look at the simple, one-way case first.

One-Way Trust Relationships

Figure 12.1 shows an example of a trust relationship that involves only two domains. In the figure, TRUSTED is the trusted domain, and TRUSTING is—do I really need to say it?—the trusting domain. So what does the trust relationship accomplish?

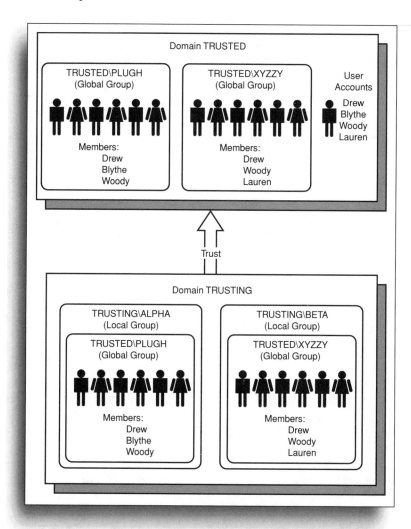

FIGURE 12.1

A one-way trust relationship.

Suppose you log on to the domain named TRUSTED. You have the following user and group memberships in TRUSTED:

- You have the user account Drew
- You are a member of the global group PLUGH
- You are a member of the global group XYZZY

Okay, so you're logged on to TRUSTED. Now you attempt to access resources in TRUSTING. You're not logged on to TRUSTING, but thanks to the trust relationship, TRUSTING can use security information from TRUSTED. This enables TRUSTING to verify that you were properly authenticated by a logon to TRUSTED. It also enables TRUSTING to learn your user account identity and your group memberships.

The administrator of TRUSTING has made the following assignments:

- The global group TRUSTED\PLUGH is a member of the local group TRUSTING\ALPHA
- The global group TRUSTING\XYZZY is a member of the local group TRUSTING\BETA

You want to access the share \\TRUSTING1\APPS. The group TRUSTING\BETA has Full Control share permissions and Change directory permissions for the files in that share. So you gain access as follows:

1. You have been given the user account Drew in the TRUSTED domain.

2. TRUSTED\Drew is a member of the global group TRUSTED\PLUGH.

3. TRUSTED\PLUGH is a member of the local group TRUSTING\ALPHA.

4. TRUSTING\ALPHA has the sharing and directory permissions you need to access files in the \\TRUSTING1\APPS share.

Remember these essential characteristics of groups:

- *Global groups* can have users as members, but global groups cannot have groups as members. Global groups can be exported to other domains that trust the domain in which the global group was created.

- *Local groups* can have global groups and users as members. The global groups and user accounts can be created in the same domain as the local group, or they can be created in a separate domain that is trusted by the domain that has the local group.

SEE ALSO

➤ *Global and local groups are introduced in Chapter 5, "Adding Users and Groups."*

Now you can really see the significance of global and local groups and how they help you meet the larger goal of setting up multi-domain networks. In the example, you must belong to a global entity in TRUSTED to be given permissions in TRUST-ING. You can belong to two types of global entities:

- *Global user accounts.* All normal Windows NT user accounts are global, so that's a possibility in the present scenario.

- *Global groups.* Group type is up to the administrator, who must create the correct one for the situation.

In either case, you can be given local permissions in TRUST-ING. Permissions can be assigned in three ways:

- Permissions can be assigned directly to your global user account.

- Permissions can be assigned directly to the TRUSTED\PLUGH or TRUSTED\XYZZY global groups, of which you are a member.

- Permissions can be assigned to local groups in the TRUST-ING domain, which in turn have your user account or your global group accounts as members.

By far the best alternative is the third. If you set up a local group account, you can collect global users and groups from as many domains as you want. Then you can change all permissions for all the collected objects simply by changing permissions for the single local group.

Figure 12.2 shows how local groups can improve management efficiency. Now the domain TRUSTING has two trusted

domains: TRUSTED1 and TRUSTED2. The local group
TRUSTING\ALPHA collects global groups from both trusted
domains.

FIGURE 12.2

A trusting domain that trusts
two domains.

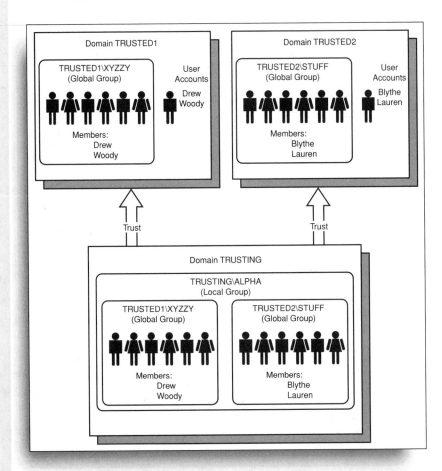

Trusts: An Analogy

Trust relationships are difficult to understand, so let's try to find an analogy. Suppose
that your company has offices in Chicago and Boston. Each office has its own security
staff and keeps its own security access logs.

Albert, from the Boston office, is visiting Chicago and needs access to the Xyzzy project. Here's how things might work:

1. The security officer in Chicago calls Boston and says, "I've got Albert here. His
   badge number is 231956. Can you authenticate him?"

2. Boston looks up Albert's records and verifies that he is an employee with Level 2
   security access. This information is relayed back to Chicago.

Trusts: An Analogy
continued

3. Because Chicago trusts Boston, the security officer in Chicago accepts Albert's credentials. Albert's Level 2 security clearance is sufficient to give him access to the
Xyzzy project, so Albert gets in.

Albert has no local records in Chicago. But because Chicago trusts Boston, records in
Boston can be used to authenticate Albert and establish his security group memberships.

You could assign individual permissions to TRUSTED1\Drew,
TRUSTED2\Blythe, TRUSTED1\XYZZY, and
TRUSTED2\STUFF but it would be a darn nuisance
if the permissions changed. If everything is a member of
TRUSTING\ALPHA, one change affects everyone.

Two-Way Trust Relationships

A trust relationship is a one-way street. In Figure 12.1,
TRUSTED *does not* trust TRUSTING. Suppose that users log
on to TRUSTING. The administrator of TRUSTED cannot
perform the same magic that you just saw in the TRUSTING
domain.

Figure 12.3 shows an important relationship between trusted
and trusting domains. Users in the trusted domain can use
resources in the trusting domain. But users in the trusting
domain cannot use resources in the trusted domain.

Two-way trusts require two trust relationships. In Figure 12.4,
BLIVETS trusts WIDGETS and WIDGETS trusts BLIVETS.
This allows the administrator of either domain to assign permissions based on user and group memberships created in the other
domain.

Pass-Through Authentication

Pass-through authentication permits a bit of logon sleight of
hand. Figure 12.5 illustrates a common network situation. User
Marie has a user account in Widgets but is not currently logged
on. She attempts to log on to the domain Blivets, but does not

have a user account in Blivets. Thanks to pass-through authentication, Marie is able to log on to Blivets without taking any special steps. It works like this:

1. Marie logs on to the Blivets domain, entering her user name and password from Widgets.

FIGURE 12.3
Trusting and usage between domains.

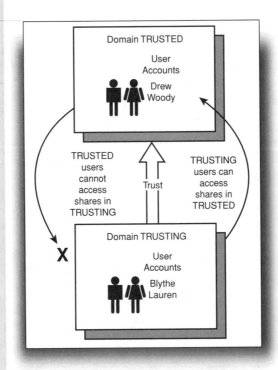

2. Blivets doesn't know anything about a user named Marie, but Blivets does trust Widgets, which has a user account named Marie.

3. Blivets sends the user name Marie to Widgets, along with Marie's password, to Widgets for authentication.

4. If Widgets validates Marie's logon, Blivets is notified that Marie is authenticated.

5. Blivets uses the trust relationship, accepts the logon authentication from Widgets, and gives Marie appropriate local permission.

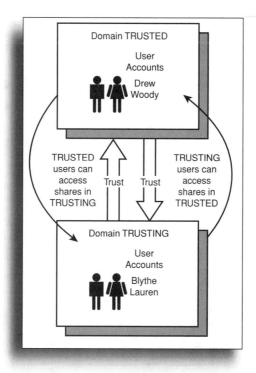

FIGURE 12.4
Two trust relationships establish a two-way trust.

Pass-through authentication makes a potentially sticky situation a piece of cake.

Pass-through authentication can also take place after a user has logged on. Suppose that a user requires access to a resource in a trusting domain. If the user has not been authenticated, the trusting domain will attempt to authenticate the user through its trusted domains. If the user has the same username and password in another domain, pass-through authentication is completely transparent. If the trusting domain cannot locate a matching user account, it will present a logon dialog box, enabling the user to log on using a different username.

Trusts Are Not Transitive

An important thing to remember about trusts is that they are not transitive. Figure 12.6 shows what that means:

- Domain B trusts A
- Domain C trusts B
- Domain C does not trust A

FIGURE 12.5

Pass-through authentication.

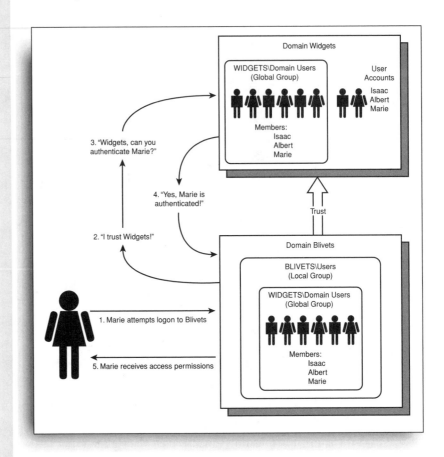

FIGURE 12.6

Because trusts are not transitive, domain C does not trust A.

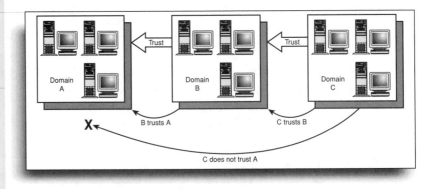

In other words, the trust relationship does not flow through domain B. If domain C must trust domain A, an explicit trust relationship must be established as in Figure 12.7.

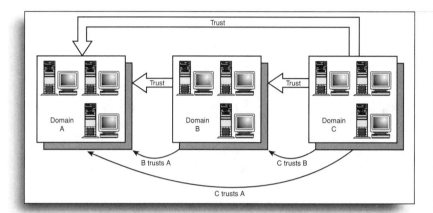

FIGURE 12.7

An explicit trust relationship enables C to trust A.

Multi-Domain Models

Until now, we have focused primarily on single-domain networks, a design Microsoft refers to as the *single-domain model*. If you must expand your network to multiple domains, it is useful to be aware of some basic models that suggest how multi-domain networks can be organized.

Microsoft has defined three models for multi-domain networks:

- **Master domain model**. One domain is used to authenticate user logons. Additional domains contain shared resources.

- **Multiple-master domain model**. Two or more domains authenticate user logons. Separate domains contain shared resources.

- **Complete trust**. Many domains trust each other to authenticate user logons in a fairly informal relationship.

As you might suspect, each model has advantages and disadvantages, so you need to investigate each in turn.

The Master Domain Model

The primary function of the master domain model is to allow domains to specialize. One domain is devoted entirely to processing user logons. Additional domains are devoted to sharing resources. With this division of labor, the processing of logons does not slow down computers that are serving files, printers, or applications.

Figure 12.8 shows a master domain network. The domain Malaprop is the master domain, used to authenticate all logons. The domains Widgets and Blivets are *resource* domains, which users access for shared resources.

FIGURE **12.8**

A network with a single master domain.

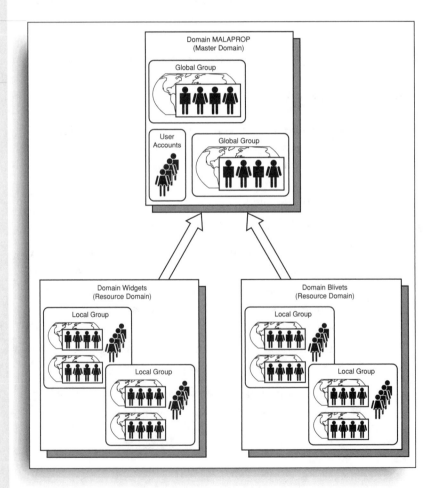

Because Malaprop authenticates all logons, the domains Widgets and Blivets do not require any user accounts of their own. They each have an Administrator user account (which cannot be disabled), although it is not typically used to administer the domains. The Guest account is disabled.

So, if the local Administrator user is not employed to manage Widgets and Blivets, who administers the resource domains? Anyone who is a member of the Malaprop\Domain Admins can be made an administrator of Widgets and Blivets simply by adding Malaprop\Domain Admins to the memberships of the Administrators groups in Widgets and Blivets. Recall that Domain Admins is a global group and can, therefore, be referenced in trusting domains. And Administrators is a local group that can have global groups as members.

If you want general users in Malaprop to be users in Widgets and Blivets, you simply include Malaprop\Domain Users in the Users groups of Widgets and Blivets. The principle is the same as you saw with Domain Admins: global groups can be members of local groups in any trusting domain.

In some cases, departments might want to administer their own resource domains. They have two choices:

- They can create their own administrator user accounts in the resource domains, in which case their administrators must log on to the resource domains separately.

- They can add individual users from the Malaprop domain into the Administrators groups of the resource domains, instead of including all members of Domain Admins.

By and large, I prefer the second alternative, which retains the concept of a single, central security database.

Master domain networks have several advantages:

- Security management is centralized.

- Resource domains can be established as required to organize resources logically.

- Browsing activity is distributed through the resource domains.

- Global groups in the master domain can be easily used to establish permissions in the resource domains.

- Departments have the option of managing their own resources without the need to administer user accounts for all users in the organization.

The chief limitation of a master domain network is that all logon activity is focused on a single domain, raising the possibility of performance bottlenecks at times of peak logon activity. You might need more than one master domain to make the master domain concept work in a large organization. Typically, a master domain can support at most 26,000 user and computer accounts.

For the right organization, however, a single master domain approach will result in better performance than is possible with a single domain. If you feel your organization is outgrowing a single domain, adding a master logon domain should be one of the first corrective techniques you try.

The Multiple Master Domain Model

The multiple master domain model extends on the single master domain model by adding logon domains. This is the primary technique that enables Windows NT Server networks to meet the needs of large organizations.

Figure 12.9 shows a simple network that is organized around two master domains with each master domain supporting about half the network accounts.

Your first reaction may be that you are starting to get a lot of trust relationships. Well, trust relationships proliferate quite readily as domains are added to a network. This network is simple compared to some you will encounter. Let's analyze the trust networks that are required.

A two-way trust relationship has been established between the two master domains, Malaprop1 and Malaprop2. This enables administrators of either domain to manage the other master domain. Also, to enable administrators to manage either domain, the following group memberships are assigned:

- Malaprop2\Domain Admins is a member of Malaprop1\Administrators.

- Malaprop1\Domain Admins is a member of Malaprop2\Administrators.

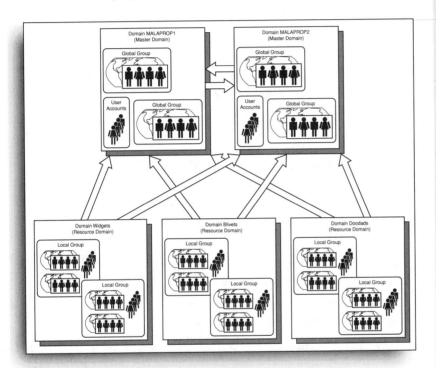

FIGURE 12.9
A network with two master domains.

Each resource domain must trust each master domain so that either master domain can authenticate logons. The following group memberships enable administrators of Malaprop1 and Malaprop2 to manage all the resource domains:

- Malaprop1\Domain Admins is a member of Widgets\Administrators.

- Malaprop1\Domain Admins is a member of Blivets\Administrators.

- Malaprop1\Domain Admins is a member of Doodads\Administrators.

- Malaprop2\Domain Admins is a member of Widgets\Administrators.
- Malaprop2\Domain Admins is a member of Blivets\Administrators.
- Malaprop2\Domain Admins is a member of Doodads\Administrators.

Similarly, the Domain Users groups for Malaprop1 and Malaprop2 must be added to the Users groups for Widgets, Blivets, and Doodads. That will enable users to access files in any resource domain, regardless of the domain they use to log on.

The sample network, with two master domains and three resource domains, requires eight trust relationships. Let's see what a simple network expansion does to the trust relationship count. Figure 12.10 shows a network with three master domains and four resource domains. To fully configure the network, you need

- Two trust relationships between each pair of master domains, for a total of six
- Three trust relationships per resource domain, one each for each master domain, for a total of 12

So, a slight network expansion has taken you from eight to 18 trust relationships! The moral is, add domains only when necessary. Typically, you should let performance be your guide. Add master domains when logon performance lags.

The multiple master domain model has several desirable features:

- It is scalable to organizations of any size.
- Security is managed centrally.
- Departments can manage resource domains if that is desired.
- Related users, groups, and resources can be grouped logically into domains.

Add your own groups

If this were your network, you might want to add other global groups to the master domains. You might add global groups for specialized departments, for example, such as Personnel, Sales, or Accounting. These global groups can then be used to grant access to specific shares in the resource domains.

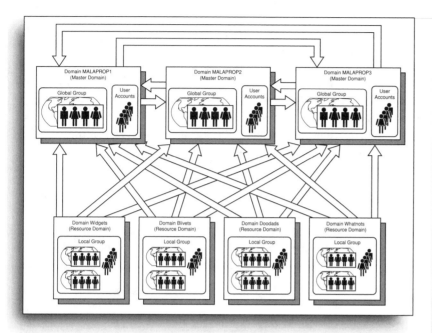

FIGURE 12.10
A network with three master domains.

There are some disadvantages, however:

- Trust relationships multiply rapidly as the number of domains increases.

- Accounts are not concentrated in a single SAM database, so you must document the relationships between user accounts, groups, and master domains.

If expanded unwarily, a multiple master domain network can become unwieldy. Certainly three or four master domains is a desirable maximum, but recall that a logon domain theoretically can support 26,000 users, enabling a network with three master domains to support 78,000 users.

The Complete Trust Model

When Windows NT was fairly new, Microsoft presented the complete trust model as an argument for the flexibility of the domain model. Microsoft has since backed away from this model because it can quickly become overly complex and it poses significant security concerns. Nevertheless, you'll learn about the complete trust model here for completeness.

The complete trust model comes into play when an organization does not have a central network management department. Then, either because they want to or because they have to, departments manage their own domains, establishing trust relationships with other departments as required.

Figure 12.11 shows a network with four domains that is organized around the complete trust model. Each domain can function as an independent entity. It has its own user accounts, groups, and shared resources. When users need to use resources in another domain, a trust relationship is put in and the administrators cooperate to set up the required groups and permissions.

FIGURE 12.11

A four-domain network that uses the complete trust model.

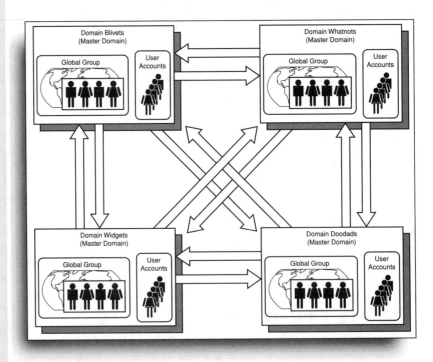

Trusts are fully developed in Figure 12.11. Each domain has a two-way trust with every other domain. If you tally up the trust relationships, you will arrive at a total of 12 for this four-domain network. That's not too bad.

Add another domain and things start to escalate, however. A five-domain network requires 20 trusts. If n is the number of domains, $n \times (n - 1)$ trust relationships are required if each domain trusts each. The numbers can quickly get out of hand.

However, the number of trust relationships isn't the big problem with the complete trust model. The problems arise because domain administration will almost certainly be inconsistent. Some domains will be managed with tight security policies, while others will be lax.

As a believer in tight network security, I prefer to avoid the complete trust model much as I prefer to avoid bubonic plague. I would be reluctant to let users access resources in my domain based on the policies and management skills of another department.

There are other complications with the complete trust model. Because it does not establish a central network management location, several tasks are made more complicated, including the following:

- Backup
- Network infrastructure management
- Email management
- User account naming standards
- Access security enforcement

Few departments have trained staff who can perform all these tasks well, and without a central network staff keeping a large network healthy is nearly impossible.

Although I don't put much stock in the complete trust model, here are some of the theoretical advantages Microsoft attributes to it:

- No central IS department is required.
- The model can be scaled to organizations of any size.
- Departments retain control of their users and resources.
- Users and groups are grouped departments.

Microsoft concedes these disadvantages:

- No central security authority is established.
- Many trust relationships are required.
- Departments are dependent on the management practices of other departments.

The disadvantages are, I believe, fatal. A network based on the complete trust model will almost certainly be plagued with inconsistent policies and practices, and it is difficult to see how it could function well.

Establishing Trust Relationships

Each trust relationship is established by two events, which occur in the following order:

1. A domain, known as the *trusted* domain, permits itself to be trusted by another domain, known as the *trusting* domain.

2. The trusting domain is configured to trust the trusted domain.

To illustrate, configure a trust relationship between Malaprop and Blivets. Malaprop is a master domain that will permit itself to be trusted by the Blivets resource domain.

Permitting Blivets to Trust Malaprop

First, an administrator of Malaprop must add Blivets to the list of domains that are permitted to trust Malaprop. The following steps show you how to permit a domain to trust another:

Permitting a domain to trust

1. Start the User Manager for Domains utility in the Administrative Tools folder.

2. Examine the title bar of User Manager to verify that you are managing the trusted domain. If you are not managing the trusted domain:

    a. Choose **Select Domain** from the **User** menu to open the Select Domain dialog box, shown in Figure 12.12.

Selecting domains

If your network has multiple domains, you must always ensure that you are managing the proper one. Always verify the domain in the title bar for User Manager for Domains before you perform any management actions. Change your domain by choosing the **Select Domain** command from the **User** menu.

FIGURE 12.12
Selecting the domain to be
managed.

b. Browse the domain list in the **Select Domains** box and
   select the trusted domain.

c. Click **OK** to exit the Select Domain dialog box.

3. Choose **Trust Relationships** from the **Policies** menu. The
Trust Relationships dialog box, shown in Figure 12.13,
appears.

FIGURE 12.13
The Trust Relationships dialog
box.

4. Click the **Add** button beside the **Trusting Domains** list.
This brings up the Add Trusting Domain dialog box. The
example shown in Figure 12.14 is adding Blivets to the list
of domains that trust the Malaprop domain.

FIGURE 12.14
Adding a trusting domain.

5. An optional password can be specified. If a password is specified, the password must be entered to enable the trusting
domain to complete the establishment of the trust relationship. If a password is specified, it must be entered in the
Initial P̲assword and **C̲onfirm Password** fields.

6. Click **OK**. When you return to the Trust Relationships dialog box, the domain you specified is added to the **Tr̲usting
Domains** list.

7. The **Cancel** button changes to **Close** after a domain has
been added or removed. Click **Close** to exit the dialog box.

Trusting Malaprop

Next, an administrator must add Malaprop to the list of trusted
domains for the Blivets domain. To complete the trust relationship in the trusting domain, perform the following actions:

Trusting a domain

1. Start the User Manager for Domains utility.

2. Examine the title bar of User Manager to verify that you are
managing the trusted domain. If you are not managing the
trusted domain:

    a. Choose **S̲elect Domain** from the **U̲ser** menu to open
the Select Domain dialog box, shown in Figure 12.12.

    b. Browse the domain list in the **S̲elect Domains** box and
select the trusted domain.

    c. Click **OK** to exit the Select Domain dialog box.

3. Choose **T̲rust Relationships** from the **P̲olicies** menu to
display the Trust Relationships dialog box.

4. Click the **A̲dd** button next to **Trusted Domains**. The Add
Trusted Domain dialog box, shown in Figure 12.15, appears.

FIGURE 12.15

The Add Trusted Domain
dialog box.

5. Enter the name of the domain to be trusted in the **Domain** field. If a password is specified by the trusted domain, enter the password in the **Password** field. Figure 12.15 shows a completed dialog box that adds Keystone to the domains that are trusted by Widgets.

6. Click **OK** to return to the Trust Relationships dialog box.

7. If all goes well, a message is displayed stating that `Trust Relationship with MALAPROP successfully established.`

   An error message results if the domains are unable to establish contact to confirm the trust relationship. An error also results if you have specified a domain name that does not exist or a password that does not match the password specified by the trusted domain.

8. Confirm that the domain has been added to the domains listed in the **Trusted Domains** box.

9. Click **Close** to close the Trust Relationships dialog box.

Granting Inter-Domain Permissions

Trusting another domain does not immediately give users in the trusted domain access to resources in the trusting domain. You also must grant permissions that enable users who log on through the trusted domain to access resources in the trusting domain. In most cases, you will add users or global groups in the trusted domain to local groups in the trusting domain.

Suppose that Malaprop includes a global group named All Engineers. The Blivets administrator wants to permit members of All Engineers to access specification documents in the \\Blivets1\Specs share, which shares files in C:\Specifications. This could be done in two ways:

- By explicitly granting permissions to Malaprop\All Engineers

- By adding Malaprop\All Engineers to a local group in the Blivets domain that has the required permission

Let's briefly look at both options.

Granting a Global Group Local Permissions

Assume that the Blivets\Specs share gives Full Control Permissions to Everyone. The NTFS permissions are more restricted, however, and group Everyone has no permissions to view files in C:\Specifications. As a consequence, even though the share offers Full Control permissions, no one has NTFS permissions to actually view the directory contents.

To let members of All Engineers view files in C:\Specifications, they must be given Read permissions to the folder. In this example, Read permissions are being assigned directly to the All Engineers group.

SEE ALSO

➤ *For more information on NTFS Permissions, see Chapter 10, "File Storage Systems."*

To give a remote global group permissions for a local folder, do the following:

Giving a global group local permissions

1. Log on with ownership or Full Control permissions for the directory being shared.

2. Access the folder in Explorer or My Computer.

3. Right-click the folder and select **Properties** from the context menu.

4. Select the **Security** tab and click the **Permissions** button.

5. In the Directory Permissions dialog box, click **Add** to open the Add Users and Groups dialog box, shown in Figure 12.16.

6. Open the **List Names From** list box and select the domain that contains the desired global group.

7. Select the global group in the **Names** list.

8. Click **Add** to copy the group name to the **Add Names** list.

9. Select the desired access permissions from the **Type of Access** list box.

10. Click **OK**.

A reminder about no access

Remember, you can't block Everyone by using the No Access permission because doing so would prevent all users from accessing the files, regardless of other permissions they might have.

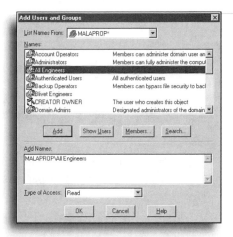

FIGURE 12.16
Adding a global group from another domain to local directory permissions.

Adding a Global Group to a Local Group

Rather than granting a global group permissions in a local domain, it is preferable to create a local group that is given the required permissions. Then you can add global groups from other domains to the local group. This works better because the local group serves as a collecting point for groups and users from all trusted domains, enabling you to focus permission assignments on a single entity.

To make a global group a member of a local group, do the following:

Making a global group or user a member of a local group

1. Log on as an Administrator.

2. Open User Manager for Domains

3. Create the local group.

4. Select the local group and choose **Properties** from the **User** menu.

5. In the Local Group Properties dialog box, click **Add** to open the Add Users and Groups dialog box, shown in Figure 12.16.

6. Pull down the **List Names From** list box and select the domain that has the global group or user you want to add.

7. Select the group or user and click **A**dd.

8. Repeat steps 6 and 7 for each group or user to be added.

9. Click **OK** when all groups and users have been added.

Removing Trust Relationships

Two steps are required to remove a trust relationship. The trusting domain must stop trusting the trusted domain, and the trusted domain must cancel its permission to be trusted.

Removing a Trust Relationship

Removing a domain from the trust relationships is accomplished by following these steps:

Removing a trust relationship

1. Log on as a domain administrator for the trusting domain Widgets and start the User Manager for Domains utility.

2. Choose **S**elect **Domain** from the **U**ser menu. In the Select Domain dialog box, select the trusting domain whose trust relationship is to be removed.

3. Choose **T**rust Relationships from the **Policies** menu to display the Trust Relationships dialog box.

4. In the **T**rusted Domains list, select the domain to be removed. Then click **R**emove (located beside the **Trusted Domains** list).

   Because canceling a trust relationship can have far-reaching effects, User Manager for Domains displays the warning shown in Figure 12.17.

FIGURE 12.17

You see this warning when canceling a trust relationship.

5. Click **Yes** to complete the action. You are returned to the Trust Relationships dialog box, and the domain you removed is no longer listed.

6. Click **Close** to exit the Trust Relationships dialog box.

Canceling Permission to Trust a Domain

Next, an administrator on the trusted domain must cancel permission to trust the domain. Canceling a trust permission is accomplished with this procedure:

Canceling a trust permission

1. Log on to the trusted domain as a domain administrator and start the User Manager for Domains utility in the Administrative Tools folder.

2. Choose **Trust Relationships** from the **Policies** menu to display the Trust Relationships dialog box.

3. In the **Trusting Domains** list, select the domain to be removed. Then click **Remove** (located beside the **Trusting Domains** list).

   Because this action also can create havoc on the LAN, User Manager for Domains displays a warning message.

4. Click **Yes** to complete the action. You are returned to the Trust Relationships dialog box, and the domain you removed no longer is listed.

5. Click **Close** to exit the Trust Relationships dialog box.

After the trust relationship has been removed on both the trusting and the trusted server, the complete trust relationship has been removed.

Planning Multi-Domain Networks with WANs

When you were introduced to domains in Chapter 4, "Building a Domain," you learned that WANs impose special requirements on domain setup. Specifically, to reduce traffic through the WAN link, it is highly desirable to place a BDC at each remote site so that users are enabled to log on locally. Now you have a network with multiple domains. How does a WAN affect a multi-domain network?

Essentially, you still should locate a BDC for each master domain at each remote site. Figure 12.18 shows a WAN that incorporates three domains:

- Malaprop is the master domain, which all users use to log on.
- Widgets is a local resource domain that is used only by users in the Widgets division, which is located at the main site for Malaprop.
- Blivets is a remote resource domain that is separated from the Malaprop site by a WAN link.

The network is not very complex. The only special twist is that a BDC for Malaprop has been placed at the remote Blivets site so that Blivets users do not generate WAN traffic when logging on. Because users do not log on to the Blivets domain, it is unnecessary to locate a Blivets BDC at the main Malaprop site.

Now for the Big Time

You are now ready to start building really big networks. The master domain model enables you to differentiate between the security and resource functions of the network. Master domains control user logon and authentication, and you can distribute domain controllers throughout your network to allow users to log on to local domain controllers. Resource domains can be placed close to users so that the majority of required resources are "nearby" in network terms; that is, they can be accessed without crossing a WAN link.

That brings you to the question of building WANs. What if your network must grow beyond the confines of a single site? Although you can configure WANs using the tools you have seen so far, using the NWLink protocol, the overwhelming choice for WAN protocols is TCP/IP. The TCP/IP suite protocols make the Internet work, so you know they can run really big networks. And, because there is a high likelihood that you will want your network to talk to the Internet in any case, you must face up to the task of learning TCP/IP.

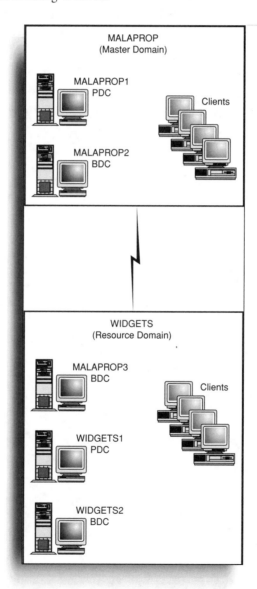

FIGURE 12.18

Implementing a master domain model on a WAN.

NWLink is practically a gimme. You must learn how to assign network numbers and activate routing, but that's about as complex as network configuration gets with NWLink. TCP/IP is a completely different story. You must know TCP/IP at several levels. That's why the next five chapters are devoted to setting up the TCP/IP network infrastructure. So, take a break, relax with Solitaire for a bit, and then we will embark into the world of TCP/IP.

Essential TCP/IP Concepts

Microsoft's TCP/IP architecture

Computer addressing on TCP/IP networks

Computer names on Microsoft TCP/IP networks

Computer names on the Internet

TCP/IP routing

TCP/IP is the common language of the network world. These days, when computers need to talk to computers, it's a safe assumption that they will communicate using TCP/IP.

The TCP/IP protocols did not always display the exalted and omnipresent aura they show today. In the 1980s, TCP/IP was considered by many to be a nonstandard set of informal protocols that were found primarily in the esoteric realm of the Internet, an environment frequented by educators, computer wizards, and defense contractors. International standards bodies were developing official protocols that were expected to put TCP/IP out to pasture before too long.

Today, however, TCP/IP has become the dominant network protocol suite with hardly a viable competitor in sight, the international effort to establish competing protocols having died a quiet death. The difference has been the stodginess of the international standards process versus the vitality of the Internet. Indeed, the success of TCP/IP is a market-driven phenomenon, propelled by consumer demand and the desire to make a buck.

TCP/IP has become so dominant that sooner or later your network is going to need to talk TCP/IP, because sooner or later it is going to need to talk to another network—the Internet or some other—that talks only TCP/IP. That's good and bad; good because TCP/IP is an excellent protocol suite, offering good performance and use of network bandwidth. It's bad because until you are used to it, TCP/IP is a lot of trouble to set up and manage.

Until this chapter, we have been working in a Plug-and-Play world where network protocols are concerned. As you learned in Chapter 3, "Configuring Network Adapters, Services, and Protocols," NetBEUI requires no configuration at all, whereas NWLink must be configured only when routing is required. There is so much to configuring TCP/IP, on the other hand, that we need a chapter of background information before we can even begin to set up TCP/IP on a network.

My intention is to keep things as simple and practical as possible. I'll have to give you some theory, but it will be theory that you will immediately put into practice, not theory that you will put into practice "someday."

This is the theory chapter, and we're going to cover five specific topics:

- Microsoft's TCP/IP architecture
- How computer addresses are assigned
- How computer names work on Microsoft TCP/IP networks
- How computer names are managed on the Internet
- How TCP/IP handles routing

Those five topics—and I'll keep the discussion as short as possible—establish a foundation that will take us through the subsequent chapters, which cover TCP/IP implementation.

SEE ALSO

➤ *The material in this chapter simplifies—perhaps over-simplifies—TCP/IP technology. I'm telling you enough to get started, but more could be said. If you live for detail, please see my book* Networking with Microsoft TCP/IP, *available from New Riders Publishing.*

Microsoft's TCP/IP Architecture

Microsoft has a somewhat unique way of organizing protocol suites. The architecture is organized around two key requirements:

- The need to support TCP/IP alongside NWLink and NetBEUI
- The need to support NetBIOS applications in the TCP/IP environment

SEE ALSO

➤ *To review material on Managing NetBEUI and NWLink Networks, turn to page 83.*

Figure 13.1 shows how the pieces of the Microsoft network architecture fit together.

One component of the network protocol architecture is NDIS, the Network Driver Interface Specification, which lets any network protocol communicate with any network adapter. NDIS lets all NT protocols communicate through a single network adapter should the need arise.

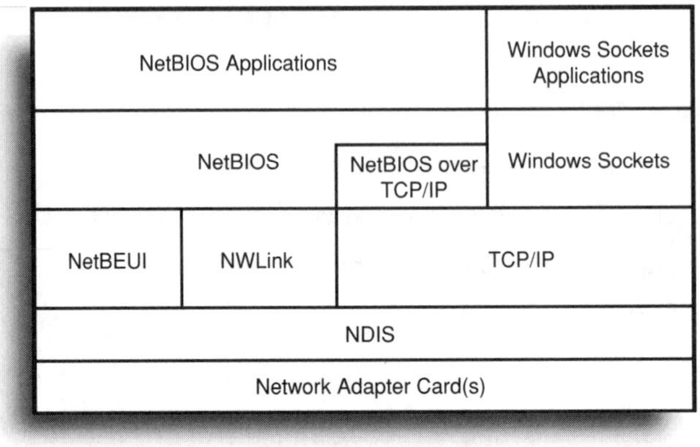

FIGURE 13.1

Microsoft's network protocol architecture.

NetBIOS Applications		Windows Sockets Applications
NetBIOS	NetBIOS over TCP/IP	Windows Sockets
NetBEUI	NWLink	TCP/IP
NDIS		
Network Adapter Card(s)		

Microsoft provides *application programming interfaces* (APIs) that developers use to adapt their programs to the network environment. Notice that Microsoft's architecture supports two APIs:

- **NetBIOS** is the *network basic input/output system*, a fairly old API that has long been the primary API for applications running on Microsoft networks. Most applications written to network on Microsoft networks are written to the NetBIOS API.

- **Windows Sockets** (WinSock) is Microsoft's implementation of the *sockets* API that has become the primary API for TCP/IP applications. The applications you think of as Internet applications, such as Web browsers and FTP clients, are written for the Windows Sockets interface.

But that leaves a hole. What if I want to run only TCP/IP protocols on my network, but I don't want to abandon my venerable NetBIOS applications? Well, Microsoft has an answer for that as well, called *NetBIOS over TCP/IP* (*NetBT* or *NBT* for short). Thanks to NetBT, any Windows application can network over TCP/IP with no adaptation whatsoever.

Computer Addressing on TCP/IP Networks

TCP/IP predates just about all other networking standards that remain in common use. When the Internet was still a project of the United States Department of Defense and was named ARPAnet (for Advanced Research Projects Agency Network), the idea of a global network that embraced many different brands of computers was as exotic as interstellar travel. No one had formed even a fuzzy vision of how such a network might be implemented. So, the gurus had complete freedom to design a network solution. But freedom brings with it the opportunity to be unique, and some of the technologies on the Internet are definitely unique.

One unique characteristic of the Internet is the way computers are identified. The designers of the Internet protocols wanted an identification scheme that was independent of any one computer or network equipment design. So they established a scheme of *IP addresses*. (IP, or Internet protocol, is one of the two most prominent TCP/IP protocols, and is the protocol in the TCP/IP protocol suite that is most intimately concerned with addressing.)

You've almost certainly seen IP addresses while surfing the Web, numbers like 192.168.153.80. As you administer TCP/IP on your network, a considerable part of your time will be devoted to IP address assignment, because IP addresses don't just happen. They have to be entered manually into the configuration of each TCP/IP computer on your network. When a computer is added to your network, it needs an IP address. When it moves, it probably needs a new IP address.

So, you have to understand how IP addresses work. Unfortunately, IP address rules are a bit subtle, and errors are common. I will hazard a guess that IP address misconfiguration will be the most common cause of difficulty you will experience with TCP/IP networking.

IP Addresses and Dotted-Decimal Notation

An IP address is really a pretty simple thing. It is just a 32-bit binary like the following:

11001101101101110010001001101110

Did I say simple? How would you like to remember a few dozen of those? Well, even network gurus blanch at the thought of committing 32-bit numbers to memory, so they devised a system that codes IP addresses in more familiar binary numbers.

To display an IP address in decimal form, the first step is to break the binary address into four 8-bit fields, like this:

`11001101 10110111 00100010 01101110`

Each of these 8-bit fields—they're usually called *octets*, incidentally—can be represented by a decimal number in the range of 0 through 255. If you're not comfortable with number conversions, take a look at Figure 13.2. Notice that each digit position corresponds to a power of 2. For example, the third digit from the right corresponds to 2^2, or 4.

FIGURE 13.2

Converting an 8-bit binary number to decimal.

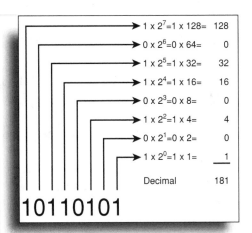

To convert a binary number to decimal, examine each bit position. If the bit is a 1, the corresponding decimal number is included in the decimal total. If the bit is a 0, that bit does not affect the decimal total. Add up the decimal values corresponding to each 1 bit and you arrive at the decimal equivalent of the 8-bit binary number.

Fortunately, you don't need to convert more than 8 bits, because IP addresses are commonly represented in *dotted-decimal notation* where a decimal number represents each 8-bit group. Figure 13.3 shows an example.

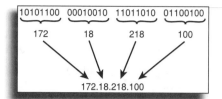

FIGURE 13.3
Converting an IP address to dotted-decimal notation.

Isn't that simple? Well, perhaps not. At least not simple enough to make the head math easy for most of us. Fortunately, Windows includes a shortcut. The Windows Calculator applet has a scientific mode that includes number base conversion functions. Figure 13.4 shows Calculator after it has been placed in scientific mode.

FIGURE 13.4
Converting numbers in the Windows Calculator applet.

To convert a number to another base, do the following:

Converting a number to another base

1. Open the Calculator applet and choose **Scientific** from the **View** menu.

2. Select the radio button that matches the base of the number you want to convert (**Hex**adecimal, **Dec**imal, **Oct**al, or **Bin**ary).

3. Enter the number to be converted. (You can paste a number you have copied from another application.)

4. Select the radio button that matches the base you want to convert to (**Hex**adecimal, **Dec**imal, **Oct**al, or **Bin**ary). The result is displayed in the number entry field. (You can copy the results from Calculator and paste them elsewhere if you want.)

Although users see dotted-decimal addresses if they see addresses at all, as an administrator you must be aware of the binary equivalents of IP addresses. This is particularly the case when you get involved with subnet addressing, where the binary bit patterns are crucial information.

Address Classes

Each host on a TCP/IP network—*host* is another term for a device that is attached to a TCP/IP network—must have a unique IP address that distinguishes it from all other hosts on that network. That means that every host that can communicate with the Internet must have an IP address that is unique on the entire Internet.

Actually, a host's IP address contains two pieces of information:

- netid is the network to which the host is attached.
- hostid is the host's unique ID on its network.

Because the IP address serves two functions, the Internet designers had to decide how many bits of the IP address would serve as the netid and how many bits would serve as the hostid. Did the Internet need a few networks with many hosts per network, or did it need a large number of networks with few hosts per network? Well, the answer was, "Both, and we need something in between as well." That answer resulted in the establishment of *address classes*.

You will encounter three address classes: A, B, and C. Class A defines a few networks, each of which can contain a vast number of hosts. Class C defines many networks, each of which can contain a couple hundred hosts. Class B falls somewhere between A and C.

Figure 13.5 shows how the IP address classes are defined. The key differences between the classes are the numbers of bits that are allocated to the netid and hostid portions of the address. Here's how the address classes play out:

- **Class A** addresses have 8 bits in the netid portion and 24 bits in the hostid portion. There are 126 class A networks available, each of which accommodates 16,777,214 hosts. A class A address has a 0 for the initial bit, and the first octet will have a decimal value between 1 and 126. (Networks 0 and 127 have special uses.)

- **Class B** addresses have 16 bits in the netid portion and 16 bits in the hostid portion. 16,384 class B networks are possible, each supporting 65,534 hosts. A class B address begins with the bits 10, and the value of the first octet falls in the range 128 through 191.

- **Class C** addresses have 24 bits in the netid portion and 8 bits in the hostid portion. Consequently, 2,097,152 class C network addresses are available, each of which can have 254 hosts. A class C address begins with the bits 110, and the value of the first octet falls in the range 192 through 223.

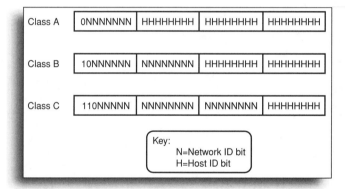

FIGURE 13.5
IP network address classes.

If you take a close look at the bits and try to confirm my totals for netids and hostids, you'll find that the sums aren't what you might expect. That's because some bit patterns aren't available for hosts. Here are some restrictions.

- Address 255 (all 1s in binary) is used to address *broadcast* messages, which are received by all hosts on a given network. The most common broadcast address is 255.255.255.255, which addresses messages that are to be received by all hosts on the local network.

- The fourth octet cannot be all 1s or all 0s in binary. A hostid that is all 0s refers to this network. So, the IP address

155.38.0.0 refers to the entire network with the netid 155.38. A hostid that is all 1s is a broadcast address, referring to all hosts on a specific network.

- The netid cannot be all 0s because all 0s means "this network." That's why the class A network number 0 is unavailable.

- Netid 127 is a reserved address called the *loopback address*, and is used in testing.

Figure 13.6 shows a network that demonstrates the use of IP addresses. This network consists of four network segments that communicate through routers. Although it is improbable, I have included examples of all three classes of network addresses in the figure. You can freely mix address classes on your networks. The routers will sort things out.

FIGURE 13.6

A TCP/IP network that includes addresses from all IP address classes.

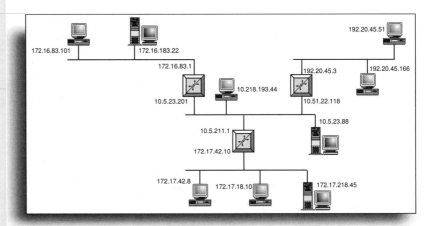

Notice that each network segment is associated with a single netid. All hosts on a given network segment are given IP addresses that share a common netid.

Routers attach to the network as ordinary hosts. A router is assigned an IP address on each network to which it is attached. Actually, and this is an important distinction, the IP address isn't assigned to the router, but to the interface in the router. So, a router has at least two interfaces, each of which is assigned its own IP address.

Networks 172.16.0.0 and 172.17.0.0 were included to illustrate how class B and C netids work. Even though both networks have 172 as the first octet of their IP addresses, these are class B networks (first octet 128 through 192). Therefore, the netid is defined by two octets, and 155.38.0.0 and 155.39.0.0 function as separate network segments. Because a class C netid is defined by three octets, any difference in the first three octets of a class C address refer to different networks.

IP Address Assignment

If you are running a private TCP/IP network, you can choose any IP addresses you want for your hosts. If, on the other hand, your network will be connecting to the Internet, you must use assigned IP addresses that don't conflict with anyone else.

Until fairly recently, organizations requested IP addresses directly from the Internet Network Information Center (InterNIC), but that seldom happens these days because the Internet has simply grown too big for a single point of contact to handle the demand for access. The current practice for most organizations wanting to connect to the Internet is to obtain access from an Internet service provider (ISP) that provides you with an Internet hookup (for a fee, of course) and assigns you a block of IP addresses. The InterNIC prefers to work with a relatively few ISPs, assigning them blocks of addresses that they in turn allocate to their customers.

You can no longer obtain a class A or B address. In fact, class C addresses are scarce. Your ISP probably won't assign you a complete class C address unless you really need it. You may be given use of a portion of a class C address. OK, so how do you use part of an address range? Thanks for asking, because the technique for subdividing address ranges is my next topic.

Subnet Addressing

As you might suspect, a class A or B address is a pretty big thing. It is difficult to imagine a network with 16 million hosts—or even 65,000 hosts—and not a single router, but that is what it would take to use up a class A or B address.

Now that they had an address space, the Internet community discovered that many of the IP address ranges were too large. A way was needed to subdivide the addresses so that portions of the address space could be allocated to multiple network segments. The mechanism they arrived at is called *subnet addressing*.

We come now to one of the most challenging topics in this book. Many TCP/IP newbies find subnet addressing the highest hurdle they must clear, so don't be surprised if you find this material difficult. Just hang in, and I'll make sure you get a grasp of the concept.

Subnet addressing is a method for "borrowing" bits from the hostid portion of an IP address so that the bits can be applied to the network ID.

SEE ALSO

➤ *For more information on subnetting and routing, see page 471.*

Subnetting a Class B Address

Suppose that you have been assigned the Class B address 172.16.0.0. You need to create four separate networks from your one IP address range. The technique is to borrow three bits from the hostid field. These three bits let you configure six separate subnets. (Why not eight? I'll tell you later.)

To see how subnet addressing works, let's first convert the IP address to binary form:

```
10101100 00010000 00000000 00000000
```

Remember, in a class B address, the first 16 bits are the netid and the last 16 bits are the hostid.

To indicate that bits are being borrowed from the hostid, we make use of a *subnet mask*, which is also a 32-bit binary number. To make the purpose of the subnet mask clear, we need to examine it beside the binary IP address, like this:

```
10101100 00010000 00000000 00000000

11111111 11111111 11100000 00000000
```

Subnet masks are typically represented just like IP addresses, in dotted-decimal notation. The subnet mask used in the example is

`11111111 11111111 11100000 00000000`

That has the dotted-decimal equivalent of 255.255.224.0.

There are only a few common subnet masks, making them easy to remember. Here they are, with their decimal equivalents:

Subnet Mask	Decimal
10000000	128
11000000	196
11100000	224
11110000	240
11111000	248
11111100	252
11111110	254
11111111	255

The rules of subnet masking are extremely simple:

- **1** in the network mask indicates that a bit in the IP address is part of the netid.

- **0** in the network mask indicates that a bit in the IP address is part of the hostid.

Because there are 19 bits in the network mask, we now have 19 bits to work with in the netid. This lets us generate the following subnetwork IDs (subnetids) from the class B address:

`10101100 00010000 00100000 00000000`

`10101100 00010000 01000000 00000000`

`10101100 00010000 01100000 00000000`

`10101100 00010000 10000000 00000000`

```
10101100 00010000 10100000 00000000

10101100 00010000 11000000 00000000
```

Why only six subnets? We have to avoid two "forbidden" subnets (000 and 111), which are explained in an upcoming section.

If you do the math to convert the binary addresses to decimal, you find that the subnet mask 255.255.224.0 lets us construct six subnets with the following address ranges:

172.16.32.1 through 172.16.63.254

through 172.16.95.254

through 172.16.127.254

through 172.16.159.254

through 172.16.191.25

172.16.192.1 through 172.16.223.254

The subnet mask actually becomes part of the configuration of each host on the network, enabling the hosts to discriminate netid, subnetid, and hostid.

Let's put subnetting to work. Figure 13.7 shows an example of a network that is entirely based on the IP address 172.16.0.0. To determine what network segment a host is connected to, you must apply the subnet mask to its IP address.

A word about subnets

The terms *subnet* and *subnetwork* are used a bit inconsistently. Often, they refer to a part of a network where subnet addressing has been employed. However, the terms are used more generally to describe any section of a network that is bounded by routers, even if the network section is identified by a nonsubnetted IP address.

FIGURE 13.7

Subnet addressing with a class B address.

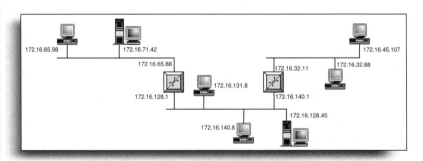

Take host 172.16.89.33, for example. Because this is a class B address, the netid consists of the first two octets and is 172.16. To figure out the subnetid, we need to apply the subnet mask to the third octet, which is binary 1011001. Here's the address octet next to the subnet mask:

10110001

11100000

So the subnetid portion is 101 and the hostid portion is 10001.

Which hosts can occupy the same subnet? The third octet for the subnet can have a value between 10100000 and 10111111, or between 160 and 191 decimal. In other words, any host with an IP address between 172.16.160.1 and 172.16.191.254 can be on the same subnet.

Netids, Subnetids, and Routers

To enable two hosts to communicate without a router, four conditions must be met:

- The hosts must be connected to the same network segment
- The host's IP addresses must have the same netid
- The hosts must be configured with the same subnet mask
- The hosts must have the same subnetid

Failing any of these conditions, a router is required to allow the hosts to communicate.

SEE ALSO

➤ *For more information on IP routing, see page 471.*

➤ *For more information on networks, see Chapter 1, "Setting Up Your Network."*

"Forbidden" Subnets

I've alluded a couple of times to the fact that some subnets are not permitted by the Internet standard that defines subnetwork addressing.

The first restriction applies to all TCP/IP implementations: the subnetid cannot consist entirely of 1s because all-1s addresses are used to address broadcast messages.

A second restriction is that the subnetid cannot consist entirely of 0s. Actually, there really isn't a good reason to prohibit the all-0s subnet, and avoiding the all-0s subnet wastes valuable address space. So in practice many have chosen to support the all-0s subnets on their products. Windows NT permits use of the all-0s subnet, although I have never seen the fact stated in Microsoft documentation.

More Subnet Examples

Because it is so important for you to understand subnet addressing, let's do some exercises.

Exercise 1

Problem: For the IP address 10.86.45.3 and subnet mask 255.255.0.0, answer the following questions:

- What is the netid of the IP address?
- What is the subnetid of the IP address?
- What is the hostid of the IP address?
- What host IP addresses permit hosts to communicate directly with this host, assuming all hosts are connected to the same network segment?

Solution: The first step is to determine the class of the IP address. Because the first octet has the value 10, it is a class A address, and the netid consists of the first octet. Therefore, the netid is 10.

The subnet mask reserves 16 bits for the network address. The first 8 bits are the netid, so the next 8 bits, the entire second octet, make up the subnet ID. Now we know that the subnetid is 86.

The subnet mask leaves 16 bits for host addressing. Consequently, the hostid of this host is 45.3.

This host can communicate with hosts having IP addresses 10.86.0.1 through 10.86.255.254, assuming that all the hosts can communicate without crossing a router.

Example 2

Problem: For the IP address 192.168.45.109 and subnet mask 255.255.255.240, answer the following questions:

- What is the netid of the IP address?
- What is the subnetid of the IP address?
- What is the hostid of the IP address?

- What host IP addresses permit hosts to communicate directly with this host, assuming all hosts are connected to the same network segment?

Solution: Because the first octet has the value 192, this is a class C address, and the netid consists of the first three octets. Therefore, the netid is 192.168.45.

The subnet mask 11110000 reserves 4 bits for the network address. The fourth octet is 01101101 binary, making the subnetid 0110.

The subnet mask leaves 4 bits for host addressing. Consequently, the hostid of this host is 1101 decimal.

With this subnet mask, the fourth octet can have binary values 01100000 through 01101111. But a hostid cannot be all 0s or all 1s. Therefore, valid values for the fourth octet are 01100001 through 01101110. Consequently, this host can communicate with hosts having IP addresses 192.168.45.97 through 192.168.45.110, assuming that all the hosts can communicate without crossing a router.

Example 3

Problem: For the IP address 192.168.87.95 and subnet mask 255.255.255.224, answer the following questions:

- What is the netid of the IP address?
- What is the subnetid of the IP address?
- What is the hostid of the IP address?
- What host IP addresses permit hosts to communicate directly with this host, assuming all hosts are connected to the same network segment?

Solution: Because the first octet has the value 192, this is a class C address, and the netid consists of the first three octets. Therefore, the netid is 192.168.87.

The subnet mask 11100000 reserves 3 bits for the network address. The fourth octet is 01011111 binary, making the subnetid 010.

The subnet mask leaves 5 bits for host addressing. Consequently, the hostid of this host is 11111 decimal.

Oops, this was a trick question, wasn't it? Given that IP address and subnet mask, the netid is invalid because a netid cannot consist entirely of 1s. Now you can see why it is so important to dig down to the binary bare metal when you assign IP addresses. Unless you do, address errors are inevitable.

Trouble with Subnets

Subnet addressing is one area where network administrators are likely to encounter trouble. Suppose that a subnet contains the following hosts and uses the subnet mask 255.255.234.0:

172.16.161.80

172.16.180.153

172.16.192.209

172.16.177.44

Do you see a problem? Host 172.16.223.153 will be unable to communicate because it has a different subnetid from the other hosts. That isn't extremely obvious until you examine the binary values of the third octets (I've set out the subnet bits in bold type):

10100001

10110100

11000000

10110001

Oh, my! 172.16.192.209 is on another subnet, a fact you could easily miss if you relied on the dotted-decimal addresses.

Default Subnet Masks

A subnet mask is part of every host's configuration. What, even if no subnetting is taking place? Yes, always. When the network address isn't subnetted, the host is configured with a *default subnet mask*, in which the 1 bits match the standard netid bits for the class of the network class. If the network is using a class A address, for example, the default subnet mask is 255.0.0.0. Here are the default subnet masks:

- Class A: 255.0.0.0
- Class B: 255.255.0.0
- Class C: 255.255.255.0

Subnets: Some Observations

Taking all the rules for subnetting into account, it appears that some subnet masks have more potential than others. After some discussion, I'll give you some tables that make it easy to evaluate the usefulness of various subnet options.

Take the subnet mask 128 (10000000), which in theory ought to permit you to set up two subnets. But one of those subnets would be the all-1s subnet, which is prohibited. So your payoff for giving up a bit of hostid is one subnet, exactly where you started off.

A subnet mask of 196 (11000000) gets you three subnets, not four as you might expect, again because the all-1s subnet isn't permitted. You only get three subnets because Microsoft permits use of the all-0s subnet.

Subnetting a class C address—yes, as small as it is, you may need to subnet a class C address if it is all you've got—has some special concerns because you have so few bits to work with. Suppose you are subnetting a class C address with the subnet mask 255.255.255.248. Here's the binary subnet mask:

`11111111 11111111 11111111 11111000`

The goal is to create a lot of subnetworks. Although you do in fact make it possible to configure 30 subnets, each subnet accommodates only six hosts! Besides resulting in itty-bitty subnets, you waste a lot of your potential addresses. A class C address can support a maximum of 254 hosts without subnetting. With the subnet mask 255.255.255.248, the same address supports only 180 hosts, 210 if you use the all-0s subnet. It is unfortunate that Internet address space has become so tight that it is necessary to subnet class C addresses, but it is often necessary to do so.

Tables 13.1, 13.2, and 13.3 summarize subnet options for class A, B, and C networks. Some options are marked "invalid" because they don't result in useful subnetwork configurations.

TABLE 13.1 **Class A subnetting**

Subnet Bits	Maximum Subnets	Maximum Number of Hosts Per Subnet	Subnet Mask
0	0	16,777,214	255.0.0.0
1	invalid	invalid	invalid
2	2	4,194,302	255.192.0.0
3	6	2,097,150	255.224.0.0
4	14	1,048,574	255.240.0.0
5	30	524,286	255.248.0.0
6	62	262,142	255.252.0.0
7	126	131,070	255.254.0.0
8	254	65,534	255.255.0.0

TABLE 13.2 **Class B subnetting**

Subnet Bits	Maximum Subnets	Maximum Number of Hosts Per Subnet	Subnet Mask
0	0	65,534	255.255.0.0
1	invalid	invalid	invalid
2	2	16,382	255.255.192.0
3	6	8,190	255.255.224.0
4	14	4,094	255.255.240.0
5	30	2,046	255.255.248.0
6	62	1,022	255.255.252.0
7	126	510	255.255.254.0
8	254	254	255.255.255.0

TABLE 13.3 **Class C subnetting**

Subnet Bits	Maximum Subnets	Maximum Number of Hosts Per Subnet	Subnet Mask
0	0	254	255.255.255.0
1	invalid	invalid	invalid
2	2	62	255.255.255.192
3	6	30	255.255.255.224
4	14	14	255.255.255.240
5	30	6	255.255.255.248
6	62	2	255.255.255.252
7	invalid	invalid	255.255.255.254
8	invalid	invalid	255.255.255.255

Computer Names on Microsoft TCP/IP Networks

Networked computers are identified by numbers. On TCP/IP networks they are identified by IP numbers. On NWLink and NetBEUI networks they are identified by numbers defined by the underlying network such as Ethernet. But the rule is the same: to send a message to another device, a computer must know the numeric ID of the destination device.

But people hate referring to computers by numbers, particularly the long numbers commonly used to identify network computers, so it has long been the practice of network designers to provide a mechanism that identifies computers by names. Ideally, computer naming should be completely transparent, requiring no intervention on the part of users and little on the part of network administrators. People use the names, and in the background computers figure out the numbers they require to communicate.

To meet those goals, Microsoft has long based its network products on NetBIOS names, which are cataloged by a browser

Unsupported Internet addresses

Throughout this book I illustrate IP addressing using addresses that cannot be used on the Internet so that you can try the examples without conflicting with existing hosts. These addresses can be used on private networks but are blocked by Internet routers. The nonroutable IP address ranges are

- Class A: 10.0.0.0 through 10.255.255.255

- Class B: 172.16.0.0 through 172.31.255.255

- Class C: 192.168.0.0 through 192.168.255.255

Resolving names

The process of determining the network address that is associated with a computer name is called *name resolution*.

service. The NetBIOS name is the name you enter into the computer's configuration when you install the operating system. The Browser service collects the NetBIOS names of all servers on the network. A server is any computer that is sharing files or printers. Each Windows NT computer runs a Server service that makes itself known on the network by a special NetBIOS name

Ordinarily, the Browser service runs transparently in the background, and even administrators are unaware of its existence. Unfortunately, the Browser mechanism breaks down on TCP/IP networks. To comprehend why browsing has difficulty in TCP/IP environments and Microsoft's remedy to the problem, you need to understand how browsing works.

The Browser Service

Browsing is based on a hierarchy of browse servers. Basically, there are three levels of browse servers:

- A *domain browse master* serves as a central repository for the browsing database, called a *browse list*, for an entire domain. The browse list identifies all servers in the domain as well as any other domains associated with the domain through trust relationships. The PDC is always the domain browse master.

- A *master browser* is established for each subnetwork. It maintains a master copy of the browse list for use on that subnetwork only. The browse master is selected through an election process.

- A *backup browser* is a computer that receives a copy of the browser database from a master *browser*.

When any computer enters the Microsoft network, one of its first actions is to identify a master browser. Because it doesn't know the name of the master browser, it sends a broadcast message that is seen by all computers. The master browser responds by sending the client information about the browsers that are available.

When a computer needs to send a message to another computer it can do so in two ways:

- If it knows the identification of the destination computer it can send a directed message that will be received only by the destination computer.

- If it doesn't know the identification of the destination computer it can send a broadcast message that is received by all computers. Only the desired computer will respond to the broadcast message.

Broadcast messages are necessary in many cases, but they are undesirable because every computer on the network must spend time processing the message. If broadcasts dominate network traffic, computers can waste a lot of CPU cycles rejecting messages that aren't intended for them.

Another undesirable aspect of broadcast messages is that they don't cross routers. If they did, entire internetworks could be overwhelmed with broadcast messages.

Directed messages can be routed, however. Any message that must communicate through a router must originate as a directed message.

Every network segment on a Microsoft network is configured with a *master browser*, a server that stores the master copy of the browser database for that network segment. The browse master is selected through an election process. As clients are added to the network, *backup browsers* are automatically designated.

When a server enters the Microsoft network, it sends a directed message to the master browser called a *server advertisement*. Upon receiving the server advertisement, the master browser adds the server to its browse list. Backup browsers contact the master browser at 15 minute intervals to obtain an updated copy of the browse list.

When a workstation enters the network, it contacts the master browser to obtain a list of backup browsers. It then contacts a browser (usually a backup browser) when it needs to obtain a copy of the browse list.

From a user perspective, the following events take place:

1. Open a browser interface such as Network Neighborhood which connects with a backup or master browser. The

browser server returns a list of the domains and servers that are in its database.

2. Click a domain to open it up to expose servers in the domain.

3. Click a server. Your client contacts the server to obtain a list of shared resources.

The NetBIOS browser mechanism is highly dependent on broadcast messages that don't cross routers, and this is its Achilles heel. The practical upshot is that browsing works very differently depending on the network protocol that is employed.

NetBEUI doesn't support routing at all. Therefore, browser messages are confined to the local subnet. If two computers reside on different subnets, they cannot exchange browsing information.

NWLink has been adapted to forward browser messages. As a result, a single master browser is maintained for an entire domain, regardless of the number of subnetworks that are involved.

TCP/IP routers don't forward broadcast messages. Therefore, browsing functions independently on each subnet. If a domain spans multiple subnets, there is no domain master browser. Consequently, the standard browser mechanism lets a computer browse only the servers that are connected to the local subnet.

Clearly, that is an unacceptable restriction, so Microsoft has devised two mechanisms that let clients access Microsoft servers that are on remote subnets:

- Static database files called LMHOSTS files
- The dynamic Windows Internet Naming Service

Let's briefly look at each approach.

SEE ALSO
➤ *For more information on network browsing, see page 595.*

➤ *For more information on WINS, see page 485.*

LMHOSTS Files

An LMHOSTS file is a text file, maintained using any text editor, that maps host names to IP addresses. A typical entry in an LMHOSTS file looks like this:

```
192.168.143.8      Drew
```

Each computer must have an LMHOSTS file that contains an entry for each server. That sounds simple, but it turns out to be a significant administrative hassle.

You see, someone must not only update the LMHOSTS file, but also take responsibility for ensuring that a fresh copy is distributed to every computer every time a change takes place in the network configuration. That's fine on small networks that seldom change, but it's a recipe for indigestion on a large or dynamic network.

SEE ALSO

➤ *LMHOSTS files are discussed on page 505.*

Windows Internet Naming Service

So Microsoft needed a dynamic service that would keep itself up to date, and they came up with the Windows Internet Naming Service or WINS. The WINS system consists of one or more WINS servers that maintain copies of the network name database. Clients register their NetBIOS names and addresses with WINS. And, when a client needs to communicate with a server, it queries WINS for the server's address.

WINS appears to solve the TCP/IP naming problem. As clients enter the network, WINS is automatically apprised of any changes. That's better than LMHOSTS files. After WINS is configured, it can be pretty much ignored by the administrator. And, because all WINS communication takes place through directed messages, routers don't interfere with WINS operation.

There's only one problem with WINS. Nobody but Microsoft uses it. Everyone else uses Internet-based naming systems. So we need to look at the Internet side of things next.

SEE ALSO

➤ *WINS is discussed on page 485.*

Computer Names on the Internet

The Internet faces a problem much like the problem Microsoft solves with NetBIOS names, LMHOSTS, and WINS. Users cannot remember more than a few IP addresses, so they need names. As with Microsoft's approach, two techniques have been used to simplify host naming on TCP/IP networks: HOSTS files and the Domain Name Service.

HOSTS Files

HOSTS files work just like LMHOSTS files. They are text files with entries that match host names with IP addresses. An entry in a HOSTS file looks like this:

```
192.168.143.8      drew ws1 blivets99
```

An entry in a HOSTS file isn't that different from an entry in LMHOSTS except that a HOSTS file lets a host have more than one name, called an *alias*. (Also, LMHOSTS files have some special features specific to the Microsoft environment.)

HOSTS files have the same disadvantages cited for LMHOSTS files. They are tedious and, because each host must receive a new copy each time the file is updated, HOSTS files are time-consuming to maintain and distribute. Consequently, most TCP/IP administrators rely on the Domain Name Service to provide name resolution support.

SEE ALSO

➤ *HOSTS files are discussed on page 529.*

Domain Name Service

Like WINS, the Domain Name Service (DNS) deploys servers that can be queried by network clients to resolve names to IP addresses. But that is about all the similarity there is between DNS and WINS.

The DNS name database is big, and it can be distributed in chunks across many, many name servers. On a network as big as the Internet, it would be inefficient to maintain the complete database on one computer. For one thing, the computer would be overwhelmed with the data and with servicing name resolution queries. For another, a single database would be impossible to maintain because every organization would need to submit name changes to a central authority, a bureaucratic nightmare when millions of organizations are involved. The Internet needed a naming system that let each organization maintain its own chunk of the database. DNS meets that goal. It is expandable without limit, and it permits local control of portions of the database.

But there are problems with DNS in the Microsoft environment. For one thing, DNS isn't Microsoft's native method of maintaining a name database. For another, DNS isn't dynamic. Administrators modify the DNS database by manually making entries to database files. On most DNS servers, changes don't take effect until the DNS server is stopped and restarted. That's definitely not in keeping with the dynamic nature of naming on Microsoft networks.

So Microsoft has built a DNS server of its own, which is included with Windows NT Server 4.0. The Microsoft DNS server has three distinct advantages:

- Entries can be modified interactively through a graphic interface.

- It isn't necessary to restart a Microsoft DNS Server to activate database changes.

- The Microsoft DNS Server can obtain names from WINS, allowing it to keep pace with the dynamic Windows naming environment.

SEE ALSO

➤ *The Microsoft DNS Server is discussed on page 529.*

TCP/IP Routing

TCP/IP routing is also a bit more involved than anything you have seen so far in the book. The only thing you need to do to configure routing with NWLink is to install RIP for NWLink. With TCP/IP you have two options: static routing and RIP.

Static Routing

Static routing makes use of a static routing database that resides on each computer. You maintain some entries in the static routing table using entries in the Network applet in the Control Panel. Other entries are managed using the route command-line utility.

Every TCP/IP computer has a static routing table. An important entry in the static routing table is the *default router*. If a host doesn't know where to send a message, it will send the message to its default router, which is presumed to know how to deliver the message to its final destination.

All TCP/IP routing can be handled through static routing, but it can be a hassle to maintain static routing when the network configuration changes frequently. On large networks it is more common to use a dynamic routing protocol such as the Routing Information Protocol.

Routers and gateways

In the TCP/IP environment, routers are often known by the older term *gateway*. When you configure a Microsoft TCP/IP client, you enter the default router IP address in a field labeled *default gateway*.

Routing Information Protocol

You have already encountered a version of the Routing Information Protocol (RIP) that is used to configure routers for NWLink. Microsoft includes RIP for TCP/IP with Windows NT 4.0.

RIP is a dynamic routing protocol that updates routing tables based on information exchanged with other RIP routers. The dynamic nature of RIP lets routers update their routing tables as the network configuration changes. RIP, or another dynamic routing protocol, is deployed on most large TCP/IP networks because the task of maintaining static routing tables would be overwhelming.

SEE ALSO

➤ *Detailed information on TCP/IP routing can be found starting on page 471.*

That's It for TCP/IP Theory

I promised you I'd keep the theory to a minimum, and I've done my best. You now have the basic knowledge you need to begin setting up TCP/IP on your network. And so, without further ado, let's put theory into practice. In the next chapter, you learn how to configure the basic features of a Microsoft TCP/IP client.

Building a Basic TCP/IP Network

Planning a TCP/IP network

Installing and configuring TCP/IP on Windows NT computers

Testing TCP/IP communication

Installing and configuring TCP/IP on Windows 95 and 98 computers

Installing and configuring TCP/IP on Windows for Workgroups 3.11

Installing and configuring TCP/IP on MS-DOS and Windows 3.1 computers

Now that you've integrated some TCP/IP into your network knowledge structure, you can proceed to set up your first, basic TCP/IP network. This chapter keeps things simple by sticking with a single network segment. That lets us avoid the issues involved with routing.

First, we'll go through a planning phase, examining the configuration information you need to obtain prior to setting up TCP/IP. Then we'll look at the procedure for setting up TCP/IP support on Windows NT. Finally, you need to know a few basic testing procedures.

Planning Your TCP/IP Network

The preceding chapter introduced you to the principle TCP/IP planning issues. For a simple network, there is only one real concern: What IP addresses will be used?

If you will be connecting to the Internet, be sure to obtain your own Internet addresses. If you don't, you will need to reconfigure all your hosts when you make the Internet connection.

For this first network, we will use the class C address 192.168.45.0 with the subnet mask 255.255.255.0. I can use hostids ranging from 1 through 254. Which ones should I use first?

The best idea is to allocate hostids starting at the bottom of the address range. That way you are using the rightmost bits in the IP address. If you leave the leftmost bit alone, you simplify matters if you need to subnet your IP address range in the future, because subnetting starts with the leftmost bits. Because you have been using the rightmost bits for hostids, there is less disruption when subnetting is added to your network scheme.

You should establish some conventions for assigning netids. Here are some suggestions:

- Use low hostids for hosts you want to remember easily, such as routers and servers. You will quickly commit your netid to memory, but you will have many hostids; so make the important ones easy to remember. DNS and WINS servers are good candidates for low hostids because you will frequently be required to enter their IP addresses into host configurations.

- I like to reserve the first two or three hostids for routers. The first router I add to the sample network would have the IP address 192.168.45.1, for example. If I have an Internet connection, I like to use hostid 1 for the Internet router.

- I like to number servers after routers. Typically, my name servers come first. I may start numbering name servers with hostid 4, for example, to leave space for two local routers and an Internet connection.

- I typically start numbering users' workstations at hostid 10. That leaves me room for six servers.

The sample network has three hosts, as shown in Figure 14.1:

- A Windows NT Server, with IP address 192.168.45.4. This computer is the domain PDC. And, when we set up an Internet connection, this computer will be the DNS server.

- Another Windows NT Server, with IP address 192.168.45.5. This server is the BDC. If the network expands, this computer will be set up as a WINS server.

- A Windows NT Workstation, with IP address 192.168.45.10. This will be the first user workstation.

That's all the planning that is required. Now you can install TCP/IP support on the computers.

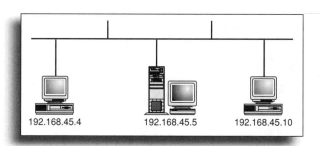

FIGURE 14.1
The sample network for this chapter.

A tip before you start

Before you attempt to configure TCP/IP for the first time, use NWLink or NetBEUI to test out the network. You can't misconfigure those protocols, so any errors you encounter will be due to hardware problems. Correct the hardware problems and continue until you can communicate.

After you are sure the network is functioning, attempt to install TCP/IP. If you cannot get hosts to communicate, you can be fairly sure that the problem stems from TCP/IP configuration errors, not from hardware.

Installing and Configuring TCP/IP on Windows NT Computers

The TCP/IP protocols are installed using the Network applet in the Control Panel. The procedure is as follows:

Installing TCP/IP protocols on Windows NT computers

1. Open the Network applet and select the **Protocols** tab.

2. Choose **Add** to open the Select Network Protocol dialog box.

3. In the **Network Protocol** list box, select **TCP/IP Protocol**. Then click **OK**.

4. The next prompt asks, Is there a DHCP server on your network? If this network does not have a DHCP server, as is the case with the sample network, click **No**.

5. Setup needs to copy files from the Windows NT installation CD. Supply file paths and disks as requested.

6. Close the Network applet.

7. After bindings are established, you will be shown the Microsoft TCP/IP Properties dialog box. Only the **IP Address** tab must be configured at this time. It is shown in Figure 14.2.

FIGURE 14.2

TCP/IP Protocol IP Address properties.

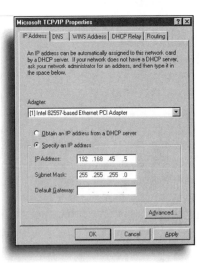

8. In this chapter, we will be using static IP addresses. Click the **S̲pecify an IP address** radio button.

9. Complete the **I̲P Address** field, which is a required field for all TCP/IP computers that are assigned static IP addresses.

10. Complete the **Su̲bnet Mask** field, which is also required for statically configured TCP/IP computers.

11. The simple network used in this chapter does not have a router. Therefore you do not need to complete the **Default G̲ateway** field. Similarly, it is unnecessary to configure any advanced properties, which are accessed through the **A̲dvanced** button.

12. Close the Microsoft TCP/IP Properties dialog box and exit the Network applet.

13. Shut down and restart the computer to activate the settings.

In this chapter, IP addresses and other configuration parameters will be manually configured. A computer with a manually configured IP address is said to have a static IP address. Name servers (DNS and WINS) must always be configured with static IP addresses. It is useful to assign static addresses to any computer that you will frequently reference by its IP address. To assign static IP addresses, you click the **S̲pecify an IP address** radio button.

Later in the book, you will learn how to use DHCP, the Domain Host Configuration Protocol, to simplify the tasks of assigning network addresses and configuring host TCP/IP properties. If a DHCP server were being used on this network, you would select this radio button to force this host to obtain its TCP/IP configuration from DHCP. If this radio button is selected, the **I̲P Address, Su̲bnet Mask**, and **Default G̲ateway** fields are not active.

SEE ALSO

➤ *DHCP is covered in Chapter 17, "Simplifying Administration with DHCP," starting on page 511.*

Now configure at least one other computer with TCP/IP. After that is done, you can test TCP/IP communication on your network.

IP address conflicts

Communications become snarled when two hosts have the same IP address, so Windows NT won't let you activate an IP address if it is already in use. After you configure the TCP/IP properties, NT polls the network to determine whether the IP address you entered is in use. If it is, NT notifies you of the problem and disables the interface that has the conflicting address. You must enter a non-conflicting address before TCP/IP will be activated on the interface.

Testing TCP/IP Communication

Although you can perform some tests on a single host, it is best to have two hosts configured and running. The primary tool for testing TCP/IP communication is the ping command, which is used at the command line.

The ping utility sends out a series of packets to the IP address that is specified. If the specified device receives the packets, it transmits responses that are displayed for your examination. A response to a ping indicates that TCP/IP is operational between this host and the destination. (*Ping* is often used as a verb, as in, "Now ping 192.168.45.85.")

Figure 14.3 shows the results of two ping commands. The command ping 192.168.45.4 succeeded in eliciting a response from the target IP address. The response indicates the approximate time required for the response to be received. The hosts used in this example are connected through a LAN, so the response time is very short. Longer response times would be expected if the hosts were separated by a slower WAN link.

The second ping command attempts to reach an IP address that does not exist. Because ping does not receive a response in a required time interval, it displays the response Request timed out.

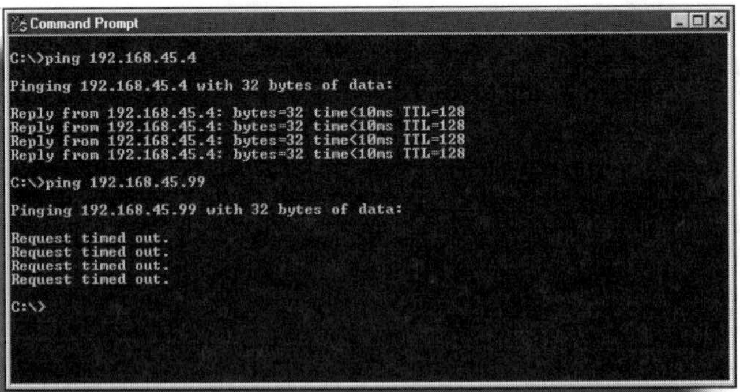

FIGURE 14.3

Successfully and unsuccess-fully pinging an IP address.

```
Command Prompt                                          _ □ ×

C:\>ping 192.168.45.4

Pinging 192.168.45.4 with 32 bytes of data:

Reply from 192.168.45.4: bytes=32 time<10ms TTL=128
Reply from 192.168.45.4: bytes=32 time<10ms TTL=128
Reply from 192.168.45.4: bytes=32 time<10ms TTL=128
Reply from 192.168.45.4: bytes=32 time<10ms TTL=128

C:\>ping 192.168.45.99

Pinging 192.168.45.99 with 32 bytes of data:

Request timed out.
Request timed out.
Request timed out.
Request timed out.

C:\>
```

Ping tests can fail for a variety of reasons:

- The destination IP address does not exist.

- The destination IP address may be correct, but the subnet mask may be incorrect on the source or destination host. If both hosts are on the subnet, they must have correctly configured IP addresses and they must have the same subnet mask.

- The network connection may have failed between the two hosts.

- The TCP/IP protocols may be improperly configured on either host.

- The network hardware may have malfunctioned or it may be misconfigured in either host.

When you configure a new TCP/IP host, you should test it with ping. Start by running the following tests in the order specified:

Testing a host's TCP/IP configuration

1. **Ping 127.0.0.1.** The address 127.0.0.1 is a special address called the *loopback address*. When you ping the loopback address, the ping request is responded to by the TCP/IP on the local computer. If ping is successful, you can be fairly sure that the TCP/IP protocols are working properly.

2. **Ping the local network interface.** If your network adapter has the IP address 192.168.45.6, enter the command ping 192.168.45.6. If ping is successful, you can be fairly sure that the network adapter and network drivers are working properly.

3. **Ping other hosts on the local network.** If you can ping some hosts but not others, you may have problems with your network. Try pinging different combinations of hosts to isolate the problem.

Network troubleshooting is chiefly a matter of careful detective work. If you suspect the network, see whether the computers can communicate with NWLink or NetBEUI, which are much easier to configure. Unless you have sophisticated equipment, network troubleshooting is primarily a matter of substituting components until you find the failed item.

After you are sure the network is functioning, check your TCP/IP configurations very carefully. It is very easy to mistype a digit in an IP address or to get the subnet masks wrong.

Configuring Your Clients

Before you configure TCP/IP support on your clients, you should be comfortable with the basic client configuration procedures discussed in Chapter 8, "Activating Network Clients." In this section, I am going to assume that you are adding TCP/IP support to existing network clients. However, the procedures aren't very different if you are configuring TCP/IP during the initial installation of the network client software.

SEE ALSO

➤ *See Chapter 8, "Activating Network Clients," page 247, for the basic procedures for configuring Windows 95 and 98, 3.x, and MS-DOS clients.*

Installing and Configuring TCP/IP on Windows 95 and 98 Clients

Both Windows 95 and 98 are configured using the Network applet in the Control Panel, which you became familiar with in Chapter 8. To add TCP/IP protocols to a Windows 95 and 98 computer, do the following:

Installing TCP/IP protocols on Windows 95 and 98

1. Open the Network applet in the Control Panel.

2. To add TCP/IP, choose **Add** in the Network tool dialog box. This will open the **Select Network Component Type** dialog box.

3. Select **Protocol** and choose **Add** to open the **Select Network Protocol** dialog box.

4. In the **Manufacturers** box, select **Microsoft** to open a list of Microsoft protocols. Then, in the **Network Protocols** box, select **TCP/IP**. Click **OK** to continue. The focus returns to the Network tool dialog box. Now TCP/IP is listed as a protocol.

5. The TCP/IP protocols have been installed, but currently are configured with default properties. To review the protocol properties, select **TCP/IP** in the box labeled **The following network components are installed:**. Then choose **Properties** to open the **TCP/IP Properties** dialog box (see Figure 14.4).

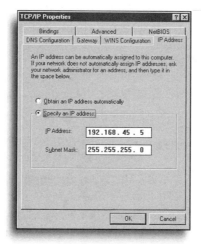

FIGURE 14.4

Configuring TCP/IP properties for Windows 95 and 98.

6. The **TCP/IP Properties** dialog box has several tabs that enable you to configure various aspects of the TCP/IP configuration. The information on these tabs is similar to the information that appears in the Windows NT protocol dialog boxes, although information is arranged on the tabs differently. After configuring the protocols, click **OK** to return to the Network tool main dialog box.

7. After you exit the Network tool, you might need to supply disks and file paths required to copy files to the computer. After copying the files, restart the computer to activate the new protocols.

Installing and Configuring TCP/IP on Windows for Workgroups 3.11 Clients

Although WfW is network-ready, the standard package does not include TCP/IP protocols. You need to build a **TCP/IP 32 for Windows for Workgroups 3.11** client installation disk using the Windows NT Server Client Administrator.

SEE ALSO

➤ *The procedure for creating client installation disks using Client Administrator is discussed in Chapter 8, "Activating Network Clients," page 247. See the section titled "Creating an Installation Disk" for instructions.*

The following procedures assume that WfW has been installed and that a network adapter card has been configured. Only procedures for adding TCP/IP client support are covered.

To add TCP/IP to a WfW network configuration, perform the following steps:

Installing TCP/IP protocols on Windows for Workgroups

1. Start the Windows Setup utility.

2. In the **Windows Setup** dialog box, choose the **Change Network Settings** command in the **Options** menu.

3. The **Network Setup** dialog box should resemble Figure 14.5. The dialog box should specify support for **Microsoft Windows Network (version 3.11)**. Also, the Network Drivers dialog box should specify the network adapter that is installed in this computer.

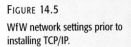

FIGURE 14.5
WfW network settings prior to installing TCP/IP.

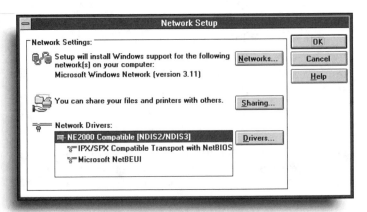

4. To install TCP/IP client support, choose the **Drivers** button to open the **Network Drivers** dialog box.

5. In the **Network Drivers** dialog box, choose the **Add Protocol** button.

6. In the **Add Network Protocol** dialog box, choose **Unlisted or Updated Protocol** in the protocol box and click **OK**.

7. When prompted for the location of the protocol files, insert the **TCP/IP 32 Client for Windows for Workgroups** disk in a disk drive. Specify the drive path, and then click **OK**.

8. After the Unlisted or Updated Protocol dialog box appears, choose **Microsoft TCP/IP-32 3.11** and click **OK**. Files are copied from the client disk and Setup returns to the Network Drivers dialog box, which now shows **Microsoft TCP/IP-32 3.11** as an installed network driver.

9. To configure the TCP/IP protocols, in the Network Drivers dialog box select **Microsoft TCP/IP-32 3.11** and choose **Setup** to open the Microsoft TCP/IP Configuration dialog box (see Figure 14.6).

The WfW TCP/IP protocol configuration dialog boxes are nearly identical to the dialog boxes used for Windows NT.

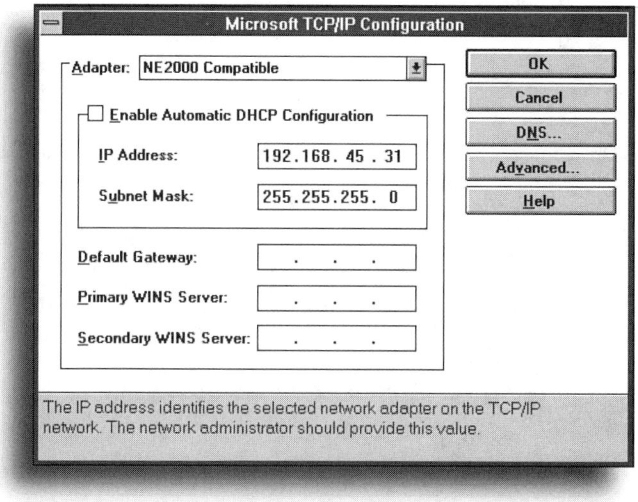

FIGURE 14.6
The Microsoft TCP/IP Configuration dialog box.

10. After entering the TCP/IP configuration, click **OK**, exit the Windows Setup utility, and restart the computer.

Icons for the TCP/IP utilities **ftp** and **telnet** are installed in the newly created Microsoft TCP/IP-32 program group. Also installed in this program group are icons for Microsoft TCP/IP help and for a Release Notes file.

The Windows NT Server installation CD contains a number of files that upgrade Windows for Workgroups networking capabilities. The files should be copied to WfW from the directory \Clients\Update.wfw on the installation CD. Copy the files as follows:

- Copy NET.EXE and NET.MSG to the Windows directory, usually C:\WINDOWS.

- Copy all other files (with DLL and 386 extensions) to the SYSTEM directory, usually C:\WINDOWS\SYSTEM.

Installing and Configuring TCP/IP on MS-DOS and Windows 3.1 Computers

TCP/IP support for MS-DOS and Windows 3.1 is installed from the disks used to install Network Client v3.0 for MS-DOS. To install the MS-DOS client, exit to an MS-DOS prompt, insert Disk 1 of the Network Client v3.0 disk set in a disk drive, and do the following:

SEE ALSO

➤ *The procedure for creating client installation disks using Client Administrator is discussed in Chapter 8, "Activating Network Clients," page 247. See the section titled "Creating an Installation Disk" for instructions.*

➤ *The procedure for installing the MS-DOS client software is described in Chapter 8, page 271, in the section titled "Installing Network Client for MS-DOS."*

To install TCP/IP protocol support on an MS-DOS computer, follow these steps:

Installing TCP/IP protocols on MS-DOS Clients

1. Install the MS-DOS client software as described in Chapter 8. Proceed until you see the Client Configuration dialog screen.

2. To add the TCP/IP protocol, choose **Change Network Configuration**. The network adapter and protocol configuration screen will display.

3. By default, adapters are configured with the NWLink protocols. These are not required on a purely TCP/IP network and can be removed. To remove the protocols, select **NWLink IPX Compatible Transport** and then choose **Remove** in the **Options** box.

4. To add the TCP/IP protocols, select the adapter in the **Installed Network Adapter(s)** box. Then choose **Add Protocol** in the **Options** box. Select the **Microsoft TCP/IP** protocol in the list. You are returned to the main menu. The TCP/IP protocol is shown in the **Installed Network Adapter(s) and Protocol(s)** box.

5. TCP/IP must be configured. Select the TCP/IP protocol in the **Installed Protocol(s)** list (see Figure 14.7) and click **Change Settings** in the **Options** box. Figure 14.8 shows the TCP/IP settings.

To configure the client to obtain an IP address from DHCP, retain the default setting of 0 for **Disable Automatic Configuration**. Set this parameter to 1 to manually configure addresses.

If addresses are manually configured, enter appropriate information in the **IP Address**, **IP Subnet Mask**, and **Default Gateway** sessions.

Click **The listed options are correct** after completing the settings.

6. When adapters and protocols have been configured, click **Network configuration is correct** and press Enter to return to the Setup main menu.

7. When all configuration options are as desired, return to the Setup main menu, click **The listed options are correct**, and press Enter.

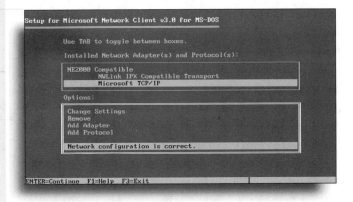

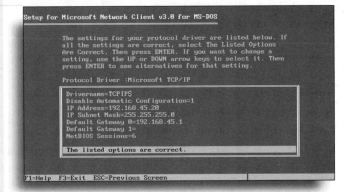

Even if you selected one of the prepackaged network adapter drivers, you are asked to insert an OEM drivers disk. Insert Disk 2 of the client installation set to supply the driver files. For drivers not included with the client disk set, insert the OEM disk.

After copying files, restart the computer to activate the client software.

Apart from the procedures described in Chapter 8, no special procedures are required to configure Windows 3.1 for TCP/IP.

That's It for Basic TCP/IP

A single, brief chapter and you have TCP/IP running on a simple network. As you can see, the essentials aren't difficult at all. Be aware, however, that a great many of the problems you will encounter relate to tasks covered in this chapter.

With the basics out of the way, we need to move on to some heavy duty stuff. The first step is to see how routers are used to extend TCP/IP networks. These days, few LANs don't have a router or two. You will have one if you connect to the Internet, for example. And because many other things are complicated by the presence of routers, we need to add routing techniques to your repertoire.

Building TCP/IP Internetworks

Chapter 14, "Building a Basic TCP/IP Network," assumed a simple network that didn't require routing. But few TCP/IP networks remain that simple. For one thing, most eventually connect to the Internet. For another, most eventually run into the physical limits of their LANs. Either they have too many computers, or there is too much traffic, or users are distributed across too great an area. These are all constraints that call for dividing your network into smaller subnetworks.

Designing Routed Networks

In the preceding chapter, you learned that every TCP/IP host is assigned a 32-bit IP address, and that each IP address consists of the following three components:

- Network ID (netid)
- Subnetwork ID (subnetid)
- Host ID (hostid)

The size of the netid component is determined by the class of the IP address. The netid component of a class A address is 8 bits, of a class B address is 16 bits, and of a class C address is 24 bits.

The remaining bits belong to the hostid. However, some bits can be borrowed from the hostid to establish a subnetid. A subnet mask determines how many bits are allocated to the subnetid.

Two hosts are considered to be on the same subnet if all the following conditions are true:

- The hosts are connected to the same network segment.
- The hosts have the same host ID.
- The hosts have the same subnet mask.
- The hosts have the same subnetid.

If two hosts are on the same subnet, delivery is a piece of cake. The host originating the message just places it on the correct subnet, where the destination host picks it up. It's a lot like

Speaking of Routing...

I'm keeping the discussion about routing quite simple in this chapter. A lot of theory has been avoided, and I have pretty much ignored the fairly complex topic of static route configuration. All these topics receive more thorough coverage in my book *Networking with Microsoft TCP/IP, 2nd Edition* from New Riders Publishing.

passing a note in school to a student whose desk is next to yours—you simply hand the note over.

When two hosts are not on the same subnet, they must communicate through routers. A *router* is a network device that receives messages from one subnet and delivers the messages to the correct subnet destination. Suppose you are a student who wants to pass a note across the room. You pass the note to a "default neighbor" who is presumed to be reliable. From then on, you don't know what route the note will take. It's up to your default neighbor to keep it moving toward its destination.

Routers and Routing Tables

Typically a host knows two crucial pieces of information:

- **The netid and subnetid addresses of any networks to which the host is directly attached**. These networks are local to the host. If the host needs to send a message to a host on a local network, it just transmits the message on the correct subnet.

- **The IP address of a default router, which must be attached to a local subnet**. If the host needs to send a message that is not connected to a local subnet, the host sends the message to the default router on the assumption that the router knows how to deliver the message.

Figure 15.1 shows a simple internetwork that requires two routers. Suppose that host 172.16.0.100 needs to communicate with host 172.18.0.100. How does that communication take place? Let's trace the events:

1. 172.16.0.100 examines its netid (172.16) and the netid of the destination (172.18) and determines that the netids are different. Therefore, 172.16.0.100 knows that the message must be routed.

2. Because 172.16.0.100 cannot deliver the message locally, it sends the message to the default router specified in its configuration. 172.16.0.100 examines its TCP/IP configuration and determines that its default router is 172.16.0.1.

3. Host 172.16.0.100 addresses the message to its default router and sends the message to 172.16.0.1 along with a request to forward the message to 172.18.0.100.

4. Router A receives the message through interface 172.16.0.1. Router A consults its configuration to determine whether it knows how to deliver a message to network 172.18.0.0.

5. Router A does not know how to route to network 172.18.0.0, so Router A sends the message to its own default router, which is 172.17.0.2.

6. Router B is directly attached to network 172.18.0.0. Therefore Router B can deliver the message to host 172.18.0.100.

FIGURE 15.1

Routing on this network makes use of default routers.

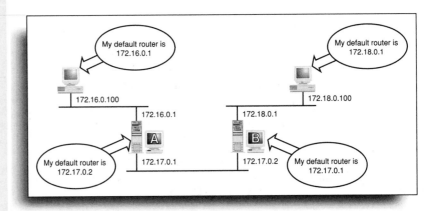

Routing decisions are kept simple because all routing decisions are made ahead of time and recorded in a *routing table*. The routing table on a host includes entries for the locally attached networks and for the default router. The routing table for a router can be far more elaborate. Typically the routing table for a router includes routes to all subnets on the internetwork.

In Figure 15.1, I documented the default route for Router B as well. This enables all hosts on this network to communicate. There are six possibilities:

■ A host on network 172.16.0.0 that wants to communicate with networks 172.17.0.0 sends messages to the default router at 172.16.0.1. Router A can deliver messages to network 172.17.0.0 directly.

■ A host on network 172.16.0.0 that wants to communicate with networks 172.18.0.0 sends messages to the default router at 172.16.0.1. Router B can deliver messages to network 172.18.0.0 through its default router.

■ A host on network 172.18.0.0 that wants to communicate with networks 172.17.0.0 sends messages to the default router at 172.16.0.1. Router B can deliver messages to network 172.17.0.0 directly.

■ A host on network 172.18.0.0 that wants to communicate with networks 172.16.0.0 sends messages to the default router at 172.18.0.1. Router B can deliver messages to network 172.16.0.0 through its default router.

■ A host on network 172.17.0.0 that wants to communicate with network 172.16.0.0 might have 172.17.0.1 as its default router. When Router A receives the message it can deliver it directly to network 172.16.0.0.

■ A host on network 172.17.0.0 that wants to communicate with network 172.18.0.0 and has 172.17.0.1 as its default router will send the message to its default router, Router A. Router A cannot deliver the message directly to the destination network, so Router A sends the message to its default router, Router B. Router B can deliver the message to the destination network.

As you can see, the simple default router mechanism can handle a network with two routers and three subnets quite easily.

It's worth looking at a simpler case to make a point. The network in Figure 15.2 has a single router and two subnets. Because this router is directly connected to both subnets, it can route all messages on this internetwork. There is, therefore, no need to configure the router with a default router. The hosts on both subnets must have default routers, however, or they cannot direct messages to the router for delivery to the other subnet.

FIGURE 15.2

This router does not need a default gateway.

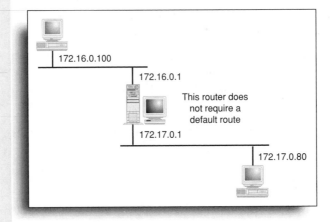

172.16.0.100

172.16.0.1

This router does not require a default route

172.17.0.1

172.17.0.80

Specifying a Default Route

Ordinarily you don't need to directly manage entries in the routing table, although you do manage some entries indirectly. You place a default route in the routing table, for example, by configuring the default gateway parameter in the host's TCP/IP protocol configuration.

Every host on an internetwork should be configured with a default gateway. On Microsoft TCP/IP clients, you define the default gateway by completing the **Default Gateway** field on the TCP/IP IP Address property page. (Remember from the discussion in Chapter 14 that *gateway* is an older term for *router*.) Figure 15.3 shows the IP Address property page for host 172.16.0.100 in Figure 15.1.

Routing Protocols

On complex networks, default routes are insufficient to support all possible routes. Consider the network in Figure 15.4. If host 172.16.0.100 sends a message to 172.18.0.50, it will send the message to Router A. The default router for Router A is 172.17.0.2, but if Router A sends the message to Router B it will not be delivered. Because Router A can have only one default router, it is unable to route messages that must be delivered through Router C.

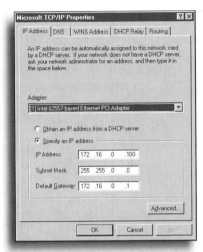

FIGURE 15.3
IP address properties showing
a default router.

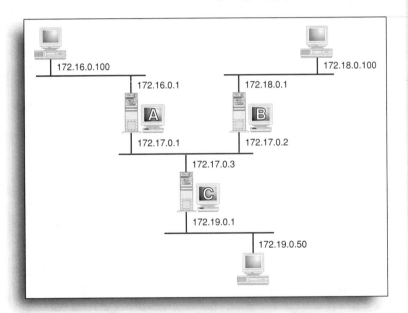

FIGURE 15.4
Default routers cannot support
this network.

What is required to make Router A smarter? Specifically, we
need to add an entry to Router A's routing table that says, "To
reach a destination on network 172.18.0.0, send messages to
172.17.0.3." That enables Router A to send messages to Router
C when appropriate.

On any complex network, it is necessary to supplement routing tables with specific routes to specific networks. That can be done manually. You can add fixed routes called *static routes* to routing tables using the route command line utility. But it takes expertise and time to manage static routes. You have to really understand how routing works and how to troubleshoot problems.

My goal in this book, on the other hand, is to make your life as easy as possible. So I'm going to show you how to use a dynamic routing protocol to automatically distribute routing information on complex networks.

Routing Information Protocol

Routing Information Protocol (RIP) is a dynamic routing protocol that automatically updates routing tables as the routing configuration changes on the internetwork. Essentially, RIP routers talk to each other and exchange routes. Then each router stuffs its routing table with the routes it learns. When routes change, routers notify each other, and the routing tables are updated automatically.

Figure 15.5 shows how RIP works. Each router broadcasts its routing table, which announces the networks that the router can reach and the cost to reach the destinations. As routers exchange these messages, they learn which networks they can receive through other routers, until eventually they learn how to reach every destination on the Internet.

To make one thing clear, RIP does not perform routing—that is to say, RIP does not forward messages between networks. Message forwarding is performed by the Internet Protocol when it is running on a computer that has two interfaces. You don't need RIP to have a router. All you need to make a TCP/IP router is a computer that has two network interfaces and TCP/IP installed.

All RIP does is exchange messages between routers that enable the routers to share the information in their routing tables. Consequently, there is no point in installing RIP on a router when it is the only router on the network. The router has no peers to exchange routing information with and will just pollute the network with RIP route advertisements that no other router will use.

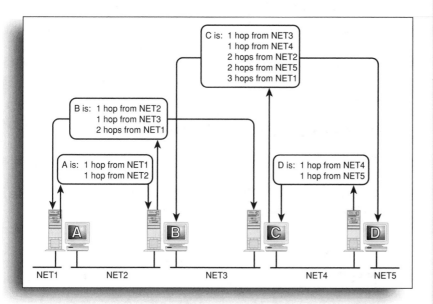

FIGURE 15.5
Default routers cannot support this network.

Actually there is probably no need for RIP unless you have at least three routers. As the network in Figure 15.1 illustrates, routing with two routers can be handled adequately with default routes. But RIP is the easier approach on most networks with three or more routers.

Limitations of RIP

RIP is not a perfect protocol, and it has some limitations and liabilities. One problem is that RIP routers are pretty talkative. Each router announces its routing table every 30 seconds. On a big network, these announcements generate a lot of network traffic.

Another problem is that RIP is slow to adjust to changes in the network, particularly when network connections fail. It can take several minutes for all the routers to learn that the connection is down and whether an alternative route exists. The process of updating all the routers on the current state of the network is called *convergence*, and slow convergence is one of RIP's major shortcomings.

A number of tricks have been introduced to speed RIP convergence. One trick imposes a maximum size on RIP networks. No message can cross more than 15 networks to reach its destination. Any destination that is more than 15 networks away is considered to be "at infinity" and unreachable. Consequently, you need to be very careful when planning networks that approach the 15-hop limit.

Installing RIP for Internet Protocol

After you have concluded that you need to install RIP on a router, the task of installation is a no brainer. Just install the RIP for Internet Protocol service as follows:

Installing RIP for Internet Protocol

1. Install a second network adapter if one is not already installed.

SEE ALSO

➤ *The procedure for installing network adapters is covered in Chapter 3, "Configuring Network Adapters, Services, and Protocols," page 83 in the section titled "Adding and Removing Network Adapters."*

2. Open the Network applet in the Control Panel.

3. Select the **Services** tab.

4. Click **Add** to open the Select Network Service dialog box.

5. Select **RIP for Internet Protocol** in the **Network Service** list box.

6. When prompted, supply the path to the Windows NT installation files (for example, f:\i386).

7. Close the Network applet.

8. Restart the computer.

RIP for IP requires no configuration.

Limitations of RIP for Internet Protocol

The version of RIP for IP that is included with Windows NT Server 4 is version 1 of the RIP protocol, typically referred to as RIP I. An important limitation of RIP I is that it does not directly support subnetwork addressing. RIP I routers can learn subnetwork addresses only of the subnets to which they are directly attached. If your network uses IP subnetwork addressing, you should consider upgrading to Microsoft's Routing and Remote Access Service, a free Windows NT upgrade that is included with the *Windows NT Option Pack*. Consult www.microsoft.com for information about downloading the Option Pack. My book *Inside Windows NT Server 4, 2nd Edition* (New Riders Publishing) includes a chapter on Routing and Remote Access Service.

Testing Your Router

You test a routed network just as you test a non-routed network, with the ping command. You can ping any host, whether you communicate with it locally or through a router. Unless you get involved with network packet analysis, ping and a good investigative spirit are your best tools for troubleshooting router connections.

The procedure is a simple extension of the procedure for testing local communications:

Using *ping* to test a router

1. Ping the loopback address (127.0.0.1).
2. Ping the local IP address.
3. Ping the default router.
4. Ping any intervening routers.
5. Ping the remote host.

If several routers intervene between your computer and the remote host, you may need to ping each router in turn to determine where communications problems lie. The process is just a matter of testing communication from one end of the connection to the other until you isolate a problem.

Connecting to a Wide Area Network

Let's make this real easy. Unless you know a great deal more about telecommunications than you will learn in this book, you won't take any part in actually setting up your WAN connections. You will be contracting with a telecommunications provider who will do all the hard work for you and will provide you with a box on your end to which you connect your network. It's really that simple. The hard tasks on your end are defining your requirements, comparing plans, selecting a vendor, and paying the (Ouch!) bill.

If you are connecting with the Internet, you can usually arrange for the entire connection package through your ISP. Typically, you will consider three choices:

- **ISDN**. A switched digital service that typically offers network bandwidth up to 128 Kbps.

- **Frame relay**. A WAN technology that offers service in 64 Kbps increments. You purchase a basic service level called a *committed information rate* (CIR) for a fixed monthly fee. Some services will permit you to temporarily exceed your CIR for a surcharge, so frame relay can be a flexible way to meet changing bandwidth requirements.

- **A digital dedicated line** (such as a T1 line, which offers a data rate of 1.544 Mbps). Digital dedicated lines have fixed bandwidth, and you pay for all the bandwidth regardless of whether you use it. You should be very clear about your requirements before you commit to a dedicated digital connection.

Establishing a digital connection is a complex affair that typically involves two or three vendors. Unless you want a crash course in telecommunications, let a telecommunications provider or an Internet service provider plan your connection and monitor its installation.

A WAN connection turns your network into an instant internetwork because at least one router will be added to your network to route traffic to and from the WAN. Figure 15.6 illustrates a typical Internet connection. Note that the router that connects to the WAN must be able to route messages back to your local hosts. In most cases, that means you will run RIP on the WAN router and on your local routers so that the routers communicate and stay current on any changes to the network. (In many cases the router and the WAN interface will be part of the same piece of equipment. I wanted to distinguish between the routing and interface functions in the figure.)

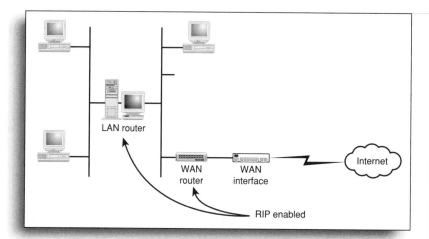

FIGURE 15.6
Routing with a WAN connection.

Your Internetwork's Up

As you can see, NT makes it pretty easy to set up an internetwork. You use ordinary NT computers as routers, and the toughest part is adding the extra network adapters. After that, it's a matter of configuring default routes and adding RIP if your network requires it.

Now that you can build really big networks, you have a problem. Windows NetBIOS names won't cross a TCP/IP router, so your users can no longer browse the network. That's one of the hurdles Microsoft had to leap when they deployed TCP/IP on Windows networks. The solution they developed is WINS, the Windows Internet Name Service—our next stop along your way to Windows NT Server mastery.

Supporting Windows Naming with WINS

TCP/IP support in a network is a good thing, even a vital thing. It's difficult to even consider functioning in today's connected world without TCP/IP. But when Microsoft began to add TCP/IP support to its LAN server products, it had a problem, because the naming system used on Microsoft networks doesn't function on TCP/IP networks that include routers.

Microsoft network computers are known by their NetBIOS names. From the administrator's perspective, NetBIOS names are pretty cool because they automatically advertise servers' identities on the network with no effort on the part of the administrator. Simply install a server and, shazam, it shows up in users' browse lists.

But NetBIOS has a design limitation that shows up in routed networks, because NetBIOS relies heavily on broadcast messages to spread the word about servers and their shared resources. *Broadcast messages* are messages that are received by every computer within earshot, rather than by a specific computer. Broadcasting is a lot like shouting in a restaurant—everyone else must stop talking to listen to one loud person. That's fine if the message is important ("Fire!") but not if it's just someone complaining about his clam chowder.

To confine the impact of broadcast messages, networks typically don't forward broadcast messages through routers. If they did, the broadcast message could echo throughout the internetwork and take over the whole thing. Microsoft specifically designed their NWLink routing protocol to forward NetBIOS messages, but TCP/IP is another matter. TCP/IP is standardized, and Microsoft's TCP/IP router has to be like everyone else's TCP/IP router. So Microsoft had to find a way to make NetBIOS naming work in a standard TCP/IP network.

Microsoft's first solution, introduced in its older LAN Manager server, was to use files named LMHOSTS, which consisted of records matching NetBIOS names to IP addresses. When a computer couldn't find a particular NetBIOS computer on the local network it would consult its LMHOSTS file to see if the computer could be found elsewhere.

LMHOSTS files fall in the category of "static name databases." An LMHOSTS file is a text file that must be edited manually. After creating a master LMHOSTS file, an administrator must copy the file to every computer on the network. Every time a computer was installed or removed, the master LMHOSTS file had to be updated and redistributed. Doesn't that sound like fun? (You will briefly examine the structure of the LMHOSTS file later in this chapter, but I doubt that LMHOSTS will be your chief naming mechanism.)

So Microsoft needed a dynamic name service that would keep itself current on computers on the network. A name service that could work in routed TCP/IP environments. A name service that they dubbed the *Windows Internet Naming Service* (WINS). Although you could support naming on your TCP/IP network using LMHOSTS, you don't want to unless you have lots of free time. It is far better to set up WINS and let it do the work for you. And that's what this chapter will teach you to do.

NetBIOS Node Types

There are two ways computers can communicate on a network:

- Through broadcast messages, which every computer hears
- Through directed messages, which are sent to a specific computer

Whenever possible, it is preferable to communicate through directed messages. And directed messages will propagate across routers. So, Microsoft needed a name service that relied primarily on directed messages. It took awhile to arrive at that goal, however, and you need to examine the various naming methods that can be used on Microsoft networks.

These naming methods are referred to as *node types*. A node, you will recall, is simply a device on a network. Every computer on a Microsoft computer is configured with one of four node types that determines whether the computer will learn names through broadcast messages, directed messages, or some combination of

The WINS essentials

As with almost everything else about TCP/IP, there's a lot more I could tell you about WINS. This chapter contains the essentials, which is all that most administrators need to know. If you want to get down to the bare metal of WINS, see my book *Networking with Microsoft TCP/IP* from New Riders Publishing.

broadcast and directed messages. Before you can work with WINS, you need to know what the node types are and when they are used:

- **B-node** (broadcast node) relies exclusively on broadcast messages and is the oldest name resolution mode. A host needing to resolve a name request sends a message to every host within earshot, requesting the address associated with a host name. B-node has two shortcomings: Broadcast traffic is undesirable and becomes a significant user of network bandwidths, and TCP/IP routers don't forward broadcast messages, which restricts b-node operation to a single network segment.

- **P-node** (point-to-point node) relies on WINS servers. Clients register themselves with a WINS server and contact the WINS server with name resolution requests. WINS servers communicate using directed messages, which can cross routers, so P-node can operate on large networks. Unfortunately, if the WINS server is unavailable, or if a node isn't configured to contact a WINS server, p-node name resolution fails.

- **M-node** (modified node) is a hybrid mode that first attempts to resolve names using b-node. If that fails, an attempt is made to use p-node name resolution. M-node was historically the first hybrid mode put into operation, but it has the disadvantage of favoring b-node operation, which is associated with high levels of broadcast traffic.

- **H-node** (hybrid node) is also a hybrid mode that favors WINS. First, an attempt is made to use p-node to resolve a name via WINS. Only if WINS resolution fails does the host resort to b-node to resolve the name via broadcasts. Because it typically results in the best network utilization, h-node is the default mode of operation for Microsoft TCP/IP clients configured to use WINS for name resolution.

Although networks can be organized using a mixture of node types, Microsoft recommends against it. B-node clients ignore p-node directed messages, and p-node clients ignore b-node broadcasts. Therefore, it is conceivable that two clients could separately be established with the same NetBIOS name.

Elements of a WINS Network

Figure 16.1 illustrates clients and WINS servers on a routed network. Four types of computers appear in the figure:

- **WINS Servers.** When WINS clients enter the network, they contact a WINS server using a directed message. The client registers its name with the WINS server, and uses the WINS server to resolve NetBIOS names to IP addresses.

- **WINS Clients.** WINS clients use directed (p-node) messages to communicate with WINS servers, and are typically configured to use h-node communication. Windows NT, Windows 95 and 98, and Windows for Workgroups computers can be WINS clients.

- **Non-WINS Clients.** Older Microsoft network clients that can't use p-node can still benefit from WINS. Their broadcast messages are intercepted by WINS proxy computers that act as intermediaries between the b-node clients and WINS servers. MS-DOS and Windows 3.1 clients function as non-WINS clients.

- **WINS Proxies.** Windows NT, Windows 95 and 98, and Windows for Workgroups clients can function as WINS proxies. They intercept b-node broadcasts on their local subnet and communicate with a WINS server on behalf of the b-node client.

Notice that two WINS servers are found on the sample network. Both WINS servers can register client names when a client enters the network. Periodically, the WINS servers replicate their databases so that each WINS server comprehends the entire network. Whenever possible it is desirable to have at least two WINS servers. This lets name resolution take place when one name server is down. It also lets administrators distribute WINS activity across multiple servers to balance the processing loads.

FIGURE 16.1

A routed network that uses
WINS.

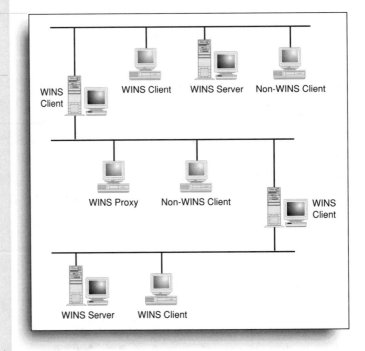

FIGURE 16.1

A routed network that uses
WINS.

Installing the WINS Service

Any Windows NT Server computer can be configured as a
WINS server. To install the WINS service, do the following:

Installing the WINS service

1. Open the Network applet in the Control Panel and select
   the Services tab.

2. Click **Add** to open the Select Network Services dialog box.

3. Select Windows Internet Name Service from the **Network
   Services** list box and click **OK**.

4. When prompted, supply a file path to the installation CD-
   ROM. Files will be copied to the server.

5. Review the configuration in the Microsoft TCP/IP
   Properties window.

6. Restart the computer to activate the new service.

Managing the WINS Server

When the WINS service is installed, a shortcut to the WINS Manager application is added to the Administrative Tools program group in the **Start** menu. The WINS Manager is used to monitor and manage all WINS functions.

Adding WINS Servers to WINS Manager

Figure 16.2 shows the WINS Manager. In the example, the network is configured with two WINS servers, which are listed in the **WINS Servers** pane. The right-hand pane displays summary statistics for the selected WINS server. You can view statistics for any WINS server by double-clicking the server in the **WINS Servers** pane.

If a WINS server doesn't appear in the **WINS Servers** pane, select the **Add WINS Server** command from the **Server** menu, and specify the IP address of the WINS server in the dialog box that is provided.

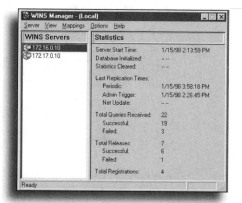

FIGURE 16.2

The main dialog box for WINS Manager.

Configuring the WINS Service

Several properties on a WINS server can be adjusted. To configure a WINS server, select a server in the WINS Servers pane of the WINS Manager main window. Then choose the **Configuration** command from the **Server** menu to display the WINS Server Configuration dialog box, shown in Figure 16.3.

WINS servers can't be routers

A WINS server can't be equipped with more than one network interface adapter because WINS permits a computer to be registered on only one network. Therefore, you cannot configure routers as WINS servers.

In this figure, the **Advanced** button has been pressed to open
the **Advanced WINS Server Configuration** properties at the
bottom of the dialog box.

FIGURE 16.3

Configurable properties for a
WINS server.

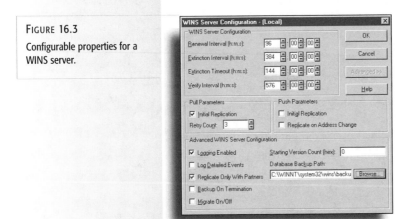

The WINS Server Configuration box includes four properties
that affect WINS client name resolution:

- **Renewal Interval** specifies the intervals at which a WINS
  client must reregister its name. A name that isn't reregis-
  tered is marked as released in the WINS database. A good
  renewal interval value is four days (96 hours), which ensures
  a client retains its registration over a long weekend. If
  clients are forced to renew very frequently (more often than
  three days), network traffic is increased.

- **Extinction Interval** specifies the interval between the time
  a name is marked released and when it is marked extinct.
  Extinct records are eligible to be purged. Try setting this
  value to four times the renewal interval.

- **Extinction Timeout** specifies the interval between the time
  a name is marked extinct and when the name is actually
  purged from the database. The minimum value is one day.

- **Verify Interval** specifies the interval after which a WINS
  server must verify that names it doesn't own are still active.
  The maximum value is 24 days (576 hours).

SEE ALSO

➤ *Properties in the **Pull Parameters** and **Push Parameters** are discussed in the section "Configuring WINS Database Replication" later in this chapter on page 494.*

The **Advanced WINS Server Configuration** properties are revealed by clicking the **Advanced** button. The following advanced properties are available:

- **Logging Enabled** is checked if logging to should be turned on. Log messages are recorded in a file named Jet.log.

- **Log Detailed Events** is checked to turn on detailed logging. Because verbose logging can consume considerable resources, it should be turned on only during performance tuning.

- **Replicate Only With Partners** is checked if replication should take place only with push and pull partners specifically configured for this server. If this option isn't checked, an administrator can force push or pull replication with this server.

- **Backup On Termination** is checked if the database should be backed up automatically when WINS Manager is stopped (except when the server is shutting down).

- **Backup Path** accepts a path to a file that is used to back up the database. Backup can be initiated automatically, as discussed in step 8, or manually by using the **Backup Database** command from the **Mappings** menu. Click **Browse** to browse for a path if desired.

- **Migrate On/Off** is checked if you are upgrading non-Windows NT systems to Windows NT. This option allows static records to be treated as dynamic and reassigned to eliminate conflicts.

You should complete the **Backup Path** field to enable WINS database backup. Otherwise, WINS will work fine with default settings, so you may never need to visit the configuration dialog box.

Configuring WINS Database Replication

As mentioned earlier, if your network has two or more WINS servers they can be configured to replicate their databases. This lets you have multiple copies of the WINS database, so that WINS name resolution continues to function if a WINS server goes down. Because every network subnet should be equipped with a WINS server or a WINS proxy, the best approach is to place WINS servers on separate subnets.

WINS servers replicate their databases through two operations: *pushing* and *pulling*. To replicate data, two WINS servers form a partnership that works like this:

- A *replication push partner* is a WINS server that notifies other WINS servers that it has recorded changes in its database. It then sends these changes upon request from a pull partner.

- A *replication pull partner* is a WINS server that requests data from a push partner and then accepts the data that the push partner sends.

Figure 16.4 shows how replication is configured when there are two WINS servers. Notice that replication must be configured in both directions. Each computer must be a pull partner to the other's push partner.

FIGURE 16.4

Replicating WINS data between two WINS servers.

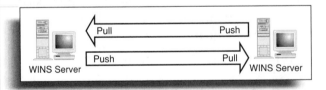

Figure 16.5 shows three WINS servers that form replication partnerships. These servers form a ring in which each server has one push partner and one pull partner.

You should avoid constructing replication rings that are two large, however, or it may take too long for a change to be replicated to all servers. If you have more than three or four WINS servers you may want to use a combination of two-way and one-way replication, as shown in Figure 16.6.

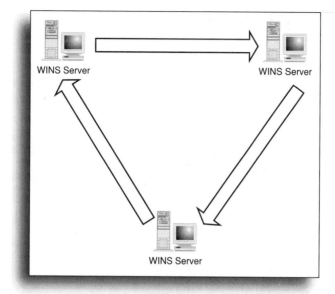

FIGURE 16.5
Replicating WINS data in a ring configuration.

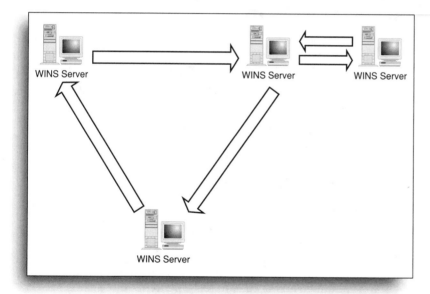

FIGURE 16.6
WINS resolution using a combination of one-way and two-way relationships.

To set up a WINS replication relationship, you must configure a push partner and a pull partner.

Configuring a Push Partner

To configure a push partner, do the following:

Configuring a push partner

1. Open WINS Manager and select a WINS server in the main window.

2. Choose **Replication Partners** from the **Server** menu to open the Replication Partners dialog box, shown in Figure 16.7.

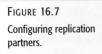

FIGURE 16.7

Configuring replication partners.

3. Select another WINS server in the **WINS Server** list of the Replication Partners dialog box.

4. Check the **Push Partner** check box in the **Replication Options** box.

5. Click **Configure** to open the Push Partner Properties dialog box, shown in Figure 16.8.

FIGURE 16.8

Configuring a push partner.

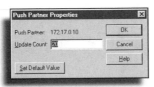

6. If desired, enter a value in the **Update Count** field. This parameter specifies the number of updates that must be made to the local database before it will notify its pull partners. (Entries pulled from other partners don't count in this context. Only local updates are taken into consideration.)

Configuring a Pull Partner

To configure a pull partner, do the following:

Configuring a pull partner

1. Open WINS Manager and select a WINS server in the main window.

2. Choose **Replication Partners** from the **Server** menu to open the Replication Partners dialog box, shown in Figure 16.7.

3. Select another WINS server in the **WINS Server** list of the Replication Partners dialog box.

4. Check the **Pull Partner** check box in the **Replication Options** box.

5. Click **Configure** to open the Pull Partner Properties dialog box, shown in Figure 16.9.

Avoid forcing frequent updates

If you force updates to occur too frequently, WINS can generate excess network traffic. The minimum value for the **Update Count** is 20.

FIGURE 16.9

Configuring a pull partner.

6. In the **Start Time** field boxes, specify the earliest time in the day when database replication should be performed. If you don't specify a start time, replication takes place 24 hours a day.

7. In the **Replication Interval** spin boxes, specify the intervals at which this server should pull data from its push server.

Replication and network traffic

Ideally, changes to the WINS database should be replicated as soon as they occur, but immediate replication could generate too much network traffic. When configuring WINS replication, you are establishing a compromise between timeliness and network traffic load.

Forcing Database Replication

Although WINS replication takes place automatically, you may want to force replication from time to time. You can initiate replication by sending push or pull triggers.

To send a push replication trigger, do the following:

Sending a push replication trigger

1. Select a pull replication partner in the Replication Partners dialog box.

2. Check the **Push with Propagation** box if the selected server should send a push trigger to its pull partners after it has pulled replicas from this server.

   Leave the box unchecked if the selected pull partner should not send a push trigger to its pull partners.

3. Click **Push** in the **Send Replication Trigger Now** box to send a replication trigger to the selected pull partner. This trigger takes effect only for other servers that have been configured as pull partners.

To send a pull replication trigger, do the following:

Sending a pull replication trigger

1. Select a replication partner in the Replication Partners dialog box.

2. Click **Pull** in the **Send Replication Trigger Now** box to send a replication trigger to the selected push partner. This trigger takes effect only for other servers that have been configured as push partners.

3. To start immediate replication, click **Replicate Now**.

Managing WINS Preferences

You can configure several WINS preferences by choosing the **Preferences** command from the **WINS Manager Options** menu. The Preferences dialog box is shown in Figure 16.10. This figure shows how the window appears after the Partners box has been checked to display options for configuring new pull and push partners. The following list contains the available options:

- Options in the **Address Display** box specify whether the address should be displayed in the main window by IP address, computer name, or both.

- Check **Auto Re_f_resh** to specify that statistics should be updated automatically at the interval specified.

- The **_L_AN Manager-Compatible** box should always be checked unless your network will be receiving NetBIOS names from sources other than Microsoft networks. (All Microsoft network clients use LAN Manager compatible names.)

- Check **_V_alidate Cache of Known WINS Servers at Startup Time** if this server should query its list of known WINS servers each time Windows NT Server starts up. Ordinarily, this option isn't required.

- Check **Confirm _D_eletion of Static Mappings & Cached WINS servers** if warnings should be displayed when you delete a static mapping or the cached name of a WINS server. This option is recommended.

- Specify default options for pull partners in the **New Pull Partner Default Configuration** box.

- Specify default options for push partners in the **New Push Partner Default Configuration** box.

FIGURE 16.10

You can establish several WINS preferences in this dialog box.

Managing the WINS Database

Prior to Windows NT Server 4.0, you needed to perform several periodic maintenance tasks on the WINS database. Now nearly everything is done automatically. This section will focus on two management tasks you may need to perform: monitoring and backing up the database.

Monitoring the WINS Database

To view the contents of a WINS server's database, select the server in the WINS Manager main window and select **Show Database** from the **Mappings** menu. Figure 16.11 shows a sample of entries in the WINS database.

FIGURE 16.11

Sample contents of a WINS database.

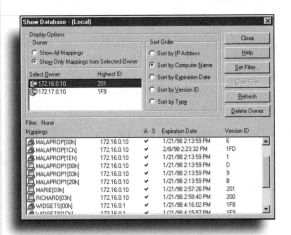

With WINS, the owner of a mapping is the WINS server that originated the mapping, not a particular user account.

To view mappings owned by a particular server, do the following:

Viewing mappings owned by a particular server

1. Select **Show Only Mappings from Selected Owner** in the **Owner** box.

2. Select a WINS server in the **Select Owner** list.

If you want to view all mappings in the database, select **Show All Mappings**.

If you want to view only mappings for a particular computer, follow these steps:

Viewing only mappings for a particular computer

1. Click **Set Filter**.

2. In the Set Filter dialog box, specify a value in the **Computer Name** or **IP Address** field.

3. Click **OK**.

You can't delete individual entries from the WINS database.

To delete all mappings owned by a particular WINS server, follow these steps:

Deleting all mappings owned by a particular WINS server

1. Select a WINS server from the **Select Owner** list.

2. Click **Delete Owner**.

NetBIOS Names

In Figure 16.11, notice that many computers appear more than once in the mappings table. In fact, a given NetBIOS computer can be identified by as many as 16 names, which consist of two parts:

- A text name up to 15 characters. This is the name you specify when you configure the computer name when setting up networking.

- A 16-bit hexadecimal number suffix that describes the program with which the name is associated.

WINS is one of the few places where you will observe NetBIOS names complete with their numeric suffixes. In Figure 16.11, the computer MALAPROP1 is linked to four NetBIOS names:

- **MALAPROP1[00h]** is the name associated with the Workstation service. Every Microsoft network client will be associated with at least one Workstation service name.

- **MALAPROP1[03h]** is the name associated with the Messenger service, the name used to send messages to this computer. This name is observed if the Messenger service is active.

- **MALAPROP1[20h]** is associated with the Server service, and is seen on any Microsoft computer that is configured to share resources with the network.

Also of interest are the entries for the MALAPROP domain. Domains also have NetBIOS names, and you can learn something about the domain structure by examining the WINS database. For example:

- **MALAPROP[1Ch]** indicates that the computer with the IP address specified is a domain controller for the MALAPROP domain.

- **MALAPROP[1Eh]** indicates that the computer is a potential browser.

continues…

NetBIOS Names
continued

You can observe the NetBIOS names associated with a computer by entering the command `nbtstat -n` from a command prompt.

It isn't all that important that you be able to interpret NetBIOS names. All the important work is done in the background for you. I'm including this information because it is visible in WINS Manager, and I thought you might be curious about the multiple entries.

Backing Up and Restoring the WINS Database

One potential problem with WINS is that WINS keeps its database open whenever it is running, and open files can't be backed up. As a result, if there is a system crash, you will lose the WINS database file. This forces WINS clients to reregister and could result in some clients being unable to use their accustomed names.

To avoid this problem, the WINS database is backed up automatically every 24 hours, creating files that can be backed up to tape. The backup directory is specified in the WINS Server Configuration dialog box.

SEE ALSO

> *The WINS Server Configuration dialog box is discussed in this chapter, page 491, in the section, "Configuring the WINS Service."*

You may want to force a backup of the database to take place, for ensurance or to capture the WINS database at a particular point in time. And you certainly need to know how to restore the database from its backup in case you ever need to restore an entire server from tape.

Backing Up the WINS Database

Backing up a WINS database must be performed on the computer running the WINS Server service.

Backing up the WINS database

1. Choose the **Backup Database** command from the **Mappings** menu to open a **Select Backup Directory** dialog box.

2. If desired, select a disk drive in the **Dri̲ves** box. The best location is another hard disk so that the database files remain available if the primary hard disk fails.

3. Specify the directory in which backup files should be stored. WINS Manager proposes the directory you specify in the WINS Server Configuration dialog box.

4. If desired, specify a new directory name to be created in the directory chosen in Step 3. By default, a subdirectory named wins_bak is created to store the backup files.

5. Click **OK** to make the backup.

Restoring the WINS Database

If users can't connect to a server running the WINS Server service, the WINS database probably has become corrupted. In that case, you might need to restore the database from a backup copy. This can be done manually or by using menu commands. The procedure must be performed on the computer running the WINS service.

To restore the WINS database using menu commands, do the following:

Restoring the WINS database

1. Stop the WINS Service using one of these methods:

   - Stop the Windows Internet Server Service using the Services tool in the Control Panel.

   - Open a command prompt and enter the command net stop wins.

2. Start the WINS Manager. Ignore any warning message that says The Windows Internet Naming Service is not running on the target machine, or The target machine is not accessible.

3. Choose the **R̲estore Local Database** command from the **M̲appings** menu.

4. In the **Select Directory To Restore From** dialog box, specify the directory from which to restore.

5. Click **OK** to restore the database.

6. Start the WINS service using one of the following methods:

- Start the Windows Internet Server Service using the **Services** tool in the Control Panel.

- Open a command prompt and enter the command `net start wins`.

Configuring WINS Clients

Each Microsoft client can be configured with the IP addresses of two WINS servers. On Windows NT clients, the WINS server properties are on the WINS tab of the Microsoft TCP/IP Properties dialog box, shown in Figure 16.12. You can specify two IP addresses in the **Pri̱mary WINS Server** and **Ṣecondary WINS Server** boxes.

FIGURE 16.12

Entering WINS servers in a client's TCP/IP properties.

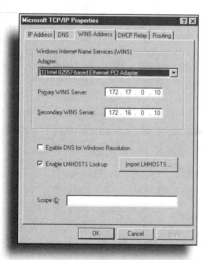

The client will prefer the primary WINS server. If your network has two or more WINS servers, you should configure clients so that all WINS servers will be used about equally.

To configure a client to function as a WINS proxy, do the following:

Configuring a client as a WINS proxy

1. Display the TCP/IP properties dialog box for the client.

2. Click **Advanced** to display the Advanced Microsoft TCP/IP Configuration dialog box.

3. Check **Enable WINS Proxy Agent**.

SEE ALSO

➤ *To learn more about proxies turn to page 489 in this chapter.*

Configuring Name Resolution with LMHOSTS

If for some reason you don't want to configure WINS on your network, or if you want to have a backup in case a single WINS server fails, you can use LMHOSTS files to provide naming support for Microsoft network clients.

An LMHOSTS file has a very simple structure, as with the following:

```
172.16.0.1        MALAPROP1

172.16.0.50       ISAAC

172.17.0.25       ALBERT

172.17.0.100      MARIE
```

Each entry in LMHOSTS appears on a separate line and consists of two fields: an IP address and a name. The fields must be separated with at least one space or tab character. You will find a sample LMHOSTS file in the directory C:\Winnt\system32\etc.

LMHOSTS Files Keywords

Several keywords can appear in LMHOSTS files. Here is an example of a file with keywords:

```
172.16.0.1        MALAPROP1      #PRE         #DOM:MALAPROP

172.16.0.5        MALAPROP2      #PRE

#BEGIN_ALTERNATE
```

```
#INCLUDE  \\MALAPROP1\PUBLIC\LMHOSTS

#INCLUDE  \\MALAPROP2\PUBLIC\LMHOSTS

#END_ALTERNATE
```

The #PRE keyword specifies that the entry should be preloaded into the name cache. Ordinarily, LMHOSTS is consulted for name resolution only after WINS and b-node broadcasts have failed. Preloading the entry ensures that the mapping will be available at the start of the name-resolution process.

The #DOM: keyword associates an entry with a domain. This may be useful in determining how browsers and logon services behave on a routed TCP/IP network. #DOM entries may be preloaded in cache by including the #PRE keyword.

The #INCLUDE keyword makes it possible to load mappings from a remote file. One use for #INCLUDE is to support a master LMHOSTS file that is stored on logon servers and is accessed by TCP/IP clients when they start up. Entries in the remote LMHOSTS file are examined only when TCP/IP is started. Therefore, entries in the remote LMHOSTS file must be tagged with the #PRE keyword to force them to be loaded into cache.

If several copies of the included LMHOSTS file are available on different servers, you can force the computer to search several locations until a file is successfully loaded. This is accomplished by bracketing #INCLUDE keywords between the keywords #BEGIN_ALTERNATE and #END_ALTERNATE, as was done in the preceding sample file. Any successful #INCLUDE causes the group to succeed.

Using host names as parameters

In the sample listing, note that the hosts MALAPROP1 and MALAPROP2 were explicitly defined so that the names could be used in the parameters of the #INCLUDE keywords.

Using the #INCLUDE Statement

There is a catch to the #INCLUDE statement. The LMHOSTS file is processed before the user is logged in. Therefore, when LMHOSTS is processed, the user isn't authenticated and doesn't have access to the share where the included LMHOSTS file is stored.

The solution to this problem is to make the share a *null share* that can be accessed by clients who have not logged in. Null shares are defined in the Registry. On the server that has the share, use the Registry Editor to open the following Registry value:

Using the #INCLUDE
Statement **continued**

```
HKEY_LOCAL_MACHINE\   System\   CurrentControlSet\   Services\
LanManServer\   Parameters\   NullSessionShares
```

NullSessionShares is a value entry of type REG_MULTI_SZ. The value consists of a list of shares that are designated as null shares. In the example, PUBLIC would be added to the strings already present in the value array. This would be done on the MALAPROP1 and MALAPROP2 servers.

SEE ALSO

➤ *For a more detailed discussion of Registry concepts turn to page 657.*

Enabling Clients to Use LMHOSTS Files

Generally speaking, LMHOSTS files are unnecessary on networks that have a properly functioning WINS name service. If an internetwork will not be using WINS, LMHOSTS lookups should be enabled and LMHOSTS files should be configured to help computers find critical hosts.

Any TCP/IP client can be enabled to use LMHOSTS files by checking the **Enable LMHOSTS Lookup** check box in the WINS tab of the Microsoft TCP/IP Properties dialog box (see Figure 16.13).

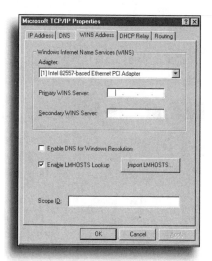

FIGURE 16.13
Enabling LMHOSTS lookups.

Guidelines for Establishing LMHOSTS Name Resolution

B-node computers that are not configured to use WINS name resolution can use LMHOSTS to resolve names on remote networks. If the majority of name queries are on the local network, it isn't generally necessary to preload mappings in the LMHOSTS file. Frequently accessed hosts on remote networks may be preloaded with the #PRE keyword.

#DOM keywords should be used to help non-WINS clients locate domain controllers on remote networks. The LMHOSTS file for every computer in the domain should include #DOM entries for all domain controllers that don't reside on the local network. This ensures that domain activities such as logon authentication continue to function.

To browse a domain other than the logon domain, LMHOSTS must include the name and IP address of the primary domain controller of the domain to be browsed. Include backup domain controllers in case the primary fails or in case a backup domain controller is promoted to primary.

LMHOSTS files on backup domain controllers should include mappings to the primary domain controller name and IP address, as well as mappings to all other backup domain controllers.

All domain controllers in trusted domains should be included in the local LMHOSTS file.

End of the Identity Crisis

Now, thanks to WINS, everyone knows everyone else on your TCP/IP network. That's a major crisis averted, and in a very real sense you now have a completely functional TCP/IP network.

But that doesn't make it easy to manage. If your network is of any size at all, you are probably getting a bit ticked off by now. Every change to a host's TCP/IP configuration requires you to visit the computer and make configuration changes. If a WINS server moves, you have to visit every computer to make a configuration change. Unfortunately, your job doesn't include a shoe leather bonus. So what's a frazzled LAN administrator to do?

That's where the Dynamic Host Configuration Protocol (DHCP) comes in. Using DHCP, you can automate a lot of the client configuration that you have performed manually until now. So the next chapter might save you quite a few Tylenols and Tums.

Simplifying Administration with DHCP

How DHCP works

Installing DHCP

Configuring routers to support DHCP

Managing DHCP scopes

Configuring DHCP options

Backing up and restoring the DHCP database

Managing DHCP clients

As a fledgling TCP/IP administrator, you might be freaking out about the amount of configuration required to keep your network clients happy. Move a WINS server, and you have to reconfigure every client. Move a client to a new subnet, and you have to update its IP address—and the manager who plugs his notebook into a new location every day definitely won't be in your good graces. Every change to the network requires a visit to one or more computers to update configuration properties. As if running a LAN isn't tough enough, you're too busy swatting mosquitoes to take aim at that grizzly that's charging out of the bushes.

Well, the Internet community has long been aware of the hassles of host configuration, so they came up with the *Dynamic Host Configuration Protocol* (DHCP). DHCP can save a tremendous amount of wear and tear on you and on your shoes. It takes a bit of time to set things up at first, but not all that much, and the rewards can be generous.

How DHCP Works

Figure 17.1 shows a DHCP network that has two DHCP servers. Although a single DHCP server can support a network of any size, it is often useful to have two. Here's what happens when a DHCP client enters the network:

1. The client broadcasts a DHCP discover message that is forwarded to DHCP servers on the network.

2. Each DHCP server that receives the discover message responds with a DHCP offer message that includes an IP address that is appropriate for the subnet where the client is attached.

3. The client considers the offer message and selects one. It sends a request to use that address to the DHCP server that originated the offer.

4. The DHCP server acknowledges the request and grants the client a lease to use the address.

5. The client uses the IP address to bind to the network. If the
IP address is associated with any configuration parameters,
the parameters are incorporated into the client's TCP/IP
configuration.

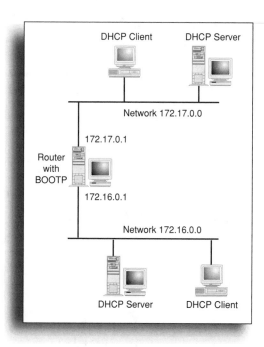

DHCP Client   DHCP Server

Network 172.17.0.0

172.17.0.1

Router
with
BOOTP

172.16.0.1

Network 172.16.0.0

DHCP Server   DHCP Client

FIGURE 17.1

A network with two DHCP
servers.

In step 1 I told you that DHCP clients request their addresses
using broadcast messages. The preceding chapters have pointed
out several times that broadcast messages don't cross TCP/IP
routers. Does that mean that a DHCP client can't obtain an IP
address from a DHCP server on another subnet?

No, not if you configure routers with the BOOTP protocol.
BOOTP is an older protocol that assigns IP addresses, and it
remains in use to allow DHCP broadcasts to propagate across
routers. Thanks to BOOTP, a DHCP server can service clients
on any number of subnets.

In Figure 17.1, BOOTP is enabled on the router, which must, of
course, be configured to route TCP/IP traffic. When the client
broadcasts a request for an IP address, BOOTP receives the
request and sends a directed message to any DHCP server that it
knows about. This allows a DHCP server on a remote subnet to

receive the request. The DHCP server responds through a directed message, so there is no problem with routing the response back to the client.

Installing DHCP

DHCP is installed as a service. After installing the DHCP service, you need to configure BOOTP on any routers and then define subnet configurations on the DHCP server.

To support DHCP on a network, one or more computers must be running the DHCP service. A DHCP server can't also be a DHCP client. Therefore, computers running the DHCP Server service must be configured with fixed IP addresses.

To install the DHCP server service, follow these steps:

Installing the DHCP Server service

1. Open the Network applet in the Control Panel.

2. Review the TCP/IP Properties page and confirm that the computer is configured with a fixed IP address.

3. Select the **Services** tab.

4. Click **Add** to open the Select Network Services dialog box.

5. Select **Microsoft DHCP Server** from the **Network Services** list box and click **OK**.

6. When prompted, supply a file path to the installation CD-ROM. Files will be copied to the server.

7. Next you will see a message that states If any adapters are using DHCP to obtain IP addresses, they are required to use a static IP address. Click **OK**.

8. Close the Network applet. Review the configuration in the Microsoft TCP/IP Properties window.

9. Restart the computer to activate the new service.

Configuring BOOTP Forwarding

You must enable BOOTP forwarding on any router that must pass DHCP discover messages. To enable BOOTP forwarding, open the TCP/IP Properties page and select the **DHCP Relay** tab, shown in Figure 17.2.

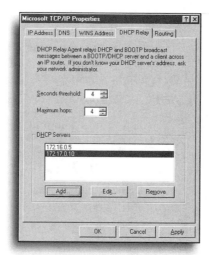

FIGURE 17.2

Configuring DHCP forwarding.

The **DHCP Servers** list must be configured with the IP address of at least one DHCP server. You should include in this list the IP addresses of all the DHCP servers on your network. Click **Add** to open a dialog box where you can specify an IP address.

The **Seconds threshold** field determines how long DHCP broadcast messages will be permitted to remain on the network.

The **Maximum hops** field determines the maximum number of networks a DHCP discover message can cross before it is removed from the network. DHCP discover messages that exceed the maximum hop count will not be delivered. The maximum hop count determines how far DHCP clients can reach in their quest for a DHCP server.

After you have configured BOOTP forwarding, restart the computer to activate the changes.

Managing DHCP Scope

A *scope* is a range of IP addresses that can be assigned to clients on a given subnet. A scope can also include a set of configuration parameters that are assigned to clients that obtain their IP addresses from the scope. After installing the DHCP service, you must define at least one scope on the server.

Creating Scopes

Scopes are managed using DHCP Manager. An icon for DHCP Manager is added to the Administrative Tools program group when the DHCP Server service is installed. Figure 17.3 shows DHCP Manager after two scopes have been defined.

To create a scope, do the following:

Creating a scope

1. Open DHCP Manager. At least one computer should be displayed in the left DHCP Servers pane. The computer on which DHCP Manager is running will be listed as Local Machine.

2. Double-click the server on which the scope will be created. Then choose **Create** from the **Scope** menu to display the Create Scope dialog box, shown in Figure 17.3.

FIGURE 17.3

Creating a scope.

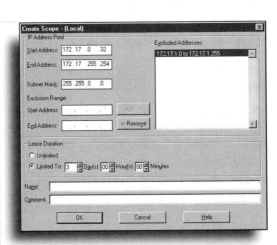

3. A **Start Address** and an **End Address** field define the address range of a scope. Enter a valid IP address range in these two fields. The IP addresses in the scope include the values you enter.

4. Click **Set Range** to save the address range.

5. Specify a subnet mask in the **Subnet Mask** box. Unless you are using address subranges, this entry will be the default mask for the address class you entered in the **Start Address** and **End Address** boxes.

6. If you don't want to have some of the addresses in the scope range assigned to DHCP clients, you can exclude ranges of addresses from the scope.

    To exclude a range, under **Exclusion Range**, enter a **Start Address** and an **End Address**. Then click **Add**.

    To exclude a single address, enter the address in the **Start Address** box and click **Add**.

    To remove an excluded address or range, select it in the **Excluded Addresses** list and click **Remove**.

7. Specify the lease duration for this scope.

    If leases should not expire, select **Unlimited**.

    If leases should expire, select **Limited To** and specify a lease duration in days, hours, and minutes.

8. Optionally, you can complete the **Name** and **Comment** fields for this scope. The name you enter will help identify the scope in the DHCP Manager window.

9. When the scope has been defined, click **OK**. DHCP Manager displays this message: `The scope has been success-fully created, but has not yet been activated. Activate the new scope now?` Click **Yes** to activate the scope.

10. When the DHCP Manager window is displayed, the new scope will appear. The light bulb icon will be lit (yellow), indicating that the scope is active.

Guidelines for Defining Scopes

You must define at least one scope, on at least one DHCP server, for each subnet that contains DHCP clients. You might wonder how the DHCP server knows which subnet a client is attached to. After all, the client doesn't know its IP address, so it can't very well know its subnet.

Lease duration

It is tempting to assign leases a long duration on the assumption that this will cause less work for the administrator, but just the opposite can be true. If a configuration change is made to a scope, clients of the scope won't learn of the change until they renew their leases. Consequently, it's wise to have clients renew their leases every few days. I recommend a three- or four-day lease duration.

We can thank BOOTP forwarding for sorting out this mess. When BOOTP forwards a DHCP discover message, it tags the message with the address information of the subnet from which the request was received. This lets the DHCP server assign an IP address for the correct subnet.

On a network, it is always useful to have two of anything important so that life goes on if one thing fails. Because you can have multiple DHCP servers, you might be tempted to assign two DHCP servers scopes for the same subnet. Then clients from the subnet can obtain their leases even if one DHCP server goes down.

Suppose that you configure two DHCP servers to support subnet 192.168.48.0, for example. You create scopes on both DHCP servers that offer IP addresses in the range 192.168.48.1 through 192.168.48.254. How does that work out?

Pretty badly, as a matter of fact. The design of DHCP doesn't let the DHCP servers exchange information about active leases. Therefore, it's possible—probable, in fact—for each DHCP server to assign the same IP address. If you want disaster on a network, having two hosts with the same IP address is a good start.

To avoid this, you need to assign different IP address ranges to the scopes on each server. One server could assign IP addresses 192.168.48.1 through 192.168.48.127, for example, while the other server offers 192.168.48.128 through 192.168.48.254. It doesn't matter how you divvy up the addresses, so long as the ranges don't overlap.

It might look like you're wasting addresses if you choose this approach, but you aren't. Both servers respond to DHCP requests for the subnet and offer IP address leases. All the IP addresses remain available for assignment. Only when one server is down does part of the address range become unavailable.

Modifying Scopes

To modify an existing scope, follow these steps:

Modifying an existing scope

1. Select the scope in the DHCP Manager window.

2. Choose **Properties** from the **Scope** menu.

3. Make the required changes in the Scope Properties dialog box, which is nearly identical in content to the Create Scope dialog box, shown in Figure 17.3. The sole difference is that a **Set Range** button is added to this dialog box.

4. If you change the **Start Address** or **End Address** values, click the **Set Range** button to save the changes to the IP address pool.

5. Click **OK** to save the changes to the scope.

Activating, Deactivating, and Deleting Scopes

To activate a deactivated scope, follow these steps:

1. Select the scope in the DHCP Manager window.

2. Choose **Activate** from the **Scope** menu.

To deactivate an active scope, follow these steps:

1. Select the scope in the DHCP Manager window.

2. Choose **Deactivate** from the **Scope** menu.

To delete an active scope, follow these steps:

1. Deactivate the scope.

2. Verify that active leases have been released. You can wait for leases to expire or have users disconnect from the DHCP server.

3. Select the scope in the DHCP Manager window.

4. Choose **Delete** in the **Scope** menu.

Viewing and Managing Active Leases

To view or manage the leases that are active for a scope, do the following:

Viewing or managing active leases in a scope

1. Select the scope in the DHCP Manager window.

2. Choose **Active Leases** from the **Scope** menu to display the Active Leases dialog box, shown in Figure 17.4.

Activating DHCP clients

Now that DHCP scopes are active, you can activate DHCP clients. When you configure TCP/IP on the clients, check **Obtain an IP address from a DHCP server** in the Microsoft TCP/IP Properties window. Chapter 14, "Building a Basic TCP/IP Network," explains how to configure all Microsoft clients for TCP/IP.

It is not necessary to specify an IP address or subnet mask. In fact, most of the static client configuration parameters have no effect on DHCP clients. Restart the client, and it should connect to the DHCP server and lease an address.

Deactivating scopes

Deactivating a scope won't disconnect active leases, but it will cause DHCP to stop leasing addresses from that scope.

Information at the top of the dialog box lets you determine how many of the addresses in the scope are available.

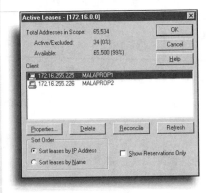

3. To delete a client and terminate the lease, select the lease and click **Delete**. DHCP Manager knows that this can cause problems, so it asks you to confirm.

    Delete only entries that are no longer in use. If you delete an active client, deleted addresses can be reassigned to new clients and duplicate IP addresses can be created on the network.

4. To review the properties for the lease, select the lease and click **Properties**. The Client Properties dialog box, shown in Figure 17.5, appears.

    You can't edit any properties for an active lease, but you can review the following items:

    - **Client Name.** This doesn't necessarily match the user's computer name, and changing the client name won't affect the computer name.

    - **Unique Identifier.** This is the hardware MAC address for the client and is determined automatically when the lease is established.

    - **Client Comment.** Any comment text you want to add.

FIGURE 17.5

Client properties for an active DHCP client.

What's your IP address?

You can determine the IP address assigned to a DHCP client by entering the command `ipconfig` at a command prompt on the client. The `ipconfig` utility is installed when you install TCP/IP on a computer.

You can also cut and paste the address within DHCP Manager. First, view a client that doesn't have a reservation in the Client Properties box. Although you can't edit the **Unique Identifier** field, you can select it and copy its contents (press Ctrl+C). Then you can paste the value to the **Unique Identifier** field of the Add Reserved Clients dialog box when creating the reservation.

Reserving DHCP Addresses

It's almost fun to configure clients with DHCP. It can feel like magic when you plug in a client and it hooks up to the network with no configuration whatsoever. But sometimes you need to assign fixed IP addresses. Can you assign a dedicated IP address but retain the ability to reconfigure clients using DHCP? Yes, you can, and it's not at all difficult.

To reserve an address for a client, follow these steps:

Reserving an IP address for a client

1. Start DHCP Manager.

2. Select a scope and choose **Add Reservations** from the **Scope** menu. This will display the Add Reserved Clients dialog box, shown in Figure 17.6.

FIGURE 17.6

Reserving an IP address for a client.

3. In the **IP Address** field, enter an IP address that falls within the range of addresses reserved for this scope.

4. In the **Unique Identifier** field, enter the hardware address for the client that will use this IP address. You can determine this address by typing the command net config wksta at

a command prompt on the client. For Ethernet or token ring, this will be a 12-digit hexadecimal number. The unique identifier, not the client name, is the crucial bit of information that lets a client access the reserved address. Other information is informational only.

5. Enter a client name in the **Client Name** field. This doesn't have to match the user's account name. It's entered here for informational purposes only.

6. If desired, add a comment in the **Client Comment** field.

7. Click **Add**.

If you select this scope and choose **Active Leases** from the **Scope** menu, you will see the reservation listed in the Active Leases box, as shown in Figure 17.7. A reservation that is actively being used is labeled as Reservation in use.

Determining the TCP/IP configuration of Windows 95 and 98

Windows 95 and 98 include the winipcfg utility, a graphic utility that reports TCP/IP configuration settings. You can start winipcfg from a command prompt or by selecting the **Run** command from the **Start** menu.

FIGURE 17.7

The active leases on this server include an address reservation.

Managing active reservations

Once a reservation has been created, its properties are managed from the Active Leases dialog box. Select the reservation and click **Properties** to display information about the reservation.

Configuring DHCP Options

DHCP can do more than assign IP addresses. It can also assign a variety of configuration options such as default gateway and WINS server addresses.

Options are assigned at three levels:

- **Default options** apply to all scopes unless they are specifically overridden by options that are assigned globally or to a specific scope.

- **Global options** apply to all scopes and override default options. Global options are overridden by specific scope options.

- **Scope options** apply to clients of a specific scope and override default and global options.

Assigning a Scope Option

As an example, we will add a default router option to a scope. To assign an option to a scope, do the following:

Assigning an option to a scope

1. Select the scope in the DHCP Manager main window.

2. Choose the **Scope** command from the **DHCP Options** menu. The DHCP Options dialog box appears, as shown in Figure 17.8.

FIGURE **17.8**
Adding a scope option.

3. Select an option in the **Unused Options** list and click **Add**. The option will be moved to the **Active Options** list. In Figure 17.8, the 003 Router option has been added.

4. For options that must be configured, select the option in the **Active Options** list and click **Value**. An Options dialog box will be added to the DHCP Options window, as shown in Figure 17.8. At first, the **IP Address** box contains the legend <None>, indicating that no entries have been made. Figure 17.9 shows the list after one address has been added.

5. Some options can be edited directly in this box. Options that accept multiple values require you to display another dialog box by clicking **Edit Array**. Figure 17.10 shows the IP Address Array Editor.

To configure a default router, follow these steps:

- Remove the initial value of 0.0.0.0 by selecting it in the **IP Addresses** list and clicking **Remove**.

- Add a value by entering the default router address in the **New IP Address** field and clicking **Add**.

Figure 17.10 shows the dialog box after an address of 172.16.0.1 has been added.

6. Click **OK** twice to save the option and return to the DHCP Manager main window.

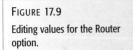

FIGURE 17.9

Editing values for the Router option.

FIGURE 17.10

Editing an array of values for a DHCP option.

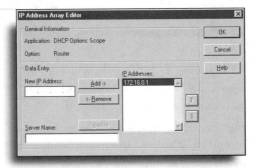

Default and global options are defined in much the same manner. You will find **Default** and **Global** commands on the **DHCP Options** menu.

Useful DHCP Options

Your network is likely to require these options:

- **003 Router**. Specifies one or more default routers for the subnet.

SEE ALSO

➤ *Default routers are discussed in Chapter 15, page 471. See the section "Specifying a Default Route."*

- **006 DNS Servers**. Specifies an address list of available DNS servers.
- **015 Domain Name**. Specifies the DNS domain name that the client should use for DNS host name resolution.

SEE ALSO

➤ *DNS is discussed in Chapter 18, "Supporting the Domain Name Service," page 529.*

If the scope includes WINS clients, you will need to add two options to the scope:

- **044 WINS/NBNS Servers**. Specifies the IP addresses of WINS servers that are to be used by the client.
- **046 WINS/NBT Node Type.** This option specifies the WINS client node type. The preferred value is 0×8, which configures the client for h-node address resolution.

SEE ALSO

➤ *For more information about WINS, see Chapter 16, page 485. WINS node types are described in the section "NetBIOS Node Types."*

Managing Options for a DHCP Reservation

To manage options for a DHCP reservation, follow these steps:

Managing options for a DHCP reservation

1. Select the scope that supports the reservation in the DHCP Manager main window.
2. Choose **Active Leases** from the **Scope** menu.
3. Select the reservation from the **Active Leases** list box.
4. Click **Properties**.

5. Click **Options** to display the DHCP Options: Reservation dialog box. This dialog box lets you manage options for a reservation using the procedures to manage options for a scope.

Backing Up and Restoring the DHCP Database

Once clients are registered with DHCP, the contents of the DHCP database become quite valuable. To preserve its contents, Windows NT Server periodically makes a backup copy of the database in the directory `C:\Winnt\system32\dhcp\backup\jet\new`. The copy of the database can be backed up to tape.

If the DHCP service is started but clients can't obtain leases, it's possible that the DHCP database might have been corrupted, in which case it might be possible to restore the backup database.

The first thing to try is to simply stop and start the DHCP service. If DHCP attempts to start and discovers that its database is corrupted, it will automatically attempt to recover the backup database.

SEE ALSO

➤ *The procedure for starting and stopping services is covered in Chapter 23, page 673, "Managing the Server."*

If that fails, try the following:

1. Stop the Microsoft DHCP Server service using the Services applet in the Control Panel.

2. Copy all files in `C:\Winnt\system32\dhcp\backup\jet\new` to `C:\Winnt\system32\dhcp`.

3. Start the Microsoft DHCP Server service using the Services applet in the Control Panel.

After you restore the database, you need to make it current on active leases that have been recorded since the backup was made—a procedure called *reconciling the DHCP database*. To reconcile the DHCP database, do the following:

1. Start DHCP Manager.

2. Select a scope from the **DHCP Scopes** pane.

3. Choose **Active Leases** from the **Scope** menu.

4. Click the **Reconcile** button in the Active Leases dialog box.

5. Repeat steps 2 through 4 for each scope.

Managing DHCP Clients

There might be times when you need to visit a client and review or renew its DHCP configuration manually. The tool you use is actually a general-purpose TCP/IP client tool named ipconfig.

If you want to know a client's TCP/IP configuration, you can go for the short form by opening a command prompt on the client and entering the command ipconfig. But I'm going to show you the long form. Enter the command ipconfig /all to see all the intimate details of a client's configuration. A sample configuration looks like this:

```
Windows NT IP Configuration

        Host Name . . . . . . . . . : malaprop1
        DNS Servers . . . . . . . . :
        Node Type . . . . . . . . . : Hybrid
        NetBIOS Scope ID. . . . . . :
        IP Routing Enabled. . . . . : No
        WINS Proxy Enabled. . . . . : No
        NetBIOS Resolution Uses DNS : No


Ethernet adapter E100B1:

        Description . . . . . . . . : Intel 82557-based
        ➥Ethernet PCI Adapter
        Physical Address. . . . . . : 00-A0-C9-22-E8-D9
        DHCP Enabled. . . . . . . . : Yes
        IP Address. . . . . . . . . : 172.16.255.225
        Subnet Mask . . . . . . . . : 255.255.0.0
        Default Gateway . . . . . . :
        DHCP Server . . . . . . . . : 172.16.0.1
        Primary WINS Server . . . . : 172.17.0.10
```

```
Secondary WINS Server . . . : 172.16.0.10
Lease Obtained. . . . . . . : Thursday, January 15,
➥1998 11:00:50 PM
Lease Expires . . . . . . . : Sunday, January 18, 1998
➥11:00:50 PM
```

This listing reports just about anything you would want to know about a client's TCP/IP settings. It sure beats visiting all the TCP/IP property tabs!

Here are a couple of other useful things to do with ipconfig:

- To force a DHCP client to give up its lease on an IP address, enter the command ipconfig /release.
- To force a DHCP client to renew its lease or to obtain one if it doesn't have one, enter the command ipconfig /renew.

That's How I Spell Relief!

DHCP can be one of the biggest time- and frustration-savers you can add to your network, but you have to design your DHCP support carefully. Be sure clients can communicate with the DHCP servers through routers. And plan your scopes carefully so that DHCP servers can't assign conflicting IP addresses. It takes a bit of work, but there is a significant payoff for your effort.

Now we'll move on to a new TCP/IP administration task—supporting a conventional TCP/IP name service. WINS is used only on Microsoft networks. If you want to share your network with non-Microsoft clients, or if you want your users to be able to resolve names on the Internet, you need to set up an Internet name service called the Domain Name Service (DNS). DNS is quite a bit different from WINS, so we need to consider the two separately. You already know WINS, so let's move on to DNS.

CHAPTER 1

Supporting the Domain Name Service

Name services are invisible but essential components of user-friendly networks. Users cannot be expected to remember dozens of IP addresses. In a purely Windows environment, you can rely on WINS, but the world isn't a purely Windows environment. The moment you add an Internet connection or a UNIX computer, you leave WINS behind and must embrace the Domain Name Service (DNS), the standard naming service in the TCP/IP world.

DNS is more complex than WINS because DNS was designed with the capability of naming every computer on the Internet, and that's a lot of computers—potentially, in the neighborhood of four billion! No single computer now in existence could handle that number of host names, particularly given that every minute millions of users are querying the name database.

Consequently, DNS was designed as a distributed database. Parts of the overall name database are placed on separate computers so that the data storage and query loads are distributed throughout the Internet. Hundreds of thousands of computers share the responsibility of providing naming support on the Internet.

DNS was designed for power and flexibility, not for easy administration. A minimum Windows naming service can be configured by installing WINS on one server, but managing DNS is considerably more involved than installing the DNS server. You must manually configure entries in the DNS database, and you must link your DNS server with the other DNS servers on the Internet so that your users have access to the entire Internet name database.

To administer DNS, you must have an understanding of DNS theory. You must understand the DNS name space architecture and how individual DNS servers support their portions of the overall name space.

After you have a picture of DNS as a whole, you'll be ready to look at the specifics of supporting DNS with the Microsoft DNS server. Windows NT Server 4 includes a DNS server service that is reasonably easy to administer because it has a graphic management interface. It also has a unique benefit on Windows networks because the Microsoft DNS server can obtain names from WINS, allowing you to support a dynamic DNS name database that is constantly updated as the names of Windows computers change.

How the Domain Name Service Works

If you have ever used the Internet, you have seen DNS names. In most cases, a Web URL contains a domain name, as in **http://www.microsoft.com**. You don't need to learn a foreign language here. Domain names are the stuff of everyday experience.

However, the DNS name space is more complex than WINS because the DNS name space isn't a flat database. DNS names compose a *hierarchical database* that functions much like the directories in a file system. Hierarchies are powerful database structures because they can store tremendous amounts of data while making it easy to search for specific bits of information. Before examining the specifics of the DNS name space hierarchy, let's review some rules about hierarchies in general.

The Structure of Hierarchies

You are intimately acquainted with hierarchies if you have been working with computers for more than a few days; all modern computers use hierarchical structures for organizing file storage. It's too chaotic to store all files together on a homogenous hard drive. Files need to be stored in related groups. The best approach is the hierarchical one, and PCs have been using hierarchical file systems since MS-DOS version 2.

Figure 18.1 illustrates a common file system hierarchy. You have undoubtedly seen hierarchies referred to as *trees*. I commonly refer to a *directory tree*, for example. Technically, the tree in Figure 18.1 is an *inverted tree* because it is oriented with the branches pointing down, but inverted trees have become so commonplace that one seldom thinks of their unusual orientation. Well before computers were invented, genealogies were referred to as family trees, even though the root ancestor is typically at the top of the diagram.

FIGURE 18.1

Directory trees illustrate the
rules for constructing hierarchies.

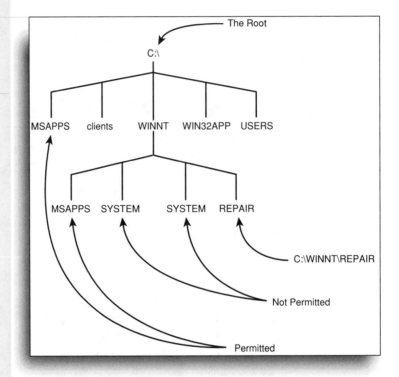

In file systems, the intersections of the branches are called *directories* or *folders*, of course. A directory can contain files and other directories. The capability of placing directories in directories allows you to extend the file system nearly without limit, adding categories and subcategories as the application demands.

In practical terms, hierarchies become unwieldy if they sprout too many levels. There are no hard and fast rules to this. A lot depends on whether applications or users must cope with the levels. A computer program can remember a file pathname of indefinite length, but humans have difficulty remembering more than four or five levels.

There are several rules for constructing hierarchies:

- Every hierarchy has exactly one top container, usually called the *root*. On a file system, this is the root directory. All other containers are subcontainers of the root container.

- Every item within a container must have a unique name within the container.

- The full name of an item includes its own name as well as the names of all the containers that connect it with the root. This full name is often referred to as a *fully qualified name*.

- Items in different containers can have the same name because they will have different fully qualified names.

Now that you've reviewed the rules for constructing hierarchies, you will now see how they apply to DNS.

The DNS Name Space Hierarchy

Figure 18.2 illustrates a small part of the DNS name hierarchy.

The containers in the DNS hierarchy are called *domains*. The hierarchy starts with a root container, of course, referred to as the *root domain*. The root domain doesn't have a name, so it is typically represented by a single period.

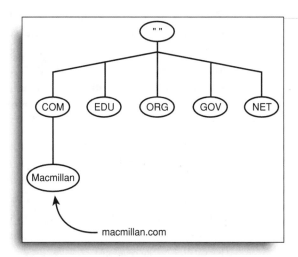

FIGURE **18.2**

Part of the DNS name hierarchy.

Directly below the root domain are the *top-level* or *first-level* domains. Lower-level domains are *second-level*, *third-level*, and so on.

Figure 18.2 depicts the commonest top-level domains, the ones you are most likely to encounter, but the list is only partial. For one thing, each country is assigned a top-level domain name, and there are too many of those to list. Also, there are specialized top-level domains such as MIL (reserved for the United States military) that few of us will encounter. Finally, new general-purpose domain names are being added because some domains are becoming so full that it is difficult to invent new names within the domains. For this discussion, though, you'll stick with the most common top-level domains:

- **COM.** Originally, the COM domain was supposed to contain commercial entities, but COM has become the overwhelming favorite top-level domain, and everyone wants his personal subdomains to be in COM. Because COM has been overused and abused, it's nearly impossible to come up with a sensible new name for a COM subdomain. Crowding in COM is the main impetus behind the definition of new top-level domains. (Example: mcp.com)

- **ORG.** This domain is supposed to accommodate organizations that are noncommercial in nature. Although many noncommercial organizations have registered in the COM domain, most have respected the intent of this domain. This is a good place for nonprofit organizations, professional groups, churches, and other such organizations. (Example: npr.org)

- **EDU.** This domain was originally supposed to embrace all types of educational institutions, but it began to fill up quickly as schools gained access to the Internet. Now it is primarily reserved for higher education institutions. Primary and secondary schools are supposed to register in their state domains, which are subdomains of their country domains. (Example: berkeley.edu)

- **GOV.** This domain contains agencies of the United States Federal government, apart from the military, which has the MIL domain. (Example: whitehouse.gov)

- **NET.** This domain supports Internet Service Providers and Internet administrative computers. (Example: internic.net)

Every host named on the Internet will have a host name in the Internet DNS name hierarchy. Typically, host names are listed to include every domain that connects the host with the root, for example, `isaac.widgets.malaprop.com`. A domain name that includes all domains between the host and the root is a *fully qualified domain name* (FQDN).

When an organization wants to establish a domain name on the Internet, the domain name must be registered with the InterNIC Registration Services. You can research new domain names and access registration forms at **http://www.internic.net**.

Establishing a domain name

1. Search the Internet Directory to identify a domain name that isn't already in use.

2. Determine the IP addresses of two name servers—a master and a backup—that will be authoritative for your domain. If your ISP will be providing your name servers, obtain the IP addresses from your ISP.

3. Register the domain name with the InterNIC. The Web site includes online forms for registering and changing domain names.

4. Pay the registration fee, which is currently $100 per domain name for the first year and $50 per domain per year there-after.

At some point, you'll need to host your domain on the name servers you have identified. Before you learn how to do that, let's examine how your name servers will fit into the overall process of name resolution on the Internet.

Resolving Host Names Through DNS

Many computers provide DNS name services, each supporting a small portion of the overall DNS name space. A name server that resolves names for a domain is said to be *authoritative* for the domain. A name server can be authoritative for one or many domains, located anywhere in the DNS hierarchy.

Zones

When a DNS server is authoritative for a domain, the domain is referred to as a *zone*.

Of special interest are the *root name servers* that support the root of the name space hierarchy. At present, there are ten computers supporting the root domain. As you'll see in a moment, the root name servers are critical to the name resolution process. When a local name server can't resolve a name, it refers the name to a root name server, which begins the process of searching for a name server that can resolve the name.

Every client is configured with the IP address of at least one DNS server. When the client needs to send data to a host, it must learn the IP address of the host. To resolve the host name to an IP address, the client sends the host name to its name server, as shown in Figure 18.3.

FIGURE 18.3

The process of resolving a DNS name.

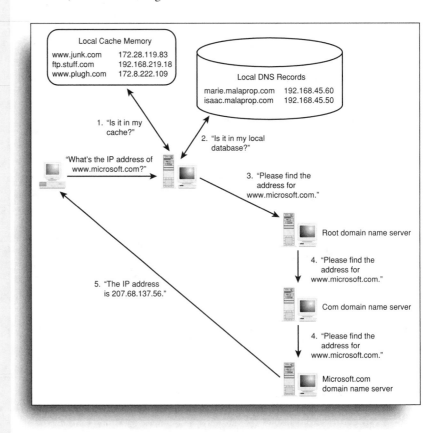

The DNS name server resolves a name to an IP address

1. The name server looks in a local memory cache for names it has recently resolved. If the name is found in the local cache, the name server can provide the IP address the client requires.

2. The name server looks in local static tables to see whether the administrator has added an entry that maps the host name to an IP address. If a static entry exists, the name server forwards the IP address to the client.

3. The name server refers the request to a root name server.

4. The root name server refers the request to a name server for the first-level domain in the host name. The first-level domain name server refers the request to a name server for the second-level domain in the host name, and so on, until a name server is encountered that can resolve the complete host name.

5. The first name server that can resolve the host name to an IP address reports the IP address to the client.

As the administrator of a TCP/IP network, you must ensure that your local users have access to at least one, and preferably two, DNS name servers. These name servers can be private ones you configure on your own network or name servers provided by your ISP. Which should you choose?

If you elect to use DNS name servers provided by your ISP, this relieves you of the responsibility for maintaining a DNS server. An ISP will always offer at least two name servers because the InterNIC requires that every Internet domain be hosted on at least two name servers. Name servers operated by ISPs are typically UNIX servers running BIND, the application that is the overwhelming choice for providing DNS name services in the UNIX environment. Changes made to the name database on BIND servers are entered in text database files and go into effect only when the name server is stopped and restarted. Consequently, it usually takes 24–48 hours to make a change to the name database of an ISP's DNS servers. However, BIND

For more information about DNS

See my book *Networking with Microsoft TCP/IP, Second Edition* (New Riders Publishing) for a much more thorough discussion of the Microsoft DNS Server. There I explain the BIND database files and show you how to move data between the two types of name servers.

The definitive source for information about DNS and BIND is *DNS and Bind* by Paul Albitz and Cricket Liu (O'Reilly & Associates, Inc.).

running on UNIX provides better name server performance than the Microsoft DNS server, an important factor on the Internet, where name servers take huge numbers of queries.

If you elect to operate your own DNS servers using the Microsoft DNS Server service that is included with Windows NT Server 4.0, you gain two distinct advantages. Host names that are entered manually go into effect automatically; there is no need to wait until the name service can be stopped and restarted. Also, the Microsoft DNS Server can communicate with WINS so that NetBIOS names are automatically registered in the DNS name space.

Because the Microsoft DNS Server is easy to administer and has particular advantages on Microsoft networks, you'll probably elect to configure your own name servers. In that case, you must have at least two Windows NT Server 4 computers on your network so that you can have a master and a backup name server.

Administering the Microsoft DNS Server

I'm going to focus on the essentials of managing the Microsoft DNS Server and avoid some advanced topics, such as the method for exchanging static database files between the Microsoft DNS Server and BIND. Explaining the syntax of the BIND database files would double the size of this chapter.

The tasks I will cover are

- Installing the Microsoft DNS Server service
- Adding DNS servers to DNS Manager
- Creating domain name zones
- Creating reverse-naming zones
- Adding and modifying resource records
- Creating subzones
- Linking the Microsoft DNS Server with WINS
- Configuring a backup name server for a zone

Installing the Microsoft DNS Server Service

Installing the Microsoft DNS Server Service

1. Open the Network applet in the Control Panel and select the **Services** tab.

2. Choose **Add** to open the Select Network Services dialog box.

3. Select **Microsoft DNS Server** in the Network Services list box and choose **OK**.

4. When prompted, supply a file path to the installation CD-ROM. Files will be copied to the server.

5. Review the configuration in the Microsoft TCP/IP Properties window.

6. Restart the computer to activate the new service.

In addition to installing the DNS service, the setup program adds a shortcut to the DNS Manager utility to the **Administrative Tools** group in the **Start** menu.

Adding DNS Servers to DNS Manager

Before you can manage a DNS server, you must add it to the DNS Manager's configuration. Figure 18.4 shows the DNS Manager after a DNS server has been added.

Adding a DNS server to DNS Manager

1. Select the **New Server** command in the **DNS** menu.

2. In the Add DNS Server dialog box, enter the IP address or the NetBIOS name of a computer that is running the Microsoft DNS Server service.

It's worth taking a moment to examine the configuration of a brand-new DNS server. In Figure 18.4, a DNS server on Malaprop1 has been added to the DNS Manager. I expanded the Malaprop1 entry in the Server List tree to show the Cache zone, which is created automatically for each new server.

If DNS Manager Cannot Communicate with a Remote DNS Server

If DNS Manager can communicate with a remote DNS server that you add, the server will be tagged with an icon that has a green light. If DNS Manager cannot communicate with the DNS server you add, the server icon will be marked with a red *X*, and you'll see the following message in the Server Statistics pane: The RPC server is unavailable.

RPC refers to the Remote Procedure Call protocol used to support communication between processes running on different computers. The message means that the remote DNS server is unavailable, probably because of a communication problem. You must determine why the computers can't communicate and correct the problem. Then press **F5** to try to connect DNS Manager with the remote DNS server.

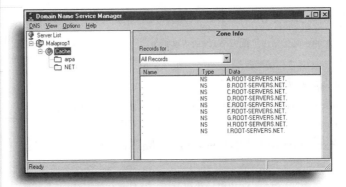

FIGURE 18.4

DNS Manager after a server has been added.

Recall from earlier discussions what happens when a DNS server can't resolve a name request from information that is available locally. It refers the name request to a name server that is authoritative for the root domain, which initiates a full-network search for the name. How does the local name server know which name servers are authoritative for the root domain?

The root name servers are listed in the Cache zone, which is automatically configured with a list of the Internet root name servers. In Figure 18.4, I have selected the Cache zone icon so that the root name servers appear in the Zone Info pane. Nested deeper in the Cache database are the IP addresses of the name servers. You'll probably never be required to edit entries in the Cache zone.

Creating Primary Zones

To allow the DNS server to be authoritative for a domain, you must create a zone for the domain. There are two types of zones:

- **Primary zones** contain the master database records for a zone.

- **Secondary zones** contain duplicates of the database records for a zone, which are obtained by copying the records from a primary zone, a process that is called a *zone transfer*.

Creating the primary zone for a domain

  1. In the Server List pane, right-click the server that will host the primary zone.

Automatically created zones

Besides the Cache zone, three other zones are automatically created for each new DNS server. The names of the automatically created zones are `0.in-addr.arpa`, `127.in-addr.arpa`, and `255.in-addr.arpa`. Because these zones typically require no administration, they are not normally shown in the Server List.

To view the hidden, automatically created zones, select **Preferences** in the **Options** menu and check **Show Automatically Created Zones**. Ordinarily, you'll find it convenient to hide the automatically created zones.

2. Choose **New Zone** from the context menu to open the Create New Zone dialog box.

3. The first Create New Zone dialog box has two option buttons:

- **Primary**. Select this option button to create a primary zone.

- **Secondary**. Select this option button to create a secondary zone.

Because you are creating a primary zone, this procedure assumes that the **Primary** option button is selected. Click **Next** to proceed.

4. The next dialog box is reproduced in Figure 18.5. To complete this dialog box, do the following:

a. Enter the zone name in the **Zone Name** field.

b. Press the **Tab** key to move to the **Zone File** field. If you move to this field by pressing **Tab**, the field is automatically completed with a filename that follows Microsoft's conventions (the extension .dns is added to the domain name).

c. Click **Next**.

Server List context menu

All objects in the Server List are associated with context menus, which you reveal by right-clicking the object. These context menus contain commands that allow you to add and delete objects and to modify their properties.

FIGURE 18.5
Defining a primary zone.

5. Click **Finish** to create the zone.

Figure 18.6 shows DNS Manager after a zone has been created for `malaprop.com`. In the figure, I selected the `malaprop.com` zone so that you could see the records that are automatically added to the database of a new zone. The right pane contains two records of type SOA and NS.

FIGURE 18.6

The primary zone `mala-prop.com` has been created on the Malaprop1 DNS server.

SEE ALSO

➤ *To create secondary zones, page 582.*

➤ *See the description of SOA and NS resource records, page 544.*

Creating Reverse-Naming Zones

The previous section describes the creation of a primary zone that is matched to the name of a domain. This type of zone is called a *forward-naming zone* because it is used to look up the IP address associated with a particular host's domain name. That sort of lookup is the primary business of DNS.

There are times, however, when it is necessary to start with the IP address and determine the domain name of the host that has that IP address, a process that is called a *reverse-lookup*. The DNS name space includes special *reverse-naming zones* that are used to look up the host name associated with an IP address. These reverse-naming zones are also called `in-addr.arpa` zones.

For more information about `in-addr.arpa`

I'm not going into the details of the `in-addr.arpa` zones because you don't need to know how reverse lookups work in order to configure the reverse-naming zones. If you want to know how the whole shebang works, see my book *Networking with Microsoft TCP/IP*.

The process of looking up a host name involves examining the IP address an octet at a time in special zone database files. The database files are named to reflect the IP address of the zone, with the octets arranged in reverse order. Here are some examples:

- The reverse-naming database file for network 192.168.48.0 (a class C address) is named 48.168.192.in-addr.arpa.

- The reverse-naming database file for network 172.16.0.0 (a class B address) is named 16.172.in-addr.arpa.

- The reverse-naming database file for network 10.0.0.0 (a class A address) is named 10.in-addr.arpa.

Creating a reverse-naming zone

1. In the Server List pane, right-click the server that will host the primary forward-naming zone.

2. Choose **New Zone** from the context menu to open the Create New Zone dialog box.

3. In the first Create New Zone dialog box, select the **Primary** option button. Click **Next** to proceed.

4. The next dialog box is reproduced in Figure 18.7. To complete this dialog box, do the following:

   a. Enter the zone name in the **Zone Name** field.

   b. Press the **Tab** key to move to the **Zone File** field. The name of the database file is automatically entered.

   c. Click **Next**.

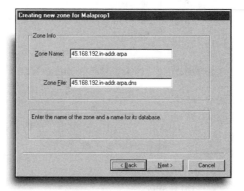

FIGURE 18.7
Defining a reverse-naming zone.

5. Click **Finish** to create the zone.

Figure 18.8 shows a newly created reverse-naming zone. You should create a reverse-naming zone for each range of IP addresses that is used by hosts defined in your forward-naming zones.

FIGURE 18.8

A newly created reverse-naming zone.

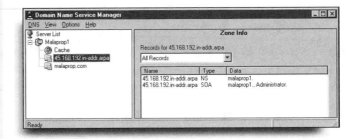

Adding Resource Records

Now that you have created a forward-naming zone for the domain, along with any required reverse-naming zones, it is time to add records to the zones. These records are called *resource records*, of which there are many types. This book mentions only a few of the available types, but the ones not mentioned are ones you're unlikely to encounter unless you become a serious DNS expert.

Let's add a typical resource record so that you can see how it is done. Then you'll look at the various types of resource records you are likely to need.

Adding an Address Resource Record

Address resource records are the core of DNS. Each address record matches an IP address to a host name, and except for host names that are obtained from WINS, every host will be defined in an address resource record.

There is nothing mysterious about resource records, as you'll see.

Creating an address resource record

1. Right-click a forward-naming zone.

2. Choose the **New Record** command in the context menu to open the New Resource Record dialog box shown in Figure 18.9.

3. In the **Record Type** list box, select **A Record** where an A record is an address resource record.

4. Review the **Domain** field to verify the A record is being created in the correct domain. You cannot modify this field.

5. In the **Host Name** field, enter the host's name only. Do not include the host's domain name. For the host `isaac.mala-prop.com`, you would enter `isaac` in the **Host Name** field.

6. In the **Host IP Address** field, enter the host's complete IP address.

7. If the correct reverse-naming zone has been created, check **Create Associated PTR Record**.

8. Choose **OK** to create the record.

> **A shortcut for creating A records**
>
> DNS Manager offers a New Host dialog box that provides a slightly more efficient method of adding A records. You can open the New Host dialog box by selecting the **New Host** command from the context menu that opens when you right-click a domain in the Server List. The **New Host** also appears in a context menu that pops up when you right-click the database pane while a domain is selected in the Server List.

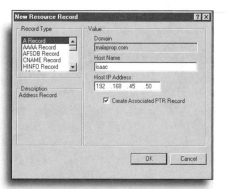

FIGURE 18.9
Creating an address resource record.

If you examine the forward-naming zone after creating the A record, you'll see an entry like the one in Figure 18.10.

FIGURE 18.10
The zone `malaprop.com` contains an A record for the host `issac.malaprop.com`.

Every name server must have an address record

Every name server must be defined in an A record. Sometimes DNS Manager will create the A record when the zone is created, but sometimes it won't. I haven't figured out why the A record isn't created consistently. Be sure to review the resource records and to add an A record for the name server if one has not been created.

If the reverse-naming zone was properly configured and you checked **Create Associated PTR Record**, you'll also see an entry in the reverse-naming zone that resembles this:

```
192.168.48.24              PTR      isaac.malaprop.com
```

If the PTR record was not created automatically, you'll need to add it manually. Let's see how you can add the most common types of resource records.

Common Resource Records

Each resource record is identified by a type abbreviation. For example, address records are identified by the type abbreviation *A*. You'll also need to be familiar with start of authority (SOA), name server (NS), pointer (PTR), alias (CNAME), and mail exchanger (MX) records. Each is examined in the following sections. Figure 18.11 shows a zone that contains at least one of each type of resource record discussed in this chapter (with the exception of the PTR record, which can appear only in a reverse-naming zone).

FIGURE 18.11

This zone illustrates a variety of resource records.

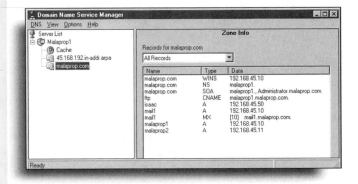

Modifying resource records

To modify a resource record, double-click its entry in the database. This opens a dialog box where you can edit the properties of the resource record.

All resource records can be entered by using a procedure similar to the one discussed for the address record. You will not need to add the SOA record because it is automatically created with the zone. However, you might need to modify the contents of the SOA record.

Start of Authority (SOA) Records

Each zone will have a start of authority record that identifies the zone and defines several zone operational parameters. Figure 18.12 shows the properties dialog box for the SOA resource record. The following properties are defined:

- **Primary Name Server DNS Name.** This is the FQDN name of the primary DNS server for this zone. I recommend that you edit this field to contain the FQDN of the host, including a trailing dot (see the note "Specifying Host Names in Resource Records").

- **Responsible Person Mailbox DNS Name.** This record defines the email address of the user who is responsible for this zone. Because the @ character has other uses in resource records, it can't appear in a resource record data field. If, for example, you enter the name Administrator and the record is in the malaprop.com zone, you are specifying the mail address **Administrator@malaprop.com**, which appears as Administrator.malaprop.com in the resource record.

- **Serial Number.** This number should be incremented every time the SOA record properties are modified. The serial number is used in some situations when zone record data is copied between name servers. DNS Manager updates this field when changes are made to the zone, and you should not need to manually edit the field.

- **Refresh Interval.** These fields specify the frequency with which a secondary name server checks in to download a copy of the zone data from the primary name server.

- **Retry Interval.** These fields specify the interval at which a secondary name server waits after a failed zone transfer before attempting to make the zone transfer again.

- **Expire Time.** These fields specify how long a secondary name server will retain records learned in a zone transfer. If the record isn't refreshed in a zone transfer before the expiration time, the record is considered invalid and is discarded.

- **Minimum Default TTL.** The minimum time a resource record is retained in the name server database. After the TTL expires, the name server discards the record.

Typically, you will not find it necessary to modify the timing parameters in the SOA resource record.

FIGURE 18.12

Properties for the SOA record.

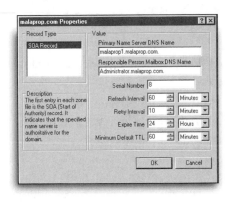

Specifying Host Names in Resource Records

When you specify a host name in a resource record, you have two choices for entering the name. You can enter a FQDN, or you can enter a name in the record's domain context. It is very important that you enter host names correctly.

If you enter a host name alone, without a trailing dot, the host name takes its context from the zone in which the record is defined. If you enter the host name `isaac` in a resource record for the `malaprop.com` domain, you are by implication referring to the host with the FQDN `isaac.malaprop.com`.

If you enter a FQDN, in most cases you must include a trailing dot after the name— `isaac.malaprop.com.`, for example. This unusual use of the trailing dot is necessary to prevent the DNS server from placing the FQDN in the zone's context domain. In many records, if you omit the trailing dot, `isaac.malaprop.com` is understood as `isaac.mala-prop.com.malaprop.com`. When discussing the various record types, I will prompt you on the instances when you should supply the trailing dot.

Name Server (NS) Records

Each primary and secondary name server must be defined in an NS record. Figure 18.13 shows the properties dialog box for the NS record. This dialog box has two fields, only one of which can be edited:

- **Domain**. This field specifies the domain that owns the resource record. The value of the **Domain** field is established when the resource record is created; it cannot be edited.
- **Name Server DNS Name**. This field specifies the FQDN host name of a name server for the zone that contains the resource record. When the zone is created, DNS Manager specifies only the host name with a trailing dot. I recommend you edit this field to specify the FQDN of the name server, including the trailing dot, as in the figure.

Every DNS name server must also be defined in an address (A) resource record as well.

FIGURE 18.13

The properties dialog box for an NS record.

Pointer (PTR) Records

PTR records appear only in reverse-naming zones and are functional mirror images of address records. Whereas an A record maps a name to an IP address, a PTR record maps an IP address to a name. Figure 18.14 shows the properties dialog box for a PTR record, which has two data entry fields:

- **IP Address.** The complete IP address of the host.
- **Host DNS Name.** The FQDN of the host. You must include a trailing dot after the FQDN.

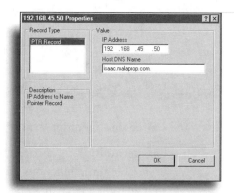

FIGURE 18.14

The properties dialog box for a PTR record.

Alias (CNAME) Records

Creating aliases for hosts is frequently useful. Suppose that the same computer is serving as a domain controller and is also a World Wide Web server. It might be useful to refer to that computer as both `malaprop1.malaprop.com` and as `www.malaprop.com`. The abbreviation CNAME stands for *canonical name*, a fancy expression for *alias*. You can use CNAME records to establish as many alias names as you want for an IP address.

Figure 18.15 shows the properties dialog box for a CNAME record, which has three fields:

- **Domain.** The value of this field is defined by the zone in which the CNAME record is created.

- **Alias Name.** The alias name. This name is understood to be in the domain specified by the **Domain** field. If the **Domain** field has the value `malaprop.com` and the **Alias Name** has the value `www`, the FQDN of the alias is `www.malaprop.com`.

- **For Host DNS Name.** The FQDN of the host that this alias refers to. You must include a trailing dot after this name.

FIGURE 18.15

The properties dialog box for a *CNAME* record.

You can establish multiple names for an IP address in two ways:

- **Create multiple A records for the IP address.** This is preferable if the functions are logically separate and might split apart at a later time. If you later plan to create a dedicated Web server, give the Web server its own A record, which you can later edit to point to the dedicated mail server computer.

- **Create one A record for the IP address and then one or more CNAME entries for the host name.** This is preferable if the names will probably remain together on the same computer in the future. If you edit the IP address of the A record, the CNAMEs follow because they are associated with the host name, not the IP address.

Mail Exchanger (MX) Records

Mail systems based on TCP/IP standards can consult DNS to determine which hosts provide mail delivery for a particular domain. Suppose that the mail server `mail.widgets.com` must deliver a message that is addressed to **marie@malaprop.com**. The `mail.widgets.com` mail server queries DNS to determine which computers are mail servers for the `malaprop.com` domain. Mail exchanger (MX) resource records provide the information that is required.

If you are setting up a mail server that is based on TCP/IP standards, you should add an MX record to the domain for each mail server. Figure 18.16 shows the properties form for an MX record. This form has the following fields:

- **Domain.** The value of this field is defined by the zone in which the MX record is created.

- **Host Name.** The host name of the mail server. This field is optional.

- **Mail Exchange Server DNS Name.** The FQDN of the mail server. You must include a trailing dot after this name.

- **Preference Number.** This number has no effect unless multiple mail servers service a domain. If the mail servers have different preference numbers, the mail server with the lowest preference number will be the preferred mail server. If the mail servers have the same preference numbers, they will receive mail in approximately equal amounts.

Notice that the MX record specifies only the host name of the mail server. You must also create an A or CNAME record that maps the mail server's host name to an IP address.

FIGURE 18.16

The properties dialog box for an *MX* record.

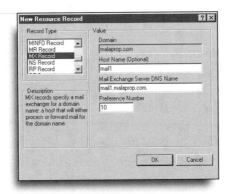

Creating Subzones

In many cases, you'll have subdomains of your primary DNS domain. It would be reasonable, for example, for malaprop.com to have the subdomains widgets.malaprop.com and blivets.malaprop.com, establishing a subdomain for each company division.

Adding subdomains after the zone has been created for the primary domain

1. Right-click the zone in the Server List.

2. Choose the **New Domain** command from the context menu.

3. In the New Domain dialog box, enter the name of the subdomain in the **Domain Name** field.

4. Choose **OK** to create the subdomain.

After the subdomain has been created, add A and CNAME records, just as you would add them in the primary domain. In Figure 18.17, two subdomains have been created in the malaprop.com zone: widgets.malaprop.com and blivets.malaprop.com.

If you check **Create Associated PTR Record** when creating the A record, the host name in the PTR record reflects the subdomain in which the host is created.

FIGURE 18.17
The malaprop.com zone
has two subdomains.

Linking the Microsoft DNS Server with WINS

If you have WINS running on your network, you can automatically include data from WINS in address records for a domain.
There are two catches:

- The primary DNS server for the domain must be a
  Microsoft DNS Server.

- All records obtained from WINS will appear in the same
  domain.

Configuring a primary DNS server to accept address records from WINS

1. Right-click the primary zone in the Server List.

2. Select **Properties** from the context menu.

3. Select the **WINS Lookup** tab in the Zone Properties dialog
   box. Figure 18.18 shows the **WINS Lookup** tab.

FIGURE 18.18
Configuring WINS lookup.

4. Check **U̲se WINS Resolution** to configure the DNS server so that it will obtain host address records from WINS.

5. In most cases, you will not check **Settings only affect local server.** When the box isn't checked, WINS records that are transferred to secondary name servers can't be overridden by records on the secondary DNS server.

   If you check this box, WINS records that are transferred to secondary DNS servers can be overridden by records created on the secondary DNS server.

6. You must add the IP address of at least one WINS server to the **W̲INS Servers** list. If more than one WINS server is specified, they will be consulted in the order they appear in the list. Use the **Move Up** and **Move Down** buttons to adjust the order of multiple entries.

7. Choose **OK** to complete configuration of WINS lookup.

After WINS lookup is configured, a WINS resource record is added to the zone. Figure 18.11 includes an example of a WINS resource record.

Configuring a Backup Name Server for a Zone

It is always a good idea to support each zone on at least one backup name server, referred to as a *secondary DNS server*. A secondary DNS server doesn't have its own copy of the zone data but downloads the zone data from the primary name server, a process called a *zone transfer*.

Creating a secondary DNS server requires three operations:

1. Adding an NS record to the zone

2. Installing the DNS server on a second computer and configuring the secondary zone

3. Configuring DNS notification on the primary DNS server

Creating an NS Record for the Secondary DNS Server

Every name server must be defined in an NS record for each zone that the name server supports. Therefore, the first step in setting up a secondary DNS server is to add an NS record to the zone on the primary DNS server.

Configuring the Secondary DNS Server

Microsoft has made it extremely easy to configure secondary name servers.

Configuring secondary name servers

1. Install the Microsoft DNS Server service on the primary DNS server and configure the primary zone.

2. Install the Microsoft DNS Server service on the secondary DNS server.

3. Start DNS Manager on either DNS server.

4. Add both DNS servers to the Server List of DNS Manager. Ensure that DNS Manager can communicate with both servers.

5. Expand the listings under the primary DNS server to reveal the primary zone. DNS Manager will now resemble Figure 18.19.

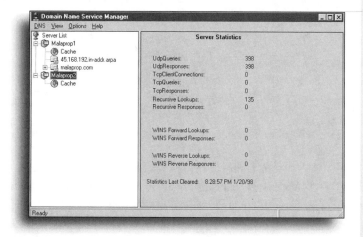

FIGURE 18.19

DNS Manager has been prepared for the creation of a secondary zone on server Malaprop2.

6. Right-click the secondary server in the Server List.

7. Choose **New Zone** from the context menu.

8. Select the **Secondary** option button in the Creating New Zone dialog box. Figure 18.20 shows DNS Manager in the process of creating a secondary zone. Note the hand icon, which will be used to simplify creation of the secondary zone.

FIGURE 18.20

Creating a secondary zone.

9. If necessary, relocate the Creating New Zone dialog box so that you can see the primary zone in the Server List.

10. Use the mouse to drag the hand icon and drop in on the primary zone in the Server List. The **Zone** and **Server** fields will be completed so that they correctly refer to the primary name server. The final result is shown in Figure 18.20.

11. Choose **Next** to open the next dialog box, which is the same as Figure 18.5. The **Zone Name** and **Zone File** fields are completed automatically.

12. Choose **Next** to open the dialog box shown in Figure 18.21. An *IP master* is a DNS server from which the secondary name server transfers zone records. Ordinarily, a secondary server has a single IP master, but a secondary server can be configured with more than one IP master. For example, a secondary server can have a primary server and another secondary server as its IP masters. In that case, if the primary server is down, the secondary server can transfer zone records from another secondary server.

You must add the IP address of at least one IP master to the IP Master(s) list. If you specify more than one IP master, arrange the IP addresses in the order of preference by using the **Move Up** and **Move Down** buttons.

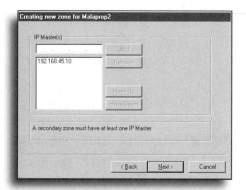

FIGURE 18.21
Defining the IP masters for a secondary zone.

13. After defining the IP masters, choose **Next**. Then choose **Finish** to create the secondary zone.

You can create secondary zones for reverse-naming zones in the same manner. Figure 18.22 illustrates DNS Manager after Malaprop2 has been configured as a secondary DNS server for malaprop.com and 48.168.192.in-addr.arpa. You might need to wait a few minutes before a zone transfer populates the database of a secondary zone.

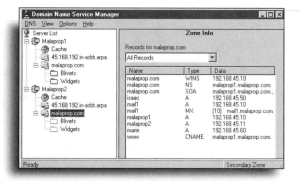

FIGURE 18.22
Malaprop2 has been config-ured with two secondary zones.

Configuring Secondary Server Notification

Ordinarily, secondary name servers initiate zone transfers only at intervals specified in the SOA record. To improve timeliness, you might want to configure a notify list on the primary name server, allowing the primary name server to notify its secondaries when changes have been made to the zone database.

Setting up a notify list

1. Right-click the primary zone and choose **Properties** from the context menu. Then select the **Notify** tab shown in Figure 18.23.

FIGURE 18.23

Configuring DNS notification on the primary name server.

DNS security

The IP addresses of your name servers are public knowledge, easily obtained by a hacker who can use the information to attempt to download your DNS zone information in a zone transfer. Simply knowing your working IP addresses and host names gives a hacker an advantage when trying to penetrate your network. It's a good idea to check **Only Allow Access from Secondaries Included on Notify List** to prevent unauthorized zone transfers.

2. In the **Notify** tab, add the IP address of the secondary name server. This information allows the primary name server to notify the secondary name server when changes are made to the zone database.

3. Ordinarily, any secondary name server can contact any primary name server to initiate a zone transfer. Check **Only Allow Access from Secondaries Included on Notify List** if you want to restrict the secondary name servers to those you specify in this dialog box.

4. Choose **OK** to save the notify list.

Configuring Microsoft DNS Clients

After you have enabled a DNS server, you must configure clients to take advantage of it. All Microsoft clients accept similar configuration properties.

Windows NT clients are configured to use DNS by editing the TCP/IP Protocol properties in the Network applet of the Control Panel. On the **WINS Address** tab, check the **Enable DNS for Windows Resolution** check box. Also, complete the **DNS** tab, shown in Figure 18.24.

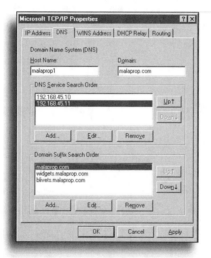

FIGURE 18.24
Configuring Windows NT DNS properties.

The DNS properties tab has the following fields:

- **Host Name**. With Windows NT, the default DNS host name is the same as the NetBIOS computer name after removing the 16th hexadecimal character that designates the service type. You can change this default name by editing the **Host Name** property.
- **Domain.** In this field, specify the domain name under which the host appears in the DNS name space.

Defining the FQDN

The 15-character NetBIOS name is combined with the specified domain name to establish the FQDN for the host.

- **DNS <u>S</u>ervice Search Order.** In this list, specify the IP addresses of one or more DNS name servers. Resolution attempts will query name servers in the order they appear in the search order list. Use the <u>**Up**</u> and **Do<u>w</u>n** buttons to adjust the search order.

Configuring the domain suffix search order

Always include at least one domain name in the **Domain Suffix Search Order** list, even if it is the same as the domain specified in the **Domain** field. Some processes will not work properly without a domain suffix list.

- **Domain Su<u>f</u>fix Search Order.** In this list, specify one or more domain names that are to be used as suffixes during attempts to resolve names that are not entered as fully qualified domain names. (A name that includes a period is regarded as an FQDN.) If keystone.com appears in this list and an attempt is made to resolve the name oliver, the resolver will query DNS with the name oliver.keystone.com. The suffixes are used in the order they appear in the search order list. Use the <u>**Up**</u> and **Do<u>w</u>n** buttons to adjust the search order.

Testing the DNS Server

After you have configured the DNS server and client, you can use ping to determine whether the client can resolve names. Figure 18.25 shows two examples in which hosts are pinged by name. In the first case, the ping is successful. In the second, the ping is unsuccessful because the name could not be resolved to an IP address.

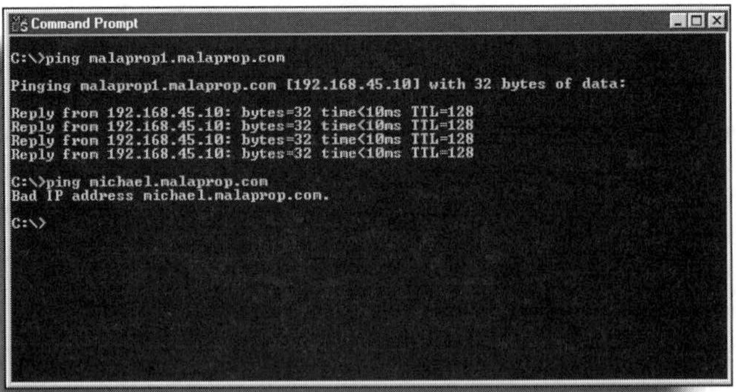

FIGURE 18.25

Pinging a host by name.

Another way to test the DNS server is to use the nslookup command. Figure 18.26 shows two examples of nslookup queries. The first is by host name, the second by host address. nslookup queries the DNS server specified in the client's DNS properties to attempt to resolve host names and IP addresses. Notice that nslookup reports the information for the target host as well as the identity of the name server that serviced the request.

FIGURE 18.26
Using nslookup.

Now Everyone Is Acquainted

Between WINS and DNS, everyone is now acquainted with everyone else, and you have a friendly network. I'm sorry it took so much work, but it's the nature of TCP/IP that many services require manual configuration.

That's it for setting up the TCP/IP infrastructure. Now that hosts can communicate, you probably want to put TCP/IP to work. These days, that means setting up a World Wide Web server. In the next chapter, you'll learn how to build a Web server, using Microsoft's Internet Information Server.

Setting Up a World Wide Web Server

It is impossible to overstate the effect of the World Wide Web on modern communication. Equally as much as television or radio, the Web promises to revolutionize the way we access information.

In this chapter, I will show you how easy it is to construct a Web server by using Microsoft's Internet Information Server (IIS) add-in for Windows NT. IIS is free if you have NT, it's easy to administer, it's capable, and it's fast becoming one of the dominant Web servers on the Internet.

In the brief time since the first release of IIS, Microsoft has already released four versions of the product. Version 2 is included with Windows NT Server 4.0, but IIS version 2 is old hat because version 4 is available as a free download from Microsoft's Web site. Because version 4 is more mature and capable than version 2, and because version 4 is just as free as version 2, there seems little reason not to focus on version 4.

IIS version 4 is a big software package. It includes World Wide Web and File Transfer Protocol (FTP) servers, a Simple Mail Transfer Protocol (SMTP) server, and facilities for setting up key-based encryption for Internet communication. That's too much for a chapter. Thorough coverage of the Web server alone is too much for a chapter. Therefore, this chapter has a tightly focused agenda. By the end of it, you'll be able to set up and manage a no-frills World Wide Web server.

A Few Words About Web Servers

The life of a Web server has become very complicated in recent years, now that Web pages are expected to move, interact, and have sound. I can't provide you with even a basic tutorial on Web development in this chapter, but you'll have no problem finding scads of material on the topic. In fact, here are a few books from Macmillan that can help you:

- *Teach Yourself Web Publishing with HTML 3.2 in a Week, Third Edition*, by Laura Lemay. Published by Sams.net.
- *Creating Killer Web Sites, Second Edition*, by David Siegel. Published by Hayden Books.

- *Web Designer's Guide to Style Sheets*, by Steven Mulder. Published by Hayden Books.

Despite all the hoopla, a Web server's job is to send documents to user computers, where they are displayed on a Web browser. These documents are somewhat peculiar because they consist of hypertext; that is, they contain more than text. Besides text and text formatting, a hypertext document can contain links to other documents. That's the magic of the World Wide Web: Documents' hypertext links can be other hypertext documents, or they can contain sound, graphic, animation, or applications. Name a type of content, and someone is probably working on a way to adapt it to the Web. Can touch and smell be far away for the Web?

For the purposes of this chapter, I am going to keep things simple, relying on documents written in the Hypertext Markup Language (HTML) to illustrate the capabilities of the IIS Web server.

Obtaining and Installing IIS Version 4

IIS Version 4 is distributed as part of the *Windows NT 4.0 Option Pack*, a massive package of Windows NT 4 add-ons. You can learn about the Option Pack and download it from Microsoft's Web site. You can learn about IIS and start a download from **http://www.microsoft.com/iis/**.

You can download the Option Pack through the Internet, but be warned that it is big. Very big. Almost 10MB. Unless you have a direct connection to the Internet, you should probably order a CD-ROM.

Prerequisites for IIS Version 4

Before you install IIS 4, you must install the following software, in this order:

1. Service Pack 3 (or later) for Windows NT 4.

2. Internet Explorer 3.02 (or later). (You also need Internet Explorer 3.02 or later to download the Option Pack.)

The Default Document

The default document is an important object on a Web server. When a directory on a Web server is accessed with a URL that doesn't include a filename, the server looks for a default document in the directory that is accessed.

When IIS looks for a default document, it looks first for a document with the name `default.htm` where `.html` and `.htm` are the conventional extensions for documents written in HTML. (The default document name can be changed if you want.)

If IIS doesn't find a document named `default.htm`, it looks for a document named `default.asp`. (The default document name can be changed if you want.) Documents with the extension `.asp` are *Active Server Pages (ASP)* documents. ASP is a Microsoft technology that enhances Web pages, enabling functions such as interaction and database access.

Don't even try to install the Option Pack until both Service Pack 3 and a supported version of Internet Explorer are in place. The Option Pack will attempt to install, but there will be a few dozen errors and the resulting installation won't work. Both the Service Pack and Internet Explorer can be downloaded from Microsoft's Web site. You can download Service Pack 3 when you download the Option Pack.

Here are some other things you should do to prepare:

- Configure TCP/IP in the computers that will be participating.

- Identify a Windows NT Server computer that will host IIS. If you expect IIS to be heavily used, this server should be dedicated to the task of providing IIS services.

- Disable any WWW, FTP, or Gopher servers that might be running on the IIS server. (IIS 4.0 installation will remove earlier versions of IIS from the host system.)

- Just in case, back up any WWW or FTP content directories currently on the server.

- Format the volumes to be used by IIS with NTFS, or convert them from FAT to NTFS. This ensures the highest possible level of security.

- Enable auditing if you feel you need to closely monitor the server for security breaches.

- Set up a name resolution method. You have several choices:
  - **DNS** is best if you'll be connected to the Internet or if your network includes non-Microsoft hosts.
  - **WINS** is probably easiest to maintain because it will automatically cope with network changes, particularly if IP addresses are assigned by DHCP. However, WINS can't supply names to non-Microsoft hosts unless it is configured to work in conjunction with the Windows NT DNS server. Also, WINS doesn't allow you to host multiple Web sites on the same Web server.
  - **HOSTS files** can be used to support Microsoft and non-Microsoft hosts. HOSTS files are static, though,

and any change to the network means updating everyone's HOSTS files. Also, HOSTS files won't allow outsiders to access your Web and FTP servers by name.

- **LMHOSTS files** can provide static naming for Microsoft hosts.

SEE ALSO

➤ *Learn about file system management, page 319.*

➤ *Learn how to convert FAT volumes to NTFS, page 319.*

➤ *Learn the procedure for auditing, page 673.*

➤ *Learn the procedures for setting up WINS and LMHOSTS files, page 485.*

➤ *Learn how to manage a DNS server, page 529.*

Installing IIS Version 4

After you install Service Pack 3 and Internet Explorer 3 (or later), you can install the Option Pack. The procedure is extremely simple, so I won't take you through each step, partly because the details change from time to time. Simply execute the Setup.exe program that is included with the Option Pack. A wizard will take you through the entire process.

If you obtain the Option Pack on CD-ROM and insert the CD-ROM on a computer that has a working browser, the autorun program initiates a browser-based installation. From there, you can install Service Pack 3 and Internet Explorer 4. Install those options if needed, restart the CD-ROM, and initiate installation of the Option Pack from your browser.

Selecting the Type of Installation

At one point, the Wizard offers you three installation options:

- **Minimum.** This option installs the minimum files required to establish a Web site.

- **Typical.** In addition to the components included in a minimum installation, this option includes documentation and several components that support Web application development.

- **Custom.** This option leads you to a dialog box where you can select the Option Pack components you want to install.

Before you begin

Before you begin to install IIS, be sure that the computer can communicate with the PDC for its domain. The Setup program needs access to the PDC to create user accounts and security required by IIS.

This chapter assumes that you have selected a Typical installation. For the sake of thoroughness, however, let's briefly look at what happens when you select **Custom.** The dialog box shown in Figure 19.1 allows you to select the components you want to install. In some cases, components have interdependencies. If you select a component that depends on another component, all required components will be selected for you by the wizard.

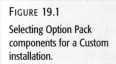

FIGURE 19.1

Selecting Option Pack components for a Custom installation.

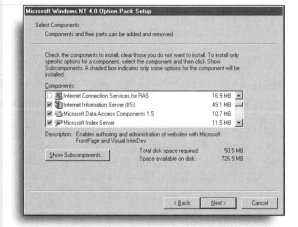

Viewing component descriptions

If you select a component in the **Components** list of the Setup Wizard, a brief description appears below the list.

Don't be concerned about selecting components at this time. You can always rerun the Setup program and install components you missed.

As I said before, everything in this chapter can be performed from a Typical installation.

Specifying Product Directories

After you select the components to be installed, the wizard prompts you to specify the root directories for the various services that will be configured. Figure 19.2 shows the Setup Wizard dialog box.

Each product has a product root directory that appears to be the server's root directory to users. For the WWW Service, the default product root directory is C:\Inetpub\wwwroot. The content files that will be published are placed in the WWW Service root directory, but to users of the Web server, they appear to be in a root directory. Users don't see C:\Inetpub\wwwroot at all.

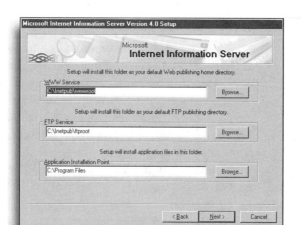

FIGURE 19.2
Specifying product directories.

I recommend that you use the default directories proposed by the Setup Wizard. You can change the server root directories at a later time if you want.

As for the **Application Installation Point**, this specifies the parent directory in which IIS directories will be established. IIS is not installed directly in the `C:\Program Files` directory.

Completing the Installation

A later dialog box prompts you for a root directory for the mail service. You can accept the default, but you won't be examining the mail service in this chapter.

After you accept the mail service root directory, files will be copied and the product directories will be created. The entire procedure is automatic, so sit back and wait for the configuration procedures to be completed. Restart the computer when prompted to complete the installation and activate IIS.

After installing the Option Pack, take a moment to examine the **Start** menu. Look for **Start | Programs | Windows NT 4.0 Option Pack** to locate the shortcuts and menu folders related to IIS. In particular, look for the shortcut **Start | Programs | Windows NT 4.0 Option Pack | Microsoft Internet Information Server | Internet Server Manager**. The Internet Service Manager is the primary tool used for managing the IIS.

IIS user accounts

The IIS Setup program must have access to the PDC during installation because it creates two user accounts.

`IUSR_servername` is used to define security permissions for anonymous users of the Web server, users who don't connect to the Web server using a user name and password. (`servername` is replaced by the name of the computer on which IIS is installed.)

`IWAM_servername` is used to provide permissions used by managers of Web applications.

Testing the Installation

A Web server should be running as soon as you reboot the computer after installation is completed. A quick way to test is to open Internet Explorer on the computer that is running IIS. (That way there can't be any problems with routing or name resolution.) Then enter the computer's NetBIOS name in the **Address** field. Internet Explorer will supply the remaining components of the URL. If the Web server is functioning properly, you'll see its default document. Figure 19.3 shows an example of the default document.

FIGURE 19.3

Viewing the default document for the default Web site.

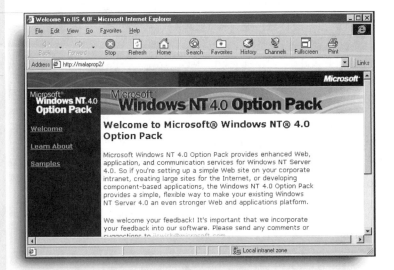

Introducing the Microsoft Management Console

If you select the Internet Server Manager shortcut in the Start menu, the application that greets you isn't called *Internet Service Manager* at all. Instead, you see the Microsoft Management Console (MMC), shown in Figure 19.4. The MMC is more than just another new NT management utility. It is an extensible utility that will eventually become the cornerstone of your Windows NT management activities. MMC connects with several existing utilities and accepts plug-in components that extend its capabilities.

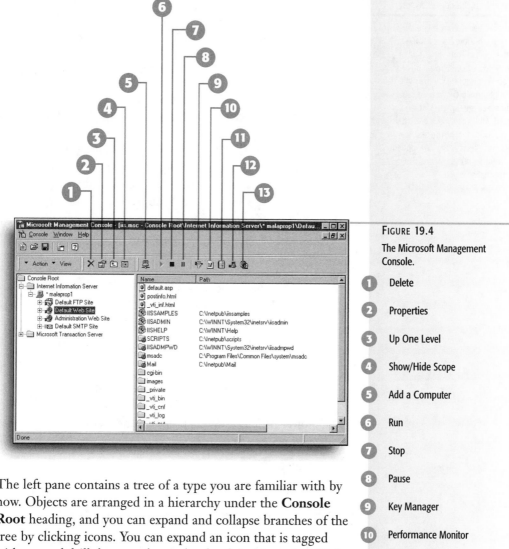

FIGURE 19.4

The Microsoft Management Console.

1. Delete
2. Properties
3. Up One Level
4. Show/Hide Scope
5. Add a Computer
6. Run
7. Stop
8. Pause
9. Key Manager
10. Performance Monitor
11. Event Viewer
12. Server Manager
13. User Manager

The left pane contains a tree of a type you are familiar with by now. Objects are arranged in a hierarchy under the **Console Root** heading, and you can expand and collapse branches of the tree by clicking icons. You can expand an icon that is tagged with a **+** and drill down to deeper levels of the hierarchy. Click the **–** symbol to collapse a branch. The tree in the left pane is also referred to as the *scope*.

The right pane contains objects for the level below the object selected in the Console hierarchy, just as in Explorer, which shows a folder's contents in the right pane when you select a folder in the left pane.

Customizing the objects display

You can open a **View** menu by clicking the **View** button at the end of the toolbar. From the **View** menu, you can customize the way objects are displayed in the right pane of the MMC. You have four options: **Large**, **Small**, **List**, and **Detail**. All figures in this book display the detail view. The best way to learn the effects of the view options is to try them until you find the choice that suits you.

Under the Internet Information Server heading in the **Console** list are several entries tied to sites. To users, each site is an independent server, but one IIS server can support multiple sites. Initially, a default site is configured for each service supported by IIS. Later in this chapter you'll learn how to create your own Web site.

An IIS server can have several Web sites, but all the sites are supported by the same service, which appears in the Services applet as the **World Wide Web Publishing Service**. You can manage each site individually without affecting other sites, an advantage that is new with IIS version 4. If you stop or start the **World Wide Web Publishing Service**, however, you affect all sites.

Figure 19.4 shows the **Default Web Server** object selected, which produces two effects:

- The objects below **Default Web Server** in the hierarchy are displayed in the right pane. As you can see, the default Web site is elaborate.

- The toolbar is customized with functions that match the selected object.

You'll become intimately acquainted with MMC as you manage IIS, so take a moment to familiarize yourself with the features shown in Figure 19.4. I'll discuss the features in the next few sections.

SEE ALSO

➤ See a description of the Services applet, page 673.

MMC: Changing the State of a Service

Three buttons in the MMC toolbar allow you to change the state of a site:

- The **Start** button starts a service that is paused or stopped. When a service is started, no comment appears beside the service object in the Console hierarchy.

- The **Stop** button stops the service. When you stop a service, connected users are disconnected, and new users aren't permitted to connect. A stopped service is tagged with the legend (Stopped) beside its entry in the Console hierarchy.

- The **Pause** button pauses a service. When you pause a service, connected users aren't affected and can continue to access the service. New users, however, aren't permitted to connect with the service. A stopped service is tagged with the legend (Paused) beside its entry in the Console hierarchy.

In some instances, you must stop a service in order to make configuration changes. You can wait until after hours to stop the service, but you might not have that option. If you don't want to force users off the service, pause the service and wait until all users have disconnected. You can then stop the service without disrupting users.

MMC: Accessing Other Utilities

Five buttons in the toolbar access other management utilities:

- **Key Manager** is a utility for creating digital certificates, which provide a means of authenticating network users. Many organizations use a third party to provide digital certificates, but you can manage your own. Unfortunately, digital certificates are far beyond the scope of this book.

- **Performance Monitor** opens Performance Monitor with some special counters tailored to IIS.

- **Event Viewer** opens the event log viewer.

- **Server Manager** opens Server Manager.

- **User Manager** opens User Manager For Domains.

SEE ALSO

➤ *Learn about the Performance Monitor, page 690.*

➤ *See a discussion of the Event Viewer, page 707.*

➤ *Learn about the Server Manager, page 674.*

The Action menu

At the left end of the toolbar is a button that expands the **Action** menu. This menu includes a variety of commands, many of which duplicate functions that can be performed by using toolbar buttons. You can, for example, start, stop, and pause sites by using commands in the **Action** menu.

MMC: Other Toolbar Utilities

You'll find several other buttons on the toolbar:

- **Delete** deletes the object selected in the Console tree.
- **Properties** opens dialog boxes for editing the properties of the object selected in the Console tree.
- **Up one level** moves the current context up one level in the Console tree.
- **Show/Hide Scope** shows or hides the scope pane (the left pane) of the MMC.
- **Add a computer to the list** adds a server to the Console hierarchy. The MMC can manage more than one server, allowing you to manage several servers from one place.

Using the Product Documentation

To access the documentation from the server running IIS, select the **Product Documentation** option in the **Windows NT 4.0 Option Pack** group of the **Start** menu.

The product documentation is actually served up by the WWW server, part of the reason why the WWW server must be installed and running as part of every IIS system. You can access the documentation from a browser on a remote system as well. If the workstation is logged on to the server's NT domain, you can access the documentation by using the following URL, where *server* is the server's NetBIOS name:

```
http://server/iisHelp/iis/misc/default.asp
```

If the server is named in DNS, you can also use its domain name in the URL. The following URL assumes the help files are on server www.malaprop2.com:

```
http://www.malaprop2.com/iisHelp/iis/misc/default.asp
```

Figure 19.5 shows the product documentation, viewed from Internet Explorer 4. If the documentation displays correctly, you can presume that your Web server is functioning.

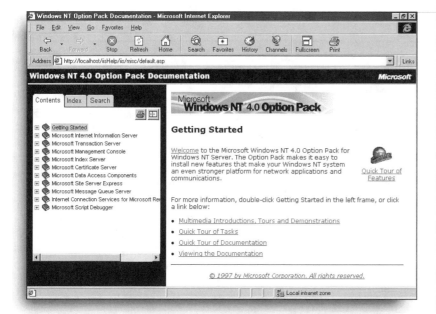

FIGURE 19.5

Viewing the product documentation in Internet Explorer.

Tips on using the product documentation

The product documentation is easiest to view on a monitor that has resolution of 800×600 or greater.

The product documentation makes frequent use of Active Server Pages, a Microsoft technology that enhances Web pages but is currently supported only on Microsoft's Internet Explorer browser, versions 3.0 and later. Some features in the documentation will be unavailable if you are using another brand of browser.

Uniform Resource Locators

Uniform Resource Locators (URLs) are used to request access to directories, files, and services on the World Wide Web. A URL specifies four categories of information:

- The **protocol** to be used. The protocol name is followed by the characters **://**. Protocol specifiers you'll encounter in this chapter are

  - **http://.** Hypertext Transport Protocol, the protocol used to display WWW documents formatted with Hypertext Markup Language.

  - **ftp://.** File Transfer Protocol, a protocol that allows users to receive files from and send files to the server.

- The **domain name** or **IP address** that the user wants to access. Typically, users will specify a domain name. If a WWW server is running on the local computer, you can refer to it as `localhost`.

- Optionally, the **port** that is to be used to connect with the server.

- The **path** to the information the user wants to retrieve. A path can specify directories, subdirectories, and a file to be accessed. The path is optional. If a path is not specified, the WWW server opens its root directory.

continues…

Uniform Resource Locators continued

The following URL accesses the root directory of the WWW server at www.microsoft.com:

http://www.microsoft.com

Here is an example that opens a specific subdirectory for FTP transfer:

ftp://www.widgets.com/public

This example opens a specific file on a Web server:

`http://www.keystone.com/public/information/goodstuf.htm`

The default port for a Web server is 80. If the Web server uses a different port, the port must be specified in the URL. This example opens a Web server with port 8080:

`http://www.malaprop.com:8080/`

For more information on URLs, check out

`http://www.w3.org/hypertext/WWW/addressing/addressing.html`

Creating a Web Site

Now let's see how easy it is to create a Web site. In doing so, you are going to leave the default Web site intact. That will enable you to examine the technique for supporting multiple Web sites on the same IIS server installation.

Creating a new Web server

1. Establish a unique identity for the new Web site.
2. Ensure that existing Web sites don't conflict with the new site's identity.
3. Create the new Web site.
4. Identify the new Web site in DNS.
5. Supply content for the new Web site.
6. Test the new Web site.

I'll expand on each of these subtasks in the following sections.

Identifying the New Web Site

A Web server can support multiple sites, provided each site has a unique identity that consists of one of the following characteristics:

- **A unique IP address.** You can assign multiple IP addresses to the same host, and each IP address can support a distinct Web site.

- **A unique port number.** Each TCP/IP process is identified with a port number. You can enable a new Web site by providing it with a port number that is unique on the computer running IIS.

- **A unique combination of an IP address and port number.** If you want, you can change both the IP address and port.

Configuring a Unique IP Address

The most common technique for distinguishing a site is to provide it with its own IP address. This approach simplifies the user's life because the user must specify a port in the URL if a site is not identified by the default Web port of 80. Fortunately, it is a simple matter to configure more than one IP address for a TCP/IP network adapter.

Adding an IP address to an adapter

1. Open the Network applet and select the **Protocols** tab.

2. Double-click **TCP/IP Protocol** to open the Microsoft TCP/IP Protocols dialog box.

3. Select the **IP Address** tab and click the **Advanced** button to open the Advanced IP Addressing dialog box, shown in Figure 19.6.

4. If the computer is equipped with more than one network adapter, open the **Adapter** list and select the adapter to be configured.

5. Click the **Add** button under the **IP Addresses** list.

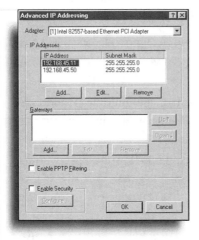

FIGURE 19.6

Adding a second IP address to a TCP/IP interface.

6. In the TCP/IP Address dialog box, complete the **IP Address** and **Subnet Mask** fields to specify the IP address to be added to the adapter.

7. Click **Add** to return to the Advanced IP Addressing dialog box.

8. Add more addresses, if required, by repeating steps 4 through 7.

9. Exit the Network applet and restart the computer.

Reconfiguring Conflicting Sites

No two computers can share the same IP address, even if Web servers on those computers are configured with different port numbers.

No two Web sites on the same computer can use the IP address that will be assigned to this Web site, unless the sites have different port numbers.

IP address limits

You can assign as many as six IP addresses with this method.

One Web site on an IIS server can be assigned the IP address (All Unassigned), which is the property that establishes the site as the default Web site, not the name. Only the default Web site can have the IP address (All Unassigned).

The default Web site—the site with the IP address (All Unassigned)—will respond to all Web service requests directed to all IP addresses on this computer, unless the IP address is specifically assigned to another Web site. As a result, the default Web site can't conflict with other Web sites that have explicit IP address assignments.

Because the default Web site will service all IP addresses that aren't explicitly directed to an operating Web site, you should be careful what you put on the default Web site. ISPs, for example, should use the default Web site as their own so that users will not be directed to another organization's Web site if their intended Web site is not functioning.

Before you install a new Web site, you should review the configurations of existing Web sites running on the IIS server. Reconfigure IP addresses and ports to eliminate conflicts, and identify an IP address/port number combination that can be used to uniquely identify the new Web site.

Reviewing the IP addresses of existing Web sites

1. Open the **Microsoft Management Console** and expand the Console tree to reveal the Web sites.

2. Right-click a **Web Site** object and choose **Properties** from the context menu. Figure 19.7 shows the Web Site Properties dialog box.

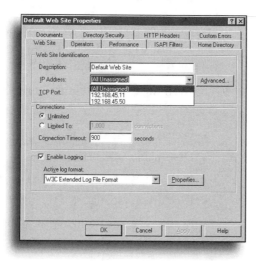

FIGURE 19.7

Examining the IP addresses for Web sites.

3. Select the **Web Site** tab.

4. Note the value of the **IP Address** field. (You can see the available options in the drop-down selection list.) Ensure that this value doesn't conflict with the IP address of any other site (unless the sites sharing the IP address use different ports).

The default Web site created when IIS was initially installed has the value (All Unassigned) for this property. As explained previously, this is the property that defines the default Web site. If you assign the (All Unassigned) address to another Web site, that site becomes the default Web site.

5. Repeat steps 2 through 4 for all Web sites on the server to ensure that no IP addresses conflict with the IP address of the new site.

Creating the New Web Site

The next step is to create the new Web site. The process is surprisingly simple. Before you create the site, you should establish its basic characteristics. The Web server must have a DNS name, a root directory, and an IP address.

While you plan, you must determine where its root directory will be located. It is often best to add a new subfolder to the \Inetpub folder. On large sites, you should create a separate volume to host your Web site. To improve performance, place the volume on a separate SCSI disk.

The Web site illustrated in this chapter will have the following characteristics:

- Web server: MALAPROP2.
- DNS name: www.malaprop.com.
- Web server root directory: C:\Inetpub\www2root.
- IP address: 192.168.45.11.
- Access security: Anonymous connections are permitted.

Configuring the new Web site

1. Log on as an administrator.

2. Use your favorite file management tool to create the root directory for the new Web site.

3. Open the MMC and expand the Console tree to reveal the server that will host the new Web site.

4. Right-click the server that will host the new Web site and select **New|Web Site** from the context menu. This will kick off the New Web Site Wizard.

5. In the first dialog box of the New Web Site Wizard, enter a description of the Web site in the **We̲b Site Description** field.

6. Click **Next** to open the Web site identity dialog box, shown in Figure 19.8.

Add a server to the Console list

If a server doesn't appear in the **Console** list, add it by clicking the **Add a computer to list** button, which is identified in Figure 19.4.

FIGURE 19.8
This Wizard dialog box establishes the Web server's unique identity.

7. Select an IP address for this site in the field **Select the IP Address to use for this Web Site**. Remember that the site with the address (All Assigned) is the default Web site.

8. Verify that the port value is correct in the field **TCP Port this Web Site should use**. This example uses the default Web port of 80.

9. Choose **Next** to open the next wizard dialog box, shown in Figure 19.9.

FIGURE 19.9

Specifying the root directory
for a new Web site.

10. Enter the Web site's root directory in the field **Enter the
    path for your home directory**. The directory must have
    been previously created, as described in step 2.

11. To permit anonymous access, leave the check mark in the
    field **Allow anonymous access to the web site.**

12. Click **Next** to open the next wizard dialog box, shown in
    Figure 19.10.

FIGURE 19.10

Specifying access for the
anonymous user.

13. Check the access permissions to be assigned to
    IUSR_*servername*. The following permissions are available:

    • **Allow Read Access.** This option allows users to
      retrieve documents from the Web server and is enabled
      by default.

    • **Allow Script Access.** This option permits users to exe-
      cute ASP (Active Server Pages) scripts and is enabled
      by default.

- **Allow <u>E</u>xecute Access.** This option permits execution of any executable file, including `.dll` and `.exe` files. This option includes script access.

- **Allow <u>W</u>rite Access.** This option permits users to write to files in the Web server directory.

- **Allow <u>D</u>irectory Browsing.** If this option is checked, IIS will generate a browsing document whenever it's asked to serve a directory that doesn't contain the document specified in the URL (or doesn't contain a default document if no document is specified in the URL).

14. Choose **Finish** to complete creation of the Web site.

15. The Web has been created, but it is stopped. To start it, select the new Web site in the Console tree. Then click the **Start** button in the toolbar.

Identifying the New Web Site in DNS

Next you must give the new Web site an identity in the DNS name space. Although you can support basic Web services using NetBIOS names, these names don't permit you to establish multiple Web sites on a Web server—a given NT computer can have only one NetBIOS name. DNS, on the other hand, allows you to define a different host name for each IP address on the computer.

Identifying the Web Site with an Address Record

Normally, you'll define an address (A) record for the Web server. You could, for example, add the following A record to the `malaprop.com` domain:

```
www              A        192.168.45.11
```

Identifying the Web Site with an Alias

If you have already established a name for the IP address, however, you might want to create an alias (CNAME) record instead. Suppose that the following resource record was previously added to the `malaprop.com` zone:

```
malaprop2        A        192.168.45.11
```

Assigning Web permissions

Usually, users of Web sites are given Read and Script permissions to a Web server. Execute, Write, and Directory Browsing permissions each introduce security concerns because they create an opportunity for the user to directly manipulate files and data on the server. Careful attention to security is essential if you open up your server to any permissions beyond Read and Script.

This record associates `malaprop2.malaprop.com` with the IP address `192.168.45.11`. The following CNAME record associates `www.malaprop.com` with the same IP address by making `www.malaprop.com` an alias for `malaprop2.malaprop.com`:

```
www                    CNAME    malaprop2.malaprop.com
```

Supplying Content for the New Web Site

Web content is a big subject, deserving about a dozen books, so I can't explain much here. Simply put, Web content consists of documents written in the Hypertext Markup Language (HTML); they are nothing more than text documents you create with any editor.

Here is a simple HTML document you can add to the root directory of your new Web server:

```
<HTML><HEAD><TITLE>Hello!</TITLE></HEAD><BODY>
Hello! Welcome to my new Web site.<BR>
</BODY>
</HTML>
```

Create this file with any text editor and save it in the Web server's root directory with the filename `default.htm`.

After you have created the `default.html` document, it will appear in the Web site contents, as shown in Figure 19.11.

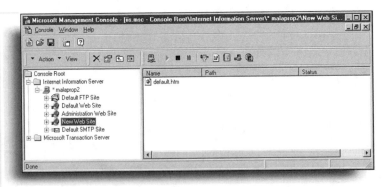

Actually, almost no one edits HTML in a text editor these days. There is a wide variety of tools that include intelligent HTML editors to help you with the command formats and check your HTML documents for errors. Most will let you preview your pages to double-check your layout.

There are also many WYSIWIG tools that let you develop Web pages in a fully graphic environment. Microsoft Word 97 can generate a limited range of HTML documents. Microsoft FrontPage is a more versatile tool, specifically designed for Web publishing. IIS 4.0 has special links with FrontPage that enable you to manage your Web site contents from FrontPage.

Testing the New Web Site

The first thing to do is test the DNS naming. Start by pinging the Web server by name. For example, enter the command ping www.malaprop.com. If the ping doesn't succeed, start debugging DNS. Make sure you have added a correct A record for the Web server. Also, check the DNS configuration of the client you are using. Can it ping other hosts by name? If not, visit the **DNS** tab of the Microsoft TCP/IP properties page and ensure that the client is properly configured.

After you have debugged DNS naming, open a browser and attempt to connect with the Web site. In the case of the sample Web site, you would enter the URL **http://www.malaprop. com/**. If you are successful, you'll see the sample Web page that appears in Figure 19.12.

FIGURE 19.12
The sample Web page.

SEE ALSO

➤ *Learn more about configuring DNS properties of TCP/IP clients, page 559.*

Configuring Site Properties

There are a great many properties that can be configured to customize a Web site. Some properties address advanced features that are beyond the scope of this chapter, but there are a few that you should review before moving on.

To open the properties page for a site, right-click the site in the **Console** list and choose **Properties** from the context menu. Figure 19.13 shows the Web site Properties page with the **Web Site** tab selected. Let's selectively examine some of the available properties.

FIGURE 19.13

Web site properties: The **Web Site** tab.

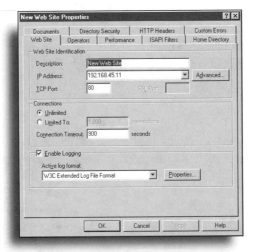

Web Site Identification Properties

The **Web Site** tab has three fields that identify the Web site:

- **Description.** This field serves only to identify the Web site in the MMC Console tree.
- **IP Address.** You can change the IP address associated with the Web site by editing this field.

■ **TCP Port.** You can modify the port that is associated with the Web site.

Connection Limit Properties

Also on the **Web Site** tab are properties that determine the numbers of users who can connect with the Web site. Although by default the **Unlimited** option button is selected, it is an unrealistic setting because all server hardware has performance limits. If too many users connect with a server, all users will suffer because of inadequate performance.

For this reason, you'll probably want to select the **Limited To** option button and specify a maximum number of connections. If users complain about performance, you can then reduce the number of connections allowed, until an acceptable performance level is reached.

The **Connection Timeout** value prevents users no longer actively using the Web site from monopolizing connections. Inactive users will be disconnected when the connection time-out expires.

Operator Properties

The **Operators** tab allows you to specify which groups and users are permitted to administer the Web server. By default, members of the Administrators local group have access to the Web server administration tools.

Performance Properties

Figure 19.14 displays the **Performance** tab. This tab has two settings that you should be aware of.

The **Performance Tuning** slider adjusts the memory that is allocated to the Web server based on the anticipated number of page hits. If memory use is not a concern, set the slider to the **More than 100,000** end of the control. Otherwise, adjust the control appropriately to achieve a compromise between performance and memory demand.

Activating Web site changes

If you modify any properties that affect operation of the Web site, you must stop and start the Web site to activate the changes. Remember, stopping and starting a Web site doesn't affect the Web service, and other sites are unaffected.

FIGURE 19.14

Web site properties: The
Performance Tab.

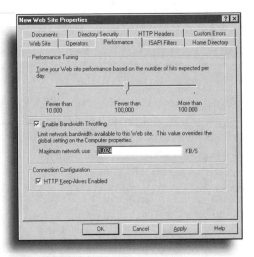

Web servers can generate very high traffic levels. When outsiders access your Web server through a WAN link, Web traffic
can dominate the WAN link. To reduce traffic generated by the
Web server, you should check **Enable Bandwidth Throttling**
and then specify a maximum traffic level in the **Maximum network use** field.

Home Directory Properties

The **Home Directory** tab is shown in Figure 19.15. One option
is to modify the source of the home directory (also referred to as
the *Web server root directory*). The **Home Directory** tab will be
modified depending on of the following choices you select as the
home directory source:

- A directory located on this computer
- A share located on another computer
- A redirection to a URL

Assuming that the directory is located on this computer, let's
review some of the available properties.

The **Read** and **Write** check boxes determine the operations that
can be performed by anonymous users.

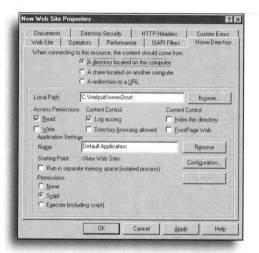

FIGURE 19.15

Web site properties: The **Home Directory** tab.

Directory browsing is a useful feature in some situations. When a user accesses a directory, several things can happen:

- If the URL specifies a particular file and the Web server finds the file, the file is sent to the user's browser.

- If the URL doesn't specify a file or specifies a file that isn't present, a default document is presented.

- If the URL specifies a file that is not present or doesn't specify a file, and if a default document is not found, the Web site can optionally generate a browsing document.

If you want the Web server to generate a browsing document when the Web server can't provide a requested or default document, check **Directory browsing allowed**. The browsing document is essentially a directory listing that shows files and folders in the specified directory. The user can browse the directory by clicking entries in the browser. Figure 19.16 shows an example of a browsing document. The root folder for `www.malaprop.com` contains three files and one directory. I right-clicked a file to show you the context menu that Internet Explorer provides for manipulating files in browsing documents.

FIGURE 19.16

A browsing document generated by the Web server.

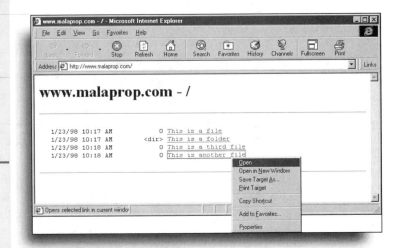

The perils of directory browsing

Directory browsing provides a possible back door that allows users to access your Web site content in ways you hadn't anticipated. If you permit directory browsing, carefully review your file and directory security to ensure that browsing users can't perform unwanted actions.

Browsing in Internet Explorer

Internet Explorer is well-equipped to browse directories. You can navigate through directories by clicking their hyperlinks. Also, you can perform a variety of file operations by right-clicking a file and selecting a function from the context menu.

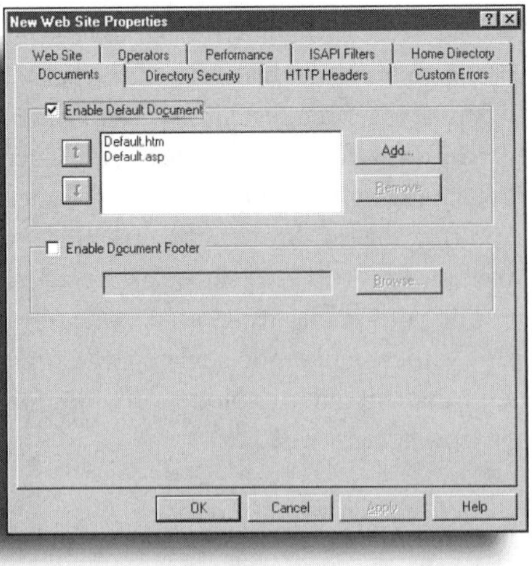

FIGURE 19.17

Defining the default documents.

Default Document Properties

The **Documents** tab specifies the names of documents that qualify as default documents. As shown in Figure 19.17, the standard default documents are `default.htm` and `default.asp`, in that order. If the Web server encounters several potential default files in a target directory, it will serve the one that appears first in the default documents list. You can add or modify the default documents and adjust their order of preference.

You've Only Just Begun

I wish I could tell you that you've taken a big step in this chapter, but unfortunately it is just the first step of many. The big deal with the Web server isn't the server itself—it's the content you publish, and Web content is a complex subject, almost without limits. Now it's time to get some books on Web authoring and a Web publishing tool or two and become really involved in generating material for your Web site. A good start is Microsoft's FrontPage 98 because Microsoft has taken pains to make it easy to manage your Web site content from FrontPage.

This chapter concludes the focus on TCP/IP. It is now time to move on to some more general topics. In the next chapter, you'll learn how to configure Dial-Up Networking and the Remote Access Server to support dial-out and dial-in capabilities on your network.

Setting Up a Remote Access Server

More and more workers are spending less and less time in their offices. Executive, sales, and marketing staffs have long been used to traveling to do their jobs. These days, increasing numbers of workers are working in virtual offices in their homes, seldom visiting the main office.

Increasingly, remote users are keeping in touch through the Internet. They can, for example, connect with the Internet and receive their mail from a company email server. Also, they can connect their browsers to a company Web site and get the latest news. There is little doubt that the Internet has been a prime motivator of the virtual office, providing a worldwide communication infrastructure that didn't exist a few years ago.

However, there remain times when users need to connect directly with the office network. Perhaps they need to retrieve report files from a coworker's workstation or to leave a spreadsheet where their boss can examine it. In such situations, dial-in access remains a viable method of connecting with the LAN in the home office.

Remote Access Server (RAS) is a dial-in server that is gradually becoming a general communication server. Eventually, you'll be able to use RAS to connect through dial-up lines, conventional Internet connections, or private networks that communicate through the public Internet.

This chapter concentrates on the dial-up capabilities of RAS. You'll learn how to set up your own RAS server to let users dial in to your network. You'll also learn how to set up the dial-out capabilities of NT to become a dial-in remote client on your organization's network.

Understanding Remote Access Server

RAS enables clients to dial in to a Windows NT Server computer and communicate as remote network nodes. Figure 20.1 shows a computer that has dialed in through a modem. I said that the computer is connected as a remote network node. That means that, apart from the fact that the modem connection is orders of magnitude slower than a direct network connection, the client functions exactly as though it has a direct connection. Any traffic that would flow through its network adapter when connected directly will flow through its modem when connected through RAS.

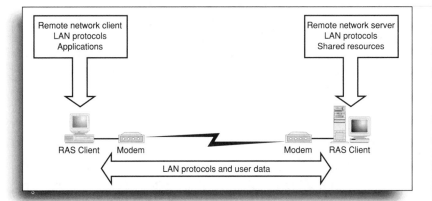

FIGURE 20.1

Operation of a client connected through RAS.

The fact that a client is a remote node means that very little is required to configure the client to operate remotely. It doesn't need to run any special software, other than the dial-out component, and the user works on the dial-in client as if it were directly connected to the network.

Because the dial-in connection is considerably slower than the LAN connection, you need to take certain precautions when setting up the client. It is perfectly reasonable to install applications on a LAN server and let clients access the program files through the network. It is much easier to manage applications that are installed one time on a LAN server than if they are installed a thousand times on a thousand clients. The drawback of running applications from the LAN server is that considerable network traffic is generated.

Unlike LANs, modems are slow, and right now there seems no way around it. The new 56Kbps modems help, provided compatible modems are operating at both ends of the connection, but poor line conditions often limit modem performance, particularly on long-distance connections. When you consider that an

Ethernet user can frequently pump a burst of data through a LAN at 4–5Mbps, the best modems are slow by comparison.

Because dial-in clients are connected at modem speeds, don't attempt to run applications from the server. All applications should be installed directly on the client so that only data files are transferred through the dial-up connection. The user might copy a .DOC file, for example, and edit it locally. However, all the files required for the Microsoft Word application should be installed directly on the user's workstation. Do everything you can to reduce the data that must be transferred through the dial-up connection.

Even application files are big these days. Excel spreadsheets and documents are frequently larger than 1MB. Document sizes are measured in mega*bytes*, and line speeds are measured in kilo*bits*, so a 1MB document is huge from the perspective of a 33.6Kbps modem. Consequently, it is often useful to use a file compression program to reduce the size of files that are to be transferred through dial-up connections.

When setting up a Remote Access Server, design is everything. Pay careful attention to detail. Keep the traffic levels as low as possible.

Features of the Remote Access Service

RAS consists of two components. The server component is what you usually think of when you use the term *Remote Access Service*. The client component often goes by the name of *Dial-Up Networking*. The server and client components are configured separately.

Before looking at RAS configuration, let's examine some features so that you understand some of the installation questions that face you.

Communication Technologies

By far the most common connection method used with RAS is to use modems. However, RAS supports other dial-up technologies as well. I will examine the options in the following sections.

Analog Modems

Windows NT can support up to 256 modems. This enables RAS to serve as a powerful, dial-up server. RAS supports three modem protocols:

- **SLIP.** The *Serial-Line Internet Protocol* (SLIP) is an old and very basic protocol that operates without error checking, flow control, or security. SLIP has slipped in popularity of late and is less frequently encountered in commercial settings. RAS supports SLIP so that RAS clients can dial in to SLIP servers such as those found in some UNIX environments, but RAS doesn't support SLIP as a dial-in protocol.

- **PPP.** The *Point-to-Point Protocol* (PPP) is a significant improvement over SLIP. PPP performs error checking and recovery, enabling it to operate on noisier communication lines than SLIP. Although the extra overhead associated with PPP results in lower performance compared to SLIP, its advantages have gradually made PPP the dominant protocol. RAS supports PPP for dial-in and dial-out functions.

- **RAS Protocol.** Microsoft has long supported this proprietary protocol and continues to do so in RAS. The RAS Protocol is required to support the NetBEUI protocol.

Note

Officially, Microsoft recommends that you select your modems from the Windows NT hardware compatibility list and that you use the same modems on both ends of a connection. That isn't realistic these days, when most computers come with built-in modems. Don't be too concerned, however. I've used RAS with a variety of modems, usually mismatched ones, and have had little trouble.

If your modems support some exotic new technology such as 56Kbps, you must match standards at each end to benefit from the feature. Preferably, with new technologies, match brands and models as well. There are, for example, two competing and incompatible 56Kbps standards.

Null Modem

Although it is most common to make serial connections through modems, it is also possible for computers to communicate through two directly wired serial ports, a configuration that is called a *null modem* because the cable that connects the computers fools them into thinking they are communicating through modems. Using null modems, RAS lets two computers communicate without the need for network cards. Null modem cables and adapters are sold in a better computer store near you.

X.25

X.25 is an old, clunky, wide area network protocol based on packet switching. X.25 is limited to data rates of 56Kbps and is rapidly being eclipsed by newer technologies such as frame relay. I mention X.25 because you'll see the tabs where RAS can be configured to support X.25. It is unlikely, however, that you'll be implementing a RAS network using X.25.

ISDN

Integrated Services Digital Network (ISDN) is a digital, dial-up technology that offers better performance than analog modems. A typical ISDN connection supports two 64Kbps channels and one 16Kbps channel. With the right equipment and software, the 64Kbps channels can be aggregated to provide a total bandwidth of 128Kbps.

Telecommunications providers have been slow to deploy ISDN, and availability remains spotty. ISDN requires end-to-end ISDN capability and special hardware. This is another problem with ISDN. You might be able to obtain ISDN service at one end but not at the other end of a proposed connection.

Just as ISDN is beginning to become readily available, increased competition from new technologies such as television cable modems threaten its very existence. It now appears that ISDN will be obsolete before it is fully deployed.

Supported Clients

Microsoft supports several clients that can dial in to RAS:

- **Windows NT and Windows 95 and 98.** These clients include RAS server capability and also support the PPP protocol. The clients can dial in and negotiate security with

RAS servers supporting RAS, PPP, and SLIP protocols. They can also dial in to UNIX and Internet servers, using PPP or SLIP.

- **Windows for Workgroups.** Windows for Workgroups includes RAS. You can upgrade the network client software to support TCP/IP, PPP, and SLIP with the TCP/IP client for Windows for Workgroups (WfW).

- **MS-DOS and Windows 3.1.** The Microsoft Network Client version 3.0 provides RAS support. You must enable the full redirector and access RAS using the `rasphone` command. RAS for MS-DOS supports only NetBEUI applications and doesn't support TCP/IP or IPX. Given the limitations, you should probably consider Windows for Workgroups the minimum RAS client.

- **PPP clients.** Any terminal or workstation that supports PPP can dial in to a RAS server. The RAS server will automatically initiate an authentication dialog. This allows UNIX and other non-Microsoft clients to access files on the RAS server or an attached network.

Installing and Configuring RAS

RAS is configured as a network service. In many ways, installation and configuration procedures resemble the procedures used with a network adapter card, so much of the material in this chapter will be familiar to you from earlier chapters.

The RAS installation and configuration procedure involves these major stages:

1. Hardware installation
2. Configuration of serial ports
3. Configuration of the modems
4. Installation of the RAS software
5. Configuration of RAS LAN protocols
6. Configuration of RAS user accounts

Hardware Installation

Because hardware installation is highly varied, it won't be addressed here; it is beyond the scope of this book. I will mention, however, that the chief limitation of setting up a RAS server on an Intel x86 computer is the limited number of serial ports that the x86 architecture supports. (The limitations I am discussing don't apply to RISC computers.)

Officially, you can add four serial ports to an x86 computer, COM1–COM4. There's a rub, though: COM1 and COM3 ordinarily share IRQ 4, which prevents both ports from being used simultaneously. Similarly, IRQ 3 is shared by COM2 and COM4, and those ports can't be operated at the same time. You must find four free interrupts to have four COM ports. Many serial adapters support only the default IRQs, so even if you can find four free interrupts, your hardware might prevent you from using them.

A variety of vendors have brought out multiport serial communication adapters that allow many serial ports to share a single interrupt. These adapters are your only options if you need to support a RAS solution with more than three or four modems.

X.25 PADs are installed as serial devices on RS-232C ports.

ISDN adapters should be installed according to the manufacturer's instructions. Installation of this hardware is beyond the scope of this book.

Interrupt priorities

IRQ 3 has a higher priority than IRQ 4. To provide the best support for a mode, connect your mouse to COM 1 so that it will use IRQ 4. Then connect your modem to COM 2. If your computer uses a PS/2 style mouse, the mouse probably uses IRQ 12, so this note doesn't apply.

Incidentally, IRQ 9–15 cascade off IRQ 2. Therefore, IRQs 9 and above have a higher priority than IRQs 3–8. A multiport serial adapter that uses a high interrupt will offer better performance than a serial port that uses IRQ 3 or 4.

Configuring Serial Ports

Serial ports are configured using the Ports utility of the Control Panel. If you run the Ports applet, you see the Ports window shown in Figure 20.2. This window shows the ports that Windows NT knows about. If your computer uses a COM port to support a mouse, the mouse's COM port will not appear in this list.

The Ports window displays only information for COM1 and COM2. If you have added COM port hardware, you need to choose **Add** and specify the advanced port settings as described in the following sections.

FIGURE 20.2

Configuring a serial port with the Ports applet.

Configuring Serial Port Settings

If you select a port and choose the Settings In The Ports window, you access the Settings dialog box shown in Figure 20.3. This box lets you configure serial communication parameters for the port you selected.

Serial ports must be configured with a variety of parameters, which must match settings in the communications software. These settings follow:

- **Baud Rate.** A measure of the bits-per-second rate at which the port will operate. When connecting through a modem, the software will negotiate a rate, starting at the value you specify and working toward slower speeds until a compatible rate is found. You should, therefore, set this parameter to the highest value that is supported by your modems.

UART performance

It is never a problem on newer equipment, but if you're using older computers to support RAS, you should ensure that the serial ports are configured with 16550A UARTs. The Universal Asynchronous Receiver/Transmitter is the heart of the serial port, and you need the 16550A version to support modems faster than 9600bps. The 16550A also supports FIFO buffering.

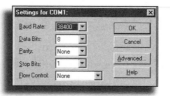

FIGURE 20.3

Settings for a COM port.

- **Data Bits.** Serial communication takes place one character at a time. Each character contains 4–8 bits of data. In almost all cases, you'll want to work with 8 data bits, which support advanced character sets and graphics.

- **Parity.** Parity is a rudimentary form of error detection that seldom is employed. In general, you can configure both devices for **None**. Other options are **Even**, **Odd**, **Mark**, and **Space**.

- **Stop Bits.** One or more stop bits signal the end of a serial character. It isn't important how many are used, as long as the computers at both ends agree. (However, extra stop bits do waste a bit of the communication bandwidth, and one stop bit will do fine.) One stop bit is by far the most widely used setting.

- **Flow Control.** This parameter determines how the computer and modem inform each other when data is ready to transmit and when the modem's input buffer is full. Options for this setting follow:

  - **Hardware.** The computer and modem communicate through extra wires in the serial cable. This is the most commonly implemented handshaking method.

  - **XON/XOFF.** Software handshaking transmits control characters called *XON* and *XOFF* to start and stop transmission. This setting is used when flow control must take place between the computers, but it's seldom required.

  - **None.** Risky if the volume of data potentially could overflow the modem's input buffer, which is often the case.

Choose **OK** to save settings. Click **Advanced** to configure hardware settings for the port.

Configuring Advanced Serial Port Settings

Click the **Advanced** button in the Settings For COMx window to configure additional settings for a serial port. The Advanced Settings For COMx dialog box, shown in Figure 20.4, can be used to configure Windows NT if your serial ports use nonstandard hardware settings or exceed the COM1 and COM2 port configurations that Windows NT knows by default.

FIGURE 20.4

Configuring advanced modem settings.

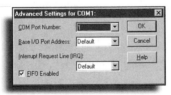

The settings in the Advanced Settings window follow:

- **<u>C</u>OM Port Number.** This field allows you to specify the COM port that you want to configure. If you add a new port, it should be numbered COM3 or above.

- **<u>B</u>ase I/O Port Address.** COM ports must be configured with an address in the memory range 2E0h–3ffh. This address supports communication between the OS and the port. Avoid changing the default settings for COM1 through COM4, which have standard and nonconflicting port addresses.

- **<u>I</u>nterrupt Request Line (IRQ).** If your serial port hardware permits you to configure custom interrupts, you can configure NT for those interrupts here. To use COM1 and COM3 at the same time (or COM2 and COM4), you need to configure custom, nonconflicting interrupts. Interrupts must be in the range of 2–15, although most of the interrupts in this range are unavailable.

- **<u>F</u>IFO Enabled.** This field allows Windows NT to take advantage of the capability of some advanced serial chips (called UARTs) to buffer incoming signals. Check your serial port documentation before you enable this feature.

Choose **OK** to save the settings.

Install Modems

Before attempting to install RAS, you must install at least one communications device. Modems are installed by using the Modem utility in the Control Panel. Here is the procedure:

Installing a modem with the Modem Wizard

1. Open the Modem applet in the Control Panel.

2. If no modems have been installed, the Install New Modem Wizard will be invoked.

3. Windows NT is very adept at detecting modem hardware. In the majority of cases, you should *not* check **<u>D</u>on't detect my modem; I will select it from a list**, which is found in the first window of the installation wizard.

4. Choose **Next**. The wizard will scan your COM ports and attempt to identify a modem. The modem might not be identified by brand. A standard Hayes-compatible modem is identified as a Standard Modem.

5. If you don't like the modem choice, choose **Change**. You can then select a specific make and model.

6. Choose **Next** when you're satisfied with the modem choice.

7. Choose **Finish** when you're informed Your modem has been set up successfully.

If at least one modem has been installed, the Modem utility looks like Figure 20.5. You can use this window to add, remove, and change the properties of modems. Choosing **Add** starts the Install New Modem Wizard.

Note

To enable RAS to communicate through a null-modem cable, the computers at both ends of the connection must be configured to use null-modem connections. To install null-modem support, select the modem manually. In the Install New Modem dialog box, specify **(Standard Modem Types)** in the **Manufacturers** list, and specify **Dial-Up Networking Serial Cable between 2 PCs** in the **Models** list.

Advanced Modem Configuration

The Modem utility is used to configure the configuration properties for modems (see Figure 20.5).

FIGURE 20.5

The Modem applet in the Control Panel.

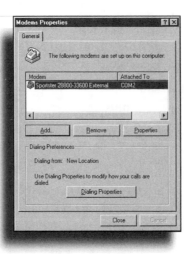

Configuring a modem

1. Select a modem in the **Modem** list of the Network utility and choose **Properties** to open the Modem Properties window, shown in Figure 20.6.

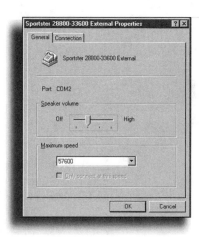

FIGURE 20.6
Configuring properties for a modem.

2. The **General** properties tab (refer to Figure 20.6) has three settings:

    - **Port.** Describes the COM port to which the modem is connected.

    - **Speaker volume.** Determines the loudness of the modem speaker.

    - **Maximum speed.** Specifies the maximum speed at which software should attempt to operate the modem.

3. The **Connection** properties tab, shown in Figure 20.7, defines a number of modem communications characteristics.

    - **Data bits.** Specifies the size of the data character to be used. 8 bits is the most common setting and is configured by default.

    - **Parity.** Specifies the type of parity checking to be used. The most common setting is **None**, which is specified by default.

    - **Stop bits.** Specifies the stop bits to be sent after a data character is sent. One stop bit is the most common choice and is the default setting.

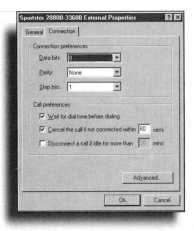

FIGURE 20.7

Configuring modem connection properties.

- **W̲ait for dial tone before dialing.** When checked (the default), the modem will not commence dialing until a dial tone is detected.

- **C̲ancel the call if not connected within ... secs.** Check this option if calls should time out when a specified number of seconds elapse before a connection is established.

- **D̲isconnect a call if idle for more than ... mins.** Check this option if connections should be terminated when no traffic is generated within a specified period of time.

4. Choose **A̲dvanced** on the **Connection** tab to open the Advanced Connection Settings dialog box (see Figure 20.8). This dialog box has a variety of options.

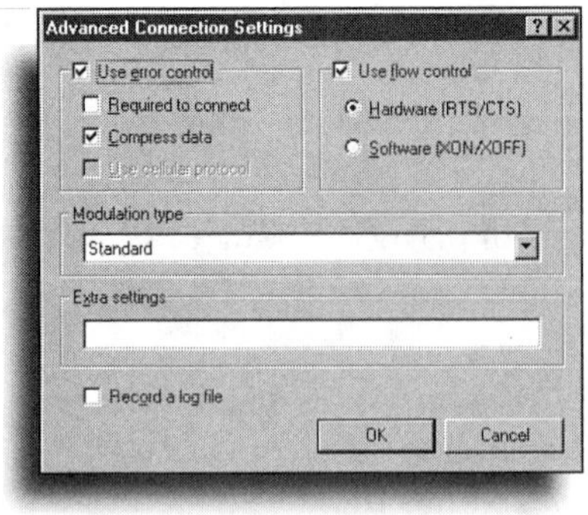

FIGURE 20.8

Configuring advanced modem properties.

- **Use error control.** Check this option if the modem's hardware error control should be used. Modems at both ends of the connection must be capable of performing the same type of error control. Typically, error control is provided by the RAS communication protocol. Checking this box allows you to configure the next three options.

- **Required to connect.** If hardware error control is enabled, check this option if error control is required to establish a connection. If this option isn't checked, connections can be established without error control in effect.

- **Compress data.** If hardware error control is enabled, check this option if hardware data compression should be used. Modems at both ends of the connection must be capable of performing the same type of compression.

- **Use cellular protocol.** If the modem is capable of communicating through a cellular telephone link, check this option to enable cellular communication.

- **Use flow control.** Check this option to enable flow control. Flow control techniques smooth the process of communication between a serial interface and the modem, preventing either device from overwhelming the other with excess traffic. If you check this option, the next two check boxes are enabled.

- **Hardware (RTS/CTS).** Hardware flow control uses two wires in the serial interface cable to signal when the modem is ready to receive data. This is more efficient than software error control because extra traffic isn't generated.

- **Software (XON/XOFF).** Software flow control consists of sending special XON and XOFF characters to start and stop data transmission. Software flow control is generally used only when hardware flow control isn't supported.

- The **Modulation type** field can be used to specify nonstandard modulating techniques if required in certain circumstances.

- The **Extra settings** field accepts special product-specific settings. Consult your hardware manuals for suitable settings.

- **Record a log file**. Check this box if you want modem activity to be recorded in a log file. A log file can be a valuable troubleshooting tool.

5. Choose **OK** when advanced settings are completed.

6. Choose **OK** to exit the Modem applet.

Installing RAS Software

As with all network services, RAS is installed, and its protocols are configured by using the Network utility in the Control Panel. To install the RAS software:

Installing the Remote Access Service

1. Open the Network utility in the Control Panel and select the **Services** tab.

2. Choose **Add** and select **Remote Access Service** in the **Network Service** box.

3. Choose **OK**.

4. When prompted, supply the path where files can be found on the installation CD-ROM. Files will be copied and the adapter software will be installed. You'll be returned to the Network utility window.

5. After files are copied, the Add RAS Device dialog box appears, as shown in Figure 20.9. Review the current configuration by pulling down the **RAS Capable Devices** list. Then do the following:

   a. Choose **Install Modem** to add a modem to the configuration. This will start the Install New Modem Wizard.

   b. Choose **Install X25 Pad** to add an X.25 packet assembler-disassembler.

   c. Choose **OK** to accept the RAS device configuration.

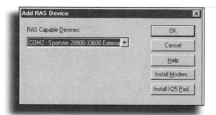

FIGURE 20.9
Adding a RAS device.

6. Next, the Remote Access Setup dialog box appears (see
Figure 20.10). In this dialog box, you add ports and devices
to the RAS configuration. At this point, you should configure any ports that are currently installed. The procedure is
as follows:

   a. Select a port and choose **Configure** to open the
     Configure Port Usage dialog box (see Figure 20.11).
     Select one of the following options to configure the
     port:

       • **Dial out only**

       • **Receive calls only**

       • **Dial out and Receive calls**

   b. Review the configuration in the Remote Access Setup
     dialog box and choose **Continue** when satisfied.

7. If NetBEUI protocol support is installed on the computer,
the RAS Server NetBEUI Configuration dialog box appears
next.

8. If TCP/IP protocol support is installed on the computer, the
RAS Server TCP/IP Configuration dialog box appears next.

**Installing modem-pooling
equipment**

Configure the equipment to
function as one of the modem
types supported by RAS. The
equipment must interface via
standard RS-232 signals.

Connect a COM port to the
equipment and configure RAS
with the same modem type that
was configured for the modem-
pooling equipment.

Microsoft recommends configuring modem-pooling equipment as standard
Hayes-compatible modem
devices.

ISDN adapters are installed as
network adapters by using the
Network utility in the Control
Panel.

FIGURE 20.10

Use the Remote Access Setup
dialog box to configure RAS
ports.

FIGURE 20.11

Configuring usage for a port.

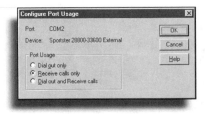

9. If IPX protocol support is installed on the computer, the RAS Server IPX Configuration dialog box appears.

10. If NWLink is installed on the computer, you'll see the message `Netbios Broadcast Propagation (broadcast of type 20 packets) is currently disabled. Do you want to enable it?`. Typically, NWLink isn't configured to propagate NetBIOS broadcast packets (type 20 packets), that is, to forward NetBIOS broadcast packets over routers and throughout a network. In most cases, you can accept the default response of **N**o. Select **Y**es if browsers will be located on the dial-up side of the connection.

11. Choose **OK** when you see the message `Remote Access Service has been successfully installed`.

12. Close the Network applet and restart the server.

When RAS is installed, two new programs are installed:

- **Dial-Up Monitor** echoes status lights for several of the modems' most critical lines. It is especially useful with internal modems. The icon is installed in the Control Panel.

- **Remote Access Admin** configures a RAS server. You can also use it to start a RAS server. It is located in the **Administrative Tools** submenu of the **Start** menu.

The Dial-Up Networking utility is installed in a standard Windows NT setup. This is the RAS dial-out program, which is installed in the **Start** menu. Look in the **P**rograms/**A**ccessories submenu.

SEE ALSO

➤ *Examine the Network applet features, page 83.*

➤ *Learn the procedures for installing RAS, page 88.*

RAS Authentication Protocols

RAS supports several authentication protocols, and you'll need to select one when you configure a port.

CHAP (challenge handshake authentication protocol) adds considerable security to the RAS session. When a connection is being established, the CHAP server sends a random challenge to the client. The challenge is used to encrypt the user's password, which is returned to the server. This has two advantages: The password is encrypted in transit, and an eavesdropper can't forge the authentication and play it back to the server at a later time because the challenge is different for each call.

MS-CHAP is the most secure encryption protocol supported by RAS. MS-CHAP, also known as RSA Message Digest 4 (MD4), uses the RC4 algorithm to encrypt all user data during the RAS session.

PAP (*Password Authentication Protocol*) is a clear-text authentication protocol that is associated with the PPP protocol. PAP authentication should be used only when dialing in to servers that don't support encrypted authentication, such as SLIP and PPP servers.

SPAP (*Shiva Password Authentication Protocol*) is supported on the RAS server only and is an implementation of PAP on Shiva remote client software.

Configuring RAS Ports

The Network utility in the Control Panel is used to reconfigure RAS ports.

Configuring a RAS port

1. Open the Network utility in the Control Panel and select the **Services** tab.

2. Select **Remote Access Service** in the Network Services box and choose **Properties** to open the Remote Access Setup dialog box (refer to Figure 20.10).

3. Use the Remote Access Setup dialog box to add, remove, and configure ports.

4. To configure port usage, select a port and choose **Configure** to open the Configure Port Usage dialog box (refer to Figure 20.11). After configuring ports, choose **OK** to close the dialog box.

5. The **Network** button in the Remote Access Setup dialog box is used to configure the protocols that RAS will support. Choose this button to display the dialog box shown in Figure 20.12.

FIGURE 20.12

Use the Configure Report Usage dialog box to configure the network properties of RAS ports.

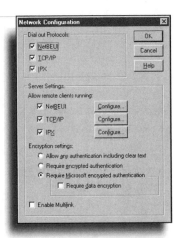

6. Check the protocols that will be supported for dial-in and dial-out operation.

7. In the Dial Out Protocols box, check the protocols to be supported by RAS.

8. In the Server Settings box, select the encryption setting:

   • **Require Microsoft encrypted authentication.** For clients that support Microsoft encryption (MS-CHAP), this is the preferred setting. If you check the box **Require data encryption**, all data transferred between the client and server is encrypted using the RSA Data Security Incorporated RC4 algorithm.

   • **Require encrypted authentication.** This option allows users to connect with MS-CHAP, MD5-CHAP, and SPAP.

   • **Allow any authentication including clear text.** This choice permits clear text authentication as well as encrypted authentication using MS-CHAP, MD5-CHAP, SPAP, and PAP. This setting is useful with clients that don't support data encryption.

9. Dial-up multilink capability allows RAS to aggregate multiple physical links into a logical bundle. Bundling is a common technique used with ISDN links. Check **Enable Multilink** to support the feature.

10. Choose **OK** when the Network Configuration settings are complete.

11. Exit the Network utility when RAS ports have been configured.

Configuring RAS LAN Protocols

When you're installing RAS, you need to configure the protocols that RAS will support. It is important to remember that RAS clients must be running a network protocol—NetBEUI, IPX, or TCP/IP—that is supported by RAS. If you accept the default values, little protocol configuration is required. RAS will make most address assignments.

If you need to reconfigure RAS LAN protocol support, return to the Network utility in the Control Panel and open the properties for the Remote Access Service. In the Remote Access

---

RAS client support

Windows 3.x clients can use only NetBEUI with RAS.

Windows NT and Windows 95 and 98 clients can use NetBEUI, NWLink, and TCP/IP with RAS.

The cost of encryption

Encryption requires extra processing at both ends of the connection and hence results in slower communication. Use encryption only when sensitive data is being transmitted. Passwords are very sensitive, and encrypted authentication is preferred.

Setup dialog box (refer to Figure 20.10), choose **Network** to open the Network Configuration dialog box (refer to Figure 20.12). Access the configuration dialog boxes of the RAS protocols by choosing the appropriate **Configure** button.

RAS Server Configuration for NetBEUI

Configuring a port for NetBEUI

1. Choose **Configure** in the Network Configuration dialog box to open the RAS Server NetBEUI Configuration dialog box (see Figure 20.13). In this dialog box, choose the network access that will be granted to RAS users. Your choices are

   - **Entire network**
   - **This computer only**

2. After you make your selection, choose **OK**.

FIGURE 20.13

Configuring NetBEUI properties for a port.

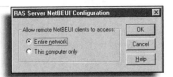

RAS Server Configuration for TCP/IP

Configuring a port for TCP/IP

1. Choose **Configure** in the Network TCP/IP Configuration dialog box (see Figure 20.14).

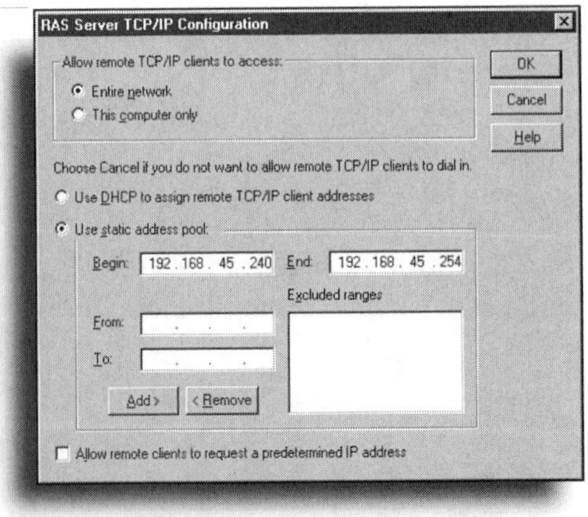

FIGURE 20.14

Configuring TCP/IP properties for a port.

2. Specify the network access that will be granted to users on this port by selecting one of the following radio buttons:

- **Entire _n_etwork**
- **This _c_omputer only**

3. Select one of the following radio buttons to specify the technique that will be used to assign IP addresses to users on this port:

- **Use _D_HCP to assign remote TCP/IP client addresses.** If the Dynamic Host Configuration Protocol (DHCP) is running on your network, this is the most satisfactory approach because no further address configuration is required.

- **Use _s_tatic address pool.** You can select a range of addresses from which an address will be assigned to dial-in users. You'll need to specify the address range in the **_B_egin** and **_E_nd** fields.

4. If you selected **Use _s_tatic address pool**, you must specify a range from which addresses will be selected. To prevent address conflicts, this range of addresses should be the exclusive property of this port.

- a. Specify the starting address in the address pool in the **_B_egin** field.
- b. Specify the ending address in the address pool in the **_E_nd** field.
- c. If you want, you can exempt some addresses from the address pool. Specify a range of addresses in the **_F_rom** and **_T_o** fields and choose **_A_dd** to exclude that address range from the address pool.

5. Check **A_l_low remote clients to request a predetermined IP address** only if users must have control over their IP address. This is seldom the case.

6. Choose **OK** when the port has been configured.

SEE ALSO

➤ *Learn about TCP/IP addressing, page 428.*

➤ *Learn about DHCP, page 511.*

RAS Server Configuration for IPX

If a port will support NWLink (IPX), configure it as follows:

Configuring a port for IPX

1. Choose **Configure** in the Network IPX Configuration dialog box, shown in Figure 20.15.

2. Determine the access that will be granted to IPX clients by selecting one of the following radio buttons:

    - **Entire network**
    - **This computer only**

3. Choose **OK** to save the port configuration.

FIGURE 20.15

Configuring IPX properties for a port.

If you configure network and node number settings as shown in Figure 20.15 (the default settings), no further IPX configuration is required. If you must assign IPX network or node numbers, read the following sections.

Assigning IPX Network Numbers

IPX requires all clients to be associated with a network number for routing purposes. In most cases, a given network segment is assigned a single network ID for each protocol and frame type that the segment supports. An IPX network number is a hexadecimal number up to 8 digits.

The *IPX Routing Information Protocol* (RIP), similar in principle to TCP/IP RIP, advertises network numbers by having routers announce them at one-minute intervals. As the quantity of network numbers increases, RIP traffic increases rapidly. It is preferable to minimize the number of network numbers whenever possible.

Therefore, the default setting is to check **Assign <u>s</u>ame network number to all IPX clients**.

You can choose two methods of assigning network numbers:

- **Allocate network numbers <u>a</u>utomatically.** RAS will assign a network number that doesn't conflict with existing network numbers.

- **Alloca<u>t</u>e network numbers.** Use this option to specify a range of addresses from which network numbers will be assigned.

Assigning IPX Node Numbers

Each device on a network has a node number, a hexadecimal number up to 16 digits. For clients that are attached to the network, this number is usually derived from the hardware address of the Ethernet or token-ring card.

You can, if you want, allow users to specify their own IPX node address by checking **Allow remote clients to request <u>I</u>PX node number**. This is a risky option because it can permit users to impersonate other users by using their node numbers.

Configuration of RAS User Accounts

Before users can use a RAS server, you must use Remote Access Admin to set up user permissions. The main window for Remote Access Admin is shown in Figure 20.16. This window displays the status of each RAS communication channel and is used to access RAS administration functions. Here is the procedure for assigning users RAS permissions:

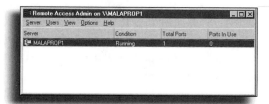

FIGURE 20.16

The Remote Access Admin utility.

Assigning RAS permissions to users

1. Open the Remote Access Admin utility.

2. Choose the **Permissions** command in the **Users** menu. The Remote Access Permissions dialog box appears (see Figure 20.17). In this dialog box, you can administer remote access permissions for individuals or for all network users.

FIGURE 20.17

Granting users RAS permissions.

3. To revoke RAS permissions from all users, choose **Revoke All**.

4. Check the **Grant dialin permission to user** box to grant RAS dial-in access.

5. Select one of the following permissions options:

    • **No Call Back.** This option lets users call in and connect with the network on the same call.

    • **Set By Caller.** With this option, the caller will be asked to enter a telephone number. RAS will disconnect, call the user at the number specified, and connect the user to the network.

    • **Preset To.** This option requires you to specify a number that RAS will call to connect the user. Using a specified number enhances security because a user must have physical access to a particular telephone to enter a remote session.

6. To grant the same permissions to all users, set the permissions and choose **Grant All**.

7. To grant permissions to an individual user, select the user account name in the **U**sers box. Then set the permissions to apply to that user.

8. After making the required settings, choose **OK**.

Managing the Remote Access Server

The Remote Access Admin utility can be left active to monitor RAS operation. The main window lists the status of active RAS servers in the current domain (refer to Figure 20.16). The status indicates the number of ports that are configured for each server, as well as the number of active connections.

Starting and Stopping the Server

After RAS has been installed and the server has been restarted, the Remote Access Service should be started. The **Server** menu in Remote Access Admin has four options for starting, stopping, and pausing the RAS server:

- **S**tart **Remote Access Service.** Starts the Remote Access Service.
- **St**op **Remote Access Service.** Stops the Remote Access Service.
- **P**ause **Remote Access Service.** This action prevents users from accessing the service but leaves it enabled for administrators and server operators.
- **Co**ntinue **Remote Access Service.** Changes the status of the service from Paused to Started.

SEE ALSO
➤ *All these actions can also be performed using the Services utility in the Control Panel, as described in Chapter 23. See the section "Service Manager" on page 681. When the RAS software is installed, the Remote Access Service is configured to start automatically when Windows NT Server is restarted.*

Managing Server Ports

To obtain details about server ports, double-click the entry in the main window, or select the server and choose the **C**ommunication Ports command in the **S**erver menu. Figure

---

Setting dial-in permissions in User Manager For Domains

You can also manage user dial-in permissions in User Manager For Domains. Open the User Properties dialog box and choose **Di**alin to open the Dialin Information dialog box, which has the options shown in Figure 20.17.

Warning: Avoid using the Guest account for dial-in access

Because the Guest account doesn't ordinarily have a password, you should avoid giving this account dial-in permissions. If you intend to grant guests dial-in access, either strictly restrict permissions assigned to this account or assign a password.

Managing remote RAS servers

Remote Access Admin can manage RAS servers in any domain on the network. Use the **Select Domain or Server** command in the **Server** menu to change domains.

If you're managing another domain through a modem or other slow connection, choose the **Low Speed Connection** option in the **Options** menu to reduce the amount of data that will be transmitted through the communication link.

20.18 shows an example of a Communication Ports display. Four buttons can be used to access port management features:

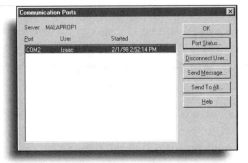

FIGURE 20.18

Port information for a RAS server.

- **Port Status.** This button displays a detailed status report for the selected port. An example is shown in Figure 20.19. Click the **Reset** button to zero out the statistics. This display is extremely useful for troubleshooting RAS connections. (Much of this information is also available in the Dial-Up Networking Monitor in the Control Panel.)

- **Disconnect User.** Select a user and click this button to break a remote connection.

- **Send Message.** Use this option to send a message to the selected port.

- **Send To All.** Use this option to send a message to all users connected to this server.

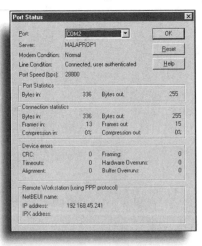

FIGURE 20.19

Status information for a port.

A similar display is available for connected users. Choose the **Active Users** command in the **Users** menu to display the Remote Access Users dialog box (see Figure 20.20). Options are similar to the detailed port status display, with the exception of the **User Account** button, which displays information about the user's account.

FIGURE 20.20
Active RAS users.

Dialing Out with RAS

If you're familiar with Windows 95, you'll be comfortable with Dial-Up Networking. They aren't identical, unfortunately, but they are similar enough that you won't feel as though you're on another planet.

Configuring Telephony Services

You have the option to configure Telephony Services, which establishes contexts for dialing out from various locations.

Configuring locations in Telephony Services

1. Open the Telephony applet in the Control Panel. The window is shown in Figure 20.21.

2. In the **I am dialing from** field, enter a name for a new location, or choose an existing location to be modified.

3. Enter the local area code in the field **The area code is**. When dialing, an area code will not be added to the phone numbers of calls placed in this area code.

4. Select the country for this location in the **I am in** field.

Logging on through dial-up networking

When RAS is installed on a computer, a **Logon using Dial-Up Networking** option is added to the Logon Information dialog box. This allows you to log on to a remote network during the standard logon procedure.

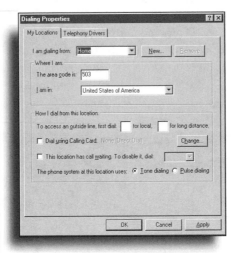

FIGURE 20.21

Adding a new location to
Telephony Services.

5. In the **To access an outside line, 1st dial ..._for local,
..._for long distance.** fields, enter any dialing prefixes
required to obtain a local and a long distance outside line.

6. If your long-distance charges are to go on a calling card,
check **Dial using Calling Card** to open the Change Calling
Card dialog box. Select the service in the **Calling Card to
use** field and enter your PIN in the **Calling Card number**
field. Choose **OK** to save the entry.

7. If your location has call waiting, disable the feature by
checking **This location has call waiting. To disable it,
dial.** Then enter the code to disable call waiting in the field
provided.

8. Specify the dialing mode by selecting **Tone dialing** or
Pulse dialing.

9. Choose **Apply** to save the entry, and choose **OK** to exit.

Using Dial-Up Networking

The Dial-Up Networking application is used to manage your
dial-up configurations and to connect to remote locations. After
you learn how to manage phone book entries, you're ready to
dial out to RAS and other servers.

Installing Dial-Up Networking

The first time you start Dial-Up Networking, you see the message The phonebook is empty. Press **OK** to add an entry. When you choose **OK**, you're shown the New Phonebook Entry Wizard. You need to configure at least one phonebook entry to use Dial-Up Networking. The following information is required:

- A name for the new phonebook entry
- Whether you're calling the Internet
- Whether it is okay to send your password in plain text if requested by the server
- If you're calling a non-Windows NT server, whether the server expects you to enter login information after connecting
- The phone number (and alternative phone numbers, if available)
- Whether the phonebook entry will use telephony dialing properties

When the phonebook entry is completed, it will appear in the Dial-Up Networking dialog box (see Figure 20.22).

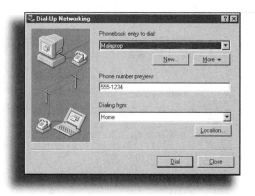

FIGURE 20.22
A completed phonebook entry.

To edit the phonebook entry, choose **More** to open a menu. Select **Edit entry and modem** properties from the menu to open the Edit Phonebook Entry dialog box (see Figure 20.23).

The Edit Phonebook Entry dialog box has five tabs. A thorough discussion of the tabs is beyond the scope of this book, but basic configuration isn't at all difficult.

FIGURE 20.23

Editing a phonebook entry: Basic properties.

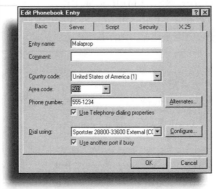

Basic Dialing Properties

The **Basic** tab, shown in Figure 20.23, defines the basic dial-out configuration. If you want to use settings established in your Telephony configuration, check **Use Telephony dialing properties**. The entries for this tab should require no explanation.

Choose **Configure** to open a dialog box in which you can configure the following modem properties:

- **Initial speed (bps).** This setting specifies the first speed at which the modem will attempt to connect. Lower speeds will be attempted if a connection can't be negotiated at the speed you specify.

- **Enable hardware flow control.** Hardware flow control is enabled by default.

- **Enable modem error control.** Modem error control is enabled by default.

- **Enable modem compression.** Modem compression is enabled by default.

- **Disable modem speaker.** Speaker is enabled by default.

Server Protocol Properties

The **Server** tab defines the protocols that will be used to communicate with the server (see Figure 20.24).

Using data compression

Compressed data can't be further compressed, and it is a waste of processing to enable both hardware and software data compression. Typically, on today's faster computers, because software data compression outperforms hardware data compression, hardware data compression should be disabled.

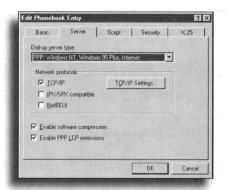

FIGURE 20.24
Editing a phonebook entry:
Server protocol properties.

Selecting the Dial-Up Server Type

In the **Dial-up server type** field of the **Server** tab (refer to
Figure 20.24), you can select one of three types of dial-up
servers:

- **PPP: Windows NT, Windows 95 Plus, Internet.** This is
  the default and the best all-around choice. When PPP is
  selected, you can select any or all of the available protocols.

- **SLIP: Internet.** When SLIP is selected, only TCP/IP is
  available as a protocol option.

- **Windows NT 3.1, Windows for Workgroups 3.11.** This
  option selects the RAS protocol that was standard before
  Windows NT 3.5. It should be used only when backward
  compatibility is required. When the RAS protocol is selected, only the NetBEUI protocol is available.

SEE ALSO
➤ For descriptions of the dial-up protocols, page 599.

Configuring the Dial-Up Network Protocols

In the Network protocols box of the **Server** tab (refer to Figure
20.24), check the protocols that are to be supported. Only PPP
gives you a choice. TCP/IP is required for SLIP, and NetBEUI
is required for the RAS protocol.

If **TCP/IP** is selected in the Network protocols box, the
TCP/IP Settings dialog box can be accessed by clicking the
TCP/IP Settings button. The options you see depend on
whether the PPP or SLIP protocol is selected.

Figure 20.25 shows the PPP TCP/IP Settings dialog box. The options in this window are as follows:

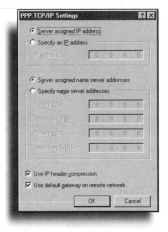

- **Server assigned IP address.** Select this option if the PPP dial-in server will assign an IP address for you; this is the most common situation.

- **Specify an IP address.** Select this option and specify an IP address in the IP address field if the PPP server doesn't assign an IP address.

- **Server assigned name server addresses.** Select this option if the PPP dial-in server adds the address of a DNS server to your configuration when you dial in. This is less commonly done than automatic IP address assignment.

- **Specify name server addresses.** Select this option to manually specify the IP addresses of DNS and WINS name servers.

- **Use IP header compression.** Header compression—also known as *Van Jacobson IP header compression* or *VJ header compression*—is almost always used to reduce the amount of traffic. Check with the manager of the dial-in server to determine whether header compression is used.

- **Use default gateway on remote network.** This option applies to computers connected to local networks at the same time they are dialing remotely. When this option is checked, packets that can't be routed to the local network are routed to the default gateway on the remote network.

Figure 20.26 shows the SLIP TCP/IP Settings dialog box. The options in this window are as follows:

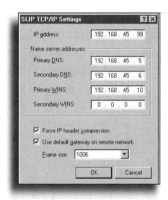

FIGURE 20.26

TCP/IP properties for dialing a SLIP server.

- **IP address.** You must specify an IP address. SLIP servers cannot assign addresses.
- **Name server addresses.** You must specify IP addresses for the applicable DNS and WINS name servers.
- **Force IP header compression.** Check this option if the SLIP server uses header compression.
- **Use default gateway on remote network.** This option applies to computers that are connected to local networks at the same time they are dialing remotely. When this option is checked, packets that can't be routed to the local network are routed to the default gateway on the remote network.
- **Frame size.** This value determines the size of frames that will be used. Adjust this value, if required, for the SLIP server. Frame sizes of 1006 and 1500 can be selected.

Other Server Protocol Settings

Returning to the **Server** tab (refer to Figure 20.24), there are two other options of which you should be aware:

- **Enable software compression.** When this option is checked (the default), the communication software will compress and decompress communications data. It is unproductive and unnecessary to enable both hardware (modem) and software (protocol) compression. Typically, software compression is more efficient, particularly on higher end computers. Software compression isn't supported by the SLIP protocol.

- **Enable PPP LCP extensions.** LCP is a component of newer PPP implementations but isn't supported by older PPP servers. Try deselecting this box if problems occur when using PPP.

Script Properties

Figure 20.27 shows the **Script** tab. *Scripts* are text files that contain commands that automate dial-in events such as logon. The details of scripts are beyond the scope of this book and are discussed in the Windows NT Server documentation.

FIGURE 20.27

Editing a phonebook entry: Script properties.

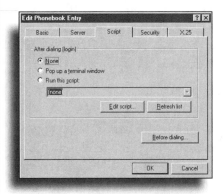

Scripts are typically unnecessary when dialing into PPP servers. PPP includes the Password Authentication Protocol (PAP), which automates the acceptance of user IDs and passwords. Because no automation is available for SLIP, however, scripts can be of benefit.

The **Script** tab provides options for scripts to be executed after dialing. The options are

- **None**. No script will be executed. This is the default and will work with most PPP servers.

- **Pop up a terminal window.** If this option is selected, a terminal window will be opened when a connection is established. The terminal will be used to accept the user's password and other required logon information.

- **Run this script.** If this option is selected, enter the pathname for a script. You can choose **Edit scripts** to create and modify script files.

You can also specify scripting to take place before dialing. Choose **Before dialing** to open the Before Dialing Script dialog box, which is practically identical to the After Dialing box shown in Figure 20.27.

Security Properties

The **Security** tab, shown in Figure 20.28, determines the types of encryption that will be used. The option chosen must match the requirements of the server.

SEE ALSO

➤ *For descriptions of the RAS security options, page 613.*

FIGURE 20.28
Editing a phonebook entry: Security properties.

If you want to use your username and password on the Windows NT network, check **Use current username and password**. This option is available only if you select **Accept only Microsoft encrypted authentication**.

X.25 Properties

If you're connecting to an X.25 network, select the X.25 tab, shown in Figure 20.29. Entries on this tab are as follows:

- **N**etwork. Select the name of the X.25 network you are calling.

- **A**ddress. Specify the X.25 address supplied by the X.25 network provider.

- **U**ser Data. Enter additional connection data supplied by the X.25 network provider. This field can be left blank.

- **F**acilities. Enter parameters to request facilities from your X.25 provider. Consult the provider for appropriate parameters. This field is optional.

FIGURE 20.29

Editing a phonebook entry: X.25 properties.

Dialing with a Phonebook Entry

After you have entered a phonebook entry, choose **OK** in the New Phonebook Entry window to open the Dial-Up Networking window (refer to Figure 20.22). The actual events that take place depend on

- Whether the host is a RAS server or a TCP/IP network
- Whether the host is configured for dial-back operation

Dialing a RAS server

1. Open Dial-Up Networking.

2. Select a phonebook entry in the **Phonebook entry to dial** field.

3. Verify the entry in the **Dialing from** field. You can select another location by choosing **Location**. (New locations must be entered using the Telephony utility in the Control Panel.)

4. Verify the number in the **Phone number preview** field. If the number isn't complete and correct, check the configuration for the location.

5. Choose **Dial** to open the Connect dialog box shown in Figure 20.30.

FIGURE 20.30

Completing dial-up account properties.

6. Complete the fields in the Connect dialog box as follows:

   - **User name.** Enter your username on the destination network. This field and the **Password** field will be completed with your Windows network username if you checked **Use current username and password** in the **Security** tab when configuring this phonebook entry.

   - **Password.** Enter your password on the destination network.

   - **Domain.** If you're dialing to a RAS server, enter the domain you want to log on to. If you're dialing a non-RAS server, clear this field.

   - **Save password.** Check this field if you want to have your password saved with the phonebook entry. This can be hazardous. Saving your password allows any user to dial your remote account without entering a password.

7. Choose **OK** when you have configured the Connect dialog box.

8. The client dials and enters a conversation with the RAS server.

9. The RAS server sends a challenge to the client.

10. The client sends an encrypted response.

11. The server checks the response against its database.

12. If the response is valid, the server checks for remote access permission.

13. If the user has been given remote access permission, the client is connected.

14. If callback is enabled, the server disconnects, calls the client, and completes steps 8–13 again.

15. If the server doesn't support all the protocols that you enabled in the **Protocols** tab for the phonebook entry, you'll see the message One or more requested network protocols did not connect successfully. If you check **Do not request the failed protocols next time**, the protocols will be removed from the phonebook entry. Typically, because these protocols are unnecessary, you can safely remove them.

16. Choose **Accept** to continue the connection with the supported protocols. Choose **Hang Up** if a required protocol isn't supported and you want to try another server.

17. Next, a message box informs you that the connection is complete. At this point, you can specify two actions that will take place when you make future connections:

- **Close on dial.** If this box is checked, the Dial-Up Network application will be closed when a connection is established. Your connection remains active after the Dial-Up Network application is closed.

- **Do not display this message again.** If this box is checked, you will not see this message in the future when a connection is completed.

18. When the session is complete, choose the **Hang Up** button in the Dial-Up Networking application. You'll need to reopen the application if you checked **Close on dial** in step 17.

You're now connected. The connection mimics a direct network connection, and you can use any applications that are appropriate to the environment. For example, you can use Windows NT applications to access files on a RAS server. Also, you can use Winsock-compatible TCP/IP to access remote TCP/IP services, such as those offered by the Internet.

Disconnecting from a Dial-Up Server

When the session is finished, disconnect as follows:

Disconnecting from a dial-up server

  1. Reopen the Dial-Up Networking application.

  2. Choose **Hang Up** in the Dial-Up Networking dialog box.

More Options in the Dial-Up Networking Application

To see additional dial-up networking options, return to Dial-Up Networking and choose the **More** button. A menu opens with the following options:

- **Edit entry and modem properties.** Choose this option to use the phonebook editor to modify this phonebook entry.

- **Clone entry and modem properties.** Use this option as a shortcut for creating a new phonebook entry that has similar settings to an existing entry.

- **Delete entry.** Use this option to remove the entry shown in the Phonebook entry to dial field.

- **Create shortcut to entry.** This option opens a dialog box that allows you to create a shortcut. To put the shortcut on your desktop, place it in `C:\Winnt\Profiles\`*username*`\Desktop`. To put the shortcut in the **Start** menu, place it in `C:\Winnt\Profiles\username\Desktop\Start Menu\Programs\`*folder*, where *folder* is the submenu that should contain the shortcut.

- **Monitor status.** This option opens the Dial-Up Networking Monitor, shown in Figure 20.31. This utility, which can also be started from the Control Panel, displays a variety of information about the dial-up session and lets you

configure certain options for the dial-up session. In the
Preferences tab, you can determine whether status lights
will be displayed as a taskbar icon or as a window on the
desktop. See the "Troubleshooting RAS" section for more
information about the status lights.

FIGURE 20.31

The Dial-Up Networking
Monitor.

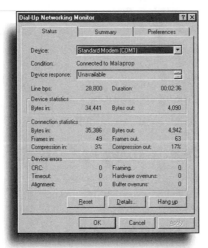

FIGURE 20.31

The Dial-Up Networking
Monitor.

- **Operator assisted or manual dialing.** Use this option if
  the phone number must be entered manually or by an operator.

- **Logon preferences.** This option opens the Logon
  Preferences utility, shown in Figure 20.32. Use this utility to
  configure a variety of options that affect the dial-up process.
  Of particular interest is the **Callback** tab, shown in the figure. You must configure this tab to enable callback
  operation.

Using RAS Automatic Dialing

With Windows NT 4, an automatic dialing feature has been
added to RAS. When a connection is established, automatic dialing associates a network address with a phonebook entry. RAS
AutoDial also learns about every connection that is established
over a RAS link.

FIGURE 20.32
Setting callback options in the
Logon Preferences utility.

If you aren't connected to a dial-up network, whenever the address is referenced, RAS will automatically be invoked and will attempt to connect, using the appropriate phonebook entry.

Under certain circumstances, you might want to disable the AutoDial feature:

1. Choose **More** in the Dial-Up Networking dialog box and select the **Logon Preferences** option in the **Options** menu.

2. Select the **Appearance** tab.

3. Deselect the **Always prompt before auto-dialing** entry.

Installing the RAS Clients for Windows for Workgroups

RAS client software is included with Windows for Workgroups. As with Windows NT, RAS is considered a network service. To install RAS on WfW, use the following steps:

Installing RAS on WfW

1. Start the Windows Setup utility.

2. Choose **Change Network Settings** in the **Options** menu.

3. In the Network Settings dialog box, choose **Drivers**.

4. In the Network Drivers dialog box, choose **Add Adapter**.

5. In the Add Network Adapter box, scroll the adapters in the **Select a Network Adapter to Install** list until you find **Remote Access Service**. Select that option and choose **OK**.

6. When installation begins, supply the pathname for files and change disks as requested.

7. In the Remote Access Configuration dialog box, select a COM port in the **Port** box. Then pull down the **Device** list and select a communication device. Then choose **OK**.

8. Choose **Close** in the Network Drivers box. Then choose **OK** to close Network Setup.

9. In the Microsoft Windows Network Names box, specify

- **User Name.** The username to be used to access the network
- **Workgroup.** The workgroup or domain to be accessed
- **Computer Name.** A name for this computer that isn't in use on the network to be accessed

Choose OK when this information has been entered. Remote Access files will be copied to the computer.

10. Restart the computer when prompted.

The Remote Access program icon will be installed in the Network program group.

Troubleshooting RAS

By far the most common problems you'll have, at least while you're learning RAS, will result from misconfiguration of the client or the server. Start with a basic setup, get everything working, and then add modem pools and other fancy features.

If possible, do your initial testing with two identical modems. If that works and other modems don't, you can be sure the modems are incompatible with RAS.

The Dial-Up Networking Monitor (see Figure 20.33) is an extremely useful tool for testing flaky connections; it pops up when dialing commences. The Dial-Up Monitor displays modem status lights during a session, either in a window or as an icon on the taskbar. The window version is more informative, showing the status of the TX (transmit data), RX (receive data), and CD (carrier detect) lines, and whether errors are detected.

Especially look for high error rates that might be causing lost connections.

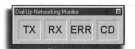

Logging RAS Events

You can enable two RAS logs by changing Registry entries. The PPP log can be used to troubleshoot problems with PPP connections. To enable the PPP log, change the Logging parameter to 0x1 in the following Registry key:

```
HKEY_LOCAL_MACHINE
   \SYSTEM
   \CurrentControlSet
   \Services
   \RasMan
   \PPP
```

The device log records all communication from serial ports to connected devices when modem commands are being executed. To enable the device log, change the Logging parameter to 0x1 in the following Registry key:

```
HKEY_LOCAL_MACHINE
   \SYSTEM
   \CurrentControlSet
   \Services
   \RasMan
   \Parameters
```

Log data is stored in the file DEVICE.LOG in the C:\Winnt\system32\ras directory.

By default, the logs are stored in the directory C:\Winnt\system32\ras. The PPP log file is named PPP.LOG and the device log is named DEVICE.LOG. You can view these files using the Windows Write program.

640

SEE ALSO

➤ *Learn more about changing values in the Registry, page 657.*

Are We Remotely Connected?

If you did your homework in this chapter, your users now have a new way to connect with the network by dialing in from an outside computer. It's really pretty painless to configure RAS, and it greatly improves the usefulness of your network.

It's becoming harder and harder to think up transitions between chapters as we fill in the cracks by examining diverse NT Server technologies. I don't have a good transition for the next chapter, so I'll have to settle for "The next chapter shows you how to manage the Microsoft network browser environment." Pretty clever, huh?

Managing the
Browser Environment

Browsing is a peculiarity of Microsoft networks. Computers cooperate to build a database of shared directories and printers that is somehow magically made available to users, who browse the list using Network Neighborhood, Explorer, or other tools. The entire process works so invisibly that we take it for granted while using the network. Browsing just happens.

Except when it doesn't happen. You might encounter times when two users' browsers show completely different views of the network. And WINS was invented because browsing doesn't work on a routed TCP/IP internetwork. Because browsing can break down, you need to know how it works so that you can deal with the fallout and correct the problems.

Browser Roles

Several types of computers participate in the maintenance of the browser database. Computers can have five roles, sometimes having several roles at one time. For example, a master browser can also be a server, and it can be a browser client for another domain. Here are the computer browser roles:

- Master browser
- Backup browser
- Potential browser
- Servers
- Browser client, or nonbrowser

There are subtle differences in the ways that computers are assigned browser roles, depending on the underlying network protocol. Let's start with some definitions and general discussion and then look at the specifics for NetBEUI, NWLink, and TCP/IP.

There are also some differences depending on whether the user is browsing a domain or a workgroup. We'll look at these differences as well.

The Master Browser

Each domain has a *master browser* (also sometimes called a *browse master*). The master browser collects browser announcements for the entire domain, including all network segments, and provides a master browser list for the domain. The master browser list contains information about all servers in the domain.

Any Windows NT computer that is running the Server service (or its equivalent on earlier versions of Windows) is advertised via the browser mechanism. When a server comes onto the network, it announces itself to the master browser. Periodically, the server checks in with the master browser, decreasing the frequency until it's checking in about every 12 minutes.

The master browser is selected in an election process. For a domain, the election process is highly biased and guarantees that if the primary domain controller is active, it is always the master browser. If the PDC isn't running, an election takes place, and a BDC will be selected from among the list of backup and potential browsers.

If a master browser announces that it is shutting down, other computers hold an election to determine which one is best able to become the domain master browser. If a client can't find a browser, it can force an election of a new master browser.

Backup Browsers

As additional computers are added to the network, they may become backup browsers. By default, Windows NT computers become backup browsers, although computers can be configured as standby browsers. The master browser can instruct standby browsers to become backup browsers, attempting to maintain about one backup browser per 31 computers. Backup browsers spread the work of browsing around, because browse clients can access the browse database through any backup browser.

Backup browsers check in with the master browser every 15 minutes to update their databases. Consequently, it can be up to 15 minutes before a backup browser learns of a change to the backup browser's database.

Backup browsers serve two functions. They contain backup copies of the browser database. They can also be consulted by nonbrowsers to browse the domain server database.

When a master browser fails, it might be 15 minutes before backup browsers detect the failure. The first backup browser to detect the failure forces an election to select a new master browser.

Potential Browsers

Many servers can become browsers when they are called on to do so by the master browser. Potential browsers include Windows NT, Windows 95 and 98, and Windows for Workgroups computers. A computer must be configured as a server to be a potential, backup, or master browser.

Servers

A server is a computer that can potentially share file and printer resources. Servers can function as master browsers, backup browsers, or potential browsers, or they can be configured to always be nonbrowsers.

On Windows NT, a server is a computer that is running the Server service. Windows 95 and 98 and Windows for Workgroups computers can also function as servers and have functionality similar to the Windows NT Server service.

When a server enters the network, it transmits a broadcast message that announces its presence. These announcements are repeated periodically to inform browsers that the server remains available. The server announces its presence at increasing intervals of 1, 2, 4, 8, and 12 minutes. Thereafter, the server announces itself at 12-minute intervals.

If the master browser doesn't hear from a server after three announcement intervals, the master browser removes the server from its browse list. In the worst case, the master browser will not remove a server from its browse list for 36 minutes. Because backup browsers obtain browse lists from the master browser at

15 minutes, it can take up to 51 minutes for backup browsers to learn that a server has been removed from the network. This delay is one reason why different backup browsers can have different browse lists.

Browser Clients

When clients browse the network, they use a browser client such as Explorer or Network Neighborhood, which uses an API call to identify browsers on the network, select a browser, and browse the database in the browser.

Determining Computers' Browser Roles

You might want to configure the browser behavior of specific computers. The following sections describe the configuration procedures for Windows NT, Windows 95 and 98, and Windows for Workgroups.

Windows NT

A Windows NT computer's browser behavior is determined by a value under the following Registry key:

```
HKEY_LOCAL_MACHINE\SYSTEM\CurrentControlSet\Services\
Browser\Parameters
```

Under that key, the MaintainServerList value entry can have three values:

- **No**. Indicates that the computer will never be a browser.

- **Yes**. Indicates that the computer will be a browser. It will attempt to contact the master browser and become a backup browser. If no master browser is found, the computer forces an election for a master browser. Yes is the default value for Windows NT computers.

- **Auto**. Indicates that the computer is a standby browser and can become a backup browser if a master browser notifies it to do so.

Hiding servers from browse lists

In rare instances, you might have a Windows NT computer that is configured as a server (it is running the Server service) but that you don't want to be advertised in browse lists. To prevent the server from appearing in browse lists, use the Registry editor to add a value to the key `HKEY_LOCAL_MACHINE\System\CurrentControlSet\Services\LanManServer\Parameters`. Add a value entry with the name Hidden and the type `REG_ DWORD`. Set the value to 1 to remove the computer from browse lists. Set the value to 0 to have the computer appear in browse lists.

SEE ALSO

➤ *See Chapter 22 for information about the Registry, starting on page 657.*

Windows 95 and 98

Windows 95 and 98 computers are configured through the Network applet in the Control Panel. A Windows 95 or 98 computer can function as a browser only if file or print sharing is enabled, because only then does the computer appear as a server on the network.

Configuring the browser role of a Windows 95 or 98 computer

1. Open the Network applet.

2. Examine the list of network components. If the list doesn't contain the entry File and printer sharing for Microsoft Networks, click **File and Print Sharing** and check either or both of the following check boxes:

   - **I want to be able to give others access to my files**
   - **I want to allow others to print to my printer(s)**

   Click **OK** to return to the Network applet.

3. Select File and printer sharing for Microsoft Networks.

4. Click **Properties** to open the Advanced dialog box, shown in Figure 21.1.

FIGURE 21.1

Configuring the browser behavior for a Windows 95 or 98 computer.

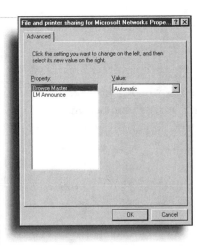

5. Select Browse Master from the **Property** list.

6. Select one of the following browser behaviors from the
   Value list:

   - **Automatic**. The computer is a potential browser.
   - **Enabled**. The computer will be a browser for its
     domain or workgroup.
   - **Disabled**. The computer will never be a browser.

7. Exit the Network applet. If you're configuring file and printer sharing for the first time, you will need to specify a directory path so that the required files can be installed.

8. Restart the computer to activate the changes.

Windows for Workgroups

With a Windows for Workgroups computer, you can control the
computer's browser behavior by adding a line to the [network]
section of the system.ini file. To prevent the computer from
functioning as a browser, add the following line:

```
MaintainServerList=No
```

Browser Protocol Dependencies

Browser operation differs significantly, depending on the underlying network protocol. You need to be aware of the protocol
dependencies so that you can troubleshoot the browser environment.

Browsing and NetBEUI

NetBEUI messages can't be routed. Therefore, every subnetwork functions as an independent browsing environment. Figure
21.2 shows a NetBEUI network that includes two subnets. The
router is deceiving, because the computers function as though
they are on completely separate networks.

**Domain and workgroup size
limitations**

Prior to Windows NT Server
version 4, the list of servers
maintained by a master browser was limited to 64KB of data.
As a result, a domain or workgroup is limited to about 2,000
to 3,000 computers.

FIGURE 21.2

Browsing on a NetBEUI network.

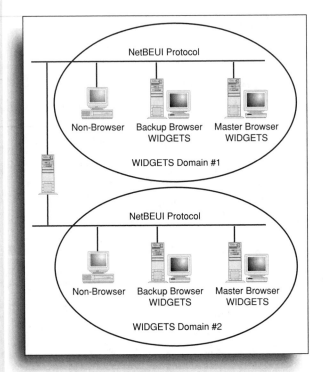

Notice that each subnet has a master browser and a backup browser for the WIDGETS domain. In fact, there are *two* WIDGETS domains on this network, and they are completely isolated from each other.

Browsing with NWLink

NWLink is a routable protocol, and NetBIOS broadcast forwarding can be enabled on Windows NT routers that are configured with the NWLink protocol. As a consequence, the browsing mechanism is not fragmented when routers are introduced to the network. Figure 21.3 illustrates browsing on a routed NWLink network.

SEE ALSO

➤ *Configuration of NWLink routing is covered in Chapter 3, in the section "Configuring IPX Routing" on page 99.*

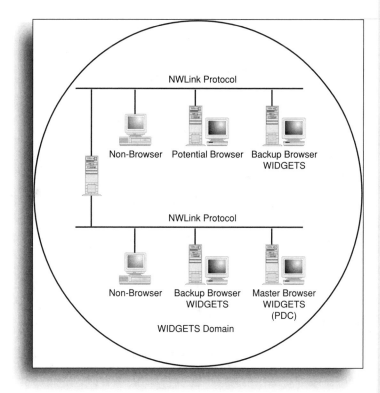

FIGURE 21.3
Browsing on an NWLink network.

Notice that a single master browser services the entire network. This master browser receives service announcements from all servers and creates a master browse database for the domain. Backup browsers contact the master browser at 15-minute intervals to obtain copies of the domain browse database.

Because NWLink supports a single master browser per domain, it is often undesirable to distribute domains across WAN links when using the NWLink protocols. Backup browsers that are separated from the master browser by the WAN link generate considerable WAN traffic as they poll the master browser for updated browsing information. The traffic required to maintain the browse databases can eat into the available WAN bandwidth.

Browsing with TCP/IP

Although TCP/IP is a routable protocol, IP routers do not forward NetBEUI broadcasts. Consequently, routers fragment browsing on TCP/IP networks. As Figure 21.4 shows, each sub-net is configured with a master browser.

FIGURE 21.4

Browsing on TCP/IP networks.

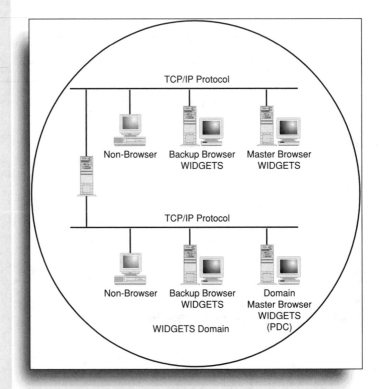

On TCP/IP networks, a new twist is added to the browser mechanism. The PDC for a domain functions as a *domain master browser* for the domain. Each client registers with the domain master browser, which constructs a master domain browse data-base. Master browsers periodically contact the domain master browser to obtain copies of the master domain browse database. To let nonbrowsers browse the entire domain, each subnet must be configured with at least one computer that can function as a master browser.

In order for the domain master browser mechanism to work, routers must be configured to forward broadcasts sent to UDP port 137. UDP is a protocol in the TCP/IP protocol suite, and port 137 is the service address for the NetBT Name Service.

Routers based on Windows NT computers meet this requirement, as do some routers from other vendors. If all routers meet this specification, you can configure a naming service without resorting to WINS.

SEE ALSO

➤ *TCP/IP routing configuration is covered in Chapter 15, "Building TCP/IP Internetworks," starting on page 471.*

➤ *WINS is the subject of Chapter 16, "Supporting Windows Naming with WINS," starting on page 485.*

Nevertheless, Microsoft recommends that WINS be configured to support TCP/IP browsing on internetworks. In my experience, WINS seems to learn the network faster and more reliably than browsers based solely on the domain master browser approach. It often seems to take an eternity for master browsers to obtain complete domain information from the domain master browser, and sometimes master browsers don't synchronize at all. I have successfully configured fully browsable, routed TCP/IP networks without WINS, but I never know how long it will take to get the browsers to converge on the same picture of the network.

WINS servers, on the other hand, are triggered to replicate when minimum numbers of changes are made to their databases. WINS replication can also be triggered manually to speed the dispersal of server information.

Browsing on Multi-Protocol Networks

When multiple protocols are installed on a network, a separate browsing environment is maintained for each protocol. If, for example, a subnet is running NWLink and TCP/IP, the subnet will have an NWLink master browser and a TCP/IP master browser, which may or may not be the same computer.

Browsing Domains and Workgroups

Nearly everything I have said applies to browsing domains and workgroups alike. There is a restriction, however, in that workgroups can't span routers. If computers on a routed network are configured to use the same workgroup name, each subnet has a separate workgroup. The workgroups might share names, but they don't share browse databases. If you require a browsing strategy that spans routers, you must implement a domain.

Because confusion can result when the same workgroup name is used on several subnets of an internetwork, it's best to avoid reusing a workgroup name. The first step is to name workgroups individually and avoid using the default name WORKGROUP.

Monitoring Browser Status

The Windows NT Resource Kit includes a Browser Monitor that can be used to monitor the status of browsers on a network. The icon for this program is installed in the Resource Kit program group.

When you start the Browser Monitor utility, you must tell it which domain or domains to display. Choose the **Add Domain** command from the **Domain** menu, and then select a domain from the **Select Domain** list. Workgroups count as well as Windows NT domains; you can add either or both. After you have added domains, you should have a list similar to the one shown in Figure 21.5. A blue icon in the **Domain** column identifies a network that has a functioning browser environment. A red icon in the **Domain** column identifies a network that doesn't support browsing.

FIGURE 21.5

Browser Monitor.

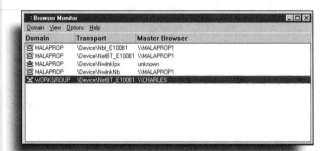

Figure 21.5 depicts a contrived situation in which I have installed all three network protocols. Each protocol that

supports browsing should show a master browser. This figure shows master browsers for each of the following protocols:

- **NetBT.** NetBIOS over TCP/IP.
- **Nbf**. NetBIOS Frame protocol, also known as NetBEUI.
- **NwlnkNb.** NetBIOS over NWLink.

You can determine from this window which computer is functioning as the master browser for each domain. MALAPROP1 is the master browser for the MALAPROP domain, which isn't surprising, because it is the primary domain controller. The Windows 95 computer named Charles is the master browser for WORKGROUP.

Each of these entries can be used to access a separate browser status window, which you can examine by selecting an entry and choosing the **Properties** command from the **Domain** menu. Figure 21.6 shows the browser status for the MALAPROP domain NetBT protocol. From this window, you can determine that MALAPROP1 is the master browser for the domain. (Its icon has a little red dot at the top, but this doesn't really show up in a black-and-white figure.) MALAPROP2 is a backup domain controller for the MALAPROP domain. Notice that server MALAPROP1 is also serving as a browser in the BLIVETS and WORKGROUP domains.

The raw NWLink network in Browser Monitor

If your network is running NWLink, there will also be a network entry for NwlnkIpx, the raw IPX network. Because the raw IPX network doesn't support NetBEUI, it doesn't have a master browser. You can remove this entry by selecting it and using the **Remove Domain** command on the **Domain** menu.

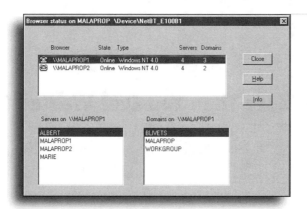

FIGURE 21.6

Browser status for the NetBT protocol on the MALAPROP domain.

The **Servers on \\MALAPROP1** list announces the servers that are known to the selected browser. You can compare this list on different browsers to ensure that server information is being distributed to the various browsers in a domain.

Remember that it takes some time for backup browsers and servers to register their presence with the master browser. If you're running Browser Manager immediately after starting computers on the network, it might take a while before the data catches up with your expectations.

If you want to see details about one of the browsers, double-click its entry in the **Browser** list. You will see a list containing more statistics than you care to know, as shown in Figure 21.7.

FIGURE 21.7
Details about a browser.

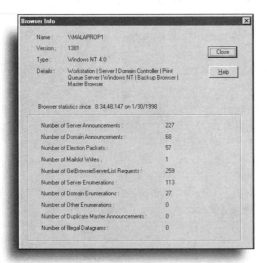

More Than You Ever Wanted to Know

You have probably learned more than you ever wanted to know about browsers. But if you remember two main rules, you will never need to concern yourself with browser operation:

- Don't use NetBEUI on routed networks.
- Use WINS on routed TCP/IP networks.

I have used the term "Registry" throughout this book. Earlier in this chapter, I mentioned a Registry parameter you can modify to configure the browsing behavior of a Windows NT computer. Well, it's time to see what the Registry is all about. In the next chapter, we'll explore the database that configures nearly every aspect of Windows NT behavior.

Editing the Registry

The Registry is a database that records most of the parameters that configure Windows NT and applications designed for Microsoft 32-bit operating systems. Windows NT still supports .INI files for the sake of compatibility with 16-bit Windows applications written for Windows 3.x environments, but with Windows NT and Windows 95 and 98, the emphasis is on storing configuration data in the Registry.

The Registry is designed to be more robust than older text-file configuration files. It is difficult to damage Registry files because changes are recorded in log files, enabling NT to back out of incomplete changes and repair damage.

Perhaps the chief disadvantage of the Registry is that it is big, and it takes a bit of time to become oriented so that you can find the parameters you need. Consequently, the bulk of this chapter will be devoted to exploring the Registry structure. Once you locate what you require, the mechanics of editing the Registry contents are not difficult at all.

Viewing the Registry

With NT 4 you get a bonus of two Registry viewers. One is window-oriented, and the other is tree-oriented. Let's take a quick look at the Registry in each viewer.

First is the old-style Registry editor, shown in Figure 22.1, which has changed very little since Windows NT 3.5x. You start this editor by executing the command regedt32.exe from the **Run** prompt on the **Start** menu. Initially, the windows cascade, but I have rearranged things a bit so that you can see some of the contents of each window.

Windows NT 4 includes a new tree-oriented Registry editor that you start by entering the command regedit.exe from the **Run** prompt on the **Start** menu. This editor, shown in Figure 22.2, works a lot more like Windows NT Explorer. I have expanded one branch so that you can see what the data entries look like. The data entries shown aren't particularly significant, but I had to find values that weren't too deep in the tree so that you could see a variety of values as well as the overall tree structure.

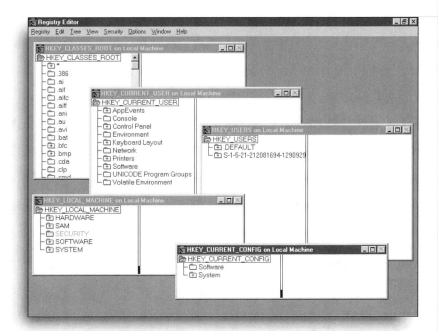

FIGURE 22.1

Viewing the Registry in the `Regedt32.exe` Registry Editor.

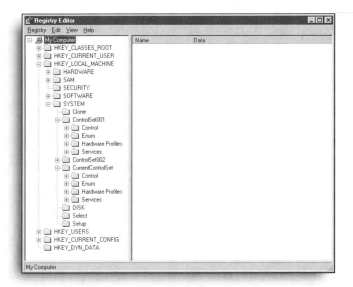

FIGURE 22.2

Viewing the Registry in the `Regedit.exe` Registry Editor.

Unfortunately, neither Registry editor has a corner on features. Regedit has better search capabilities and unifies the Registry into a single tree, so on the surface it appears superior. But Regedt32 makes it easier to edit data values, and its entries look more like the entries you will encounter in reference books. So, despite my general preference for the user interface of Regedit, I will use Regedt32 to illustrate Registry concepts in this chapter.

The Registry's Structure

The Registry is structured as a hierarchy consisting of containers that contain data. The containers are called *Registry keys*, and the data is called *value entries*. Registry keys are represented as folders in the Registry editor, and value entries appear in the right-hand pane of the Registry editor as keys are selected.

Registry Subtrees

Entries in the Registry are grouped under five keys, each of which comprises a subtree of the overall Registry:

- **HKEY_LOCAL_MACHINE.** Contains computer hardware information and configuration information for software installed on the computer. Part of this subtree is reconstructed each time the computer is started to reflect the current hardware configuration.

- **HKEY_CURRENT_CONFIG.** Contains the current hardware configuration, derived from the configuration used to boot Windows NT.

- **HKEY_CLASSES_ROOT.** Contains object linking and embedding (OLE) and file-class association data. Information in this subtree is duplicated in HKEY_LOCAL_MACHINE.

- **HKEY_CURRENT_USER.** Contains user-profile data for the currently logged-on user.

- **HKEY_USERS.** Contains all actively loaded user profiles, including the default profile and a duplicate of information in HKEY_CURRENT_USER. Profiles for remotely logged-on users are stored in the Registries of their local computers.

Registry precautions

The Registry contains valuable data, so you shouldn't navigate through it without care. While you're learning about the Registry, you can place Regedt32.exe into read-only mode by choosing **Read Only Mode** from the **Options** menu. While you're in read-only mode, changes can't be saved, and you can't inadvertently damage the Registry.

Edit with Regedt32

I haven't confirmed the problem, but some authors of Registry references warn that Regedit can damage your Registry. Since I know Regedt32 is reliable, I recommend that you use it for making Registry modifications. But Regedit can be so nice for searching that I wanted you to be aware of its existence.

You will become most acquainted with HKEY_LOCAL_MACHINE, which contains most of the parameters you will want to configure. So let's dig deeper into the Registry, using HKEY_LOCAL_MACHINE as the vehicle for discussion.

In Figure 22.3, the HKEY_LOCAL_MACHINE key is expanded and drilled down to reveal some content details. The technique is identical to that of browsing the file system in Windows NT Explorer, so I won't go into the details of how I arrived here.

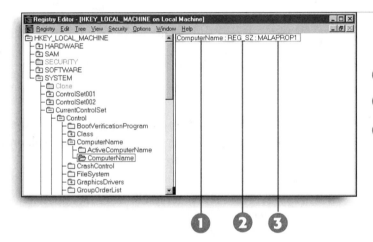

FIGURE 22.3

Expanding HKEY_LOCAL_MACHINE.

1 Name

2 Data type

3 Data

As you can see, keys can contain subkeys, just as folders can contain folders in the file system. Any subkey can contain other subkeys and can also contain values.

Values

Each key and subkey can be assigned one or more values, which are displayed in the right-hand pane of the window. These values have a specific structure. The ComputerName value has only one data entry, but you will see examples of values that have many data entries. As Figure 22.3 illustrates, a value has three fields:

- **Name.** The name of the value entry.
- **Data type.** Programmers are familiar with the concept that data has a type that restricts the information that the data can display. Each data type is discussed in the next section.

Representing Registry values

Registry values are represented much like file paths, using back-slashes to separate the keys, although the keys are often put on separate lines for clarity. The following represents the Registry value that is isolated in Figure 22.3:

HKEY_LOCAL_MACHINE\
SYSTEM\

CurrentControlSet\
Control\

ComputerName\
ComputerName\

ComputerName

- **Data.** The actual data. The type of data stored depends on the data type.

Data Types

Each data entry is classified by a data type that describes the types of values that can be stored. You'll encounter some other data types if you browse around, but these five types are the ones that most concern you:

- **REG_BINARY.** This data type describes raw binary data, the form used to store most hardware data, which can be viewed in more readable form in WINMSD. An example of such an entry follows:

  ```
  Video:REG_BINARY:00 00 00 00
  ```

- **REG_DWORD.** Data represented by a number up to 4 bytes long. This data can be displayed in binary, hexadecimal, or decimal form. An example follows:

  ```
  ErrorMode:REG_DWORD:0
  ```

- **REG_EXPAND_SZ.** Data represented in an expandable data string, which contains a system variable. The following example makes use of the %SystemRoot% variable:

  ```
  SystemDirectory:REG_EXPAND_SZ:%SystemRoot%\system32
  ```

- **REG_MULTI_SZ.** Data represented in a multiple string consisting of lists or multiple values. Most human-readable text is of this type. Here is an example that has three values (autocheck, autochk, and *):

  ```
  BootExecute:REG_MULTI_SZ:autocheck autochk *
  ```

- **REG_SZ.** Character data used to store human-readable text. For example:

  ```
  DaylightName:REG_SZ:US Eastern Standard Time
  ```

Editing Registry Value Entries

In several places in this book you will encounter settings that can only be changed by editing Registry values. You will encounter many other settings in the Windows NT documentation, magazine articles, and elsewhere. All NT administrators should be familiar with the procedures for adding and editing Registry values.

Let's try something harmless by making a change to the desktop. The current user's personal environment settings are stored in HKEY_CURRENT_USER. Let's make a simple change by modifying the current user's wallpaper.

Editing a Registry value entry

1. Start the Registry Editor. Choose the **Run** command from the **Start** menu. Enter regedt32 in the **Open** field and click **OK**.

2. After the Registry Editor starts, check the **Options** menu. If the **Read Only Mode** option is checked, remove the check mark. Otherwise, you will be unable to save changes.

3. If the HKEY_CURRENT_USER window isn't open, open it by doing one of the following:
   * Choose HKEY_CURRENT_USER from the **Window** menu.
   * Double-click the HKEY_CURRENT_USER icon.

4. Double-click the Control Panel key. After this key opens, you see the subkeys shown in Figure 22.4. In this figure, the Desktop subkey has been selected. It contains the field you will be editing.

5. Double-click the Desktop key to display its values.

6. Double-click the entry named Wallpaper. A dialog box opens that contains the value of the current wallpaper file. Figure 22.5 shows an example of a Registry value editor—in this case, the editor for a REG_SZ data type. Edit this entry to read lanmannt.bmp, which will configure the wallpaper file to a file that should exist on your system. (The change has already been made in Figure 22.5.)

Update your emergency repair disk

Before you experiment with the Registry, update your ERD. When you do this, you make a backup snapshot of the Registry. If you accidentally damage the Registry, you can use the ERD to return the Registry to an earlier state.

See the section "Making Emergency Repairs" in Chapter 2, "Installing Windows NT Server 4," for instructions on updating the ERD and using it to repair the Registry.

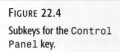

FIGURE 22.4

Subkeys for the Control Panel key.

FIGURE 22.5

The Registry Editor dialog box for a REG_SZ value entry.

7. Click **OK** to save the entry.

8. Quit Registry Editor and restart Windows NT. When Windows NT starts, the wallpaper will have changed.

Other Registry entries are edited in a similar fashion, although you will be shown different dialog boxes depending on the data type of the value entry.

Adding Registry Value Entries

Registry changes take effect when the computer restarts

Notice that the change made to the Registry didn't take effect immediately. Changes made to the computer configuration in the Registry take effect when the computer restarts. Changes made to a user's environment take effect when the user next logs on.

In some cases, you might be called on to add a Registry value entry. Let's illustrate this process by adding a Registry value that automates the entry of a password during logon. The value will be added to the following Registry key:

HKEY_LOCAL_MACHINE\SOFTWARE\ Microsoft\Windows NT\
➥CurrentVersion\Winlogon

The value entry is as follows:

DefaultPassword:REG_SZ:*password*

Adding a Registry value entry

1. Start Regedt32 and select the HKEY_LOCAL_MACHINE window.

2. Drill down in the subtree and select the Winlogon subkey.

3. Examine the DefaultUserName value entry in the right-hand pane. This Registry key holds the user name that is used as the default when logging on. Normally, this is the last user name used to successfully log on to the system.

   If the user name specified is not the desired user name, double-click the DefaultUserName value to open the String Editor. Edit the data field so that it has the value of the user account that will be used to automatically log on. Click **OK** to save the change to the value.

4. Choose **Add Value** from the **Edit** menu to open the Add Value dialog box, shown in Figure 22.6.

FIGURE 22.6
Adding a value to the Registry.

5. Enter DefaultPassword (no spaces) in the **Value Name** field.

6. Select REG_SZ from the **Data Type** field.

7. Click **OK**. This will open the String Editor Dialog box.

8. In the **String** field, enter the password associated with the user account you identified in step 3.

9. Click **OK** to save the new Registry value.

You can test the new Registry value by restarting the computer. This time the logon should be completed automatically.

Don't make automated logins a habit

For your first exercise in Registry editing, I wanted to include an example that was easy to perform and easy to test. But I want to warn you that automated logons can compromise your security when used in the wrong situation. This change is strictly for use on test servers and other servers that contain no critical data.

Finding Registry Entries

The Registry is a big place, and you might be wondering how you can locate specific keys. After you become familiar with the Registry structure, you can find a great deal by browsing, but the Registry Editor does have a **Find Key** command. The catch is that you need to know which subtree to look in. After that, it's pretty straightforward.

As an example, look for entries regarding installed printers. Because this is hardware, the keys appear in the HKEY_LOCAL_MACHINE subtree.

Searching for a Registry key

1. Open the HKEY_LOCAL_MACHINE window.

2. Select the root key of the tree HKEY_LOCAL_MACHINE.

3. Choose the **Find Key** command from the **View** menu. You see the Find dialog, box shown in Figure 22.7.

FIGURE 22.7

An example of a Registry search.

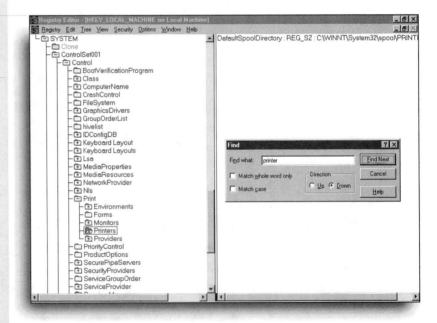

4. Type printer in the **Find what** box.

5. Do not check the **Match whole word only** box, because many key names are compound words, and printer might be only part of the key name.

6. Don't check **Match case** unless you're trying to find a specific entry for which the case of the letters is known.

7. Select **Down** if it is not already selected.

8. Click **Find Next** to initiate the search.

9. The search result is shown in Figure 22.7. (I opened the Printers key after it was found to ensure that it held the information I wanted.) The specific printer information probably differs on your computer, but the key under which the information is located should be found without trouble.

Searches are one area where the tree-oriented Regedit editor excels. For one thing, you don't need to know which subtree holds the object you're searching for, because you can start searching from the top of the Registry tree. For another thing, you can search for keys, values, and data. Figure 22.8 shows the Find dialog box for Regedit. In many cases, you will use Regedit to find the data you want and then use Regedt32 to make the desired changes.

FIGURE 22.8
Search options in Regedit.

Hives and the Registry

The data in the Registry subtrees are derived from six or more sets of files, called *hives*. The term *hive* was coined by a Microsoft systems programmer to reflect the way Registry data is stored in compartmentalized forms. Each hive consists of a

data file and a log file. The log file is responsible for the
Registry's fault tolerance. It's described in greater detail later.

Each hive represents a group of keys, subkeys, and values that
are rooted at the top of the Registry tree. It's easy to identify the
Registry keys that are associated with each hive. Figure 22.9
shows a composite of two windows: the HKEY_LOCAL_MACHINE window from the Registry Editor, and a File Manager window that
shows the C:\Winnt\system32\config subdirectory.

FIGURE 22.9

Hive files in the config subdirectory are related to Registry
keys.

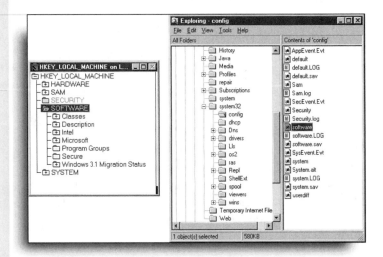

You can easily identify files in the directory that are related to
keys in the Registry. The SOFTWARE key, for example, is associated
with the files software and software.LOG.

The Registry hives and files are summarized in Table 22.1.

TABLE 22.1 Registry hives and associated files

Registry Hive	Associated Files
HKEY_LOCAL_MACHINE\SAM	Sam and Sam.LOG
HKEY_LOCAL_MACHINE\SECURITY	Security and Security.LOG
HKEY_LOCAL_MACHINE\SOFTWARE	software and software.LOG
HKEY_LOCAL_MACHINE\SYSTEM	system, system.LOG, and System.ALT

Registry Hive	Associated Files
HKEY_USERS\DEFAULT	default and default.LOG
HKEY_CURRENT_USER	Ntuser.dat and ntuser.dat.LOG

Beginning with Windows NT 4, the user part of the Registry, corresponding to HKEY_CURRENT_USER, is stored in the files Ntuser.dat and ntuser.dat.LOG in the user's profile directory. In prior versions of Windows NT, the user profile files were stored in the config subdirectory.

Notice that in Figure 22.9, hives are associated with all the subtrees in HKEY_ LOCAL_MACHINE except HARDWARE. The information in the HARDWARE subtree is regenerated each time the computer is booted and therefore is not stored permanently in hives. On Intel x86 computers, the information is gathered by the NTDE-TECT program. On Advanced RISC computers, the information is gathered by the ARC configuration database.

The hives are responsible for storing different categories of information:

- **HKEY_LOCAL_MACHINE\SAM.** Stores security information for user and group accounts. This information is used by the Windows NT Server Security Account Manager (SAM).

- **HKEY_LOCAL_MACHINE\SECURITY.** Security information regarding local account policy, used by the Windows NT security subsystem.

- **HKEY_LOCAL_MACHINE\SOFTWARE.** The configuration database for locally installed software. Serves the same purpose as application .INI files for Windows NT applications.

- **HKEY_LOCAL_MACHINE\SYSTEM.** The system startup database. Data is configured during installation and when the computer is reconfigured. The computer can't start without this information.

- **HKEY_USERS\DEFAULT.** The default user profile.

- **HKEY_CURRENT_USER.** The profile for the current user of the computer. This information is duplicated in the HKEY_LOCAL_MACHINE\SYSTEM hive. If entries in the hives disagree, HKEY_CURRENT_USER takes precedence.

Editing a Remote Registry

If you need to, you can edit the Registry of a remote Windows NT computer. The command **Select Computer** on the **Registry** menu opens a dialog box where you can select another Windows NT computer. After you do so, two keys of the remote computer's Registry will be loaded into windows in the Registry Editor.

In Figure 22.10, Registry Editor is running on computer MALAPROP1. I have selected the Registry of MALAPROP2 with the result that two windows are added to the Registry Editor:

- HKEY_LOCAL_MACHINE on MALAPROP2

- HKEY_USERS on MALAPROP2

FIGURE 22.10

Editing Registry keys on the remote computer MALAPROP2.

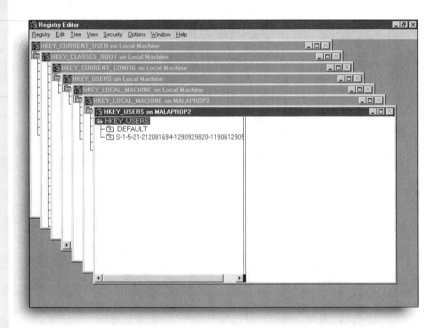

HKEY_LOCAL_MACHINE and HKEY_USERS are the only keys you can access in this way, but then again, they are the only keys you are ever likely to edit.

When you have finished viewing or editing data in a window, select the window and choose **Close** from the **Registry** menu.

The ability to edit a remote Registry is of occasional value. In some cases, it can save you a trip to the user's computer. In other cases, it can help you repair damage to the user's environment that prevents you from working on the user's computer directly.

Learning About Registry Keys

The Registry is so big that it is unlikely that a comprehensive list of Registry keys and values will ever exist. Several books have been published that are good resources for Registry information.

The *Windows NT Resource Kit* for Windows NT Server 3.5 included a volume called *Optimizing Windows NT.* Appendix B of that volume contains many pages of Registry value entries. To my knowledge, Microsoft hasn't published anything comparable for Windows NT 4, but fortunately, most of the information is still applicable. This volume is available in electronic form on the TechNet CD-ROM. To find it (as of the January 1998 version of TechNet), drill down to MS BackOffice and Enterprise Systems\MS Windows NT Workstation\Resource Kit Version 3.5\Appendix B Registry Value Entries.

You're a Registered NT Expert

The Registry isn't a difficult place to work in, but it's large and a bit dangerous. It's one place where you have the power to totally trash NT. So be careful, pay attention to detail, and keep your Emergency Repair Disk current.

Now it's time to fill in the holes in your system management skills by examining a variety of tools that help you keep NT happy and healthy.

Managing the Server

Server management is, of course, an almost omnipresent topic in this book, which is, after all, about Windows NT *Server*. But this chapter collects several tasks that relate specifically to managing the server itself, as opposed to the services that it offers. It's a bit of a grab bag, but I think you will see the overall theme.

Server Manager

Figure 23.1 shows the main window of Server Manager, which is used to manage Windows NT Servers and Workstations. Server Manager has three command menus, each of which has features that still require further discussion. Each menu is described in the following sections.

FIGURE 23.1

The main window of Server Manager.

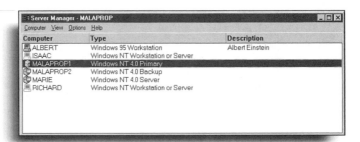

The Computer Menu

The **Computer** menu contains commands that enable you to manage Windows NT computers on the network. To manage a computer with commands in the **Computer** menu, first select the computer in the Server Manager window.

SEE ALSO

➤ *To refamiliarize yourself with the features of Server Manager that have already been discussed, turn to page 117.*

Managing Windows NT Computer Properties

The **Properties** command displays the computer Properties dialog box shown in Figure 23.2. This dialog box is used both to view and to manage properties of computers. The Properties dialog box has one input box that enables you to enter a description of the server. It also has five buttons you can use to manage specific categories of computer properties.

Viewing and Disconnecting Users Connected to a Server

The **U**sers button calls up the User Sessions dialog box shown in Figure 23.3. Each user who is connected to the computer is listed in the **Connected Users** scroll box. When you select a user, any shares that it has connected are listed in the Resource box.

For each user, the following information is displayed:

- **Opens.** The number of files the user has open.
- **Time.** The time that has elapsed since the connection was established.
- **Idle.** The time that has elapsed since the user accessed this connection.
- **Guest.** Whether the user is logged on as Guest.
- **Resource.** Shares to which the user is connected.

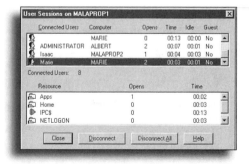

Administrators and Server Managers can take the following actions with connected users displayed in this window:

- To disconnect a single user from this computer, select the user in the **C**onnected **U**sers box and choose the **D**isconnect button. You will need to confirm this action.

- To disconnect all users from this computer, choose **Disconnect A**ll.

Disconnecting a user doesn't log the user out. Disconnecting simply closes any resources to which the user is connected.

Viewing and Disconnecting Users Connected to a Share

The **S**hares button reveals the Shared Resources dialog box shown in Figure 23.4. In many ways, the Shared Resources dialog box does the opposite duty of the User Sessions dialog box. Instead of displaying users first and then their shares after users are selected, the Shared Resources box enables you to select a share and see who is connected to it. For each share, you see how many users are attached and the path to which the share is assigned.

Administrators and Server Managers can take the following actions with connected users displayed in this window:

- To disconnect a single user from all connected resources, select the user in the **C**onnected **U**sers box and click the **D**isconnect button. You will need to confirm this action.

- To disconnect all users from a share, select the share in the **S**harename box and choose **Disconnect A**ll.

Disconnecting a user doesn't log out the user. Disconnecting simply closes any resources to which the user is connected.

Viewing and Closing Open Resources

After a user opens a shared resource, it is listed in the Open Resources dialog box (see Figure 23.5) that is displayed by choosing **I**n **U**se in the computer Properties dialog box.

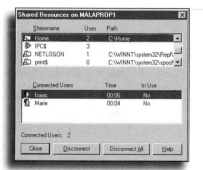

FIGURE 23.4
The Shared Resources dialog box for a server.

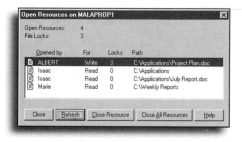

FIGURE 23.5
Viewing open resources.

Unlike the User Sessions and Shared Resources dialog boxes, the Open Resources dialog box displays resources that are actually opened by users. This information is especially useful when you are attempting to manage an open resource because open resources cannot be copied, deleted, or modified. With the Open Resources dialog box, you can identify users who are holding a resource open so that you can ask them to release it.

If you must force users off a resource, you have two button choices:

- **Close Resource.** Closes a single, selected resource.
- **Close All Resources.** Forces all resources on the server to close.

Managing Directory Replication

The directory-replication feature accessed by the **Replication** button in the computer Properties dialog box brings up the Directory Replication dialog box.

SEE ALSO

➤ *This feature is thoroughly explained in Chapter 25, "Managing Directory Replication," starting on page 727.*

Configuring Computer Alerts

The **A**lerts button in the computer Properties dialog box reveals the Alerts dialog box shown in Figure 23.6. In this box, you determine which users and computers receive administrative alerts that are generated by this computer.

- To have a user or computer receive alerts from this computer, type the user or computer name in the **New Computer or Username** box and choose **A**dd.

- To disable alerts for a user or computer, select the user or computer in the **Send Administrative Alerts To** box and choose **R**emove.

FIGURE 23.6

Configuring administrative alerts.

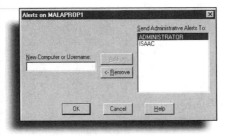

Services required for alerts

The Alert and Messenger services must be running for alerts to be sent. Clients must be running the Messenger service to receive alerts.

SEE ALSO

➤ *For instructions about starting and stopping services turn to page 681.*

Managing Shared Directories

Shared directories can be managed with Explorer or with the Shared Directories dialog box, which is accessed by choosing the **Shared Directories** command from the **Computer** menu of Server Manager. The Shared Directories dialog box is shown in Figure 23.7.

This is the place where you can see all the shares on a server. Each share type has a distinctive symbol, as you can see in Figure 23.7. You can manage these shares using techniques similar to those used with Windows NT Explorer and the Printer management windows.

FIGURE 23.7
Managing shared directories.

Managing Computer Services

You can start the Service Manager by choosing the Services command from the Computer menu.

SEE ALSO
➤ *The Service Manager is described on page 681.*

Sending Messages to Users

You can choose the **Send Message** command from the **Computer** menu to communicate with users on the network. Simply enter the text of the message in the Send Message dialog box, as shown in Figure 23.8, and click **OK** to send the message to all users who are connected to the server. Only connected users receive the message—not all users in the domain.

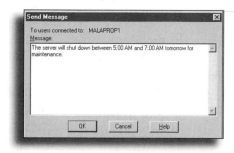

FIGURE 23.8
Sending a message to connected users.

SEE ALSO
➤ *Users of Windows 3.x must be running the Windows Popup program. For information on configuring this option, see page 247.*

Promoting a Domain Controller

The next option on the **Computers** menu is **Promote to Primary Domain Controller**.

SEE ALSO

➤ *For more information on promoting a backup domain controller, turn to page 103.*

Synchronizing the Domain Database

On rare occasions, the copies of the domain database on the various backup domain controllers can get out of synchronization with the database on the primary domain controller. Synchronization is performed automatically, but also can be initiated manually.

Synchronizing a backup domain controller

1. Select the computer name of the BDC in the Server Manager window.

2. Choose **Synchronize with Primary Domain Controller** from the **Computer** menu.

The database on the BDC is resynchronized with the database on the domain PDC.

Synchronizing all backup domain controllers

1. Select the computer name of the domain PDC in the Server Manager window.

2. Choose **Synchronize Entire Domain** from the **Computer** menu.

The database is copied from the PDC to all BDCs in the domain, which can be a time-consuming process.

Adding and Removing Domain Computers

The **Add to Domain** and **Remove from Domain** commands on the **Computer** menu are used to create and remove domain accounts for Windows NT computers.

SEE ALSO

➤ *For more information on using server manager to add a computer account to a domain, turn to page 127.*

Selecting a Domain to Manage

By default, Server Manager selects your logon domain to manage. You can change to another trusting domain by choosing the **Select Domain** command from the **Computer** menu.

The View Menu

Use options in the View menu to determine which computers are displayed in the Server Manager window. You have the following choices:

- **Servers.** Choose to display only Windows NT Servers.
- **Workstations.** Choose to display only Windows NT Workstations.
- **All.** Choose to display all Windows NT computers.
- **Show Domain Members Only.** Check this option to limit displayed computers to computers that are members of the current domain.

The Options Menu

Commands in the **Options** menu enable you to configure the operation of Server Manager. Two of the commands on this menu follow:

- **Save Settings on Exit.** If you want Server Manager to retain your current setup each time you quit, check this option. If you want to have Server Manager restore default settings or savings you saved at an earlier time, remove the check.
- **Font.** Use this option to select a new font to be used in Server Manager. A good use of this option is to select an enlarged font for an administrator who has a vision impairment.

Service Manager

The Service Manager applet can be started in two ways:

- Choosing the **Services** command from the Server Manager **Computers** menu.
- Double-clicking the Services icon in the Control Panel.

Starting Service Manager displays the Services dialog box, shown in Figure 23.9.

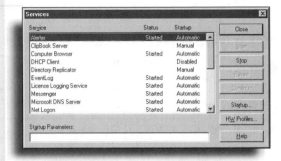

FIGURE 23.9
The Services applet.

Stopping the Server service

The Server service supports all remote user connections. Stopping the Server service disconnects all users, including Administrators. Therefore, remote Administrators cannot stop and restart this service; it must be restarted locally.

Before stopping the Server service, use the **Send Message** command to alert users so that they can close open files and prepare to be disconnected.

When the Server service is paused, members of the Administrators and Server Operators groups can establish new connections with the server, but other users cannot.

SEE ALSO

➤ *The Schedule service is discussed on page 382.*

➤ *The UPS service is discussed in Chapter 24, starting on page 715.*

➤ *The Directory Replicator service is discussed in Chapter 25, starting on page 727.*

Starting, Stopping, and Pausing Services

Select a service and choose the **Start**, **Stop**, or **Pause** button to change the status of the service.

To pass arguments to a service, type them in the Startup Parameters box before choosing Start.

Configuring Services

Define the characteristics of a service

1. Select a service in the Services window.

2. Choose **Startup** to display the service startup dialog box shown in Figure 23.10.

FIGURE 23.10
Configuring startup settings for a service.

3. Choose the service startup type from the following:

- **Automatic.** The service starts when the server is booted.
- **Manual.** The service must be started manually from the Services dialog box.
- **Disabled.** The service cannot be started.

4. Choose **System Account** if the service should log on using the system account. This setting is used for almost all services.

5. Choose **This Account** to have the service log on with a user account. Only the Directory Replicator and Schedule services log on using other accounts.

If **This Account** has been chosen, enter a user account and passwords in the appropriate boxes.

6. Choose **OK**.

7. Start the service.

Service startup settings take effect only when the service is started. A running service must be stopped and restarted if startup settings change.

SEE ALSO

➤ *For information about setting up the Schedule service see Chapter 13, starting on page 425.*

➤ *For information about setting up the Directory Replicator service see Chapter 18, starting on page 529.*

➤ *To learn how the Schedule service can be made to log on with a user account, enabling it to perform tasks in the background, see page 382.*

The System Utility

The System applet in the Control Panel is shown in Figure 23.11. This window has six tabs that are used to configure several Windows NT settings.

FIGURE 23.11

The System Applet: The
Environment Tab.

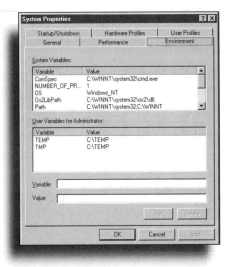

FIGURE 23.11

The System Applet: The
Environment Tab.

Environment

The Environment tab is shown in Figure 23.11. Windows NT is
much less dependent on environment variables than is Windows
3.x or DOS. Nevertheless, a few environment variables are
maintained. In fact, two sets are available:

- **System variables.** Used by the system regardless of the user
  who is logged on.

- **User variables.** Can be customized for each user.

To delete a variable, select the variable and choose **Delete**. The
following step by step procedures show you how to add and edit
environment variables.

Adding an environment variable

1. Select the **System Variables** or the **User Variables** box.

2. Enter the variable name in the **Variable** box.

3. Enter a value for the variable in the **Value** box.

4. Choose **Set**.

Editing an environment variable

1. Select the variable.

2. Change the value in the **Value** box.

3. Choose **Set**.

Changes made to system environment variables take effect the next time the computer is started.

Changes made to user environment variables take effect the next time the user logs on to the computer.

General Properties

The **General** tab, shown in Figure 23.12, is informational only, displaying information about the operating system, the registered owner, and the computer.

Hardware Profiles

The **Hardware Profiles** tab supports the capability of Windows NT to define multiple hardware profiles, which may be selected when the system is booted. Hardware profiles enable a user to, for example, have one configuration for a laptop PC when it is docked at a desk and another configuration when the computer is undocked and mobile.

Hardware profiles are not very applicable to network servers and are not considered in this book.

Learning about system environment variables

It is instructive to select a system environment variable and observe the value in the Value box. Notice that the values make extensive use of Windows NT variables such as %SystemRoot%.

Use extreme caution when changing system environment variables. Most are vital to the proper functioning of Windows NT.

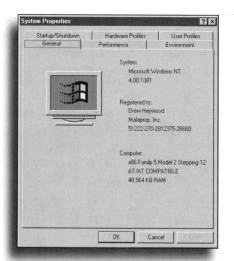

FIGURE 23.12

The System Applet: The General tab.

User Profiles

The **User Profiles** tab is used to copy user profiles, as described in Chapter 9, "Advanced Client Features."

Performance

The **Performance** tab is shown in Figure 23.13. This tab has one setting and enables you to access the window where virtual memory is configured.

FIGURE 23.13

The Performance tab on the System Applet.

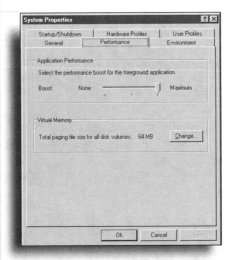

The **Application Performance** setting determines the responsiveness of the foreground Windows application, that is, of the application whose Window has the focus. Set the **Boost** to **Maximum** if the foreground application should be given the greatest share of available processing. Set the **Boost** to **None** if you require background Windows to receive improved service. If, for example, you are programming and want to compile programs in the background, you would lower the Boost setting to ensure that compilation receives reasonable access to the processor.

The **Change** button in the Virtual Memory area opens the Virtual Memory dialog box shown in Figure 23.14. Windows NT uses the *virtual memory* capability of Intel 386 and later processors to significantly increase the memory that is available to the operating system. Virtual memory uses disk storage to simulate RAM—a process called *paging*, which uses a *paging file* to create virtual memory. Although virtual memory is much slower than RAM, it is much better to have slow memory than to run out.

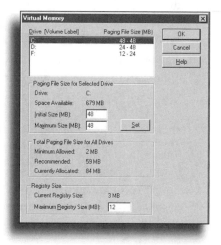

Microsoft recommends that you create a paging file for each volume. Depending on the capabilities of the computer hard drive controller, multiple paging files can enhance virtual memory performance.

A paging file is created automatically when the system disk is created. Paging files for other disks must be created manually. A minimum and maximum size is declared for each paging file. With NTFS volumes, Windows NT automatically increases the sizes of paging files as required. If multiple paging files exist, size increases are distributed across all paging files.

Create or modify the paging file for a volume

1. Select a volume in the **Drive** box.

2. Enter the paging file parameters in the **Paging File Size for Selected Drive** box. A recommended total value is displayed in the **Total Paging File Size for All Drives** box.

The virtual memory paging file

Virtual memory is stored in a file named **pagefile.sys**, which cannot be deleted under Windows NT. If the file is deleted under another operating system, it is re-created when Windows NT is restarted.

Limiting Registry size

The Virtual Memory dialog box also includes the **Maximum Registry Size** field which is used to set a limit to the growth of the Registry, and sets an upper bound both for the page pool (in RAM) and for the Registry disk space. This parameter doesn't allocate space, and space will be used only as required. Also, this parameter doesn't guarantee that the memory specified will be available.

3. Choose **Set** to save the changes.

4. Restart the system to have the changes go into effect.

Startup/Shutdown Properties

The **Startup/Shutdown** tab, shown in Figure 23.15, contains two categories of settings: system startup and recovery.

Specifying Startup Options

The properties in the System Startup area determine two options in the BOOT.INI file. The **Startup** property determines which startup option in the BOOT.INI file will be the default. Each option in the [operating systems] section of the BOOT.INI file appears as a choice in the Startup field.

To specify the time that the startup configuration menu is displayed, edit the time in the **Show List For...Seconds** spin box. I don't recommend that you set this value to 0 because that will make it difficult to start the computer in default VGA mode.

SEE ALSO

➤ *The structure of the* BOOT.INI *file is described on page 74.*

FIGURE 23.15

The System Applet: The Startup/Shutdown tab.

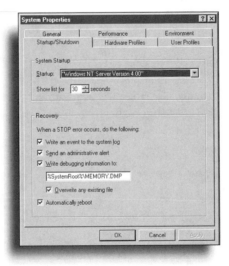

Specifying Recovery Options

When Windows NT Server encounters a critical error, called a STOP error or a fatal system error, the system records an event in the System log, transmits an Administrator alert, and optionally reboots itself. Because Windows NT Server reboots itself without waiting for an Administrator to intervene, downtime is reduced.

The Recovery box includes several fields that determine what will happen when a STOP error occurs. The fields in this box are as follows:

- **Write An Event In The System Log.** The system log can be examined using the Event Viewer, which is described later in this chapter.

- **Send An Administrative Alert.** Check this option if administrators should receive an alert message through the network.

- **Write Debugging Information To Filename.** Debugging can assist Microsoft with the diagnosis of your problem. If you select this option, you must specify a file name.

- **Overwrite Any Existing File.** If this option is checked, an existing debugging file will be overwritten if a new STOP error occurs.

- **Automatically Reboot.** Check this option if the server should attempt to reboot after STOP error actions have been executed.

Task Manager

One of the most useful tools is also among the simplest to use. When you press Ctrl+Alt+Delete while logged on to Windows NT, one of the options available in the Windows NT Security box is **Task Manager**. When you select that option, you access the Task Manager, shown in Figure 23.16.

FIGURE 23.16

Task Manager: The
Performance tab.

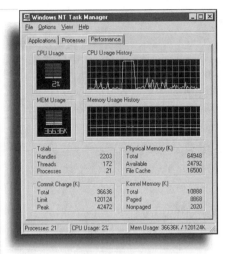

The Performance Tab

The first thing you see in Task Manager is the **Performance** tab, shown in Figure 23.16. This tab displays running graphs of CPU and memory usage. These graphs provide quick checks to determine whether your CPU or memory resources are tight.

Incidentally, the CPU usage values represent actual work being performed by the CPU. When it isn't busy with meaningful tasks, the CPU runs a thread called the *idle thread*. Time spent running the idle thread isn't reflected in the CPU Usage graph.

Most of the data on the Performance tab relate to memory usage. Recall that system memory comes from two sources: physical memory (RAM) and virtual memory (disk cache). The computer used to prepare the Figure has 64MB of RAM and was configured with 75MB of virtual memory, resulting in a total of 120204KB of available memory. (If the system is configured with an expandable paging file, the total available memory reflected in the Performance tab represents the minimum or current size of the paging file, whichever is greater, not the maximum size of the paging file.)

Kernel Memory

A portion of the operating system kernel must operate in RAM, and cannot be swapped out to virtual memory. This memory requirement is referred to as *Nonpaged* Kernel Memory, and represents RAM that is always dedicated to the operating system. (The process of swapping data between physical and virtual memory is called *paging*.)

Other portions of the operating system kernel can be paged to virtual memory if necessary. This is referred to as *Paged* Kernel Memory. The total memory requirement for the kernel is the sum of paged and nonpaged kernel memory.

Commit Charge

Total memory usage for the system is described in the entries headed **Commit Charge (K)**. The **Total** entry represents all memory currently in use, and matches the value shown in the MEM Usage graph. Due to the use of virtual memory, the **Total** Commit Charge memory can exceed physical RAM, in which case the system uses virtual memory to provide the needed memory space.

The **Limit** parameter represents the sum of physical and virtual memory.

The **Peak** parameter records the maximum memory use of this system since it was started.

Physical Memory

The Total value in the Physical Memory section describes, of course, the total random access memory installed in the system, and the Available memory represents the amount of memory not currently in use by an application.

The **File Cache** entry describes the amount of memory that is released to control of the file cache. This value may expand as the demand for virtual memory grows.

The example system has plenty of memory to handle current requirements by the kernel together with loaded services and applications. You might think that MEM Usage + Available Physical Memory would equal Total Memory. Because the sum is greater than Total Memory, it is clear that even on this lightly loaded system, Windows NT is paging some data to virtual memory.

Virtual or physical?

The **Commit Charge** parameters are a good way to determine the degree to which the system is relying on virtual memory. Some use of virtual memory is normal with Windows NT, and is no cause for concern. If the normal Total Commit Charge value exceeds available physical memory, however, it is time to add some physical memory to the system.

Memory leaks

Some poorly-written programs result in memory leaks, memory that the program doesn't free up when it terminates. If it seems that available memory has decreased on a Windows NT computer, you may want to start looking for memory leaks.

Reboot the system so that you start clean, and use Task Manager to determine the baseline memory usage. Then load a suspect application, let it work a bit, and unload it. Return to Task Manager to see if memory use has returned to its baseline level. If it hasn't, you have a memory leak. Either get a fix from the application's provider or get a new application.

The Applications Tab

The **Applications** tab is shown in Figure 23.17. Items listed on this tab are foreground applications. The status of each application is shown.

You can stop an application by selecting the application and clicking **End Task**.

You can switch to an application, giving the focus to the application's window, by selecting the application and clicking **Switch To**.

The **New Task** button opens a Create New Task dialog box that is the functional equivalent of a Run prompt, enabling you to enter a command to be executed.

The Processes Tab

The **Processes** tab, shown in Figure 23.18, lists all processes running on the computer. This screen is a great place to identify CPU and memory hogs. It is also a way to determine whether an application leaves any processes running after it terminates, which, of course, should not be the case.

FIGURE 23.17

Task Manager: The Applications tab.

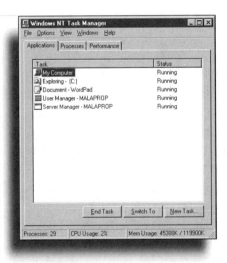

You can stop a process by selecting the process and clicking **End Process**. Be aware that this doesn't always result in a smooth process shutdown. Open files might not be properly closed, or other processes dependent on the process might be jeopardized.

FIGURE 23.18
Task Manager: The Processes tab.

Using Windows NT Diagnostics

The Windows NT Diagnostics (WINMSD) program enables you to observe configuration information for some features of the server hardware and software. It isn't a full-blown diagnostics program. In particular, Windows NT Diagnostics isn't capable of testing hardware. For that, you should obtain a third-party program. However, third-party programs generally are oriented around DOS, so you would need to bring the server down to perform any diagnostics. Windows NT Diagnostics is a Windows NT program that can be run while the server is operating and, of course, it is free.

The Windows NT Diagnostics icon isn't installed in the Start menu, although you can do so if you want. Start the program by executing the command WINMSD at the Run prompt in the Start menu. When you run the utility, you will see the window shown in Figure 23.19. This window has nine tabs that access different categories of data.

FIGURE 23.19

Windows NT Diagnostics: The
Version tab.

The following sections cover entries on the various tabs.

Version

The **Version** tab (refer to Figure 23.19) describes the processor,
the Windows NT serial number, and the registered owner.

System

The **System** tab (see Figure 23.20) describes the BIOS version
and the microprocessor in greater detail. In the figure, an x86
Family 5 CPU describes an Intel Pentium processor.

The item labeled "HAL" refers to the Hardware Abstraction
Layer, the component of Windows NT that interfaces the operating system to the computer hardware. Although the operating
system code remains the same from platform to platform, a HAL
must be designed for each type of computer hardware. In this
case, the HAL is designed for a PC-compatible.

Display

The **Display** tab describes the video adapter, current video settings, and the video driver that is installed.

FIGURE 23.20

Windows NT Diagnostics: The System tab.

Drives

The **Drives** tab displays a hierarchy consisting of all disk drives on the system. Figure 23.21 shows the basic display, opened to reveal the entries for the hard drives. Two buttons enable you to determine the order in which drives will be listed:

- Drives by Type
- Drives by Letter

FIGURE 23.21

Windows NT Diagnostics: The Drives Tab.

If you open a drive entry, you are shown the properties for that device. Figure 23.22 shows the details for the C: drive. The **General** tab shown in the figure describes the storage utilization, whereas the File System tab (see Figure 23.23) describes the file system with which the drive is formatted.

FIGURE 23.22

Properties of a hard disk.

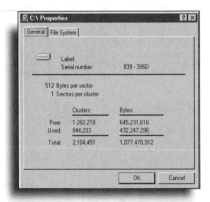

FIGURE 23.23

Properties of the file system on a hard disk.

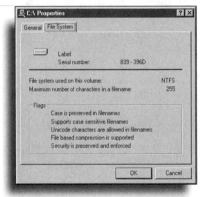

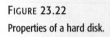

Support for unicode characters

NTFS is the only Windows NT file system in which Unicode characters are allowed in file names. Unicode is a means of representing many different character sets so that applications can be written to support languages that could not be comprehended by ASCII.

Memory

The **Memory** tab shows details of the system memory including available memory and memory in use by various resources. As Figure 23.24 shows, the **Memory** tab is a good way to keep track of the use of physical and virtual memory to determine whether memory should be added or the pagefile size should be increased. You can also determine pagefile location and sizes.

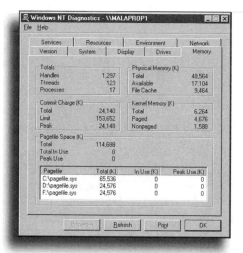

FIGURE 23.24

Windows NT Diagnostics: The Memory tab.

Services

The **Services** tab displays listings of all services and devices that are installed on the computer. The display in Figure 23.25 lists services. Choose the **Devices** button to switch to a listing of devices.

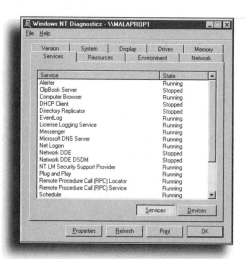

FIGURE 23.25

Windows NT Diagnostics: The Services tab.

You can double-click any service or device to obtain more detail. Figure 23.26 shows properties for the NetLogon service. The **Dependencies** tab lists any other services that this service depends on for its operation.

FIGURE 23.26

Example of service properties: The NetLogon service.

Resources

The **Resources** tab (see Figure 23.27) provides information about various characteristics of hardware that has been added to the Windows NT configuration. Unlike Windows 95, Windows NT doesn't automatically detect most devices. Devices are added to the configuration during installation and manually by using various Control Panel utilities. Therefore, hardware may be present in the system that isn't reported in this list. A sound card that has not been added to the configuration, for example, will not be reported in this list.

Five buttons display different categories of information. Use the information in these lists to identify available resources and to determine when resource conflicts exist:

- **IRQ.** Displays the IRQ, bus, and bus type for each installed device, as shown in Figure 23.27.

- **I/O Port.** Displays the I/O port addresses associated with installed devices.

- **DMA.** Displays the DMA channel, port, bus, and bus type for any installed DMA-driven device.

- **Memory.** Displays any blocks of memory that have been dedicated to specific hardware devices.

- **Devices.** Lists the installed hardware devices.

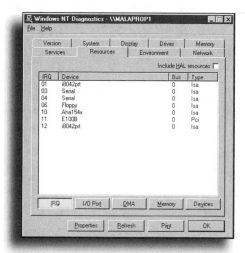

FIGURE 23.27
Windows NT Diagnostics: The Resources tab.

You can display properties for all the entries in the five categories by selecting an entry and choosing **Properties**. Figure 23.28 shows the properties for the Adaptek Aha154x SCSI adapter installed in this computer. First, the Devices button was chosen to list installed hardware, and then **Properties** was chosen to produce the window shown in the figure.

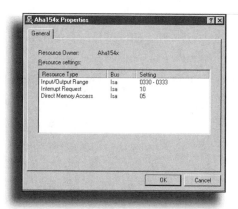

FIGURE 23.28
Example of device properties.

Environment

The **Environment** tab, shown in Figure 23.29, lists the environment variables that are in memory. Choose **System** to display system variables, and choose **Local User** to display variables for the currently logged-on user.

FIGURE 23.29

Windows NT Diagnostics: The Environment tab.

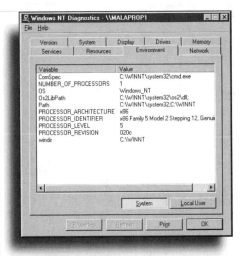

Network

Figure 23.30 shows the **Network** tab, which displays information that isn't readily available elsewhere. It is extremely useful for you to examine this screen as you configure and reconfigure your server. If you are running a service in the background with its own logon name, it appears as a logon count in the Network Info for box, for example.

Four buttons access different categories of information:

- **General.** This button lists information about the computer's network configuration and currently logged-on users.

- **Transports.** This gives descriptions about the transport protocol layers that are installed along with configuration information.

- **Settings.** Shows the current values of numerous Windows NT Server settings.

- **Statistics.** WINMSD keeps a running total of dozens of events that occur as the server operates. Of particular interest are various reports of errors. If you see that the Network Errors statistic is climbing, for example, you might suspect a problem in your network hardware or cabling.

FIGURE 23.30

Windows NT Diagnostics: The Network tab.

Auditing Files and Printers

Auditing is a useful function in any large LAN. Auditing is a way of gathering statistics about how resources are being used. More important, auditing is a way to determine who is responsible if resources are being misused. As LANs take on increasingly critical tasks, it becomes more desirable to implement auditing.

Windows NT Server enables you to audit the use of domains, files, directories, and printers.

Auditing Domains

Domain auditing is configured through User Manager for Domains. In some ways, domain auditing is the most important auditing category, particularly if your network is part of a wide area network. WANs, particularly when they participate in the Internet, are more vulnerable to intruders than networks that are

Auditing security requirements

You must be logged on as a member of the Administrators group to audit files and directories.

confined to a company's own buildings. Domain auditing can tell you whether large numbers of attempted security breeches are taking place, which might indicate that someone is trying to break into your system.

Defining a domain audit policy

1. Open User Manager for Domains.

2. Choose the **Select Domain** command from the **User** menu to select the domain to be audited.

3. Choose the **Audit** command from the **Policies** menu to display the Audit Policy dialog box shown in Figure 23.31.

4. Choose **Audit These Events** to activate auditing for the domain.

5. Check the events to be audited.

6. Choose **OK** to save the auditing policy.

FIGURE 23.31

Defining the Domain audit policy.

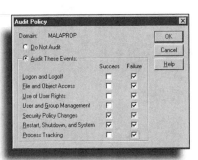

The following domain events can be audited:

- **Logon and Logoff.** A user logs on, logs off, or makes a connection through the network.

- **File and Object Access.** A directory or file was accessed that had been configured for auditing in File Manager. A print job was sent to a printer that was configured for auditing in Print Manager.

- **Use of User Rights.** Use of a user right apart from rights related to logging on or off.

- **User and Group Management.** The following activities are audited with respect to user accounts or groups: creation, changing, deleting, renaming, disabling or enabling, and password changes.

- **Security Policy Changes.** Any change to user rights, audit, or trust relationships policies.

- **Restart, Shutdown, and System.** Shutting down or restarting the server. Any action that affects system security or the security log.

- **Process Tracking.** Program activation, process exit, handle duplication, and indirect object access.

Auditing Directories and Files

The auditing of directories and files is managed through File Manager. Setting up auditing is a simple matter of declaring the groups or users whose use of a file or directory will be audited along with the events to be audited. Auditing is available only for NTFS volumes.

Defining auditing for a directory or file

1. Right-click the directory or file to be audited in Windows NT Explorer, My Computer, or Network Neighborhood.

2. Choose **Properties** from the context menu and open the Security tab.

3. Choose **Auditing** from the **Security** tab to display the Directory Auditing dialog box shown in Figure 23.32.

4. Check **Replace Auditing on Subdirectories** if all subdirectories of this directory are to be audited in the same fashion.

5. Check **Replace Auditing on Existing Files** if existing files should be audited in the same fashion. If this box isn't checked, auditing affects only the directory.

6. To add a user or group, choose the **Add** button to display a Browse list. Select each name to be added in the Browse list and choose **Add**. Choose **OK** when all desired names have been added. When you return to the Auditing window, the names are listed in the **Name** box.

Tip: getting started with auditing

When you are setting up auditing, audit the success and failure of everything to make it easy to determine that you have set up your auditing to track the resources you want. When you are confident that you are tracking the correct resources, pare back the audited events to the events you really want to know about.

FIGURE 23.32
Defining directory auditing.

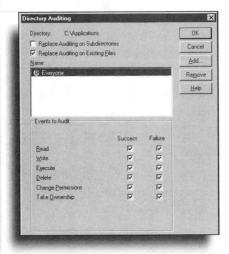

7. To remove a user or group, select the entry in the **Name** box and choose **Remove**.

8. For each event that is to be audited, check the appropriate box in the Events to Audit box.

9. Choose **OK** to save the auditing information.

Tables 23.1 and 23.2 summarize the actions that are audited by each event that can be checked in the Auditing dialog box.

TABLE 23.1 **Actions audited by directory audit events**

	Read	Write	Execute	Delete	Change Permissions	Take Ownership
Display attributes	●	○	●	○	○	○
Display filenames	●	○	○	○	○	○
Change attributes	○	●	○	○	○	○
Create subdirectories and files	○	●	○	○	○	○
Go to a subdirectory	○	○	●	○	○	○
Display owner and permissions	●	●	●	○	○	○
Delete directory	○	○	○	●	○	○
Change directory permissions	○	○	○	○	●	○
Change directory ownership	○	○	○	○	○	●

TABLE 23.2 Actions audited by file audit events

	Read	Write	Execute	Delete	Change Permissions	Take Ownership
Display file attributes	●	○	●	○	○	○
Read file data	●	○	○	○	○	○
Display owner and permissions	●	●	●	○	○	○
Change file attributes	○	●	○	○	○	○
Change file attributes	○	●	○	○	○	○
Change file data	○	○	●	○	○	○
Execute program file	○	○	○	●	○	○
Change file permissions	○	○	○	○	●	○
Change file ownership	○	○	○	○	○	●

Auditing Printers

Printing is a service that often is abused. If you don't want users printing football pools on the $10,000 color printer, or if you want to know which user is going through all those reams of paper, printer auditing might give you the support you need.

Printer auditing is configured with Print Manager.

Defining auditing for printers

1. Open the printer window for the printer to be audited.

2. Choose the **Properties** command from the **Printer** menu and select the **Security** tab.

3. Choose **Auditing** from the **Security** tab. The Printer Auditing dialog box appears, as shown in Figure 23.33.

4. To add a user or group, choose **Add** to display a Browse list. Select each name to be added in the Browse list and choose **Add**. Choose **OK** when all desired names have been added. When you return to the Auditing window, the names are listed in the Name box.

5. To remove a user or group, select the entry in the **Name** box and choose **Remove**.

Requirements for auditing directory and file events

Directory and file events are audited only if you have activated **File and Object Access** auditing in the Audit Policy for the domain. The procedure for setting the domain audit policy is described in the preceding section.

FIGURE 23.33

Defining auditing for a printer.

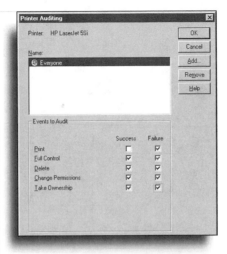

6. For each event that is to be audited, check the appropriate box in the **Events to Audit** box.

7. Choose **OK** to save the auditing information.

The printer events that can be audited are as follows:

- **Print.** Printing documents.
- **Full Control.** Changing document job settings. Pausing, restarting, moving, and deleting documents.
- **Delete.** Deleting a printer.
- **Change Permissions.** Changing printer permissions.
- **Take Ownership.** Taking ownership of a printer.

Reviewing the Security Log

All the auditing facilities record their messages in the Security log, which is examined by using the Event Viewer. Figure 23.34 shows an example of Security log entries. Use of the Event Viewer is described in the following section.

Security log entries are identified with two icons. A key designates a successful action, and a lock designates an unsuccessful action. In the figure, the user BUSTER attempted an action for which he did not have the required permissions, resulting in several entries in the Security log.

Requirements for auditing printer events

Printer events are audited only if you have activated **File and Object Access** auditing in the Audit Policy for the domain. The procedure for setting the domain audit policy is described in the section "Auditing Domains," earlier in this chapter.

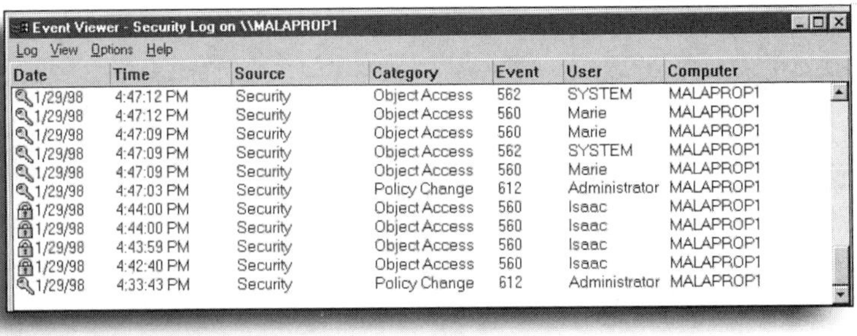

FIGURE 23.34
The Security Log as viewed in
Event Viewer.

Event Viewer

The Event Viewer is used to examine three Windows NT Server
logs:

- **System log.** Records events logged by the Windows NT
  system.

- **Application log.** Records events logged by applications. A
  Windows NT Server-aware application, for example, might
  log a message when a file error is encountered.

- **Security log.** Records events that have been selected for
  auditing in User Manager for Domains, File Manager, or
  Print Manager.

Viewing Event Logs

To view a log, choose **System**, **Security**, or **Application** from
the **Log** menu of the Event Viewer. Figure 23.35 shows an
example of a System log.

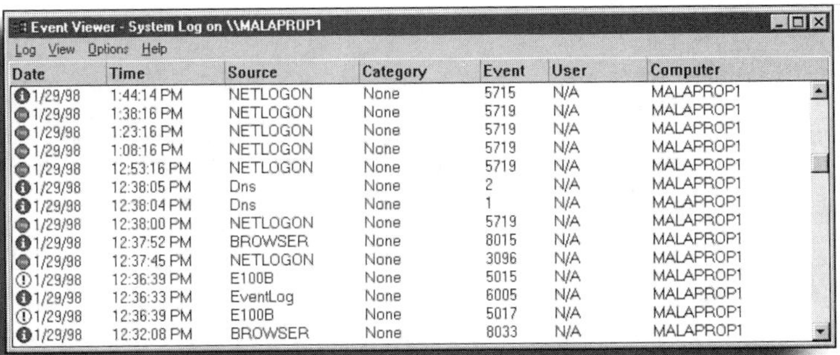

FIGURE 23.35
Events in the System Log.

For each entry, you see the following information in addition to the date and time when the log entry was recorded:

- **Source.** The software that logged the event—either an application name or a component of Windows NT.

- **Category.** An event classification.

- **Event.** Each source is assigned a unique number, which appears in this column.

- **User.** The user name of the account that was logged in when the event was logged.

- **Computer.** The computer name where the event occurred.

To make it easy to scan events visually, each event is labeled with an icon. Figure 23.36 identifies the icons and their meanings.

FIGURE 23.36

Icons appearing in the Event Log.

Here are more complete descriptions of the events:

- **Information.** Infrequent significant events that describe the successful operation of Windows NT Server services.

- **Warning.** Noncritical errors that may predict future problems.

- **Critical Error.** Data loss or failure of major functions.

- **Success Audit.** Audit events that are associated with the successful execution of an action.

- **Failure Audit.** Audit events that are associated with the unsuccessful execution of an action.

You can display a detailed view of each event by double-clicking the event entry. An example of a detailed display is shown in Figure 23.37.

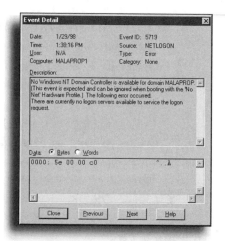

FIGURE 23.37

The detailed description of an event.

Configuring Event Log Options

The Event Log Settings dialog box enables you to determine how large log files will grow (see Figure 23.38). Unless they are properly controlled, log files can grow to a significant percentage of server file capacity.

FIGURE 23.38

The Event Log Settings dialog box.

Configuring event log settings

1. Choose Log Settings from the **Log** menu to access the Event Log Settings dialog box.

2. Select a log in the **Change Settings For...Log** list box.

3. Enter a maximum size in the **Maximum Log Size** spin box. If the log reaches this size and you have not specified a means of trimming old records, event logging ceases.

4. To have new events overwrite old events after the log is full, choose **Overwrite Events as Needed**.

5. To limit the log by discarding old records, choose **Overwrite Events Older Than...Days** and specify a number in the box. If logs will be archived weekly, a good choice is seven days.

6. To clear the log manually, choose **Do Not Overwrite Events (Clear Log Manually)**. Avoid using this option unless there are events you cannot afford to miss. Security on a critical server might be an example of such information.

7. Choose **OK** after the Event log settings are entered.

Clearing a Log

Clearing the event log

1. Select the log to be cleared from the Log menu.

2. Choose **Clear All Events** from the **Log** menu. You are asked to verify your decision to clear the log.

Viewing Specific Events

Event Viewer has several tools that enable you to more easily identify specific events. You can change the order for sorting events and add filters to determine which events are displayed.

Sorting Events

To change the sorting order for events, choose either **Newest First** or **Oldest First** from the **View** menu.

Filtering Events

Event logs can grow to be quite large, and you might find your-self wanting to limit the events that are displayed, or limiting yourself to a specific type of event to enable you to focus on a problem. Event Viewer enables you to filter events in a wide variety of ways.

To filter events, follow these steps:

Filtering log events

1. Choose **Filter Events** from the **View** menu to display the Filter dialog box shown in Figure 23.39.

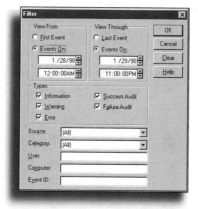

FIGURE 23.39
Filtering Event Viewer events.

2. To restore default filters, choose **Clear**.
3. Specify the filters to be used. The various filters are dis-cussed in the following list.
4. Choose **OK** to activate the filters.

The following event filters can be selected:

- **View From.** Specifies a date of the oldest records that should be displayed. Choose First Event to display events starting from the beginning of the log. Choose Events On to start displaying events occurring on the specified day.

- **View Through.** Specifies a date of the newest records that should be displayed. Choose Last Event to display events through the end of the log. Choose Events On to display events through the specified day.

- **Information.** Infrequent significant events that describe successful operation of Windows NT Server services.

- **Warning.** Noncritical errors that may predict future problems.

- **Error.** Critical errors. Data loss or failure of major functions.

- **Success Audit.** Audit events that are associated with the successful execution of an action.

- **Failure Audit.** Audit events that are associated with the unsuccessful execution of an action.

- **Source.** The application, computer, or driver that originated the log entry.

- **Category.** Event categories specific to the log source.

- **User.** User name of the account that was logged on when the log entry was generated (not case sensitive).

- **Computer.** Computer from which the log message originated (not case sensitive).

- **Event ID.** The number that corresponds to the specific type of event.

To disable event filtering, choose **All Events** from the **View** menu.

Searching for Events

You can search for specific events. This capability is useful when it is necessary to locate specific events in large log files.

Searching for log events

1. Choose **Find** from the **View** menu to display the Find dialog box shown in Figure 23.40.

2. Choose **Clear** to restore default values to the dialog box.

3. Enter the criteria of the events to be found.

4. Select **Up** or **Down** to specify the search direction.

5. Choose **Find Next** to locate successive records that meet the criteria.

6. Choose **Cancel** to exit the dialog box.

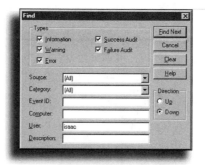

FIGURE 23.40
Finding events in Event Viewer.

Archiving Event Logs

Logs can be archived in three forms:

- **Event log format**, which you can review later in the Event log
- **Text Files**, which may be read by any text editor
- **Comma-delimited format**, which can be read by many other programs for analysis of the data

Archiving log events

1. Select the log in the **Log** menu.
2. Choose **Save As** from the **Log** menu.
3. In the Save As dialog box, select a directory and a log file name. By default, log files have the .EVT file name extension.
4. Select the file format in the **Save as Type** list box.
5. Choose **OK** to save the file.

Viewing an archived log

1. Choose **Open** from the **Log** menu.
2. Select the directory and file name in the **File Name** list of the dialog box.
3. Choose **OK** to retrieve the archive file.
4. In the Open File Type dialog box, specify the type of log you are retrieving: **System**, **Security**, or **Application**.

Logs that are archived in text file or comma-delimited format include data in the
following fields:

1. Date
2. Time
3. Source
4. Type
5. Category
6. Event
7. User
8. Computer
9. Description

Comma-delimited files can be imported by most spreadsheet and database applications.

Keeping a Server Healthy

It takes a bit of effort to keep a server healthy. Mostly it takes
attention to the server's vital signs and critical events. In this
chapter I've described several tools that are easy to use and provide quite a bit of useful information about the server. But the
information is of no value if you don't take the time to monitor
the server.

Your best approach is to monitor the server when demand is
moderate and the network seems to be performing well. This
information provides a baseline description of the server. By
comparing baseline measurements to measurements taken when
problems are being encountered, you can begin to isolate the
server component that may be at the root of current problems.

The next chapter looks at the prevention of a very specific
source of server problems: power problems. You will learn how
to condition the power that feeds your server to reduce the
effects of erratic power conditions. You will also learn how to use
an uninterruptible power supply to protect your server and its
data in the event of a power failure.

Protecting Servers with a UPS

Equipment for surges, spikes, noise, and power fluctuations

Uninterruptible Power Supplies

Connecting the UPS to the server

Configuring the UPS service

An operating system is a complex, almost living thing. It is constantly monitoring its world, generating output, and making internal adjustments to itself. As a result, any number of processes can be in progress at a given time. A job might be printing, for example, or a database update might be partially completed, or a vital configuration file might be taking place. Given all these critical processes, it becomes clear that interrupting a computer with a power failure can have consequences that are at best inconvenient and at worst disastrous. In some cases, vital files can be corrupted because incomplete updates put the file in an inconsistent state.

Power problems create havoc on computers. Here are just a few of the problems a computer must contend with:

- **Power outages.** Complete losses of power.
- **Voltage variations.** You know how the lights in your house dim when you start the vacuum cleaner? Power-hungry systems can cause the voltage at an AC outlet to vary by a surprising degree. I've seen more than one server problem caused by these periodic "brownouts." Brownouts are also stressful for equipment. Repeated brownouts can burn out power supplies.
- **Voltage spikes and surges.** Equipment can be damaged by a voltage spike so short that you might not even notice it. Lightning is a prime cause of voltage spikes.
- **Noise.** Radio frequency noise on the AC line might get past the filtering in your computer power supply, which is really only designed to cope with the 50 to 60 Hz frequency of line current. Noise can also cause computers to act erratically.

This chapter looks at equipment that deals with all these problems. We will end up by configuring the Uninterruptible Power Supply (UPS) utility that lets Windows NT monitor an uninterruptible power supply and undertake a smooth shutdown in the event of a power failure.

Equipment for Surges, Spikes, Noise, and Power Fluctuations

Depending on your equipment, you might need more than one device to deal with all these problems. Many UPS units don't provide spike protection or filtering, and most can't protect against voltage variations in the AC line.

At a minimum, every computer should be plugged into a surge and spike protector, and you need to plug your UPS into one unless the UPS provides surge and spike protection. Don't even think about using a $10 special. Expect to spend about $50 for a spike and surge suppressor—particularly one that also filters out high-frequency noise. This device is a must.

A surge and spike suppressor is designed to eliminate relatively short voltage changes. If your power line experiences periodic brownouts or overvoltages, you need a power-line conditioner. These devices can level off low and high voltages, maintaining a constant output voltage within a reasonable range of line fluctuations. Expect to spend about $300 for a power-line conditioner. If possible, have an electrician install a dedicated conditioned power line for your server. I used to think that power-line conditioning was seldom required, but the proliferation of electronic equipment (copiers and laser printers are particular culprits) connected to the power lines of a typical office often results in a very dirty power system that must be shared by a server. A server is an expensive investment, and a few hundred dollars for a power-line conditioner seems a small added cost.

Uninterruptible Power Supplies

All UPS devices work by charging a battery during normal operation. The power in the battery can be converted to AC current that can be used to power a computer. A UPS can be designed to operate with the battery either online or offline. Figure 24.1 shows how the two types of UPS devices work.

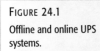

FIGURE 24.1

Offline and online UPS systems.

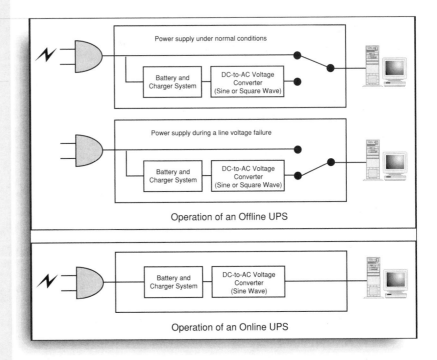

The majority of UPSs use the offline approach. Under normal conditions, the AC line is switched directly to the outlets that service the computer. AC power is also directed to the battery system, which is kept constantly charged. When power fails, an electronic switch connects the UPS outlets to the inverter circuits that convert DC power from the battery into AC power that can run the computer.

The most significant problem with an offline UPS is the period of time that is required to switch from direct AC power to the inverter. Most UPS devices are now designed to make the switch rapidly enough that few computers are bothered, but this was once a common problem.

The online UPS makes it unnecessary to switch power, because the computer is always connected to the battery/inverter system. The outside AC power runs the charging circuits that keep the battery topped off, but it is never directly connected to the computer. Because there is no switch-over, a power outage is handled much more smoothly. Because the AC line voltages are never connected to the computer, an offline UPS inherently functions as a surge, spike, and power-line conditioner.

Every battery-powered UPS must be capable of converting battery-direct current (DC) into the alternating current (AC) required by the protected computer. In the majority of UPS devices, the AC voltage produced is not a true sine wave, like the AC current you get from the wall. Most UPS devices produce a square wave that can cause problems with some computer equipment. Some manufacturers design their equipment to produce a simulated sine wave, which is a stepped-square wave. Simulated sine waves are acceptable to most equipment. Figure 24.2 illustrates the various waveforms.

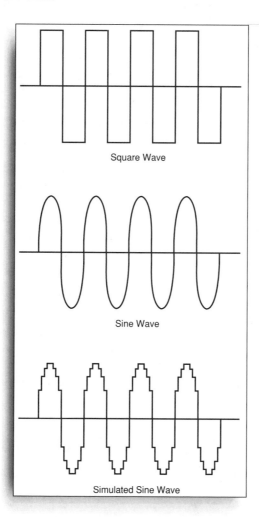

Square Wave

Sine Wave

Simulated Sine Wave

FIGURE 24.2
Waveforms produced by UPS systems.

Because an online UPS is constantly supplying the computer with remanufactured AC, it must produce a true sine wave. Equipment operating too long on a square-wave AC will be damaged.

Most offline UPS systems produce square-wave voltages, which can be used to operate the majority of computers for relatively short periods of time, such as the few minutes it takes to shut down the server properly in the event of a long power failure.

UPS systems can power a server for only a limited time before their batteries are depleted. Therefore, it's desirable to have a means of automatically monitoring the UPS and shutting down the server before the UPS can no longer sustain the required operating voltage. Windows NT includes a UPS service that can provide UPS monitoring with many UPS systems.

Connecting the UPS to the Server

To use the UPS service, your UPS must be equipped with a monitoring interface—usually a DB-9 connector that uses RS-232 serial interface signaling. A cable is used to connect the UPS to a serial port on the computer.

Unfortunately, there are no standards for how UPS monitoring should be done, and every manufacturer seems to have a different way of configuring the monitoring port. Therefore, it's always best to obtain a cable that is designed to match your UPS to Windows NT Server. Contact the manufacturer of the UPS to obtain cables or cable specifications.

In a pinch, you might be able to reverse-engineer the hardware and build a cable yourself. Be aware, however, that this might not be straightforward or even possible. For example, the cable for one of my UPS devices requires a CMOS integrated circuit to support Windows NT Server. In case you want to attempt it, Table 24.1 shows the pin requirements for Windows NT Server.

TABLE 24.1 **Pin requirements for Windows NT Server**

Signal	DB25	DB9	Purpose
CTS	5	8	The UPS can supply a positive or negative voltage at this pin to signal the UPS service that a power failure has occurred.
DCD	8	1	The UPS can supply a positive or negative voltage at this pin to signal the UPS service that a low-battery condition exists.
DTR	20	4	Windows NT can send a positive voltage at this pin to signal the UPS that it can shut itself off.
TXD	2	3	Windows NT maintains a negative voltage at this pin for use with contact-closure signaling from some UPSs.
RTS	4	7	Windows NT maintains a positive voltage at this pin for use with contact-closure signaling from some UPSs.

Before you can configure the UPS service, you must know whether your UPS will generate a positive or a negative signal at the CTS and DCD pins. This information might be available in the documentation for your UPS, or you might need to contact the manufacturer.

After you connect the UPS to your server with a suitable cable, you can configure the UPS service.

Configuring the UPS Service

You access the configuration dialog box from the UPS service through the UPS applet in the Control Panel.

Configuring the UPS monitor

1. Open the UPS applet in the Control Panel. The UPS dialog box is shown in Figure 24.3.

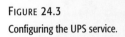

FIGURE 24.3
Configuring the UPS service.

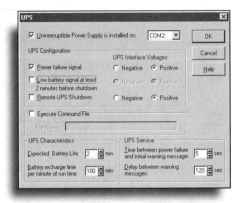

2. Check the **Uninterruptible Power Supply is installed on** check box to activate the other options in the window.

3. Select a COM port. You might need to use the Ports applet in the Control Panel to activate the port you need.

4. If your UPS can send a signal indicating that a power failure has taken place, check the **Power failure signal** check box. Select the **Negative** or **Positive** radio button to indicate whether the UPS sends a negative or positive voltage to signal a power failure condition.

5. If your UPS can send a signal indicating that its battery is low, check the **Low battery signal at least 2 minutes before shutdown** check box. Select the **Negative** or **Positive** radio button to indicate whether the UPS sends a negative or positive voltage to signal a low-battery condition.

6. If your UPS can accept a signal that orders it to shut itself off, check the **Remote UPS Shutdown** box. Select the **Negative** or **Positive** radio button to indicate whether the UPS accepts a negative or positive voltage to trigger it to shut off.

7. If you didn't check the **Low battery signal at least 2 minutes before shutdown** check box, options in the UPS Characteristics box will be active.

   • Enter a conservative estimate of how long the UPS can power the server in the **Expected Battery Life** spin box.

- Enter a conservative estimate of the time required to recharge the UPS battery in the **Battery recharge time per minute of run time** spin box.

The manufacturer of your UPS is the best source of information for the values to put in these fields. Because the UPS can't signal a low-battery condition, the UPS service uses these values to estimate when a low battery condition is likely.

8. Most UPSs send a power failure warning immediately, even for a very short loss of service. If the UPS service interprets such a short loss as the start of a serious outage, it often notifies network users to log off when logging off is unnecessary.

You can specify a delay in the signaling of a power failure by entering a value in seconds in the **Time between power failure and initial warning message** spin box. If power is restored within this time period, no message is sent.

9. The UPS service sends periodic messages as long as the power outage continues. You can specify the delay between these messages by entering a value in seconds in the **Delay between warning messages** spin box.

10. You can instruct the UPS service to execute a command file when a low-battery condition exists. This command file could be a batch file that shuts down special applications, such as a database server. The UPS service will shut down most server functions normally, so a command file is required only in special instances.

To activate the feature, follow these steps:

- Check the **Execute Command File** check box.
- Enter a command filename in the **File Name** field.

11. When you have configured the service, click **OK**.

When you activate the UPS service, it automatically configures its own startup parameters so that it will start automatically when the server boots. The UPS service configuration also ensures that the Alerter, Messenger, and EventLog services are started.

When the UPS service starts up, it tests the interface to the UPS hardware by assuming that normal power conditions prevail. If you have specified a positive voltage at the CTS pin to signal a power failure, the UPS service assumes that a negative voltage will be found at the pin. Each pin you have activated in the UPS Control Panel will be tested. If the expected voltages aren't found, the UPS service won't start.

Testing the UPS

Never assume that your UPS works. After you have configured the UPS service, plan a test. If the server is being used, schedule the test for after hours. You can use the Send Message command in Server Manager to notify users that a test will take place. Users must log out for the duration of the test.

Testing is simple. Pull the plug on your UPS and see what happens.

After the delay you specified (in the **Time between power failure and initial warning message** box), a message is broadcast to the domain, as shown in Figure 24.4. This message repeats at the intervals you specified. During this period, new users can't attach to the server.

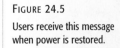
FIGURE 24.4

This message notifies users of a power failure.

At this time, the server can resume normal function if power is restored. When power comes back up and the UPS hardware clears the power failure signal to the UPS service, users receive the message shown in Figure 24.5. Users can reconnect to the server and resume their work.

FIGURE 24.5

Users receive this message when power is restored.

The next step is initiated in one of two ways:

- If you configured the UPS service to expect a low battery signal, the UPS initiates the next phase of the shutdown.
- If you configured the UPS service to use a timed shutdown (**E**xpected battery life), the next phase starts when the shutdown timer expires.

After a low-battery condition occurs, UPS executes any command you specified in the UPS command screen. This command must execute in 30 seconds or less if the server is to be shut down smoothly within two minutes.

After executing the command, the UPS service starts a controlled shutdown of the server. After it begins, the shutdown process can't be aborted.

You should let your test continue until the UPS service shuts down the server.

More Power to You

If you have configured your UPS supply, you have given your Windows NT computer a valuable insurance policy. You can now relax a bit, knowing that a power failure at 2:00 a.m. won't trash the data on your server. You might be called in after power is restored at 4:00 to get the server up and running, but that's better than having to do panic file restores to recover the data needed by the CEO for a 10:00 a.m. meeting.

The next chapter goes off in a completely different direction. What if you need to have the exact same data on several computers, and you need the data to be constantly kept up-to-date? You could attempt to automate some copy commands, but there's another way: the Windows NT directory replicator service. It's one of the most interesting extras in NT.

Managing Directory Replication

Directory replication is a special bonus feature of Windows NT. Network administrators often encounter the need to distribute files across multiple servers. Although you can just copy files using connections to directory shares, between copy operations the directories will probably drift out of synchronization. Multiply the problem by several servers and you can begin to appreciate the value of an automated directory replication service.

Directory replication does not perform one-time copies. It provides an automated, easy-to-manage mechanism that keeps the files in two directories in sync. When any change is made to a file in a master directory, the changes are replicated to a replica directory automatically, within a few minutes.

I alluded to the Directory Replication service in Chapter 9, "Advanced Client Features," where directory replication is used to keep users' logon scripts synchronized. By synchronizing copies of logon scripts on all the domain controllers in a domain, a user can log on to any server and still access a copy of his or her logon script.

But directory replication can be used as a general-purpose directory synchronization tool. For example, you might use it to distribute copies of policy statements, project documents, announcements, phone lists, or newsletters. By distributing copies, users can retrieve the files from their local servers rather than hitting on a single, central server. This can improve performance by distributing file service requests and can reduce WAN traffic by enabling users to retrieve copies of files locally rather than through the WAN.

How NT Directory Replication Works

Two types of computers participate in directory replication. *Export servers* contain master copies of directories called *export directories*. The contents of these directories are copied to *import directories* on *import computers*.

When you configure an export server, you configure two things:

- An **export directory**. The directory that contains all files and subdirectories eligible for export.

- A **list of import computers**. Computers that receive replicas of the export computer. An export computer can export to individual computers or it can export to a domain, in which case files will be replicated to every computer in the domain that is configured as an import computer.

For an import computer, you must configure similar characteristics:

- An import directory that receives all imported files and subdirectories.

- A list of export servers from which replication files will be accepted.

Figure 25.1 illustrates the relationship between an export and an import directory. The default location for the export directory is `%SystemRoot%\system32\Repl\Export` and the default location for the import directory is `%SystemRoot%\system32\Repl\Import`. The scripts subdirectory is created when Windows NT Server is installed. I have created the `phonelst` and `docs` subdirectories to make replication a bit more interesting. Using the default directories, the `Import` subdirectory on the import computer will mirror the `Export` subdirectory of the export server.

Note that directory synchronization is one-way. You cannot both export from directory A to directory B and export from B to A. In other words, any given replication relationship will have one master directory only. All other directories will be replicas. Changes made directly to replicas will not be copied to the master directory. In fact, changes made directly to an import directory will be obliterated the next time the import directory is replicated to its export directory.

One export directory

A given computer can have only one export directory. All exported files must reside in the export directory or in subdirectories of the export directory.

FIGURE 25.1

The default export and import directories.

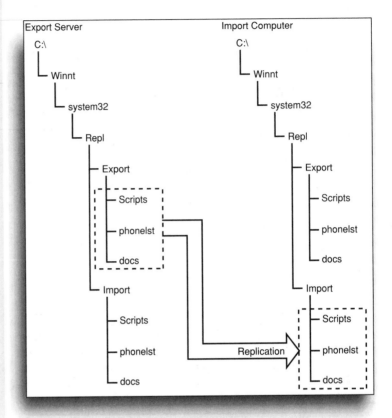

Exports and time stamps

To determine whether files should be exported, the Replicator Service examines the data and time stamps on files in the export directory, exporting files that are newer than corresponding files in the import directory. For this approach to work well, the system clocks on the export and import computers must be set to approximately the same time.

A computer can function as an export server and as an import computer, raising many possible configurations for directory replication. Figure 25.2 suggests a few.

You need to do four things to configure a replication link:

- Start the Directory Replicator service on the export server and on the import computer.
- Configure trust relationships.
- Configure the export server.
- Configure the import computer.

Let's take those four tasks in order.

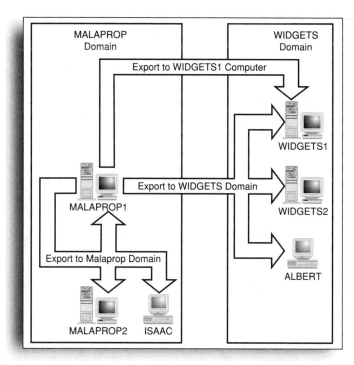

FIGURE 25.2
Possible replication scenarios.

Starting the Directory Replicator Service

The Directory Replicator service runs in the background and is responsible for synchronizing export and import directories. The Directory Replicator service logs on with a special user. First you must create the user account. Then you can configure the Directory Replicator service.

Setting Up the Directory Replicator Service User Account

Create a user account in each domain that will be using the Directory Replicator service. The user account must have the following properties:

- **Password Never Expires** has been checked.
- Account logon hours are configured to permit it to log on 24 hours a day, 7 days a week.

■ The account is a member of the Backup Operators local group. (Remember, members of Backup Operators can back up and restore files that they cannot actually access, a characteristic that is perfect for the Directory Replicator service.)

SEE ALSO

➤ *Backup Operators is a built-in group. You can refresh your memory about built-in groups by referring to the section "Built-In Groups" on page 139 in Chapter 5, "Adding Users and Groups."*

You cannot use the name Replicator for the user account because that name already belongs to a built-in local group. I use the name RepUser for this account.

Setting Up the Directory Replicator Service

After you have set up the Replicator user account, you can start the Directory Replicator service. The procedure is as follows:

Starting the Directory Replicator service

1. On a computer that will be an export server or an import computer, open the Services applet in the Control Panel. As shown in Figure 25.3, the Directory Replicator service is listed in the **Ser_vice** column. Initially, the corresponding entry in the **Status** column will be blank and the entry in the **Startup** column will be **Manual**.

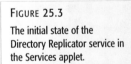

FIGURE 25.3

The initial state of the Directory Replicator service in the Services applet.

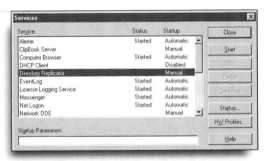

2. Select the **Directory Replicator service** entry and click **Sta_rtup** to open the Service dialog box shown in Figure 25.4. In the figure, the dialog box has been completed with the information required to configure the Directory Replicator service.

FIGURE 25.4

Configuring the Directory Replicator service.

3. In the **Startup Type** box, click the **A**utomatic radio button.

4. In the **Log On As** box, click the **T**his Account radio button.

5. Enter the Directory Replicator user account name in the **T**his Account field. If you wish, you can click the **...** button to browse for the user account.

6. Enter the user account password in the **Password** and **C**onfirm Password fields.

7. Click **OK** to return the **Services** list. You will be shown the message box that appears in Figure 25.5. As you can see, the Directory Replicator user account is given some special system permissions that enable the Directory Replicator service function.

FIGURE 25.5

When you set up the Replication service, this message verifies changes made to the Replication service user account.

8. Select **Directory Replicator** in the Ser**v**ice list and click **S**tart. You will see the message Attempting to Start the Directory Replicator service.

The status of the Directory Replicator service should now be **Started**.

Repeat the preceding procedure on each computer that will function as an export server or an import computer.

Setting Up Trust Relationships

Every domain that will be importing files from another domain must trust the export domain. Be sure that an export domain permits the import domain to trust it. Then configure the import domain to trust the exporting domain.

SEE ALSO

➤ *Chapter 12, "Extending Multi-Domain Networks," discusses trust relationships. See the section titled "Establishing Trust Relationships" on page 412 for specific procedures on setting up a trust relationship.*

If directories will be replicated in both directions between domains, two-way trust relationships must be configured.

Configuring an Export Server

Only Windows NT Server computers that function as domain controllers can be configured as export servers. A default export directory is established when Windows NT Server is installed, and I recommend you use it. If you want to change the export directory, however, be sure to assign Full Control permissions for the directory to the Replicator local group.

You must also assign appropriate permissions to any users who will access files in the export directory. Typically, some users will need permissions that enable them to create the files that will be exported.

To configure an export server, follow these steps:

Configuring an export server

  1. Open the properties dialog box for the server to be configured. You can open the server properties dialog box in two ways:

   ■ Run the Server applet in the Control Panel if you are working on the server being configured.

- In Server Manager, select a server in the computer list. Then choose **Properties** in the **Computer** menu.

Figure 25.6 shows the Server properties dialog box.

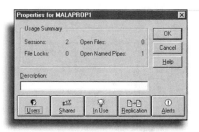

2. In the Server properties dialog box, click the **Replication** button to display the Directory Replication dialog box shown in Figure 25.7. In the figure, the computer has been configured as an export server.

3. Click the **Export Directories** radio button.

4. If you are not using the default export directory, edit the directory path in the **From Path** field.

5. You must add at least one import computer or domain to the **To List** list box. To add an import destination:

- Click **Add** to display the Select Domain dialog box shown in Figure 25.8. This dialog box lists this computer's domain and domains that trust this computer's domain.

Configuring Windows NT Workstation

If you open the Replication properties for a Windows NT Workstation computer or a standalone Windows NT Server, you will see only the properties related to directory importing. Only a Windows NT Server domain controller can be an export server.

- Browse the **Select Domain** list to locate the import domain or computer. If the domain is not shown, you can enter the domain manually in the **Domain** field.

- Click **OK** to accept the import domain or computer and return to the Directory Replication dialog box.

FIGURE 25.8

Browsing for an import destination.

Exporting through a WAN

Replication to a domain is problematic if the export and import domains are connected through a wide area network. When a WAN connection is involved, you should export to individual computers in the import domain.

6. Repeat step 5 to add any other desired import destinations to the **To List** list box.

7. Click **OK** to save the server properties.

Configuring an Import Computer

Import computers can be Windows NT Workstation computers, Windows NT Server domain controllers, or Windows NT Server stand-alone servers.

To configure an import computer, follow these steps:

Configuring an import computer

1. Open the properties dialog box for the server to be configured. You can open the server properties dialog box in two ways:

- Run the Server applet in the Control Panel if you are working on the server being configured.

- In Server Manager, select a server in the computer list. Then choose **Properties** in the **Computer** menu.

2. In the Server properties dialog box, click the **Replication** button to display the Directory Replication dialog box. In Figure 25.9, the computer has been configured as a replication import computer.

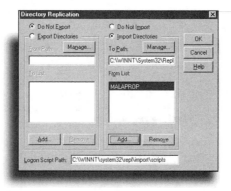

FIGURE 25.9
Replication properties for an import computer.

3. Click the **Import Directories** radio button.

4. If you are not using the default export directory, edit the directory path in the **To Path** field.

5. You must add at least one export computer or domain to the **From List** list box. To add an export source:

- Click **Add** to display the Select Domain dialog. This dialog box lists this computer's domain and domains that trust this computer's domain.

- Browse the **Select Domain** list to locate the import domain or computer. In many cases, the export domain does not trust the import domain and you must enter the domain manually in the **Domain** field.

- Click **OK** to accept the export domain or computer and return to the Directory Replication dialog box.

6. Repeat step 5 to add any other desired export sources to the **From List** list box.

7. Click **OK** to save the server properties.

At this point, directory replication is fully configured. You can now proceed to test the replication connection.

When domains aren't listed

In most cases, you will be exporting from a master domain to a resource domain. In such cases, when you are setting up the export server, the import domain or computer will be listed in the **Select Domain** list.

Because the master domain does not typically trust resource domains, however, if you are setting up an import domain or computer in a resource domain, the master domain will not appear in the **Select Domain** list. It will then be necessary to specify the export domain manually in the **Domain** field.

Testing Directory Replication

Directory replication does not happen immediately, so you must be patient when testing replication operation. Replication takes place only after a stabilization interval configured by the administrator.

SEE ALSO

➤ *The section "Managing Replication Servers" on page 740 explains the stabilization property.*

To verify that replication is working, follow these steps:

Testing replication

1. On the export computer, open a window in File Manager or My Computer to view the export directory.

2. On the import computer, open a window in File Manager or My Computer to view the import directory.

3. Create a file in the export directory, either by copying an existing file to the directory or by using an application to create a new data or text file.

4. Create a subdirectory in the export directory.

5. Wait at least 10 minutes. After a few minutes, the file and directory you created should be mirrored on the import computer.

If directory replication does not take place in 10 minutes or so, you should begin to troubleshoot the replication configuration.

Troubleshooting

Directory replication errors are recorded in the Applications log. Examine the Applications log in the Event Viewer. Choose **Applications** from the **Log** menu to view directory replication messages.

SEE ALSO

➤ *Chapter 23, "Managing the Server," describes the Event Viewer in the section titled "Viewing Event Logs" on page 707.*

If directory replication is not working, check the following items:

- Verify that the user account used for the Directory Replicator service is a member of the Backup Operators group.

- Verify that the Directory Replicator service has been configured on each export and import computer, and that the following properties are established:

  - Startup Type: **Automatic**.

  - **This Account** is selected.

  - The **This Account** field contains the name of the user account configured for the Directory Replicator service.

  - The proper passwords have been specified.

- Verify that the Directory Replicator service is started on each export and import computer.

- Verify that the system clocks on the export and import computers are reasonably close in their time settings.

- Verify that the export domain allows itself to be trusted by each import domain.

- Verify that each import domain trusts the export domain.

- If the export or import directories reside on NTFS volumes, verify that the Directory Replicator account has Full Control permissions for the directories, either through direct assignment or through group membership.

- If replication takes place but some files are not replicated, verify that the files are not locked open by an application. Only closed files can be replicated.

Replication Registry Settings

You can adjust several replication parameters in the Registry. The value entries are located in the following Registry key:

```
HKEY_LOCAL_MACHINE\
   SYSTEM\
   CurrentControlSet\
   Services\
   Replicator\
   Parameters
```

SEE ALSO

> *The Registry is covered in Chapter 22, "Editing the Registry," starting on page 657.*

The following entries must be added to the Parameters subkey. All are of type REG_DWORD.

- **Interval**. This value entry determines the interval in minutes at which the export server checks replicated directories for changes. Range: 1–60 (minutes); default: 5.

- **Pulse.** This value entry specifies the frequency with which the export server repeats sending the last update notice. To ensure that no import server misses the notice, the export server continues to send change notices even when no changes have occurred. The server waits `Pulse'Interval` minutes between notices. Range: 1–10; default: 3.

- **Guard Time.** This value entry determines the number of minutes the export directory must be stable before the import server can import its files. Range: 0–½ of Interval (minutes); default: 3.

When you change these parameters, you must stop and restart the Directory Replicator service to put the changes into effect.

Managing Replication Servers

You can manage several characteristics of export servers and import computers.

Managing Export Servers

To manage an export server, open the server's Directory Replication dialog box (refer to Figure 25.7). Then choose the **Manage** button in the Export Directories box to display the Manage Exported Directories dialog box, shown in Figure 25.10. An entry is listed for each subdirectory that is in the export directory. The following information is displayed for each subdirectory:

- **Locks.** Unless the lock count is 0, this subdirectory will not be exported. Locks are added with the **Add Lock** button, discussed in the next list.

- **Stabilize.** Indicates whether the **Wait Until Stabilized** option has been selected. If this field is No, files are eligible to be exported as soon as they are modified. If this field is Yes, modified files will be allowed to stabilize for at least two minutes.

- **Subtree.** Indicates whether the **Entire Subtree** option has been selected. If this field is No, subdirectories of this directory will not be exported. If this field says Yes, subdirectories will be exported.

- **Locked Since.** For locked subdirectories, indicates the time and date when locks were applied.

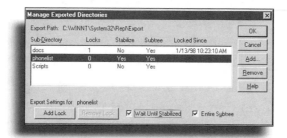

FIGURE 25.10

Managing an export server.

To manage a subdirectory, select it in the **Sub-Directory** list. Then use the following controls:

- **Add Lock.** If a lock is added to a subdirectory, nothing will be exported from it or from its subdirectories. You can add more than one lock (although Microsoft does not explain why you would want to do so). Exporting will not resume until all locks are removed.

- **Remove Lock.** Choose this option to reduce the lock count by one. Exporting resumes when the lock count is 0.

- **Wait Until Stabilized.** Check this box to force Directory Replication to wait at least two minutes after a file is modified before exporting the file. Use this option to help eliminate partial replication. If this box is checked, the **Stabilize** column will indicate Yes for this subdirectory.

- **Entire Subtree.** If this box is checked, subdirectories of this directory will be exported whenever this directory is exported. If the box is not checked, only this directory will be exported, without its subdirectories.

- **Add.** If a subdirectory in the export directory is not listed in the Manage Export Directories window, click the **Add** button to add it to the display. In most cases, subdirectories will be added and removed by the system.

- **Remove.** To remove a subdirectory from the window, select the subdirectory and click **Remove**.

Managing Import Computers

The **Manage** button in the Import Directories box displays a slightly different window, as shown in Figure 25.11. The following information is displayed for each subdirectory:

- **Locks.** Unless the lock count is 0, this subdirectory will not be imported. Locks are added with the **Add Lock** button, discussed in the next list.

- **Status.** This field can have the following values:

  - OK indicates that the subdirectory is receiving regular imports.

  - No Master indicates that imports are not being received. The export server may not be running or a configuration error may exist.

  - No Sync indicates that imports have taken place, but that data is not current. This condition can result from communication error or incorrect permissions at the export server.

  - If the field is blank, replication has not occurred in this subdirectory.

- **Last Update.** The date and time the subdirectory last received an import.

- **Locked Since.** For locked subdirectories, this field indicates the time and date when locks were applied.

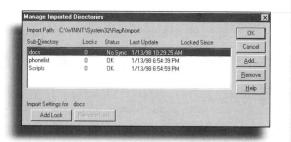

FIGURE 25.11
Managing an import computer.

The Manage Imported Directories window has these controls:

- **Add Lock.** As with export directories, you can place locks on import subdirectories. Files will not be imported to a subdirectory if any locks are applied.

- **Remove Lock.** Select this button to remove a lock from the selected subdirectory.

- **Add.** If a subdirectory in the export directory is not listed in the Manage Export Directories window, click the **Add** button to add it to the display. In most cases, subdirectories will be added and removed by the system.

- **Remove.** To remove a subdirectory from the window, select the subdirectory and choose Remove.

Directory Replication and Logon Scripts

SEE ALSO

➤ *You were introduced to logon scripts in Chapters 8 and 9, "Activating Network Clients" and "Advanced Client Features," starting on pages 247 and 291, respectively.*

One difficulty with logon scripts is that the user does not access a logon script through a share. Instead, the logon script must be stored in a directory that is local on the domain controller that authenticates the user's logon. This is complicated by the fact that a user may log on using any domain controller in the domain. Therefore, each domain controller in a logon domain must be configured with a copy of the logon scripts. The Directory Replicator service makes it easy to distribute logon scripts from one computer to the other domain controllers.

The Directory Replication dialog box is used to declare the location of logon scripts for the server (refer to Figure 25.7). Directory replication is commonly used to replicate master copies of logon scripts to all domain controllers in a domain or on the entire network.

The logon script path is a subdirectory of the default export directory. By default, the logon script path is `C:\Winnt\system32\Repl\Import\Scripts`. To replicate logon script files, the master copies should be placed in the same subdirectory of the export subdirectory. The default subdirectory for master logon scripts to be exported is `C:\Winnt\system32\Repl\Export\Scripts`.

Users whose logons are replicated by the master export server must be able to access logon scripts in the `Import\Scripts` subdirectory. The easiest way to achieve this is to configure the master export server to export to its own domain. This configuration causes scripts to be replicated to the `Import\Scripts` directory on the master export server at the same time it is replicated to other import computers in the domain.

Almost at the End

We're almost at the end of our tour of Windows NT networking. In fact, for many of you, this is the end. If you don't need to connect with NetWare networks, you are done, and you can pick up your diploma at the Registrar's office. Congratulations on getting this far. I have tried to make this book a career booster, one that will jump-start your efforts to become a Windows NT network administrator. But I can only do so much, and it's your perseverance at reaching the end and at honing your skills that are the crucial ingredients required to make you a network professional. If you made it to the end, give yourself a pat on the back. Many thanks for giving me the opportunity to work with you.

If you need to connect with NetWare, you need to digest one more chapter. The following chapter gives you the tools you need to enable users on your Windows NT network to access files and printers on NetWare servers.

Connecting with NetWare

Technologies for accessing multiple LAN environments

Preparing NetWare to support the gateway for NetWare

Installing the gateway for NetWare

Activating the gateway and sharing NetWare files with users

Sharing NetWare printers with Microsoft users

Migrating users from NetWare to Windows NT

Although Windows NT Server has become extremely popular, most of the world's network servers still run Novell NetWare. So it's not at all unlikely that you will need to make your Windows NT Server network coexist with NetWare servers and clients. You can bridge the gap between NetWare and NT in several ways:

- You can install both Microsoft and NetWare client components. This enables a client computer to participate on NT and NetWare networks simultaneously.

- You can install a gateway that allows users on the NT Server network to access files and printers on the NetWare server as though the files and printers are shared by an NT server.

- You can migrate user accounts and files on your NetWare servers over to Windows NT Server.

This chapter examines all three approaches.

Accessing Different Environments with Multiple Client Protocol Stacks

You have seen how easy it is to install more than one protocol on a Windows NT computer. It is just as easy to install multiple protocols on other Microsoft clients as well. Clearly, Microsoft has designed a flexible network protocol architecture that can be enhanced just by plugging in new features.

One component required to connect with NetWare is the NWLink protocol, which enables Microsoft clients to converse with NetWare servers running Novell's IPX/SPX protocols. Compatibility with NetWare is the chief reason Microsoft developed NWLink.

SEE ALSO

➤ *NWLink is described in Chapter 3, "Configuring Network Adapters, Services, and Protocols," starting on page 83.*

In addition to protocol compatibility, a computer needs a NetWare client so that it can log in and communicate with the NetWare server.

On Windows 95 and 98, a NetWare client is installed by default when you set up networking.

SEE ALSO

➤ *For more information about the Windows 95 and 98 client, see the section titled "Enabling Windows 95 and Windows 98 as Network Clients" in Chapter 8, "Activating Network Clients," page 247.*

On Windows NT Server, you install a NetWare client when you install the Gateway (and Client) Services for NetWare, which is the subject of this chapter.

Accessing Different Environments with a Gateway

A *gateway* is a heavy-duty translator that allows two very different computer environments to communicate. Windows NT Server includes the Gateway Services for NetWare that enables Microsoft network clients to access services on NetWare servers.

The great thing about a gateway is that you don't need to make any changes to the clients. When viewed through the gateway, a NetWare server looks like a Microsoft server. Clients run the same Microsoft network client they are used to, which saves you the trouble of installing client software on network client computers. It also eliminates the need to train your users on the changes they will encounter when logging on to two servers.

Figure 26.1 shows a network that incorporates a Windows NT NetWare gateway. On the Windows side of the gateway, clients communicate using any protocol supported by Windows NT Server, and use Microsoft's techniques for exchanging data between servers. The gateway translates client messages into IPX/SPX format and communicates with the NetWare server using Novell's network conventions.

"Log in" and "Log on"

You may notice that I use "log in" when I'm talking about connecting to a NetWare server and "log on" when connecting to a Microsoft server. Among the many niggling inconsistencies in the network industry is the use of two words for the same action. But NetWare has the **LOGIN** command, whereas Microsoft uses **NET LOGON**; so I've tried to use the term that originates in each environment.

FIGURE 26.1

The Gateway for NetWare translates protocols between Novell and Microsoft environments.

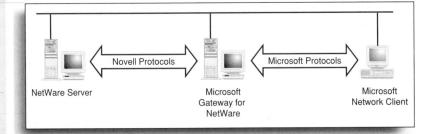

The interesting thing about the gateway approach is that the NetWare server appears to users as just another shared resource on a Windows NT server. No changes to Windows network clients are required to enable them to access the NetWare server through the gateway.

Using a gateway to connect your users with a NetWare server has several attractive features:

- It is easier to set up and maintain users' computers because they require only one network client.

- Users do not need to learn new techniques for accessing network resources.

- Very few changes are required on the NetWare side.

- There is a single point at which the Microsoft network talks to the NetWare network.

But you need to be aware of some disadvantages of gateways:

- The translations the gateway must perform are extensive, and performance is generally slower than a connection with the proper protocols.

- Some features on the NetWare host might not be available. In particular, the NetWare gateway cannot access NetWare 4.x Novell Directory Services, and users must access NetWare 4.x servers in Bindery mode.

Opinions on gateways differ. I'll give you mine, but you will need to study the pros and cons in light of your organization's needs.

I have operated Windows networks with multiple protocol stacks with no real trouble. It is extremely easy to add support for a second network with Windows NT, Windows 95, or Windows for Workgroups clients. Performance doesn't take a significant hit with multiple protocols, and I haven't seen a user yet who wasn't performance-conscious. I also prefer native NetWare security to the share-level security available with the Windows NT Gateway. Yes, it means extra administration, but good security is worth the effort.

Consider using a gateway if your users require fairly casual access to NetWare, particularly if they need to access printers on the NetWare network. Thanks to print queues and spooling, printing performance isn't as critical to most users as application performance. A gateway also is an easy way to enable users to pass files between the two networks.

Setting Up a Gateway

To configure a gateway for NetWare, you must do the following:

1. Prepare NetWare to support the gateway.
2. Install the gateway.
3. Activate the gateway and share NetWare files with users.
4. Share NetWare printers with users.

These steps are discussed in the following sections. To avoid writing another book as large as this one, I'm assuming you are familiar with NetWare techniques and terminology.

Preparing the NetWare Server to Support a Gateway

To set up the NetWare server to support Gateway Services for NetWare, a NetWare administrator must use SYSCON to create the following entities:

- **A group named NTGATEWAY.** Grant this group the rights that should be available to users who access the server

For more about NetWare, check out these books:

Novell IntranetWare Professional Reference, Fifth Edition. Published by New Riders.

Special Edition Using IntranetWare. Published by Que.

through the gateway. Remember, all users of the gateway access the NetWare server with the same rights.

- **A user account with the same username that is used to log on to the Windows NT network from the gateway computer.** Give this user the appropriate rights. Because I'm logging in as the Windows NT Administrator user, I created a user account named ADMINISTRATOR on the NetWare server. Configure passwords so that they are the same on the Windows NT Server and the NetWare server. (Several accounts might be necessary if the gateway computer is shared.)

- **A user account that is used by the gateway service.** I named my user account GATEWAY. Make this user account a member of the NTGATEWAY group. To create other gateways, create a user account for each gateway and add each account to the NTGATEWAY group. Only one user account is required per gateway computer.

Installing the Gateway Service

When you set up the Gateway Services for NetWare, two components are installed:

- A client service enables the user of the gateway computer to log directly in to the NetWare server, providing the user with a normal NetWare client environment.

- A gateway service enables Microsoft network clients to access shared NetWare resources.

You can configure each of these services to access the NetWare server through a separate NetWare user account.

For the smoothest operation, users should log on to the Windows and NetWare networks with the same username, which should have the same password on each server. After this is done, Windows can automatically log the user on to each service environment when the username and password are specified.

Gateway Service for NetWare is installed from the Network utility in the Windows NT Server Control Panel. To install the service, follow these steps:

Bindery mode is required

Clients can only access NetWare servers that use NDS in Bindery mode. If you will be using the Gateway Service for NetWare to access a NetWare server that uses NDS (NetWare 4.x or IntranetWare), you must establish a bindery context so that the Gateway Service can access the NetWare server in Bindery mode. That requires a statement similar to the following in the AUTOEXEC.NCF file:

```
set bindery context =
.ou=widgets.o=malaprop
```

The gateway user accounts

I do not recommend using the same user account for both the client service and the gateway service. You might be using the client service account as a NetWare supervisor account, with privileges you don't want to make available to gateway users. Create a separate user account that has only the permissions required by gateway users for the gateway service.

Installing Gateway Service for NetWare

1. Open the Network applet in the Control Panel and select the **Services** tab.

2. Click **A̲dd** and select **Gateway (and Client) Service for NetWare** in the Network Service box.

3. Click **OK**.

4. When prompted, supply the path where files can be found on the installation CD-ROM. Files are copied, and the adapter software is installed. You will be returned to the Network utility window.

5. Exit the Network applet and restart the computer to activate the changes.

SEE ALSO

➤ *Consult Chapter 3, "Configuring Network Adapters, Services, and Protocols," for information about configuring NWLink. See the section titled "Building Networks with NWLink" on page 83.*

Activating the Gateway Server and Adding Shares

After the server reboots and you log on within the Welcome dialog box, you are shown a new dialog box titled Select Preferred Server for NetWare. In this window, you can specify the first NetWare server that the login process attempts to connect you with. You can name a preferred server for a Bindery-mode NetWare server or a default tree for an NDS network. The server or tree you select will be the preference for your personal NetWare user ID.

The dialog box that appears at logon resembles the dialog box in Gateway Service for NetWare, shown in Figure 26.2. The specifics are discussed in this chapter in the section titled "NetWare Login Preferences." If you wish, you can click **Cancel** to skip the logon dialog box and use Gateway Services for NetWare to establish the NetWare connection configuration.

If you specify a preferred server or a default tree, Windows NT attempts to authenticate you on the NetWare server by using your Windows NT account name and password. If the login fails, you are asked to enter a username and password for NetWare.

NWLink is installed with the gateway

If NWLink was not previously installed on the computer, it is added when you install Gateway Service for NetWare. Unless your network has specific protocol requirements, no configuration should be needed.

Configuring the NetWare User Account Information

When Gateway Service for NetWare (GSNW) is installed, a new GSNW applet is added to the Control Panel. GSNW is used to configure two different things:

- Your preferences for logging directly in to the NetWare server as a NetWare client
- The Gateway Service for NetWare that is used by gateway clients to access the NetWare server

This tool is used to configure NetWare services on the computer and is shown in Figure 26.2. Information in the Gateway Service for NetWare dialog box determines the login preferences for the user whose name is shown after **Username**. This information is used to configure this user's personal NetWare environment.

FIGURE 26.2

Entering user account information for the Gateway Service for NetWare.

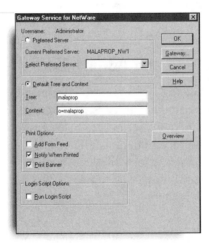

NetWare Login Preferences

The following fields specify the user's login preferences:

- **Preferred Server.** Click this radio button to establish a Bindery-mode server as the default server. Specify a server name in the **Select Preferred Server** field. Use this option when connecting to NetWare 3.x or to NetWare 4.x in Bindery mode.

- **Default Tree and Context.** Click this radio button to connect to a Novell Directory Services tree in NDS mode. Specify the tree name in the **Tree** field and the user context in the **Context** field.

- Check **Run Login Script** if a NetWare login script is to be executed when logging in to NetWare.

The preceding fields are the same that you see when you first log on to Windows NT Server after installing Gateway Service for NetWare. The first-time logon process was discussed in the preceding section. You can change these parameters. Changes take effect the next time you log on.

NetWare Printer Preferences

You can also configure your printing preferences in this dialog box. Print options for printing to NetWare printers can be set as follows:

- **Add Form Feed.** Check this box if NetWare should force a form feed at the end of print jobs. Most software sends a form feed, and this option should not be checked in most cases.

- **Notify When Printed.** Check this box if you want to receive a message when a job has been sent to a printer.

- **Print Banner.** When this option is checked, NetWare prints a banner page before each job. Do not check this option if printing to a PostScript printer. Most organizations do not find it necessary to activate banners, but large organizations may find banners make it easier to identify users' print jobs.

At this point, you have configured your personal preferences for NetWare. These settings do not affect gateway operation. If you will not be configuring a gateway, click **OK** to exit the utility.

Synchronizing Account Passwords

When the NetWare account was set up for the locally logged in user, the password was probably not synchronized to the user's password on the Windows network. As a result, the user is asked to enter a password each time a connection is established with the NetWare server. For greatest convenience, you should change the password on the NetWare server so that it is the same as the password in NT.

To change the password on the NetWare server, follow these steps:

Changing the password on the NetWare server

1. Open a command prompt.

2. Use the `net use` command to connect a drive to the NetWare SYS volume. For example, if your NetWare server is named NW4, you would enter the following command:

   `net use s: \\nw4\sys`

3. Change to the connected drive.

4. `CD` to the `\PUBLIC` directory.

5. Enter the command `setpass`. Follow the prompts to change the NetWare password.

After passwords match in Windows NT and NetWare, you need to enter your password only once when logging on to the network.

Configuring the NetWare Gateway and Sharing Directories

To configure the gateway, click the **Gateway** button in the Gateway Service for NetWare dialog box to open the Configure Gateway dialog box, shown in Figure 26.3. At first, the **Add**, **Remove**, and **Permissions** options are not active because the gateway service has not been started.

Configuring a NetWare gateway

To configure a gateway, use these steps:

1. Check **Enable Gateway**. Checking this option instructs Windows NT Server to start the gateway service when the server starts. You can disable the gateway without removing the software by removing the check mark from this box.

Warning: Stopping the Gateway Service for NetWare

Do not stop the Gateway Service for NetWare service using the Service applet in the Control Panel. Several other vital services are stopped with it. Instead, disable the gateway in the GSNW utility.

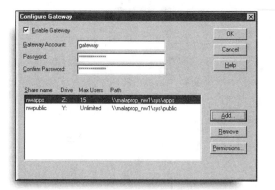

FIGURE 26.3
Configuring the gateway.

2. Enter the NetWare user account name that you created for the gateway server in the **Gateway Account** box. When an account name has been entered, the **Add** button is activated.

3. Enter the password for the NetWare user account in the **Password** and **Confirm Password** boxes.

4. To make directories on the NetWare server available to gateway users, you must define them as shares. To add a share, click **Add** to display the New Share dialog box shown in Figure 26.4. Complete the following information for the share you are adding:

- **Share Name**. Enter the name by which the share will be known to gateway users.

- **Network Path**. Enter the path to the NetWare directory that will be shared. The utility accepts uniform naming convention (UNC) names. For NetWare servers accessed through the gateway, UNC names have the following format:

  `\\server\volume\directory\subdirectory...`

Figure 26.4 shows the UNC name for the APPS directory on the SYS volume of the NW4 server.

SEE ALSO

▶ *UNC names are explained in the note titled "UNC Names" on page 166 in Chapter 5, "Adding Users and Groups."*

FIGURE 26.4
Creating a gateway share.

Modifying gateway shares

Unfortunately you cannot modify a gateway share after it is added. To make changes, you must remove the existing share and add a new share with the desired settings.

- **Comment**. You can add a comment to describe the share if desired. This comment will be shown when the share is listed in users' browse lists.

- **Use Drive**. Select an available drive letter from the list. Drive letters that correspond to physical drives on the computer are not available, and available drives are usually limited to the letters *E* through *Z* because a gateway can provide access to at most 22 or 23 directory shares.

- **Unlimited**. Choose this option if you do not want to restrict the number of users who can access the share.

- **Allow**. Choose this option and specify a number to restrict the number of users who can access the share. Because performance will suffer if too many users connect to a given share, a limit is desirable.

  Click **OK** when you have configured the share. The gateway service will attempt to locate the shared directory on the specified NetWare server. If the share can be validated, it will be added to the **Share name** list in the Configure Gateway dialog box.

5. By default, the group Everyone is given Full Control permissions to a newly created gateway share. If you want to change the default permissions, select the entry in the **Share name** box and choose **Permissions**. The Access Through Share Permissions dialog box, shown in Figure 26.5, functions like the Share Permissions dialog boxes in File Manager.

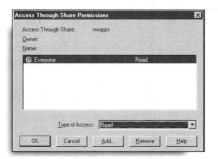

FIGURE 26.5
Managing permissions for the gateway share.

SEE ALSO

➤ *Consult Chapter 6, "Sharing Files and Managing File Security," for details about setting share permissions. See the section titled "Share Permissions" on page 190.*

6. After you have configured the desired gateway shares, click **OK** to quit the Gateway Service for NetWare applet.

More About Gateway Shares

The Gateway Services for NetWare applet is used to create gateway shares and assign share permissions. Gateway file shares cannot be managed in File Manager. As a result, you cannot use File Manager to fine-tune directory and file permissions.

You can, however, use NetWare administration tools to assign detailed NetWare rights to the NTGATEWAY group. Directory and file rights will set maximum permissions for all gateway users, regardless of the share permissions that may be assigned by the Gateway Service for NetWare.

As a result, NetWare directories accessed through the gateway should generally be regarded as group directories, not personal directories. You can add a share that grants permissions to only one user, but because you are restricted to 22 gateway shares, assigning private shared directories on the gateway is not very practical.

If any users require personal directories on the NetWare server, you should assign them individual NetWare accounts and equip their computers with NetWare client software.

Sharing NetWare Printers

NetWare users do not print directly to printers. They print to print queue files, from which jobs are printed by a print server. Gateway Service for NetWare enables users on the Windows network to connect to NetWare print queues and print to NetWare-managed printers.

Although NetWare directory sharing is managed with the GSNW utility rather than File Manager, NetWare printers are shared using fairly standard procedures in the Print Manager.

To share a NetWare-based printer, follow these steps:

Sharing a NetWare-based printer

1. Log in to the NetWare network from the gateway computer. The account you use must have NetWare rights to use the desired print queue.
2. Open the Printers icon in the Control Panel.
3. Double-click **Add Printer** to open the Add Printer Wizard.
4. Choose **Network printer server**. Then click **Next**.
5. Next a Connect to Printer dialog box opens a browse list similar to the one shown in Figure 26.6. Browse the network and select a shared printer. Click **Next**.

FIGURE 26.6

Connecting to a shared printer.

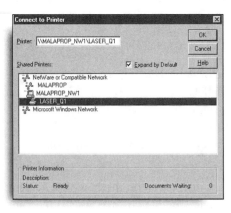

6. Windows NT ordinarily expects to find a suitable printer driver on the computer to which it is connecting. Because NetWare servers don't come equipped with Windows print drivers, you will see the warning The server on which the printer resides does not have a suitable printer driver installed. Before you can print to the NetWare queue, a suitable printer driver must be added to the local computer. Click **OK** in this message box and go through the steps of selecting and installing a print driver.

SEE ALSO

➤ *See Chapter 7, "Sharing Printers," starting on page 213 if you want more information about network printing.*

7. After the print driver has been installed, the printer is added to the local printer configuration and an icon is added to the Printers window. The locally connected user can now print to the printer. Before gateway users can use the printer, however, it must be shared.

8. To share the printer with the gateway, select the printer in the Printer window. Then choose the **Properties** command in the **Printer** menu. Figure 26.7 shows the **Sharing** tab of the Printer Properties dialog box.

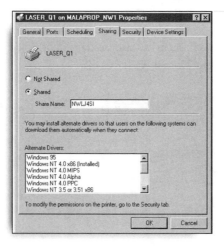

FIGURE 26.7

Configuring properties for a printer shared through the Gateway for NetWare.

9. To share the printer, click **Shared**. Enter a share name in the **Share Name** field. Select any additional drivers to be supported in the **Alternate Drivers** list. You can, if desired, configure the other properties for the share, such as security.

10. Click **OK** when the share properties are specified.

Windows users can now access this shared printer as though it were directly attached to the gateway computer.

Accessing NetWare Resources from the Gateway Server

Shared printers and directories are advertised in the browse list for the gateway computer, just as though they resided physically on that computer. As a result, most of the NetWare gateway mechanism is invisible to network users.

A user who logs on to the Windows NT Server Gateway for NetWare is logged in to the NetWare server as a NetWare client. As a result, resources offered by the NetWare server are available using standard browsing tools.

Figure 26.8 shows the Network Neighborhood dialog box of a gateway computer. Notice that entries appear for the NetWare 4.11 server, a printer, and for the two volumes. When logged in to NetWare, your access is controlled by standard NetWare security, and you are unaffected by permissions assigned to the gateway shares.

FIGURE 26.8

The logged-in user sees this view of the NetWare server.

After gateway shares are established, they appear in your My Computer window as shared volumes. Figure 26.9 shows some examples.

Using NetWare Applications Through the Gateway

A wide variety of NetWare MS-DOS utilities can be run through the gateway:

chkvol	grant	pconsole	rights	slist
colorpal	help	psc	security	syscon
dspace	listdir	pstat	send	tlist
flag	map	rconsole	session	userlist
flagdir	ncopy	remove	setpass	volinfo
fconsole	ndir	revoke	settts	whoami
filer				

NetWare menu utilities, such as RCONSOLE, require access to files such as SYS$MSG.DAT, which is installed in the SYS:PUBLIC directory. To access these files, either make SYS:PUBLIC your default directory before running the utility or add SYS:PUBLIC to your search path.

Not all NetWare-aware applications run in a Windows NT gateway environment. Consult your program documentation for information about supported environments. Some applications may require that the NWLink (IPX/SPX) protocol be loaded on the client.

Many NetWare-aware applications that are written for 16-bit Windows require DLL files that are provided by Novell. The NWIPXSPX.DLL file is included with the NetWare DOS client software. If the NetWare client software has ever been installed on the client, this file should have been installed. To make the file available to gateway clients, obtain NWIPXSPX.DLL and copy it to the directory C:\Winnt\system32.

Some NetWare-aware applications directly send and receive Novell network protocol packets. These applications might require a copy of NETWARE.DRV, which is copied to the C:\Winnt\system32 directory when the gateway service is installed. NETWARE.DRV is used in combination with either NWNE-TAPI.DLL or NWCALLS.DLL, depending on the version of NetWare being used. Consult the NetWare documentation for the correct file to use. Copy these files to the directory C:\Winnt\system32.

For MIPS and ALPHA AXP clients, the file TBMI2.COM must be copied to the directory C:\Winnt\system32. Also, add the following line to the AUTOEXEC.NT file and restart the computer:

```
lh winnt\system32\tbmi2.com
```

Applications do not generally perform as well through the gateway as they would with a direct logon connection. This is particularly true if large amounts of data must flow through the gateway. Gateway translation takes time.

Tape Backup Incompatibilities

One particular area of incompatibility is tape backup. You might be tempted to use the backup program from Windows NT Server because it's already included with the product. When backing up NetWare, however, you must use a backup product that is aware of the existence of the NetWare bindery files. Windows NT Backup was written for Windows NT, not for NetWare.

Translation of File Attributes

Gateway Service for NetWare must translate several file system characteristics when users access NetWare files. Among the features that require translation are file attributes. Table 26.1 describes Windows NT file attributes and the way they are translated for NetWare files.

TABLE 26.1 Translation of Windows NT attributes to NetWare attributes

Windows NT Attribute	NetWare Attribute
R (Read Only)	Ro, Di (Delete Inhibit), Ri (Rename Inhibit)
A (Archive)	A
S (System)	Sy
H (Hidden)	H

The NetWare Ci (Copy Inhibit), P (Purge), RW (Read Write), S (Shareable), T (Transactional), Ra (Read Audit), and Wa (Write Audit) attributes are not supported by the gateway, although they do restrict the operations that gateway users can perform on NetWare-based files.

Migrating Users from NetWare to Windows NT

If you dislike the idea of maintaining two types of servers and have decided to move all your servers over to Windows NT Server, you are faced with the big problem of moving user accounts from NetWare to Windows NT. If you have a large number of NetWare users, you might decide that the task of creating new accounts in the Windows NT Server environment is too daunting.

Microsoft includes the Migration Tool for NetWare with Windows NT Server. This tool reduces the pain of moving users to Windows NT networks. The Migration Tool is not installed as an icon; and, because you will probably not be running it frequently, you will probably choose to run it from a Run command.

The server running the migration must meet the following conditions:

- Volumes to which NetWare files will be migrated must be formatted with the NTFS file system so that NetWare directory and security information can be migrated.
- The NWLink protocols must be installed.
- The Gateway Service for NetWare must be installed. The Gateway Service enables the Migration Tool to access the NetWare server from which you are migrating.

The icon for Migration Tool for NetWare is installed in the Administrative Tools program group when you install Gateway Service for NetWare. The first dialog box you see, Select Servers for Migration, is shown in Figure 26.10. Specify the names of the NetWare and Windows NT Server computers and click **OK**. If you need to log on to either server, you are prompted for a username and a password. The NetWare user account should be secured as a Supervisor equivalent. The Windows NT user account should have Administrator permissions on the target server.

FIGURE 26.10

Selecting a file server to be migrated.

After logging on to the source and destination servers, the main Migration Tool dialog box is displayed (see Figure 26.11). The **Add** and **Delete** buttons are used to add and delete source and destination servers.

Setting Migration User Options

The **User Options** button in the Migration Tool is used to access the User and Group Options dialog box, shown in Figure 26.12. The dialog box has four sub-boxes that are accessed by clicking tabs: **Passwords**, **Usernames**, **Group Names**, and **Defaults**. Each of these boxes is covered in turn.

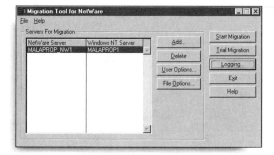

FIGURE 26.11

The Migration Tool for NetWare.

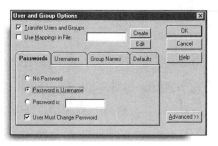

FIGURE 26.12

User and group options for the Migration Tool.

Selecting the Transfer Option

Check **Transfer Users and Groups** if you want to migrate NetWare groups and users. If you wish, you can turn this option off to transfer only files.

Using a Mappings File

If you want to control how names of users and groups are handled during the migration, use a mappings file. To use a migration mapping file, do the following:

Migrating with a mappings file

1. Check **Use Mappings in File**.

2. Enter a filename in the box. The file the Migration Tool creates is a text file that will have a .MAP extension.

3. After you click **OK** in the User and Group Options window, you are shown this message: Mapping file created successfully. Do you want to edit it? If you click **Yes**, Notepad is started, and the mapping file is loaded for editing. Figure

26.13 shows an example. The example was kept very simple. As you can see, you can map the user's NetWare account name to a new name on the Windows NT server. You can also change user group names and specify an initial user password.

FIGURE 26.13

Example of a migration mappings file.

Selecting Password Options

Not even a NetWare Supervisor can discover user passwords, so passwords cannot be migrated to Windows NT. The passwords box has three options for creating passwords:

- **No Password.** This option makes it unnecessary for you to distribute passwords to users.
- **Password is Username.** The password for the user account will be the same as the username.
- **Password is.** The initial password will be the password you specify.

It is recommended that you check **User Must Change Password** if you use the **No Password** option so that users will be forced to change or create a password when they first log on.

Selecting Username Options

Select the **Usernames** tab in the User and Group Options box to display the **Usernames** options shown in Figure 26.14. Options in this box specify the action that will be taken if a username on the NetWare server is duplicated by an existing name on the Windows NT Server.

- **Log Error.** This option records conflicts in the ERROR.LOG file created during migration.

- **Ignore.** This option ignores accounts on the NetWare server that already exist on the Windows NT Server.

- **Overwrite with new Info.** This option replaces account information on the Windows NT Server with account information from NetWare.

- **Add prefix.** You can specify a prefix that is appended to the NetWare name if a conflict occurs.

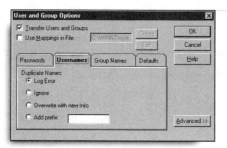

FIGURE 26.14

Specifying actions to be taken when usernames conflict during migration.

Selecting Group Name Options

Click the **Group Names** tab to display the box shown in Figure 26.15. Because these options duplicate options on the **Usernames** tab, they require no discussion.

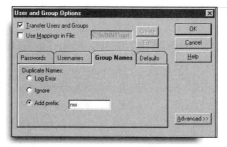

FIGURE 26.15

Specifying actions to be taking when group names conflict during migration.

Selecting Supervisor Defaults

Click the **Defaults** tab to determine how supervisor rights will
be transferred to the Windows NT Server environment. The
option you choose depends on whether NetWare administrators
will be established as administrators of your Windows NT network. Options are shown in Figure 26.16.

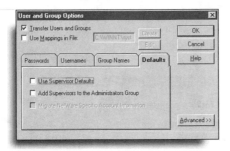

- **Use Supervisor Defaults.** Check this box to transfer
  account restrictions from NetWare to Windows NT Server.
  Remove the check mark if Windows NT account policy settings should be used.

- **Add Supervisors to the Administrators Group.** Check
  this box if users who are user-equivalent to the NetWare
  Supervisor should be added to the Administrators group.
  Remove the check mark if supervisor equivalents should not
  be made administrators of the Windows NT Server.

Setting Migration File Options

The **File Options** button in the Migration Tool main window
produces the File Options dialog box shown in Figure 26.17.
This box enables you to control where files will be placed on the
Windows NT Server. The NetWare server used in this example
has only one volume, named SYS. All the volumes on the
NetWare server should be listed, and the **Add** button will only
be activated if you delete a volume.

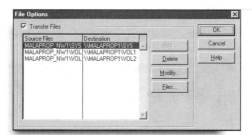

FIGURE 26.17

Specifying file migration
options.

The **Modify** button displays the Modify Destination dialog box
shown in Figure 26.18. By default, files in a NetWare volume
are copied to a directory with the same name as the volume. The
share name assigned to the directory will be the same as the
original volume name.

FIGURE 26.18

Specifying the file migration
destination.

You can modify the destination directory and share name in this
dialog box. Change the **Share** entry to specify the share name
that is assigned to the directory to which these files are copied.
You can also specify a different directory by clicking **Properties**.

If you want to select specific files and directories to be transferred, click the **Files** button in the File Options dialog box to
display the Files To Transfer dialog box shown in Figure 26.19.
Select directories and files much as you would in File Manager.
Double-click a closed folder icon to examine the directory contents. Check the directories and files to be transferred and clear
check marks for items that should not be migrated. In Figure
26.17, the SYS volume was opened to reveal the first-level directories. By default, several directories are not checked. It would
make no sense to migrate the SYSTEM directory, for example,
which contains the NetWare system files. You can go down to
the file level if you want to exercise that much control over files

that will migrate. You will probably want, for example, to exclude most if not all of the files in the PUBLIC directory.

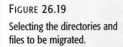

FIGURE 26.19

Selecting the directories and files to be migrated.

The **Transfer** menu in the Files To Transfer dialog box contains two options, **Hidden Files** and **System Files**, that determine whether these files will be transferred.

Setting Migration Logging Options

You can determine the amount of logging that will take place during migration by choosing the **Logging** button in the Migration Tool main window. Figure 26.20 shows logging options.

FIGURE 26.20

Specifying the migration logging options.

The **View Log Files** button is only active if log files have been created.

Running a Trial Migration

Before you perform an actual migration, run a trial by clicking the **Trial Migration** button in the Migration Tool main window. Your migration settings will be tested without actually migrating anything.

After the trial migration is completed, a summary box reports the results, which will resemble those shown in Figure 26.21.

FIGURE 26.21
Summary statistics for a trial migration.

A trial migration creates log files just as would be created by an actual migration. Three log files are created:

- `LOGFILE.LOG` contains information about users, groups, and files.

- `SUMMARY.LOG` contains an overview of the migration process.

- `ERROR.LOG` reports any migration errors that were encountered.

You can view these logs by clicking the **View Log Files** button in the Transfer Completed box. The LogView utility, shown in Figure 26.22, includes windows for the three migration logs. You can select logs for review as required.

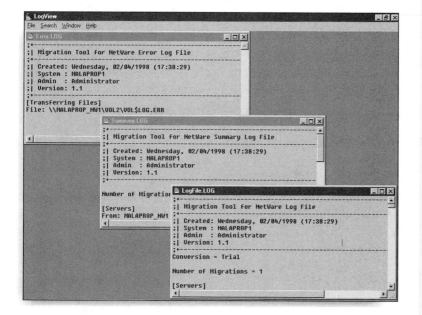

FIGURE 26.22
Viewing the trial migration logs.

Be especially sure that the ERROR.LOG file does not report critical errors, such as the following:

- User and group names that did not transfer
- Network errors, such as a failure to access the source server
- System errors, such as insufficient space for transferred files on the destination drives

The following listing contains part of the LOGFILE.LOG file that is created. This file was created with the **Verbose User/Group Logging** option and contains a detailed record of the migration.

```
;+-----------------------------------------------------------------
➡----------------+
;¦ Migration Tool for NetWare Log File
➡¦
;+-----------------------------------------------------------------
----------------+
;¦ Created: Wednesday, 02/04/1998 (17:38:29)
➡¦
;¦ System : MALAPROP1
➡¦
;¦ Admin   : Administrator
➡¦
;¦ Version: 1.1
➡¦
;+-----------------------------------------------------------------
➡----------------+
Conversion = Trial

Number of Migrations = 1

[Servers]
    From: MALAPROP_NW1    To: MALAPROP1


;+-----------------------------------------------------------------
➡----------------+
;¦ Server Information
➡¦
;+-----------------------------------------------------------------
➡----------------+

[MALAPROP1]
    Windows NT(R) Server
```

```
    Version: 4.0

    [Drives]
        C: [NTFS]
            Free Space: 722,910,720
        E: [CDFS]
            Free Space: 0

    [Shares]
        NETLOGON
            Path: C:\WINNT\system32\Repl\Import\Scripts
        Apps
            Path: C:\Applications
        Reports
            Path: C:\Weekly Reports
        nwapps
            Path: Z:\
        nwpublic
            Path: Y:\
        Home
            Path: C:\Home

[MALAPROP_NW1]
    NetWare(R) Server
    Version: 4.11

    [Shares]
        SYS
        VOL1
        VOL2


;+------------------------------------------------------------
➥------------------+
;¦ Setting User Defaults from Supervisor Defaults
➥¦
;+------------------------------------------------------------
➥------------------+
;+------------------------------------------------------------
➥------------------+
;¦ From: MALAPROP_NW1
➥¦
;¦ To:   MALAPROP1
➥¦
```

```
;+----------------------------------------------------------
➡-----------------+
;¦ Converted: Wednesday, 02/04/1998 (17:38:29)
➡¦
;+----------------------------------------------------------
➡-----------------+
```

[Transfer Options]
    Convert Users and Groups: Yes

    User Transfer Options:
        Use mapping file: No
        Passwords: 2 - Password is username
            User must change password: Yes
        Duplicate Names: Log Error

        Duplicate Groups: Pre-pend constant: nw

        Use supervisor defaults: No
        Add Supervisors to the Administrators Group: No

    [File Options]
        Convert Files: Yes

    [New Shares]
        SYS
            Path: C:\SYS
        VOL1
            Path: C:\VOL1
        VOL2
            Path: C:\VOL2

    [Users]
        Number of Users = 2

        Users to Transfer
        +---+
         GATEWAY
         ISAAC

```
    [GATEWAY]
➡(Added)
    Original Account Info:
        Name:
        Account disabled: No
        Account expires: (Never)
        Password expires: (Never)
        Grace Logins: (Unlimited)
        Initial Grace Logins: (Unlimited)
        Minimum Password Length: 0
        # days to Password Expiration: (Never)
        Maximum Number of Connections: (Unlimited)
        Restrictions:
            Anyone who knows password can change it
            Unique passwords required: No
        Number of login failures: 0
        Max Disk Blocks: (Unlimited)


    Login Times:
        Midnight                  AM                    Noon
➡PM
            12 1  2  3  4  5  6  7  8  9  10 11 12 1  2  3  4
➡5   6   7   8   9   10 11
            +------------------------------------------------------
➡------------------+
        Sun **  **  **  **  **  **  **  **  **  **  **  **  **  **  **  **  **
➡** ** ** ** ** ** **
        Mon **  **  **  **  **  **  **  **  **  **  **  **  **  **  **  **  **
➡** ** ** ** ** ** **
        Tue **  **  **  **  **  **  **  **  **  **  **  **  **  **  **  **  **
➡** ** ** ** ** ** **
        Wed **  **  **  **  **  **  **  **  **  **  **  **  **  **  **  **  **
➡** ** ** ** ** ** **
        Thu **  **  **  **  **  **  **  **  **  **  **  **  **  **  **  **  **
➡** ** ** ** ** ** **
        Fri **  **  **  **  **  **  **  **  **  **  **  **  **  **  **  **  **
➡** ** ** ** ** ** **
        Sat **  **  **  **  **  **  **  **  **  **  **  **  **  **  **  **  **
➡** ** ** ** ** ** **


    New Account Info:
        Name:
```

```
Password: GATEWAY
Privilege: User
Home Dir:
Comment:
Flags:
    Execute login script: Yes
    Account disabled: No
    Deleting prohibited: No
    Home dir required: No
    Password required: Yes
    User can change password: Yes
Script path:
Full Name:
Logon Server:


Logon Hours:
    Midnight                    AM                    Noon
➡PM

        12 1  2  3  4  5  6  7  8  9  10 11 12 1  2  3  4
➡5  6  7  8  9  10 11

    +---------------------------------------------------
➡-------------------+

Sun ** ** ** ** ** ** ** ** ** ** ** ** ** ** ** ** **
➡** ** ** ** ** ** **

Mon ** ** ** ** ** ** ** ** ** ** ** ** ** ** ** ** **
➡** ** ** ** ** ** **

Tue ** ** ** ** ** ** ** ** ** ** ** ** ** ** ** ** **
➡** ** ** ** ** ** **

Wed ** ** ** ** ** ** ** ** ** ** ** ** ** ** ** ** **
➡** ** ** ** ** ** **

Thu ** ** ** ** ** ** ** ** ** ** ** ** ** ** ** ** **
➡** ** ** ** ** ** **

Fri ** ** ** ** ** ** ** ** ** ** ** ** ** ** ** ** **
➡** ** ** ** ** ** **

Sat ** ** ** ** ** ** ** ** ** ** ** ** ** ** ** ** **
➡** ** ** ** ** ** **



[ISAAC]
➡(Added)
    Original Account Info:
        Name:
```

```
    Account disabled: No
    Account expires: (Never)
    Password expires: (Never)
    Grace Logins: (Unlimited)
    Initial Grace Logins: (Unlimited)
    Minimum Password Length: 0
    # days to Password Expiration: (Never)
    Maximum Number of Connections: (Unlimited)
    Restrictions:
        Anyone who knows password can change it
        Unique passwords required: No
    Number of login failures: 0
    Max Disk Blocks: (Unlimited)


  Login Times:
   Midnight                  AM                    Noon
➥PM
            12 1  2  3  4  5  6  7  8  9  10 11 12 1  2  3  4
➥5  6  7  8  9  10 11

        +----------------------------------------------------
➥--------------------+
   Sun ** ** ** ** ** ** ** ** ** ** ** ** ** ** ** ** ** **
➥** ** ** ** ** ** **
   Mon ** ** ** ** ** ** ** ** ** ** ** ** ** ** ** ** ** **
➥** ** ** ** ** ** **
   Tue ** ** ** ** ** ** ** ** ** ** ** ** ** ** ** ** ** **
➥** ** ** ** ** ** **
   Wed ** ** ** ** ** ** ** ** ** ** ** ** ** ** ** ** ** **
➥** ** ** ** ** ** **
   Thu ** ** ** ** ** ** ** ** ** ** ** ** ** ** ** ** ** **
➥** ** ** ** ** ** **
   Fri ** ** ** ** ** ** ** ** ** ** ** ** ** ** ** ** ** **
➥** ** ** ** ** ** **
   Sat ** ** ** ** ** ** ** ** ** ** ** ** ** ** ** ** ** **
➥** ** ** ** ** ** **


  New Account Info:
    Name:
    Password: ISAAC
    Privilege: User
    Home Dir:
    Comment:
    Flags:
```

```
                    Execute login script: Yes
                    Account disabled: No
                    Deleting prohibited: No
                    Home dir required: No
                    Password required: Yes
                    User can change password: Yes
            Script path:
            Full Name:
            Logon Server:

       Logon Hours:
          Midnight                    AM                    Noon
   ➥PM
                12 1  2  3  4  5  6  7  8  9  10 11 12 1  2  3  4
   ➥5  6  7  8  9  10 11

             +------------------------------------------------------
   ➥-----------------+
          Sun ** ** ** ** ** ** ** ** ** ** ** ** ** ** ** ** **
   ➥** ** ** ** ** ** **

          Mon ** ** ** ** ** ** ** ** ** ** ** ** ** ** ** ** **
   ➥** ** ** ** ** ** **

          Tue ** ** ** ** ** ** ** ** ** ** ** ** ** ** ** ** **
   ➥** ** ** ** ** ** **

          Wed ** ** ** ** ** ** ** ** ** ** ** ** ** ** ** ** **
   ➥** ** ** ** ** ** **

          Thu ** ** ** ** ** ** ** ** ** ** ** ** ** ** ** ** **
   ➥** ** ** ** ** ** **

          Fri ** ** ** ** ** ** ** ** ** ** ** ** ** ** ** ** **
   ➥** ** ** ** ** ** **

          Sat ** ** ** ** ** ** ** ** ** ** ** ** ** ** ** ** **
   ➥** ** ** ** ** ** **


   [Groups]
      Number Groups = 2
      NTGATEWAY
   (Added)
        WIDGETS
   (Added)

        [NTGATEWAY]
          GATEWAY
```

```
    [WIDGETS]
        ISAAC


[Security Equivalences]
    [GATEWAY]
        NTGATEWAY

    [ISAAC]
        WIDGETS


[Print Operators]
        Domain Admins
[Files]

    Copying Files From Volume: SYS
    To Share: SYS
        [Files]
        [Files]
        [Files]
        [Files]
        [Files]
        [Files]
        [Files]
        [Files]
        [Files]


    Copying Files From Volume: VOL1
    To Share: VOL1
        [Files]


    Copying Files From Volume: VOL2
    To Share: VOL2
        [Files]



Conversion Finished: Wednesday, 02/04/1998 (17:38:33)
```

Completing the Migration

When the trial migration runs satisfactorily, use the **Start Migration** button in the Migration Tool main window to start the actual migration.

Welcome to NT Enlightenment

You have now completed the 26 steps to Windows NT Server enlightenment and are now entitled to wear the green T-shirt of the NT initiate. It has been a pleasure and a privilege to share with you the experience of learning Windows NT Server administration, and I wish you all success for the future. There's a lot more about NT Server; but if you have absorbed the material in this book, you will be well on your way to mastery of Windows NT Server.

Appendixes

Tips on the Windows NT User Interface

If you have significant experience with the Windows 95 interface, you probably don't need this appendix. If you are new to the interface, however, the tips offered here will shorten your learning curve.

Running Commands from the Run Prompt

The **Run** prompt enables you to execute a single typed command. Just click **Start** and then click **Run** in the **Start** menu to open the Run dialog box shown in Figure A.1. Enter a command in the **Open** field and click **OK** or press Enter to execute the command. The Run dialog box remembers the last command you entered.

FIGURE A.1

The Run dialog box.

Running Commands from a Command Prompt

A command prompt is a dialog box where you can interact with NT using a command-line interface. Some commands must be executed in a command prompt so that you can see the results. To open a command prompt, click **Start** to open the **Start** menu. Then click **Program** and **Command Prompt** in the **Start** menu. Figure A.2 shows a command prompt dialog box.

FIGURE A.2

A command prompt dialog box.

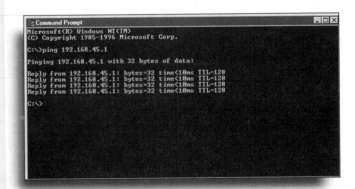

Copying Objects

You can use a variety of methods to copy files or folders in Windows NT Explorer, My Computer, or Network Neighborhood.

The easiest method is drag and drop. Just click the mouse on the item(s) to be copied or moved. Hold down the mouse button, and drag the item(s) to the new location. For this method to work, both the source and destination locations must be visible on the desktop, and you may need to open multiple windows in the Windows NT Explorer, My Computer, or Network Neighborhood.

When you drag items with the mouse, be aware of the following:

- Dragging a directory or files to a different disk drive makes a copy of the items on the new drive. If you want to move an item(s) to a new drive, removing the item(s) from the original drive, hold the Shift key while dragging and dropping.
- Dragging a directory or files to a location on the same drive moves them. The directories and files are removed from the old location and stored in the new location.
- To copy files to a new location on the same drive, you must hold down the Ctrl key as you drag the files.

When you drag an executable file (EXE or COM), three results are possible:

- If the destination folder is on the same disk as the source folder, the executable file remains in the original location and a shortcut icon is created in the destination.
- If the destination folder is on a different disk than the source folder, the executable file is moved to the destination folder.
- If you hold down Ctrl+Shift while dragging, a shortcut is created in the destination folder.
- If you hold down the Ctrl key while dragging, a copy of the file is placed in the destination and the original file remains in the source location.
- If you hold down the Shift key while dragging, the file is always moved to the new location.

You can also use cut-and-paste techniques:

- To cut an item or items, select the items and choose **Cut** in the **Edit** menu. Cutting removes the original items, placing a copy in the Clipboard.
- To copy an item or items, select the items and choose **Copy** in the **Edit** menu. Copying places a copy in the Clipboard, leaving the original items intact.

- To paste the contents of the Clipboard, select the destination folder and choose **Paste** in the **Edit** menu. The contents of the Clipboard will be placed in the selected folder.

Right-clicking files and folders

If you right-click a file or folder, a context menu is displayed that offers options for manipulating the object.

Moving Objects

You can move most objects just by dragging them to a new folder. When you drag and drop an EXE file to a new location on the same volume, however, you create a shortcut to the EXE file, which remains in its original location.

To move an EXE or COM file using drag and drop, hold down the Shift key while you drag the object. The EXE or COM file will move and no shortcut will be created.

Creating Shortcuts

You will find it handy to add shortcuts to your desktop or to your **Start** menu. To add a shortcut, right-click on the desktop or the destination folder. Choose **New** from the context menu, and then choose **Shortcut**. A wizard takes you through the entire process of creating the shortcut.

SEE ALSO

➤ *Windows NT maintains personal **Start** menu settings for each user that logs on to a computer. Chapter 9, "Advanced Client Features," explains the structure of the **Start** menu folders in the section titled "User Profiles" on page 292.*

Selecting Multiple Objects in a List

Often you will want to select more than one item in a list, such as a list of files in Explorer or a list of users in User Manager for Domains. Here are two useful techniques:

- Select a range of objects by first selecting an object at one end of a range. Then hold down the Shift key as you click the object at the other end of the range. Selecting a range deselects any objects not in the range.

- Select individual objects, holding down the Ctrl key as you click on each one. Previously selected objects will remain selected as you Ctrl+click additional objects. You can use Ctrl+clicking to add objects to a range that was previously selected.

In some utilities, you can drag a selection frame around a block of objects. That works in Explorer, which is more attuned to the newer "Windows 95" interface. But it doesn't work in older tools such as User Manager for Domains, which has essentially the same design it had in Windows NT 3.5x, which was pre-Windows 95.

Tips on Windows NT Explorer

Windows NT Explorer is a versatile tool, and you will probably spend quite a bit of time with it as you manage Windows NT Server. This section covers some basic procedures that will help you get the most out of Explorer.

Browsing the Desktop

Figure A.3 shows the Windows NT Explorer, which is my favorite tool for managing files. In the left-side All Folders pane of Explorer, the desktop is displayed as a large tree which contains both local and network resources. Thus the Explorer provides one-stop shopping for all available resources. Windows NT uses a "folders" metaphor for directories, and directories in the file system are typically referred to as folders when they are displayed graphically.

The right-side Contents pane shows the contents of the folder that is selected in the All Folders pane.

Items displayed in the Explorer are identified by icons. Some of the icons you will encounter are described in this appendix and are labeled in Figure A.3. Many resources can contain other resources. A hard drive can contain folders, for example. By default, the contents of many resources are not expanded in All

Explorer vs. My Computer

You can obtain all the results described in this section by using the My Computer tool as well. However, I'm most comfortable with the tree-oriented approach of Windows NT Explorer as opposed to the many windows that must often be navigated in My Computer. Try working with both tools and choose the one that fits your style.

Folders. A resource that is not expanded is tagged with a plus sign (+). A resource that has been expanded is tagged with a minus sign (–). Click a resource to expand it and display its contents.

FIGURE A.3

Windows NT Explorer.

SEE ALSO

➤ *See the section titled "Selecting Multiple Objects in a List" on page 786 for tips on selecting files and directories.*

Creating Folders

To create a folder, follow these steps:

Creating a folder

1. In the All Folders pane, select the parent directory that will contain the new directory.

2. Right-click in the Contents pane and choose **New** in the **Options** menu. Then choose **Folder** in the context menu. A new folder will be added to the Contents pane. It will be named **New Folder**, and the name will be selected for editing.

3. Edit the name of the folder and press Enter.

Deleting Directories and Files

To delete directories or files, select the items and then press the Delete key or choose **Delete** in the **File** menu.

Opening Additional File Management Windows

You will often find it handy to have two or more folders open. If you are doing a drag and drop, for example, the source and destination folders must be visible on the desktop. You can open any combination of the following:

- Multiple copies of Explorer
- Windows opened in My Computer
- Windows opened in Network Neighborhood

Just drag and drop between any two visible locations.

Customizing the View

You might want to customize the manner in which Explorer displays directories and files. The **View** menu supplies a number of options that enable you to tailor your display.

Check the **Toolbar** option to display an icon bar at the top of the Explorer window. By default, the toolbar is disabled, but it was enabled when Figure A.4 was prepared.

Check the **Status Bar** option to display a status bar at the bottom of the display. The status bar describes the current action when you are accessing a menu. At other times, it displays information about the objects selected in the All Folders pane. By default, the status bar is enabled.

Three commands specify whether Explorer should display icons or a list in the Contents pane. **List**, the default option, displays a vertical listing. If you prefer another format, choose **Large Icons** or **Small Icons**. If you have specified an icon display, the **Line up Icons** command is active and can be used to clean up the arrangement of the icons in the Contents pane.

The Recycle Bin

When you delete items from the Network Neighborhood or the Windows NT Explorer, they are not deleted; they are moved to the Recycle Bin, which has an icon on the desktop. You can recover items from the Recycle Bin until it has been emptied.

To empty the Recycle Bin, right-click the Recycle Bin icon on the desktop. Then choose **Empty Recycle Bin** from the context menu.

FIGURE A.4

Windows NT Explorer with details enabled.

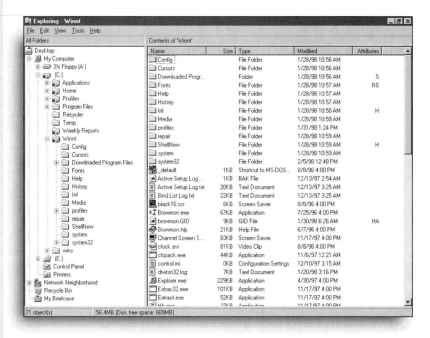

By default, only folder and file names are listed in the Contents pane. If you want to see more information, check **Details** in the **View** menu. Figure A.4 illustrates a detailed display. You can change the widths of the columns in the Contents pane by dragging the dividers between the column headers. In the figure, the divider between the All Folders and the Utilities panes was dragged to permit more space for the detailed display.

The **Arrange Icons** option opens a submenu where commands determine whether files are sorted by name, type, size, or date. An **Auto Arrange** option is available only when large or small icons are displayed. Choose this option if you want Explorer to clean up the icons arrangement as changes are made.

Windows NT Explorer will update its display to reflect changes made locally, but it does not check the network to determine whether changes have been made elsewhere. If you want to bring the contents of the Explorer displays up to date, click **Refresh** or press F5.

The final command in the **View** menu is **Options**, which is important enough to deserve a section of its own.

Selecting Explorer Options

The **Options** command in the **View** menu produces the
Options utility shown in Figure A.5. The Options dialog box has
two functions: determining which files will be excluded from the
Explorer lists, and registering file types to associate them with
applications.

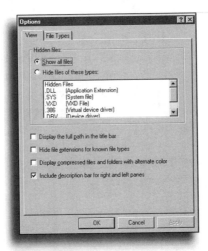

FIGURE A.5

Configuring the File view in
Explorer Options.

The following options are available in the **View** tab:

- **Show all files.** Select this option if all files should be listed
  in Explorer, including system files.

- **Hide files of these types.** Select this option to exclude system files from the Explorer display. The types of excluded
  files are listed in the scroll box. This is the default value.

- **Display the full path in the title bar.** Check this option to
  display the full path of the selected resource in the Explorer
  title bar. By default, this option is not checked.

- **Hide the extensions for known file types.** If you have
  added an extension to the list of known file types, check this
  option to prevent Explorer from displaying the extension in
  listings. Extensions are so important in the Windows environment that you will find it difficult to work when they are
  not shown. In most cases, you will want to remove the check
  from this option.

- **Display compressed files and folders with alternate color.** If you want to display compressed folders and files in a distinctive color, check this option.

- **Include description bar for right and left panes.** This option determines whether the panes will be labeled with the All Folders and Contents legends. Remove the check mark to permit a bit more room for data display.

Figure A.6 shows the **File Types** tab. Using this tab, you can associate filename extensions with particular applications. Doing so informs Windows NT to run the associated application whenever you open the data file. If files with the extension DOC are associated with Microsoft Word for Windows, for example, the Word application is launched whenever you open a file with a DOC extension.

FIGURE A.6

Examining file type registrations.

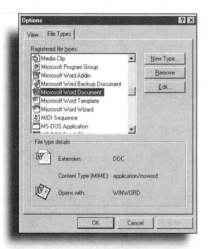

Figure A.6 shows an association between the DOC filename extension and the Microsoft Word for Windows application. From this display, you can examine associations in the **Registered file types** list. You can also remove an association by selecting it and clicking **Remove**.

Although it is possible to add your own file-type registrations, the details are beyond the scope of this book, often requiring a knowledge of DDE. Typically, when Windows applications are installed, the related file-type registrations are established for you.

Managing Directory and File Properties and Attributes

Files and directories can also be assigned several attributes that determine actions that can be performed with them. To display the properties for a folder or a file, follow these steps:

Managing file and folder properties

1. Right-click on the folder or file and choose the **Properties** command from the **Options** menu.

2. Select the **General** tab. Figure A.7 shows the **General** tab for a folder.

3. Check the attributes you want to assign to the folder or file. The attributes are described following this procedure.

4. Click **OK**.

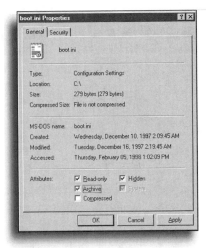

The attributes are as follows:

- **Archive.** Assigned by the operating system to indicate that a file has been modified since it was backed up. Backup software usually clears the archive attribute. The Archive attribute makes it possible to identify modified files when performing incremental backups.

- **Compressed.** Identifies folders and files that have been or should be compressed. This option is available only on NTFS partitions.

- **Hidden.** Files and directories do not usually appear in directory lists. You can direct Explorer to display hidden files by choosing the **Options** command in the **View** menu and checking the **Show all files** box.

- **Read-Only.** Files and directories cannot be erased or modified.

- **System.** Files usually are given this attribute by the operating system or by the OS Setup program. This attribute rarely is modified by administrators or users. System files and directories behave as if they have both the Read-Only and Hidden attributes. You can display the attributes in Explorer listings by using the technique described for hidden files.

Formatting and Copying Floppy Disks

You can format and copy disks from Explorer. To format or copy a disk, follow these steps:

Formatting and copying disks

1. If necessary, insert the disk to be formatted.

2. You cannot format the selected drive. If the floppy drive is selected, select another drive.

3. Right-click the disk icon in the All Folders pane.

4. To format a disk, choose the **Format** command in the **Options** menu and follow the prompts.

5. To copy a disk, choose the **Copy Disk** command in the **Options** menu and follow the prompts.

Searching for Files

Servers typically have many files in large directories on very large drives. If you had to remember where every file was

---

The Compressed attribute

Assign the Compressed attribute to directories or files that you want Windows NT to compress. Compression takes place in the background and can dramatically reduce the space required to store files. Some performance penalty attaches because compressed files must be decompressed before use; however, the cost is reasonable in most cases, considering the storage savings that result. Do not, however, compress files that are used frequently, such as large data files that many users share. Compression/ decompression will reduce file access performance, and, because the file will spend most of the time in a decompressed state, nothing of real benefit is gained.

located, you would be in trouble. Fortunately, Windows NT Explorer provides a search option. To search for a file, follow these steps:

Searching for a file

1. Right-click on the object in the All Folders pane where you would like to begin the search. The search will proceed down the tree from this point.

2. Choose the **Find** command in the **Options** menu to open the Find: All Files window shown in Figure A.8.

You cannot format the system partitions (usually C:) from Explorer.

FIGURE A.8
Searching for a file.

3. Select the **Name & Location** tab.

4. In the **Named** field, enter a filename, which can include the ? and * wildcards. You can pull down a list of typical file name search targets.

5. You can change the starting point for the search by pulling down the **Look in** field to select another disk object. If desired, choose **Browse** to browse for a particular directory.

6. Select the **Date Modified** tab, shown in Figure A.9.

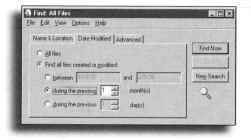

FIGURE A.9
Specifying a data parameter for a file search.

7. Select **All files** to search all files, regardless of their date stamps.

8. Select **Find all files created or modified** to search for files with specific date stamps. Select one of the available date criteria and enter the required parameters.

9. Select the **Advanced** tab, shown in Figure A.10, if it is necessary to further narrow the search.

FIGURE A.10

Specifying advanced parameters for a file search.

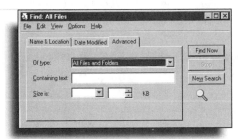

10. To narrow the search to a particular file type, pull down the **Of type** field and select a file type from the list. These file types reflect the file type registrations that have been established on this computer.

11. To search for a specific text string in the file contents, enter the text in the **Containing text** field.

12. To search for files in a particular size range, select **At least** or **At most** in the **Size is** field. Then specify a file size in the **KB** field.

13. Choose **Find Now** to initiate the search.

When the search is complete, Explorer displays a list of files that meet your specifications. You can perform any operation on files in this list that you could perform in the Contents pane of Windows NT Explorer.

Running Applications from Windows NT Explorer

You can start applications directly from Explorer. An application file is any file with an extension of EXE, COM, BAT, or PIF. (PIF files are Program Information Files that can be used to configure the operating environment for an EXE or COM file. Running a PIF file automatically executes the program file specified in the PIF file.) Several techniques can be used to run an application from Explorer:

- Double-click on the icon for the application file.

- Right-click on the icon and choose **Open** from the context menu.

- Drag a data file icon to the icon for the appropriate application file. This approach works only if both icons are visible and is difficult to perform in Windows NT Explorer when the file and application are in different folders. You may need to open a second copy of Explorer to have both file icons visible.

- Double-click on a data file that has been registered for a particular application, as described earlier in this appendix.

Windows NT Terms

%SystemRoot% A universal reference to the directory in which the Windows NT system files are installed. Typically, %SystemRoot% is C:\Winnt. If multiple copies of Windows NT are installed in a multiboot system, each copy will have its own %SystemRoot% directory.

archive attribute A file attribute that is set when the file has been modified since it was last backed up.

archive bit *See* archive attribute.

authentication The process of verifying a user's identity on a network.

authoritative When a DNS name server supports the name database for a domain, it is said to be authoritative for that domain.

backup browser A computer that stores a copy of the master browser database. Browse clients can browse the domain or workgroup by querying the backup browser for the browse database.

binding A connective relationship between network adapters, drivers, and protocols in a computer's network communication configuration.

browse client A computer that doesn't store a copy of the domain or workgroup database and must browse the network by querying the browse database on a backup or master browser.

client A computer that accesses resources that are shared on a network. Or, the software component of a computer that lets the computer access resources shared on a network.

default router When a host needs to transmit a packet to a destination not on the local network, it sends the packet to a default router, which is then responsible for routing the packet to its destination network.

disk drives, duplexing A configuration of mirrored disk drives in which each disk drive is serviced by a separate drive adapter. This arrangement lets one drive of the pair continue functioning if there is a failure in a disk drive adapter.

disk drives, mirroring A configuration of two disk drives in which both drives store the same data. A mirrored disk drive set can continue to function when one of the disk drives malfunctions.

disk drives, stripe set A configuration of three or more disk drives in which data is written in blocks sequentially to each drive. Stripe sets have better storage and retrieval times than single hard disks with comparable specifications but also are more subject to hardware failure.

disk drives, stripe set with parity A stripe set where one record in each set contains parity data. The parity data can be used to recover data if any one drive in the stripe set fails. A stripe set with parity can continue to function despite the failure of a single disk drive.

DNS *See* Domain Name Service.

domain A container in the DNS name hierarchy.

domain master browser A browser on Microsoft TCP/IP networks that collects service announcements from all servers in a domain and creates a master browser database for the domain. Master browsers on other subnets can obtain the domain master browser database for use by browse clients on the local subnets.

Domain Name Service (DNS) A database service used to resolve names on TCP/IP networks.

duplexing *See* disk drives, duplexing.

extended partition A partition that can be configured with one or more logical drives. MS-DOS supports extended partitions as the means of configuring more than one volume on a hard disk.

FQDN *See* fully qualified domain name.

frame One term for a basic unit of network communication, consisting of a message and the information required for delivery. Also referred to as a packet.

fully qualified domain name (FQDN) The complete DNS name of a host, including the host name and all domains that connect the host to the root domain. Typically expressed without a trailing period, with the root domain assumed.

fully qualified name The name of a container or data object in a hierarchy, consisting of the object's name and the names of all containers that connect the object to the root container.

hierarchy A database structure based on the principle of categories and subcategories, typically represented in the form of an inverted tree. Each hierarchy has exactly one master category, typically called the root, and all other categories are subcategories of the root category. Categories can contain subcategories as well as data.

hive Registry data is stored in six or more sets of files called hives. Each hive consists of two files: a data file and a log file.

hop A common metric used with routing protocols, in which one hop is counted for each network a message traverses on a route.

host A device that is attached to a TCP/IP network.

host A static database file used to resolve names on TCP/IP networks.

hostid The portion of an IP address that uniquely identifies a host on its local TCP/IP network.

internal network number On IPX networks, each server must have an internal network number, an eight-digit hexadecimal number used to deliver data to the correct process within the server.

Internet The worldwide network that has evolved out of the ARPANET developed by the United States Department of Defense.

Internet Service Provider A vendor that provides network connectivity to the Internet as well as support services such as name, news, and electronic mail.

internetwork An extended network consisting of discrete networks that communicate through routers. A "network of networks." Also called an internet.

InterNIC Internet Network Information Center. The organization that has overall responsibility for assigning Internet domain names and IP addresses.

IP address A 32-bit address that uniquely identifies a host on a TCP/IP network.

IP master A DNS server that is the source of the zone transfer that transfers records to a secondary DNS server.

ISP *See* Internet Service Provider.

lmhosts A static database file used to resolve names on Microsoft TCP/IP networks.

logical drive A portion of an extended partition that can be formatted as a volume.

master browser A computer that collects service announcements from servers and constructs a browse list. Backup browsers periodically contact the master browser to obtain an updated copy of the master browser database.

medium The vehicle that carries data between a server and a client. Network media include copper cable, optical fiber, microwaves, and light pulses.

metric With routing protocols, a number that assigns a preference to a route. The route with the lowest metric is the preferred route.

mirroring *See* disk drives, mirroring.

name resolution The process of determining the network address associated with a computer name.

netid The portion of an IP address that identifies the network to which a host is attached.

network number On IPX networks, each network is identified by an eight-digit hexadecimal number that uniquely identifies the computer on an internetwork.

node On networks, a device that communicates on the network and is identified by a unique address. In hierarchies, a container that contains other containers and data.

null modem A cable that lets computers communicate through serial ports by simulating a modem connection.

octet Commonly used to refer to groups of eight bits in network addresses, such as IP addresses. A 32-bit IP address consists of four octets.

paging The process of swapping data between RAM and disk-based virtual memory.

paging file A temporary file used to support virtual memory.

partition A physical subdivision of a disk drive that can be formatted with a file system.

port, hardware A hardware component that lets a computer communicate with other devices. Examples are printer ports, serial ports, and network ports.

port, TCP A software address that lets the TCP/IP protocols deliver messages to the correct process on a computer. Each process running on a TCP/IP computer must be associated with a unique combination of an IP address and a port number. The combination of an IP address and a port number is referred to as a socket.

primary partition A partition that can be used to boot an operating system. NT can also use primary partitions for file storage. It permits up to four primary partitions per hard disk. MS-DOS permits one primary partition per hard disk.

primary zone A DNS zone that contains the master copies of resource records for a domain.

print server A computer configured to share its printer through the network. Windows NT computers become print servers when their printers are shared.

profile *See* user profile.

profile, local A user profile stored on the user's workstation.

profile, locally cached *See* profile, local.

profile, mandatory A user profile that can be accessed from any workstation on a network. Users can't save changes made to a mandatory profile.

profile, roaming A personal user profile that can be accessed from any workstation on a network. Users can change settings in roaming profiles.

protocol A standard set of rules for communicating between computers.

Registry key A container for data in the Registry data hierarchy.

resource record A data record in a DNS zone. For example, an address resource record is the data record that describes the address-to-name relationship for a host. Many types of resource records are available.

root In a hierarchy, the container that holds all other containers.

routing table Each TCP/IP host maintains a routing table that describes routing decisions the host can make. Minimum entries in the routing table include routes to each local network and a default route.

SAM *See* Security Access Manager.

secondary zone A DNS zone that obtains copies of the resource records for a domain through a zone transfer from a primary zone.

Security Access Manager (SAM) The component of Windows NT that manages the security database and all security functions.

Security ID (SID) An alphanumeric code used internally by Windows NT to identify computers, users, and other objects described in the SAM database.

server A computer that shares resources on a network.

SID *See* Security ID (SID).

site On an Internet server such as a World Wide Web server, a site is a logical server. Each site must be defined by a unique combination of properties. For example, each Web site running on a given computer must be defined by a unique combination of an IP address and a TCP port.

socket The unique combination of an IP address and a TCP port number that identifies a particular process running on a particular TCP/IP computer.

spanning The practice of continuing backup jobs on additional tapes when the amount of data to be archived exceeds the capacity of a single tape.

static route An item in a routing table that is entered manually and that doesn't change based on information received from a routing protocol.

stripe set *See* disk drives, stripe set.

stripe set with parity *See* disk drives, stripe set with parity.

subnet A subdivision of a TCP/IP internetwork that communicates with other subnets through routers.

TCP port *See* port, TCP.

trusted domain A domain that allows another domain to share its security database.

trusting domain A domain that assigns user permissions based on user account and group memberships in another domain that it trusts.

twisted pair Cable in which pairs of wires are twisted to reduce sensitivity to electronic noise.

user profile A database that stores a user's personal computer settings so that the settings are available each time the user logs on.

virtual memory A technique for simulating RAM by swapping memory contents between RAM and disk-based files.

volume A portion of one or more disk drives that can be formatted as a single storage unit. Volumes are usually identified by a drive letter from A: through Z:.

Web server On IIS, a single computer can run one instance of the World Wide Web Server service and functions as one Web server.

Web site A Web server can support multiple Web sites. Each Web site must be identified by a unique combination of an IP address and port number.

zone A domain for which a Microsoft DNS server is authoritative.

zone transfer The process of copying DNS resource records from a primary zone to a secondary zone.

Configuring Servers and Clients

Every LAN administrator needs to know something about the hardware on his or her LAN. Emergencies always happen when your contract support people are unavailable (in fact, they write into their contracts that support can be called only when support is unavailable). Hardware vendors will attempt to sell you more hardware than you need, or they will push their favorite products rather than the products you really need. Ignorance is not bliss as far as network hardware is concerned.

Parameters Used to Configure Microcomputers

As you add devices to microcomputers, you need to ensure that they don't step on each other's toes. Each device needs to obtain access to certain system resources to get attention or exchange data. To have devices cooperate without conflicting, you need to attend to four system settings:

- Interrupts
- I/O addresses
- Shared memory addresses
- DMA channels

Interrupts

An interrupt is often referred to as an IRQ, which stands for interrupt request. Each device that might need attention is assigned an interrupt. When it wants to signal the CPU, the device *asserts* the interrupt. This interrupt signals the CPU to stop what it's doing and come to the aid of the device.

If two devices are configured with the same interrupt, considerable confusion can arise. An important step in system configuration is ensuring that each device in the system has a unique interrupt. Unfortunately, this can be more difficult than you might think.

All Intel PCs now being manufactured inherit their basic interrupt mechanisms from the 16-bit ISA bus of the 1985 IBM AT. Table C.1 lists the interrupts as defined by the AT architecture (interrupts 0 and 1 aren't listed because they are reserved for the system).

TABLE C.1 Interrupts used in IBM PC compatibles

IRQ	Use
2	Cascade to IRQ 9
3	COM2 and COM4
4	COM1 and COM3
5	LPT2
6	Floppy disk controller
7	LPT1
8	Real-time clock
9	Cascade from IRQ2
10	Available
11	Available
12	PS/2 and Inport mice (if present)
13	Math coprocessor
14	Hard disk controller
15	Available

Lower-numbered interrupts have higher priorities. That's why interrupts 0 and 1 are reserved for the system clock and keyboard. You can free up some of the low interrupts by disabling I/O ports. If your system doesn't support a directly attached printer, disable the LPT ports. Some ports are deactivated by removing jumpers on I/O cards. Newer systems usually let you disable ports from the BIOS setup program.

Interrupts 2 and 9 are special interrupts. When designing the model AT computer, IBM chose to control a second interrupt controller by connecting IRQ 2 of the first controller to IRQ 9 of the new controller. IRQ 2 is called a *cascade interrupt* because it lets interrupts 8 through 15 cascade down through IRQ 2 to get system attention.

When interrupts 8 through 15 fire, IRQ 9 is asserted, which cascades to IRQ 2. When the system is interrupted by IRQ 2, it knows that the real interrupt comes from the second 8259. It then checks to determine which of the interrupts 8 through 15 was actually asserted.

Because of this cascade mechanism, some operating systems, such as MS-DOS, have trouble with interrupts 2 and 9. In most cases, Windows NT can handle devices using IRQ 9, but if you can avoid it, don't configure option cards for these interrupts. They might work, but you might get a flaky system if you try.

Because IRQ 2 has a high system priority, interrupts 8 through 15 inherit that priority. If possible, put your most critical option cards, such as NICs, in these interrupts. SCSI adapters generally use IRQs 10 or 11.

Although Intel-based computers equipped with the PCI bus are still limited to 15 interrupts, PCI devices are often able to share interrupts without conflict.

I/O Addresses

After an expansion card has the CPU's attention, it needs to be able to communicate data. This is done by assigning memory blocks that can be used to exchange data. Two types of memory assignments can be made:

■ **I/O addresses or ports**—small addresses that are located in lower system memory

■ **Shared memory addresses** that let expansion cards use larger amounts of system RAM

I/O addresses (also called *ports*) are found in the memory range 100h through 3FFh. Typically, a port will be 8 bytes to 32 bytes. Unfortunately, the documentation for many option cards doesn't tell you how big a port the card requires. In general, assume that an 8-bit card requires 8 bits and that a 16-bit card requires 16 bits. If two cards overlap I/O address ranges, some very strange things can happen, so always suspect I/O address conflicts when two cards have neighboring addresses. Table C.2 lists some common I/O ports.

TABLE C.2 Common I/O port assignments

Base Address	Device	Typical Address Range
200	Game port (joystick)	200 to 20F
260	LPT2	260 to 27F
2E8	COM4	2E8 to 2EF
2F8	COM2	2F8 to 2FF
300	Common factory setting for many network cards	300 to 31F/n
330	Adaptec and other SCSI adapters	330 to 33F/n
360	LPT1	360 to 37F
3CD	EGA video display	3C0 to 3CF
3D0	CGA video display	3D0 to 3DF
3E8	COM3	3E8 to 3EF
3F8	COM1	3F8 to 3FF

Shared memory addresses are found in memory above the DOS 640 KB line. Actually, not much memory is available in that range, as shown in Figure C.1. A0000 to BFFFFh are used by video systems, and F0000 to FFFFFh are used by the system's ROM BIOS.

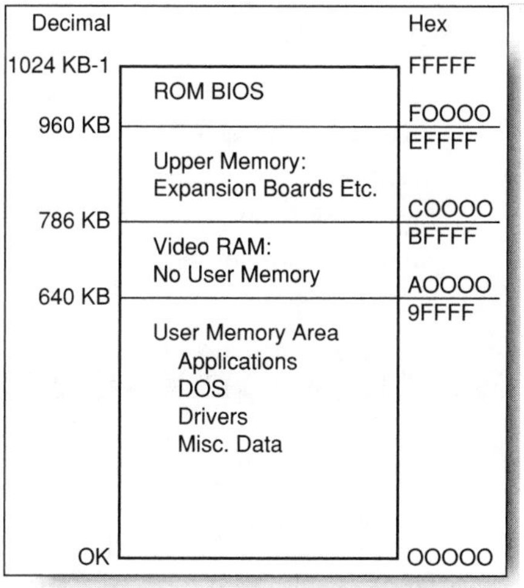

FIGURE C.1
DOS memory usage.

Consequently, shared memory addresses generally need to fit in the range of C0000h through EFFFFh. As with I/O ports, it is essential that shared memory addresses don't overlap. Table C.3 lists some common shared memory addresses.

TABLE C.3 **Common shared memory addresses**

Device	Memory Range
Mono Video	B0000 to B1000
CGA	B8000 to C0000
EGA	A0000 to C0
VGA	A0000 to C4000
BIOS	F0000 to FFFFF

DOS PCs that use expanded memory also require that an area above 640 KB be set aside as a page frame for swapping memory in and out of expanded memory. The location of this memory is declared as a parameter of the EMM386.EXE memory manager. Be sure that this page frame doesn't conflict with memory used by your expansion cards. Windows NT provides automatic emulation of expanded memory as required by applications.

Excluding memory on DOS PCs

You should also exclude expansion card shared memory from the extended memory used by your system. This is achieved by including the X= parameter when EMM386.EXE is run in CONFIG.SYS. Consult a DOS manual for more complete instructions.

DMA Channels

DMA channels let peripherals communicate with memory directly without bothering the CPU. Eight DMA channels are available, numbered 0 through 7. Lower-numbered channels have higher priority. The DMA address 0 is reserved for DRAM memory refresh.

Installing Expansion Cards

Modern PCs generally include many options that were rare not too long ago. Practically every PC manufactured today has a CD-ROM drive and sound card, for example. As a result, interrupts and memory addresses represent some pretty precious real estate in many PCs. When you buy an expansion option, it makes sense to obtain cards that support as many interrupt and address options as possible. Things to look for when buying an expansion card include support for IRQs 8 through 15 (whenever possible) and easy setup procedures.

Configuring Cards with Jumpers and Switches

Many cards still configure with jumpers and switches. Figure C.2 illustrates both options. Setting jumpers and switches is usually the pits. Many vendors don't provide clear instructions, and the pins and switches usually aren't labeled in any sensible way. For example, you might be told to add a jumper to pins 14 and 15 to set a memory address of 360h. So, unless you work with a particular card every day, you need to consult the manual each time you set up a card. Don't lose the manual, or you're sunk.

When you need to disable a jumper setting, don't completely remove the jumper. You might need it later when you reconfigure the card. Instead, place the jumper over one pin of the pair to keep the jumper with the card. Never throw a jumper away! Put it in your junk drawer. You will need it someday. And there are at least two sizes of jumpers, so be alert to the difference, and save some of both sizes.

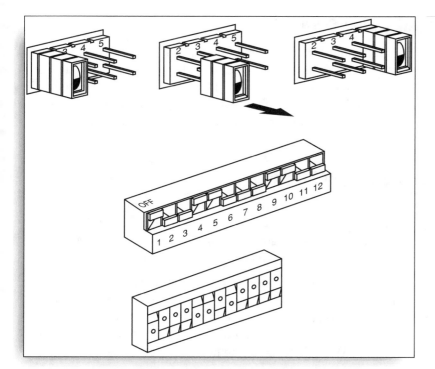

FIGURE C.2

Examples of jumpers and switches for setting expansion options.

Switches are easier to set and can't be lost. They are called DIP switches because they are packaged in *dual-inline pin* assemblies, not because the guy who designed them was a dip.

Before you start reconfiguring a card, write down its settings so that you can restore them easily if things don't work. Much trial and error is involved in configuring a PC, and proper documentation can save you a great deal of hassle.

Software-Configurable Cards

Most cards are available in configurations that have replaced switches and jumpers with nonvolatile memory that is configured with a setup program. Many setup programs can examine systems to determine a configuration that won't conflict with existing options.

Configuring ROM BIOS

Some options are configured from the ROM BIOS. Most new motherboards include many features that used to be located on expansion cards, including COM and LPT ports and disk controllers. In most cases, the ROM BIOS routine has an option for disabling or reconfiguring the settings for some or all of these features.

Configuring PCI Devices

Actually, you can't do much, if anything, to configure a PCI device. PCI was designed as a Plug-and-Play bus, and it's supposed to be self-configuring. In most computers, you take the settings you get when you put a card in a PCI slot.

In most cases, this means that you don't know the hardware configuration for a PCI card until it's installed and running. Then you can look at it to determine its settings. You can use Windows NT Diagnostics, described in Chapter 19, "Setting Up a World Wide Web Server," to determine the hardware settings.

After you know the resources being used by your PCI cards, you can use the remaining available settings to configure your ISA adapters.

Installing Hard Drives

Only IDE and SCSI drives will be considered here. If you have older drives, you probably can't buy replacement controllers or drives. Besides, the performance improvements of IDE and SCSI more than justify the cost of upgrading.

Installation Considerations

This section gives you some general guidelines that will be of interest when you're installing any type of hard drive.

Drive Bays

Desktop PCs are including fewer and fewer drive bays these days. If you will be adding many options to a desktop system, look for a minitower case.

Servers should always have full-tower cases with as many drive bays as possible. Be sure that the case design provides proper ventilation. Large hard drives put out considerable heat, and you want to ensure that they will have good air circulation. It's often best to mount hard drives in individual external drive cabinets. Then each drive has its own power supply and ventilation fan.

Some cases require drive rails in order to mount drives, but the best approach is to select a tower case that doesn't require drive rails. Then you will have more options for where you can install equipment. Drive rails don't really simplify much. You still have to screw something to the drive to hold it in place.

Be sure that your server cabinet provides plenty of ventilation. A second fan is a useful precaution. Also, with Pentium processors, it's a good idea to mount a cooling fan on the processor itself. Such a fan generally is included on better Pentium systems.

Power and Power Connectors

A server generally should be equipped with a power supply that has at least a 300-watt capacity. The power supply should be fitted with a large number of power connectors.

PCs use two power connectors, both of which are shown in Figure C.3. The larger connector is more common, but you will encounter the smaller connector on devices that are designed with a 3½-inch form factor.

IDE Drives

IDE drives couldn't be much easier to install. Most new PC motherboards are equipped with an IDE connector.

If your system includes only one IDE controller, the addresses are preset and standard. The I/O address for the first controller is always 1FE hex, and the interrupt is always 14.

FIGURE C.3
Power connectors used in PCs.

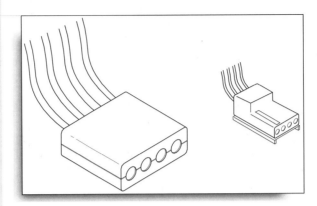

If you need more than two IDE drives, you can include a second IDE controller if one isn't present on your motherboard. IDE controllers are available for ISA, VESA, and PCI slots. The address for the second controller is usually 170 hex. You will need to determine an available interrupt.

You must configure each IDE drive as a master or a slave, usually by setting jumpers. The first drive is always configured as a master and is seen by your system as drive C. If you add a second drive, set its jumpers to the slave setting.

A single ribbon cable with two drive connectors supports both the master and the slave drive. Drives can be connected to the cable in any order. Be sure that line 1 of the ribbon cable attaches to pin 1 of the drive connector. Line 1 is usually identified by a stripe along one edge of the cable.

SCSI Adapters and Drives

You have to work a bit harder to install a SCSI subsystem. Each SCSI subsystem consists of a SCSI adapter (also called a *SCSI host bus adapter*), one or more SCSI devices, and a series of cables that connect the adapter and devices in a daisy chain configuration. There are a fair number of rules, but they are pretty easy to follow:

- SCSI is configured as a bus, and each device on the bus must be assigned a unique address in the range of 0 to 7. (Wide SCSI buses can support addresses ranging from 0 to 15. Consult the documentation for your SCSI adapter.)

- The SCSI adapter will always be assigned address 7, which is the factory default.

- Most SCSI adapters expect device 0 to be the hard drive that boots the system. Adapters also might expect drive 1 to be a hard drive. If this is the case, don't assign address 0 or 1 to other types of devices.

- Lower-numbered SCSI addresses have higher priorities. If your server has hard drives and a CD-ROM, assign the hard drives lower addresses.

- A system can support up to four SCSI adapters. Of course, you must ensure that each adapter is assigned unique settings for interrupts, memory, and so on.

- Most SCSI adapters are equipped with floppy drive connectors. If your floppy drives are attached to other controllers, be sure to disable floppy drive support on the SCSI adapter.

- You add devices to the SCSI bus by daisy-chaining cables from device to device.

- The first and last devices in the SCSI daisy chain must be terminated.

- Devices in the middle of the daisy chain must not be terminated.

- External SCSI devices must be separated by at least .3 meter of cable.

- The total length of the SCSI cable daisy chain can't exceed 6 meters.

- At least one device must supply power to the SCSI bus. In most cases, this will be the SCSI adapter. All devices are protected by diodes, and it doesn't matter if more than one device supplies power to the bus.

SCSI Addressing

SCSI is an attractive technology because one controller can manage seven devices (or more with Wide SCSI). Each device is identified on the SCSI bus by a unique SCSI address. Several precautions were mentioned in the preceding list.

A PC can support four SCSI buses, and devices on separate buses can share the same address.

The addresses of internal devices usually are set with jumpers. Many external devices are equipped with switches that make it easy to set the addresses.

Connecting SCSI Devices

Internal SCSI devices connect to a 50-pin or 68-pin ribbon cable. The cable is simply daisy-chained from one device to the next. Be sure that line 1 of the ribbon cable attaches to pin 1 of the SCSI connector. Line 1 is usually identified by a stripe along one edge of the cable. If you're lucky, when you reverse a cable, the attached device will only complain. If you're unlucky, it will die.

Figure C.4 illustrates three common connectors:

- The top connector is a 25-pin D connector.
- The middle connector resembles a Centronics printer connector but has 50 contacts.
- The bottom connector is a miniaturized connector with 50 pins. This connector is sometimes called a SCSI-2 connector.

FIGURE **C.4**

Connectors used with external SCSI devices.

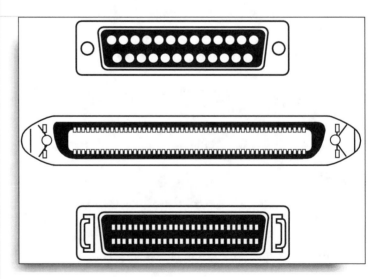

If you're using Wide SCSI-2, you will encounter a connector much like the bottom connector in Figure C.4, but with 68 pins.

External devices are generally equipped with two connectors, which are used to daisy-chain cables between devices. You can use either of the connectors in any order. There is no "in" or "out." Just connect a cable to one connector and use the other connector to daisy-chain to the next device.

Each connector will have some mechanism for being secured, which can consist of clips or screws. Be sure that the connector is secured properly. Most problems with external SCSI devices can be traced to loose connectors. If one connector lets go, the entire bus shuts down.

Figure C.5 shows a complete installation with internal and external devices.

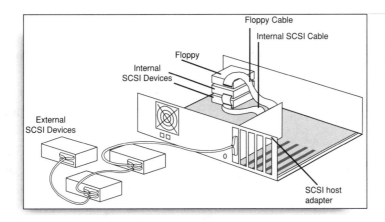

FIGURE C.5

A SCSI system with internal and external devices.

Terminating the SCSI Bus

SCSI devices are terminated in several ways:

- Some SCSI devices, particularly internal devices, incorporate *resistor packs*. These are little inline packages that plug into connectors on the device. You will find three resistor packs on most devices; some will have two. Resistor packs are delicate and nearly impossible to replace. Be careful when you remove or install them, and don't lose the ones you remove. It's a good idea to tape resistor packs to the drive from which they were removed.

- Banks of switches or jumpers can be used. Some devices use a single switch to control termination.

- External devices can use *external terminators*—special connectors that include the termination resistors. A terminator is just plugged into the open connector of the last device in a daisy chain.

- Some all-too-rare devices know where they are in the daisy chain and set their termination characteristics automatically.

- Adapters that are at the ends of daisy chains also must be terminated. Some use resistor packs, but most newer adapters let you use a setup program to enable or disable termination.

SCSI buses can be configured in three ways:

- If only external devices are used, as shown in Figure C.6, the SCSI adapter is terminated, as is the last device in the daisy chain.

- If only internal devices are used, as shown in Figure C.7, the SCSI adapter is terminated, as is the last internal device in the daisy chain.

- If both external and internal devices are used, as shown in Figure C.8, the SCSI adapter is not terminated. The last external device is terminated, as well as the last internal device.

Configuring the Adapter

SCSI configuration options can be set in several ways:

- Using switches or jumpers on the adapter. SCSI adapters for the ISA bus will always have at least a few switches or jumpers.

- Through a configuration program, which is often stored on ROM and is accessed by pressing some keys when the adapter is initializing.

- Through the EISA or MicroChannel setup programs on systems using those buses. Adapters for these buses typically do not require jumpers or switches.

- Through the Plug-and-Play feature of a PCI bus. The PCI bus can typically configure nonconflicting interrupts and memory addresses. Some adapter features, however, must be configured manually.

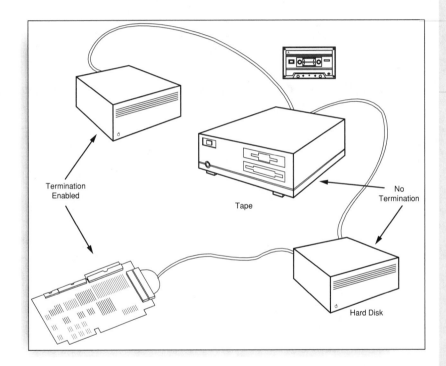

FIGURE C.7

SCSI termination with internal devices only.

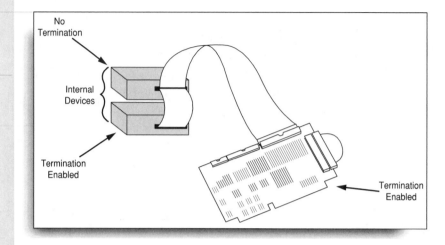

FIGURE C.8

SCSI termination with internal and external devices.

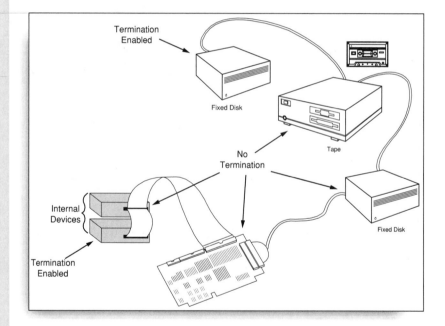

SCSI BIOS

When you use an IBM-compatible PC, the SCSI adapter has an interesting and difficult job. Access to the disk drives is usually performed via the computer's BIOS (basic input/output system), which is a set of programs that is installed in the hardware ROMs that control the computer boot process. The BIOS on an IBM-compatible PC wasn't defined with SCSI in mind. It's used to directly manipulate drive hardware to read and write specific sectors on specific tracks. To start the operating system after completing the startup tests, the PC's BIOS locates the boot drive and positions the heads over a specific track called the *boot track*. In the boot track is the operating system boot loader, which begins the process of starting the OS. Once the boot loader has been located and executed, the operating system takes over control of the PC.

On a SCSI disk, the operating system doesn't directly access tracks and sectors. Instead, data is stored in blocks and is retrieved simply by requesting a given block. This presents a problem on an IBM-compatible, because the BIOS can access data on disks via tracks and sectors. Somehow, the SCSI adapter must translate between the SCSI block-oriented storage and the track-sector storage favored by the PC BIOS.

This could be accomplished by installing a software driver that interfaces the OS with the SCSI adapter, but the driver program must be read from a hard disk. And the PC BIOS can't read the driver from a SCSI disk until the driver is loaded. Clearly there's a catch. The SCSI adapter must perform a trick or two to let the PC access the SCSI disk and boot the operating system.

This sleight of hand is performed by a SCSI BIOS that is loaded after the system test and prior to attempting to start the operating system. After the system test, you will typically see a message indicating that the SCSI BIOS is installed and identifying the devices that are attached. The SCSI BIOS lets the ROM BIOS locate the boot track and start the operating system.

The SCSI BIOS is required only to let the computer boot from a SCSI disk. If the PC is booting from an IDE or ESCI hard disk, the operating system can load appropriate SCSI drivers that let it access nonbootable SCSI devices, such as additional hard drives and CD-ROMs. If the PC isn't booting from a SCSI hard drive, you can disable the SCSI BIOS. You will save a bit of memory. More importantly, you will speed up the boot process, because it is unnecessary for the SCSI adapter to initialize and scan the bus to identify devices. With ISA SCSI adapters, the SCSI BIOS is enabled using a jumper or a switch.

On many recent adapters, when the SCSI BIOS initializes, you're given the option of pressing a key to enter a SCSI setup program. Some of the settings you might see in the setup program are discussed in the following section. *The ROM-based setup program is available only when the SCSI BIOS is enabled.* To configure the adapter, you must enable the SCSI BIOS, run the configuration program, and then disable the SCSI BIOS.

SCSI Adapter Hardware Settings

Many SCSI adapters are equipped with floppy-disk controllers, allowing them to replace the floppy/hard drive controller that was common in early PCs. The majority of modern PCs are equipped with floppy disk controllers on the motherboard. If your SCSI adapter has a floppy drive port, you must disable floppy support on either the motherboard or the SCSI adapter. Floppy support is usually configured via a switch or jumper on the adapter card.

SCSI adapters require sole access to an interrupt and a range of memory addresses that functions as an I/O port. Many also require a DMA address. If your system has a single SCSI adapter, chances are the factory settings will work without alteration, although you should double-check the IRQ. If you need to install multiple SCSI adapters—up to four can be supported— ensure that each adapter is set up with a unique set of communication parameters.

When the SCSI BIOS is enabled, you must specify the starting address for a memory range where the BIOS will be loaded. If multiple SCSI adapters are being installed, the BIOS must usually be enabled only on the adapter that supports the boot disk. The BIOS on other adapters needs to be enabled only when those adapters are being configured or when features requiring the SCSI BIOS are enabled.

You must determine whether termination should be enabled or disabled. On many newer adapters, an automatic termination mode is available that lets the adapter configure itself depending on its position in the SCSI daisy chain.

Some new SCSI adapters are equipped with a Plug-and-Play feature that lets them be configured automatically by some operating systems. Plug and Play is supported by Windows 95 but not by Windows NT. You should disable Plug and Play if the adapter will be running under Windows NT.

Configuring SCSI Drive Startup

Hard drives consume the most power when they are spinning up to their operating speed. When a computer is equipped with several hard drives, it might exceed the capacity of the power supply to spin all drives when the system is turned on. In these cases, it's possible to spin the drives individually, under the control of the SCSI adapter. Two configuration changes are required:

- You must configure the *remote start* capability of the hard drive by changing the appropriate jumper. Most hard drives are configured at the factory to start when power is applied.

- You must configure the SCSI adapter to send a *start unit command* to the drive. The SCSI BIOS must be enabled to send this command, even though this might not be the first SCSI adapter.

These procedures are required only for hard drives, and then only when several drives are present. In most cases, the boot drive will be configured to start automatically, and other hard drives will be started remotely. Other types of SCSI devices, such as CD-ROMs and tape drives, don't require configuration of remote startup.

Configuring older SCSI-1 devices

Caution is required when configuring older SCSI-1 devices to operate on some Fast SCSI adapters. SCSI-1 devices can function only at a 5MBps transfer rate. A Fast SCSI controller, however, will attempt to negotiate 10MBps transfers. Consult the documentation for your SCSI adapter if you are installing SCSI-1 devices.

Index